Photographic Collections in Texas

Photographic Collections in Texas

A UNION GUIDE

COMPILED BY

Richard Pearce-Moses

Published for the Texas Historical Foundation by
Texas A&M University Press, College Station

Library of Congress Cataloging-in-Publication Data

Pearce-Moses, Richard.
    Photographic Collections in Texas.

    Includes indexes.
    1. Photograph collections--Texas--Directories.
I. Texas Historical Foundation. II. Title.
TR12.P43 1987   026'.779'025764   87-9979
ISBN 0-89096-351-7

This book is made possible

by generous grants from

The Robert J. Kleberg, Jr. and Helen C. Kleberg Foundation

and from

E. I. du Pont de Nemours, and its energy subsidiary, Conoco Inc.

CONTENTS

PREFACE

In 1982 the Texas Historical Foundation hosted a workshop for professional curators, librarians, and historians in the state who had an interest in photography as a historical medium. At that meeting Martha A. Sandweiss, Curator of Photographs at the Amon Carter Museum in Fort Worth, suggested that the foundation develop a descriptive directory of photographic collections in the state. Such a guide would serve a variety of purposes: curators would be better able to assess their holdings, donors would know the best place to give their materials, and researchers would be able to locate materials pertinent to their topics.

One result of the workshop was a questionnaire mailed around the state seeking out which institutions had photographic holdings, a first step to assembling a guide. The responses were gathered for the foundation under the supervision of Roy Flukinger, Curator of Photographs, Harry Ransom Humanities Research Center, the University of Texas at Austin. The guide project took new life in 1984 with money received from Conoco Inc. and E. I. du Pont de Nemours, and in 1985 the foundation received additional funds from the Robert J. Kleberg, Jr. and Helen C. Kleberg Foundation for the completion of the project.

These grants enabled the Texas Historical Foundation to hire a project archivist to work on the project full-time. As archivist I was able to build on the questionnaire responses through additional mail surveys. These responses were the basis for many of the collection descriptions. In addition, I was able to visit major repositories, so that those collections could be given more complete descriptions than their staffs alone could be expected to provide on a form.

Photographic Collections in Texas: A Union Guide is the outcome of the diverse and generous efforts of all the many individuals, collection staffs, and foundations: Dr. Sandweiss and Mr. Flukinger, for their early efforts; Bill Wright, Chairman of the Photography Committee and Member of the Board of Directors of the Texas Historical Foundation, for his on-going supervision of the project; foundation staff members, Mark Trowbridge, Pat Olvera, Tanya Fain, Elizabeth Vair, and Mary Ellen Graf, who helped throughout the project; Dr. Kenneth Foote, of the University of Texas at Austin, who assisted in the format of entries. Mark Longley edited the manuscript. Rixon Reed of Photo-Eye Books provided typesetting services. Countless staff members at the many collections described in this guide gave time, energy, and care to assist in the description of their holdings and checking the entries for correctness.

Finally, I wish to offer a word of personal thanks to Lisa Jones and to Sue Borowicz and Mike Nazar. Without their encouragement and support, I could never have undertaken this project.

Although no second edition of this guide is planned, a supplement or some revised edition is inevitable. Corrections and additions to existing entries should be directed to the Texas Historical Foundation, Historic Photography Project Coordinator; collections not included in this edition who wish to participate in future guide publications should contact the coordinator for a survey form.

Richard Pearce-Moses

Historic Photography Project Coordinator
January 1987

INTRODUCTION

This guide lists photographs in the state of Texas held by libraries, historical societies, universities, museums, government agencies, corporations, and other public entities (generically referred to here as *collections*). No private individual's collection is included, nor are collections held by commercial picture agencies, newspaper photo morgues, or the files of active, professional photographers, as these collections can be accessed through business references. Subject matter was not a criterion for inclusion. As a result, the photographs described in this guide range from snapshots and fine art photography to cartographic data and production stills of television programs. Such a potpourri is valuable: photography, as a medium, is useful for research in many disciplines, the same image often being valued by different persons for very different reasons.

Creating this guide was not the simple interfiling of catalog entries from participating collections. More often than not, the photographs held by these collections had been ignored as ephemeral materials and had not been cataloged, inventoried, or indexed in any fashion. Where a catalog did exist, it was often incomplete, inaccurate, or so poorly constructed as to be of no practical use. Hence, the first task usually was the description of the collection's photographs.

The varied nature of the collections' holdings presented a wide range of problems to overcome in their description. Size, availability of information about the images, importance of the material, content of the photographs, and other factors sometimes seemed insurmountable. The solution was a two-part schematic for describing the materials generally under several broad categories and particularly according to provenance or the intellectual divisions of the materials. (The structure of the entries is described in detail in the next section.)

It was not possible to visit and describe all the collections, so many of the descriptions were provided by the collection staffs. The descriptions vary because of the different degrees of expertise and helpfulness of the staffs. Often these staffs were volunteers who had the best of intentions, usually no formal training in collection management, but more importantly, had elbow grease and an enthusiasm for their materials. In three instances individuals went above and beyond the call of duty, providing great quantities of excellent information, often working against formidable time and staff constraints; they are noted in their collections but should be thanked again here: Robert Schaadt of the Sam Houston Regional Library and Research Center in Liberty, Martha Utterback of the Library of the Daughters of the Republic of Texas in San Antonio, and Kathryn Davidson of the Menil Foundation in Houston.

Organization of the Guide

Because of the limited time and resources of the project, equal attention could not be given to every collection, nor to every photograph within those collections treated. A number of collections stood out from the beginning as preeminent because of the historical or aesthetic value of the material, the large number of images, or the breadth of scope. Many more collections contained materials that were considerably more limited in their interest or contained materials that were entirely expected; for example, local history collections traced the economic and social development of the community and business archives documented the activities of the company. Collections whose materials justified detailed analysis are described in the Abstracted Collections section; the remaining collections, generally smaller and more focused and typical in their subjects, are described tersely in the Unabstracted Collections section. A few borderline collections were treated as an Abstracted Collection to suggest the types of materials that smaller or tightly focused collections may hold. In no way should unabstracted be interpreted as unimportant: many unabstracted collections hold photographs of great value but which could be described in few words because of their limited scope.

Within each section, the entries are arranged alphabetically by city. Within cities, collections are arranged alphabetically; collections that are part of a larger institution are placed hierarchically under the name of the larger institution—for example, the Eugene C. Barker Texas History Center is listed under the University of Texas. Following the entries are the indices. Separate indices are provided for geographic location, personal name, photographer, and subject.

Other parts of the guide include a description of the format of entries, which contains a glossary of abbreviations and words used in a particular and restricted sense by this guide. Researchers are encouraged to read this section closely to understand the method with which collections are described.

Some additional notes: Cross references within an entry are noted (v.i.) and (v.s.) and to other areas in the guide are noted (q.v.). References to citations in the Bibliography are under the same name as the Record Group title unless otherwise indicated. Parallel titles, pseudonyms, and other variant names are indicated in parentheses with an equal sign—for example, Lewis Carroll (= Charles Lutwidge Dodgson). Headings are alphabetized according to common library rules; the most important of these rules include the disregarding of initial article adjectives, the placement of nothing before something (new ton before Newton), the interfiling of *Mc* as *Mac*, and the placing of corporate names formed from personal names under the last name (Eugene C. Barker Texas History Center under B).

ORGANIZATION OF THE ENTRIES

Abstracted collections are described in terms of their policies and their content. Policy is described under the headings of hours, assistance, finding aids, and publication restriction. Content is described first under the broad categories of bibliography, physical scope, geographic places, generic and proper impersonal subjects, people, and photographers. Holdings are then described more particularly by the record groups or logical divisions in which they are maintained by the collections. Record group descriptions contain essential information on provenance whenever it could be easily captured; generic and proper subjects; geographic locations; photographers; quantity of the materials; photographic processes; related non-photographic materials; capture dates; and collection reference numbers. Unabstracted collections generally contain no access information beyond the address, and the collection's holdings are treated as a single record group. When noteworthy, additional information is given, such as extraordinary access conditions, bibliography notes, or treating the holdings as more than one record group.

PURPOSE: The collecting institution's nature and the types of materials it collects, including non-photographic materials.

HOURS: Notes on when the materials may be viewed, distinguishing between exhibition space and reserve collection hours for collections with a public viewing space; whether an appointment is necessary; whether any research or admission fees are charged.

ASSISTANCE: How the collection is staffed—professional indicates formal training in library, museum, or archive practice; specialized indicates formal training in the collection's area of specialization; experienced indicates educated at the School of Hard Knocks. Whether written or phone inquiries are accepted. Whether electrostatic copies (e.g., Xeroxes) of photographs are available, and the availablity of photographic copy prints (referred to as photoduplications). In all collections, a charge should be assumed for electrostatic copies and photoduplications, and the availability of such copies will depend on the physical condition of the materials.

PUBLICATION: Requirements of the collection for publication of its photographs, including permission fees and collection credit. Whether third-party permission is needed to publish the material (e.g., from the copyright holder).

FINDING AIDS: Types of catalogs, indices, inventories, or other devices to maintain intellectual control over and gain access to the holdings.

BIBLIOGRAPHY: Publications that reproduce a significant number of photographs from the collection. In addition, researchers should consult the works cited below for picture essay books that contain many photographs from many different collections. The list also notes bibliographies that list county histories which often have a few illustrations. Works listed in the Bibliography section may no longer be in print but should be available through interlibrary loan and are frequently represented on OCLC and in the *National Union Catalog.*

> Baker, T. Lindsay. *Building the Lone Star: An illustrated guide to historic sites.* College Station: Texas A&M Press, 1986.
>
> Cruz, Gilberto R., and James A. Irby. *Texas bibliography: A manual on history research materials.* Austin: Eakin Press, 1982.
>
> Haley, Jim. *Texas: An album of history* . Garden City NY: Doubleday, 1985.
>
> Holmes, Jon. *Texas: A self-portrait.* New York: Harry N. Abrams, 1983.
>
> McQuaid, James, and Paulette Privitera Wilson. *An index to American photographic collections.* Boston: G. K. Hall, 1982.
>
> Munnerlyn, Tom. *Texas local history: A source book for available town and county histories, local memoirs, and genealogical records.* Austin: Eakin Press, 1983.
>
> Sandweiss, Martha A., Roy Flukinger, Anne Tucker, William A. Owens, and Richard Pearce-Moses. *Historic Texas: A photographic portrait.* Austin: Texas Monthly Press, 1986.
>
> Willoughby, Larry. *Texas, Our Texas.* Austin: Learned & Tested, 1987. A public-school textbook available from the publisher.

SCOPE: Notes in broad terms the number of photographs, the processes represented, the inclusive dates of the images, and other materials pertinent to the photographic holdings. Scope is often followed by a table listing quantity by process and date.

GEOGRAPHIC: Locales represented in the collection. Locales should be assumed to be Texas, unless otherwise noted, with the exception of major cities such as Boston, Chicago, Los Angeles, London, New York, Philadelphia, and San Francisco. When used as a heading, the names of US states are spelled out; when used as modifiers of headings, the two-letter postal abbrevation is used—for example, "Maine" indicates photographs from the state of Maine, while Portsmouth ME indicates photographs from the town of Portsmouth in Maine. TX is used to distinguish ambiguous headings—for example, Palestine TX and Palestine.

SUBJECTS: General subjects followed by the proper names of inanimate subjects, such as organizations and buildings, held in quantity by the collection. Listings of headings are drawn from the collection's subject list, when one was available; otherwise, headings are generated from a standard subject heading list used for the subject index.

PEOPLE: Proper names of individuals held in quantity in the collection. Photographs of family members and associates of individuals listed are often present in a collection's holdings but in quantities too small to be mentioned. Generalizations such as occupations and other personal characteristics of the individuals in the collection are noted.

Ethnicity (including race) is mentioned only when the collection has significantly broad holdings or is actively collecting along the lines of ethnic origins. Few collections hold more than a scattering of items pertinent to non-Caucasian settlers of Texas, and hence fall outside the scope of this guide. The Houston Metropolitan Research Center of the Houston Public Library and the Institute of Texan Cultures in San Antonio are to be commended for the extraordinary efforts to preserve the heritage of the many diverse ethnic groups that make up the state's history. The Texas Historical Foundation encourages a supplement to this guide that will inventory specifically those small caches of photographs along the lines of ethnicity.

PHOTOGRAPHERS: Names of photographers, photographic studios, and other corporate identities responsible for the creation of the photographs in the collection. When possible, a photographer's primary place of operation is indicated parenthetically. Most entries indicate names held in quantity by the collection, but significant photographers may be listed even if the collection holds only a few works by that photographer. When possible, quantities are also listed. Bias was given to Texas photographers, to collections with the archives of photographers, and fine art photographers. See glossary for a note on the stylistic distinctions between snapshot and amateur photographers, and the treatment of various and unidentified photographers. Authoritative forms for names and dates were drawn from *International Center for Photography Encyclopedia of Photography* (New York: Crown Press, 1984) and *The Photograph Collector's Guide*, Lee D. Witkin and Barbara London (Boston: New York Graphic Society, 1979).

RECORD GROUPS: This section describes the arrangement of the materials in the collection in terms of their physical, provenance, or logical order at the collection. Elements of the record group description include, in broad terms, identification, subject, responsibility, physical description, and span dates. Identification includes the guide reference number, the record group title used by the collection; life dates of persons and a biographical or explanatory note about the persons or organizations in the title are provided when such information is available. Subjects are presented in a narrative statement about the contents of the photographs, including proper names of people and inanimate objects, and capture locations. Responsibility covers photographers and other individuals associated with the creation of the photographs or their compilation into the record group. Physical description includes the quantity and processes of materials, related nonphotographic materials, and finding aids specific to this collection. Span dates of the materials denote when the image was captured, and when available, information about later editions of the prints. References to the Bibliography and collection identification numbers are reproduced at the end of the record group description when they were provided by the collection. Not all elements are present in each description, although every effort was made to obtain information in each area. Some very large record groups have descendant subrecord groups; these subrecord groups are indented and appear below the introduction to the record group.

Additional Rules:

Formally published materials, such as books with vintage photographs bound in, are described in a more traditional bibliographic format, and are distinguished by having the record group title set in upper and lower case. Collections of unpublished materials have the title set in capital letters.

Record groups are arranged alphabetically by title. Some collections with large quantities of materials have record groups of like nature described together; in these cases, an introductory note describes the order in which the material appears.

Glossary:

A few words are used with restricted definitions in the guide. Definitions of processes, styles, and other technical terms not listed here can be found in standard photographic reference works, such as the *Encyclopedia of Photography*, noted above.

amateur A photographer who has passed beyond the realm of a snapshooter, exhibiting a sophistication of aesthetic and technique in their images, but not practicing the craft as a vocation. *Amateur* should not be read with any derogatory connotation suggesting second-rate work. See *snapshooter.*

anonymous Distinguished from *unidentified*; *anonymous* suggests the presence of names while the identity of the person is little known. *Unidentified* indicates that no name of the person is known.

coverage Quantity modifiers such as *few, many, some, most,* and the like, are relative to the quantity of the material being described at hand. *Broad, substantial, major,* and *minor,* when modifying coverage, indicate a collection's signficance relative to all collections in Texas. For example, "100 photographs, a few in color," points to a small number of color photographs within that record group; "extensive coverage of the Trans-Pecos" indicates that the collection is a primary reference place for this type of material.

economic and social development A phrase indicating broad subject coverage in historical collections, but pertinent to that community alone.

in situ Portraits made in a non-studio environment that usually is characteristic of the sitter; for example, in a home or work environment.

late-Pictorialism A term used to suggest reliance on painterly devices for aesthetic effect. Late-Pictorialism was common to many studio portrait photographers in the twentieth century, long after the Pictorialism of H. P. Robinson and O. G. Rejlander had lost popularity.

retrospective views indicates photographs of historical structures made significantly later than the historical moment. For example, photographs of the state Capitol made in 1954 would be retrospective views, but those made at the dedication would not be so designated.

snapshooter (also *snapshot*) A photographer who takes pictures primarily for their mnemonic value, with little regard to aesthetic or technique.

unidentified Without any identifying information. See *anonymous* and *various.*

various Like anonymous, *various* is used to indicate the presence of many identities, none of whom are widely recognized.

Photographic Collections in Texas

ABSTRACTED COLLECTIONS

Archives of the Big Bend (A16)

Sul Ross University
Bryan Wildenthal Memorial Library
P.O. Box C-149
Alpine, Texas 79830

915-837-8127. Contact: Assistant Archivist.

PURPOSE: A research archive housed in a university library devoted to the cultural and political history of the Trans-Pecos area and its people. The archive collects manuscripts, oral history, rare and recent books, and photographs.

HOURS: Weekdays, 8:00-5:00. Closed major and academic holidays. Appointments required.

ASSISTANCE: Professional staff. Written inquiries accepted; phone inquiries accepted on a limited basis. Electrostatic copies available. Photoduplications may be made by patron or ordered through the archive.

PUBLICATION: Publication fee. Collection credit required. Free copy of publication to archive. Third-party permission required on a few items.

FINDING AIDS: Card index; access by general subject heading and by personal name; computerized index being developed. Published descriptive guide.

BIBLIOGRAPHY:
Perry, Kenneth D. *Guide to manuscript collections*. Alpine: Sul Ross University, 1981.

SCOPE: 10,000 photographs and negatives, most silver gelatin prints. Many collections have associated manuscripts. 1860s to present, most 1900 to 1940.

Type of photo	Pre-1880	1880-1899	1900-1919	1920-1939	1940-1959	1960-1986
D/A/T-types	20					
Glass negs		12				
Film negs					1,000	1,000
Vintage prints	500	1,500	3,000	3,000	1,000	1,000
Copy prints	100	100	100	100	50	
Photo albums		5	5			

GEOGRAPHIC: Central America. Cuba. Italy. Mexico (Chihuahua, Ojinaga). South Africa. South America. US.

Texas: Alpine. Boquillas. Candelaria. Castolon. El Paso. Fort Davis. Fort Stockton. Glen Springs. Guadalupe Peak. Haymond. Kent. Lajitas. Langtry. Marathon. Marfa. Pecos. Presidio. Ruidoso. San Angelo. San Antonio. San Vicente. Sanderson. Study Butte. Terlingua. Terrell Wells. Trans-Pecos (Brewster, Jeff Davis, and Presidio counties). Van Horn.

SUBJECTS: Major subject headings used in the Archives:

Agriculture. Anthropology. Business and industry. Cultural and social activities. Disasters. Domestic life. Education. Fauna and wildlife. Foreign countries. Geography (landforms). Government. Law enforcement. Man-made environment (divided by locale). Military—US. Mineral resources—mining. Ranching. Recreation—sport. Religion. Transportation.

Academia (university). Agriculture (farming—cotton, ranching—sheep, —goat, —cattle). Animals (cattle, wildlife). Architecture (commercial, domestic, religious). Economic and social development (Alpine). Events (Mexican Revolution). Government (law enforcement, US Customs). Industry (candelilla wax, general commerce, mining—quicksilver, oil). Landscape (aerial, arid, mountains). Military (US Army encampment—Ruidoso TX—1916). Services (hotel). Social life and customs (Sul Ross students). Sports and amusements (bull fights, circuses, hunting, rodeo). Transportation (aviation, railroad).

Big Bend National Park. Camp Holland. Camp Kent. Camp La Noria. Civilian Conservation Corps. Davis Mountains State Park. Fort D. A. Russell. Fort Davis. Fort Leaton. La Tuna Federal Prison. McDonald Observatory. Marfa Army Air Field. Mexican Army. Paisano Hotel (Marfa). Sul Ross State University. US Army and US Army Cavalry. [E. A.] Waldron Quicksilver Mine.

PEOPLE: Iva Lee Bales. May Bennett. Steve Bennett. Chandler family. W. R. "Willie" Green family. General Obregon. Thomas V. Skaggs family.

PHOTOGRAPHERS: Austin Studios (CA). A. Beasley (Remington IN). Boone (Austin). Glenn Burgess (Alpine). Dudley Studio (Alpine). Frank Duncan (Marfa). O. T. Ericson (Vermillon SD). Sergio Franco (Ojinaga, Mexico). Harper and Company (Houston). Hillyer and Son (Belton and Taylor). Charles M. Hunter (Alpine). Jordan (Austin). Lippe's Studio (Del Rio). Roberto Lopez (Chihuahua, Mexico). Mecca (San Antonio). Metcalfe (El Paso). Paris and Rothwell (San Antonio). L T. Rice (Wabash IN). Rodgers (Brownwood). Sanders and Lenox (Brownwood). H. S. Shuster (Salem OR). J. Sterling Skaggs. Thomas V. Skaggs. W. D. Smithers (Alpine). Standiford (Louisville KY). W. F. Stuart (El Paso). Mr. and Mrs. J. C. Thain (Alpine). US Army Air Corps, 22nd Photo Section. Walton's Studio (Cisco).

RECORD GROUPS:

A16.1 ALDRICH (ROY W.; 1869-1955) COLLECTION. Soldier in Spanish-American War, Texas Ranger, and banker. Most snapshots, some commercial views of the Big Bend (possibly photographed by W. D. Smithers), Spanish-American War, safari and natives in Africa, commercial travel views and snapshots of Mexican cities, landscape, and natives; portraits of Aldrich, relatives, and friends, prisoners, Spanish-American War, and Texas Rangers.

    A16.1.1 [*Aldrich family album I.*] Unidentified studio portraits by various US Midwest photographers, especially from Golden City and Kansas City MO. 64 gelatino-chloride and collodio-chloride cabinets. 1890s.

    A16.1.2 [*Aldrich family album II.*] Studio portraits of Roy Aldrich and unidentified sitters by various US Midwest photographers. 35 albumen and collodio-chloride cabinets. 1890s.

A16.1.3 [*Aldrich family album III.*] Unidentified studio portraits by various US Midwest photographers. 21 silver gelatin and albumen cabinets and cartes. 1870s to 1890s.

666 photo prints, mostly silver gelatin snapshots and many photo postcards; 16 negatives; 3 albums. 1892 to 1953, most 1910s to mid-1950s.

A16.2 CASEY (CLIFFORD B.; 1897-1986) COLLECTION. Commercial views and some snapshots; Alpine, Fort Davis, Marathon, and Marfa, including early cityscapes, businesses, and aerial views; Mexican Americans, including Revolutionaries; ranch life and customs; and Sul Ross State University. 3 cubic feet including 1,000 vintage and copy photo prints, some color; negatives. 1882 to 1976, most 1910s to 1930s.

A16.3 CROSSON RANCH COLLECTION. Crosson family and friends, Crosson Ranch, Marfa vicinity, and snapshots of Cuba. 34 vintage and 235 copy prints. 1891 to 1974, most 1900 to 1919.

A16.4 HUNTER (CHARLES) COLLECTION. Alpine studio and commercial photographer. Alpine businesses, churches, and organizations, including First National Bank (Alpine); Alpine Cowboys (baseball club); Apollo astronauts visiting Big Bend and Marfa; Big Bend National Park; Brewster County Memorial Hospital; Camino del Rio; Camp Holland; Castolon vicinity; deer hunting; Fort Davis National Historical Site and centennial celebration; Stillwell family and ranch; and studio portraits of area residents, including the Casner, Forchheimer, and Herbert L. Kokernot families. Some coverage of Lajitas, Presidio, and Terlingua. 1,600 prints and negatives. 1940s to 1969s. Itemized card index.

A16.5 LIVINGSTON (CHARLES WESLEY; 1901-1985) COLLECTION. Operated the Livingston Funeral Home in Alpine and amateur photographer who worked with W. D. Smithers. Landscapes of Big Bend; family photographs; schools and school activities in Marfa, Alpine, and Fort Davis, including Sul Ross University; churches, landscapes, residences, and people in Mexico; residences and commercial structures in Alpine, Fort Davis, Marfa, Shafter, Langtry, Castolon, and Study Butte; military encampments at Fort Davis, Camp Holland, and Camp Glenn Springs; Livingston Ranch in Tom Green County; and Paisano and Bloys camp meetings. 3,655 silver gelatin prints, 385 safety negatives, 2,226 nitrate negatives, 8—8mm movies.

A16.6 MITCHELL (W. B.; 1896-1969) COLLECTION. Cattle breeder and rancher. Family members, professional associates, cattle sales, and ranch life. 86 vintage silver gelatin and copy prints. 1913 to 1958.

A16.7 SHIPMAN (Mrs. O. L., = ALICE JACK; 1890-1972) COLLECTION. W. H. Cleveland family, First US Cavalry, Fort Davis, W. B. Mitchell family, and outlaw "Black Jack" Ketchum; landscapes photographed by Frank Duncan. 56 silver gelatin prints, some copies. 1865 to 1950, most 1930s.

A16.8 SKAGGS (THOMAS V.; 1887-1945) COLLECTION. Snapshot portraits and landscapes.

Skaggs, J. Sterling, photog. [*Skaggs photo album*.] Amateur views of ranch life and customs on the ranch of the Jim P. Wilson family in Green Valley and the Wilson ranch near Alpine. 110 silver gelatin prints. Ca. 1906.

295 photo prints, most silver gelatin, some cabinets and cyanotypes; 367 film negatives; 1 album (v.s.). 1878 to 1960, most 1900s to 1910s.

A16.9 SMITH (ED R.; b. 1860) ALBUMS. Owner of Elgin Brick company and insurance agent. Commercial views of Austin vicinity landscapes photographed by S. B. Hill.

A16.9.1 *Moffett album.* Studio portraits of the Moffett family by various Indiana photographer(s). 15 cabinets and 16 albumen cartes. Late 1860s to 1900s.

A16.9.2 *Mr. & Mrs. Ed R. Smith: Compliments of the Arion Club.* Studio portraits by various Indiana photographer(s) including J. Harry Swaine (Richmond IN) and Stigleman (Richmond IN). 20 albumen cabinets and 38 albumen cartes. 1881.

6 silver gelatin prints; 2 albums (v.s.). 1890s.

A16.10 TOWNSEND (E. E.) COLLECTION. Family photographs, including E. E. and Alice Augusta Jones Townsend and various others in the Alpine and Big Bend area. 337 photo prints, including four albums and some postcards; itemized inventory; associated papers. 1860s to 1940s.

A16.11 WALTON (D. A. T.; 1837-1915) COLLECTION. Snapshot portraits and grave markers. 18 silver gelatin prints, 1 ambrotype, 3 tintypes. 1860s to 1911.

Unprocessed collections:

A16.12 BEARD (Mrs. RUTH) COLLECTION. Early Alpine and area residents. 60 photographs. 1886 to 1930. ABB# 1982.36.

A16.13 BEARD (Mrs. T. A.) COLLECTION. Personal and business photographs. 2 cubic feet total material. 1914 to 1982. ABB# 1984.5.

A16.14 FROMAN (BONNIE JEWEL) COLLECTION. Portraits. One-half cubic foot glass negatives. Ca. 1910. ABB# 1984.57.

A16.15 HARRISON (DUDLEY) COLLECTION. Politics and family photographs. 4 cubic feet total materials. 1978 to 1982. ABB# 1983.62.

A16.16 HOLMAN (J. D.) COLLECTION. Jackson/Harmon Ranch and Jackson family. Early Alpine, including Casner Motor Company and the First Christian Church. 1 cubic foot total material. 1886 to 1966. ABB# 1982.33, 1984.51.

A16.17 LIVINGSTON (GEORGE M.) COLLECTION. 21 photographs. 1900 to 1950. ABB# 1985.15.

A16.18 McLAIN (Mrs. FAY) COLLECTION. Yarboro family and ranch photographs. 26 leaves. ABB# 1982.52.

A16.19 McSPADDEN COLLECTION. Portraits, received from Martha Elms. 2 cubic feet total materials. 1910 to 1981. ABB# 1984.50.

A16.20 MEADOR (MATT) COLLECTION. Operated a photography studio in Alpine in the 1920s and 1930s. Studio portraits, many of babies and school groups, photographed by Meador. 528 glass negatives. 1920s to 1930s.

A16.21 NEWS AND INFORMATION SERVICE COLLECTION. Sul Ross State University football games, buildings, and class favorites; students and activities. 6 cubic feet negatives and positives; movie film, negatives and contact prints. 1973 to 1983. ABB# 1982.64, 1983.68, 1984.36.

Museum of the Big Bend (A18)

Sul Ross University
US 67/90 entrance
Alpine, Texas 79830

915-837-8145. Contact: Director.

PURPOSE: A museum with regional and natural history exhibits and reserve collections of material culture artifacts, costumes, and vintage and copy photographs.

HOURS: Tuesday through Saturday, 9:00-5:00; Sunday, 1:00-5:00. Closed major and academic holidays. Appointment necessary for use of reserve collections.

ASSISTANCE: Professional, experienced staff. Written inquiries accepted; phone inquiries accepted on a limited basis. Electrostatic copies available. Photoduplications may be made by patron or ordered through the museum.

PUBLICATION: Publication fee. Collection credit required. Free copy of publication to museum. Third-party permission required on a few items.

FINDING AIDS: Card index; access by general subject heading and personal name; computerized index being developed.

SCOPE: 400 vintage and 2,000 copy photographs in major formats. Late 1840s to present, most 1900 to 1940s.

Type of photo	Pre-1880	1880-1899	1900-1919	1920-1939	1940-1959	1960-1986
D/A/T-types	34	16				
Film negs				75		
Vintage prints		10	60	100	75	15
Copy prints	100	300	600	600	200	200

GEOGRAPHIC: Emphasis is on the Big Bend National Park and Trans-Pecos region of Texas (Brewster, Jeff Davis, and Presidio counties).

Alpine. Fort Davis. Fort Stockton. Marfa.

SUBJECTS: Economic and social development of the region.

Agriculture (ranching—sheep). Archaeology (Big Bend region cave shelters). Industry (mining). Landscape. Military.

PEOPLE: Snapshots and studio portraits of area residents. Substantial coverage of Caucasians and Hispanics.

PHOTOGRAPHERS: N. H. Rose. V. J. Smith. W. D. Smithers.

RECORD GROUPS:

A18.1 MEXICAN-AMERICAN COPYPRINT COLLECTION. A collection gathered by the museum documenting the Hispanic population in the region. Portraits, Mexican-American social life and customs. 2,000 silver gelatin copyprints. Ca. 1900 to 1950s.

A18.2 SMITHERS (W. D.; 1895-1951) COLLECTION. Mexican Revolution along Texas border; mining at Terlingua. 78 copy prints from University of Texas at Austin, HRHRC, Photography Collection (q.v.). 1920s to 1930s.

University of Texas at Arlington
Libraries, Special Collections (A26)

University of Texas at Arlington
P.O. Box 19497
Arlington, Texas 76019

817-273-3393. Contact: Assistant Director for Special Collections.

PURPOSE: A special-collections division within an academic library collecting rare books and periodicals, manuscripts and records, rare maps, oral history, and photography. Special attention is given to the labor movement in Texas and to the history of the Southwest with an emphasis on Texas.

HOURS: Weekdays, 8:00-5:00; Saturday, 10:00-2:00. Closed on major holidays.

ASSISTANCE: Professional, experienced staff. Written inquiries accepted on a limited basis. Electrostatic copies available. Photoduplications must be ordered through the library.

PUBLICATION: Publication fee for commercial use. Collection credit required. Free copy of publication to the library. Third-party permission required for some materials.

FINDING AIDS: Card index; access to photographs by subject and access to collections by subject, organization, city, and date, although presence of photographs not specified in collection indices; collection inventory.

BIBLIOGRAPHY:
Meek, Philip J. *The Fort Worth Star-Telegram: Where the West begins.* New York: The Newcomen Society in North America, 1981.

SCOPE: The Special Collections Division is composed of several separate collections with photographic holdings totaling some 200,000 photographic prints, most vintage, and some 120,000 original negatives. 1890s to 1960s, many 1920s to 1940s, most after the 1940s.

Type of photo	Pre-1880	1880-1899	1900-1919	1920-1939	1940-1959	1960-1986
D/A/T-types	24	24				
Film negs		10	5,000	40,000	55,000	50,000
Vintage prints		300	5,000	30,000	45,000	35,000
Copy prints			100		200	

GEOGRAPHIC: Extensive coverage of Fort Worth and Tarrant County with some coverage of Dallas, El Paso, San Antonio, Thurber, and of Starr County.

SUBJECTS: Major topics include the history and development of organized labor in Texas, the history of the University of Texas at Arlington, and journalistic coverage of Fort Worth. See Record Groups for subject headings.

PEOPLE: Many state and national labor leaders, Texas politicians, especially those who sought the labor vote, and Democratic party members. See Record Groups for names.

PHOTOGRAPHERS: Many unidentified photographers. *Fort Worth Star-Telegram* staff.

RECORD GROUPS: Holdings are broadly divided into three areas: the Labor and University Archives, Special Collections, and the Jenkins Garrett Manuscript Collection.

Labor and University Archives: Many record groups contain small numbers of photographs; they are arranged under the library's headings of labor, miscellaneous, political papers, and the University of Texas at Arlington history collections. The Texas AFL-CIO Archives are listed at the end of this area.

A26.1 LABOR COLLECTIONS. Ruth Allen papers (#31). Amalgamated Transit Union, Local 694, San Antonio (#7). American Federation of Musicians, Local 72, Fort Worth (#10). Communication Workers of America photographs (#270). Dallas AFL-CIO Council (#5). Edward L. Dato papers (#241). Eugene V. and Theodore Debs papers (#185). Harvey C. Fremming papers (#136). John W. "Preacher" Hayes papers (#9). International Alliance of Theatrical Stage Employees and Motion Picture Operators Local 249A (#65). International Brotherhood of Electrical Workers, Local 850, Lubbock (#92). International Ladies Garment Workers Union, Local 214, Houston (#29-30). Clyde Johnson collection (#213). George and Latane Lambert papers (#127). Lee Andrew Lewis papers (#154). F. F. "Pancho" Medrano papers (#55). Frank E. Morton papers (#111, 262). M. M. and Reecy McKnight collection (#24, 215). Office and Professional Employees International Union, Local 277, Fort Worth (#242). Retail, Wholesale, and Department Store Union, Sabine Area Industrial Union, Local 1814, Port Arthur (#53). Wallace C. Reilly papers (#115). Sam Twedell papers (#44). Texas State Federation of Labor, Austin (#182). Thurber Coal Miners collection (#88). United Automobile, Aerospace, and Agricultural Implements Workers of America, Arlington (#186). United Packinghouse Workers of America, District 8 (#51). Blanche Wells papers (#59).

A26.2 MISCELLANEOUS COLLECTIONS. Anna C. Leahy papers (#76, 214). Bernard Rapoport papers (#200). Committee on the History and Heritage of American Civil Engineering records (#209, 231).

A26.3 POLITICAL PAPERS. Betty Andujar papers (#254, 272). Jack Parrish Avery papers (#238). Joe B. Cannon papers (#248). Margaret B. Carter papers (#265). John Hill Campaign Headquarters records (#253). Don Kennard papers (#128). Oscar H. Mauzy papers (#218). Dale Milford papers (#234).

A26.4 UNIVERSITY OF TEXAS AT ARLINGTON HISTORY COLLECTIONS. Dr. Clarence P. Denman collection (#199). Ex-students Association of North Texas Agricultural College (#177, 216, 243). Howard and Arista Joyner collection (#195). L. G. Meier papers (#193). Duncan Robinson papers (#210). Rebel Theme Controversy collection (#232). Rusty Russell papers (#190). University of Texas at Arlington Library records (#236). University of Texas at Arlington R.O.T.C. Scrapbook collection. (#225). University of Texas at Arlington 75th Anniversary collection (#271). Walter Prescott Webb Memorial Lectures, Arlington (#192). Glenn O. Wilson collection (#206).

Subject headings used in the Labor and University Archives index: Anti-unionism. Blacks. Collective bargaining. Community affairs. Conventions. Education. Farm labor. Individual organizations. Industrial labor—craft, —general. Mergers. Mexican-American affairs. Leaders. Parades.

Political activities. Specific events. Strikes. Texas AFL-CIO. Wartime activities. Women. Work, daily affairs. Cities.

Areas of specific interest: United Farm Workers Strike, Starr County (1966-67). Peyton Packing Company Strike, El Paso (1959-1962). International Ladies Garment Workers Strike, Dallas (1935). Tex-son Strike, San Antonio (1959-1960).

Total for above record groups is 5,290 photo prints. 1900 to present, most 1920s to 1960s.

A26.5 TEXAS AFL-CIO ARCHIVES. The official repository of the union and its affiliates, consisting primarily of records and publications, with some photographs interfiled. Subjects include conventions, meetings of affiliated organizations, labor leaders and politicians:

> William B. Arnold. Al Barkan. Edgar L. Berlin. Jack Brooks. H. S. "Hank" Brown. N. E. Coward. Roy R. Evans. Lester Graham. William J. Harris. Jerry Holleman. Hubert H. Humphrey. A. R. Johnson. Texas legislature. M. M. McKnight. Sherman A. Miles. Henry Munoz Jr. Antonio Orendain. Harry O'Reilly. Fred H. Schmidt. Paul C. Sparks. Rosa Walker. L. N. D. Wells Jr. Senator Ralph Yarborough.

1,500 photographs, primarily silver gelatin prints, some negatives, some slides. 1952 to 1973, most 1950 to 1967. UTA# 110, 256, 275-277.

Special Collections: Two collections, each with substantial numbers of photographs.

A26.6 *FORT WORTH STAR-TELEGRAM* PHOTO MORGUE. A paper formed by the merger of the *Star* and the *Telegram* in 1909, owned by Amon Carter. Extensive emphasis on Fort Worth business and social life; substantial coverage of Texas, the Panhandle, and West Texas, emphasizing the cattle and oil industry; some coverage of national and international topics through news agency photographs.

> Fort Worth subjects: Aerial views. Bell Helicopter. Buildings (businesses, churches, Continental Plaza, firehouses, hospitals, hotels, jail, Masonic Temple, municipal buildings, museums, Tarrant County Courthouse). Businesses (Burrus Mill and Elevator Company, helium plant, Swift and Company). Dams (Whitney, Eagle Mountain, and Denison). Early Fort Worth. Fort Worth Fat Stock Show. General Dynamics (airplanes and missiles). Local disasters. Military camps (Camp Bowie and various airfields). Parks (Botanic Gardens, Fort Worth Zoo). Van Cliburn International Piano Competition.

> People: Many prominent Fort Worth individuals held in quantity, including the Bass Brothers, Amon Carter and family. Area retailers, oilmen, cattlemen and cowboys, employees and other businessmen. British royal family. Fat Stock show participants. Local, state, and national politicians, including presidents Franklin Roosevelt, Harry Truman, Dwight Eisenhower, John Kennedy, Lyndon Johnson, and Richard Nixon and Vice-President John Garner. Socialites. Sports figures, coaches, and teams. Texas Boys Choir. Texas National Guard. Will Rogers.

Approximately half the images are from the major news services or are publicity photographs; the remaining half are by staff photographers. 180,000 photo prints; 900 glass and 112,000 film negatives; clippings; descriptive essay by Kenneth Rendell. Prints 1870s to present, most 1920s to 1960s; negatives 1929 to 1949. See Bibliography—Meek.

A26.7 CLEMONS (BASIL EDWIN; 1887-1964) COLLECTION. Commercial photographer active in Breckenridge from 1919 to ca. 1954. Subject headings used in the collection:

Automobiles. Carbon black plant. Children. Churches, groups, camps. Circuses. Clubs (Red Cross, KKK, Masons, Salvation Army). Courthouses, court and law officers. Davis Dancers. Family groups. Fires. Funerals and funeral homes. High school graduates. Men. Mexican town. Mule teams for oil. Odd ones [miscellany]. Oil Belt fairs. Oil fields. Ouida Wildman and Wesley Tuttle [minstrels]. Parades and July 4th. Pep squads and school clubs. Possum Kingdom and lakes. Ranches, dairy, cattle, chickens. Rodeos. School groups, schools, class-rooms. School plays. Snow. Soldiers. Sports. Store and window displays. Street builders. Waterworks and water parks. Weddings and anniversaries. Wild West shows. Women.

12,300 silver gelatin prints; 4,566 nitrate and safety negatives. 1919 to 1948, most 1920s to 1930s.

A26.8 Jenkins Garrett Manuscript collections: Record groups are not related to one another. Record groups that contain a few photographs include: Ben Capps. Cyrus Moore Durham papers. Goliad College collection. John Howard Griffin collection (5 folders). Irion family papers. Albert Sidney Johnston collection. Ruby Mixon collection. Robertson Colony collection. Santerre photographs. Texas Legislature History Project.

A26.9 GOGGINS PHOTOGRAPH COLLECTION. Early Fort Worth residents. Studio portraits, most unidentified. 62 photo prints, most cabinets. Ca. 1890s.

A26.10 GREEN (BEN KING) PAPERS. Texas rancher and western author. Horses and other animals, portraits of Green and family. 307 photographs. Ca. 1930 to 1970.

A26.11 PADDOCK (B. B.) PAPERS. Fort Worth businessman. Texas Spring Palace, portraits, group portraits of family and veterans. 16 photographs. Ca. 1880s to 1920s.

A26.12 POLLACK-CAPPS PAPERS. Portraits of family groups and friends. 98 photographs. Ca. 1900s.

A26.13 TRUSSEL FAMILY PAPERS. Pioneer, Texas Hill Country family. Portraits of family and friends, train wreck, and European cities. Various commercial and snapshot photographers. 170 photographs. 1848 to 1945.

Archives of the Episcopal Church (A28)

Episcopal Church in America
606 Rathervue Place
P.O. Box 2247
Austin, Texas 78768

512-472-6816. Contact: Archivist.

PURPOSE: Archive for the Protestant Episcopal Church in the United States of America (= PECUSA = Domestic and Foreign Mission Society of the Episcopal Church); the official repository for the records of the church.

HOURS: Weekdays, 8:30-12:00 and 1:00-4:00. Closed major holidays. Appointment required.

ASSISTANCE: Professional staff. Written and phone inquiries accepted for historical research. Electrostatic copies available (limited quantity). Photoduplications (limited quantity) must be ordered through the archive.

PUBLICATION: No publication fee. Prior permission required for publication. Collection credit required. Third-party permission occasionally required.

FINDING AIDS: Complete inventory of holdings, partial itemized, descriptive list and partial computerized data base; access by geographic location.

BIBLIOGRAPHY:

Spirit of missions. Philadelphia: W. Staverly, edited for the Domestic and Foreign Missionary Society of the Protestant Episcopal Church in the USA (1833-1949); New York: Domestic and Foreign Missionary Society of the Protestant Episcopal Church in the USA, 1950 to present.

SCOPE: 50,000 vintage and 150 copy photographs, including 300 glass lantern slides and 7,000 film transparencies. 1850 to present.

Type of photo	Pre-1880	1880-1899	1900-1919	1920-1939	1940-1959	1960-1986
D/A/T-types	31	5				
Glass negs	20	20	200			
Film negs			600	1,000	1,000	2,000
Vintage prints		100	10,000	10,000	10,000	20,000
Copy prints	50	50	25	25		
Photo albums		15	15	15		

GEOGRAPHIC: Photographs from all the Episcopal missions around the world. Texas is broadly covered by many photographs from Houston.

Asia. Africa. South and Central America. Caribbean. England. India. United States (all states, including Alaska and Hawaii).

SUBJECTS: Most photographs relate to the Episcopal church in some fashion.

Academia. Architecture. Cityscape. Events. Landscape. Organizations. Religion (missionaries). Transportation.

PEOPLE: Bishops and missionaries of the Episcopal church. Social life and customs, domestic activities, and studio portraits. Ethnic groups are predominantly Caucasian, with substantial numbers of Amerind, Black, Chinese, Hispanic, Japanese, and Liberian persons.

PHOTOGRAPHERS: John Chapman. Hudson Stuck.

RECORD GROUPS:

A28.1 CHAPMAN (Reverend JOHN W.) COLLECTION. Missionary in Alaska from 1887 to 1930. Amateur views of mission at Anvik AK, including landscapes and Eskimos. 300 lantern slides, most hand-colored. 1895 to 1920s.

A28.2 DOMESTIC AND FOREIGN MISSION SOCIETY ARCHIVES. Received in three large groups covering, with some overlap, the periods 1900 to 1940, 1940 to 1960, and the 1960s. The archives receives additions more frequently now. The photographic materials in these archives were generated largely by missionaries and sent back to the society offices. The photographs depict in general something of the people and land in which they were stationed and more specifically the mission activities at churches, schools, and hospitals.

A28.2.1 D.F.M.S. I. Locations and subjects:

Alaska, including Anvik, Christ Church mission and school, Allakaket, Fairbanks, Fort Yukon, Ketchikan, Nenana, Point Hope, Sitka, Tanan. 400 photographs. Ca. 1925.

China, including ancient Chinese temples, gates, and other structures; schools; children, including orphans, Boy Scouts, and students; agriculture; famine and relief; soldiers of the revolutionary army; Chinese clergy; and various Anglican conventions and bishops in China. Locales include Anking (Saint James Hospital, Cathedral of the Holy Savior and School, Grace Church and School, Saint Agnes School), Changsha (Trinity Girls School), Changshu, Fukai (Yamen Refugee Camp), Hankow (Saint Paul's Cathedral, Saint Louis School), Kuling province (American School), Nanching (Saint Matthew's Church and School), Wuchang (Saint Michael's Church, Saint Savior's Church, Church General Hospital, Boone College, Saint Hilda's School), Shanghai (Saint Paul's Church, Saint John's Pro Cathedral, Saint Luke's Hospital, Saint Elizabeth's Hospital, Saint John's University—faculty, —students, Saint Mary's Hall, Saint Mary's Orphanage), Soochow, Tsingpoo (Church of the Transfiguration), Wusih (views, Holy Cross Church, Saint Andrew's Hospital), Yangchow (views, Emmanuel Church, Saint Faith's School). 5 boxes (2,000 photographs, most prints and some negatives). 1891 to 1930s, most 1905 to 1925.

Cuba, including Bacuramo, Bolondron (San Pablo Church), Céspedes, Camaguey (Church of the Holy Apostles), Cienfuegas, Guantánamo and Guantánamo Bay (US military ships, All Saints Church and School), Havana (Holy Trinity Cathedral and Jesú del Monte Mission), La Gloria (Holy Trinity Mission), Santiago, and Woodin. 1 box (350 photographs). 1916 to 1939.

Dominican Republic and Haiti, including San Pedro de Macoris (Saint Stephen's Church), Santo Domingo (Epiphany Church and School), Archaie (Saint Thomas Church), and Port au Prince. 325 photographs. 1916 to 1932.

Honolulu, including Saint Andrew's Cathedral and Priory, Iolani School, Saint Mary's Mission; Kaphulu and Saint Mark's missions. 200 photographs. 1912 to 1932.

Japan, including Buddhists, workers, city views, economic and social customs; locales include Tokyo (earthquake—1923, Bishop Motoda, Bishop J. De Wolf Perry, Saint Luke's Hospital, Saint Timothy's Church, True Light Church; North Tokyo; Ikebukuro, Saint Paul's University), Kyoto (Saint Agnes Mission, Church of Resurrection), Osaka (typhoon—1934), Kanazawa, Koriyama, Kusatsu, Nara, Obama, and Takaidomura (Saint Margaret's School). 4 boxes (1,625 photographs). 1900 to 1930s.

Liberia, including Cape Mount. 175 photographs. 1900 to 1930.

Mexico, including Guadalajara (Saint Andrew's Industrial School), Mexico City (Hooker School), and San Pedro Martir. 400 photographs. 1906 to 1937.

Near East, including Jerusalem (Saint George's Cathedral, Saint James' Monastery), and Mosul. 100 photographs. 1920s to 1930s.

Panama Canal Zone, including part of Colombia, Bella Vista, Colón (Christ Church), and Las Sabanas. 100 photographs. 1907 to 1920s.

Philippine Islands, including Besao, Guam, Manila (Saint Luke's Church and Hospital), Sagada (Saint Mary the Virgin Mission), and Zamboanga (Moro Mission). 325 photographs. 1900 to 1930s.

Puerto Rico, including hurricane—1928, San Juan, Barahona, El Coto de Manati (Church of Resurrection and the New World School), Mayaguez (Saint Andrew's Church and School), and Ponce (Saint Luke's Hospital). 325 photographs. 1900 to 1930s.

Southern Brazil, including Livramento (Church of Nazarene) Pelotas, Porto Alegre (Trinity Church, Church of Ascension, Southern Cross School), and Rio Grande do Sul. 225 photographs. 1900s to 1930s.

US, including domestic work of the D.F.M.S., grouped by diocese and then by population served, including foreign born, Indian, Negro, and white; services provided include health care and education for the poor. Extensive coverage of the nation with concentration on Boise ID, Nixon NV (Amerind), Raleigh NC, Ethete WY (Saint Michael's Mission, Arapahoe), Wind River WY (Shoshoni), La Grange GA, Arizona, Berkeley CA (School for Christian Service), Colorado, eastern Oregon, Pan American Conference in Evanston IL, and the General Convention of 1934. 925 photographs. 1900 to 1930.

Virgin Islands, including Fredericksted. 150 photographs. 1900s to 1930s.

A28.2.2 D.F.M.S. II. Continuation of the first series, with similar subjects in addition to General Conventions held in 1938, 1955, 1958, and 1961. Missions (to the Amerind and in the locales Alaska, Brazil, China, Colombia, Costa Rica, Cuba, Dominican Republic, El Salvador, Guatemala, Haiti, Hawaii, Honduras, Japan, Liberia, Mexico, Nicaragua, Okinawa, Panama Canal Zone, Philippines, Puerto Rico, Taiwan, and the Virgin Islands), dioceses in the US, Church of England (including Great Britain, Africa, Australia, Far East, India, Near East, South America, West Indies, Anglican church in Canada, and the Church in Wales); subject files include art, bishops, chaplains, armed forces, child life, Christian education, Christian social relations, churches in Europe, conventions and conferences, contests, Eisenhower inauguration, Girls' Friendly Society, Inside the Church, Institute of Pastoral Care, laymen's training program, National Council [= Executive Council] buildings, organizations and staff, offerings and funds, posters, publication covers, radio, Red Cross, relief and rehabilitation, transportation and industries, universities, seminaries, colleges and schools, women's auxiliaries. 64 boxes (25,600 photographs). 1940 to 1960.

A28.2.3 D.F.M.S. III. Continuation of the first two series with similar subjects; locales include China (missions, schools, and WW II destruction and refugees; Anking—Saint James' Church and Hospital; Hankow; Hong Kong; Shanghai); Japan (Tokyo, WW II aftermath); Philippines; US (industries, Virginia—Christ Church, western North Carolina; consecration of various bishops and portraits of bishops and clergy; presidents Truman, Eisenhower, and Franklin D. Roosevelt; Blacks in the South; promotions, public relations, and church photo contests; General Conventions 1922 to 1967; US armed forces); and Trieste (refugee camps). 28 boxes (11,200 photographs). 1920s to 1960s, most 1940s and 1960s.

[End of Domestic and Foreign Missionary Society archives.]

A28.3 PECUSA EXECUTIVE COUNCIL COMMUNICATIONS OFFICE ARCHIVES. Organizational branch of the church producing religious publications for populations in and outside the church. Subjects include recording sessions of the serial radio programs "The Search" and "Viewpoint"; extensive coverage of installation of and studio portraits of bishops Lane Wickham Barton, Alexander Hugo Blankenship, Hugo Heber, John Elbridge Hines, Arthur Carl Lichtenberger, Lyman Cunningham Ogilby, Ephraín Salinas y Velasco, and Henry Knox Sherrill, with some coverage of other members of the Episcopal clergy; General Conventions, overseas districts, camps and conferences, "Church Serving in the World," geographic, "World in Which We Live," and photographic displays. 11 boxes (8,620 photographs), including 35mm transparencies, photo prints, and safety negatives. 1960s to 1970s.

Albums in the archives:

A28.4 [*Carte portrait album.*] Predominantly portraits of male Episcopal religious and British intellectual figures. 16 albumen cartes. 1860s.

A28.5 [*Carte portrait album.*] Christ Church (Philadelphia PA) and studio portraits of male Episcopal clergy by various Philadelphia and New York photographers; includes a series published by F. Gutekunst. 13 albumen cartes. 1880s.

A28.6 *Friends and classmates of Reverend Charles E. Phelps.* Studio portraits and some art reproductions of various male religious figures by various northeastern US studio photographers. 73 albumen cartes. 1875 to 1885.

A28.7 Gurney, J., and Sons, photog. *The House of Bishops of the Protestant Episcopal Church of the United States from life during the Triennial Convention.* New York: T. Porter Shaw, 1862. 24 albumen cartes with printed legends. AEC# 72.111.

A28.8 *House of Bishops at General Convention, Cleveland.* Studio portraits of all but one bishop of the church, "secured by Silas Wood of Newport, Kentucky." 1 whole-plate and 25 half-plate daguerreotypes, later mounted in an album. 1850.

A28.9 [*Photographs presented to J.C.B. by Rev. Mr. and Mrs. G. W. Anderson.*] Studio portraits of male Episcopal clergy, intellectual figures, prominent persons, and travel views by various European photographers, including John Watkins (London). 45 albumen cartes. Ca. 1875.

Austin History Center (A32)

Austin Public Library
810 Guadalupe
P.O. Box 2287
Austin, Texas 78768-2287

512-473-4280. Contact: Photographic Manager.

PURPOSE: A research archives and library with an exhibit space specializing in local history and collecting books and journals, manuscripts, artworks, artifacts, audio and video tapes, maps, architectural drawings, and photographs.

HOURS: Monday through Thursday, 9:00-8:45; Friday and Saturday, 9:00-5:45; Sunday 12:00-5:45. Closed major holidays.

ASSISTANCE: Experienced, professional staff. Written and phone inquiries accepted. Electrostatic copies available. Photoduplications must be ordered through the center.

PUBLICATION: No publication fee. Collection credit and collection identification required. Free copy of publication to center. Third-party permission needed on a few items.

FINDING AIDS: Printed index by LC subject heading, decade, personal and proper name, and location. Computerized database being developed with same access points plus photographers and process. Artificial collections stored by subject; other photographs stored by record group.

BIBLIOGRAPHY:

Austin seen: A juried photography exhibit April 6-June 10, 1984. Austin: Waterloo Press, 1984. Exhibition catalog.

Bateman, Audray, ed. *An Austin album.* Austin: Encino Press, 1978.

Caro, Robert A. *The path to power.* New York: Alfred A. Knopf, 1982.

Clark, Sara. *The capitols of Texas: A visual history.* Austin: Encino Press, 1975.

Daniel, Jean Houston, Price Daniel, and Dorothy Blodgett. *The Texas Governor's Mansion.* Austin: Whitley Company, 1984.

Farenthold, Lisa, and Sara Rider. *Admissions: The extraordinary history of Brackenridge Hospital.* Austin: City of Austin, 1984.

The Governor's Mansion of Texas: A historic tour. Austin: Friends of the Governor's Mansion, 1985.

Hart, Katherine. *Austin and Travis County: A pictorial history, 1839-1939.* Austin: Encino Press, 1975.

Humphrey, David C.; picture research by Allison Beck. *Austin: An illustrated album.* Northridge CA: Windsor Publications, 1985.

Manry, Joe Edgar. *Curtain call: The history of the theater in Austin, Texas, 1839-1905.* Austin: Waterloo Press, 1985.

One hundred years of education: The centennial history of Austin High School. Austin: Stephen F. Austin High School 1980.

Waterloo scrapbook. Austin: Friends of the Austin Public Library, 1968 and following.

Welch, June Rayfield. *The Texas governor.* Dallas: G.L.A. Press, 1977.

Willoughby, Larry. *Austin: A historical portrait.* Norfolk and Virginia Beach VA: Donning Company, 1980.

SCOPE: More than 500,000 vintage and 50,000 copy photographs, including 300 stereographs, 500 panoramic prints, glass lantern slides, 9,000 film transparencies, 640 motion pictures, 1,000 videotapes, and a small collection of photographic equipment and ephemera. Some photographs have supporting manuscripts or other related archival materials. Many negatives have modern prints.

Type of photo	Pre-1880	1880-1899	1900-1919	1920-1939	1940-1959	1960-1986
D/A/T-types	300					
Glass negs	1,000	2,000	1,500			
Film negs	13,000	17,000	24,000	15,000	207,000	193,000
Vintage prints	11,000	18,000	18,000	17,000	20,000	26,000
Copy images	3,000	3,000	3,000	3,000	3,000	2,500
Photo albums	75	100	75	25	25	

GEOGRAPHIC: The center collects material pertinent to Travis County; there is a small amount of material from surrounding counties. Occasionally, geographic regions from outside the area appear as the result of being collected by a Travis County resident when traveling.

Travis County: Austin. Barton Creek. Bull Creek. Colorado River. Govalle. Lake Austin. Lake

McDonald. Lake Travis. Lakeway. Manor. Oak Hill. Nameless. Pflugerville. Shoal Creek. Town Lake. Waller Creek.

Texas: Bastrop, Blanco, Burnet, Caldwell, Hays, and Williamson counties. Round Rock.

SUBJECTS: Extensive coverage of the economic and social development of the community and news events in the community. Subject headings (many overlapping) used in the collection:

Aeronautics (airlines, airplanes). Agriculture. Amusements. Animals. Art (art reproduction, exhibitions). [Austin] city council. [Austin] city hall. [Austin] fire department. [Austin] municipal buildings. [Austin] police department. [Austin] post office. [Austin] public utilities. Automobiles (parking, racing, service stations). Banks. Baseball. Birds. Boats. Book (booksellers). Bridges. Buildings. Business. Carriages and carts. Cattle. Celebrations. Cemeteries. Children. Christmas. Churches (by denomination). Circus. Creeks. Cycling (motor and bicycling). Dam breaks. Dancing. Department stores. Fires. Fishing. Floods. Flowers. Food. Football. Fountains. Freemasons. Gardens. Golf. Groceries. Highways. Hike and bike trails. Hitching posts. Holidays. Horses. Hospitals. Hotels and taverns. Houses. Log cabins. Lumberyards. Mills. Monuments. Motels. Motion picture theaters. Motorbuses. Museums. Music. Nursing. Parades. Parks. Politics and government (Austin, Travis County, Texas). Prisons. Private schools. Protests and demonstrations. Public schools. Public welfare. Public works. Railroads. Rain. Refuse and disposal. Restaurants. Roads. Rural schools. Saengerrunde. Sailing. Saloons. Sewer disposal. Shopping centers. Slavery. Social life and customs. Sports. Steamboats. Streetlights. Street parking. Street railroad. Street vendors. Streets. Swimming. Theater. Traffic (accidents, signs). [Travis County] courthouse. Transportation. US Army. US Centennial. University of Texas at Austin (athletics, buildings, grounds, social life and customs, students). Veterans. Views (aerial). Water and Wastewater Department. Weather. Women. WW I. WW II.

Alamo Hotel. AquaFest. Austin Braves [baseball team]. Austin High School. Austin Hotel. Austin Pioneers [baseball team]. Austin Dam. Austin Public Library. Barton Springs Pool. Bergstrom AFB. Boy Scouts of America. Brackenridge Hospital. Buchanan Dam. Calcasieu Lumber Company. Camp Mabry. Capitol (1853, 1881, 1884). Civil War. Driskill Hotel. Elisabet Ney Museum. French Legation. General Land Office building. Governor's Mansion. Juneteenth. Laguna Gloria Museum. Lower Colorado River Authority. Mansfield Dam. Millett Opera House. Robert Mueller Municipal Airport. Saint David's Hospital. Saint Edward's University. Seton Hospital. Texas Governor's Mansion. Texas School for the Deaf. Texas State Hospital. Texas Supreme Court. Treaty Oak. University of Texas at Austin.

PEOPLE: Many local residents; state, county, and local politicians and employees. Although predominantly Caucasian, the center holds some material relating to Blacks (including ex-slaves), Kiowa Amerinds, German, Hispanic, and Swedish ethnicities. Substantial coverage of the families and descendents of (individuals are filed under the names of the first family member to come to Austin):

Charles H. Alff. James V. Allred. John Hy Armstrong. Robert Stafford Bacon. George Begg. Oscar Richard Bertram. Jacob Bickler. Walter Bacon Black. John Bremond. Dolph Briscoe. Vander Clyde Broadway. Brooks family. John Houghton Brownlee. Albert Sidney Burleson. Michael Butler. Roy Anderson Butler. William Thomas Caswell. Price Daniel. John Know Donnan. William Sherman Drake. Alfred Ellison. James Edward "Pa" and Miriam A. "Ma" Ferguson. Fischer family. Goeth family. Graham family. Collier Read Grandbury. Gross family. Harrison family. James Pickney Hart. Henry Louis Hilgartner. William Hickman Hill. Henry

Hirschfeld. James Stephen Hogg. Samuel Houston. Otto Koock. Hermann Lungkwitz. Frank Wilkins McBee. Henry Maerk. Peter Mansbendel. Robert Thomas Miller. Daniel J. Moody. Robert Mueller. Joseph Nagle. Pat Morris Neff. Elisabet Ney. W. Lee O'Daniel. Michael Paggi. Elisha Marshall Pease. Edgar Howard Perry. William Sydney Porter. John Robb Reed. John William Robbins. Allan Shivers. Edward Tips. William Von Rosenberg. Thomas Benton Wheeler. Michael Ziller.

PHOTOGRAPHERS: Many local commercial and studio photographers as well as many unidentified snapshot and amateur photographers. See Record Groups for additional photographers.

Nicholas Ankenman. Walter Barnes. George H. Berner. Amy Blakemore. Boone Photo Company. Reagan Bradshaw. Christianson-Leberman Studios. J. P. Crowe. Keith Dannemiller. Brad Doherty. Jim Dougherty. Neal Douglass.* The Elliotts (Jane and Martyn). Mike Flahive. Barbara Hagen. Harper and Company. Samuel B. Hill.* Hamilton Biscoe Hillyer. Thomas Jensen. E. P. Jordan.* William O. Journeay. Luck Brothers. Bill Malone. Douglas Manger. Harvey R. Marks. Van Redin. Jack Rehm. George Schuwirth. Les Simon. Lawrence Kelley Smoot. Jack Tisdale. George F. Townsend. University Studio (Ava Crofford). Nolan Williamson.

*See Record Groups.

RECORD GROUPS: The House and Building File (5,000 photographs), the Austin File (general subjects, 15,000 photographs), and the Biography File (12,000 photographs) are artificial collections; other record groups listed below are maintained as discrete collections. Many archival collections of manuscripts contain photographs not represented here.

A32.1 *AUSTIN AMERICAN-STATESMAN* PHOTO MORGUE. Journalistic coverage of local events by staff photographers. 300,000—35mm negatives; arranged by date; limited access. 1958 to 1975.

A32.2 *AUSTIN CITIZEN* PHOTO COLLECTION. Journalistic coverage of local people and events by staff photographers. 5,000—35mm negatives with contact sheets, and 2,000 silver gelatin prints; arranged by subject. 1973 to 1981.

A32.3 AUSTIN PARKS AND RECREATION DEPARTMENT COLLECTION. Institutional picture archive of this city agency representing facilities, activities, staff, and officials photographed by an unidentified staff photographer. 6,000 silver gelatin prints and 3,600 negatives; arranged by subject. 1928 to 1975.

A32.4 AUSTIN PUBLIC INFORMATION OFFICE COLLECTION. City facilities, public works, events, and officials by an unidentified staff photographer. 5,000 prints, 15,000 negatives; arranged by department's original subject headings. 1953 to 1979. Limited access.

A32.5 "AUSTIN SEEN" COLLECTION. A 1984 exhibition juried by Russell Lee, Roy Flukinger, and Stanley Farrar showing work by 58 local, amateur and professional photographers. Artistic and documentary interpretation of contemporary life in Austin. 114 exhibition prints, 300 additional submitted prints; most silver gelatin, some color. 1960s to 1984, most ca. 1984. See Bibliography.

A32.6 BRACKENRIDGE HOSPITAL COLLECTION. Facilities, programs, and officials; centennial celebration; and many images from the institution's archives. Staff and city photographers.

4,500 original negatives with 2,000 modern prints, 6,500 contact sheets, and 2,000 vintage silver gelatin prints. See Bibliography—Farenthold.

A32.7 CHAMBER OF COMMERCE COLLECTION. Commercial cityscapes of Austin buildings and street scenes, parks, roads, and portraits of community leaders. 450 lantern slides. 1920s.

A32.8 COLSON (J. B.) WEST CAMPUS NEIGHBORHOOD DOCUMENTARY PROJECT COLLECTION. Social life and customs of the residential and business area west of the University of Texas at Austin campus, including fraternities, businesses, and residents. Photographed by a documentary photography class in the university's journalism department under Professor Colson's direction, including Bill Boulton, Gail Chavez, Terry Gregston, Ronald Cortes, Karen Luzius, Leslie Tallant, Jim Trotman, and Tim Wentworth. 372 prints, 65 contact sheets, 480 negatives, 15 manuscripts, and 16 printed items.

A32.9 CROWE (J. P.) COLLECTION. Commercial views of social events, business interiors, people, and street scenes in Austin photographed by Crowe. 659 vintage silver gelatin prints, 729 safety negatives. 1940s to 1950s.

A32.10 DOUGLASS (NEAL) COLLECTION. Austin studio and commercial photographer, news photographer for the *Austin American-Statesman*, and photographer for the Texas legislature. 20,000 vintage silver gelatin prints; 3,000 nitrate and 40,000 safety negatives; limited access. 1940s to 1960s.

A32.11 ELLISON-CHALBERG ARCHIVES. Ellison Studios archives (operated under direction of Jordan, Jordan-Ellison, Ellison, and now by Chalberg, from whom this collection was acquired). Commercial views of architecture, cityscapes, news, wedding, and studio portraiture by E. P. Jordan, Alfred Ellison, and unidentified photographers. 9,000 copy, 8,000 vintage, and 1,000 modern prints; 11,000 glass, nitrate, and safety negatives. 1870s to 1960s.

A32.12 GETHSEMANE COLLECTION. Donated by the Gethsemane Lutheran Church. Views in Austin. 53 mounted albumen prints. Mid-1860s.

A32.13 GOODMAN (MARK; b. 1946) WEST CAMPUS DOCUMENTARY PROJECT II COLLECTION. Western portion of the University of Texas at Austin campus photographed by a documentary photography class in the university's art department under Goodman's direction; photographers include Amy Blakemore, David Wharton, and Barbara Hagen. 108 color and silver gelatin prints. 1984.

A32.14 Hill, Samuel B., photog. *Views of Texas*. Austin: S. B. Hill, [ca. 1887.]. Mostly Austin cityscapes, homes and commercial buildings, street scenes; some landscape, including Fort Stockton Springs. 2 variant volumes, each with 22 albumen prints.

A32.15 JENSEN-ELLIOTT COLLECTION. Predominantly studio portraiture from two separate studios. 10,000 negatives and 30,000 photo prints. 1900 to 1940s. Limited access.

A32.16 JONES (Mrs. HUBERT) COLLECTION. Social life and customs by an unidentified photographer. 300—5x7 glass negatives with modern prints; some stereographs. Ca. 1890s.

A32.17 LONG (WALTER; 1886-1973) COLLECTION. Manager of the Austin Chamber of Commerce and the city's historian. Economic and social development of the city. 8,000 photo graphs, many copy prints, most silver gelatin prints and negatives, a few tintypes and daguerreotypes. 1850s to 1960s.

A32.18 LOWCOCK (FORD; b. 1957) PORTFOLIO. *Barton Creek portfolio.* [Austin: 1984.] Limited edition portfolio of landscapes and details of the natural environment along Barton Creek. 8 color dye-transfer prints.

A32.19 MALONE (BILL) COLLECTION. Austin commercial photographer and official photographer for the Texas legislature. Studio portraiture, commercial photography, and documents of state functions. 30,000 negatives; Malone's index. 1945 and 1981.

A32.20 SOIL SURVEY FIELD SHEETS. Aerial photographs of Travis County (no city views), many with soil types indicated in ink. 3,000 photographs. August to November 1940.

A32.21 SYKES (THOMAS J.) COLLECTION. Street scenes along Sixth Street in Austin. 18 silver gelatin prints. 1974.

A32.22 "WATERWORKS 1985" COLLECTION. An aquadance choreographed by Dee McCandless and Gene Menger at Barton Springs Pool, photographed by Scott Van Osdol and Doug Manger. 23 silver gelatin prints. 1985.

Catholic Archives of Texas (A34)

1600 Congress Avenue
P.O. Box 13327
Austin, Texas 78711

512-476-4888. Contact: Archivist.

PURPOSE: A repository collecting artworks, manuscripts, artifacts, books and journals, and photographs pertinent to the history and heritage of the Roman Catholic church in Texas. Maintains a working relationship with the Texas Catholic Historical Society.

HOURS: Weekdays, 8:30-5:30. Closed major, state, federal, and religious holidays. Appointments highly recommended.

ASSISTANCE: Professional staff. Written and phone inquiries accepted for limited research; fee charged for lengthy inquiries. Electrostatic copies available. Patron may make photoduplications or order them through the archives.

PUBLICATION: No publication fee. Collection credit required.

FINDING AIDS: Card index, inventory, and descriptive, itemized listing of photographs; access by general subject, geographic location, and personal name. Photographs arranged by subject.

SCOPE: 5,000 photographs; most vintage prints and some stereographs, albums, film transparencies, and motion pictures. Ca. 1863 to present.

Type of photo	Pre-1880	1880-1899	1900-1919	1920-1939	1940-1959	1960-1986
Vintage prints	5	50	100	1,000	1,500	2,000
Copy prints		200	200			
Photo albums			10	10	10	10

GEOGRAPHIC: Predominantly Texas; some snapshot travel views from France, Germany, Italy, Mexico, and Vatican City.

SUBJECTS: Documentation of Catholic history and heritage in Texas.

Academia. Architecture (religious). Documents. Events (ceremonies, parades, parties). Monuments/memorials. Organizations (fraternal). Religion (congregations, services). Services (medical).

Catholic religious congregations and organizations, including the Dominican Sisters, Knights of Columbus, and Sisters of Charity.

PEOPLE: Predominantly Catholic clergy and religious who served in Texas, some coverage of laity, especially lay fraternal organizations.

PHOTOGRAPHERS: Mary M. Clayton.

RECORD GROUPS: Many photographs are associated with manuscript collections, although the archive maintains an artificial collection of photographs received in small quantities without associated materials. The Records of the Knights of Columbus Historical Commission contains the most substantial number of photographs; other record groups with photographs include the Bishops of Texas collection, Clergy files, Parish files, and Religious Congregations files.

Lyndon Baines Johnson Presidential Library (A42)

2313 Red River
Austin, Texas 78705

512-482-5137. Contact: Audiovisual Archives.

PURPOSE: A research library and exhibiting museum specializing in materials related to President Lyndon Baines Johnson (1908-1973), his administration (1963-1969) and political career (1937-1969), his associates, and his family. The library holds extensive government records, manuscripts, books and journals, audio and video recordings, artworks, artifacts, and photographs. A division of the National Archives and Records Administration.

HOURS: Exhibition area—daily except Christmas, 9:00-5:00. Audiovisual Archives—weekdays, 9:00-5:00 during the winter, 8:30-4:30 during the summer. Reading Room—same hours and Saturday, by appointment 9:00-1:00. Audiovisual Archives and Reading Room are closed federal holidays.

ASSISTANCE: Professional, experienced, specialized staff. Written and phone inquiries accepted. Electrostatic copies available. Photoduplications must be ordered through the Audiovisual Archives.

PUBLICATION: No publication fee. Third-party permission required on a few photographs (especially the Pre-Presidential collection).

FINDING AIDS: Visual card index for White House collection and card index for other images; access by date, proper name, subject, geographic location.

BIBLIOGRAPHY:
Johnson, Lady Bird. *A White House diary.* New York: Holt, Rinehart, and Winston, 1970.
Johnson, Lyndon Baines. *The vantage point.* New York: Holt, Rinehart, and Winston, 1971.

SCOPE: More than 600,000 photographs: most 35mm color and black-and-white negatives with contact prints; some slides and vintage prints; 825,000 feet of motion picture stock. Ca. 1908 to present; most from Johnson's administration, 1963 to 1969.

GEOGRAPHIC: Many locations visited by President Johnson; images show little of the landscape or country, but concentrate on crowds greeting the President and those leaders with whom he met.

Australia. Canada. Costa Rica. El Salvador. Germany. Guam. Guatemala. Honduras. India. Italy. Korea. Malaysia. Mexico. New Zealand. Nicaragua. Pakistan. Philippines. Surinam. Thailand. Uruguay. Vietnam.

Virtually all of the United States is covered, with substantial coverage of Texas (the President's home state).

Austin. Beaumont. Dallas. El Paso. Floresville. Fredericksburg. Houston. Johnson City and the LBJ Ranch. Killeen. Mount Pleasant. San Antonio. San Marcos. Stonewall. Waco.

SUBJECTS: All subjects are related to the President and his tenure in office, especially the official and ceremonial activities of the President and First Lady; for example "church attendence" relates to the President's own church attendence, not church attendence in general. There is virtually no coverage of the culture or events not directly connected with the President. Subject headings used in the archive:

Aircraft (especially Air Force One interiors). Ambassadors. Animals (pets, livestock; Yuki). Armed Forces (military reviews, personnel). Awards and decorations (Congressional Medal of Honor winners). Bill and treaty signing. Boating (on board the *Sequoia*). Business Council and groups. Cabinet meetings. Children. Church attendance. Congressional leadership. Congressional meetings. Crowds. Dancing. Entertainment. Ethnic groups (especially Black). Family portraits. Farm leaders. Flowers. Funerals. Governors. Handicapped. Historical site (Boyhood home). Inauguration. LBJ candid studies. Joint Chiefs of Staff. Labor leaders and groups. Luncheons, weekly. National Security Council. Oaths of Office. Prayer breakfast. Press. Press conferences. Press walks. Secret Service. Senior citizens. Speaking. Telephone [LBJ on the]. Television [LBJ viewing]. Travel (domestic, foreign). Visitors, foreign. Weddings (Luci Baines Johnson to Pat Nugent; Lynda Byrd Johnson to Charles Robb). White House.

PEOPLE: Many important foreign heads of state and US politicians; White House staff, cabinet members, and governmental agency heads; business and civil rights leaders; Johnson family. Most are in groups. Almost all are meeting with the President, frequently in the Oval Office. Many entries are represented by several photographs at a single event. Thousands of individuals appear with the President in single "handshake" poses.

Extensive coverage of: Joseph Califano. George Christian. Secretary Henry Fowler. Vice President Hubert and Muriel Humphrey. Johnson family: Lady Byrd Johnson, with the President, on her own official and ceremonial visits around the country and world, her beautification campaign; Luci Baines Johnson, her husband Patrick Nugent, and their child; Lynda Byrd Johnson, her husband Charles Robb, and their child; Sam Houston Johnson. Secretary Robert MacNamara.

Major entries (family members frequently appear): Tyler and Bess Abell. General Creighton Abrams. Dean Acheson. Gardner Ackley. King Adulyadej Bhumibol. Senator George Aiken. US Rep. Carl Albert. Clifford Alexander. Senator Clinton Anderson. US Rep. Leslie Arends.

Ambassador George Ball. Donald Barns. Undersecretary Joe Barr. Francis Bator. David Bell. Justice Eugene Black. US Rep. Hale Boggs. Phyliss Bonanno. President Bourguiba Babib. US Rep. Frank T. Bow. Secretary Alan Boyd. Chancellor Willy Brandt. US Rep. Jack Brooks. Governor Farris Bryant. Ralphe Bunche. McGeorge Bundy. Secretary William Bundy. Ambassador Ellsworth Bunker. Horace Busby. Senator Robert Byrd.

Liz Carpenter. Doug Cater. Secretary Anthony J. Celebreeze. General Leonard Chapman. Attorney General Ramsey Clark. Justice Tom Clark. Secretary Clark Clifford. General Chester V. Clifton. Secretary Wilbur Cohen. Colonel J. B. Comny. Secretary John Connor. Colonel James Cross.

Mayor Richard Daley. Price Daniel. Captain William Douglas Davidson. Ambassador Sir Patrick Dean. Undersecretary Frederick Deming. Ambassador Alexsy Dobrinin. Justice William O. Douglas. Secretary Douglas Dillon. Senator Everett Dirksen. William Driver. Angier Biddle Duke. James Dussenberry.

Prime Minister Mohamed Egal. Dwight Eisenhower. Chancellor Ludwig Erhard. Prime Minister Eshkol. Marie Fehmer. Secretary Robert Fleming. US Rep. Gerald Ford. Justice Abe Fortas. Secretary Orville Freeman. Secretary Edward Fried. Senator J. W. Fulbright. Betty Furness.

Prime Minister Indira Gandhi. Secretary John Gardner. William Gaud. Ambassador Arthur Goldberg. Ernest Goldstein. Prime Minister John Gorton. Reverend Billy Graham. General Wallace Greene. Ambassador John Gronouski.

Lloyd Hand. Robert Hardesty. Ambassador Averell Harriman. Senator Carl Hayden. Richard Helms. President Fidel Sanches Hernandez. Senator Bourke B. Hicklenlooper. Clint Hill. Senator Lister Hill. Prime Minister Harold Holt. Prime Minister Keith Holyoake. J. Edgar Hoover. Bob Hope. Dr. Donald Hornig. Governor Richard Hughes. King Hussein.

Prime Minister Il-Kuong Chung. Senator Daniel Inouye. Senator Henry Jackson. Jake Jacobsen. Lem Johns. Harold Johnson. Tom Johnson. James Jones. William Jordan.

Undersecretary Nicholas Katzenbach. Senator Edward Kennedy. Senator Robert Kennedy. President Ayub Khan. Chancellor Kurt Kiesinger. Martin Luther King Jr. Robert Kintner. Prime Minister Kittikachorn Thanom. Jerry Kivett. Chancellor Joseph Klaus. Robert Komer. Chairman Alexsy Kosygin. Prime Minister Jens Otto Krag. Arthur Krim. Senator Thomas Kuchel. Prime Minister Nguyen Cao Ky.

Mrs. Mary Lasker. Larry Levinson. Mayor John V. Lindsay. Peter Lisagor. Ambassador Henry Cabot Lodge. Senator Russell Long.

Prime Minister Diosado Macapagal. Senator Eugene McCarthy. Senator John McConnell. US Rep. John McCormack. Harry McPherson. John Macy. Senator Warren Magnuson. Charles Maguire. US Rep. George Mahon. Mike Manatos. Senator Mike Mansfield. President Ferdinand Marcos. Leonard Marks. Justice Thurgood Marshall. William McChesney Martin. George Meaney. Harry Middleton. US Rep. Wilbur Mills. Admiral Thomas H. Moorer. Senator Wayne Morse. Bill Moyers. Charles Murphy. Senator Edmund Muskie.

Ambassador B. K. Nehru. Undersecretary Paul Nitze. President-Elect Richard Nixon. Lawrence O'Brien. Yoichi Okamoto. Arthur Okun. Covey Oliver. President Diaz Ordaz.

Shah Mohammed Reza Pahlavi. Senator John Pastore. US Rep. Wright Patman. Prime Minister Lester Pearson. DeVier Pierson. Pope Paul VI. Admiral William Raborn. Prime Minister Tunku Abdul Rahman. Senator Jennings Randolph. Dan Rather. George Reedy. Secretary Stanley Resor. Walter Reuther. US Rep. Mendel Rivers. Juanita Roberts. Colonel Hugh Robinson. Dr. John Roche. Governor Nelson Rockefeller. Eugene Rostow. Walt Rostow. Secretary Dean Rusk. Senator Richard Russell.

Pierre Salinger. Barefoot Sanders. President Giuseppe Saragat. Prime Minister Eisaku Sato. Ray Scherer. Charles Schultze. Governor William Scranton. Dr. Glenn T. Seaborg. Emperor Haile Selassie. Guillermo Sevilla-Secasa. Admiral Ulysses S. Sharp. President Zalman Shazar. Ambassador Sargeant Shriver. Hugh Sidey. Joseph Sisco. Queen Sirikit Thail. Senator George Smathers. Bromley Smith. Secretary C. R. Smith. Howard K. Smith. Merriman Smith. Senator John Sparkman. Irvine Sprague. Major General Ben Sternberger. Adlai Stevenson. Reverned Leon Sullivan. President Cevdet Sunay. James Symington.

Robert Taylor. Larry Temple. President Nguyen Van Thieu. Ambassador Llewellyn Thompson. Secretary Alexander Trowbridge. Harry S. Truman. President William Tubman. Secretary Stewart Udall. U Thant. Jack Valenti. Cyrus Vance.

Justice Earl Warren. Mayor Walter Washington. Marvin Watson. General Earl Weaver. Secretary Robert Weaver. General William C. Westmoreland. Roy Wilkins. Prime Minister Harold Wilson. Secretary Willard Wirtz. Robert Wood. Senator Ralph Yarborough. Whitney Young. Rufus Youngblood. US Rep. Clement Zablocki. Charles Zwick.

PHOTOGRAPHERS: *Austin American-Stateman* staff. Jack Kightlinger. Robert Knudsen. Art Kowert. Frank Muto. National Park Service. Y. R. Okamoto. Abbie Rowe. Cecil Stoughton. US Intelligence Agency staff. Frank Wolfe.

RECORD GROUPS:

A42.1 PRE-PRESIDENTIAL COLLECTION. Photos taken, commissioned, and collected by family and staff. 8,600 negatives and prints. Ca. 1900 to 1963.

A42.2 POST-PRESIDENTIAL COLLECTION. Photos furnished by individuals and organizations to Johnson after his retirement. 4 feet of prints. 1963 to ca. 1973.

A42.3 WHITE HOUSE COLLECTION. President, family, friends and associates in public and in private. 500,000 negatives with contact prints, some color; visual card index for approximately twenty percent of total take, photographs arranged by date, by personal name, and by subject headings. 1963 to 1969.

Private collections:

A42.4 INTERNATIONAL MACHINISTS COLLECTION. 1,000 prints. 1963 to 1969.

A42.5 KOWERT (ART) COLLECTION. LBJ Ranch activities and Fredericksburg during the pre-presidential years. 500 negatives.

A42.6 MUTO (FRANK) COLLECTION. Johnson in the US senate. 10,000 negatives. Ca. 1937 to 1960.

A42.7 WOOD (SAM) COLLECTION. Johnson's early years in and around Austin. 400 negatives.

Collections from government agencies:

A42.8 LBJ LIBRARY PHOTOGRAPHS COLLECTION. Johnson, family, library events and activities. 40,000 negatives.

A42.9 NATIONAL PARK SERVICE COLLECTION. Johnson around Johnson City. 127 prints.

A42.10 US INTELLIGENCE AGENCY COLLECTION. Johnson as vice-president overseas. 20,000 prints. 1960 to 1963.

Texas Department of Highways and Public Transportation (A54)

Thirty-fifth and Jackson streets
P.O. Box 5064
Austin, Texas 78763

512-465-7410. Contact: Audiovisual Manager.

PURPOSE: A working collection of file images generated for *Texas Highways* magazine and gathered through administration of the highway system.

HOURS: Weekdays, 8:00-11:45 and 1:00-4:45. Closed major and state holidays. Appointments recommended.

ASSISTANCE: Experienced, professional photographic staff. Picture service. Written and photo inquiries accepted. Electrostatic copies not available. Photoduplications must be ordered through the department.

PUBLICATION: No publication fee. Collection credit requested. Tear sheet requested. Department holds copyright on most materials.

FINDING AIDS: Filed by subject. Computerized database being developed.

BIBLIOGRAPHY:
Texas Highways. Austin: Texas Department of Highways and Public Transportation.

SCOPE: 20,000 original and 300 copy photographs, 5,000 safety negatives, 15,000 slides, and 200 color separations. 1960s to the present (an open collection).

GEOGRAPHIC: Extensive coverage of Texas, many representing tourist locales, state parks, and natural attractions in the state.

Amarillo. Austin. Beaumont. Corpus Christi. Dallas. El Paso. Fort Worth. Houston. Lubbock. San Antonio.

SUBJECTS: Photographs document Texas landmarks, portraying the state in a manner to help generate tourism and travel. Headings used in the collection vary slightly for 35mm and 4x5 transparencies:

Accommodations (food and entertainment, overnight, services). Agriculture (cattle, crops, domestic animals, horses, and cowboys; ranch and farm; windmills and water pumps). Aircraft. Art (Indian). Attractions. Beautification (Lady Bird Johnson, Beautify Texas Council). Caverns. Cities (colleges, downtown, feature). Department of Highways and Public Transportation (buildings, signs and markers, awards, personnel, events—highway week, —dedications, —hearings). Ethnic and life-style (Alabama-Coushatta Indians, Chinese, German, Latin, Lebanese, Mexican, Negroid, Tigua Indians). Events (ethnic, fairs/festivals/fiestas, folk art, food, historic/holidays, music, rodeos, theatrical). Ferries. Flora (autumn colors, bluebonnets, cactus and desert, gardens, trees and shrubs). Ghost towns. Highway construction and maintenance. Highway history (bridges). Highways (interstate, US, state, and farm to market). Historical (archaeology, buildings and homes, churches and missions, forts, museums, old West—cowboys and brands, sites). Industry (food, lumber, manufacturing, resources, shipping, shopping and retail). Landscapes (arranged by region). Mexico. Observatories. Outdoor land sports and hobbies (arts and crafts, backpacking/hiking, camping, flying and hang gliding, golf, horseback riding, hunting, jogging, mineral collecting, motor racing/bicycling, tennis). Parks and forests (national, state). Resorts and dude ranches. Safety rest areas. State Capitol complex. Tourist Bureaus. Transportation. Travel. Water and water sports (inland waters: boating, canoeing, fishing, rafting, swimming, water slide; coastal waters: beach, boating, fishing, shrimping, surfing). Weather. Wildlife (birds, deer, insects, mammals, pronghorn, refuge, reptiles). Zoos.

PEOPLE: People frequently appear in photographs as figures in a landscape, but there are few portraits. Some coverage of folklife festivals and folk traditions in communities.

Domestic and personal activities. Ethnic (Anglo, German, Hispanic).

PHOTOGRAPHERS: Staff photographers.

Willis Albarado. Geoff Appold. Bob Gates. Randy Green. Herman Kelly. Jack Lewis. Bob Parvin. Hugh Pillsbury. Griff Smith. Jack Suhrstedt. Greg White.

RECORD GROUPS: A single collection separated by format and filed by subject.

Texas Historical Commission (A60)

Commission Offices
Carrington House
1511 Colorado Street

512-463-6100. Contact: Executive Director.

National Register Program Office
Elrose Building
108 West Sixteenth Street

512-463-6094. Contact: Supervisor of Survey.

Office of the State Archeologist
Gethsemane Church Annex
105 West Sixteenth Street

512-463-6090. Contact: State Archeologist.

Texas Antiquities Committee
Gethsemane Church Annex
105 West Sixteenth Street

512-463-6098. Contact: Director.

Texas Main Street Center
Gethsemane Church
1510 North Congress Avenue

512-463-6092. Contact: Program Director.

Mailing address for all departments:
P.O. Box 12276-S
Austin, Texas 78711

PURPOSE: A state agency collecting photographs in the course of its operations; many of the commission's activities are related to surveying the state's historic resources, including buildings of historical or architectural signficance and archaeological sites of prehistoric (Amerind), Spanish colonial, and historic (postrevolutionary) civilizations in Texas. Other activities of the commission include the promotion of historic preservation and awareness through its publication, *The Medallion*, and the State Marker Program. Each department maintains a reference library of books and journals, maps, and other supporting materials.

HOURS: Weekdays, 8:00-5:00. Closed major and state holidays. Open to qualified researchers by appointment.

ASSISTANCE: Specialized staff. Written inquiries accepted on a limited basis. Electrostatic copies available. Photoduplications must be ordered through the agency.

PUBLICATION: No publication fee. Collection credit required. Free copy of publication to the agency. Third-party permission required on a few items.

FINDING AIDS: Card index and in-house inventory.

BIBLIOGRAPHY: A complete list of publications is available from the Commission.
Carlisle, John C. "Our Post Office Art." *Texas Highways* (July 1984, pp 30-35).
Fort Worth central business district: Tarrant County historic resources survey. Fort Worth: Historic Preservation Council for Tarrant County, 1983.
Goeldner, Paul, comp.; Lucy Pope Wheeler and S. Allen Chamber Jr., eds. *Texas catalog, Historic American Building Survey: A list of measured drawings, photographs and written documentation in the survey—1974.* San Antonio: Trinity University Press, [1975.]
Mansfield: Tarrant County historic resources survey. Fort Worth: Historic Preservation Council for Tarrant County, 1983.
The Medallion. Austin: Texas Historical Commission.
Steely, James Wright, comp. *A catalog of Texas properties in the National Register of Historic Places.* Austin: Texas Historical Commission, 1984. Available from the commission.

SCOPE: 500,000 photographs, including prints, negatives, and transparencies; some color material. 1940s to present, most 1966 to the present.

GEOGRAPHIC: Broad, extensive coverage of Texas. All counties are represented, including rural and urban areas. Many cities are represented, especially the larger communities of a county or locales of historic significance. Many archaeological sites are represented, including sites that have been inventoried before their destruction (for example, areas flooded by Amistad Reservoir). A small amount of material from Mexico in the files of the Office of the State Archeologist (v.i.). See Record Groups for specific headings. Extensive coverage of:

Austin. Dallas. El Paso. Fort Worth. Galveston. Houston. San Antonio.

SUBJECTS: The two major foci of the collection include historic structures and archaeological sites that document the varied cultural heritage of the state. Many of the buildings recorded have been demolished or significantly altered since these photographs were made. See Record Groups for specific sites.

Architecture (commercial, domestic interiors and exteriors; most are retrospective views). Artifacts (archeological—Amerind, —Spanish colonial, —historic [post-Revolutionary]; petroglyphs). Landscapes.

PEOPLE: Few photographs have people as subjects; some coverage of commission staff members, government officials, and public figures involved in historic preservation in Texas.

PHOTOGRAPHERS: Most photographs made by the professional staff. After 1981 National Register Department photographs were made by various photographers for contracting survey agencies.

Staff photographers: Donald Abbe. Lissa Anderson. Barbara Baskin. Ellen Beasley. Jim Bonar. Alton Briggs. Kathy Burns. Anthony Crosby. Glenna Dean. Ronald Emrich. Dennis Farmer. John Ferguson. Linda Flory. Dan Fox. Joe Freeman. Martha Freeman. Daniel Hardy. Marlene Heck. LaVerne Herrington. Margaret Howard. Hal Jenson. Carol Kennedy. Craig Kennedy. Stan Klein. Uli Kleinschmidt. Marie Landon. James Malone. Alan Mason. Peter Maxson. Pat Mercado-Allinger. Jim Merritt. David Moore. Alex Nelson. Joseph Oppermann. Wayne Roberson. Bill Sorrow. Dan Scurlock. Steve Smith. Jim Steely. de Teel Patterson Tiller. Curtis Tunnell. Sally Victor. Mike Yancey.

Contracting agencies: Bell, Klein, and Hoffmann (Austin). Hardy, Heck, and Moore, Inc. (Austin). Bob Parvin (Bastrop). Victor and Victor Consultants (Austin).

RECORD GROUPS: The commission is divided into several departments, each with its own collection of photographs: Markers Program Office, National Register Program Office, Office of the State Archeologist, Publication Office, Texas Antiquities Committee, and the Texas Main Street Center.

A60.1 MARKER PROGRAM OFFICE. Files contain applications to the commission for the placement of markers at historic sites, buildings, or cemeteries and include documentation of the place's significance, the site itself, and additional information, such as press clippings associated with the marker placement. Most applications contain photographs; many are snapshots, in a variety of processes, and some are copy prints of vintage photographs. All applications, including photographs, before 1981 have been microfilmed for easy access and originals are available to make photoduplications; 21 feet of microfiche (8,500 applications). Applications after 1981 are the original paperwork; 20 feet of materials (750 applications). 1960s to present.

A60.2 NATIONAL REGISTER PROGRAM OFFICE. The state historic preservation office established by the National Historic Preservation Act of 1966. The office works in partnership with the National Park Service to document the state's cultural resources through field surveys and to compile historical and descriptive information about significant places identified in those surveys. Places of exceptional merit are nominated for listing on the National Register of Historic Places in the categories site, structure, building, object, district, or multiple resource. Photographs in the files of the office include materials gathered in the process of executing inventories and nominating specific places to the National Register. Most photographs in the offices pertain to the built environment; photographs of the remnants of past cultures and to archaeological sites are held by the Office of the State Archeologist (v.i.) and the Texas Antiquities Committee (v.i.). Within each group of materials in the offices, photographs are generally arranged by county and by city; places in all counties are represented, as are many in larger or historically significant communities.

A60.2.1 CIVILIAN CONSERVATION CORPS BUILDINGS SURVEY. Buildings constructed by the CCC in 33 state parks and recreation areas. 1 foot of materials, including 5,000—35mm negatives with contact sheets and a few 35mm color transparencies. 1984.

A60.2.2 COMPLETION REPORTS. Documents the final restoration of 150 historic buildings around the state, including county courthouses more than 50 years old; reports contain photographs of elevations and oblique views and of significant details. 150 reports, most with silver gelatin prints. 1970s to present.

A60.2.3 HISTORIC AMERICAN BUILDING SURVEY FILES. A microfilm copy of all measured drawings, plan, photographs, and other materials gathered by this program which grew out of the New Deal Administration. 1 roll of microfilm. Images cover 1930s to 1950s. See Bibliography—Goeldner.

A60.2.4 NATIONAL REGISTER APPLICATION FILES. Applications to list a building, object, site, or structure on the National Register of Historic Places. The application minimally requires photographs of all sides and of significant details; more recent applications have photographs interfiled; photographs were not kept with older applications, but those photographs can be viewed in a set of microfiche copies of the entire Washington file. All these photographs are taken from the Survey Negative Collection (v.i.). Some 1,300 places were listed as of 1984 and are described in *A Catalog of Texas Properties in the National Register of Historic Places* (see Bibliography—Steely). 60 linear feet of materials, mostly nonphotographic.

A60.2.5 POST OFFICE MURALS. Art reproductions of murals painted in Texas post offices as a New Deal project to employ artists; 41 murals were extant at the time of the survey. Photographed in fragments when lighting fixtures of the building prevented a single overall view. Photographed by John C. Carlisle. 100 silver gelatin prints, 86—35mm slides. 1983. See Bibliography—Carlisle.

A60.2.6 SURVEY NEGATIVE COLLECTION. Retrospective views of historic places gathered in the process of conducting surveys; elevation and oblique views, many showing contextual environment, and significant details. Many counties, cities, and places; extensive coverage of:

Pre-1981, 4x5 negatives: Anderson (Palestine). Austin. Bandera (Bandera, rural). Bastrop (Bastrop, Smithville). Bell (Salado). Bexar (San Antonio—Fort Sam Houston, —King William Historic District, —missions). Blanco (Blanco). Bosque (Norse community). Bowie (Texarkana). Brazoria. Brewster (Alpine—Sul Ross State University). Burnet. Caldwell (Lockhart). Cameron (Brownsville). Cherokee. Colorado (Columbus). Comal (Gruene, New Braunfels Historic District). Concho. Dallas (Dallas—Southern Methodist University, —Swiss Avenue Historic District, —West End Historic District, —Wilson Block Historic District). De Witt (Cameron). Ellis (Waxahachie—Ellis County Courthouse and Historic District). El Paso (El Paso). Fannin (Bonham). Fayette (Flatonia, La Grange). Fort Bend (Richmond). Galveston (Galveston). Gillespie (Fredericksburg). Goliad (Mission Espiritu Santo, Presidio La Bahia). Gonzales. Grimes (Anderson). Guadalupe (Seguin). Harris (Houston). Harrison (Marshall—Ginocchio Historic District). Hays (San Marcos). Hood (Granbury). Houston (Crockett—Crook House). Johnson (Cleburne). Karnes (Panna Maria Historic District). Kendall (Boerne—Sisterdale Valley Historic District, Comfort). Kerr. Kinney (Brackettville). Lavaca (Hallettsville). Liberty (Liberty). Marion (Jefferson). Mason (Mason). Matagorda. McCulloch. McLennan (Waco). Medina (Castroville). Menard. Montgomery. Nacogdoches. Nueces (Corpus Christi). Parker (Weatherford). Presidio (Marfa, Shafter). Randall (Canyon). Robertson (Calvert Historic District). San Augustine (San Augustine). Shackelford (Albany). Smith (Tyler). Starr (Rio Grande City). Tarrant (Fort Worth). Taylor (Abilene). Tom Green (San Angelo). Travis (Austin—Bremond Block Historic District, —University of Texas at Austin). Uvalde. Val Verde (Del Rio). Washington (Brenham). Webb (Laredo). Williamson (Georgetown, Round Rock). Zapata.

Post-1981, 35mm negatives: Angelina. Bell (Belton). Brazos (Bryan). Caldwell (bridge). Cameron (Brownsville). Collin (McKinney). Cooke. Dallas (Dallas—Winetka Heights Historic District, —Swiss Avenue Historic District). De Witt (Cuero). Ellis (Ennis, Waxahachie). El Paso (El Paso, San Elizaro, Ysleta). Gillespie (Fredericksburg). Galveston (Galveston—Sealy house). Grayson (Denison, Sherman). Gregg (Gladewater, Kilgore, Longview, White Oak). Guadalupe (Seguin). Hale (Plainview). Harris (Houston—Fourth Ward, —Sixth Ward, —Sweeney, Combs, and Pilot buildings). Hill (Hillsboro). Jefferson (Beaumont). Jones (Stamford). Kleberg (Kingsville). Liberty. Lubbock. Montgomery. Nacogdoches. Nueces. Tarrant (Grapevine). Tom Green (San

Angelo). Travis (Austin). Victoria (Victoria). Walker. Waller. Washington (Brenham, Chapel Hill). Webb (Laredo). Starr. Williamson (Georgetown).

Until 1981 photographs were made by the commission staff using 4x5 black-and-white silver-gelatin safety film; after 1981 photographs were made by contract photographers using 35mm black-and-white silver-gelatin safety film and occasionally 35mm color transparency film. Because of the ease of shooting 35mm, there are frequently more diverse subjects and more images for each subject in that format. 46,000—4x5 and 150,000—35mm negatives; contacts of many 4x5 negatives with the textual documentation in the survey files and contact sheets of 35mm negatives. Extensive information about the structure in each image. 1969 to present.

A60.2.7 SURVEY SLIDE COLLECTION. Retrospective views of historic or architecturally significant structures gathered in the process of conducting surveys; elevations and oblique views, many showing contextual environment, significant details, and restoration of buildings; many Main Street programs. Many counties, cities, and places; extensive coverage of:

Bastrop (Bastrop). Bexar (San Antonio—Alamo, —King Williams Historic District, —South Saint Mary's Historic District, —Ursuline Academy). Bosque (Norse community). Cameron (Brownsville). Cooke (Gainesville—Davis house). Collin (McKinney). Dallas (Cedar Hill, Dallas, Garland, Grand Prairie, Lancaster). Eastland (Cisco). El Paso (El Paso). Ellis (Ennis, Waxahachie). Fannin (Bonham). Fayette (La Grange). Galveston (Galveston). Gillespie (Fredericksburg). Grimes (Navasota). Harris (Houston). Williamson (Georgetown, Round Rock). Harrison (Marshall). Hayes (San Marcos). Hill (Hillsboro). Jefferson. Kinney (Brackettville—Fort Clark). Lamar (Paris—Sam Bell Maxey House). Lubbock (Lubbock). Maverick (Eagle Pass—Main Street District). McLennan (Waco—Dr. Pepper Building). Nueces (Corpus Christi). Orange (Port Arthur—Lutcher Memorial Church). Palo Pinto (Mineral Wells—Baker Hotel). Potter (Amarillo—First Baptist Church, —Houghton House). Randall (Canyon—Saint Mary's Church). Robertson (Calvert—Hammond House, Hearne—R. C. Allen House). Starr (Rio Grande City, Roma). Tarrant (Fort Worth—Blackstone Hotel, —Bryce Building, —First Christian Church, —Laneri House). Taylor (Abilene). Tom Green (San Angelo). Travis (Austin—Barton Springs, —Congress Avenue District, —R. L. Batts home, —Butler house, —Carrington house, —Clarksville subdivision, —Texas Highway Department building, —Texas State Capitol-1884). Uvalde. Val Verde (Del Rio). Victoria (Victoria). Washington (Brenham). Wichita (Wichita Falls).

20,000 color transparencies; most 35mm, a few 126. Ca. 1970 to present.

A60.3 OFFICE OF THE STATE ARCHEOLOGIST. The office exists to preserve and document the material remains of past cultures that have lived within the borders of present day Texas; those cultures are generally classified as prehistoric (Paleo-Indian, Archaic, Woodland, and Neo-American cultures), Spanish colonial (ca. 1519 to 1836), and historic (post-Revolutionary). Most sites are located on private property; state properties are treated under the Texas Antiquities Committee (v.i.). Photographs in the files document artifacts, sites, and the activities of the office, and are arranged by county and then by site. Projects current at time of publication include all statewide prehistoric caches and sites (by county):

Brewster (Big Bend National Park, Buttrill Ranch, Rosillos Mountains). Brewster and Terrell (Lower Canyons of the Rio Grande). Jeff Davis (Livermore cache). Jones and Fisher (Clear Fork at Brazos River). Presidio (Redford area). Oldham (Landergin Mesa).

Past projects cover all counties and some cities; extensive coverage of:

Color transparencies: Bexar (San Antonio—Alamo, —Meyer Pottery Kiln, —Mission Concepcion, —Mission Espada, —Mission San José, —Padre Navarro House, —San Fernando Cathedral, —Ursuline Academy, —Walker Ranch, —various acequias). Bowie (Hatchell site [Caddoan Mound Builders], Texarkana Enlargement survey, Tilson site [Caddoan Mound Builders]). Brewster (Wild River Reconnaissance project—1973-1983). Cameron (Port Isabel—Fort Polk). Camp (Bob Sandlin Reservoir). Cherokee (Alto—George C. Davis Site [Caddoan Mound-builders]). Crockett (Fort Lancaster). El Paso (Hueco Mountains project, Hueco Tanks, Northeast Sewage Treatment Plant). Fisher (Upper Clear Fork Basin reconnaissance). Galveston. Gillespie. Goliad (Mission Espíritu Santo, Presidio La Bahia). Guadalupe (Wilson Kiln). Harrison (Marshall Pottery). Hays (Rutherford Ranch). Jones (Fort Phantom Hill). Kleberg (Padre Island). Lamar (Big Pine Reservoir project). Montgomery (Kirbee Kiln). Nueces (Padre Island). Oldham (Panhandle-Pastore project, Landergin Mesa project). Potter (Alibates National Park). Presidio. Randall (Buffalo Lake survey, Palo Duro Canyon State Park). Starr (Falcon Reservoir, Padre Island). Tom Green (XQZ survey). Travis (Austin—Carrington House, McKinney Falls State Park). Val Verde (Bonfire Shelter, Panther Cave, Vaquero Alcove). Willacy (Hidalgo-Willacy project). Williamson (Wilson-Leonard).

Prints and negatives: Bexar (Mission Concepcion, Mission Espada, Mission San José, Mission San Juan Capistrano, San Antonio—Alamo, —Mission Parkway, —San Fernando Cathedral). Bowie (Texarkana—prehistoric). Brewster (Bear Creek). Cameron (Fort Polk). Chambers (Presidio Orcoquizac). Cherokee (Jim Hogg birthplace). Crockett (Fort Lancaster). Culberson (Lobo Valley petroglyphs, Chispa Creek). De Witt (Cuero—prehistoric, —historic). Fisher (Adair-Steadman site—prehistoric). Gillespie (LBJ State Park). Goliad (Mission Espíritu Santo State Park). Hidalgo (Hidalgo-Willacy project). Hudspeth (Haas Ranch petroglyphs, Lower Huecos project, prehistoric natural areas survey). Irion (Fort Richardson). Jackson (Palmetto Bend). Jones (Fort Phantom Hill). Kerr (Ingram Reservoir). Montgomery (Kirbee Kiln). Oldham (Panhandle-Pastore project). Presidio (prehistoric). Sabine (Gaines-McGowan). Travis (Austin—Carrington, prehistoric). Val Verde. Washington (Washington-on-the-Brazos State Park).

Additional subjects include vandalism of archaeological sites, a few sites in Mexico, award presentations, preservation meetings, and public education efforts. 25,000—35mm color transparencies; 12 feet of prints and negatives—35mm, 120, and 4x5 formats—most black-and-white. 1960s to present.

A60.4 PUBLICATION OFFICE. Produces *The Medallion*, a newsletter covering current topics of historical interest, and other publications. Publication files contain photographs from issues produced within the past two years; general files contain many photographs not used in the newsletter and many of the photographs from issues older than two years. Subject headings:

Adobe. Annual meetings. Archeology. Main Street projects. Markers (and dedication ceremonies). Miscellaneous buildings. Museums. National Register. Oral history. Texas Antiquities Committee. Texas Historical Commission staff and administration. [Texas State] Capitol.

2,000 photographs, most silver gelatin prints and some negatives. 1970s to present.

A60.5 TEXAS ANTIQUITIES COMMITTEE. The committee maintains information about publicly owned, historic and prehistoric archaeological properties, including offshore sites.

A60.5.1 MAGNETOMETER TEST DOCUMENTS. Underwater testing using a magnetometer off Padre Island; anomalous sites suggesting concentrations of metals were explored for debris of shipwrecks. Project direction and photographs by staff archaeologist Mark Denton. 300—35mm color transparencies. Ca. 1985.

A60.5.2 INVENTORY OF HISTORIC, STATE-OWNED PROPERTIES. Photographs of buildings more than 45 years old owned by the following state agencies:

Abilene State School (Abilene). Austin State Hospital (Austin). Austin State School (Austin). Big Spring State Hospital (Big Spring). Kerrville State Hospital (Kerrville). Lake Mineral Wells (Parker County). Midwestern University (Wichita Falls). Palo Duro Canyon State Park (Randall County). Pan American University (Edinburg). Prairie View A&M University (Prairie View). Rusk State Hospital (Rusk). Sam Houston State University (Huntsville). San Angelo State School (San Angelo). San Antonio State Hospital (San Antonio). Stephen F. Austin University (Nacogdoches). Sul Ross State University (Alpine). Terrell State Hospital (Terrell). Texas A&M University (Galveston). Texas College of Osteopathic Medicine (Fort Worth). Texas Historical Commission (Austin). Texas Parks and Wildlife Department (various locales). Texas School for the Blind (Austin). Travis State School (Austin). University of Houston (Houston). University of Texas (Arlington). University of Texas M. D. Anderson Cancer Research Center (Houston). University of Texas Medical Branch (Galveston). Waco Center for Youth (Waco). Wichita Falls State Hospital (Wichita Falls).

Most agencies own more than one structure, and each is documented by several photographs. Unidentified commercial and snapshot photographers. 500 photographs, most silver gelatin prints and some color prints. Ca. 1985.

A60.5.3 PLUTORO/KEENNON/PURVIS COLLECTION. Lab and field photographs of artifacts withdrawn from and sites of the wrecks of the Spanish ships San Estéban and Espíritu Santo, which sank in 1554 off the Gulf Coast. Ownership of the Espíritu Santo was contested between the State of Texas and the Illinois excavation company, and was settled in favor of the state in 1984. Excavation of the San Estéban and photographs were made under the direction of state archaeologist Barto Arnold. 3,000—35mm color transparencies and 3,000 silver gelatin negatives with prints. Lab photographs, 1969 to 1975; field photographs, 1972 to 1975. Photographs held at the Corpus Christi Museum (q.v.).

[End of Texas Antiquities Committee.]

A60.6 TEXAS MAIN STREET CENTER. The state office supervising the Texas Main Street projects; the program attempts to revitalize downtown areas by simultaneously preserving the architectural heritage of the community and promoting business development. Photographs document the before and after condition of the downtown area buildings and environment, and the process of restoration. Cities that have participated in the program:

Alvin. Athens. Belton. Big Spring. Brenham. Brownwood. Conroe. Corsicana. Cuero. Daingerfield. Eagle Pass. Edinburg. Ennis. Floresville. Gainesville. Georgetown. Goliad. Grapevine. Greenville. Harlingen. Hillsboro. Kingsville. Lampasas. Lewisville. Longview. Lufkin. Marshall. McKinney. Mineral Wells. Navasota. Palestine. Pampa. Paris. Pittsburg. Plainview. Port Lavaca. San Marcos. Seguin. Sherman. Sinton. Stamford. Sweetwater. Taylor. Temple. Terrell. Tomball. Uvalde. Waxahachie. Wharton. Wichita Falls.

40,000—35mm color transparencies. 1981 to the present.

Texas Natural Resources Information System (A62)

Stephen F. Austin Building, Room 431
1700 North Congress Avenue
P.O. Box 13231
Austin, Texas 78711-3231

512-463-8337. Contact: Manager.

PURPOSE: The Texas Natural Resources Information System (TNRIS) is a group of state agencies pooling information on natural resources and the environment in Texas. TNRIS Central serves as the source for locating and obtaining this information from the participating agencies. The staff of TNRIS Central conducts inventories of natural resource data, develops new capabilities for data handling, and provides access to a number of automated and nonautomated natural resource data bases. Data gathered by TNRIS Central includes a working collection of aerial photographs.

HOURS: Weekdays, 8:00-12:00 and 1:00-5:00. Closed major holidays.

ASSISTANCE: Experienced, professional staff. Research fee may be charged. Written, walk-in, and phone inquiries accepted. Electrostatic copies available. Photoduplications may be made by the patron or ordered through TNRIS.

PUBLICATION: Publication fee charge for some uses. Almost all material held by TNRIS is in the public domain.

FINDING AIDS: Descriptive lists and indexes to specific collections, computerized database of many record groups; microfilm visual files. Access by geographic location.

BIBLIOGRAPHY:
File description report. Austin: Texas Natural Resources Information System, 1977, 1982, 1987. Exhaustive bibliography of information available at and through TNRIS.
Remote Sensing Data Inventory System (RSDIS). Computer listing of TNRIS holdings.

SCOPE: More than 500,000 photographs in black-and-white, color, and color infrared print and transparency processes; 2,000 rolls of aerial film, including black-and-white, color, and color infrared. Some images are in the form of photomosaics, composite images of aerial survey photographs assembled into a panoramic view of the terrain. Many Landsat images (digital imagery) and digital data tapes of areas in Texas. TNRIS Central also maintains catalogs of other, non-Texas agencies' holdings of aerial photography. 1940s to the present.

GEOGRAPHIC: Virtually all photographs are aerial and provide stereoscopic views of the earth's surface. It is possible to trace the changes in specific geographic locations over time. Extensive coverage of Texas; some coverage of the US; selected global coverage.

SUBJECTS: Cityscape (aerial). Landscape (aerial).

PHOTOGRAPHERS: Photographs acquired from various federal agencies, including US Department of Agriculture, US Geological Survey, NASA, and the Environmental Protection Agency; various state agencies, including the Texas Department of Highways and Public Transportation and the Texas Forest Service; a small amount of material by private aerial photography companies.

RECORD GROUPS: Virtually all imagery is aerial survey photography. Areas documented are often represented by many images, and each record group contains substantial numbers of photographs. Most record groups were made within the last 20 years, and many are expanding as additional, updating materials are added to them.

Materials maintained at TNRIS Central:

A62.1 BUREAU OF ECONOMIC GEOLOGY—HIGH PLAINS PHOTOGRAPHY. Aerial surveys of the Texas Panhandle; scale 1:80,000. 22 rolls of color-infrared film in original and duplicate form. September 1977.

A62.2 EROS DATA CENTER—MANNED SPACECRAFT PHOTOGRAPHY. Aerial surveys and space images gathered on various Gemini and Apollo missions; selected sites worldwide. 50,000 color and black-and-white prints. 1965 to 1969. TNRIS# 01010411.

A62.3 GENERAL LAND OFFICE AERIAL PHOTOGRAPHY. Aerial surveys covering primarily the Texas coast and state-owned lands. Several hundred rolls of large-scale, black-and-white, color, and color-infrared photography. 1970s to 1983 located at TNRIS Central; 1983 and later located at the land office.

A62.4 TNRIS AERIAL PHOTOGRAPHY ARCHIVES. Aerial surveys covering parts of Texas, arranged by county. Black-and-white, color, and color-infrared. 1930s to the present. TNRIS# 01010413.

Materials stored at the offices of TNRIS participating agencies (with microimage reproductions, catalogs, indices, and other finding aids located at TNRIS Central):

A62.5 BUREAU OF ECONOMIC GEOLOGY—CONTROLLED AERIAL MOSAICS. Aerial surveys of Texas Coastal Zone inland about fifty miles; the Nueces, San Antonio, Guadalupe, and Lavaca river basins; and the Cap Rock in the Panhandle; scale 1:24,000. 1,500 black-and-white mosaics. Ca. 1955. TNRIS# 01010425.

A62.6 BUREAU OF ECONOMIC GEOLOGY—EAST TEXAS PHOTOGRAPHY. Aerial surveys in northeastern Texas between latitudes 31°30′N and 33°N and between longitude 96°15′W and the Louisiana border, although part of western Louisiana is included; scale 1:25,000. Black-and-white and color-infrared prints. TNRIS# 01010426.

A62.7 BUREAU OF ECONOMIC GEOLOGY—STATEWIDE AERIAL PHOTOGRAPHY. Aerial surveys of most of Texas, although small areas of Crystal City and Beeville quadrangles are missing, collected for the Bureau's *Geological Atlas of Texas* project; scale 1:65,000. Black-and-white. Early 1950s. TNRIS# 01010423.

A62.8 TEXAS DEPARTMENT OF HIGHWAYS AND PUBLIC TRANSPORTATION AERIAL—PHOTOGRAPHY. Aerial surveys completely covering many counties, some cities, and various highways in the state. 1,600 rolls of large-scale black-and-white aerial film; stored at the Highway Department. Some photomosaics and indices at system offices. 1960s to present. TNRIS# 01002500.

A62.9 TEXAS FOREST SERVICE AERIAL PHOTOGRAPHY. Aerial surveys of many East Texas counties. Several hundred rolls black-and-white film; stored at the Forest service; indices and microimages at TNRIS Central. 1979 to present. TNRIS# 01012150.

Materials stored at institutions which are not part of TNRIS (TNRIS Central maintains micro-image reproductions, catalogs, indices, or other finding aids for the materials):

A62.10 COMMERCIAL AERIAL SURVEY COMPANIES. Indices only. Texas aerial surveys available through commercial aerial survey companies including black-and-white, color, color-infrared. TNRIS assists users in locating and ordering products. TNRIS# 01010412.

A62.11 DEFENSE INTELLIGENCE AGENCY (DIA) AERIAL PHOTOGRAPHY. Aerial surveys of national coverage acquired by the DIA on military training flights, and in support of the Defense Mapping Agency charting and mapping programs. Variety of film types, scales, and formats. TNRIS# 01010800.

A62.12 ENVIRONMENTAL PROTECTION AGENCY PHOTOGRAPHY. Listings of various types of aerial photography of environmental concern in Texas. TNRIS# 01010418.

A62.13 EROS DATA CENTER—AERIAL MAPPING PHOTOGRAPHY. Aerial surveys acquired by the US Geological Survey and other federal government agencies for mapping of the US; national coverage. Images have less than 5% cloud cover, and survey altitudes range from 2,000 to 40,000 feet. Black-and-white. TNRIS# 01010250.

A62.14 EROS DATA CENTER—MANNED SPACECRAFT PHOTOGRAPHY. Space photographs gathered on one unmanned and three manned Skylab missions; selected sites worldwide. Images are of extremely high resolution, made with a variety of photographic and nonphotographic systems, including a six-camera, multispectral system, an earth-terrain camera, infrared spectrometer, and L-band spectrometer. 1973 to 1974. TNRIS# 01010400.

A62.15 EROS DATA CENTER—NASA/AMES AIRCRAFT PHOTOGRAPHY. Aerial surveys gathered by NASA Earth Resources Aircraft Program using U2 and RB57F aircraft; selected sites, US and abroad. Most images have little cloud cover and survey altitudes range from a few thousand to 60,000 feet. In views over urban areas, buildings and streets are clearly visible. Color, color-infrared, and black-and-white images. TNRIS# 01010350.

A62.16 INTERNATIONAL BOUNDARY AND WATER COMMISSION PHOTOGRAPHY. Aerial surveys of the Rio Grande from the river's mouth to El Paso. 94 sheet photomosaic available at TNRIS; 1:24,000 mosaics available from USGS. 1974. TNRIS# 01010419.

A62.17 NATIONAL ARCHIVES PHOTOGRAPHY. Aerial surveys gathered by the Agricultural Stabilization and Conservation Service (ASCS); 1:20,000 scale. Most US counties represented. TNRIS# 01010415.

A62.18 NATIONAL OCEAN SURVEY (NOS) PHOTOGRAPHY. Aerial surveys gathered by NOS of the Texas coast; medium to large scale. TNRIS# 01010414.

A62.19 US ARMY CORPS OF ENGINEERS PHOTOGRAPHY. Aerial surveys gathered by the corps. Primarily Texas coasts and rivers. Mostly black-and-white and color-infrared. TNRIS# 01010411.

A62.20 US SOIL CONSERVATION SERVICE AERIAL PHOTOGRAPHY. Aerial surveys of most Texas counties; large to medium scale, most 1:20,000. Black-and-white. Various dates. TNRIS# 01010421.

Texas State Library, Archives Division (A68)

1201 Brazos
P.O. Box 12927
Austin, Texas 78711

512-463-5480. Contact: Photographic Archivist.

PURPOSE: A government archive preserving rare and recent books, journals, newspapers, manuscripts, government records, artwork, ephemera, and vintage and copy photographic prints and negatives. Emphasis is on Texas subjects; non-Texas subjects appear as they relate to the travel and activities of Texans.

HOURS: Weekdays, 8:00-5:00. Closed major holidays. Appointments recommended.

ASSISTANCE: Professional, experienced staff. Written and phone inquiries accepted on a limited basis. Electrostatic copies available. Photoduplications may be made by the patron or ordered through the archives.

PUBLICATION: No publication fee. Collection credit required. Third-party permission required on some material.

FINDING AIDS: Complete item-level description of all images accessioned before 1979 and partial through 1981; access by proper name, general subject heading, limited access by photographer and geographic region. Index to photographs published in books.

BIBLIOGRAPHY:
Daniel, Jean Houston, Price Daniel, and Dorothy Blodgett. *The Texas Governor's Mansion.* Austin: Texas State Library and Archives Commission, 1984.
Haley, James L. *Texas: An album of history.* Garden City NY: Doubleday, 1985.
Humphrey, David C.; picture research by Allison Beck. *Austin: An illustrated history.* Woodland CA: Windsor Publications, 1985.
Welch, June. *The Texas Governor.* Dallas: G. L. A. Press, 1977.

SCOPE: 60,000 vintage and 15,000 copy photographs, including 100 stereographs, 1,100 panoramic prints, 150 lantern slides, 500 film transparencies, and 150 motion pictures, and has an extensive collection of postcards, many of which are photo postcards. The photographs are interfiled with other non-photographic iconography.

Type of photo	Pre-1880	1880-1899	1900-1919	1920-1939	1940-1959	1960-1986
D/A/T-types	35	20	10			
Glass negs		170				
Film negs			1,000	5,000	5,000	6,000
Vintage prints	100	2,000	10,000	5,000	5,000	4,000
Copy prints	500	3,000	3,000	3,000	2,000	1,000
Photo albums			5	5		

GEOGRAPHIC: Extensive coverage of Texas; some coverage of all US states and foreign locales. Record groups with geographic emphasis include: Austin vicinity geological survey by Robert T. Hill (TSA# 1/34). Cameron County (TSA# 1/10). Corpus Christi, 1919 storm and turning basin (TSA# 1966/149). Glorieta Pass NM (TSA# 1/71). Old Waverly (TSA# 1963/151).

Countries: Australia. Canada. Europe. Great Britain. Mexico. Netherlands (Marken). US.

Texas: Austin. Central Texas. Galveston. Gulf Coast. Houston. Lower Rio Grande. Red River Valley. Southwest and the Big Bend.

SUBJECTS: Extensive coverage of all subjects. Record groups with a subject emphasis include: Aviation (early) in Texas (TSA# 1/183). Dress of the nineteenth century (TSA# 1/18). European intervention in Mexico, portraits (TSA# 1/131). Intercoastal canal dedication (TSA# 1/20). McVey sculpture (TSA# 1/16). Ruffini buildings (TSA# 1961/1). Eugene Savage murals and sculpture (TSA# 1/114). C. C. Slaughter Ranch (TSA# 1/9). Mexican Revolution, Francisco "Pancho" Villa, and Columbus NM (TSA# 1/108). Warwick Hotel, Houston (TSA# 1/138). Winedale Festival (TSA# 1970/100).

Agriculture. Animals. Architecture (churches, commercial, domestic, interiors). Art reproduction (paintings in the Capitol). Artifacts. Cityscapes. Documents. Events (ceremonies, Civil War, weddings, WW I, WW II). Government (Constitutional Convention—1875, —1974, state). Industry (general business). Landscape (aerial photos). Military (Hood's Texas Brigade, Texas Rangers). Monuments and memorials. Organizations. Politics. Services (law enforcement, libraries). Transportation (air, animal, auto, boat, railroad).

State capitols, 1853 to present. Governor's Mansion.

PEOPLE: Extensive coverage of Texas residents, especially Texas politicians. Montage portraits of many state legislatures. See Record Groups for additional families and individuals.

Achey family collection (TSA# 1/165). Crane family of Palestine TX (TSA# 1966/226). Charles George Freels family (TSA# 1969/10). Sam Houston. Mary Kerr Johnson relatives (daguerreotype portraits; TSA# 1957/43). John Lee and Margaret Pickle Costley family (TSA# 1969/11). Polk County Indians (TSA# 1933/10).

Ethnic (Amerind, Black, Caucasian, German, Mexican).

PHOTOGRAPHERS: Boone (Austin). S. B. Hill (Austin). H. B. Hillyer (Austin). Jordan (Austin). Bill Malone (Austin). H. R. Marks (Austin).

RECORD GROUPS: The Archives Division reserves the phrase *record group* to indicate material transferred from a state agency; other accessions are generally called *manuscripts*. This Record Groups section covers both types of material.

Artificial collections:

A68.1 GROUPS COLLECTION. Unrelated images with more than one individual represented, including composite and montage photographs. 70 photo prints, 9 photo negatives; some copy photographs. 1880s to 1960s. TSA# 1/104.

A68.2 PEOPLE COLLECTION. Unrelated portraits assembled by the archives. Predominantly studio portraits of individuals prominent in Texas history, government officials, and civic leaders. 559 photo prints, 98 negatives, 8 daguerreotypes, 2 tintypes, and some copy photographs; additional portraits in nonphotographic processes. TSA# 1/102.

A68.3 PLACES COLLECTION. Unrelated Texas scenes arranged by location. Buildings, street scenes, homes, panoramic views, historic sites, monuments, and events; many in Austin and San Antonio. 375 photo prints, 99 photo negatives; some copy photographs. 1890s to 1960s. TSA# 1/103.

A68.4 THINGS COLLECTION. Unrelated images of artifacts and natural specimens. Bluebonnets, flags, state seals, state treaties. 107 vintage and 7 copy photo prints, 6 negatives, 1—35mm color slide. TSA# 1/105.

Albums:

A68.5 Menn, Alfred E., photog. *Alfred E. Menn scrapbook.* Places and homes in Austin, prominent individuals of Austin history, including Jefferson Davis, W. H. Huddle, A. W. Terrell, A. H. Cook, Walter R. Schultz, and Swante Palm. 1 album, 114 photo prints; some color material. 1880s to 1920s. TSA# 1951/3.

A68.6 OFFICE OF THE ATTORNEY GENERAL, TEXAS-OKLAHOMA BOUNDARY DISPUTE COLLECTION. Commercial landscapes used as evidence in this US Supreme Court case; assembled by the Texas State Attorney General's Office.

> **A68.6.1** Nash, A. M., photog. [*Oklahoma vs. Texas Boundary Dispute albums.*] Wichita Falls, 1921. Primarily Big Bend area of Red River, China Creek, Electra Bridge, Hamil Island, and Goat Island; many scenes with oil derricks. 10 albums with 111 silver gelatin cirkut panoramic prints cut and hinged. 1921. TSA# 1927/7-1 to 111.

> **A68.6.2** [*Oklahoma vs. Texas Boundary Dispute album: Photographs to accompany the testimony of L. C. Glenn.*] Landscapes. 84 silver gelatin prints with typescript captions. 1921. TSA# 1927/7-172 to 263.

> **A68.6.3** [*Oklahoma vs. Texas Boundary Dispute albums: To accompany the testimony of L. L. Janes.*] Snapshot landscapes. 19 silver gelatin prints with captions. 1921. TSA# 1927/7-120 to 138.

263 silver gelatin prints in 15 albums. 1921.

A68.7 *Pictorial Brochure: One-hundredth anniversary, Fort Bliss, Texas.* El Paso: Fort Bliss, 1948. Commercial view of buildings, personnel, and events associated with the anniversary celebration of the fort. 60 silver gelatin prints, with typescript captions. 1948. TSA# 1949/5.

A68.8 Pritchett, Mrs. Roberta L., comp. *Old Coronal.* Students, faculty, and buildings of Coronal Institute in San Marcos; various Texas photographers, including H. B. Hillyer. 1 disbound scrapbook, 66 photo prints and associated ephemera. 1870s to 1890s. TSA# 1950/8.

A68.9 *Scenes of Camp Travis Military Encampment and Fort Sam Houston.* San Antonio: Fox Company, 1918. Commercial views of camp buildings and camp life. 20 Albertype prints. 1918. TSA# 1974/1.

A68.10 *Sherman, Texas: Encampment of 1900.* Social life and customs of the encampment. 12 photo prints. 1900. Dudley Dobie collection, TSA# 1939/10 to 1939/11.

Accession groups:

A68.11 ADAIR (A. GARLAND) COLLECTION. Curator of Texas Memorial Museum. Texas civic and political leaders; nineteenth-century Austin scenes; by various Texas photographers. 84 photo prints, 4 photo negatives. 1890s; 1900 to 1950s. TSA# 1963/283.

A68.12 ADAMS (CYRIL S., Sr.) COLLECTION. Commercial views of Todd Houston Ship Building Corporation with Liberty ships under construction at the Irish Bend Island Shipyards (Houston); hurricane damage in 1943. 793 silver gelatin prints. 1940s. TSA# 1972/186.

A68.13 ALLISON (Mrs. KATHRYN ACREE BEHRNS) COLLECTION. Snapshots and a few commercial portraits of Allison, friends, and relatives, including the Acree, Behrns, and Allison families; travel views of Florida, Georgia, Mississippi, and Mexico. 120 silver gelatin prints, a few color prints. 1880 to 1966. TSA# 1966/40.

A68.14 ARKANSAS HISTORICAL COMMISSION PHOTOGRAPHS. Scenes of towns along the Mexican-US Border and in the Valley, especially Mercedes and Laredo. 87 photo prints. 1927. TSA# 1977/127.

A68.15 AUSTIN STORE INTERIORS. Commercial interiors. 26 modern prints. 1910. TSA# 1973/201.

A68.16 BLUDWORTH (G. T.) COLLECTION. Monuments, tombstones, and modern views of historic sites in Texas, including the Alabama-Coushatta Indian Reservation. 83 vintage and 24 copy photo prints. 1920s to 1930s. TSA# 1926/3.

A68.17 BROOKS (MABEL H.) COLLECTION. Austin street scenes, especially along Congress Avenue; many photographed by H. B. Hillyer, S. B. Hill, and H. R. Marks, many copied by Jordan Company. 215 vintage and copy photo prints; some photomechanicals. 1866 to 1932. TSA# 1932/5.

A68.18 BUGG (WILLIAM BRADFORD) AND MILDRED WEBB BUGG COLLECTION. Bugg was daughter of Texas historian, Walter Prescott Webb, and granddaughter of William J. Oliphant, Austin photographer. Oliphant, Webb, and Bugg family pictures; many snapshots, some cartes and cabinets. 1,097 photographs. 1855 to 1964, most 1920s to 1949. TSA# 1979/9, 1979/170, 1979/224, 1981/52.

A68.19 BURLESON (EMMA KYLE) COLLECTION. Austin and the 1869 flood made by H. B. Hillyer. 14 photo prints, 14 photo negatives. Ca. 1869. TSA# 1940/7.

A68.20 CASTAÑEDA (C. E.) AND FREDRICK C. CHABOT COLLECTION. Views pertaining to early Texas history annotated by Castañeda and Chabot. 50 photo prints, many art reproductions. 1924. TSA# 1/174.

A68.21 COOK (L. L.) COLLECTION. Scenes and public buildings in smaller Texas towns used to make postcards published by the L. L. Cooke Company; extensive coverage with emphasis on Abilene, Bandera, Brownsville, Edinburg, El Paso, Junction, Kilgore, Mission, the Rio Grande Valley, and South Texas. 31 photo prints; 1,864 modern prints. Mid-1940s to early 1950s. TSA# 1968/89.

A68.22 CORBITT (HALL) COLLECTION. Cityscapes, buildings of Austin at the turn of the century. 23 vintage and 58 copy photo prints. Ca. 1900. TSA# 1/101.

A68.23 CURRENT EVENTS ACCESSIONS. In 1961 the archives began commissioning photographic documentation of state government activities to create a record for future historians. Each event is treated as a separate accession, but the different groups are described here as a whole because of their consistency. Many of these photographs are by Bill Malone Studios (Austin). Extensive coverage of the administrations of Preston Smith, Dolph Briscoe, Bill Clements, and Mark White. Typical subjects include legislative committee meetings, swearings in, Governor for a Day, appreciation dinners, and public ceremonies. Record groups of note within this collection include:

Academy of Freedom Dedication (1970/48). O. P. Carillo impeachment trial (1976/22, 23, 62, 63). Inauguration of Governor Preston Smith, January 21, 1969 (1970/143). LBJ Presidential Library Dedication (1971/139). LBJ State Park Dedication (1971/18). Medal of Valor Presentation to Astronauts (1971/22). Paris Junior College Dedication Ceremonies (1972/19)

Governor Preston Smith's Birthday Party—1970 (1970/107). Southern Governors' Conference (1978/27). Star of the Republic Museum Dedication (1970/150). Texas Boys State Convention—1970 (1970/115). Texas Institute of Letters Meeting and Dinner (1971/88). Texas State Arts and Crafts Fair (1973/17). Walter Prescott Webb International Symposium (1972/134).

5,000 photo prints and negatives, many in color. 1961 to present.

A68.24 GEDDIE (HENRY L.) COLLECTION. Commercial product illustrations distributed with press releases for Texas companies, prepared by Geddie. 187 silver gelatin prints, 2 color prints, 2 silver gelatin negatives; 161 press releases. 1940s to 1970s. 1976/94.

A68.25 GEUE (Mr. and Mrs. CHESTER WILLIAM) COLLECTION. Snapshots of bee hives, apiaries, and honey-harvesting operations of the Geue's and others; Geue family; and New Braunfels vicinity. 100 silver gelatin prints, 1 photo negative. Ca. 1930s. TSA# 1962/286.

A68.26 GRAHAM (RICHARD NILES) COLLECTION. Studio portraits and snapshots of Pease and Graham families; real estate development along Enfield Road in Austin; Trinity College in Hartford CT; New York; travels in Europe; and snapshot scenes of boot camp. 855 photo prints, many modern prints from nitrate negatives; 3 tintypes; some negatives; additional non-photographic images. 1880s to 1940s. TSA# 1964/306.

A68.27 GRANBERRY (C. READ) COLLECTION. Portraits of Granberry, the University of Texas at Austin, and the State Fair grounds in Dallas. 28 photo prints. Ca. 1920s to 1930s. TSA# 1962/189.

A68.28 GREEN (VIVIAN M.) COLLECTION. Economic and social development of Buda; these images were used to illustrate Green's thesis, *The Growth and Development of Buda, Texas, 1881-1956.* 25—3" x 4" glass negatives, some copy negatives. 1880s to 1956. TSA# 1980/147.

A68.29 GRIFFIN (Judge MEADE F.) PHOTOGRAPHS. Justice for Texas Supreme Court and Texas Court of Criminal Appeals. Griffin's service on the courts; many group portraits. 50 photo prints. 1947 to 1968. TSA# 1976/17.

A68.30 HARKRIDER COLLECTION. Portraits of Ernest Harkrider; France and Germany after WW I, including Western Front fortifications, villages, and a cemetery. 54 photo prints. Ca. 1918. TSA# 1966/86.

A68.31 HORNADAY (WILLIAM DEMING; 1868-1942) COLLECTION. Newspaper correspondent, publicity director for the Mexican National Railway, publicity director for the University of Texas; collection compiled through his work. Extensive coverage of Texas, major subjects include:

Agriculture (Mission Land Development Company, ranching—cattle). Animals (fish). Architecture (dams). Australia. China. Events (Mexican Revolution). Fiji Islands. Industry (oil). Landscape (arid). Military (forts). Hawaii. Mexico (Mexico City). New Zealand. Portraits. Transportation (railroads).

5,626 photographs, including vintage and copy prints, photoengravings, and postcards; 251 negatives with modern prints; separate finding aid and index. 1890s to 1940s, most 1910s to 1920s. TSA# 1975/70.

A68.32 HUNICUTT (J. R.) COLLECTION. Marlin High School athlete, Texas Ranger, and a soldier in WW II. Studio and snapshot portraits Hunicutt and family; his service at the 103rd

General Hospital in England during WW II; Marlin High School athletics. 546 photographs, including cabinets, silver gelatin prints, some color snapshots, and a few copy photo prints; 60 negatives. 1890s to 1940s. TSA# 1968/29.

A68.33 INDUSTRIAL ACCIDENT BOARD COLLECTION. Studio portraits of members of the board. Various Texas photographers, including Verkin (Galveston). 30 copy negatives. Ca. 1913 to 1960s. TSA# 1/14.

A68.34 KEMP (LOUIS W.) COLLECTION. Tombstones of Texas presidents and governors and their wives from Burnet to Campbell and of prominent individuals in Texas history. 55 photo prints, 15 photo negatives; captions. Pre 1928. TSA# 1928/1.

A68.35 KUHLMANN (W. H.) COLLECTION. Elisabet Ney, Edmund Montgomery, and other family members; Ney's studios in Germany and Austin; Liendo near Hempstead; art reproductions of her sculpture. 14 vintage, 133 copy photo prints. 1880s to 1900s. TSA# 1969/79, 1970/19, 1971/11, and 1971/135.

A68.36 LIBRARIES AND BOOKMOBILES COLLECTION. Commercial views of library buildings and facilities (interior and exterior) and bookmobiles in various Texas and US cities. 108 silver gelatin prints, 38 photo negatives. 1930s. TSA# 1970/144.

A68.37 LOWRY-McKINNEY COLLECTION. People, places, animals, and miscellany associated with the Thomas F. McKinney and Reynolds Lowry families, including the names Nolan, Johnson, and Blagge. Many cabinet portraits by various Austin and Galveston photographers. 225 vintage and 8 copy photo prints, one daguerreotype, one tintype. 1860s to 1940s. TSA# 1946/1.

A68.38 LUND (HARRY) COLLECTION. Studio portraits, commercial wedding photographs, parades, military, religious, organizations, commercial buildings and homes, and railroads all showing economic and social development of Brownsville, including many Hispanics; made by the Morales Studio (Brownsville). 278 silver gelatin prints, some copy photos, 10 negatives. 1900s to 1930s. TSA# 1964/263.

A68.39 MAXEY (SAM BELL) PHOTOGRAPH COLLECTION. Views of the Maxey house (interiors and exteriors) and grounds; Maxey family and friends, including commercial portraits; snapshots of family activities and travel to New York, the Yukon and Alaska, Europe, and Egypt. 1,200 albumen and silver gelatin prints. 1860s to late 1890s. TSA# 1981/177.

A68.40 MENN (ALFRED E.) COLLECTION. Retrospective views of historic buildings in Austin, San Felipe de Austin, Corpus Christi, San Antonio, Round Rock, Fredericksburg, Richmond, Paris, San Marcos, Salado, Kerrville, Belton, Temple, Georgetown, and the Diorama Oil Fields. 43 photo prints, 1 photo negative. TSA# 1/143.

A68.41 MEXICAN WAR COLLECTION. Reunions of veterans and persons associated with the Mexican War. 22 photo prints. 1901 to 1910. TSA# 1957/29.

A68.42 MORGAN (W. FESTUS, Jr.) COLLECTION. Along road from Luckenbach to Blanco; Bohls tracts and along road from Crossroads to Austin; possibly made by Morgan during his visit there in 1936. 72 photo prints. 1936. TSA# 1974/41.

A68.43 NINETEENTH-CENTURY AUSTIN COLLECTION. Private homes, businesses, and the Colorado River in Austin photographed by H. B. Hillyer. 20 stereograph negatives with modern prints. Ca. 1880s. TSA# 1/5.

A68.44 PEOPLE'S BUSINESS COLLEGE COLLECTION. Black business school founded by Mrs. E. M. Gilbert in Austin. Commercial views of class interiors with students and snapshots of student activities. 36 silver gelatin and color prints. 1950s to 1960s. TSA# 1971/156.

A68.45 POTTS (ROBERT J.) COLLECTION. Portraits of Potts and views of the Potts-Moore Gravel Company, many photographed by Gildersleeve (Waco). 23 photo prints and negatives. Ca. 1934. TSA# 1962/55.

A68.46 PRITCHARD (ZARH; b. 1866?) COLLECTION. Artist who spent his last years in Austin. Portraits of Pritchard at various periods in his life, art reproductions of his paintings, friends, and places where he lived. 453 photographs, including prints, stereographs, and color lantern slides. 1873 to 1930s. TSA# 1968/30.

A68.47 RAHT (CARLYSLE GRAHAM) COLLECTION. Raht, family, and friends. 50 photo prints, 7 negatives. 1920s to 1960s. TSA# 1968/27.

A68.48 RATCHFORD (FANNIE) COLLECTION. Snapshot and commercial retrospective views of historic structures in Texas built around the time of the Civil War. 2,569 vintage and modern silver gelatin prints; arranged by locale. 1930s to 1940s. TSA# 1970/101.

A68.49 ROBERTSON (WALTER M.) SCRAPBOOK COLLECTION. Scenes of Indian battles and Texas Ranger camps from central West Texas. 29 photo prints. Ca. 1927. TSA# 1/137.

A68.50 RUNGE (JOHANNA) COLLECTION. Views of Austin and vicinity emphasizing Congress Avenue street scenes photographed by S. B. Hill. 21 photographs. 1884. TSA# 1920/2.

A68.51 RUNGE (ROSCOE) COLLECTION. Lawyer in Mason. Scenes in Mason and vicinity, collected as evidence in his law practice. 68 photographs, 23 photo negatives. 1920s. TSA# 1968/28.

A68.52 SAN ANTONIO AND NEW BRAUNFELS PHOTOGRAPHS. People and places of significance in San Antonio and New Braunfels, including August Thiele. 64 photographs; some photomechanical postcards. 1890s to 1950s. TSA# 1/185.

A68.53 SMITH (BRAD) COLLECTION. Snapshots of events during Price Daniel's tenure as governor, including Vice-President Johnson's speech at a Rotary Club in Austin in 1962; Konrad Adenauer's visit to the state capitol in 1961; safety campaign by the Governor. 91 silver gelatin photo prints, 39 photo negatives, four motion picture films, 2 color transparencies. 1959 to 1962. TSA# 1965/162.

A68.54 SPUR RANCH COLLECTION. Branding and round-up on the Spur Ranch, views on the Throckmorton Ranch, and an unidentified ranch in Grant NM. 43 photo prints. 1915 to 1917. TSA# 1966/144.

A68.55 STUGARD (O. H.) COLLECTION. Snapshots and some studio portraits of the Stugard family in Wisconsin and at the Stugard Ranch in the Valley; commercial views and snapshots of citrus production and winter crops in Hidalgo County vicinity. 700 photo prints, many snapshots; some color snapshots; 700 postcards, many photo postcards. 1909 to 1950. TSA# 1963/185.

A68.56 TEST (NELLIE) COLLECTION. Fort Bliss, Camp Bowie, social life and customs of the US Army in Europe during WW I, military personnel, and 7th Army Corps headquarters in Wittlich, Germany. 494 silver gelatin prints and photo postcards. 1909 to 1920. TSA# 1966/185.

A68.57 TEXAS CAPITOL AND LIBRARY AND ARCHIVES BUILDING VIEWS COLLECTION. Exterior and interior views with emphasis on architectural details such as inscriptions, terracotta seals, and mosaic seals. 88—35mm color slides. 1960s. TSA# 1/132.

A68.58 TEXAS CAPITOL INTERIOR COLLECTION. Commercial views of offices, print shop, library, and the basement of the Capitol. 84 photo prints and 40 glass negatives. 1910. TSA# 1/6.

A68.59 TEXAS CAPITOL RIOT PREPARATIONS COLLECTION. Officers from Capitol security, Texas Rangers, Texas Department of Public Safety, and Austin Police Department in preparation for a riot May 6, 1970. 43 photo prints. 1970. TSA# 1970/106.

A68.60 TEXAS CENTENNIAL COLLECTION. Soft-focus, late-Pictorialist cityscapes and architecture in Austin, Dallas, Fort Worth, Houston, and San Antonio made by H. C. A. von Schoenfeldt, ARPS. 28 silver gelatin prints. 1936. TSA# 1936/8 OS.

A68.61 TEXAS CENTENNIAL CONSTRUCTION AND FESTIVITIES COLLECTION. Commercial views of the fairgrounds and ceremonies used by the Texas Department of Publicity and snapshots of desert plants. 36 photo prints. 1936. TSA# 1/163.

A68.62 TEXAS CONSTITUTIONAL CONVENTION—1974 SLIDES. The convention in session and committee meetings; made by House Media Service. 1,460—35mm color transparencies. 1974. TSA# 1975/93.

A68.63 TEXAS DEPARTMENT OF PUBLIC SAFETY COLLECTION. Governor W. Lee O'Daniel's inauguration and family photographs; governors O'Daniel, Coke Stevenson, Allan Shivers, Price Daniel, John Connally, Preston Smith during their administrations; by DPS photographers. 2,500 photographs, including prints and negatives. 1940 to 1944. TSA# 1976/8, 1976/198, 1978/23.

A68.64 TEXAS LEGISLATURE MEMBERS COLLECTION. Stylistically uniform, formal portraits; some identified. 110 salted-paper prints. Ca. 1859. TSA# 1/115.

A68.65 TEXAS NATIONAL GUARD PHOTOGRAPHS. Snapshots of the guard, including battles between Mexican Federal troops and rebel "Carranzistas"; Fort Sam Houston; and Leon Springs. 123 silver gelatin prints. 1909 to 1916. TSA# 1972/166.

A68.66 TEXAS STATE BUILDING COMMISSION COLLECTION. Construction of the San Jacinto Monument in La Porte. 5 photo prints, 63 photo negatives, 122 slides. Ca. 1936. TSA# 1964/151.

A68.67 TEXAS STATE HOSPITALS COLLECTION. Interior and exterior views of buildings and grounds of state hospitals at Abilene, Rusk, San Antonio, Terrell, and Wichita Falls. 48 photo prints. Late 1930s. TSA# 1/129.

A68.68 TEXAS STATE LIBRARY ADMINISTRATIVE DIVISION TRANSFER COLLECTION. Dedication ceremony of the library building photographed by Bill Malone. 33 vintage and 1 copy photograph. 1962. TSA# 1962/281.

A68.69 TEXAS STATE LIBRARY COLLECTION. Exterior and interior views of Texas library facilities and activities. 146 photo prints, 81 lantern slides. 1931 to 1961. TSA# 1980/219.

A68.70 TEXAS STEREOSCOPIC VIEWS COLLECTION. Published genre scenes of Galveston, Palestine TX, and Texarkana (Rome, New York: E. P. Hovey, ca. 1900). 12 stereographs. Ca. 1900. TSA# 1/28.

A68.71 THIRD ARMY MANEUVERS COLLECTION. Field ration, living quarters of officers, general staff section, telephone switchboard, interiors of supply sections, and aerial view. 79 silver gelatin prints. June to July, 1943. TSA# 1/7.

A68.72 THIRTY-SIXTH DIVISION ASSOCIATION COLLECTION. Portraits of John Hulen, pre-WW I military, WW I, interwar period and WW II, and National Guard in Texas after WW II, individual and group portraits. 9 groups of photo prints, including 1,500 prints, most silver gelatin, some tintype, albumen, and photomechanical; motion pictures. 1900 to 1940s. TSA# 1972/115.

A68.73 TILLMAN (FRANK) COLLECTION. Military views during WW I and WW II: battle scenes, soldiers in France, US Army YMCA in San Antonio and tubercular sanatorium in Kerrville, scrap-metal drives, Governor Coke Stevenson, and military personnel and operations at Fort Polk LA, Camp Bullis, Camp Travis, and Fort Sam Houston. 11 boxes of photographs, including 2,000 silver gelatin prints and 1,000 silver gelatin panoramic prints. 1918 to 1940s. TSA# 1/142.

A68.74 TOWNSEND (E. E.) COLLECTION. Brewster County and Chihuahua, Mexico, with an emphasis on geographical landmarks, towns, and the Townsend home in Alpine. 24 photo prints. 1900s to 1930s. TSA# 1936/9.

A68.75 WADE (HOUSTON) COLLECTION. La Grange and vicinity; portraits of men who took part in Dawson Massacre or Mier Expedition. 30 photo prints, some copy prints. 1860s to 1935. TSA# 1/44.

A68.76 WASSON (S. DEANE) COLLECTION. People, places, and events in Texas, including Carlos Castañeda, Austin, College Station, and the Board of Education Textbook Selection Committee; made by or for the Capital News Service. 54 photo prints; associated nonphotographic materials. 1930s. TSA# 1942/8.

A68.77 WEBB (WALTER P.; d. 1963) PAPERS. Personal photographs of Webb from his youth to the time of his death; snapshots and commercial views of Big Bend landscape; Texas Rangers; snapshot travel views of Europe; photographers include Webb, photographers associated with the National Park Commission, some possibly by W. D. Smithers. 682 vintage and copy silver gelatin prints and some photo postcards. 1900s to 1960s, most 1930s to 1960s. TSA# 1972/187.

A68.78 WEED (THURLOW B.) FUNERAL HOME COLLECTION. Commercial views of interior and exterior, hearses, and caskets. Most photographed by the Jordan Company (Ellison and Boone photographers, Austin). 21 silver gelatin prints, 6 photo negatives. 1920s. TSA# 1965/148.

A68.79 WEED (THURLOW B., Jr.) COLLECTION. Weed family and the family funeral home (v.s.) in Austin. 14 vintage and 3 copy photo prints. 1880 to 1951. TSA# 1965/87.

A68.80 WHITE (ROBERT LEON) COLLECTION. Buildings and courthouses in Texas, World's Columbian Exposition (Chicago 1893), and art reproduction. 24 photo prints. 1890 to 1910. TSA# 1/8.

A68.81 WIGGINTON (A. M.) COLLECTION. Wigginton family photographs from the southern Central Texas vicinity, especially San Antonio; most studio portraits. 39 photographs, many tintypes, cartes, and cabinets 1860s to 1900. TSA# 1/164.

A68.82 WISTER (OWEN) COLLECTION. Author of *The Virginian*. Amateur views of D. F. Savage's Ranch in Brownwood and other ranches, the San Antonio missions, and polo photographed by Wister. 143 photo prints; 114 photo negatives, many 8x10 with modern prints. Ca. 1893 to 1900s. TSA# 1969/72 and 1969/97.

A68.83 WORLD'S COLUMBIAN EXPOSITION COLLECTION. Views of this world's fair held in Chicago. 22 modern prints. 1893. TSA# 1/178.

A68.84 WRIGHT (ARVILLA) COLLECTION. Daguerreotype portraits of George Washington Wright and his wife and views of Austin and vicinity, including dam break. 2 daguerreotypes, 23 photo prints. 1860s to 1890s. TSA# 1936/10.

A68.85 WYKOFF (ROY A.) WW II PHOTOGRAPHS. Motion picture stars, military installations in Texas, Fort Crockett and Camp Wallace, and US soldiers in Guadalcanal and Solomon Islands. 24 photo prints. 1940s. TSA# 1963/108.

Architectural Drawings Collection (A74)

University of Texas
Architecture and Planning Library
Battle Hall 108
Austin, Texas 78712

512-471-1844 or 512-471-8132. Contact: Curator.

PURPOSE: A special-collections division holding original architectural drawings, students' measured drawings, research reports, blueprints, specifications, models, clippings, archival materials, and photographs covering a wide range of architecture in the US, with an emphasis on Texas and the Southwest. The Architectural and Planning Library is a division of the General Libraries of the University of Texas at Austin.

HOURS: Weekdays, 8:00-5:00. Closed major and university holidays. Appointment required.

ASSISTANCE: Specialized staff. Electrostatic copies available. Photoduplications available through the collection.

PUBLICATION: No publication fee. Collection credit required. Third-party permission required on some materials.

FINDING AIDS: Inventory for the Ayres and Ayres collection.

BIBLIOGRAPHY:
Alexander, Drury Blakeley; Todd Webb, photog. *Texas homes of the nineteenth century.* Austin and London: University of Texas Press for the Amon Carter Museum, 1979. 2nd ed.
Germany, Lisa. *Harwell Hamilton Harris.* Austin: Center for the Study of American Architecture, School of Architecture, University of Texas at Austin, 1985. Exhibition catalog.
Robinson, Willard B. *Gone from Texas: Our lost architectural heritage.* College Station: Texas A&M University Press, 1981.
Robinson, Willard B. *The people's architecture: Texas courthouses, jails, and municipal buildings.* Austin: Texas State Historical Association, 1983.
Robinson, Willard B. *Texas public buildings of the nineteenth century.* Austin and London: University of Texas Press for the Amon Carter Museum, 1974.

SCOPE: 20,000 photographs, including negatives and prints; many are copy photographs of architectural plans and renderings. 1890s to the present.

GEOGRAPHIC: Extensive coverage of the US, with an emphasis on Texas; some broad coverage of the globe.

China. Europe. India. Japan. Mexico.

SUBJECTS: Extensive coverage of architecture of all uses, including public, commercial, residential, and religious architecture. Substantial coverage of historic and vernacular architecture in Texas. See Record Groups for specific projects by the various architects.

PEOPLE: Few individuals appear in the collection outside the architects mentioned below in Record Groups; their families occasionally appear.

PHOTOGRAPHERS: Predominantly unidentified commercial photographers, although the architects themselves are frequently responsible for the photographs. The Harris collection (v.i.) contains several notable photographers.

RECORD GROUPS: Materials are maintained in record groups by provenance with photographs stored in a section at the end of each group. All record groups maintain some association, nonphotographic materials such as renderings and plans.

A74.1 AYRES (ATLEE B.; 1874-1969) AND ROBERT M. AYRES (1898-1977) COLLECTION. A San Antonio, father-son architectural partnership founded in the 1890s and joined by Robert in 1924; noted for their designs for the San Antonio Municipal Auditorium (1925, in association with Emmett Jackson and George Willis), the Smith-Young Tower (1930), and many Spanish-inspired residences, such as the Thomas Hogg and the Atkinson homes. Photographs document commercial, residential, and public buildings designed by the firm throughout Texas, with emphasis on Robert Ayres' home, the Brown residence in Oklahoma City OK, and the Engineering Building at the University of Texas at Austin. Other photographs include family trips to California, Europe, Mexico, and a world tour through China, Japan, Europe, and India, and include many buildings not designed by the firm and the family. Most are photographed by the Ayreses, but some unidentified, commercial architectural photographers are included. 4,900 film negatives, including 4x5, 5x7, and 120; some silver gelatin prints; inventory. 1920s to 1950s.

A74.2 CAMERON (RALPH; 1892-1970) COLLECTION. An architect trained at the Ecole des Beaux Arts in Paris, France, who established his practice in San Antonio in 1914; noted for his designs for the Medical Arts Building (1934) and the Federal Courthouse and Post Office (1934). Photographs of buildings designed by Cameron; the collection is not yet processed. Restricted access.

A74.3 FRONTIER ARCHITECTURE SURVEY COLLECTION. A project of the National Park Service making an early attempt to document historic and architecturally significant structures in Texas. 100 silver gelatin prints with records and associated nonphotographic text. 1937, a few later.

A74.4 GORDON (JAMES RIELY; 1863-1937) COLLECTION. Architect of 16 Texas courthouses in a Romanesque style, including the Bexar County Courthouse (1891-1896) and the Ellis County Courthouse (1892); moved to New York in 1902, where he worked with the firm of Gordon, Tracy, and Swartout, and in partnership with Hugh Tallant and Alfred Zucker, the latter noted for burning the account books and fleeing to South America. Photographs document the buildings of Gordon and his partners, including construction, interior and exterior details, and overall views; copies of plans, many of which survive only in these photographs; of note are a series of views of the interior of Gordon's office in San Antonio and a series of views of Victorian domestic interiors which also appear in the Dielmann collection at the Daughters of the Republic of Texas Library (q.v.). Many of the buildings are in New York, New Jersey, Pennsylvania, Delaware, and

Connecticut; substantial coverage of Bergen City Courthouse in New Jersey, the Connecticut Savings Bank, the Grammercy Park Apartments, and the Home Club. 1,500 photographs, including many cyanotype and silver gelatin prints, and glass negatives. 1890s to 1920. The Patton collection (v.i.) has related Gordon materials.

A74.5 HARRIS (HARWELL HAMILTON; b. 1903) COLLECTION. Harris worked for California architect Richard Neutra before establishing his own firm in Los Angeles in 1932; he was influenced by the Greene brothers and Bernard Maybeck, and developed a regional style that integrated modernist principles with sensitivity for site and materials; he was Dean of the School of Architecture, University of Texas at Austin, from 1951 to 1955. Photographs document Harris' designs for and alterations to the California residences of Mr. and Mrs. George Bauer (Glendale), Mr. and Mrs. Cecil J. Birtcher (Los Angeles), Mr. and Mrs. Lee Blair (Los Angeles), Mr. and Mrs. Robert Campbell (San Marino), Mrs. Edward DeSteiguer (Pasadena), John Entenza (Santa Monica), Greta Granstedt (Hollywood), H. H. Harris studio (Fellowship Park House, Los Angeles), Mr. Weston Havens (Berkeley), Edwin "Stan" Hawk Jr. (Los Angeles), Mr. and Mrs. Ralph Johnson (Los Angeles), Mr. and Mrs. Graham Laing (Pasadena), Pauline Lowe (Altadena), Mr. and Mrs. J. J. Mulvihill (Sierra Madre), Mr. and Mrs. Alvin Ray (Fallbrook), Mr. and Mrs. John S. Treanor (Visalia), and Mr. and Mrs. Clarence H. Wyle (Ojai). Nonresidential architecture of Harris includes commercial and religious buildings, primarily in Texas and California, including the Greenwood Mausoleum (Fort Worth), the Motel-on-the-Mountain (Mount Hillburn NY), the drive-in facilities of Security Bank and Trust Company (Owatonna MN), and various projects for Trammell Crow Company. Photographers include Fred R. Dapprich, Julius Shulman, Man Ray, Maynard L. Parker, and others, all commercial. 750 silver gelatin prints. 1930s to 1950s. See Bibliography—Germany.

A74.6 NELSON (DONALD) COLLECTION. A Chicago architect who worked on the 1933 World's Fair; moved to Dallas, where he worked on Texas Centennial Exposition buildings and sculpture and designed Love Field and many downtown Dallas high-rise buildings. Photographs document Nelson's work, especially construction shots, which were made daily. Unprocessed and restricted access. 5,000 silver gelatin prints; movies; transparencies. 1930s to 1960s.

A74.7 PATTON (GLEN) COLLECTION. Professor of art history at Trinity University in San Antonio. Buildings and materials relating to architect James Riely Gordon (v.s.) gathered in the course of researching the manuscript for an unpublished book. 400 copy photographs, including prints and negatives.

A74.8 TEXAS ARCHITECTURE ARCHIVE. A collection of reports by students of professors Blake Alexander's and Wayne Bell's courses in historic building preservation at the University of Texas School of Architecture; each student had to document a building, and most reports contain photographs. Many of the buildings are not listed in the National Register of Historic Places, nor documented by the Historic American Building Survey. 22 feet of textual and photographic materials interfiled. 1960s to present.

A74.9 TEXAS ARCHITECTURAL SURVEY COLLECTION. Retrospective views of more than 1,500 historical public and private structures in Texas; substantial coverage in Austin, Bastrop, Brownsville, Burnet, Clarksville, Columbus, Cuero, Fort Stockton, Fort Worth, Fredericksburg, Galveston, Goliad, Granbury, Hillsboro, Houston, Huntsville, Jefferson, Lampasas, Llano, Marshall, Mason, Nacogdoches, New Braunfels, Paris, Round Top, San Antonio, San Augustine, Tyler, Victoria, and Waco; various forts. 3,500 silver gelatin prints; card index arranged by city. Ca. 1964 to 1967. See Bibliography—Alexander, —Robinson.

A74.10 WEBB (Sir ASTON; 1849-1930), MAURICE E. WEBB (1880-1939), AND E. INGRESS BELL (1826-1914) COLLECTION. London architects; Aston Webb was noted for his large-scale planning projects, including the Birmingham Law Courts (1887-1891) and the Victoria and Albert Museum (1891-1909); he was associated with Bell intermittently from 1882 to 1914, and joined by his son, Maurice Webb, during his later career. Photographs document their buildings. 200 photographs. 1890s to 1920s.

A74.11 WILLIAMS (DAVE) COLLECTION. Dallas architect; toured Texas, especially Central and South Texas, with O'Neil Ford between the world wars, documenting the vernacular architecture that adapted traditional, old-world forms to the materials and environment of Texas. Photographs record the structures Williams and Ford discovered, most in rural areas and small towns; virtually all buildings are unidentified. 3,500 negatives with modern copy negatives and modern prints; 400 vintage prints. 1920s to 1930s.

Architectural Reference Center (A76)

University of Texas at Austin
School of Architecture
Sutton Hall 3.140
Austin, Texas 78712

512-471-1922. Contact: Slide librarian.

PURPOSE: A picture library maintained by the School of Architecture as a resource of didactic images. Many images circulate to professors for class lectures.

HOURS: Weekdays, 8:00-5:00. Closed major and university holidays. Appointment required. Open to faculty and students of the School of Architecture and to practicing professionals in building and design fields.

ASSISTANCE: Specialized staff. Photoduplications must be ordered through the center.

PUBLICATION: No reproduction fee. Collection credit required. Third-party permission required on approximately three-quarters of the material.

FINDING AIDS: Card index.

SCOPE: 150,000—35mm color transparencies; many are copy slides of photomechanicals in books. Buildings date from prehistoric times to the present; slides date from 1960 to present, most after 1970.

GEOGRAPHIC: Broad global coverage; extensive coverage of the US and Texas.

SUBJECTS: Architecture, with representative images of most periods, styles, and forms; some emphasis on architectural preservation and on alternative, nontraditional building techniques, such as solar technology.

PEOPLE: Few portraits appear in the collection. There is an emphasis on the work of major architects after the 1860s (see Record Groups—Architects file).

PHOTOGRAPHERS: Most commercial photographers; few identified, except Todd Webb. Many of the slides were made by professors in the School of Architecture and later donated to the collection.

RECORD GROUPS:

A76.1 ARCHITECTS FILE. Buildings by major architects of the last half of the nineteenth century to the present:

Alvar Aalto. The Architects Collaborative. Luis Barragan. Peter Behrens. Marcel Breuer. Caudill, Rowlett, Scott. Willem Dudok. Charles Eames. Peter Eisenman. O'Neil Ford. Buckminster Fuller. Frank Furness. Naum Gabo. Antonio Gaudí y Cornet. Romaldo Giurgola. Michael Graves. Walter Gropius. Hector Guimard. Charles Gwathmey. Hardy, Holtzman, and Pfeiffer. John Q. Hejduk. Hans Hollein. Victor Horta. William le Baron Jenny. Philip Johnson. Louis Kahn. Nicolai Ladocsky. Le Corbusier. Lissitsky. Adolph Loos. E. L. Lutyens. Charles R. Mackintosh. Robert Maillart. Roberto Burle Marx. Bernard Maybeck. McKim, Mead, and White. Eric Mendelsohn. Richard Meier. Mies Van der Rohe. Charles Moore. Pier Luigi Nervi. R. J. Neutra. S. O. Niemeyer. Olmstead. Otto Frei. J. J. P. Oud. I. M. Pei. Cesar Pelli. A. Perret. H. H. Richardson. G. T. Rietveld. A. Rodchenko. P. Rudolph. Eero Saarinen. Moshe Safdie. A. Sant'Elia. Sasaki. J. L. Sert. S.I.T.E. Skidmore, Owings, and Merrel. Peter and Alison Smithson. Paolo Soleri. James Stirling. E. D. Stone. Louis H. Sullivan. Deborah Sussman. Van der Leck. Van Doesberg. Van Esstern. Van de Velde. Vantongerloo. Robert Venturi. A. Vesnin. C. Voysey. Otto Wagner. Jan Wils. Frank Lloyd Wright. M. Yamasaki.

3,600—35mm color transparencies; many copy slides of photomechanical book illustrations. 1970s to present.

A76.2 CHRONOLOGICAL FILES. Buildings, arranged by period and subdivided by region:

Prehistoric. Ancient Egypt. Mesopotamian. Aegean. Minoan/Mycenean. Greek. Roman. Byzantine. Early Christian. Pre-Romanesque. Islamic. Pre-Columbian. Medieval. Romanesque. Gothic. Renaissance. Post-Renaissance [to the present].

Extensive coverage of the US and Texas; broad global coverage, with some emphasis on China, Japan, and Mexico. 22,400—35mm color transparencies; many are copy slides of photomechanical book illustrations. 1970s to present.

A76.3 LEIPZIGER-PEARCE COLLECTION. Illustrations of street scenes, city plans, and buildings in European cities rebuilt after WW II according to utopian urban-planning schemes. Many photographed by Hugo Leipziger, professor at the School of Architecture. 2,000 vintage 35mm color transparencies. 1950s to 1970s.

A76.4 PLANNING, MAPS, AND NATURAL FORMS FILES. Illustrations used for teaching. 2,000—35mm color transparencies; many copy slides of photomechanical book illustrations. 1970s to present. 1970s to present.

A76.5 STRUCTURAL MATERIALS FILE. Illustrations of buildings and construction details pertaining to engineering aspects of buildings, including stressed concrete, arches, and trusses. 1,000—35mm color transparencies; many copy slides of photomechanical book illustrations. 1970s to present.

A76.6 STUDENT WORK FILE. Art reproduction of models and plans generated by students for course assignments in the school. 3,000—35mm color transparencies. 1970s to present.

A76.7 TECHNOLOGY AND SOLAR ENERGY FILE. Illustrations of buildings and construction details pertaining to energy conservation and alternative, nontraditional energy sources. 1,000—35mm color transparencies, most vintage images. 1970s to present.

A76.8 TEXAS HISTORIC AMERICAN BUILDING SURVEY PHOTOGRAPHS. Elevations, obliques, and details of Texas buildings included in the survey; photographed by Todd Webb under the direction of preservation architect, Drury Blakeley Alexander. Arranged by county. 5,000—35mm color transparencies. 1965.

Eugene C. Barker Texas History Center (A78)

University of Texas
Sid Richardson Hall, Unit 2
Twenty-fifth and Red River
Austin, Texas 78712

512-471-5961. Contact: Director.

PURPOSE: A research library and archive holding rare and recent books, manuscripts, newspapers and journals, maps, sound recordings, ephemera, and photographs. Concentration is on Texas history and maintains the institutional archives of the University of Texas.

HOURS: Monday through Saturday, 8:00-5:00. Closed major and academic holidays. Appointments required to view uncataloged photograph collections.

ASSISTANCE: Professional, experienced, specialized staff. Written and phone inquiries accepted on a limited basis. Electrostatic copies available. Photoduplications may be made by patron with prior arrangements or ordered through the center.

PUBLICATION: No publication fee. Collection credit required. Third-party permission required on a few items.

FINDING AIDS: Indices; access by personal name, general subject heading, some major photographers. Descriptive, itemized inventories for many record groups. Published finding aid (See Bibliography—Kielman). Itemized list of proper names of people for collections received before 1967. Index to photographs in published sources. General collection arranged by subject; other collections arranged by provenance.

BIBLIOGRAPHY:
Berry, Margaret. *The University of Texas: A pictorial account of its first century.* Austin: University of Texas Press, 1980.
Duren, Almetris. *Overcoming: A history of Black integration at the University of Texas at Austin.* Austin: University of Texas, 1979.
Haley, James L. *Texas: An album of history.* Garden City NY: Doubleday, 1985.
Humphrey, David C.; picture research by Alison Beck. *Austin: An illustrated history.* Northridge CA: Windsor Publishing, 1985.
Kielman, Chester V., comp. *The University of Texas Archives: A guide to the historical manuscripts collections in the University of Texas Library.* Austin and London: University of Texas Press, 1967. Contains a brief description of 2,430 collections with subject index. Some descriptions note photographs, but many collections with photographs do not contain any such indication. Not illustrated.
Norfleet, Barbara, ed. *Championship pig: Great moments in everyday life.* Boston: Godine, 1979.
Rundell, Walter. *Early Texas oil: A photographic history.* College Station: Texas A&M Press, 1977.

SCOPE: 2,600 linear feet containing about 425,000 vintage and 7,500 copy photographs, including stereographs, autochromes, glass, nitrate and safety negatives, and albumen silver gelatin prints. Extensive book, manuscript, newspaper, and realia collections pertinent to the photographs. Nonphotographic images interfiled with photographs. 1850 to present.

Type of photo	Pre-1880	1880-1899	1900-1919	1920-1939	1940-1959	1960-1986
D/A/T-types	300	400	100			
Glass negs	100	200	10,000	1,000		
Film negs		100	2,000	40,000	60,000	100,000
Modern prints				100	100	
Vintage prints	1,000	3,000	20,000	75,000	75,000	25,000
Copy images		2,000	2,000	2,000	1,000	500

GEOGRAPHIC: Extensive coverage of the South and Southwest, including Texas, New Mexico, and Colorado. Some coverage of Mexico.

Texas cities: Austin. Brownsville. Corpus Christi. Dallas. El Paso. Fort Worth. Houston. Kerrville. Lockhart. Lubbock. Waco.

SUBJECTS: Extensive coverage. Photographs relate to the development of Texas and includes portraits of important Texans, family albums, early views of Texas cities, and images documenting the state's history. See Record Groups for additional subjects.

Academia (primary, secondary, student life and customs, university). Agriculture (ranching). Architecture (academic, domestic, historical). Industry (general commerce, oil, shipping). Landscapes. Military (WW I, WW II). Politics. Transportation (railroad).

University of Texas at Austin.

PEOPLE: Portraits of thousands of persons, most Texans or associated with Texas history; few are represented in quantity. The center has attempted to collect materials pertaining to the many diverse ethnicities in Texas, including Amerinds, Black, German, Hispanic, Jewish, and Spanish cultures. See Record Groups for names.

Occupations (cowboy, historian, military personnel, musicians, politicians, ranchers, Texas Rangers).

PHOTOGRAPHERS: Examples of the work of many major studios in Texas. See Record Groups for photographers marked with an asterisk.

Harry Annas (Lockhart).* Arthur Conrads (Kenedy and Karnes City).* Walter E. Daniel (Lubbock and Brownwood).* Jimmie A. Dodd (Kingsville, Kerrville).* R. C. Hickman (Dallas).* S. B. Hill (Austin). H. B. Hillyer (Austin). Dr. John Mathias Kuehne (Austin).* Russell Lee.* Robert Runyon (Brownsville).* Frank J. Schlueter (Houston). William S. Soule.* Edward Taulman.* Paul L. Verkin (Galveston).

RECORD GROUPS: Many record groups have itemized listings of photographs. Descriptions in quotation marks were taken from Kielman; other descriptions were provided by Alison Beck and Larry Landis of the center's staff or were paraphrased from Kielman and other finding aids. See Bibliography—Kielman for additional information about many of the record groups listed below.

A78.1 Record Groups with small amounts of photographic materials: John H. Adams papers. Elbert Macby Barron papers. R. C. Beale papers. E. H. Belcher papers. Mody C. Boatwright papers. James Perry Bryan papers. John Alton Burdine papers. Dennis W. Bushyhead papers. John Edwin Canaday papers. Katherine Pollard Carter papers. Evert Mordecai Clark papers. O. H. Clark collection. James H. Collett papers. Confederate States of America Records. Robert Bartow Cousins Sr. papers. Nellie Stedman Cox papers. Bailey Benge Crowe papers. Jon Winfield Scott Dancy. Oscar Cromwell Dancy. Nathaniel Hart Davis papers. Lorenzo de Zavala papers. Mary Decherd papers. William Gowdey Denny papers. Alexander Dienst papers. Minnie Dill papers. James Frank Dobie papers. Maurice H. Dowell papers. Mary Marshall Dunn papers. Thomas Jefferson Ely. Michael Erskine papers. Walter Christine Giesecke family papers. C. F. Goodridge papers. Robert Simonton Gould papers. Shad Graham papers. H. E. Haass papers. W. W. Hardy papers. Henry Winston Harper papers. Thomas R. Havins papers. John L. Haynes papers. Arthur R. Hays papers. Thomas Stalworth Henderson papers. George August Edward Henkel papers. Mrs. S. Lilliam Hill collection. Historical Records Survey of Texas. William E. Howard papers. Seth B. Hunt collection. Alvin Thomas Jackson papers. M. T. Jones Lumber Company records. Rudolph Kleberg collection. Richard L. Kozelka pictures. Leyendecker family papers. Addison L. Lincecum papers. William Lawrence McGill papers. Maury Madison papers. William Mahl papers. William Thompson Martin papers. John Sutherland Menefee papers. Alice G. Merchant photographs. Burchard Miller family papers. William Wallace Mills papers. Mississippi papers. A. Henry Moss papers. James Nicholson papers. Swante Palm papers. Mrs. Percy V. Pennybacker papers. Hally Ballinger Bryan Perry papers. Johnathan Edwards Pierce collection. Protestant Episcopal Church records. Grover Cleveland Ramsey papers. John H. Rogers collection. Reuben Ross family papers. Runnels County—Texas—New Deal Agencies Records. San Antonio papers. Elias "Emmett" Oliver Sanders papers. Eugene Paul Schoch papers. Walter Benona Sharp collection. Elijah L. Shettles. Morris Sheppard papers. Julia Lee Sinks papers. Ashbel Smith papers. Cecil B. Henry Smith papers. Smith papers. Samuel Henry Starr papers. Robert Sutherland papers. May Mathis Green Watson scrapbooks. Dorman Winfrey papers. Ernst William Winkler papers. Woodsville MS history. Josepha "Jodie" Wright papers.

Record Groups with substantial numbers of photographs:

A78.2 ACREE (FRED; 1878-1947) PAPERS. Poultry farmer, rancher, real estate developer, oilman, and mayor of Moody. 50 photographs. Kielman# 5.

A78.3 ADAMS (WALTER DICKSON; 1872-1961) COLLECTION. Pharmacist and editor of *Texas Druggist*. Portraits especially of Adams; Central and Northeast Texas; Texas and American Pharmaceutical associations. 187 prints, 22 oversized prints, and 16 negatives.

A78.4 ALDRICH (ARMISTEAD ALBERT; 1858-1945) PAPERS. State legislator, local historian, lay leader in his church, and county judge of Houston County. 40 prints and negatives. 1908 to 1938. Kielman# 24.

A78.5 ALDRICH (ROY WILKINSON; 1869-1955) PAPERS. Texas Ranger for 32 years. Collection has itemized, descriptive list and is divided into two periods by the date of Aldrich's move to Texas in 1907 and his joining the Texas Rangers in 1915. First period includes boyhood in Golder City MO, family, unidentified cartes, Idaho territory, Aldrich's career in Mexico as a coffee planter (1890s), Aldrich's membership in Missouri National Guard during the Spanish-American War, Georgia, Kentucky, Arizona (Tucson, Yaqui and Papago Indians; 84 photographs, 1899), Oklahoma Territory (Kiowa and Apache Indians). Second period includes Lower Rio Grande Valley and Rio Grande City (63 photographs), Big Bend (89 photographs), Mexican Revolution, Camp Mabry (Austin, 1918), law enforcement 1920s to 1930s, Texas Rangers, Aldrich as a Texas Ranger, outlaws, Old West reunions, and Aldrich after age 69 in Austin. 600 photographs. 1890s to 1930s.

A78.6 ANDREWS (WILLIE) PIONEER SCHOOLS RECORDS. Founding and history of the Pioneer Schools. 50 photographs. Kielman# 57.

A78.7 ANNAS (HARRY FORREST; 1897-1980) ARCHIVES. Studio and commercial photographer working in Lockhart. Studio portraits, school photographs, and community events photographed by Annas. 90,000 photo negatives, some nitrate. 1920s to late 1973. See Bibliography—Norfleet.

A78.8 ARMADILLO WORLD HEADQUARTERS RECORDS. Popular music establishment in Austin and the focus of much of the Austin sound in progressive country music. Promotional photographs of musicians; Armadillo World Headquarters facilities. Itemized list of artists; photographs interfiled with other materials. 100 photo prints. 1971 to 1980.

A78.9 BARKER (EUGENE CAMPBELL; 1874-1956) PAPERS. Historian, professor at the University of Texas at Austin. Personal and historical subjects. 90 photographs. Kielman# 120.

A78.10 BARLER (MILES; 1833-1907) PAPERS. Merchant, deputy sheriff, and Texas Ranger. Barler and Monroe families, Barler home, San Saba vicinity. 110 photographs. Kielman# 122.

A78.11 BATTLE (WILLIAM JAMES; 1870-1955) COLLECTION. Professor of classical languages at the University of Texas at Austin. University of Texas at Austin (100), Texas (20), R. L. Brown family (16), and reproductions of paintings and buildings (650). 786 photographs. Kielman# 142.

A78.12 BEDICHEK (ROY; 1878-1959) PAPERS. Naturalist, educator, and writer. Portraits of Bedichek and in groups, other Bedichek family members and friends, flora and fauna. 150 photographs.

A78.13 BEHRENS (FRANCIS MARION) PAPERS. Portraits of F. M. and C. L. Behrens from the Llano and San Saba vicinity. 127 photographs; 35 postcards. Ca. 1928. Kielman# 159.

A78.14 BENEDICT (HARRY YANDELL; 1869-1937) PAPERS. Professor at the University of Texas at Austin. Portraits of Benedict and others, University of Texas at Austin buildings. 106 photographs. 1884 to 1940s. Kielman# 171.

A78.15 BLACK (READING W.; 1830-1867) PAPERS. Portraits of Black and family. 13 photographs. Ca. 1870 to 1880s. Kielman# 196.

A78.16 BLACKBURN (WILLIAM A.) PAPERS AND BLACKBURN-TOWNSEND FAMILY PAPERS. Portraits of Angeline Louise, James William Culbertson, and Townsend family; views in Austin and San Antonio, Colorado, Fairmont Park, Philadephia PA, Mexico. 126 photographs. 1874 to 1903. Kielman# 198, 199.

A78.17 BLAKE (ROBERT BRUCE) PAPERS. Architecture, including Mission San Xavier del Bac (Tucson AZ), Brownsville, Old Groesbeck home, Mission San José, and San Antonio. 192 photographs. Kielman# 205.

A78.18 BONHAM (DORA DIETERICH; 1902-1973) PAPERS. Bonham, Dieterich, and Fulkes family groups, Texas State Library, Price Daniel, Daughters of the Republic of Texas members, Eugene and Lillie Bonham, and Mexican War veterans in Austin 1866-1870. Views in Austin, San

Angelo, and San Antonio, and Travis and Tom Green counties. 441 photographs, including stereographs. Kielman# 225.

A78.19 BOWER (LAWRENCE E.) PAPERS. "Senators, Governors, and Representatives from Tennessee." Portraits. 11 photographs. Kielman# 239.

A78.20 BOWNDS (MARLIN DERIC; 1888-1940) POSTCARD COLLECTION. Depicts refugees of the Mexican Revolution. 19 silver gelatin postcards. Ca. 1911.

A78.21 BOYD (BILL; 1913-1977) COLLECTION. Country-western singer; organized Bill Boyd and his Cowboy Ramblers. Predominantly publicity photographs and movie stills from Boyd's acting career. 188 silver gelatin prints; descriptive inventory. 1930s to 1940s.

A78.22 BREWSTER COUNTY PAPERS. Portraits and landscapes in West Texas. 17 photographs. 1885 to 1930. Kielman# 259.

A78.23 BROWN (JOHN HENRY; 1820-1895) COLLECTION. Soldier, politician, historian, and editor of numerous newspapers. Items relating to Brown's historical writings and to his family. 324 photographs, including daguerreotypes, photo prints, and some nonphotographic imagery; 4 postcard albums. 1850s to 1900. Kielman# 283.

A78.24 BROWN (JOHN HICKMAN) PAPERS. Cabinet maker in Corpus Christi. Portraits of Brown, his workers, shop, and home; furniture designed by him. 114 photographs. 1932 to 1959. Kielman# 284.

A78.25 BURGES (RICHARD FENNER; 1873-1945) PAPERS. Lawyer and Texas legislator (1913-1915). Fort Bliss; aerial photographs of Rio Grande near El Paso; French scenes. 22 photographs and postcards. 1915 to 1918. Kielman# 325.

A78.26 BURLESON (ALBERT SIDNEY; 1863-1937) PAPERS. Politician, district attorney in Austin, US representative, postmaster general, and the first Texan to serve in a president's cabinet (Wilson administration). Airmail inauguration, portraits of Burleson, President Woodrow Wilson, and others. 50 photographs. 1918. Kielman# 333.

A78.27 BUTTE (GEORGE CHARLES; 1877-1940) PAPERS. Educator at the University of Texas at Austin and politician who served as attorney general of Puerto Rico, acting governor general and Supreme Court justice in the Philippine Islands, and Assistant US Attorney General. Portraits of Butte family and friends, buildings, and snapshots. 33 black-and-white photo prints. 1880s to 1930s. Kielman# 354.

A78.28 CALDWELL (FRANK; 1883-1962) COLLECTION. Merchant. Historical materials compiled by Caldwell relating to Texas Rangers, outlaws, and Amerinds. 49 photo prints, 1 album with 60 photographs. Ca. 1868 to 1909.

A78.29 CALLAGHAN RANCH PHOTOGRAPH ALBUM. Images of ranching activities at the Callaghan Ranch near Encinal. 232 silver gelatin prints. 1930s to 1940s.

A78.30 CARRINGTON (JOE C.; 1895-1983) PAPERS. Businessperson, civic leader, state legislator, farmer. Portraits of Carrington made during his career in various business ventures. 100 photo prints. 1922 to 1982.

A78.31 CARRINGTON (LEONIDAS DAVIS; 1816-1881) PAPERS. Merchant and soldier. Carrington family photographs. 17 photographs. Ca. 1863 to 1942. Kielman# 385.

A78.32 CENTENNIAL OF TEXAS RECORDS. Exhibitions at the Hall of State at the Texas Centennial Exposition in Dallas, fair buildings, copies of maps used in exhibit, and Emma Kyle Burleson and children who entered the Centennial Historical Contest. 90 black-and-white photo prints. 1936. Kielman# 414.

A78.33 CHABOT (FREDERICK CHARLES; 1891-1943) PAPERS. Texas historian, helped to found the Yanaguana Society in San Antonio. Texans and Texas buildings; copies of artwork depicting people, buildings, and manuscripts all used in his publications. 60 black-and-white photo prints. Ca. 1930s to 1940s. Materials may be viewed but not reproduced. Kielman# 415.

A78.34 CIVIL WAR MISCELLANY. Battlefield scenes. 35 stereographs. 1860s. Kielman# 437.

A78.35 CLARK (ARTHUR H.) COMPANY; SOUTHWEST HISTORICAL SERIES. Materials relating to the publication of the Southwest Historical Series, edited by Ralph P. Bieber. 100 copy photos. Mid- to late nineteenth century. Kielman# 438.

A78.36 CLARK (SIMEON ENGLISH; 1868-1947) PAPERS. Educator and publisher. Clark family, educators, and pupils and teachers in front of schools in Paris TX. 20 photo prints. 1889 to 1911. Kielman# 445.

A78.37 COHEN (HENRY; 1836-1952) PAPERS. Rabbi at the Temple B'nai Israel in Galveston, influential in religious and social welfare activities in Texas, especially prison reform, hospitals, schools, and immigration. Family photograph album; portraits. 310 photographs, most prints, some negatives, and 1 tintype; postcard collection (3,289 items). Ca. 1880 to 1950s. Kielman# 464.

A78.38 COLP (DAVID E.; 1868-ca. 1936) PAPERS. Texas Highway Department official, chairman of the State Park Board. 1 album, *Bosque County's State Park Site* (ca. 1927); 2 inches photo prints and postcards of Texas outdoor scenes. Ca. 1920s. Kielman# 480.

A78.39 COLQUITT (OSCAR BRANCH; 1861-1940) PAPERS. Texas governor (1910-1915), newspaperman, state senator (1895-1899), railroad commissioner, member of US Board of Mediation and the Reconstruction Finance Corporation. Family, friends, namesakes, prisoners building roads, and architecture. Album and program of the St. Anthony Hotel, 1911. 5 inches photo prints and postcards. Ca. 1900 to 1911. Kielman# 482.

A78.40 CONRADS (ARTHUR) PHOTOGRAPH COLLECTION. Commercial photographs. Hispanic life, Hispanic-Anglo relations, architecture, and city development of Kenedy and Karnes City. Photographed by Conrads. 10,000 glass negatives, 35 photo prints. 1900 to 1940.

A78.41 COPPINI (POMPEO LUIGI; 1870-1984) AND WALDINE AMANDA TAUCH (b. 1892) PAPERS. Texas sculptors. Portraits of Coppini and Tauch, their work, and their families. 200 photo prints. 1890s to 1960s.

A78.42 COTNER (ROBERT CRAWFORD; 1906-1980) PAPERS. Professor of history at the University of Texas at Austin (1940-1977), author of *James Stephen Hogg: A Biography* (Austin: University of Texas Press, 1959). University of Texas at Austin history department, James Stephen Hogg and portraits, Ima Hogg, the Quitman house, US historic sites, illustrations for Cotner's publications, and Texas politicians. 175 photo prints and postcards; 4 canisters of film. Ca. 1951 to 1979. Kielman# 505.

A78.43 CRAFT (JUANITA JEWEL SHANKS; b. 1902) COLLECTION. NAACP activist and educator. NAACP functions and portraits of NAACP leaders, Texas Blacks, and Heman Marion Sweatt. 42 copy and vintage silver gelatin prints. 1890s (copies), vintage photographs to 1950s.

A78.44 CRANE (EDWARD; 1883-1959) PAPERS. Lawyer, professor of law at the University of Texas at Austin, and a regent of UT. Camp Funston (San Antonio), Ed Crane, UT Law School Class of 1906 fiftieth reunion, Roy Bedichek. 23 photo prints. 1917 to 1942. Martin McNulty Crane papers (v.i.) has related materials.

A78.45 CRANE (MARTIN McNULTY; 1855-1943) PAPERS. Lawyer and politician, serving as Johnson County Attorney, state representative, lieutenant governor, and state attorney general. Edward Crane, Crane family, Raymond W. Kearney. 24 photo prints. 1885 to 1918.

A78.46 CRIMMINS (MARTIN LALOR; 1876-1955) PAPERS. US Army officer, herpetologist, military historian. US military history, Texas forts, Amerinds, military officers, copies of artworks depicting battles. 139 photographs. Kielman# 525.

A78.47 CULBERSON (OLIN; 1886-1961) PAPERS. Member of the Texas Railroad Commission. Photographs document his career on the commission. 150 photo prints, 2 albums, and 6 motion picture films.

A78.48 CUMMINS (WILLIAM FLETCHER; 1840-1931) PAPERS. Methodist clergyman and geologist. Scenes near Mission; C. S. Butterfield construction project; Butterfield dredge (irrigation canal); oil fields in Mexico; San Augustin; Capote Canyon "Between Paisano Pass and Stroble"; geologic formations in Texas; identified locations in Texas and Mexico. 230 photo prints, 34 small panorama prints, 37 photo negatives. 1909 to 1933. Kielman# 542.

A78.49 DABNEY (LUCY JANE; b. 1880) NARRATIVE. Teacher. Portraits of Dabney; Huntsville, Sam Houston State Teachers College. 35 photographs. 1897 to 1934. Kielman# 549.

A78.50 DAILEY (HENRY W.) PAPERS. Portraits, C. P. Dailey store, Kenedy vicinity. 22 photographs. 1893 to 1915. Kielman# 551.

A78.51 DANIEL (WALTER LAWRENCE) PHOTOGRAPHS. Commercial photographer. Lubbock, construction of the Texas Tech University campus, oil fields, small Texas towns, WW II training camps. Photographed by Daniel. 1,500 photo prints, 1,000 negatives, 1 portfolio album. 1916 to 1968.

A78.52 DAUGHERTY (JAMES MONROE; b. 1850) PAPERS. Express rider, trail driver, rancher, and cattleman. Identified portraits. 28 photographs, including a few copy prints. 1896 to 1968. Kielman# 559.

A78.53 DAVIS (MORGAN JONES; 1898-1979) PAPERS. Chairman of Humble Oil Company. Portraits of Davis and family, Humble Oil Company. 100 photo prints, 49 negatives.

A78.54 DE ZAVALA (ADINA EMILIA; 1861-1955) PAPERS. Founder of the Daughters of the Republic of Texas, noted for her efforts to preserve the Alamo. Family photographs, missions and the Alamo, retrospective views of historic Texas structures, and portraits of notable Texans. 5 albums, 3,200 photographs, negatives, and postcards. 1930s. Kielman# 602.

A78.55 DODD (JIMMIE A.; 1917-1984) COLLECTION. Kingsville and Kerrville commercial photographer; from 1935 to 1950 Dodd had carte blanche to photograph the King Ranch. Subjects include traffic accidents taken for the police, wedding portraits, sports, celebrities, and Texas towns. Texas locales include Alice, Bishop, Kerrville, Kingsville, and Kleberg County.

> People: Abbot and Costello. Gene Autry. Wee Bonnie Baker. Lucille Ball. Macon Banner. Sarah Banner. Ann Baxter. Roy Bean. General Boatner. Eddie Byrne. E. S. Childs. K. A. Childs. E. B. Dodd. J. A. Dodd. Jimmie Dodd. Nellie B. Dodd. Wallace Ford. Judy Garland. Greer Garson. Mary Virginia Gunter. Peter Hanson. John Hodiak. President and Mrs. Lyndon B. Johnson. Jack Kidd. Ruth Ann King. Robert Justus Kleberg. Laurel and Hardy. Fred Lowery. Robert Mitchum. Tom Mix. Wayne Morris. Ed Oliver. Joe Passant. Bud Piper. Roy Rogers. Will Rogers. Mickey Rooney. Franklin Delano Roosevelt. "Babe" Ruth. Tom Sanderson. Allan Shivers. Bill Schultz. Dr. Sieblett. Ben Oris Sims. Dawson Smith. Coke Stevenson. Jimmy Stewart. Arthur Treacher. Harry S. Truman. Jake Trussell. Zack Webb. Carol Ann White.

> Subjects: Actors and actresses. American Legion. Automobiles— dealerships. Baptist church. Battleship Texas. Blacks—weddings. Boy Scouts. Business establishments and stores. Catholic church. Celanese Corporation. Central Power and Light. Chamber of Commerce. Children. Churches. Cities and towns. Clubs. Death and dying. El Jardín Club. Fairs. Family groups. Festivals—Buccaneer Days. Corpus Christi. Funerals. Future Farmers of America. Girl Scouts and Camp Fire Girls. Governors—Texas. Jersey Products. KINE Radio Station. King High School (Kingsville). King Ranch. Knights of Columbus. Lions Club. Lutheran church. Methodist church. Mexican Americans—weddings. Parades and processions—floats. Police. Poliomyelitis. Presbyterian church. Railroads—disasters, —Missouri Pacific Lines. Rodeos. Seamen. Sports—baseball, —football, —golf. Texas A&I College. Traffic accidents. US Marine Corps. Weddings.

10 feet (10,000) negatives; 40 modern prints. 1937 to 1966. Itemized inventory of names and subjects taken from Dodd's envelopes.

A78.56 DONELSON (WILLIAM A.) FAMILY PAPERS. "Relating to the social and genealogical interests of Donelson and other descendents of Rachael Donelson Jackson." 19 photographs. Kielman# 619.

A78.57 DUKE (CORDIA SLOAN; 1877-1966) PAPERS. Teacher and wife of XIT Ranch foreman, Bob Duke. XIT Ranch, ranch life, and workers. 100 photo prints. 1900 to 1940.

A78.58 DUREN (ALMETRIS) PAPERS. Black UT student advisor and housemother, author. Slide shows, "Mama Duren Overcoming" and "Innervision of Blackness"; Andrew Young, March on Washington (1983), and portraits. 146 photo prints, negatives, and slides. 1950 to 1983. See Bibliography—Duren.

A78.59 EAST TEXAS PHOTOGRAPH COLLECTION. Lumber industry, merchants, and railroads in East Texas and the Big Thicket. 58 photo prints. 1900s.

A78.60 EBERSTADT (EDWARD; 1883-1958) COLLECTION. Collector of Texana and Western Americana. Oil industry. 100 photographs, including stereographs. Ca. 1900 to 1959.

A78.61 EDWARDS (PEYTON FORBES; 1844-1918) FAMILY PAPERS. Soldier in the Civil War, attorney in Nacogdoches, judge, and politician. Family photographs. 10 photo prints, 1 daguerreotype. 1850s to 1947. Kielman# 680.

A78.62 EMMETT (CHRIS) PAPERS. Writer, lawyer, historian. Portraits, including A. H. "Shanghai" Pierce; views in Indianola and on the Gulf Coast. 51 photographs. 1873 to 1889. Kielman# 695.

A78.63 ERWIN (FRANK CRAIG, Jr.; 1920-1980) PAPERS. Regent and lobbyist for the University of Texas. Photographs depict students at the University and his service in the US Navy during WW II. 46 photographs. 1925 and early 1940s.

A78.64 FERGUSON (JAMES EDWARD; 1871-1944) COLLECTION. Ferguson and his wife, Miriam, both governors of Texas, burned their papers on leaving office, hence this collection compiled by Alex Dienst is unique. Ferguson family portraits by Howell Apex Studio (Temple) and unidentified photographers. 8 photographs. 1914 to 1924.

A78.65 FLURY (GODFREY; 1864-1936) COLLECTION. Decorative interior paintings of Saint Mary's Church in Praha and private homes and paintings executed by Flury; family photographs. Photo prints, slides. 1891 to 1926.

A78.66 GALVESTON, TEXAS WPA GUIDE ILLUSTRATIONS. Buildings and scenes in Galveston produced for this volume in the American Guide series. 122 photo prints, 29 drawings. 1930s.

A78.67 GEORGE (ANDREW W.) PAPERS. Photographer and cook. Studio portraits of Blacks and Caucasians by various nineteenth-century Austin photographers; snapshots of Llano street scenes (1880s); snapshot album of destruction of Melissa after a tornado (1921); stereographs of San Antonio by H. A. Doerr and unidentified photographer(s). 250 photographs, including 35 tintypes, 36 stereographs, cabinets and cartes. 1870s to 1920s. Kielman# 818.

A78.68 GIDEON (SAMUEL; 1875-1945) COLLECTION. Professor of architectural design and history. Papers relate to efforts to preserve historical structures. General Land Office; portraits, including W. S. Porter (= O. Henry); architecture (by county) especially Bastrop, Bexar, Gillespie, Grimes, Limestone, Marion, Mason, Medina, and Travis. 1,167 photographs, 1,547 slides, 152 glass negatives. 1886 to 1940s. Kielman# 826.

A78.69 GOODMAN (MARK; b. 1946) PHOTOGRAPH COLLECTION. Photographer, winner of Guggenheim Fellowship. Street scenes photographed by Goodman for his project, "Five Cities, Urban Texas: A View from the Street," including Dallas, El Paso, Fort Worth, Houston, and San Antonio. 50 photo prints. 1985.

A78.70 HAWKINS (WALACE EUGENE; 1895-1951) PAPERS. Personal and family portraits. 40 photographs. Kielman# 987.

A78.71 HEINSOHN (EDMUND; b. 1888) PAPERS. Pastor of University Methodist Church (Austin). Group and individual portraits of Dr. Heinsohn and parishioners, churches. 26 photo prints. Ca. 1923.

A78.72 HICKMAN (R. C.) NEGATIVES. Commercial and freelance photographer. Photographs by Hickman of Black life and the civil rights movement in Dallas. 7,000 negatives. 1950s to 1973.

A78.73 HILL (CARYL CLYDE; b. 1874) PAPERS. Portraits, West Texas. 25 photo prints, 4 negatives. Ca. 1912. Kielman# 1023.

A78.74 HINKLE (MILT D. "WRANG"; 1881-1972) PAPERS. Known as Mr. Rodeo, the South America Kid, and Uncle Milt; Hinkle's successful attempt to bulldog from a plane in Mexico in 1931 crippled him for life, hindering his career as a rodeo contestant; he was also a peace officer, Texas border patrolman, and a bodyguard for Theodore Roosevelt. Material pertains to his writings for *True West*, *Old West*, and *Frontier Times* magazines. 34 photo prints. 1964 to 1968.

A78.75 HISTORIC AMERICAN BUILDING SURVEY. Retrospective views of historical structures. 1,000 photo prints; arranged by county. 1960s. Kielman# 1036.

A78.76 HOGG (JAMES STEPHEN; 1851-1906) PAPERS. Newspaper publisher and public official serving as county attorney, state attorney general, and governor of Texas (1891-1895). 210 photographs. 1868 to 1955. Kielman# 1041.

A78.77 HOGG (WILLIAM CLIFFORD; 1871-1930) PAPERS. Son of James Stephen Hogg (v.s.), lawyer, businessperson. Family portraits, including James Stephen Hogg and Albert Sidney Burleson. 3 albums of 230 photographs, 10 loose photo prints, and 70 negatives. Kielman# 1042.

A78.78 HOLLIMAN (BLAINE S., Jr.) COLLECTION. Philippines, Turkey. 76 postcards. 1930s.

A78.79 HUNT (ROSALIS BATTLE) COLLECTION. Retrospective views of historic sites in North Carolina and Texas. 41 photographs.

A78.80 JAMES FAMILY PAPERS. Charles Albert James (1841-1875), John Garland James (1844-1930), and Fleming Wills James (1847-1918) founded the Texas Military Institute in 1868. Texas Military Institute facility; various cadets in both Bastrop and Austin. 10 photo prints. 1869 to 1879.

A78.81 JONES (JESSE HOLMAN; 1874-1956) PAPERS. Texas lumberman, banker, and statesman. Portraits of Jones and others; buildings and theaters, especially in Houston; the San Jacinto Monument. 1,000 photo prints. 1930s to 1950s.

A78.82 JONES (MARY C.) COLLECTION. Portraits, Colorado City TX, gravestones. 212 photographs. 1890 to 1910.

A78.83 KEMP (LOUIS WILTZ; 1881-1956) PAPERS. Business executive and historian. Portraits; gravesites, historic sites in Texas. 295 photographs. 1895 to 1937. Kielman# 1167.

A78.84 KREGER (EDWARD ALBERT; 1868-1955) PAPERS. Teacher, lawyer, US Army general. Portraits, Philippines. 419 photographs. 1900. Kielman# 1205.

A78.85 KREKTING (STEVEN M.) PHOTOGRAPH COLLECTION. Student at the University of Texas at Austin in the mid-1970s. Landscapes photographed by Krekting of the Rio Grande near Redford. 60 photo prints. Ca. 1976.

A78.86 KUEHNE (Dr. JOHN MATTHIAS; 1872-1960) COLLECTION. Professor of chemistry at the University of Texas at Austin. Daily life in Austin and around the university. 1,000 silver gelatin glass negatives, autochromes, and modern prints. 1880s to 1920s.

A78.87 LANHAM (FRITZ GARLAND; 1880-1965) PAPERS. UT student, lawyer, and US representative. Portraits of Lanham alone and in groups, postcards of San Antonio, the Midwest, Rocky Mountains, and Pacific Northwest. 27 photo prints, 140 postcards. 1890s to 1920s.

A78.88 LANHAM (SAMUEL WILLIS TUCKER; 1845-1908) PAPERS. Lawyer, US representative, and governor of Texas. Portraits of Lanham, family, friends, and politicians. 48 photo prints. 1890s to 1906.

A78.89 LAW (ROBERT ADGER; 1879-1961) PAPERS. Professor. English literary figures and related subjects. 19 photographs. Kielman# 1237.

A78.90 LEDBETTER (JOHN J.; 1901-1963) PAPERS. Engineer. Portraits. 25 photographs. Kielman# 1243.

A78.91 LEDBETTER (LENA DANCY) COLLECTION. Portraits from La Grange. 32 photographs.

A78.92 LEE (RUSSELL; 1903-1986) PHOTOGRAPH COLLECTION. Photographer noted for his political documents and his work for the Farm Security Adminstration. Various projects of Lee's, including his study of Spanish-speaking people in Texas (1949) and the various political campaigns of Ralph Yarborough (1954-1964); contract work for *Fortune* magazine, including photographs of Dow Chemical Company and Arkansas Power and Light Company (1952); contract work for the Arabian-American Oil Company in Saudi Arabia (1955); the Italy portfolio (1960). Other work includes various Texas subjects, his pre-FSA photographs of New York City and Woodstock NY, a trip to South America aboard a tramp steamer (1953), and the "Super University of Texas" project for the *London Observer* (1965). The collection also contains a retrospective slide show of all of Lee's photographs, including work done for the FSA, Air Transport Command, Coal Mines Administration, and Standard Oil of New Jersey that is not in this collection. 8,000 images: 35mm, 120, and 4x5 negatives, safety except for pre-FSA work; contact or modern prints of most items. Negatives are restricted; material is arranged chronologically. Associated manuscript materials include work notes and publications in which Lee's work appears. 1935 to 1977.

A78.93 LENZ (LOUIS; 1885-1967) PAPERS. Civil engineer and historian. Famous Texans and events in Texas history; portraits of Lenz. 600 photo prints.

A78.94 LIDDELL (MARK HARVEY; 1866-1943) PAPERS. Teacher, writer, editor. Portraits. 25 photographs. Kielman# 1260.

A78.95 LIPSCOMB-MYERS COLLECTION. Photographs pertain to Mance Lipscomb (d. 1976) compiled by his biographer, A. Glenn Myers (b. 1947). 169 photo prints, 44 contact prints, 1,109 negatives. 1960s to 1970s.

A78.96 LOMAX (JOHN A.; 1867-1948) COLLECTION. Texas folklorist. Portraits of Lomax and family. 200 photographs. 1900 to 1982.

A78.97 LOUISIANA PHOTOGRAPHS. Views of New Orleans LA and rural Louisiana scenes. Publishers include S. T. Blessing (New Orleans LA), Mugnier (New Orleans LA), and Woodward and Albee (Rochester NY). 30 albumen stereographs. Ca. 1885.

A78.98 McFARLANE (WILLIAM DODDRIDGE; 1894-1980) PAPERS. Lawyer, Texas representative, Texas senator, and US representative. Family photographs. 29 photo prints. Pre-1976.

A78.99 MANN (WILLIAM L.) PAPERS. Historian, retired naval officer. Portraits; Haiti, Quantico, China; corporal punishment of criminals in China. 171 photographs. 1938. Kielman# 1380.

A78.100 MARTIN (ETTA ADELE) FAMILY PAPERS. Martin and Freeman families. 127 photo prints. Ca. 1900.

A78.101 MAVERICK (MAURY, Jr.; b. 1921) PAPERS. Liberal Texas representative (1950 to 1956) known for his opposition to the Red Scare hysteria. Portraits, including two studio portraits of Maverick by Russell Lee; family snapshots; San Antonio, including La Villita Democratic Convention 1952; European and Oriental trips; photographs from his career. 96 photographs, including photo negatives and prints, slides, and album. 1860s to 1981. Kielman# 1141.

A78.102 MAVERICK (MAURY, Sr.; 1895-1954) PAPERS. Politician and lawyer. Portraits of Maverick, his political activities, and of the restoration of La Villita in San Antonio. 1,137 photo prints, 30 negatives, and 138 postcards. Ca. 1895 to 1954.

A78.103 MEEK (JAMES W.) PAPERS. Meek family portraits. 29 pictures. Kielman# 1425.

A78.104 MOOAR (JOHN WRIGHT; 1851-1940) PAPERS. WW I soldiers. 23 photographs. 1915 to 1918. Kielman# 1489.

A78.105 MOSES (HARRY BOWMAN) PAPERS. Newspaper reporter. Portraits; WW I in Italy, France, and Germany. 2 albums containing 86 photographs. 1917 to 1920. Kielman# 1526.

A78.106 NEBLETT (LIZZIE SCOTT; 1833-1917) PAPERS. Portraits and views in Colorado. 200 photographs. 1859 to 1908. Kielman# 1551.

A78.107 ORAL HISTORY OF THE TEXAS OIL INDUSTRY RECORDS. Oilfields, workers, and industry leaders. 300 photo prints. 1890s to 1950s.

A78.108 POPE (JOHN BLAND; 1914-1983) PAPERS. Certified public accountant for the Texas and federal governments. Portraits of Emma Louise Bryant; Pope family, including Jennings Bland, Clinton H., James H., Calvin, and Daniel, Charles W. Jennings, Fleming P. Jennings, John Jennings, Reverend Jacob Jewell, and Gabriel Thompson; Jennings family cemeteries. 50 photographs.

A78.109 PRESIDIO TRICENTENNIAL PHOTOGRAPHS. Views of the 300th-anniversary celebrations of the Presidio-area Catholic missions. 39 negatives, 2 contact sheets. October 1983.

A78.110 PRICE (LUCIE CLIFT; b. 1900) PAPERS. Historical researcher and genealogist. William P. Longley Historical Grove Marker dedication, Lee County Courthouse in Giddings, and a photograph of the alleged Texas Consulate on Saint James Street in London. 45 photo prints, uncounted negatives.

A78.111 PURCELL (MABELLE) PAPERS. Author of *Two Texas female seminaries* (Wichita Falls: Midwestern University Press, 1953). Live Oak Female Seminary; Stuart Seminary faculty and students; portraits, including Chief Justice John Hemphill, Judge Royal T. Wheeler, Judge Abner Lipscomb, and Melinda Rankin; churches and church schools. 194 photo prints, 100 slides, 138 glass and film photo negatives. Ca. 1870s to ca. 1899.

A78.112 PURCELL (STUART M.; b. 1890) PAPERS. Second lieutenant, 147th Aero Squadron, First Pursuit Group, American Expeditionary Forces. US servicemen in France; Eddie Rickenbacker. 4 photo prints, 1 album of photo prints, 1 photo negative. Ca. 1917 to mid-1920s.

A78.113 REASONER (LAWRENCE L.; d. 1980) PAPERS. Businessperson. Documents the development of the town of Kenedy. 576 photo prints, 40 negatives, 1 album. 1894 to 1974.

A78.114 REAUGH (FRANK; 1860-1945) PAPERS. Texas painter. Art reproductions of Reaugh's paintings. 496 color transparencies and a few photo prints. Prints ca. 1900; transparencies ca. 1966 and 1983.

A78.115 RED CROSS PAPERS. Lamar County chapter of the Red Cross during WW I, especially Paris TX; knitting. 1917 to 1919. Kielman# 1769.

A78.116 RHONE FAMILY PAPERS. Family of Calvin Lindley Rhone (1867-1921) and Lucia J. Knotts Rhone (1866-1941) was a highly regarded Black family who resided in Fayette County; teacher, church leader. Family photographs, including children Lucia, Beulah, and Lucious Rhone and Urissa Rhone Brown. 104 photo prints, some negatives. Pre-1975.

A78.117 ROCKWELL BROTHERS RECORDS. Operated M. T. Jones Lumber Company, Rockwell Brothers and Company (Houston), and retail lumber yards in Texas. Architecture and views in Austin, Boston, and Europe. 131 photographs. 1869 to 1940. Kielman# 1817.

A78.118 RUNYON (ROBERT) PHOTOGRAPH COLLECTION. Commercial photographer, politician, merchant, and botanist in Brownsville. Studio portraiture, scenes of the Mexican Revolution, Rio Grande Valley towns, trees and plants, and Runyon family members. Photographed by Runyon. 2,500 glass and 2,000 film negatives; 100 lantern slides, 2,000 photo prints. 1909 to 1947.

A78.119 SAYERS (JOSEPH DRAPER; 1841-1929) PAPERS. Texas governor (1898-1902). Portraits; scenes. 10 photographs. Ca. 1890 to 1907. Kielman# 1892.

A78.120 SHARP (Mrs. WALTER B., = ESTELLE BOUGHTON) PAPERS. Member of the Texas Federation of Women's Clubs. New Mexico, especially Santa Fe. 51 photographs. 1872 to 1916. Kielman# 1930.

A78.121 SIMMONS (DAVID A.) PAPERS. Portraits and material relating to George P. Finlay and David Antley Simmons; views in Texas, New York City, and Washington DC; Old Fort Davis, including ruins and its centennial celebration. 344 photographs, 2 albums. 1917 to 1954.

A78.122 SIMONDS (FREDERIC WILLIAM; 1853-1941) PAPERS. Professor at the University of Texas at Austin. Portraits. 52 photographs, 4 glass negatives. Kielman# 1961.

A78.123 SIMPSON (JOHN HARPER; 1854-1940) PAPERS. Family portraits. 17 photographs, 1 album. 1868 to 1936. Kielman# 1964.

A78.124 SMITH (THOMAS VERNOR; b. 1890) PAPERS. Professor of philosophy at universities of Chicago, Syracuse, and Texas. Portraits. 100 photographs. 1933. Kielman# 1994.

A78.125 SOULE (WILLIAM S.; 1836-1908) PHOTOGRAPHS. Portraits of Amerinds photographed by Soule. 1 album of albumen prints. 1870s.

A78.126 SPARKS (LYRA HAISLEY) PAPERS. Writer. Haisley family portraits. 32 photographs. 1908 to 1916. Kielman# 2015.

A78.127 STEACY (J. G.) PAPERS. Railroad contractor for Peirce, Steacy, and Yorston; executive. Unidentified portraits. 14 photographs. 1869 to ca. 1900. Kielman# 2033.

A78.128 TAULMAN (JOSEPH EDWARD; 1863-1946) COLLECTION. Linotype operator, soldier, and an itinerant photographer who settled in Clifton. Primarily studio portraiture; some pictorialist work. 2,000 vintage prints. Late nineteenth century to 1920s. Kielman# 2105.

A78.129 TAYLOR (PAT ELLIS; b. 1941) PAPERS. Author of *Border healing woman: The story of Jewel Babb* (Austin: University of Texas Press, 1981). Babb, Big Bend scenes, goats, horses, and healing scenes. 16—35mm contact sheets. Ca. 1980.

A78.130 TAYLOR (THOMAS ULVAN) PAPERS. Portraits and Austin architecture; University of Texas at Austin. 1,000 photographs and negatives. 1883 to 1939.

A78.131 TERRELL (ALEXANDER WATKINS; 1827-1912) PAPERS. Lawyer, judge, legislator, soldier, diplomat. Portraits. 38 photographs. 1881 to 1912. Kielman# 2118.

A78.132 TEXAS AERIAL PHOTOGRAPHS. Aerial landscapes produced by the US Department of Agriculture and the US Army Corps of Engineers. 1,000 photo prints. 1940 to 1974.

A78.133 TEXAS AND SOUTHWESTERN CATTLE RAISER'S ASSOCIATION RECORDS. Cattle and conventions of the association. 14 loose prints, 1 album. 1877 to 1951.

A78.134 TEXAS FILM COLLECTION. Production and scene stills from films relating to Texas. 215 photo prints. 1940 to 1984.

A78.135 TEXAS STUDENT PUBLICATION FILES. Portraits, student life, and the University of Texas at Austin campus; for such publications as *Cactus*, *The Daily Texan*, and *The Ranger*. 100,000 negatives and prints. 1895 to 1985.

A78.136 TEXAS WAR RECORDS COLLECTION. Portraits of soldiers and training camps during WW I and WW II. 500 photo prints. 1917 to 1945.

A78.137 THOMPSON (LEWIS; 1825-1888) PAPERS. Aftermath of a tornado that struck Melissa TX. 25 photographs. April 23, 1921. Kielman# 2171.

A78.138 TOWNSEND (GEORGE F.; b. 1871) PAPERS. Austin cityscapes. 35 photographs, 12 glass negatives. 1885 to 1888. Kielman# 2191.

A78.139 TROTH (FRANCIS M.) PAPERS. Service of Troth in Company I, 21st Regiment Missouri Volunteer Infantry (1862-1865); family pictures. 53 photographs in 2 albums. Associated diary. Kielman# 2201.

A78.140 TURRILL (CHARLES B.; 1854-1927) COLLECTION. Commercial photographs made for the Southern Pacific Railroad during the construction of the Sunset Limited Route depicting landscapes and railways; cityscapes of El Paso, including a 6-plate panorama. 300 silver prints, 108 glass negatives. 1898 to 1905.

A78.141 UDDEN (JOHAN A.) COLLECTION. Geologic formations in Coke and Runnels counties. 32 photo prints, 10 negatives. 1917 to 1918.

A78.142 UNIVERSITY OF TEXAS AT AUSTIN PHYSICAL TRAINING FOR WOMEN RECORDS. Department, associated women's sports organizations, intramurals, clubs, and physical education classes; archery, badminton, basketball, bowling, dance, riding; clubs such as Bit and Spur, Strike and Spare, Tee Club, and the Triggerettes. 100 photo prints, film and glass photo negatives. 1924 to 1958.

A78.143 UNIVERSITY OF TEXAS AT AUSTIN–SOCIAL ACTIVITIES PHOTOGRAPHS. Various university student organizations during social events. 810 color contact prints. 1978 to 1981.

A78.144 UNIVERSITY OF TEXAS–UNIVERSITY INTERSCHOLASTIC LEAGUE RECORDS. League events. 4,000 photo prints. 1914 to 1965.

A78.145 WEBB (WALTER PRESCOTT; 1888-1963) PAPERS. Historian, professor at the University of Texas at Austin. Portraits of Webb alone and in groups; William E. Hinds, Sam Rayburn, Rupert P. Ricker, Texas Rangers, Ranger High School. 674 photo prints and 130 negatives. Pre-1964. Kielman# 2304.

A78.146 WERDEN (FRIEDA) PAPERS. Poet, journalist, radio talk-show host, feminist, and lesbian. Austin poetry readings and images relating to the Texas Women's History Project. Ca. 1968 to 1983.

A78.147 WHITNEY (FRANCIS LUTHER; 1878-1962) PHOTOGRAPHS. Geologist, paleontologist, professor. Portraits of Whitney, his wife, and Frederic William Simonds; views of the University of Texas at Austin and natural settings in and around Austin. 110 photographs, 152 glass and film negatives. Ca. 1900 to 1910. Kielman# 2347.

A78.148 WILLRICH (GEORGE) COLLECTION. Portraits and views in Cuba and Florida. 55 photographs. 1898 to 1905.

A78.149 WINEGARTEN (RUTHE) PAPERS. Participant in the Texas Women's History Project and active in such community organizations as League of Women Voters and B'nai B'rith. Labor Day Samuel Gompers Celebration in San Antonio, 1982; and an American Nazi Party demonstration and a peace demonstration, both in Dallas, 1967. 26 photo prints. 1897 (copy) to 1982.

A78.150 WOODWARD (DUDLEY KEZER, Jr.; 1881-1967) PAPERS. Regent of the University of Texas at Austin. Portrait of W. F. Street and the University of Texas Dental Branch in Houston. 12 photo prints. 1952 to 1954.

A78.151 WORKS PROGRESS ADMINISTRATION RECORDS. Views of Texas cities made by WPA photographers. 2,000 photo prints, 1,000 negatives. 1936 to 1940.

A78.152 ZIEGLER (JESSIE D.) PAPERS. Secretary to Governor Ross Sterling 1931 to 1932; reporter in Houston; member of the Women's Advertising Club of Houston. Ziegler and friends on trips through Texas and New Mexico. 57 photo prints. Ca. 1930.

Nettie Lee Benson Latin American Collection (A80)

University of Texas
Sid Richardson Hall 1.109
Red River and Twenty-fourth Street
Austin, Texas 78712-7330

512-471-3818. Contact: Head Librarian.

PURPOSE: A research library concentrating on Latin America and the Caribbean, and Hispanics in the US. Holdings include rare and recent books and periodicals, manuscripts, maps, realia, and photographs. Photographs are maintained in the Rare Books and Manuscripts Department.

HOURS: Weekdays, 9:00-5:00; plus September through May, Saturday, 1:00-5:00. Closed major holidays.

ASSISTANCE: Professional, specialized staff. Written inquiries accepted. Electrostatic copies available. Photoduplications may be made with prior arrangement or ordered through the library.

PUBLICATION: No publication fee. Collection credit required. Free copy of publication to the library. Third-party permission required on a few items.

FINDING AIDS: Card index for record groups; subject access. Published finding aid for Mexican-American collections; see Bibliography—Flores.

BIBLIOGRAPHY:

Cordry, Donald. *Mexican masks*. Austin: University of Texas Press, 1980.

Flores, Maria G., and Laura Gutiérrez Witt. *Mexican American archives at the Benson Latin American Collection: A guide for users*. Austin: University of Texas General Libraries, 1981.

García, Genaro. *Crónica oficial de las fiestas del primer centario de la independencia de México*. Mexico: Talleres de Museo Nacional, 1911.

Hollowood, Bernard. *The story of Morro Velho*. London, 1955.

McAndrew, John. *The open-air churches of sixteenth-century Mexico*. Cambridge MA: Harvard University Press, 1965.

SCOPE: 30,500 vintage photographs, most prints. Many record groups have associated manuscript materials. 1860s to present.

Type of photo	Pre-1880	1880-1899	1900-1919	1920-1939	1940-1959	1960-1986
Film negs						10,000
Vintage prints	750	1,500	5,000	2,700	500	15,000
Photo albums		2	6			

GEOGRAPHIC: Latin America, the Caribbean, and Spanish-speaking areas of the US. Foreign countries include Brazil, Mexico, and Peru.

SUBJECTS: The collection attempts to document in general the political, economic, and social life of the Latin American region.

Architecture (Brazilian—17th century, Mexican—16th century, haciendas, religious—cathedrals, religious—missions, retrospective views). Cityscapes (travel views—19th century). Events (Mexico—Centennial and International Exposition—1910). Industry (mining). Military (Mexican Revolution—1910, Pershing's Punitive Expedition).

PEOPLE: Portraits of many prominent political, intellectual, and religious leaders in Latin America; few held in quantity. Some ethnographic material pertains to various cultural groups, including Central and South American Indians.

Ethnic (Central American Indians, South American Indians, Hispanic). Politicians. Religious (Catholic clergy).

PHOTOGRAPHERS: Various studio and amateur photographers predominantly from Mexico and some from Europe. See Record Groups for description of work by:

Adams Hnos. Aubert y Cía (Cd México). Hugo Brehme. A. Bríquet (Cd México). F. Cruces y Cía (Durango). Cruces y Campa (Cd México). Disderi (Paris). Marcel Gautherot. W. H. Horne (El Paso). Ironmonger (CA). Hans Mann. Joaquín Martínez (Puebla). Kildare. Ignacio Millán. Mora (Cd México). Motes de Oca (Cd México). F. E. Myers and Company. Patiño. Ramos. Scott. C. B. Waite.

RECORD GROUPS: Mexican-American archives with unprocessed photographic materials include: Escobar, LULAC, and Economy Furniture Company Strike Archives. Many record groups contain exclusively photo postcards from Central and South American countries and Spain (not abstracted): Laura Tausch Eiband collection, Hispanic Society of America collection, and Jeanette J. Varner collection.

A80.1 ADAMS (RICHARD NEWBOLD) COLLECTION. Aerial sequences, most unidentified, a few from Cd Chiclayo and Pachacamac, Peru. 159 silver gelatin prints. Ca. 1950.

A80.2 [*Album of Guatemala views: Presented to the Antiquarian Society by Mary L. Hammond.*] Studio portraits of prominent military and political leaders, workers, and Mayan Indians of Guatemala; commercial travel views of Guatemala City, Quezaltenango, Escuintla, and other locations. Photographed by Kildare and unidentified other(s). 82 albumen and silver gelatin prints. 1883 to 1904. Itemized list.

A80.3 *Anexo al trabajo: La lucha antituberculosa en el Estado Zulia. Su evolución y sus problemas.* Buildings, patients, and rehabilitation programs. 34 silver gelatin prints. 1958. BLAC# RA/644/T7/A552/LAC-Z.

A80.4 BARTLETT (PAUL) PHOTOGRAPHS OF MEXICAN HACIENDAS. Artist and writer. Snapshot retrospective views of Mexican haciendas used as reference for drawings. Extensive coverage of Castamay in Campeche; Puerto de Nieto in Guanajuato; Blanca, San Felipe, and Tenache in Oaxaca; and other haciendas in Hidalgo, Jalisco, Puebla, and Yucatán; many haciendas are closely documented in detail and overall perspective. 890 photo prints, transparencies; pen-and-ink drawings made from the photographs; itemized list. 1951 to 1971.

A80.5 BRAZILIAN ART AND ARCHITECTURE COLLECTION. Retrospective views of South American baroque architecture, predominantly civil and religious, and related artworks from the colonial period; substantial coverage of the regions of Rio Grande do Sul, Rio de Janeiro, Bahia, Alagoas, Ceará, Paraíba, Pernambuco, Amazônia, Minas Gerais, and Congonhas in Brazil; of Copacabana, Jesús de Machaca, Tiahuanaco, Guaicuí, and La Paz in Bolivia; and of Juli, Acora, Vilque, Pomata, and Arequipa in Peru. Photographed by Hans Mann and Marcel Gautherot. 3,186 negatives, 2,945 contact prints, 1,233 silver gelatin prints. 1967.

A80.6 Bríquet, A., photog. [*Brisbin album*]. Commercial travel views of landscapes, natives, city scenes, and the Mexican National Railroad throughout Mexico, especially the states of Mexico and Vera Cruz. 64 albumen prints with captions. Ca. 1890. Itemized list.

A80.7 CHARLES (Mrs. R. E.) ALBUM. Travel views of landscapes and architecture in Mexico and Santa Clara Island CA; photographs by Ironmonger and others. 61 silver gelatin and collodio-chloride prints. Ca. 1900.

A80.8 CORDRY (DONALD) COLLECTION. Art reproductions of ceremonial Mexican folk masks, mask makers, and people wearing the masks. 88 silver gelatin prints, 2 negatives, and 201−120 Ektachrome transparencies. 1970s. See Bibliography—Cordry.

A80.9 DULLES (JOHN FOSTER) COLLECTION. Autographed, commercial group portraits of Mexican politicians and foreign dignitaries visiting Mexico, including Dulles, and commercial portraits of Dulles alone; many relate to mining operations in Mexico. 99 silver gelatin prints. 1950s.

A80.10 ECONOMY FURNITURE COMPANY STRIKE COLLECTION. Picket lines, marches, rallies, and local and national labor leaders in Austin. 165 silver gelatin and color prints. 1968 to 1972. Unprocessed.

A80.11 ESCOBAR COLLECTION. Family and group portraits, schools, and city scenes probably in San Antonio. 150 photo prints. 1930s to 1940s. Unprocessed.

A80.12 GARCÍA (GENARO) COLLECTION. Mexican Centennial and International Exposition; portraits of prominent military, governmental, and religious figures; miscellany, generally of a historical and topographical nature.

A80.12.1 COLECCIÓN DE FOTOGRAFÍAS GENARO GARCÍA 1A. Mexico's centennial celebrations and festivities. 1) Official ceremonies, parades, identified foreign dignitaries individually and in groups. 247 gelatino-chloride and silver gelatin prints. 2) Official functions, school programs, and military parades; special night scenes of the "16 de Septiembre" celebrations. 253 gelatino-chloride and silver gelatin prints. 3) Inauguration of the Escuela Normal para Hombres, of the Manicomio General, and the laying of the cornerstone of the Palacio Legislativo; scenes of the visit of the Congreso de Americanistas, of Porfirio Díaz to munitions factory, and military parades and maneuvers. 250 gelatino-chloride and silver gelatin prints. 4) Foreign dignitaries. 251 gelatino-chloride and silver gelatin prints. 5) Studio portraits of Catholic religious figures, many photographed by Mora (Cd México). 37 silver gelatin cabinet prints. 6) Studio portraits, predominantly of military figures. 29 silver gelatin cabinet prints. Groups 1 to 4 commercial, journalistic documents, many (possibly all) by Ramos. Groups 5 and 6 are apparently unrelated to the Mexican centennial, representing "personajes civiles, eclesiásticos y militares." Total, 1,067 photo prints. 1880s, 1910.

A80.12.2 COLECCIÓN DE FOTOGRAFÍAS GENARO GARCÍA 2A. Mexican Centennial and International Exposition. 1) and 2) Commercial architectural views of interiors, exteriors with decorations, and night views with light decorations; studio portraits of "embajadores, residencias embajatorias, actos cívicos"; exposition exhibits. 298 silver gelatin and gelatino-chloride prints. 3) and 4) Commercial views of "fiestas sociales, el Día 16 (1810-1910), exposiciones, mejoras materiales, Museo Nacional." 189 silver gelatin and gelatino-chloride prints. 5) Additional centennial photographs. 133 silver gelatin and gelatino-chloride prints. Total, 620 photographs. 1910.

A80.12.3 COLECCIÓN DE FOTOGRAFÍAS GENARO GARCÍA. 1) Travel postcards. 133 silver gelatin and photomechanical postcards. 2A) Studio portrait, "Retratos de mujeres de Tehuántepec (con vestidos típicos)." 96 silver gelatin photo postcards. 2B) "Gen. Félix Díaz en Veracruz, 1912." 26 silver gelatin and photomechanical postcards. 3) Studio portraits and art reproductions of "Personajes históricos europeos" prominent literary and intellectual figures of Europe and England; by various European and English photographers. 37 cabinet prints. Total, 912 items. 1880s to 1910s.

A80.12.4 GARCÍA CARTES DE VISITE [I]. Studio portraits of various individuals, most prominent citizens, government officials, or military officers; by various Mexican photographers, including Cruces y Campa (Cd México), Joaquín Martínez (Puebla), Aubert y Cía (Cd México), F. Cruces y Cía (Durango), Motes de Oca (Cd México) and a few by Disderi (Paris, France). 464 albumen cartes. 1860s.

A80.12.5 GARCÍA CARTES DE VISITE [II]. Studio portraits of Catholic priests and bishops, both diocesan and regular, including Franciscan and Dominican; a few anonymous portraits of men and women not apparently associated with the church. By various Mexican photographers. 300 albumen cartes. 1860s to 1880s.

A80.12.6 GARCÍA CITYSCAPES. Commercial travel views of cityscapes, street scenes, and architecture of major Mexican cities, including Cd México, Guanajuato, Guadalajara, and Chihuahua. Photographs by A. S. Addis and Hijo, and by B. Velarde and unidentified photographer(s). 45 mounted albumen prints. Ca. 1880.

A80.12.7 Loose prints include "Retratos de personajes históricos, sitios y personajes históricos, fotografías etnológicas y arqueológicas, fotografías, negativas y litografías," individuals and groups; historical sites by various photographers.

Total, 3,200 items; itemized list. Mid-nineteenth to early twentieth centuries.

A80.13 D'HARNONCOURT (RENE; b. 1901) COLLECTION. Commercial travel views of street scenes and architecture; picturesque, in situ, and studio portraits of native residents of Mexico. Many from series, "Views of Mexico," by C. B. Waite (Cd México); snapshots of similar subjects. 244 photo prints, many gelatino-chloride and silver gelatin snapshots; itemized list. 1901 to 1907.

A80.14 *Historial gràfico de las actividades de la alianza de mesas Redondas Panamericanas.* Snapshots and portraits of members of the P.A.R.T. (zones 1-6) in meetings in the US and various countries in Latin America. 3 scrapbooks with clippings and 477 photo prints, some color. 1964 to 1966.

A80.15 LEWIS (SAMUEL L.) PHOTOGRAPHS. Archaeological ruins in Mexico. 24 silver gelatin prints; itemized list. 1961.

A80.16 Littlejohn, Chase, comp. *Chase Littlejohn album.* Commercial views of the Décena Trágica (1913) during the Mexican Revolution; travel snapshots of residents, landscape, and city scenes in Jalisco and unidentified locales in Mexico; snapshot portraits of Littlejohn's first wife; a few from California and New Hampshire. 295 silver gelatin prints. 1900 to 1920.

A80.17 McANDREW (JOHN) PHOTOGRAPHIC ARCHIVE OF SIXTEENTH-CENTURY MEXICAN CHURCHES. General and detailed views of cathedrals, churches, monasteries, and some nonreligious architecture in Mexico arranged by state, with substantial coverage in: Campeche; Distrito Federal, including Cd México; Guanajuato, including Celaya, Guanajuato, Salamanca, San Miguel de Allende, and Yuriria; Hidalgo, including Actopan, Epazoyucán, Ixmiquilpán, Metztitlán, Tepeapulco, Tlahuelilpa, and Zimapán); Jalisco, including Guadalajara; Mexico, including Acolman, Otumba, Tepozotlán, and Zinacantepec; Morelos, including Cuernavaca; Oaxaca, including Coixtlahuaca, Cuilapán, Oaxaca, and Teposcolula; Puebla, including San Francisco Acatepec, Acatzingo, Calpan, Cholula, Huaquechula, Huejotzingo, Puebla, Quecholac, Tecali, Tecamachalco, Tepeaca, Tochimilco, and Zacatlán; Querétaro, including Querétaro; San Luis Potosí, including San Luis Potosí; Tlaxcala, including Tepeyanco and Tlaxcala; and Zacatecas, including Zacatecas. 6,000 photographs, including prints and negatives; card index. 1960s. See Bibliography—McAndrew.

A80.18 [*Mexico = Album 1363B.*] Commercial travel views of city scenes, architecture, landscapes, and agriculture; a few Mexican archaeological artifacts in German museums. Photographers include C. B. Waite, La Rochester, Hugo Brehme, Scott, and Patiño; a few snapshots. 73 gelatino-chloride and silver gelatin prints; itemized list. 1930s.

A80.19 MÉXICO "TÍPICO E INDÍGENA" COLLECTION. Amateur, in situ portraits of workers and street life in Mexico; some architectural detail of baroque churches and landscapes. 50 silver gelatin prints. 1950s. Itemized list.

A80.20 MORELOS (JOSÉ MARÍA) COLLECTION. Cityscapes, historical buildings and sites, and art reproductions of manuscripts and texts of or related to Morelos. 2 albumen prints, 17 silver gelatin prints, 54 silver gelatin art reproductions. 1879 to 1920s. BLAC# García mss 131.

A80.21 PANAMA CANAL CONSTRUCTION COLLECTION. Construction of the canal. 83 silver gelatin prints. 1904 to 1911.

A80.22 PARÁ, BRAZIL COLLECTION. Commercial travel views of street scenes and architecture in Pará. Photographed by F. E. Meyers and Company. 14 albumen and gelatino-chloride prints on pages withdrawn from an album. Mid-1890s.

A80.23 Rickards, Constantine George. *The ruins of Mexico.* London: H. E. Shrimpton, 1910. Mayan and Aztec archaeological ruins and artifacts in the states of Chiapas, Yucatán, Tabasco, Oaxaca, and Puebla. Photographed by Rickards and Guerra (Mérida). 260 photogravures. BLAC# GZ/q972.011/R421r/v.1.

A80.24 Robelio, Cecilio A.; Conrado Castro, photog. *Album arqueológico y etnológico del estado de Morelos: Para presentarlo en las exposiciones internacionales que se han de celebrar en Madrid y Chicago en honor de Cristóbal Colón.* Cuernavaca: Gobierno de Morelos, 1892. Commercial views of archaeological ruins. 34 albumen prints. BLAC# GZ/q972.011/R54.

A80.25 ROGERS (PAUL P.) PHOTOGRAPHIC COLLECTION. Professor of Spanish. Commercial views of architecture, street scenes, and Indians in Mexico; Rancho de Taos church in New Mexico; photographed by Rogers and by I. Casasola. Commercial views of the Creole Petroleum Corporation operations in Venezuela. Late-Pictorialist still lifes and portraits, including Diego Riviera, photographed by Ignacío Millán. 92 silver gelatin prints; itemized list. 1940s to 1950s.

A80.26 ST. JOHN D'EL REY MINING COMPANY ARCHIVES. Mining operations in Minas Gerais, Brazil. All photographs are commercial views.

> **A80.26.1** *Rio de Peixe* [=*Album I*]. Construction of powerhouse at Rio de Peixe showing terrain, equipment installations, pipelines, tramroad, tunnels #1 and #2. 40 silver gelatin prints. Ca. 1920?

> **A80.26.2** *Morro Velho: Progress of surface works at Morro Velho* [=*Album II*]. General terrain, construction of physical plant, including pipelines, water-powered machinery, and buildings. 57 silver gelatin prints. 1893 to 1894.

> **A80.26.3** *Morro Velho* [=*Album III*]. Surface works, erection of giant stonebreaker, entrance to tunnel. 32 silver gelatin prints. 1894.

> **A80.26.4** *Views of drawing office, Morro Velho* [=*Album IV*]. Staff at work in office and on heavy equipment; mechanical drawings of plant and equipment. 24 silver gelatin prints, handwritten captions. 1903.

> **A80.26.5** *Album* [=*Album V*]. Work force of the "reduction" department, numerous views of the mining operation, including a stamp mill and the packing of gold bars for transport by gold troops; workers include Black men and women. 54 silver gelatin prints, handwritten captions. 1903.

> **A80.26.6** [*Album VI*]. Electrical staff and native force, with view of the operational and maintenance procedures; close-ups of interior equipment in the respective power stations at Chrystaes, Gaia, Retiro, and Rezende; generators, compressors, and switchboard panels. 32 tipped-in and 5 loose silver gelatin prints, handwritten captions. 1904.

A80.26.7 [*Album VII*]. Work forces of the woodworking shop, foundry, smithy, and fitting shop in general and detail; mechanics, surveyors, native and European personnel of the work offices, and the compressor house. 52 silver gelatin prints, handwritten captions. 1891 to 1903.

A80.26.8 [*Album VIII*]. Morro Velho, site of the mine, with views of its buildings and equipment identified; ceremony in recognition of final emancipation of the company's Black workers. 74 silver gelatin prints, handwritten captions. Ca. 1890.

A80.26.9 [*Album IX*]. Excavations to reopen the mine, company housing, officers, reduction works, workshops, view of new works, the store and brickfield, underground view of the mine, company exhibits at Chicago Exposition in 1893 and in St. Louis in 1904. 30 albumen and silver gelatin prints. 1891 to 1904.

A80.26.10 [*Album X*]. Nova Lima and Morro Velho; construction of native and European workers' housing; Morro Velho Athletic Club, the new pavilion, social events, including children's parties and the church choir; damage to cooling plant; construction at Codorna Dam and Lagoa Grande Dam; B, C, D, and F Peixe sites; visits of Prince George, the Prince of Wales, and the King of Belgium; Espírito Santo surface plant and interior views. 150 silver gelatin prints in an oversized album. 1929 to 1936.

A80.26.11 *Photographs of Morro Velho Mine, Brazil* [= Album XI]. General views of surface works; miners changing shifts; underground operations showing Caucasian and Black workers; reduction staff and works; woodworking shop; brickfield, including women workers; Morro Velho-Raposos tramway; power stations; company's general offices; hospital facilities. 239 silver gelatin prints in a mammoth volume. 1912.

A80.26.12 [*Album XII*]. Largely duplicates Album XI (v.s.), with additional views of the tennis court, the pavilion, and the Morro Velho railway station. 279 silver gelatin prints in a mammoth album. 1912 to 1920.

A80.26.13 *Gaia Scheme* [= *Album XIII*]. Fabrication and installation of pipeline, the Gaia powerhouse.

1,900 photographs total, including 789 loose photographs and 13 albums; itemized list. 1864 to mid-1950s. See Bibliography—Hollowood.

A80.27 SÁNCHEZ (GEORGE I.) PHOTOGRAPHS. Rural schools in San Miguel County and Río Arriba County NM, including Mexican Ward School/Mathis High School; Migrant Workers' Camp. 229 photo prints. 1934 to 1935.

A80.28 SCHAEFFER (NANCY) PHOTOGRAPHS. Culture of fishing villages on Peru's northern coast and traditional fishing techniques; photographed by Schaeffer. 25 photo prints, some color. 1975.

A80.29 SCHMIDT (A. J.) COLLECTION. Art reproductions of various Mexican codices; artifacts from Aztec culture, many in the National Museum of Mexico; commercial travel views, including street scenes, social life and customs; regions include Teotihuacan, Palenque, Mexico City, Guanajuato, Chihuahua. Photographed by C. B. Waite (Cd México), W. H. Horne (El Paso), and unidentified photographers. 593 lantern slides, some hand-colored; itemized list. Ca. 1910.

A80.30 TABASCO RUBBER PLANTATIONS COLLECTION. Managers, native workers, and general views of El Coco, La Constancia, and Mercedes rubber plantations in Tabasco, Mexico; photographed by C. B. Waite and Adams Hnos (Fotografía Americana). 86 collodio-chloride prints. Ca. 1901.

A80.31 TARACENA FLORES (ARTURO) COLLECTION. Revolutionary troops in Quezalte-nango, 1897; Guatemalan and foreign personalities, mainly ecclesiastic and military figures; assassination of Colonel Arana. 328 photo prints. 1890s to 1950s.

A80.32 TAYLOR (T. U.) COLLECTION. Professor of civil engineering at the University of Texas at Austin. 1 album (v.i.).

> São Paulo Tramway Light and Power Co., Ltd. *Vistas das cidades do Rio de Janeiro e São Paulo e das obras hidro-elétricas na Serra do Cubatão.* Presentation album of commercial views, including cityscapes, most of São Paulo; the company facilities, including plant and transmission lines; various dam and reservoir projects on the Rio das Pedras and Rio Grande. 37 photographs, including two hinged, cirkut panoramas. 1929 to 1936.

[End of Taylor collection.]

A80.33 VILLALONGÍN (CARLOS) THEATER COMPANY ARCHIVES. Studio portraits of performers of the company. 31 photographs; itemized list. 1890s to 1920s.

A80.34 WEISMANN (ELIZABETH WILDER) COLLECTION. Architecture of Mexico with some coverage of the states of Distrito Federal, México, Oaxaca, and Puebla; architecture of Latin American countries with some coverage of Argentina, Brazil, Colombia, Ecuador, Guatemala, Peru; art reproductions. 4,104 silver gelatin prints, 2,171−120 photo negatives. 1930s.

Library and Manuscripts Collection (A82)

University of Texas
Harry Ransom Humanities Research Center
Harry Ranson Center, Fifth floor
Twenty-first and Guadalupe streets
P.O. Box 7219
Austin, Texas 78713

512-471-9119. Contact: Research Librarian

PURPOSE: The Library and Manuscripts Collection holds some 600,000 bound volumes, many of which are incunabula, first editions, or outstanding examples of fine bindings, including a copy of the Gutenberg Bible and two copies of Copernicus' *De Revolutionibus.* The collection also holds the literary archives and personal papers of many major authors, including D. H. Lawrence and Princess Bibesco. Photographs acquired with literary collections are generally transferred to the Photography Collection of the HRHRC (q.v.), but photographs which bear manuscript information, such as photographic postcards, are not withdrawn.

HOURS: Weekdays, 9:00-5:00; Saturday, 9:00-12:00. Appointment recommended. Closed major holidays; open many university holidays.

ASSISTANCE: Professional, experienced, specialized staff. Written and phone inquiries accepted for specific personal names. Electrostatic copies available. Photoduplications must be ordered through center.

PUBLICATION: Publication fee charged. Collection credit required. Free copy of publication to the center. Most items require third-party permission.

FINDING AIDS: Partial inventory, descriptive list, and card index of collection. Access by personal name and general subject heading.

SCOPE: 3,000 photo prints; many images are photo postcards or attached to correspondence which the images are intended to illustrate. Ca. 1890 to present, most ca. 1900.

GEOGRAPHIC: Global coverage; no single place held in quantity.

SUBJECTS: Architecture. Cityscapes. Events. Landscape. Portraits.

PEOPLE: Many literary figures. See University of Texas, HRHRC, Photography Collection, Record Groups—Literary File for a partial list of names.

PHOTOGRAPHERS: Many snapshooters. Commercial photographers include Edward Sheriff Curtis and Giorgio Sommer (attrib.).

RECORD GROUPS:

A82.1 Curtis, Edward Sheriff, photog. *The North American Indian: Being a series of volumes picturing and describing the Indians of the United States and Alaska.* [Seattle WA: E. S. Curtis; Cambridge: University Press], 1907-1930. 20 octavo and folio volumes containing photogravure plates.

A82.2 TAUSCHNITZ EDITIONS. Uniform editions of nineteenth-century literature published by Tauschnitz, many extra-illustrated with photographs. Photographs attributed to Giorgio Sommer. 1,700 volumes, not all extra-illustrated. 1880s.

New York Journal-American Morgue (A84)

University of Texas
Harry Ransom Humanities Research Center
Harry Ranson Center, Fifth floor
Twenty-first and Guadalupe streets
P.O. Box 7219
Austin, Texas 78713

512-471-9119. Contact: Research Assistant.

PURPOSE: The *Journal-American* was a Hearst paper formed in 1937 with the merging of his two other New York papers, the *Morning Journal and Advertiser* (known as the *American* after 1902) and the *Evening Journal*. The *Journal-American* is occasionally referred to as the *American Journal*. The *Journal-American* continued operation until 1966. The paper's morgue contains some 9,000,000 article clippings, a complete microfilm of the *Journal-American* and its predecessors (1895 to 1966), and the photo files containing vintage negatives, prints, and wire service photos.

HOURS: Weekdays, 9:00-5:00; Saturday, 9:00-12:00. Twenty-four-hour notice required. Closed major holidays; open many university holidays.

ASSISTANCE: Experienced assistance. Written and phone inquiries accepted on a limited basis. Electrostatic copies usually available of photomechanical reproductions of prints. Photoduplications must be ordered through the HRHRC; must be returned after use.

PUBLICATION: Publication fee. Collection credit required. Free copy of publication to HRHRC. Third-party permission required on news service photos.

FINDING AIDS: Photographs maintained in original order of biography, geographic region, and general subject and subdivided within each of these categories; cross-index file for personal names.

SCOPE: 2,000,000 vintage photo prints, news photos, and a few copy prints; 1,000,000 vintage negatives. Most nitrate negative material was evidently removed and destroyed before the morgue was received by the HRHRC. Prints that were published generally have a copy of the photomechanical reproduction with cutline pasted on the back. Other prints generally have some identifying information on the back. Negatives have been rehoused in acid-free envelopes; the original envelopes with caption information and photographer's name have been saved. Many of the prints have been mocked up with white and black paint to show crop marks and enhance reproduction in letterpress reproduction. Some letterpress engravings. 1910s to 1966, most mid-1940s to 1950s.

Type of photo	Pre-1880	1880-1899	1900-1919	1920-1939	1940-1959	1960-1986
Glass negs				75,000		
Film negs				75,000	750,000	125,000
Vintage prints			2,000	150,000	950,000	750,000

GEOGRAPHIC: Emphasis of original material is New York City (36 linear feet of prints) and surrounding communities. Wire service and news photos give substantial coverage of the US (47.5 linear feet of prints) and the globe (122 linear feet of prints).

United States: California. Connecticut. Massachusetts. New Jersey. New York (New York City, Long Island). New Jersey. Pennsylvania.

Foreign Countries: Algeria. Austria. Brazil. China. Cuba. England (WW II domestic front). Ethiopia. Finland. France (WW II domestic front). Germany (post-WW II, Berlin Airlift). Greece. Hungary. India. Italy (WW II and post-WW II). Japan. Korea (Korean War). Mexico. Norway. Palestine (Israel). Philippines. Poland. Russia (post-WW II, Cold War). Spain (Franco revolution). Switzerland. Thailand.

SUBJECTS: Extensive coverage of activities of New York City and the world, with an emphasis on human interest and popular subjects; while a crusading paper, it avoided the sensationalism and vulgarity of rival *New York Daily News.* Because of its strong anti-Communist editorial position, the *Journal-American* is an excellent resource for study of the Cold War and McCarthyism.

Academia. Animals. Architecture (housing projects). Cityscapes (parks and playgrounds, street scenes). Events (crime, fires, Lindbergh kidnapping, Spanish-American War, World's Fair—1939, World's Fair—1964). Industry (banks). Labor relations. Military (atomic bomb—civilian defense, —drills, —research, —tests; Korean War, WW I, WW II). Organizations (American Nazi Party, United Nations). Religion (churches). Services (fire protection, police). Sports and amusements (baseball, beauty contests, boxing, cinema—movie stills, football, horse racing, television, theater). Transportation (aerial—balloons, —dirigible, —planes, —plane crashes, automobiles—auto shows, —driver education, —racing, —taxis, —traffic, subways, railroad, ships, space).

PEOPLE: Extensive coverage of celebrities and newsmakers, especially film and stage personalities, sports figures, and royalty; many photographed on visits to New York City. Many area residents; few held in quantity.

Astor family. Belgian royal family. Humphrey Bogart. Winston Churchill. L. Gordon Cooper. Joan Crawford. Bing Crosby. Marion Davies. Charles De Gaulle. Jack Dempsey. Governor Thomas Dewey. Joe Dimaggio. Dionne quintuplets. John Foster Dulles. Leo Durocher. President Dwight D. Eisenhower. English royal family, especially Prince Alexander, Prince Charles, King Edward VII, King Edward VIII, Edward Prince of Wales, Queen Elizabeth II and her wedding, King George V, King George VI, Princess Margaret, and the Duke and Duchess of Windsor. Eddie Fisher. Errol Flynn. Henry Ford and family. Clark Gable. The Gabor sisters. Mahatma Gandhi. Ava Gardner. Judy Garland. John Nance Garner. Bernard Gimble. Paulette Goddard. Arthur Godfrey. Judge Arthur Goldberg. Barry Goldwater. Greek royalty. Andrei Gromyko. Hubert Humphrey. Japanese royalty. Jacob Javitts. President Lyndon B. Johnson and family. President John F. Kennedy and family. Robert Kennedy and family. Nikita Khrushchev. Martin Luther King Jr. Fiorello La Guardia. Charles A. Lindbergh and family. Governor John V. Lindsay. Henry Cabot Lodge. Governor John D. Lodge. Joe Lewis. Clare Booth Luce. Senator Joseph McCarthy. General Douglas MacArthur. Rocky Marciano. General George P. Marshall. Marilyn Monroe. Benito Mussolini. President Richard M. Nixon. Jawaharlal Nehru. Pope Pius XII. Pope John XXIII. Mike Quill. Governor Nelson Rockefeller and family. Roosevelt family. Billy Rose. Ethel and Julius Rosenberg. Dean Rusk. Russian royal family. "Babe" Ruth. Walter Schirra. Joseph Stalin. Adlai Stevenson and family. Leopold Stokowski. Swedish royal family. Elizabeth Taylor. Major Gherman Titov. President Harry S. Truman. Gene Tunney. Cornelius Vanderbilt. Gloria Vanderbilt. Mayor Robert F. Wagner Jr. James J. Walker. Earl Warren. Johnny Weismuller. Grover A. Whalen. Cornelius V. Whitney. Sir Hubert Wilkins. Wendell Wilkie. Charles E. Wilson. Premier Harold Wilson. Woodrow Wilson.

PHOTOGRAPHERS: Approximately half of the photographs are by staff photographers, the other half obtained from corporate sources such as news agencies and publicity departments, including motion picture and television stills.

Corporate photographers: Associated Press. International News Photo. United Press International. US Army Signal Corps.

Staff photographers: Art Abfier. Clarence Albers. Gean Barron. John Berman. Marty Black. Mathew Black. George Brown. Charles Carson. De Lucca. John Dolan. Mel Finklestein. William Finn. Sheldon Gottesman. Roland Harvey. Bill Hearfield. John E. Hopkins. Frank Jurkowski. Bob Laird. Jack G. Layer. Vincent Lopez. James McCulla. Edward McKevitt. Art Miller. George Miller. Leonard Morgan. Pat Mulligan. Nolford. Jack O'Brien. Reidy. Ed Pickwoad [Pickwood]. Paul Rice. Frank Rino. Al Robbins. Sandhaus. Seymour Zoltorfe. Zee.

RECORD GROUPS: Original provenance of the morgue has been preserved. The morgue was arranged into three major sections: biography, geography, and subject, each of which is further subdivided.

A84.1 BIOGRAPHY PRINTS. The paper tended to file events under a personal name when possible, making it difficult to use the collection from a general subject access point; for example, one cannot research murders without knowing the names of specific cases. People (v.s.) lists individuals held in quantity. 1,500 linear feet of prints.

A84.2 GEOGRAPHY PRINTS. Major headings include foreign countries, US states, New York State, and New York City. Geographic (v.s.) lists additional locales held in quantity. 216 linear feet.

A84.3 SUBJECT PRINTS. Some subjects represented under different headings, and there is little hierarchical arrangement of subject headings. 240 linear feet.

A84.4 NEGATIVES. Negatives from the above categories have been interfiled. Predominantly 4x5 film base negatives, with some 4x5 glass negatives, and a few 120 and 35mm negatives; 630 feet.

A84.5 CLIPPINGS. No photographs, consisting of articles in Hearst publications and other newspapers and magazines. One of the largest clippings files in the world. The clippings are arranged in the same headings of biography, geography, and subject.

Photography Collection (A86)

University of Texas
Harry Ransom Humanities Research Center
Harry Ransom Center, Sixth floor
Twenty-first and Guadalupe streets
P.O. Box 7219
Austin, Texas 78713

512-471-9124. Contact: Curator.

PURPOSE: An academic research center devoted to the history of photography with an emphasis on photography in the fine arts and communications. The collection has an exhibition space and collects original and copy photographs in all major formats, an extensive library of rare and recent books and journals pertaining to photography, equipment, manuscripts, and ephemera.

HOURS: Weekdays 9:00-5:00. Closed major, academic holidays, Christmas through New Year's. Appointment recommended.

ASSISTANCE: Professional, specialized, experienced staff. Written inquiries accepted for specific questions; general inquiries answered as staff time permits. Not a picture service. Electrostatic copies not available. Photoduplications must be ordered through the collection; must be returned after use. Patrons may make hand-held copy prints for study purposes with prior permission.

PUBLICATION: Reproduction fee. Credit line required. Free copy of publication to the collection. Third-party permission required on much material.

FINDING AIDS: Inventories and visual indices for some record groups; computer database, access by name/title, photographer, date, location, subject, process, and other access points. Some albums and portfolios cataloged as books with photographer and subject access. Some represented on OCLC, many in the *National Union Catalog*.

BIBLIOGRAPHY:

Agee, James, and Walker Evans. *Let us now praise famous men*. Boston: Houghton Mifflin, 1941. 2nd ed., 1960.

Brettell, Richard, et al. *Paper and light: The calotype in France and Great Britain*. Boston: David R. Godine, 1984.

Burleson, Clyde W., and E. Jessica Hickman. *The panoramic photography of E. O. Goldbeck*. Austin: University of Texas Press, 1986.

Davenport, Marguerite. *The unpretentious pose: The work of E. O. Goldbeck, photographer.* San Antonio: Trinity University Press, 1981.

Fehl, Fred, photog. *Stars of the ballet and dance in performance photographs.* New York: Dover, 1984.

Flukinger, Roy. *The formative decades: Photography in Great Britain, 1839-1920.* Austin: University of Texas Press, 1985.

Flukinger, Roy, Larry Schaaf, and Standish Meacham. *Paul Martin: Victorian photographer.* Austin: University of Texas Press, 1977.

Gernsheim, Alison. *Fashion and reality.* London: Faber and Faber, 1963. Republished as *Victorian and Edwardian fashion: A photographic survey.* New York: Dover, 1981.

Gernsheim, Helmut. *Creative photography: Aesthetic trends 1839-1960.* London: Faber and Faber, 1962.

Gernsheim, Helmut. *Incunabula of British photographic literature: A bibliography of British photographic literature 1839-75 and British books illustrated with original photographs.* London and Berkeley: Scolar Press, 1984.

Gernsheim, Helmut. *Julia Margaret Cameron.* London: Fountain Press, 1948. 2nd ed., Millerton NY: Aperture, 1975.

Gernsheim, Helmut. *Lewis Carroll.* London: Max Parrish, 1949. Reprinted, New York: Dover, 1969.

Gernsheim, Helmut. *The origins of photography.* London: Thames and Hudson, 1983.

Gernsheim, Helmut, and Alison Gernsheim. *A concise history of photography.* London: Thames and Hudson, 1965. 2nd ed., New York: Grosset and Dunlap, 1965.

Gernsheim, Helmut, and Alison Gernsheim. *Creative photography, 1826 to the present: An exhibition from the Gernsheim collection.* Detroit MI: Wayne State University, 1963. Exhibition catalog.

Gernsheim, Helmut, and Alison Gernsheim. *Edward VII and Queen Alexandra: A biography in word and picture.* London: F. Muller, 1962.

Gernsheim, Helmut, and Alison Gernsheim. *The history of photography: From the camera obscura to the beginning of the modern era.* Oxford: Oxford University Press, 1955. 2nd ed., London: Thames and Hudson, 1969.

Gernsheim, Helmut, and Alison Gernsheim. *L. J. M. Daguerre: The history of the diorama and the daguerreotype.* London: Secker and Warburg, 1956. Reissued, New York: Dover, 1968.

Gernsheim, Helmut, and Alison Gernsheim. *Roger Fenton, photographer of the Crimean War: His photographs and his letter from the Crimea.* London: Secker and Warburg, 1954.

Gernsheim, Helmut; foreword by C. H. Gibbs-Smith. *Masterpieces of Victorian photography.* London: Phaidon, 1942.

Gernsheim, Helmut; foreword by Niklaus Pevsner. *Focus on architecture and sculpture: An original approach to the photography of architecture and sculpture.* London: Fountain Press, 1949.

Goetzmann, William H., and Kay Sloan. *Looking far North: The Harriman Expedition to Alaska, 1899.* New York: Viking, 1982. Photographs are from the Averell Harriman Collection and the Bancroft Library; the Photography Collection's Harriman photographs duplicate many of those images.

Gould, Lewis L., and Richard Greffe. *Jimmy Hare, photojournalist.* Austin: University of Texas Press, 1977.

Haynes, David Polk. *A descriptive catalogue of the filmic items in the Gernsheim collection.* Master's thesis, University of Texas at Austin, 1969.

Henle, Fritz, photog. *Casals.* Garden City NJ: American Photographic Book Publishing Company, 1975. 2nd ed., 1979.

Henle, Fritz, photog.; foreword by Allan Porter. *Fritz Henle.* Christienstead VI: Fritz Henle Publishing, 1973.

James, Lawrence. *Crimea 1854-1856: The war with Russia from contemporary photographs.* Thames, Oxfordshire: Hayes Kennedy, 1981.

Klett, Mark, et al. *Second view: The Rephotographic Survey Project.* Albuquerque NM: University of New Mexico Press, 1984.

Knight, Cynthia. *Photographic resources in the Gernsheim Collection for six nineteenth-century wars.* Master's thesis, University of Texas at Austin, 1971.

McQuaid, James, and Paulette Privitera Wilson. *An index to American photographic collections.* Boston: G. K. Hall, 1982. Not illustrated.

Miller, Sybil. *Itinerant photographer* [tentative title]. Albuquerque NM: University of New Mexico Press, forthcoming 1987.

Oliphant, Dave, and Tom Zigal, eds. *Perspectives on photography: Essays on the work of Du Camp, Dancer, Robinson, Stieglitz, Strand, and Smithers.* Austin: Humanities Research Center, 1982.

Rector, Margaret, ed.; introduction by John Graves. *Cowboy life on the Texas plains: The photographs of Ray Rector.* College Station: Texas A&M Press, 1982.

Robl, Ernest H., ed. *Picture Sources 4.* New York: Special Library Association, 1983.

Sandweiss, Martha A., Roy Flukinger, and Anne W. Tucker, eds.; introduction by Stephen Harrigan. *Contemporary Texas: A photographic portrait.* Austin: Texas Monthly Press, 1985.

Seeley, Gail. *Egypt and the Holy Land as photographic subjects, 1849-1870: A comparative study.* Master's thesis, University of Texas at Austin, 1976.

Smithers, W. D. *Chronicles of the Big Bend: A photographic memoir of life on the border.* Austin: Maduro Press, 1976.

Smithers, W. D.; foreword by Kenneth Ragsdale. *Memoirs of life on the border.* Austin: Madrona Press, 1976.

Stott, William. *Documentary expression in thirties America.* New York: Oxford University Press, 1973. 2nd ed., Chicago: University of Chicago Press, 1986.

Stott, William, with Jane Stott. *On Broadway: Performance photographs by Fred Fehl.* Austin: University of Texas Press, 1978. 2nd ed., New York: De Capo Press, 1980. 3rd ed., Chicago: University of Chicago Press, 1986.

SCOPE: 3,000,000 photographs in virtually all processes and formats, predominantly vintage prints; other formats held in quantity include stereographs, postcards, lantern and magic lantern slides, autochromes, 35mm color transparencies, and cirkut panoramic prints and negatives. 17,000 titles in 20,000 volumes ranging from the sixteenth century to the present pertaining to photography. Some record groups have supporting manuscript and ephemeral materials.

Type of photo	Pre-1880	1880-1899	1900-1919	1920-1939	1940-1959	1960-1986
D/A/T-types	250	100				
Glass negs	50	100	500	10,000		
Film negs		10	10,000	500,000	500,000	
Vintage prints	10,000	30,000	10,000	50,000	3,000	1,000
Copy prints	100	3,000	2,000	2,000		
Photo albums	100	500	500	100	100	

GEOGRAPHIC: Extensive global coverage, especially of Europe, the Middle East, and the Orient. Broad coverage of Texas.

Countries: Australia. Austria. Canada. China. Egypt. England. France. Germany. Greece. India. Ireland. Italy. Japan. Mexico. Middle East. Palestine. Russia. Scotland. Spain. Switzerland. Turkey. US.

Texas cities and regions: Austin. Big Bend. Corpus Christi. Dallas. Gatesville. Granger. New Braunfels. Plum. Robstown. San Antonio. Trans-Pecos. Waco. See Record Groups—Texas for additional locales.

SUBJECTS: Extensive coverage of all subject areas. Database catalog lists 754 subjects under 25 major headings:

Activity. Animals. Architecture (exteriors). Art reproduction. Artifact. Cityscape. Dress. Event. Genre. Industry. Interior. Landscape. Military. News. Occupation. People. Plant. Portrait. Scientific. Sport. Style. Theater. Transportation. Water.

PEOPLE: Extensive coverage of many noteworthy persons; few held in quantity. The collection is strongest in literary figures and British peerage. See Record Groups—Major—Literary File collection for names of significant writers and their associates.

Artists. Literary figures. Political leaders (European). Theater figures.

PHOTOGRAPHERS: The collection holds samples of work by more than 1,200 photographers, including many major art photographers and inventors of photographic processes, including Nicéphore Niépce. Many are represented by only a small number of images. Described in terms of daguerreotypists, print, stereo, and Texas photographers. Notes (a—g) reference an entry under the photographer's name in Record Groups; additional work by the photographer may be found in other record groups as well. Additional photographers are mentioned in descriptions of record groups.

Daguerreotypists: Richard Beard (21). Antoine Claudet (6, 20 stereo). L. J. M. Daguerre (1). William E. Kilburn (10). J. E. Mayall (5). Girault de Prangey (10). Southworth and Hawes (4).

Print photographers: Abdullah Frères (10). Ansel Adams (20/f). Robert Adamson (13; with D. O. Hill, 183/eg). Josef Albert (10). Queen Alexandra (Consort of Edward VII; 38). Alfred Brothers (11). Alinari Fratelli (50/g). Altobelli and Company (10; Altobelli and Molins, 10). Manuel Alvarez Bravo (30/f). James Anderson (10). H. Anfossi (10). J. Craig Annan (22). Thomas Annan (100/d). C. D. Arnold (50). Jean-Eugène-Auguste Atget (26/g). Alice Elizabeth Austin (21/c). Edouard-Denis Baldus (24). Luigi Bardi (75). H. Walter Barnett (147/g). Herbert Barraud (150/dg). Hippolyte Bayard (30/f). A. Beato (60/g). Cecil Beaton (56/g). Francis Bedford (125/g). Benque et Klary (11). J. Biggs (23). J. Birtles (11). Bisson Frères (25/g). Samuel Bourne (some with Charles Shepherd; 100/dg). Mathew Brady (28). F. Brandt (15). Adolphe Braun (33). Christina Broom (= Mrs. Albert Broom; 317/g). Albert Brown (39/g). William Bryans (100/d). Wynn Bullock (12/f).

Caldesi and Montecchi (100). Harry Callahan (40/f). Henry Herschel Hay Cameron (14). Julia Margaret Cameron (214/deg). Etienne Carjat (25). Henri Cartier-Bresson (16). John Christian (815/c). G. Cimetta (17/g). Larry Clark (50/f). Antoine Claudet (23). Lucien Clergue (26). Charles Clifford (89/f). Alvin Langdon Coburn (53/g). Maurice Constant (117/g). D. Constantin (50/g). Arnold Crane (50/c). William Crookes (51; with John Spiller, 20/g). Joseph Cundall (105). George S. Cundell (94/e). Edward S. Curtis (251/d). Lawrence E. Cutting (19/g). Duncan L. Dallas (17). John Benjamin Dancer (200/c). Philip Henry Delamotte (182/d). Warren DeLaRue (14). DeGaston (23). Benjamin Delessert (12). Charles Lutwidge Dodgson (= Lewis Carroll, 350/eg). Robert Doisneau (15/f). W. and D. Downey (26). C. B. Duchenne (72). Maxime Du Camp (100/d). Ducos DuHauron (13). Aimé Dupont (83).

P. H. Emerson (104/d). William England (50). Hugo Erfurth (38). Elliott Erwitt (31/f). Frank Eugene (17). Frederick H. Evans (10). Walker Evans (300/c). J. W. Falvella (100/c). Fred Fehl (50,000/a). Roger Fenton (509/dg). A. Ferrier (60). Francis Frith (& Company, 389/dg). Peter Wickens Fry (44/c). W. Ellerton Fry (150).

Alexander Gardner (25/d). D. S. George (55). Helmut Gernsheim (2,500/g). L. Ghemer Frères (13). Ralph Gibson (15/f). Major Gill (100/d). E. G. Glover (74/e). Frank Mason Good (15/c). William M. Grundy (25/d). John Hamington (38). Arno Hammacher (10). Arno Hammarskjöld (16). James H. "Jimmy" Hare (2,200/c). Sergeant John Harrold (74). Fritz Henle (1,500/af). Sir John Herschel (500/c). D. O. Hill and Robert Adamson (183/eg). Mrs. Brian Hodgson (20). E. O. Hoppe (17). Alice Hughes (116). Robert Hunt (38/g). Frank Hurley (62/g). Kurt Hutton (18).

Eugene Ives (49). C. Jung (24). Ida Kar (27). Rochard and Cherry Kearton (12). Dr. Thomas Keith (73/g). John H. Kemp Jr. (55/c). Horatio Nelson King (43/g).

Clarence John Laughlin (10). J. Laurent (150/e). Danny Lyon (30/f). Nahum Luboshez (188/g). Angus McBean (38/g). J. McDonald (330). Robert MacPherson (191/eg). Alen MacWeeney (12/f). Dr. R. L. Maddox (24). Alex Malmstrom (10). Felix H. Man (= Hans Baumann, 27). Margarite (25). Marion and Company (72). Paul Martin (1,600/ce). Maull and Polyblank (191/dg). J. E. Mayall (12). Joel Meyerowitz (9/f). Ferdinand Mulnier (20). Nickolas Muray (12/f). Eadweard Muybridge (179/d).

Nadar (= Gaspard Félix Tournachon, 28). C. Naya (21). Negretti and Zambra (40). George Oddner (20). H. Petschler and Company (85). Carlo Ponti (175/g). Herbert G. Ponting (20). Francis Edward Pratt (423/c). William Lake Price (10/d). William Pumphrey (10).

Achille Quinet (30). Oscar Gustave Rejlander (130/e). Albert Renger-Patzsch (46/g). James Robertson (55; with Beato, 94; with Sheppard/d). Henry Peach Robinson (210/g). Ralph Waldo Robinson (75). Russel and Sons (10). Sir F. P. Rutter (30).

Erich Salomon (19). Napoleon Sarony (38). A. Schranz (13). Pascal Sebah (30; Sebah and Joaillier, 49). George H. Seeley (10). William Shirriffs (127/c). August Skanda (30). A. G. Dew Smith (53/g). John Shaw Smith (95). Charles Piazzi Smyth (70/d). John Spiller (44/g). Edward J. Steichen (325/c). Otto Steinert (15). Paul Strand (57/f). Strohmeyer and Wyman (15). Jean-Pierre Sudre (12/f). Wolfgang Suschitzky (10). Sir Joseph Swan (12). W. H. Fox Talbot (76/dg). Reinhold Thiele (36). John Thomson (338/d). Linnaeus Tripe (154/d). James Valentine (47/g). Wolfgang Vennemann (32).

Carleton Watkins (53/e). Brett Weston (10). Edward Weston (12/f). H. C. White and Company (120). Clarence H. White (22). Henry White (14). George Washington Wilson (and Company, 530/g). Garry Winogrand (15/f). Walter Woodbury (32). Yorke and Company (23).

Stereograph photographers and publishers: 250 photographers and publishers of stereographs. E. and H. T. Anthony (36). Platt D. Babbitt (10). George Barker (8). Francis Bedford (23). Colonel A. S. Bennett (36). C. Bierstadt (21). Valentine Blanchard (24). James Cremer (22). Crooks and Spiller (12). William England (30). Frank Mason Good (45). Carleton H. Graves (66). George Griffith (10). D. W. Hill (19). T. W. Ingersoll (51). William Henry Jackson (11). J. F. Jarvis (10). Keystone View Company (1,000). Kilburn Brothers (40). London Stereoscopic and Photographic Company (30). Metropolitan Series (50). Eadweard Muybridge (5). William Norman (20). Petschler (82). Realistic Travels (13). Stanton (17). Underwood and Underwood (1,000). See Record Groups—Published Stereograph Sets.

Texas photographers: W. S. Adkins (5,000/b). Frank Armstrong (52/b). Fred Baldwin and Wendy Watriss (39/b). Ava Atkinson Crofford (17/b). Fred A. Gildersleeve (83/b). E. L. Goldbeck (8,000/b). E. O. Goldbeck (1,000,000/a). H. B. Hillyer. Bill Kennedy (50/b). John Frederick "Doc" McGregor (100,000/b). Nick Mersfelder. Mitchell. Michael A. Murphy (60/b). Paul Naschke (7/b). Harry Pennington Jr. (25,000/a). Ernst Raba. Ray Rector (1,000/b). W. D. Smithers (9,000/a). H. L. Summerville. Jno P. Trlica (11,000/b). William P. "Bill" Wright (12/f).

Notes:

a. See Record Groups—Major.
b. See Record Groups—Texas.
c. See Record Groups—Additional record groups.
d. See Record Groups—Published works.
e. See Record Groups—Albums.
f. See Record Groups—Portfolios.
g. See Record Groups—Major—Gernsheim collection.

RECORD GROUPS: Described in six areas (record group title indicates photographer unless otherwise noted):

— Major record groups: archives of photographers or extensive collections of photographs.
— Texas record groups: materials that are predominantly images from Texas. Texas locations may also be found in other record groups.
— Additional record groups: collections of other, unbound materials.
— Published works illustrated with photographs.
— Published stereograph sets.
— Albums: unpublished, usually unique, bound volumes of photographs.
— Portfolios: formal presentations of a photographer's work.

Major Record Groups:

A86.1 FEHL (FRED; b. 1906) COLLECTION. Broadway theater photographer noted for pioneering the use of available light photography in recording stage productions; official photographer for a wide variety of New York theatrical productions from 1930 to 1960. 1,000 Broadway and off-Broadway shows, including productions of Kazan and Balanchine, and performances by Barrymore, Brando, Ferrer, and Verdon. 2,688—35mm negative strips (50,000 images) and 5,000 silver gelatin prints. 1940 to 1978. See Bibliography—Fehl, —Stott.

A86.2 GERNSHEIM (HELMUT; b. 1913) COLLECTION. Noted historian of photography. Extensive coverage of early experimental works in the invention of photography, fine art photography, especially straight photography, and historically important subjects, emphasis on England and Europe. All work described below may be assumed to be of high quality, even when by amateur photographers. 33,000 photographs; 350 pieces of equipment; 4,000 volumes of books and journals; Gernsheim's inventory lists; associated manuscript material in HRHRC Library and Manuscripts Collection (q.v.). 1826 to present. See Bibliography—Gernsheim (numerous entries), —Flukinger, —Haynes, —Knight. Most items in Record Groups—Published Works are from Gernsheim's collection; below is an abridged list of loose prints collected by Gernsheim:

A86.2.1 ALINARI FRATELLI (est. 1852). Art reproductions and Italian architecture; some images bear Bardi's stamp. 34 mammoth albumen prints. 1865 to 1880s.

A86.2.2 ATGET (JEAN-EUGÈNE-AUGUSTE; 1857-1927). Artists' studies of Versailles and Parisian architecture. 16 silver gelatin prints. Ca. 1905.

A86.2.3 BARNETT (H. WALTER). Studio portraits of predominantly European literary and political figures, including Robert Louis Stevenson and Mark Twain. 135 silver gelatin prints and 12 safety negatives. 1900 to 1920.

A86.2.4 BARRAUD (HERBERT). Studio portraits from his series, *Men and Women of the Day* (London: Richard Bentley; Eglington, 1888-1890). 26 carbon prints. 1888 to 1890.

A86.2.5 BEATO (FELICE A.; d. 1908) AND JAMES ROBERTSON. Crimean War (156); Middle East views by Beato alone (15). 171 albumen prints. 1856 to early 1860s.

A86.2.6 BEATON (CECIL; 1904-1980). Studio portraits, many of English theater and literary figures. 68 silver gelatin prints. 1930 to 1950s.

A86.2.7 BEDFORD (FRANCIS; 1816-1894). Landscapes, travel views of Egyptian ruins, English architecture and picturesque rural scenes. 37 albumen prints. 1856 to 1870s.

A86.2.8 BISSON FRÈRES (est. 1841). French architecture and ruins, Swiss mountain scenes. 20 mammoth albumen prints. 1860s.

A86.2.9 BOURNE (SAMUEL; 1834-1912). Landscapes, architecture, and cityscapes in India. 63 mammoth albumen prints. 1863 to 1874.

A86.2.10 BROOM (CHRISTINA, = Mrs. ALBERT BROOM). News photographs made in Edwardian England. 500 silver gelatin prints, ephemera, and equipment. 1900 to 1920.

A86.2.11 BROWN (ALBERT). Portraits and cityscapes of Melbourne, Australia emphasizing the poor; produced in connection with the University of Melbourne. 39 silver gelatin prints. 1964 to 1965.

A86.2.12 CAMERON (JULIA MARGARET; 1815-1879). Tableaux vivants, portraits. 100 albumen and silver gelatin prints. 1864 to 1872. See Bibliography—Gernsheim.

A86.2.13 CIMETTA (G.). Architecture in Venice, Italy. 17 mammoth albumen prints. 1856.

A86.2.14 COBURN (ALVIN LANGDON; 1882-1966). 3 pictorial studies; 64 portraits from *Men of Mark*; and 8 portraits of Helmut Gernsheim. 75 handgravure prints. 1920, 1960.

A86.2.15 CONSTANT (MAURICE). Allied military leaders during WW II. Photographed by Constant; many marked "Official US Navy Personnel Photograph." 117 silver gelatin prints. 1940s.

A86.2.16 CONSTANTINE (D.). Acropolis ruins. 48 mammoth albumen prints, most mounted recto/verso. Ca. 1855.

A86.2.17 CROOKES (Sir WILLIAM; 1832-1919) AND JOHN SPILLER (1833-1921). Landscapes, portraits, solar and spectrographic images in early, experimental photographic processes. 133 photographs, including salted-paper and uranium prints, calotypes, other processes. 1850s.

A86.2.18 CUTTING (LAWRENCE E.). Grounds and persons associated with horse racing at York, England. 19 silver gelatin prints. Ca. 1970.

A86.2.19 DODGSON (CHARLES LUTWIDGE, = LEWIS CARROLL; 1832-1898). Portraits, especially of children, including Alexandra "Xie" Kitchin; self-portraits. 40 albumen prints, 7 collodion negatives. 1850s to 1870s. See Bibliography—Gernsheim, Lewis Carroll.

A86.2.20 FENTON (ROGER; 1819-1869). Crimean War (309); landscapes in England (15); sculpture at the British Museum (27). 351 salted-paper prints. 1854 to 1858. See Bibliography—Gernsheim, —James.

A86.2.21 FRITH (FRANCIS; 1822-1898). Picturesque rural landscapes and architectural views in England, fisherfolk. Photographs by Frith and published by his firm. 44 albumen prints. Ca. 1859 to 1891.

A86.2.22 GERNSHEIM (HELMUT) PHOTOGRAPHS. Early student work; portraits; commercial photography, including exhibition prints, of architecture and architectural detail, including Saint Paul's Cathedral, Hampton Court Palace; art reproduction of sculpture and architectural details, including monuments in Westminster Cathedral; still life; nature;

landscape; Binter's Marionette Theatre (Munich). 1,815 silver gelatin prints; 838—9x12 cm glass and 462—120 film negatives. 1940 to 1960. See Bibliography.

A86.2.23 HILL (DAVID OCTAVIUS; 1802-1870) AND ROBERT ADAMSON (1821-1848). Studio portraits, many of which were studies for Hill's painting, "The Signing of the Deed of Demission" (1866); prominent Edinburgh, Scotland, male and female sitters; genre images of Newhaven fisherfolk, scenes of Edinburgh. 37 vintage salted-paper prints, 65 modern prints, 2 oil paintings by Hill. 1843 to 1847.

A86.2.24 HUNT (ROBERT; 1807-1887). English photographic inventor. Photograms of feathers, leaves, and architecture in early experimental photographic processes. 33 photographs, including photogenic drawings, calotypes, salted-paper prints, and other rare processes. 1844 to 1853.

A86.2.25 HURLEY (FRANK; 1885-1962). Shackleton expedition to the South Pole. 62 silver gelatin prints, typescript narrative by the photographer. 1914 to 1915.

A86.2.26 KEITH (Dr. THOMAS; 1827-1885). Picturesque architecture and cityscapes in Edinburgh, Scotland, some with figures. 67 salted-paper prints, 6 paper negatives. 1840s. See Bibliography—Brettell.

A86.2.27 KING (HORATIO NELSON; 1830-1895). Active Bath, England. Studio portraits of English theater figures; English peerage; persons and architecture associated with the royal family. 33 gelatino-chloride prints. 1861 to 1870s.

A86.2.28 LUBOSHEZ (NAHUM; 1869-1925). Portraits; famine victims in Russia. 179 silver gelatin prints, 9 autochromes. Ca. 1912 to 1925.

A86.2.29 McBEAN (ANGUS; b. 1904). Contrived photographs of English theater figures, many used to illustrate *The Sketch* magazine. 40 silver gelatin prints, 12 photo Christmas cards. Ca. 1930 to 1950.

A86.2.30 MacPHERSON (ROBERT). Roman architecture, predominantly ruins; art reproduction of sculpture. 191 mammoth albumen prints. Late 1850s to early 1860s.

A86.2.31 MAULL AND POLYBLANK. Studio portraits of English men, most published in their series *Photographic Portraits of Living Celebrities*. 191 albumen prints. 1856 and following.

A86.2.32 PONTI (CARLO). Cityscapes and architecture in Venice, Italy. 31 albumen prints including 12 mammoth prints. 1860s.

A86.2.33 RENGER-PATZSCH (ALBERT; 1897-1966). Member of the 1920s German stylistic movement, *Die neue Sächlichkeit* (= the New Objectivity). Nature studies, landscapes. 46 silver gelatin prints. Ca. 1920s.

A86.2.34 ROBINSON (HENRY PEACH; 1830-1901). Prominent English Pictorialist. Genre images, including contrived and composite photographs. 66 photographs most albumen prints, some mammoth prints; 3 oil paintings, 60 watercolors, and 70 pencil sketches. Ca. 1860s to 1880s.

A86.2.35 SMITH (A. G. DEW). Portraits. 56 silver gelatin prints, 13 glass negatives. Ca. 1890.

A86.2.36 SMITH (JOHN SHAW; 1811-1873). Egyptian ruins. 113 salted-paper prints from calotype negatives; a few calotype negatives. 1850 to 1852. See Bibliography—Brettell.

A86.2.37 TALBOT (WILLIAM HENRY FOX; 1800-1877). English gentleman scholar and inventor of photography. Photograms, architecture. 53 photographs, including photogenic drawings and salted-paper prints; 6 calotype negatives. Late 1830s to late 1850s.

A86.2.38 VALENTINE (JAMES). English Gothic architecture, especially in London; picturesque views of English and Scottish landscape. 47 albumen prints. 1870s to 1880s.

A86.2.39 WILSON (GEORGE WASHINGTON; 1823-1893). Commercial photographer and publisher of photographs. Travel photographs of Australia and Africa, English architecture and interiors, including Balmoral; art reproductions; portraits. 348 silver gelatin prints, 35 photochromes, 150 lantern slides, vintage glass negatives. 1870s to 1890s.

[End of Gernsheim collection.]

A86.3 GOLDBECK (EUGENE OMAR "E. O."; 1891-1986) ARCHIVES. Commercial photographer who specialized in military subjects and cirkut panoramic photographs; founder of the National News and Photo Service in San Antonio. Military maneuvers, personnel, battalions, living insignias, equipment; WW I, WW II, Sino-Japanese War (1895); Shriners and American Legion; commercial photography, including window displays, product photography, and architecture; San Antonio, including Fiesta de San Jacinto, Battle of the Flowers, street scenes, architecture, Spanish missions, and Kool Ranch. Many group portraits. Most by Goldbeck, but also includes much of the work of photographers Mitchell, Roper, and Summerville acquired by Goldbeck. More than 1,000,000 photographs, including 60,000 safety and nitrate cirkut panoramic negatives, 10,000+ vintage panoramic prints, Goldbeck's inventories. 1,000 feet of nonphotographic materials, including business records in HRHRC Manuscripts. 1890s to present, most material 1911 to late 1960s. See Bibliography—Burleson, —Davenport.

A86.4 HENLE (FRITZ; b. 1909) ARCHIVES. Commercial and travel photographer who worked extensively for Rollei. Landscapes, travel views, and portraits of area residents made in Ceylon, China, Germany, Haiti, Hawaii, India, Japan, the Middle East, and the Virgin Islands, and in Paris, France and New York; nudes; and intimate portraits of Pablo Casals. 1,000 silver gelatin prints, 200 color prints. Early 1930s to present. See Bibliography.

A86.5 LITERARY FILE COLLECTION. Photographs withdrawn from the papers of literary figures and generally include portraits of and images collected by those figures. Major holdings include: Webster Aitken (550). Merle Armitage (334). Richard Church (220). Joseph Conrad (74). Aleister Crowley (110). e. e. cummings (116). Nancy Cunard (300). J. Frank Dobie (1,000). Arthur Conan Doyle (330). T. S. Eliot (588). C. S. Forester (73). Erle Stanley Gardner (2,000). Florence Hamilton (20). Gerald Hamilton (154). Ernest Hemingway (66) and family (200). Joseph Hergesheimer (76). Fannie Hurst (297). Robinson Jeffers (200). Robert W. Johnson (106). Spud Johnson (903). James Joyce (62). Alfred Knopf (51). Oliver LaFarge (385). D. H. Lawrence (900). Sinclair and Grace H. Lewis (300). Charles A. Lindbergh (60). Arthur Livingston (100). Willard Maas (150). Arthur Machen (126). Carson McCullers (150). Compton MacKenzie (350). John Masefield (200). Somerset Maugham (200). George Burr McCutcheon (219). Edgar Lee Masters (350). Christopher Morley (1,750). Frances Mossiker (92) Ogden Nash (85). E. A.

Parsons (300). P. S. R. Payne (250). George S. Perry (200). Edgar Allan Poe (50). Ezra Pound (100). George Bernard Shaw (500). Dame Edith Sitwell (100). John Steinbeck (50). P. Tchelitchew (100). Alfred Lord Tennyson (10). Parker Tyler (50). Carl Van Vechten (300). Walt Whitman (50). Tennessee Williams (2,000). Louis Zukovsky (60). Card index; access by proper name, photographer, and collection. More than 500,000 photographs and negatives. 1880s to 1960s. HRHRC Library and Manuscripts Collection (q.v.) holds associated manuscript material for most and additional photographic materials for some collections.

A86.6 PENNINGTON (HARRY, Jr.; 1910-197?) COLLECTION. Freelance San Antonio photographer from 1934 to 1959; photojournalist for *Life, Collier's, Saturday Evening Post*, and *Newsweek*. Social, economic, and political concerns, including community health, slum conditions, the oil and gas industry, and the migration of illegal aliens. 25,000 negatives and some motion picture material. 1934 to 1959.

A86.7 SMITHERS (WINFRED DUDLEY "W. D."; 1895-1981) ARCHIVES. Photojournalist and writer in the Big Bend area of Texas during the first third of the twentieth century. Landscapes of the Big Bend, pioneer life along the border, Mexican Americans, Mexican Revolution and Francisco "Pancho" Villa, Texas Rangers, horse cavalry, mining in Terlingua and surrounding communities, early aerial photography and early aviation, including the Stinson sisters; all border markers along the 1,900-mile US-Mexican boundary; curanderos. Most photographs are by Smithers; some copies of work by Nick Mersfelder and various others. 9,000 glass, safety, and nitrate negatives with modern prints by Smithers. 1890 to 1930. All photographs are captioned and captions are gathered into a five-volume, typescript, itemized inventory; associated manuscripts at HRHRC Library and Manuscripts Collection (q.v.) and the University of Texas at Austin, Barker Texas History Center (q.v.). See Bibliography.

Texas Record Groups:

A86.8 ADKINS (W. S.) COLLECTION: Mining in West Texas, including Chisos Mining Company, Terlingua Quicksilver District, and the Marfa and Mariposa Mining Company; oil fields in Big Spring, Mexia, Van Horn, Spindletop, and High Islands; geological formations, including Barringer Hill, American Lignite (Briquette) Company, and Chaddick's Mill; Mexico, including landscapes, aerial photography, Mayan architecture photographed in the vicinity of Mexico City, Chiapas, and Guadalajara; West Texas scenery in the Big Bend region; travel photographs from around the US; Adkins family; Texas cities, including Austin, San Antonio, Grand Saline, Fort Worth, Waco, Alpine, El Paso, Llano, and Del Rio. Photographers include Adkins, William Battle Phillips, Ellison Studios (Austin), Frank Duncan, J. F. Gandara, Elmer L. Foote, Fabian Bachrach, Knaffla Brothers, J. C. Thaine, Lippe Studio, W. H. Horne Company, Jordan Company (Austin), F. A. Gildersleeve, various and unidentified photographers. 5,000 photographs, including vintage silver gelatin prints; glass, nitrate, and safety negatives; postcards. 1890 to 1955.

A86.9 ARCHITECTURE COLLECTION. Retrospective views of historic and significant structures in Texas, organized by county. Photographed by Todd Webb and various others. 500 silver gelatin prints. 1960s. Negatives at Amon Carter Museum (q.v.) and prints at the University of Texas at Austin Architectural Drawings Collection (q.v.); card index. HRCP# DIS136.

A86.10 ARMSTRONG (FRANK; b. 1935) COLLECTION. Commercial and art photographer specializing in Southwestern subjects. Social landscapes and rural scenes in Texas. 42 silver gelatin prints. 1968 to 1976.

A86.11 BALDWIN (FRED; b. 1929) AND WENDY WATRISS (b. 1943) COLLECTION. Photojournalist team concentrating on social issues. Rural scenes and people from Grimes County. 29 silver gelatin prints. Early 1970s.

A86.12 CROFFORD (AVA ATKINSON) COLLECTION. Austin photographer and author of *The Diamond Years of Texas Photography* (Austin: W. F. Edwards, 1975). Studio portraits in a late-Pictorial style made for her PPA Master of Photography. 17 silver gelatin prints. Ca. 1940 to 1950.

A86.13 DALLAS COLLECTION. Architecture, cityscapes, store window displays, automobiles and auto races, theater fronts, telephone office and equipment, state fair and exhibits; development of Garwood and Oak Cliff by unidentified commercial photographer(s). 278 modern silver gelatin contact prints from 8x10 negatives. Ca. 1915 to 1920. HRCP# DIS12.

A86.14 FERGUSON (MIRIAM A.) PHOTOGRAPHS. Journalistic coverage of Ferguson's inauguration as Texas governor; her signing of the Sour Gas Bill; t her home in Austin and other scenes; Knights of Pythias. Photographed by Boone and unidentified photographer(s). 25 modern silver gelatin contact prints. 1930 to 1934. HRCP# DIS16.

A86.15 FORSTER (Reverend SIMON) COLLECTION. Snapshots of New Braunfels and travels. 25 silver gelatin prints. Ca. 1900.

A86.16 GILDERSLEEVE (FRED A.; 1881?-1958) COLLECTION. Commercial and industrial photography of cityscape and street scenes in Waco; architecture, especially construction shots, retail interiors. Photographed by Gildersleeve and A. A. Torrence. 70 modern and copy silver gelatin contact prints, 13 silver gelatin prints (enlargements), 6 negatives. 1925 to 1940. HRCP# DIS19.

A86.17 GOLDBECK (E. L.) COLLECTION. Son of E. O. Goldbeck (v.s.). Texas school group portraits made using cirkut panoramic camera. 8,000 safety negatives; Goldbeck's inventory. 1940s to 1970s.

A86.18 HOUSTON FLOOD PHOTOGRAPHS. Flood scenes along Buffalo Bayou in Houston, in the vicinity of Milam and Prairie streets. Unidentified photographer(s). 15 panoramic silver gelatin prints. Ca. 1900. HRCP# DIS23.

A86.19 KAROTKIN COLLECTION. Cityscapes and street scenes of San Antonio, including automobiles and trolleys, architecture, parades; aftermath of a flood; Francisco "Pancho" Villa and the Mexican Revolution. Commercial photographs by Jacobson and unidentified photographer(s). 65 copy silver gelatin photographs and copy negatives. Ca. 1900 to 1940s, most 1910 to 1920. HRCP# DIS24.

A86.20 LUBBEN (Dr. RENKE G.) COLLECTION. Snapshots of the University of Texas at Austin campus, snakes, spiders, portraits. 45 silver gelatin prints. Ca. 1920. HRCP# DIS28.

A86.21 McGREGOR (JOHN FREDERICK "DOC"; 1892-1986) ARCHIVES. Corpus Christi studio and news photographer who freelanced for the *Caller-Times*. Studio portraits, panoramic group portraits, businesses, and industrial photography. 100,000 silver gelatin prints and negatives. 1930s to early 1970s. Newspaper negatives arranged by date.

A86.22 McGREGOR BUSINESS COLLECTION. Corpus Christi business interiors made by an itinerant photographer in the month of February 1934. 354 glass negatives with modern prints. 1934. See Bibliography—Miller.

A86.23 MURPHY (MICHAEL A.; b. 1952) AND BILL KENNEDY (b. 1951) COLLECTION. Austin-based, commercial photographers no longer working together as a team. Exhibition prints documenting the Texas Prison Rodeo in Huntsville. 114 silver gelatin prints. 1976 to 1977.

A86.24 NASCHKE (PAUL; 1872-1932) COLLECTION. Commercial studio portraits, including hand-colored, late-Pictorialist work by Naschke; buildings and objects relating to the life Naschke photographed by Robert John Mihovil. 18 photographs, including 7 by Naschke; hand-colored silver gelatin prints and type-C color prints. 1930 to 1950, 1982. HRCP# DIS96; 982:042.

A86.25 NEW BRAUNFELS COLLECTION. City scenes photographed by Seidel Studios. 22 silver gelatin prints, including banquet format. 1927 to 1970. HRCP# DIS42-43.

A86.26 NEY (ELISABET; 1833-1907) COLLECTION. German-born, Texas sculptress. Ney's home, studio, and her works. Photographers include Ernst Raba and unidentified snapshooters. 200 photographs, including safety and glass negatives, silver gelatin prints, copy prints, and nonphotographic imagery; associated, nonphotographic materials in HRHRC Iconography; itemized list. Ca. 1850 to 1910. HRCP# DIS45.

A86.27 O'DANIEL (Governor W. LEE "PAPPY") PHOTOGRAPHS. Journalistic coverage of the inauguration of O'Daniel in the University of Texas at Austin stadium. Unidentified photographer(s). 12 silver gelatin prints. 1939. HRCP# DIS46.

A86.28 PLUM, TEXAS COLLECTION. Rural homestead and portraits. Unidentified amateur photographer. 26 glass negatives with modern prints. Ca. 1910. HRCP# DIS47.

A86.29 RECTOR (RAY; 1884-1933) COLLECTION. Cowboy and photographer in Stamford. Ranch life in the Stamford vicinity; SMS Flat Top Ranch; Pecos Rodeo. 1,000 nitrate negatives with modern prints. 1910 and 1940. HRCP# DIS140. See Bibliography.

A86.30 RICE FARMING IN TEXAS COLLECTION. Landscapes, especially illustrating water diversion and dam projects in Gonzales, Seguin, Marble Falls, Eureka Falls, and unidentified locations; rice farming and production, Japanese field workers. Photographers include Hoffmann, Glock, Barnett (Crowell LA), and unidentified photographer(s). From a report written by Dr. T. U. Taylor, *Rice Farming in Texas* (Washington DC: US Department of the Interior book #690, paper 71.) 49 photo prints, including silver gelatin, collodio-chloride, and gelatino-chloride processes. Ca. 1900 to 1910. HRCP# DIS50.

A86.31 ROBERTS (F. WARREN) COLLECTION. Construction of Medina Dam, Pleasanton High School; cotton gins. Unidentified photographer(s). 13 silver gelatin photo prints. Ca. 1912 to 1913. HRCP# DIS51.

A86.32 ROBSTOWN COLLECTION. People, business interiors and storefronts, farming in the Robstown vicinity. Unidentified photographer(s). 25 silver gelatin copy prints; itemized list. Ca. 1905 to 1915. HRCP# DIS52.

A86.33 SPINDLETOP MUSEUM COLLECTION. Spindletop Field and East Texas, oil-related subjects. Unidentified photographer(s). Obtained from Spindletop Museum, Lamar University (q.v.). 18 silver gelatin copy prints. Ca. 1890 to 1905. HRCP# DIS60.

A86.34 TEXAS HISTORICAL FOUNDATION COLLECTION. Ten commissioned works each by fourteen photographers and one two-person team for *Contemporary Texas: A Photographic*

Portrait. Photographers include Frank Armstrong, Fred Baldwin/Wendy Watriss, Gay Block, Ave Bonar, Jim Bones, Carol Cohen Burton, Peter Feresten, Frank Gohlke, Paul Hester, Stuart Klipper, George Krause, Skeet McAuley, Michael A. Murphy, Mary Peck, and Rick Williams. 113 silver gelatin, 30 color, 10 dye-transfer exhibition prints; work prints and contact sheets. 1984 to 1985. See Bibliography—Sandweiss.

A86.35 TEXAS MISCELLANY. Cityscapes, buildings, and businesses from Austin, Corpus Christi, and Anson. Unidentified photographer(s), some snapshots. 40 vintage silver gelatin, copy, and modern prints, nitrate and copy negatives. Ca. 1895 to 1965. HRCP# DIS61.

A86.36 TEXAS PEOPLE. Composite of Texas Senate, Seventeenth Legislature, 1881; by H. B. Hillyer. Studio portraits and group shots; by A. N. Callaway (Brenham), and unidentified photographer(s). 40 photographs, predominantly copy prints. Ca. 1880 to 1940. HRCP# DIS62.

A86.37 TRLICA (JNO P.; 1882-1978) ARCHIVE. Czech photographer and community leader in Granger. Studio portraits of area residents, including Czech, Black, and Hispanic ethnicities; personal and public events in the community, including festivals, religious ceremonies, and conventions; and corn and cotton agriculture. 10,000 glass negatives, some with modern prints, 500 nitrate negatives, 50 banquet film negatives, 700 vintage silver gelatin prints, 50 vintage panoramic prints; studio ephemera. 1909 to mid-1960s.

A86.38 UNIVERSITY OF TEXAS AT AUSTIN COLLECTIONS. Botanical subjects and landscapes, including pine forests, lumbering operations in East Texas, and scrub growth in West Texas by unidentified photographer(s). 162 gelatino-chloride prints. 1898 to 1900. Campus buildings and scenes, demolition of the Old Main building by unidentified photographer(s). 448 photographs including silver gelatin prints, color slides, safety negatives. 1935, 1938, 1950 to 1955, 1965, 1975. Graduates of the engineering department by various photographers. 100 photo prints and negatives. 1938 to 1964. Faculty and students by unidentified photographer(s). 300 silver gelatin prints and safety negatives. Ca. 1897 to 1941. Hand-colored photo prints of scenes around campus by Dr. J. M. Kuehne, University Studios, and unidentified photographer(s). 4 prints. 1900 to 1912. Opening of the Michener Gallery photographed by Walter Barnes. 6 color prints. Staff and operation of the HRHRC photographed by Frank Armstrong, Joe Coltharp, Roy Flukinger, Eric Beggs, and unidentified others. 250 photographs, including 35mm transparencies, color and silver gelatin prints. 1970 to 1979. HRCP# DIS64-76.

A86.39 UNIVERSITY OF TEXAS AT AUSTIN PETROLEUM EXTENSION SERVICE. Schools, aides, and other material in the Texas oil industry. Various and unidentified photographers. 200 photo prints and negatives. 1954 to 1962. HRCP# DIS79; 958:060.

A86.40 WACO, TEXAS COLLECTION. Street scenes, aftermath of a tornado, Tom Mix at a gravesite, and a parade. Unidentified photographer(s). 47 photo negatives, many damaged, modern prints. Ca. 1930. Itemized list. HRCP# DIS83.

Additional Record Groups:

A86.41 AMERICAN SCULPTURE PHOTOGRAPHS. Art reproductions of sculpture, statues, and friezes. Unidentified photographer(s). 127 collodio-chloride, gelatino-chloride, and silver gelatin prints. Ca. 1910 to 1920. HRCP# DIS54.

A86.42 AUSTIN (ALICE ELIZABETH; 1875?-1952) COLLECTION. Amateur pictorialist living in Boston. Studio portraits. 21 silver gelatin prints. 1880 to 1910.

A86.43 BAKER (ROGER, Jr.) COLLECTION. Experiments and inventions in photographic processes; revivals of nineteenth-century processes, including daguerreotypes and photos on glass; with some manuscript documentation. 30 items. 1970s. HRCP# DIS123.

A86.44 BARKER (Dr. PAUL) COLLECTION. Studio portraits of American Indians, including Wichitas Burgess Hunt (Qsa-hi-wa-ski-a-gi-na-us-is-sa, or Morning Star Spirit) and John Tatum; others, also probably Wichitas. Photographed by Charles Pyka. 7 silver gelatin prints. 1898. HRCP# DIS4.

A86.45 BENTLEY COLLECTION. Family and vacation photographs made in Texas, Alabama, and unidentified locales; snapshots and commercial photo postcards of WW I Navy troop carriers by International Newsreel and unidentified amateur photographers. 101 silver gelatin prints, album with 86 silver gelatin prints. Ca. 1918. HRCP# DIS3.

A86.46 BERGHEIM COLLECTION. Ruins and architecture in Jerusalem. 8 mammoth albumen prints. 1875.

A86.47 BRANT (G. EMERSON) COLLECTION. Snapshots portraits, travel views, and studio portraits. Photographers include Bryson and Son (Houlton ME), C. J. Wright (Houston), Deane (Houston), P. H. Rose (Galveston), unidentified commercial photographer(s). 135 photo prints, including cabinet, cartes, Kodak 1A snapshots, album. Early 1880s to 1910. HRCP# DIS5.

A86.48 CALLAWAY (Dr. MORGAN, Jr.; 1862-1936) COLLECTION. Professor at the University of Texas at Austin. Studio portraits. Photographers include Ashman (Baltimore MD), Blessing and Company (Baltimore MD), Fredricks (New York), S. B. Hill (Austin), Hurd and Delany's (Dalton GA), Journeay (Austin), W. Kurtz (New York), H. R. Marks (Austin), C. W. Motes (Atlanta GA), Russell (Baltimore MD), Sarony (New York), Simon (New Orleans), Smith and Motes (Atlanta GA), G. F. Ward (Abilene), and N. M. Wilcox (Georgetown). 61 photo prints, including albumen cartes, cabinet cards, and silver gelatin prints. Ca. 1861 to 1950. HRCP# DIS6; 972:002.

A86.49 CARRICK (EDWARD) COLLECTION. Ballet costume designs, predominantly by Hein Hedroth. Unidentified photographer(s). 300 silver gelatin glass negatives. Late 1940s.

A86.50 CHRISTIAN (JOHN) COLLECTION. Queretaro, Mexico, the surrounding countryside, architecture, people, marketplace, palmwork, musicians, Dance of the Conquest, Xitales Dancers; Actopan, Hidalgo market; Huastec market; and Nahut Indians. 15 silver gelatin prints and 800 Kodachrome slides; itemized inventory. 1969. HRCP# DIS7; 969:001.

A86.51 CODY (W. F. "BUFFALO BILL") COLLECTION. Portraits of Cody by Sarony, Anderson, and unidentified photographer(s); group portrait of John Y. Nelson and family, scout, guide, and interpreter of the Sioux; photographs from his "Wild West Trip to Grand Canyon of the Colorado River and Buckskin Mountain of Arizona"; photographs of a Mormon bridal party trip from Flagstaff AZ to Utah. 11 gelatino-chloride and silver gelatin prints. Ca. 1880. HRCP# DIS8; 974:006.

A86.52 COQUIOT'S (GUSTAVE) UTRILLO EXHIBITION. Art reproductions of paintings by Maurice Utrillo and an exhibition. 17 copy prints. Ca. 1950. HRCP# DIS9; 958:026.

A86.53 CRANE (ARNOLD) COLLECTION. Portraits of contemporary photographers. 50 silver gelatin prints. Late 1960s.

A86.54 CROSBY (Mrs. ROBERT C.) COLLECTION. Autographed photographs of musicians, including Joseph Stransky, George Kubilick, Lydia Lopokova, John Philip Sousa, and others by various photographers. 8 silver gelatin prints, one photogravure. Ca. 1910 to 1930. HRCP# DIS10; 958:027.

A86.55 DANCER (JOHN BENJAMIN; 1812-1887) COLLECTION. Scottish optician and photographic inventor who pioneered microphotography and stereography. Experimental photographs, subjects including family, landscape, and others. Photographed by Dancer and various others. 300 photographs, including 60 microphotographs, 56 daguerreotypes, 65 card stereographs, 46 glass stereographs, 27 ambrotypes, 30 prints in various processes; equipment; papers in the HRHRC Library, additional Dancer materials in Gernsheim collection. See Bibliography—Oliphant.

A86.56 DAVIS (ALBERT) COLLECTION. Copy photographs of Civil War battle scenes photographed by Brady, Gardner, and others; portraits of persons associated with the Civil War, especially U. S. Grant and his family; circus photographs, including clowns and acrobats photographed by Sarony and others. 345 photographs, including vintage and copy prints, cartes, cabinet cards; many severely water-damaged. Mid-1860s to 1930s.

A86.57 DULLES (JOHN FOSTER; 1888-1959) COLLECTION. US Secretary of State (1953-1959). Individual and group studio portraits of heads of state and diplomats, including Queen Elizabeth II, Prince Philip, Nehru, Arthur Vandenberg, and delegates to Versailles. Various photographers. 32 photo prints. Ca. 1915 to 1965. HRCP# DIS14, DIS145.

A86.58 EVANS (WALKER; 1903-1975) COLLECTION. Prominent photographic artist working in a documentary style, noted for his work with the Farm Security Administration and his collaboration with James Agee on *Let us now praise famous men.* 70 published and 100 unpublished documentary portraits, landscapes, and other images made in Alabama in 1936 to illustrate the book. 170 silver gelatin prints, some duplicates. 1936. See Bibliography—Agee; —Stott, *Documentary Expression . . .*

A86.59 FALVELLA (J. W.) COLLECTION. Laredo, Mexico, and the Mexican Revolution; bandits and battle scenes photographed by Falvella, Serrano (Laredo), and unidentified photographer(s). 124 silver gelatin prints and photo postcards and nitrate negatives. Ca. 1910 to 1925. HRCP# DIS15.

A86.60 FREEMAN (CHARLES M.) COLLECTION. Mexico. 170 photographs, including cartes, albumen and silver gelatin prints. Ca. 1860 to 1911. HRCP# DIS18.

A86.61 FRY (PETER WICKENS; d. 1860). Early amateur and founding member of the London Photographic Club. Informal English portraits. 44 salted-paper prints. Ca. 1850s.

A86.62 GILL (ERIC; 1882-1940) COLLECTION. English sculptor and author of a treatise on sculpture. Snapshots, studio, and commercial photo postcards (mostly Parisian?) of musicians, aviators, and others, including Granados, Alfred Bruneau, Gabriel Fauré, and others. Photographers include Henri Manuel, Brassaï, Nadar, and various others. 75 albumen, gelatino-chloride, and silver gelatin prints, including cartes and cabinets. 1895 to 1930. HRCP# DIS20; 974:003.

A86.63 GLANZ (H. H.) COLLECTION. Art reproductions and copies of images pertaining to Jewish folklore, art, history, and religion. Unidentified photographer(s). 750—35mm copy slides. Late 1950s.

A86.64 GOOD (FRANK MASON) COLLECTION. Travel photographs of the Holy Land. 15 albumen prints. Ca. 1870s.

A86.65 GOTTSMAN HEBRAICA COLLECTION. Middle Eastern landscapes. Photographed by Bonfils, Arnoux, and unidentified photographer(s). 20 albumen prints. Ca. 1870.

A86.66 HARE (JAMES H. "JIMMY"; 1856-1946) COLLECTION. American pioneer of photojournalism; worked for *Collier's* and *Leslie's Weekly*. Seven major wars from the Spanish-American War to WW I, Wright Brothers, Belmont Park Meet, Mexican Revolution, balloon ascensions, and personal images. 2,200 photographs, including silver gelatin prints, glass and film negatives, and glass lantern slides. 1890 to 1931. See Bibliography—Gould and Greffe.

A86.67 HART (WILLIAM S.; 1872-1946) COLLECTION. American stage and film actor. Production stills from many of Hart's motion pictures including, *Blue Blazes Rawden, The Border Wireless, Branding Broadway, Burglar for a Night, Claws of the Hun, The Cradle of Courage, Eaglet of White, Flare-up Sal, The Guilty Man, His Mother's Boy, John Petticoats, Kaiser's Shadow, The Narrow Trail, 9 O'clock Town, O'Malley of the Mounted, Ponjola,, Riddle Gawne, Sahara, Sand, Selfish Yates, Shark Monroe, The Silent Man, Square Deal Sanderson, The Testing Block, The Tiger Man, The Toll Gate, The Whistle, Tyrant Fear, Wagon Tracks, Wild Son of His Father, Wolves of the Rail*; studio portraits of actors and actresses, including Warner Baxter, Sylvia Breamer, Frank Brownlee, Florence Carpenter, Lon Chaney, Gertrude Claire, Maude George, Louise Glaum, Fritz (Hart's horse), Juanita Hansen, Alma Hanson, Raymond Hatton, Will Jim Hatton, Richard Headrick, Hart Hoxie, Hugh Jackson, Robert Kortman, Ann Little, Bessie Love, George McDaniel, Katherine MacDonald, Ira McFadden, Robert McKim, Mat Moore, Pat Moore, Anna Q. Nilsson, Eva Novak, G. Raymond Nye, Patricia Palmer, William Patton, Lon Poff, Charles Ray, Jack Richardson, Milton Ross, Gordon Russell, Thomas Santschi, Antrim Short, Joseph Singleton, Bertholde Sprotte, Myrtle Stedman, Edwin Stevens, Georgie Stone, Gloria Swanson, Francis Thorwalde, Mary Thurman, E. B. Tilton, George Williams, and Leo Willis. Unidentified photographer(s). 1,604 silver gelatin prints. 1917 to 1922. HRCP# DIS21; 973:001.

A86.68 HERSCHEL (Sir JOHN FREDERICK WILLIAM; 1792-1871) COLLECTION. Many unique, experimental processes, including a series of early color photograms called "flower paintings" (1834-1837, now severely faded) made with flower pigments. 500 photo prints. 1830s to 1840s. HRHRC Library and Manuscripts Collection holds extensive collection of papers on photochemical research.

A86.69 KEMP (JOHN H., Jr.) COLLECTION. Amateur, late-Pictorialist images. 55 silver gelatin prints. 1930 to 1960.

A86.70 KING (GILLIS) COLLECTION. Equipment collection focusing on prephotographic magic lantern apparatus and slides. Compiled by King; unidentified photographer(s). Itemized list.

A86.71 KHRUSHCHEV (NIKITA) COLLECTION. State visit of Khrushchev in 1956 showing US dignitaries, United Nations, crowds gathered to see Khrushchev at agricultural and factory sites, and in parades. Unidentified photographer(s), probably official US State Department photographs. 58 silver gelatin prints. 1956. HRCP# DIS25; 977:004.

A86.72 MARESH (EDWARD) COLLECTION. Czechoslovakia and Czech people; folk costume and crafts, cityscapes, architecture and interiors in Prague, Cloister Strahov, landscape, and monuments. Compiled by Maresh; various and unidentified photographer(s). 250 silver gelatin prints, 200 photographic and printed postcards. Ca. 1900 to 1930. HRCP# DIS30; 973:002.

A86.73 MARSHALL (ALEXANDER A.) COLLECTION. Head-and-shoulder portraits of unidentified sitters. Unidentified photographer(s). 10 color crayon reinforced photo prints, 2 silver gelatin prints. Ca. 1900. HRCP# DIS127; 975:013.

A86.74 MARSHALL/WALTON COLLECTION. Architecture and interiors designed by the Chicago architectural firm of Marshall and Fox, later known as Walton and Walton, including the work of architects L. B. Walton Jr. and B. H. Marshall; portraits. Various commercial photographers. 100 silver gelatin prints. 1940s. HRCP# DIS109; 982:026. Related, nonphotographic materials at the University of Texas at Austin, Architecture and Planning Library, Architectural Drawings Collection (q.v.).

A86.75 MARTIN (PAUL; 1864-1944) COLLECTION. London street people and street life; experimental night photography. 1,600 film and glass negatives, lantern slides, and photo prints by this award-winning London amateur photographer. See Bibliography—Flukinger, Schaaf, and Meacham.

A86.76 MAVERICK (JAMES S.) COLLECTION. Vacation slides from Europe and the Middle East. 2,000—35mm color slides. 1956 to 1970. HRCP# DIS115.

A86.77 MEXICAN REVOLUTION COLLECTION. Battle scenes, corpses, soldiers, connected with the insurrection led by Francisco "Pancho" Villa against Madera. Photographed by Otis A. Aultmann and unidentified photographer(s). 280 silver gelatin copy prints. Ca. 1910 to 1920. HRCP# DIS31.

A86.78 MEXICO COLLECTION. Cityscapes of Mexico City and Acapulco from the Mexican Department of Tourism. Professor William P. Glade, comp. 11 silver gelatin prints. Ca. 1975. HRCP# DIS33.

A86.79 MULLER (Colonel MARK T.) COLLECTION. Equipment collection with some photographs, mostly unidentified portraits, by George Schuwirth (Austin), by Davis and Stewart (Cleburne), Lind (Lexington), and unidentified photographer(s). 150 items, including 16 daguerreotypes, 8 tintypes, cabinet cards, silver gelatin prints. Ca. 1850s to 1920s. Exhibition prints entered in an amateur competition photographed by George A. Schwepps. 13 silver gelatin prints. Ca. 1940. HRCP# DIS37; 976:011.

A86.80 NASA COLLECTION. Space photographs, the Earth, the lunar surface, and spacecraft. From the Apollo 11 and Ranger space missions. 18 color and 17 silver gelatin prints; captions. 1964 and 1969. HRCP# DIS41.

A86.81 NASA SLIDES. Space photographs of astronauts, spacecraft, and scenes from space made during Gemini, Apollo, and Skylab missions and unmanned probes. 166 color copy slides. Early 1960 to early 1970s.

A86.82 NINETEENTH-CENTURY AMERICAN PORTRAITS. James Buchanan, Reverend William Newton, C. Vzabriskie, Sagamore Athletic Club, others photographed by Aimé Dupont, Meade Brothers, W. Kurtz (New York), and various others. 38 photo prints, including platinum prints. 1850 to 1900.

A86.83 PAGE (HOLLAND) COLLECTION. Equipment collection with books and still photographs. 1946 to 1955.

A86.84 PARNASSUS PRESERVED COLLECTION. Studio portraits and art reproduction portraits of literary figures, predominantly European. Various studio photographers. 354 albumen cartes, 4 albumen cabinet cards. 1860 to 1880. HRCP# DIS118.

A86.85 PARSONS (EDWARD ALEXANDER; 1878-1962) COLLECTION. New Orleans book collector and gentleman scholar. European architecture, interiors, architectural details, cityscapes, street scenes, and art reproductions. Photographers include Edizioni Brogi, X Phot, ND, A. G., and unidentified others. 500 albumen and silver gelatin prints. Ca. 1890 to 1920. HRCP# DIS99 and following.

A86.86 POUTIATINE FAMILY PHOTOGRAPHS. Count Eugène Poutiatine (d. 1909) moved with his five daughters, Vera, May, Olga, Dorothy, and Genia, from Moscow, Russia, to Weybridge, England, in the late 1890s. Family photographs, including snapshots and studio portraits, many from prerevolutionary Russia. Photographs by English, German, South African, Swedish, and Russian studios, and unidentified others. 250 photographs, most cartes and cabinets, but also including glass slides, silver gelatin prints; associate manuscript material and photo postcards in HRHRC Manuscripts. Ca. 1860 to 1930. HRCP# DIS 48.

A86.87 POWELL (ERNEST; d. 1951) COLLECTION. Piano intructor in Marshall. Studio portraits, predominantly of singers, including Enzo Pina, Enrico Caruso, Vladimir Horowitz, and Helen Keller. Photographers include Edward S. Curtis, Lackey (Temple), Corti Art Studio (Marshall), and various others. Many autographed by the sitter and with poems by Powell associated. 158 silver gelatin and platinum prints; itemized list. Ca. 1900 to 1950. HRCP# DIS49.

A86.88 PRATT (FRANCIS EDWARD) COLLECTION. Cityscapes, architecture, and landscapes in Mexico. 423 photo negatives with modern prints. 1908 to 1912. HRCP# DIS134; 975:004.

A86.89 REPHOTOGRAPHIC SURVEY PROJECT COLLECTION. Copy prints of landscapes and scenes from the western US made for the United States Geological Survey by noted nineteenth-century photographers, paired with modern images of the same scenes made under nearly identical situations. Nineteenth-century photographers include Jackson, O'Sullivan, Russell, Gardner, and Hiller; twentieth-century rephotographers include Mark Klett, JoAnn Verburg, Gordon Bushaw, and Rick Dingus. 120 pairs silver gelatin prints. 1870s/1970s. See Bibliography—Klett, et al. HRCP# 985:021.

A86.90 RURAL GEORGIA COLLECTION. Thomasville GA and vicinity; Black field hands; cotton farming. Photographed by Moller and by Field. 21 gelatino-chloride prints. Late 1890s. HRCP# DIS91.

A86.91 SAWARD FAMILY PHOTOGRAPHS. Studio portraits relating to Major General Michael Henry Saward (1840-1928), Governor of Guernsey and his family; snapshots of travel scenes by auto. Various English and Indian studios and unidentified photographer(s). 229 photographs, including collodio-chloride and silver gelatin prints, albumen cartes and cabinets; associated papers in HRHRC Manuscripts. Ca. 1860 to 1920. HRCP# DIS53.

A86.92 SHIRRIFFS (WILLIAM; 1886-1965) COLLECTION. Civil engineer for Texas General Land Office. 82 nitrate and 45 glass negatives. HRCP# DIS55.

A86.93 STEICHEN (EDWARD; 1879-1973) BEQUEST. Fashion photographs for Condé Nast, studio portraits. 28 photographs, including silver gelatin prints and color prints. 1922 to 1938.

A86.94 STEICHEN (EDWARD) US NAVY PHOTOGRAPHS. Work done during Steichen's Navy service as a photographer in WW II, including ships, Marines and battle scenes. 300 silver gelatin prints. Ca. 1945.

A86.95 TINKER (EDWARD LAROQUE) COLLECTION. New Orleans lawyer and newspaper editor interested in the idea that the cowboy offered a unifying concept for North, Central, and

South American cultures. Family snapshots, General Pedro Eugenio Aramburu (Provisional President of Argentina in 1959), ranch life, gauchos, El Paso, studio portraits (cartes, cabinets), Mexican Revolution (Tinker rode with Obregón's armies); late-Pictorialist renditions of New Orleans scenes. 500 photographs, including daguerreotypes, ambrotypes, tintypes, and silver gelatin prints. Ca. 1850 to 1930s. HRCP# DIS135.

A86.96 TOBENKIN (ELIAS) COLLECTION. Russian people and life following the Bolshevik Revolution; groups of writers, editor of *New Soviet Encyclopedia*; portraits of the Romanovs; portraits of Demian Bedny, Lenin, Joseph Stalin, Leon Trotsky; Selsoviet of Kopil, Trade Union of Kopil; theater stills; architecture; street scenes; peasant life; made in Russia. Photographers include Herbert Paxton, Press Cliche, and Parikas; many from the *New York Tribune*. 182 silver gelatin prints. Ca. 1917. HRCP# DIS1.

A86.97 UNITED NATIONS CHARTER CONFERENCE. Delegates and activities of the conference to form the United Nations in San Francisco. Photographers include Sam Rosenberg, Robert Eastman, Betty Cooper Lundquist, and McLaine. 21 silver gelatin prints. 1945. HRCP# DIS116; 983:020.

A86.98 US ARMY COLLECTION. History of the cavalry; Fort Hood. Unidentified photographer(s), official US Army photographs. 100 silver gelatin (many copy) and color prints. Ca. 1890 to 1975. HRCP# DIS63; 975:012.

A86.99 VALENTINE (JOHN) COLLECTION. Portraits of US political leaders, many of Franklin Delano Roosevelt and his career, Lincoln and carte cartoons of John Wilkes Booth. Various and unidentified photographers. 400 photo prints including albumen cartes, silver gelatin prints; 1—8mm film. 1870 to 1950. HRCP# DIS80; 958:051.

A86.100 VANDALE COLLECTION. Expedition of *USS Wyandot* to South Pole under command of J. J. Vandale; Panhandle ranching; turn-of-the-century Fort Worth architecture; XIT Ranch. Various and unidentified photographers. 150 silver gelatin prints, copy photos, and negatives. 1890 to 1960. HRCP# DIS82; 958:052.

A86.101 WARD (JOE) CIRCUS COLLECTION. Snapshots of clowns from Ringling Brothers Circus; Amerinds; Wichita Falls. Unidentified photographer(s). 100 silver gelatin prints, 50 negatives with modern prints. 1900 to 1940. HRCP# DIS84.

A86.102 WEINREB ARCHITECTURE COLLECTION. Architecture and details of decorative arts. Unidentified photographer(s). 25 silver gelatin prints. 1915 to 1950. HRCP# DIS92; 958:005.

A86.103 WILLIAMS (FREDERICK ALLEN; 1898-1958) COLLECTION. New England sculptor specializing in western US subjects. Studies for Williams' works, travel and landscape photographs, reproductions of artworks; predominantly Western subjects. 36 feet of silver gelatin prints, transparencies, negatives, postcards; 135 feet of lantern slides, some in color. Ca. 1920 to 1950. Unprocessed. Arranged by subject.

A86.104 WILLIAMS (SARAH) COLLECTION. Aunt of Frederick Allen Williams, this material was withdrawn from his collection (v.s.). Portraits from William's childhood in Albany NY, college days at Wellesley, as a teacher, and her world travels in her later life; genre stereographs. Various studio photographers, including Pirie McDonald (Albany NY), R. E. Churchill (Albany NY), and McDonnald and Sterry (Albany NY); unidentified other(s) and snapshooters. 500 photographs including daguerreotypes, ambrotypes, tintypes, cartes, cabinets, cyanotypes, stereographs, and silver gelatin prints. Ca. 1860s to 1940, most 1880s to 1905. HRCP# DIS94.

A86.105 WOODMAN (Colonel CHARLES) COLLECTION. Equipment collection with some photographs, including daguerreotypes and tintypes. 22 photographs. Ca. 1850s to 1900.

A86.106 WORLD WAR I COLLECTION. Aerial views of European communities and landscape, many showing effects of bombing during the war. Photographers include Fifth Photo Section, US Army Air Service, and unidentified others. 4 boxes of silver gelatin prints; most photographs captioned. 1914 to 1920. HRCP# DIS86.

A86.107 YALTA CONFERENCE COLLECTION. Delegates and site of the Yalta Conference; Roosevelt, Churchill, Stalin. Photographed by US Army Signal Corps. 50 silver gelatin prints. 1945. Most prints are captioned.

Published works illustrated with photographs: The collection holds more than 1,000 published works with vintage photographic print illustrations tipped in. Gernsheim's *Incunabula . . .* (see Bibliography) lists many books held by the Photography Collection not noted here. Main entry is photographer unless otherwise noted.

A86.108 Annan, Thomas. *Photographs of old closes, streets, &c., taken 1868-1877* [=] *Old Glasgow.* Glasgow: City Improvement Trust, 1877. 40 carbon prints. HRCP# fDA890/G5/A662.

A86.109 Barraud, Herbert. *Men and women of the day: A picture gallery of contemporary portraiture . . .* London: Richard Bentley; Eglington, 1888-1890. 3 volumes, 107 carbon prints. HRCP# fTR681/F3/M362.

A86.110 Boole, A. and J., and Henry and T. J. Dixon. *Old London.* London: Society for Photographing Relics of Old London, 1875-1886. 12 parts in 2 volumes; 120 carbon prints. HRCP# fDA683/S634.

A86.111 Bourne, Samuel, and Charles Shepherd; with historical and descriptive letterpress by James Burgess. *Photographs of architecture and scenery in Gujarat and Rajputana.* Calcutta, Bombay, and Simla: Bourne and Shepherd, 1874. 30 albumen prints. HRCP# fDS485/G8/B885.

A86.112 Bryans, William. *Antiquities of Cheshire in photograph [sic], with short descriptive notes to which are added views of several ancient buildings in Shropshire and North Wales.* Chester: Hugh Roberts, 1858. 57 albumen prints. HRCP# fDA670/C6/B882.

A86.113 Cameron, Julia Margaret. *Illustrations to Tennyson's Idylls of the King and other poems.* London: Henry S. King, 1875. 2 volumes, 26 albumen prints. The collection holds other, variant editions. HRCP# fPR5577/C264.

A86.114 Delamotte, Philip Henry. *Photographic views of the progress of the Crystal Palace, Sydenham, taken during the progress of the works, by desire of the directors.* London: Directors of the Crystal Palace Co, 1855. 2 volumes, 160 salted-paper prints. HRCP# fNA6750/S98/D354.

A86.115 Du Camp, Maxime; printed by E. Blanquart-Evrard. *Egypt, Nubia, Palestine et Syria . . .* Paris: Gide et J. Baudry, 1852. 2 volumes, 67 albumen prints. HRCP# fDT47/D823. The collection also holds an English edition (London: E. Gambart, 1852) in 25 parts. HRCP# fDT47/D822.

A86.116 Egerton, Philip Henry. *Journal of a tour through Spiti to the frontier of Chinese Tibet.* London: Cundall, Downes, and Company, 1864. 37 albumen prints. HRCP# fDS485/S74/E451.

A86.117 Emerson, Peter Henry. *Idyls of the Norfolk Broads.* London: The Autotype Company, 1887. 12 photogravures. HRCP# fNE2620/E4/1887.

A86.118 Emerson, Peter Henry. *Pictures from life in field and fen.* London: G. Bell and Sons, 1887. 20 photogravures. HRCP# fNE2615/E5.

A86.119 Emerson, Peter Henry. *Pictures of East Anglian life.* London: S. Low, Marston, Searl, and Rivington, 1888. 32 photogravures. HRCP# fDA670/E14/E648.

A86.120 Emerson, Peter Henry; descriptive text by Emerson and T. F. Goodall. *Life and landscape on the Norfolk Broads.* London: Sampson Low, Marston, Searle, and Rivington, 1886. 40 platinotypes. HRCP# fNE2620/E55.

A86.121 *Exhibition of the works of industry of all nations, 1851: Reports by the juries on the subjects in the thirty classes into which the exhibition was divided.* London: Spicer Brothers, 1851. 4 volumes with 155 salted-paper prints by Hugh Owens and G. Ferrier, printed by Nikolaas Henneman.

A86.122 Fenton, Roger. *Photographs of drawings, etc. in the British Museum.* London: Colnaghi, 1857-1858. 115 salted-paper prints. "List of photographs presented to the Right Hon. Benjamin Disraeli, M.P., by the Trustees of the British Museum." HRCP# fTR655.11/P264.

A86.123 Frith, Francis. *Egypt and Palestine.* London: J. S. Virtue, 1858-1859. 2 volumes, 76 albumen prints. The collection also holds a copy of unbound parts. HRCP# fDT54/F847.

A86.124 Frith, Francis. *The gossiping photographer at Hastings.* Reigate: Frith, 1864. 16 albumen prints. Travel views of Hastings, Saint Leonard's, Rye, and Winchelsea.

A86.125 Frith, Francis. *Lower Egypt, Thebes, and the pyramids.* London: W. Mackenzie, [ca. 1862]. 37 albumen prints. HRCP# fDT47/F7.

A86.126 Frith, Francis. *Photo-pictures, selected from the universal series.* Reigate, 1879. 20 albumen prints. HRCP# fTR652/F848.

A86.127 Frith, Francis. *Sinai and Palestine.* London: W. Mackenzie, [ca. 1862]. 37 albumen prints. HRCP# fDS180.5/F7.

A86.128 Frith, Francis; text by Joseph Bonomi and Samuel Sharpe. *Egypt, Nubia, and Ethiopia.* London: Smith, Elder and Company, 1862. 100 mounted albumen stereographs. DT54/B66.

A86.129 Frith, Francis; text by Mrs. Poole and Reginald Stuart Poole. *Egypt, Sinai and Jerusalem.* London: W. Mackenzie, 1860. 20 mammoth albumen prints. HRCP# fDT54/F848.

A86.130 *Galerie contemporaine: Littéraire, artistique.* Paris: Ludovic Baschet, 1878 and following. 124 studio portraits of leading European literary and artistic figures; 8 art reproductions. Photographers include Carjat, Mulnier, Nadar. 132 carbon prints. Late 1870s.

A86.131 Gardner, Alexander, ed. *Gardner's photographic sketchbook of the war.* Photographs by T. H. O'Sullivan (45), A. Gardner (16), John Gardner (10), and others. Washington DC: Philps and Solomons, 1865. 2 volumes, 100 albumen prints. HRCP# fE471/G19.

A86.132 Gill, Major; text by James Ferguson. *The rock-cut temples of India: One hundred illustrations of architecture and natural history in western India.* London: Cundall, Jones, and Company, 1864. 100 photo prints.

A86.133 Grundy, William M. *Sunshine in the country: A book of rural poetry embellished with photographs from nature.* London: Richard Griffin and Son, 1861. 20 albumen prints.

A86.134 Hardman, Frederick. *The Spanish campaign in Morocco.* Edinburgh and London: William Blackwood and Sons, 1860. 21 albumen prints. Gernsheim notes in his *Incunabula,* "Portraits of military personalities in the campaign, Queen Isabella and her husband, and a frontis of the author."

A86.135 Howitt, William and Mary. *Ruined abbeys and castles of Great Britain.* London: A. W. Bennett, 1862. 27 photo prints. Photographers include Fenton, Bedford, McLean and Melhuish, Sedgfield, and Wilson. The collection holds a number of other books by the Howitts illustrated with photographs.

A86.136 Lebours, N. P., et al; text by Paul de La Garenne, F. Goupil, et al. *Excursions daguerriennes: Vues et monuments les plus remarquables du globe.* Paris: Rittner et Goupil, 1842. 2 volumes, 111 plates. HRCP# fD975/E9/1842b.

A86.137 London Stereoscopic and Photographic Company, pub. *A selection of prize pictures from the London Stereoscopic and Photographic Company's amateur photographic exhibition.* London, 1885-1887. 3 volumes with 30, 57, and 93 silver gelatin prints. HRCP# fTR646/L664-666.

A86.138 Maull and Polyblank. *Photographic portraits of living celebrities.* London: Maull and Polyblank, 1856 and following. HRCP# qTR681/F3/M285.

A86.139 Muybridge, Eadweard. *Animal locomotion: An electrophotographic investigation of consecutive phases of animal movements, 1872-1885.* Published under the auspices of the University of Pennsylvania, printed by the Photogravure Company of New York. Some plates marked "Author's edition." Philadelphia, 1887. 121 collotypes. HRCP# fQP301/M882. The collection has a second copy of 38 plates, all marked "Author's Edition" (Philadelphia, 1887). HRCP# fQP301/M883.

A86.140 *The photographic album for the year 1857: Being contributions from the members of the Photographic Club.* London: Charles Whittingham, 1857. 39 albumen prints. Photographers include Bedford, Coghill, Cundall, Delamotte, Fenton, Rosling, Rejlander, Pollack, and various others. HRCP# fTR1/P568.

A86.141 *Photographs of gems of the Art Treasures Exhibition, Manchester, 1857.* Manchester: Thomas Agnew and Sons. Salted-paper and albumen prints. Photographed by Caldesi and Montecchi. HRCP# fN5056/M26/C254.

A86.142 Price, William Lake, et al. *Photographic art treasures: Or, nature and art illustrated by art and nature, by this new and beautiful art of engraving of colour and the liability to fade, so objectionable in photographs, is obviated, while the detail and touch of nature is faithfully preserved.* London: Patent Photo-galvano-graphic Company, 1856-1857. 19 photogalvanotypes. HRCP# fTR642/P468.

A86.143   Smyth, Charles Piazzi.   *Descriptive album of photographs of the Great Pyramid.*   Manchester: J. S. Pollitt, 1879. 50 albumen prints. HRCP# qDT63/S592.

A86.144   Smyth, Charles Piazzi.   *Teneriffe: An astronomer's experiment, or specialties of a residence above the clouds.*   London: Lovell Reeve, 1858.   Gernsheim notes in his *Incunabula*, "Photographs by the author depicting local flora, fauna, and members of the expedition.   This is the first book ever illustrated with stereoscopic photographs."

A86.145   South Kensington Museum.   *Turner's Liber Studiorum, photographs from the 30 original drawings by J. M. W. Turner.*   London: Cundall, Downes and Company, 1861.   30 albumen prints.   HRCP# fNE642/T987.

A86.146   Stieglitz, Alfred, ed.   *Camera work.*   New York: 1903-1917.   HRCP# TR1/C5.   The collection holds two complete runs, some with a third copy.

A86.147   Talbot, William Henry Fox.   *The pencil of nature.*   London: Longman, Brown, Green, and Longmans, 1844-1846. HRCP# fTR144/T242.

A86.148   Talbot, William Henry Fox.   *Sun pictures in Scotland.*   London, 1845.   23 salted-paper prints.   HRCP# fTR144/T245.

A86.149   [Tauschnitz editions.]   Uniform editions of nineteenth-century literature published by Tauschnitz, many extra-illustrated with photographs.   Photographs attributed to Giorgio Sommer. 1,700 volumes.   1880s.

A86.150   *The Theater.*   London: Wyman and Sons, 1877 and following.   Carbon prints.   Studio portraits, many in character, of leading stage figures.

A86.151   Thomson, John.   *The antiquities of Cambodia: A series of photographs taken on the spot.*   Edinburgh: Edmonston and Douglas; 1867.   16 mounted albumen prints, including 2, 3-plate panoramas.   HRCP# fDS567/T526.

A86.152   Thomson, John.   *Illustrations of China and her people.*   London: S. Low, Marston, Low, and Searle, 1873-1874.   4 volumes, 200 albumen prints.   HRCP# fDS709/T475.

A86.153   Thomson, John (attrib.).   *Photographic album accompanying The Ever Victorious Army.*   [London?, 1868].   To accompany the work by Andrew Wilson.   22 albumen prints.   HRCP# fDS759/P568.

A86.154   Tripe, Captain Linnaeus.   *Photographs of the Elliot Marbles and other subjects in the Central Museum, Madras.*   Madras, 1858.   84 mounted salted-paper prints.   HRCP# fNB71/M23/C368.

A86.155   Tripe, Captain Linnaeus; with descriptions by Reverend W. Tracy.   *Stereographs of Madura.*   1858.   70 salted-paper prints.   HRCP# fDS485/M29/T856.

A86.156   Wilson, Captain C. W., and H. S. Palmer, R.E.; under the direction of Colonel Sir Henry James.   *Ordnance survey of the peninsula of Sinai: Made with the sanction of the Right Hon. Sir John Packington, bart., secretary of state for war.*   London: H. M. Stationery Off., 1869.   HRHRC has part 3, volumes 1-3; 156 albumen prints.   HRCP# fDS110.5/G7.

A86.157 Woodbury, Walter B., ed. *Treasure spots of the world: A selection of the chief beauties and wonders of nature and art.* London: Ward, Lock, and Tyler, 1875. 28 woodburytypes.

Published stereograph sets: main entry is publisher.

A86.158 Keystone. *Africa.* Meadville PA, [1920?]. 80 silver gelatin stereographs.

A86.159 Keystone; accompanying text by Jospeh Mills Hanson. *World War [I] through the stereoscope.* Meadville PA, 1926. 446 silver gelatin stereographs.

A86.160 Realistic Travels. *British industries.* London, [1900?]. 100 silver gelatin stereographs.

A86.161 Realistic Travels. *The Great War.* London, [1920?]. 500 silver gelatin stereographs.

A86.162 Underwood and Underwood. *Africa.* London and New York, [190?]. 100 silver gelatin stereographs.

A86.163 Underwood and Underwood. *Greece through the stereoscope.* London, 1897-1903. 98 silver gelatin stereographs.

A86.164 Underwood and Underwood. *Japan through the stereoscope.* London, 1896-1904. 100 silver gelatin stereographs.

A86.165 Underwood and Underwood. *Palestine.* New York, [1900?]. 100 silver gelatin stereographs.

A86.166 Underwood and Underwood. *Russo-Japanese War.* New York, 1904-1905. 92 silver gelatin stereographs.

A86.167 Underwood and Underwood. *Scotland through the stereoscope.* London, 1897-1905. 84 silver gelatin stereographs.

A86.168 Underwood and Underwood; accompanying text by D. J. Ellison. *Rome through the stereoscope: Journeys in and about the eternal city.* New York, 1907. 36 silver gelatin stereographs.

A86.169 Underwood and Underwood; accompanying text by William Byron Forbush. *The travel lessons on the life of Jesus* [=] *Life of Christ.* New York, 1908. 36 silver gelatin stereographs.

A86.170 Underwood and Underwood; accompanying text by Reverend John Talbot Smith. *St. Peter's and the Vatican: A pilgrimage to the Holy Father.* New York, 1907. 36 silver gelatin stereographs.

Albums: The Photography Collection holds several hundred albums of photographs assembled for individual use or for limited distribution. Many of these albums can be grouped roughly into several classes: portrait albums, frequently commercial albums of cabinet and cartes; 19th century travel albums of commercial photographers in various countries assembled by nonphotographers on the "Grand Tour"; and amateur photographers' albums, many assembled by British military stationed in India. Albums listed here are the most significant or representative of a broader class of albums. Main entry is photographer unless otherwise noted.

A86.171 Beatrice, Princess, et al. *Tableaux vivants.* Osborne, 1888. Gernsheim notes: "Arranged by Princess Beatrice, her ladies-in-waiting, and other attendents of the royal household at Osborne, Isle of Wight, to celebrate Queen Victoria's Jubilee." 12 silver gelatin prints, 17 woodburytypes. HRCP# fTR655.11/T224.

A86.172 Blount, Sir Edward Charles, comp. *Blount album.* Designs and fantastic scenes incorporating photographic and watercolor images, many of famous personages of the time. 60 montages of albumen prints in watercolor backgrounds. 1867 to 1875. HRCP# fTR655.11/B568.

A86.173 Cameron, Julia Margaret. *Portraits and photographic studies all from life* [=] *Thackeray album.* Fresh Water Bay, Isle of Wight, 1864. Presentation album for Annie Thackeray. 61 albumen prints. HRCP# fTR655.11/C265.

A86.174 Crichton, Sir Henry, comp. *[Crichton album I.]* Travel views of India, England, Egypt, Italy, and other locations. Photographed by Bourne, Shepherd and Robertson, Saché, and others. 227 albumen prints. Ca. 1870. HRCP# fTR655.11/C853.

A86.175 Crichton, Sir Henry, comp. *[Crichton album II.]* Travel views of England, France, Ireland, India, and Switzerland; family portraits. Various photographers. 166 albumen prints. Ca. 1876. HRCP# fTR655.11/C854.

A86.176 Cundell, George S. *Cundell album.* 94 salted-paper prints. 1842 to 1847. HRCP# fTR655.11/C864.

A86.177 Dodgson, Charles Lutwidge. *[Carroll album I.]* Portraits of the Dodgson family and their friends; from Dodgson's negatives 41 to 294. 70 albumen prints. 1856. HRCP# fTR655.11/D634.

A86.178 Dodgson, Charles Lutwidge. *[Carroll album II.]* Chiefly portraits. 79 albumen prints. 1856 to 1857. HRCP# fTR655.11/D635.

A86.179 Dodgson, Charles Lutwidge. *Photographs v.III.* [= *Carroll's album III*]. Portraits, most autographed; from Dodgson's negatives 955 to 1545. 115 albumen prints. Early 1860s. HRCP# fTR655.11/D636.

A86.180 Dodgson, Charles Lutwidge, comp. *Professional and other photographs* [= *Carroll album IV*]. Photographs by Charles Lutwidge Dodgson, Lady Hawarden, O. G. Rejlander, and others. 53 photographs. Early 1860s. HRCP# fTR655.11/D637.

A86.181 Dodgson, Charles Lutwidge. *Weld family album* [= *Carroll album V.*] 10 mounted albumen prints. Ca. 1857. HRCP# fTR655.11/D638.

A86.182 *España.* Photographs by Charles Clifford (89), J. Laurent (1), and unidentified photographer(s). 1870s. 150 mammoth salted-paper and albumen prints from calotype and collodion negatives. HRCP# fDP22/E863/1870z.

A86.183 Glover, Thomas George. *The Ganges Canal.* Roorkee: Printed at Thomason Civil Engineering College Press, 1864. 42 albumen prints; author's inscribed copy. HRCP# fDS485/G5/G568.

A86.184 Glover, Thomas George. *The Ganges Canal.* Roorkee: Printed at Thomason Civil Engineering College Press, 1867. 32 albumen prints. HRCP# fDS485/G5/G569.

A86.185 Harriman, Edward Henry; photographs by Edward S. Curtis. *A souvenir of the Harriman Alaska expedition.* 1899. 2 volumes, 251 silver gelatin prints. HRCP# fF909/H377. See Bibliography-Goetzmann and Sloan.

A86.186 Hill, D. O., and Robert Adamson. *100 calotype sketches* [= *Stanfield album*]. Edinburgh, 1845. Presentation album to Clarkson Stanfield; chiefly studio portraits. 109 salted-paper prints from calotype negatives. HRCP# fTR395/H553.

A86.187 Hue, F. C. *Marlborough gems.* [1903?] Travel views of India and Kashmir, Ceylon, China, and Japan. 88 silver gelatin prints. HRCP# fTR655.11/H834.

A86.188 *Jerusalem, Bethlehem, and Jericho.* 1880s. Photographs by Felix Bonfils (41) and L. Fiorillo. 45 albumen prints. HRCP# fDS109.2/P458/1880z.

A86.189 *Kashmir.* 1860s. Photographs by Bourne (14) and unidentified photographer(s). 40 albumen prints. HRCP# fDS485/K2/B687.

A86.190 *Kashmir, Gwalior, etc.* 1860s. Photographs by Samuel Bourne (28), Shepherd and Robinson (2), and unidentified photographer(s). 56 albumen prints. HRCP# fDS485/K2/B686.

A86.191 Laurent, J. *Voyage en Espagne.* 1882. 3 volumes, 150 mammoth albumen prints. 1853 to 1862. HRCP# Album 186.

A86.192 MacPherson, Robert. *MacPherson's Vatican sculptures, 132 in all, including six interiors of halls of the Vatican.* 1862. 130 albumen prints. HRCP# fTR655.11/M236.

A86.193 Martin, Paul. *Greater London: With photographs of Whitby, England and Ramsgate, England.* 199 mounted silver gelatin prints. HRCP# fDA683/M378. 1884 to 1888.

A86.194 *Parteitag.* Nazi party function, athletic games, military reviews. 150 silver gelatin prints. 1938.

A86.195 Price, William Lake, comp. *Lake Price album.* Photographs by various photographers, many pictorialists. 74 albumen prints. 1855 to 1856. HRCP# fTR655.11/P853.

A86.196 Rejlander, Oscar Gustave. *Lawson album of Rejlander photographs.* 59 albumen prints. 1860s. HRCP# fTR655.11/R355.

A86.197 Rejlander, Oscar Gustave. *Riglander's* [sic] *album.* 49 albumen prints. 1864 to 1869. HRCP# fTR655.11/R354.

A86.198 *Victorian musical carte-de-visite album.* Photographs by various studio photographers. 27 cartes and 7 cabinet cards in an album with a music box incorporated. Late 1870s. HRCP# fTR655.11/V537.

A86.199 Watkins, Carleton. *American scenery.* 25 mammoth albumen prints, disbound. 1866. HRCP# fF868/Y6/W384.

A86.200 Wharncliffe, Lord, comp. *Franco-German War album.* 39 albumen prints. Ca. 1871. HRCP# fDC282/W537.

A86.201 Wharncliffe, Lord, comp. *Paris Commune.* Photographs possibly by Disderi or his staff. 51 albumen prints. Ca. 1872. HRCP# fDC315.5/W537.

Portfolios:

A86.202 ADAMS (ANSEL; 1902-1984) PORTFOLIO. *The Sierra Club outing 1929.* San Francisco: 1929. 25 silver gelatin prints. Rare, early portfolio of Adams. HRCP# fF786/A334.

A86.203 ADAMS (ANSEL; 1902-1984) PORTFOLIO. *What majestic word: In memory of Russell Varian.* San Francisco: Sierra Club, 1963. 15 silver gelatin prints. HRCP# fTR650/A2.

A86.204 ALVAREZ BRAVO (MANUEL; b. 1902) PORTFOLIO. *Manuel Alvarez Bravo.* Geneva: Acorn Editions, 1977. 15 modern silver gelatin prints. 1930 to 1977.

A86.205 ALVAREZ BRAVO (MANUEL; b. 1902) PORTFOLIO. *Manuel Alvarez Bravo.* Geneva: Acorn Editions, 1977. 15 modern silver gelatin prints. 1920 to 1972.

A86.206 BAYARD (HIPPOLYTE; 1801-1887) PORTFOLIO. *Bayard.* Paris: Société Française de Photographie, 1980. Modern prints by Mme. Sudre. 30 salted paper prints. 1847 to 1850.

A86.207 BULLOCK (WYNN; 1902-1975) PORTFOLIO. *Wynn Bullock.* Santa Barbara: 1973. Printed by Graham Mackintosh, with an introduction by Ansel Adams. 12 silver gelatin prints. 1951 to 1973. HRCP# fTR654/B845.

A86.208 CALLAHAN (HARRY; b. 1912) PORTFOLIO. *Harry Callahan.* 30 modern dye-transfer prints. 1960 to 1980.

A86.209 CLARK (LARRY; b. 1943) PORTFOLIO. *Tulsa.* RPG Publishing, 1980. 50 silver gelatin prints. Pre-1971. HRCP# fTR647/C52/1980.

A86.210 DOISNEAU (ROBERT; b. 1912) PORTFOLIO. *Robert Doisneau.* New York: Hyperion, 1979. 15 silver gelatin prints. 1945 to 1972. HRCP# fTR653/D637.

A86.211 ERWITT (ELLIOTT; b. 1928) PORTFOLIO. *Elliott Erwitt: The Alchan edition.* New York: Alchan Editions. 15 silver gelatin prints. 1952 to 1976. HRCP# fTR654/E784.

A86.212 ERWITT (ELLIOTT; b. 1928) PORTFOLIO. *Photographs: Elliott Erwitt.* Geneva: Acorn Editions, 1977. 15 silver gelatin prints. 1949 to 1969. fTR654/E785.

A86.213 GIBSON (RALPH; b. 1939) PORTFOLIO. *Chiaroscuro.* New York: Hyperion, 1982. 15 silver gelatin prints. 1972 to 1981. HRCP# fTR654/G522.

A86.214 HENLE (FRITZ; b. 1909) PORTFOLIO. *Mexico.* [1945?] 24 silver gelatin prints. 1936 to 1945.

A86.215 LYON (DANNY; b. 1942) PORTFOLIO. *Danny Lyon.* New York: Hyperion, 1979. 30 silver gelatin prints. 1965 to 1979. HRCP# fTR654/L855.

A86.216 MacWEENEY (ALEN) PORTFOLIO. *Alen MacWeeney.* New York: Hyperion, 1979. 12 silver gelatin prints. 1968 to 1972. HRCP# fTR654/M336.

A86.217 MEYEROWITZ (JOEL; b. 1938) PORTFOLIO. [*Paris cityscapes portfolio*]. 9 dye prints. 1983.

A86.218 MURAY (NICKOLAS; 1892-1965) PORTFOLIO. *Nickolas Muray.* Rochester NY: International Museum of Photography, 1960. 12 silver gelatin prints. Theater personalities. HRCP# fTR681/F3/M873/1960z.

A86.219 STRAND (PAUL; 1890-1976) PORTFOLIO. *Photographs of Mexico* [= *The Mexican portfolio*]. New York: V. Stevens, 1940. Introductory essay by Leo Hurwitz. 20 photogravures. HRCP# fF1215/S873.

A86.220 SUDRE (JEAN-PIERRE) PORTFOLIO. *Douze paysages matériographiques.* 1975. Abstract images. 12 photographs. HRCP# fTR654/S937.

A86.221 WESTON (EDWARD; 1886-1958) PORTFOLIO. *Edward Weston: Fiftieth anniversary portfolio, 1902-1952.* San Francisco: Grabhorn Press, 1951. 12 silver gelatin prints. HRCP# fTR653/W488.

A86.222 WINOGRAND (GARRY; 1928-1984) PORTFOLIO. *Garry Winogrand.* New York: Hyperion, 1978. 15 silver gelatin prints. 1960s to 1970s. HRCP# fTR654/W55/1978.

A86.223 WRIGHT (WILLIAM P. "BILL"; b. 1933) PORTFOLIO. *China: August 1983.* [Abilene], 1985. 12 silver gelatin prints. 1983.

Theatre Arts Collection (A88)

University of Texas
Harry Ransom Humanities Research Center
Harry Ransom Center, Seventh floor
Twenty-first and Guadalupe Street
P.O. Box 7219
Austin, Texas 78713

512-471-9122. Contact: Curator.

PURPOSE: A research collection specializing in the performing arts, including theater, motion picture, television scripts, ballet, opera, and magic, collecting rare and recent books and journals; playbills, programs, lobby cards, and broadsides; manuscripts, including correspondence, screenplays, and set and costume renderings; ephemera, including costumes, props, and stage models; two- and three-dimensional artworks; and vintage and copy photographs.

HOURS: Weekdays, 8:00-5:00. Appointment recommended. Closed major and academic holidays.

ASSISTANCE: Experienced staff. Written inquiries accepted. Electrostatic copies not generally available. Photoduplications must be ordered through the collection.

PUBLICATION: Publication fee. Collection credit required. Free copy of publication to collection. Third-party permission required on about half the materials.

FINDING AIDS: A few record groups have finding aids; most materials arranged by topic. Access is by personal and proper names.

BIBLIOGRAPHY:
Daum, Raymond W. *A visit from Gloria Swanson.* Austin: Harry Ransom Humanities Research Center, 1984. Exhibition catalog.
Geddes, Norman Bel. *Horizons.* Boston: Little, Brown, 1932. 2nd ed., New York: Dover, 1977.
Geddes, Norman Bel. *Magic motorways.* New York: Random House, 1947.
Hunter, Fredrick J. *Catalog of the Norman Bel Geddes theater collection.* Boston: G. K. Hall, 1973.
Hunter, Fredrick J. *A guide to the theater and drama collections at the University of Texas.* Austin: University of Texas Humanities Research Center, 1967.
Meikle, Jeffery L. Norman Bel Geddes and the popularization of streamlining. *Library Chronicle,* new series 13, (1980).

Meikle, Jeffrey L. *Twentieth century limited: Industrial design in America, 1925-1939.* Philadelphia: Temple University Press, 1979.

Roberts, Jennifer Davis. *Norman Bel Geddes: An exhibition of theatrical and industrial designs.* Austin: University of Texas, 1979.

Stott, William, with Jane Stott. *On Broadway: Performance photographs by Fred Fehl.* Austin: University of Texas Press, 1978. 2nd ed., New York: De Capo Press, 1980.

Swanson, Gloria. *Swanson on Swanson.* New York: Random House, 1980.

Wead, George. *Gone with the wind: The legend endures.* Austin: HRHRC, University of Texas, 1983. Exhibition catalog.

SCOPE: More than 1,000,000 photographs, including vintage prints and negatives; some collections have associated manuscript, motion picture, and ephemera materials. The collection holds many cartes, cabinets, imperials, and other standard formats popular in the late nineteenth century. Of special note are hand-colored imperial cards by Sarony. With the exception of the Selznick archives (v.i.), the collection does not actively collect motion picture footage. 1860s to the present; concentration in late nineteenth and twentieth-century materials and the 1920s.

Type of photo	Pre-1880	1880-1899	1900-1919	1920-1939	1940-1959	1960-1986
Film negs				100,000	100,000	
Vintage prints	10,000	50,000	75,000	150,000	350,000	150,000

GEOGRAPHIC: Most photographs are portraits or production stills and give little evidence of the capture location. Capture locations are international in scope with a major emphasis on Europe and America.

SUBJECTS: Artifacts (industrial design). Sports and amusement (circuses, dance, magic, motion picture, opera, theater, Wild West shows). Transportation (air, car, rail, ship).

PEOPLE: The vast majority of the collection represents people. Many movie and theater stars are represented in the collection, though most by only a few images.

Comedians. Magicians. Musicians (bands, composers, conductors, instrumental soloists, singers—opera, —popular). Performers (circus, dancers, minstrel, motion picture, stage). Ventriloquists.

Ali Hadji. Hardeen. Adelaide Hermann. Harry Houdini. Bernays Johnson.

PHOTOGRAPHERS: Many nineteenth-century studio photographers from England and the US East Coast. Many distributed by the Photograph and Press Bureau of New York.

Apeda (New York). Bruno of Hollywood. Aimé Dupont. B. J. Falk. Friedman-Abeles. Mitchell (New York). Mora (New York). Nickolas Muray. Napoleon Sarony (New York). Otto Sarony (New York). Schloss (New York). Maurice Seymour (Chicago). Edward Steichen. Carl Van Vechten.

RECORD GROUPS: Most record groups have extensive quantities of related nonphotographic material pertinent to the record group. Quantities given in linear measurement may be assumed to have some nonphotographic materials interfiled unless otherwise noted.

A88.1 Several large collections have been interfiled into several artificial collections noted below; those collections were compiled by John Gassner, Albert Davis, and Messmore Kendall. A number of other collections containing small amounts of photographs include the Jules Styne collection, the Burl Ives collection, the Magic collection, the Ernest Lehmann collection, Texas Theaters collection, Crain—P. T. Barnum collection, B. Iden Payne collection, Puppetry collection, Tobe Hooper collection, and Erle Stanley Gardner collection.

A88.2 BARTON (LUCY) COSTUME COLLECTION. Costume designer. Personal photographs and portraits of Barton; production shots of performances with costumes designed by Barton; portraits collected as reference for design of period costumes. 4 feet of cabinets, cartes, and silver gelatin prints. 1860s to 1900, 1970s.

A88.3 BEL GEDDES (NORMAN; 1893-1958) COLLECTION. Library, professional archives, and personal papers of this pioneer in stage and streamlined industrial design.

   A88.3.1 Theater collection consists of production photographs and photographs of models for productions of plays, extravaganzas, operas, and motion pictures, including *Divine Comedy*, *Eternal Road*, and *The Miracle*, designed by Bel Geddes with some commercial photographs by Francis Bruguière and a few by Edward Steichen, Goldberg, and Vandamm; personal photographs of Bel Geddes used in researching his autobiography; few photographs which were collected as reference for his design studies. 2,000 silver gelatin prints, some film negatives; some nitrate material by Bruguière has been destroyed. 1914 to 1958.

   A88.3.2 Industrial collection consists of model photography (contrived photographs), topographic models and aerial photographs, record photographs of Bel Geddes' staff executing projects, art reproductions of architectural models and renderings, as well as some photographs of completed projects: J. Walter Thompson Agency Assembly Room, Franklin Simon Company window displays, Simon bedroom furniture, Toledo Scale factory and product shots, Graham-Paige Company publicity photographs, Philco radios, Rome beds, Rockefeller Center offices, Revere Brass and Copper Company, Pan American Airways, City of Tomorrow advertising campaign done for Shell Oil Company, Futurama exhibition done for General Motors at the New York 1939 World's Fair, *Magic Motorways* research, homes in Boca Raton FL, the Toledo Tomorrow project done for the Ford Foundation, Federal Home Appliance, and various studies done for the US Navy. 13 feet silver gelatin prints and 1 inch of 8x10 Kodachrome transparencies. 1920s to 1950s.

Extensive collection of nonphotographic manuscripts and other related materials; some motion picture footage. See Bibliography—Geddes, —Hunter, —Meikle.

A88.4 BLACK THEATER COLLECTION. An artificial collection of studio portraits and publicity shots of noted Black performers, singers, and Black minstrels. 1 foot silver gelatin prints. 1900s to 1950s, most ca. 1920.

A88.5 CELEBRITY PORTRAITS ADVERTISMENT CATALOG-PRINTS COLLECTION. An artificial collection of catalog-prints (several studio portraits copied in a single image used as a catalog for commercial distributors of portraits of celebrities) by photographers: Anderson (New York), Conley (Boston), Gilbert and Bacon (Philadelphia), Houseworth's "Illustrated catalog of celebrities" (San Francisco), Mora (New York), H. Rocher (Chicago), Sparks Photo Publishing Company (Philadelphia), Sarony (New York), Schloss "Collection of Celebrities" (New York), Suddard's & Fennemore (Philadelphia), A. N. Tomlinson (Detroit MI). 500 cabinets, 100 albumen prints. 1880s.

A88.6 CIRCUS COLLECTION. Artificial collection of circus and Wild West show performers and production shots of performances; portraits of sideshows performers, many with physiological anomalies. Circuses include P. T. Barnum, Forepaugh, Hagenbeck, Ringling Brothers, Robinson's, Buffalo Bill's Wild West Show. Many photographed by E. Oisermann (New York). 6.5 feet photographs, including cabinets, cartes, and unmounted silver gelatin prints. 1860s to 1960s, most ca. 1880.

A88.7 CRAIN (WILLIAM H.) COLLECTIONS. Collections acquired for the Theatre Arts Collection by Crain include the following materials.

A88.7.1 CRAIN—JOSEPH ABELES COLLECTION. Abeles established the Talbot Studios in 1935 and joined Leo and Sy Friedman in 1957 to form Friedman-Abeles Incorporated; specialized in stage productions and commercial studio portraits. Studio portraits of some 1,200 personalities, predominantly actors:

> David Amran. Julie Andrews. Polly Bergen. Jennifer Billingsley. Richard Boone. Barry Bostwick. Dave Brubeck. Don Budge. Carol Burnett. Richard Burton. Jack Cassidy. Carol Channing. Harold Clurman. Dennis Cole. Nat "King" Cole. John Colenbeck. Jean Darling. Danielle Darrieux. Hilda Dixon. Keir Dullea. Jane Fonda. John Forsythe. Helen Gallagher. Ben Gazzara. Bob Gentry. Joyce Grenfell. Julie Harris. Teddy Hart. Julie Haydon. Bill Hayes. Helen Hayes. Mrs. William Randolph Hearst. Florence Henderson. Ron Hussman. José Iturbi and family. Christopher Jordan. Jerry Lanning. Angela Lansbury. Fredric March with Florence Eldridge. Allyn McLerie. Marion McPartland. Ralph Meeker. Robert Merrill. Raymond Middleton. Pat Morrison. Cathleen Nesbitt. James Noble. Geraldine Page. Hildy Parks. Harold Pinter. Tyrone Power. Nicholas Pryor. Chita Rivera. Tony Roberts. Sean Scully. Tonio Selwart. Maureen Stapleton. Jan Sterling. Nancy Walker. Eli Wallach and family. Sam Wannamaker. Ronny Whyte.

Commercial photographs by Abeles includes some work done for *Time* magazine and consists largely of social functions and meetings. Abeles' headings:

> Airlines. Art shows. Awards ceremonies. Buildings and restaurants. Businesses. Fashion. Film [motion picture] reviews. Health. Miscellany. Music. New York City life. Parties. Stage shows. Sylvania Corporation. Television shows. Theater related.

80,000 items, including 9 feet of portrait negatives and 3 feet of commercial negatives, most 5x7 safety film, some 120 and 35mm safety film; 10 feet of portrait prints and 3 feet of commercial prints, all silver gelatin. 1935 to 1978.

A88.7.2 CRAIN—FRED FEHL (b. 1906) THEATER COLLECTION. Live production shots of theater shows made under existing light conditions, a technique pioneered by Fehl; 360 Broadway and off-Broadway shows, including productions of Kazan and performances by Barrymore, Brando, Ferrer, and Verdon. 8 feet (5,000 items) 5x7 silver gelatin prints; original negatives in HRHRC Photography Collection (q.v.); Fehl Dance material in a separate collection (v.i.). 1940 to 1978. See Bibliography—Stott and Stott.

A88.7.3 CRAIN—LA SCALA MILANO COLLECTION. Production shots of stage design from 68 productions at La Scala. 200 silver gelatin prints. Ca. 1940s.

[End of Crain collections.]

A88.8 DANCE COLLECTION. An artificial collection of dancers, choreographers, and troupes, predominantly classical ballet, but some popular, modern, and jazz. Companies include American Ballet Theater, Martha Graham Dance Company, Harkness Ballet, Joffrey Ballet, Jerry Bywaters Cochran, Dallas Civic Ballet, Houston Ballet, Marquis de Cuevas Company, and the Royal Ballet; some 600 headings for dancers and choreographers, including Andre, Sherri and Trixie, Fred and Adele Astaire, Irene and Vernon Castle, Eva Burroughs Fontaine, Addison Fowler and Florenz Tamara, Annette Kellerman, Theodore Kosloff, Manya and Zanette, Nadji, Rudolph Nureyev, Nicholas Palajenko, Anna Pavlova, Ruth St. Denis, Ted Shawn, Mary Wigman, Andre Eglevsky, and Rosella Hightower; production shots and studio portraits; photographers include Kenn Duncan, Hixon-Connelly Studios (Kansas City MO), Bill Leidersdorf, George Platt Lynes, and Richard Tucker. 8 feet of photographs, predominantly silver gelatin prints and cabinets. 1870s to 1970s, most 1920s to 1970s.

A88.9 FEHL (FRED; b. 1906) DANCE COLLECTION. Live, existing-light production shots of performances by American Ballet Theater, New York City Ballet, Ballet Russe, and some regional companies. 46 feet of silver gelatin prints and original negatives, some color transparency material; unprocessed, arranged by performance. 1940s to 1970s.

A88.10 GOLBY (ROBERT) COLLECTION. Live productions shot of theater productions, predominantly on Broadway, some off-Broadway and in Westport CT. 750—11x14 and 15,000—5x7 silver gelatin prints with original film negatives. 1935 to 1972.

A88.11 HOWARD (G. C.) COLLECTION. Studio portraits of actor George L. Fox; studio portraits of various actors portraying characters in and production shots of different performances of *Uncle Tom's Cabin*. 1 foot photographs, including cartes, cabinets, and some silver gelatin prints. 1860s to 1900.

A88.12 JUNGE (ALFRED; 1886-1964) COLLECTION. Motion picture art director. Production stills of sets designed by Junge; art reproduction of set designs; scenic locations and architectural types collected for reference. 8,000 silver gelatin prints; some additional photomechanical postcards and nonphotographic imagery. 1930s to 1950s.

A88.13 MINSTREL COLLECTION. An artificial collection of publicity portraits of Caucasian blackface, variety troupes and minstrels, including the Arnold Brothers, Brown and Fraser, McIntyre and Heath, Frank McNish, George H. Primrose, and Billy Rice.

[*Minstrels, 1835-1891*]. Portraits of Caucasian minstrels in and out of blackface. 22 tintypes, 6 cabinets, 140 cartes. 1860s to 1891.

7 feet photographs, predominently cartes and cabinets, some silver gelatin prints; 1 album (v.s.). 1860s to 1920s.

A88.14 MOVIE BIOGRAPHY COLLECTION. An artificial collection of publicity portraits and production stills of more than 5,000 performers and persons related to the movie industry. Substantial coverage of:

A88.14.1 Actresses: May Allison. Jean Arthur. Mary Astor. Fay Bainter. Lucille Ball. Tallulah Bankhead. Lynn Bari. Florence Bates. Madge Bellamy. Constance Bennett. Joan Blondell. Clara Bow. Alice Brady. Evelyn Brent. Virginia Bruce. Madeleine Carroll. Nancy Carroll. Ruth Chatterton. Claudette Colbert. Betty Compson. Joan Crawford. Bebe Daniels. Linda Darnell. Jane Darwell. Doris Day. Alain Delon. Marlene Dietrich. Irene Dunne. Ann Dvorak. Sally Eilers. Linda Farrell. Betty Fields. Rhonda Fleming. Joan Fontaine. Kay Francis. Betty Furness. Jean Gabin. Greta Garbo. Ava Gardner. Judy Garland. Gladys George. Paulette Goddard. Betty Grable. Ann Harding. Susan Hayward. Rita Hayworth. Sonja Henie. Jean Hersholt. Miriam Hopkins. Leslie Howard. Rochelle Hudson. Pert Kelton. Deborah Kerr. Laura La Plante. Dorothy Lee. Mary Lewis. Margaret Lindsay. Sophia Loren. Ida Lupino. Helen Mack. Dorothy Malone. Jayne Mansfield. June Marlow. Virginia Mayo. Una Merkel. Gertrude Michael. Patsy Ruth Miller. Marilyn Monroe. May Murray. Maureen O'Hara. Jen Parker. Mary Pickford. Zasu Pitts. Aileen Pringle. Esther Ralston. Marion Rice. Ginger Rogers. Rosalind Russell. Norma Shearer. Anne Shirley. Barbara Stanwick. Margaret Sullavan. Gloria Swanson. Elizabeth Taylor. Shirley Temple. Claire Trevor. Lana Turner. Lois Wilson. Fay Wray.

A88.14.2 Actors and groups: Amos and Andy. Fred Astaire. Lex Barker. The Barrymore family. Richard Barthelmess. Warner Baxter. Wallace Beery. William Bendix. Jack Benny. Charles Bickford. Humphrey Bogart. John Boles. Ernest Borgnine. William Boyd. Charles Boyer. Clive Brook. Joe E. Brown. Richard Burton. Rory Calhoun. Eddie Cantor. John Carradine. Jack Carson. Lon Chaney. Charles Chaplin. Montgomery Clift. Ronald Coleman. Richard Conte. Gary Cooper. Ricardo Cortez. Donald Crisp. Richard Cromwell.

Bing Crosby. Robert Cummings. James Dean. Reginald Denny. Walt Disney. Richard Dix. Robert Donat. Kirk Douglas. James Dunn. Dan Duryea. Stuart Erwin. Douglas Fairbanks Jr. Douglas Fairbanks Sr. W. C. Fields. Barry Fitzgerald. Errol Flynn. Henry Fonda. Glenn Ford. Clark Gable. John Garfield. William Gargan. John Gilbert. James Gleason. Cary Grant. Richard Green. William Haines. Cedric Hardwick. Jack Hawkins. Van Heflin. Charleton Heston. William E. Hines and Earle Remington. William Holden. Jack Holt. Bob Hope. Edward Everett Horton. Rock Hudson. Jeffrey Hunter. Van Johnson. Al Jolson. Boris Karloff. Robert Kent. Burt Lancaster. Laurel and Hardy. Harold Lloyd. Joel McCrea. Victor McLaglen. Fred McMurray. Marx Brothers. James Mason. Victor Mature. Adolphe Menjou. Ray Milland. Robert Mitchum. Robert Montgomery. Dennis Morgan. Audie Murphy. Conrad Nagel. Paul Newman. David Niven. Lloyd Nolan. Raymond Novarro. Pat O'Brien. Sir Lawrence Olivier. John Payne. Elvis Presley. Anthony Quinn. George Raft. Basil Rathbone. Edward G. Robinson. Gilbert Roland. Cesar Romero. Mickey Rooney. Robert Ryan. George Sanders. Randolph Scott. Alan Sheridan. Frank Sinatra. Spanky and Our Gang. Jimmy Stewart. Robert Taylor. Spencer Tracy. John Wayne. Charles Winninger.

113 feet of photographs, most silver gelatin prints; some color material. 1910s to present.

A88.15 MOVIE STILLS COLLECTION. An artificial collection of production and publicity stills for 2,500 motion pictures (complete press kits for more recent titles), most by major American studios, little animation. Substantial coverage of:

The Adventures of Hadji Baba (1954). *The Adventures of Marco Polo* (1938). *The Adventures of Tom Sawyer* (1938). *Al Capone* (1954). *Algiers* (1938). *All at Sea* (1958). *Bad Company* (1931). *Bad Man of Brimstone* (1937). *Beachcomber* (1938). *Beneath the Twelve-Mile Reef* (1953). *The Betsy* (1978). *Between Two Women* (1937). *The Big Broadcast of 1938* (1937). *Blockade* (1938). *Bon Voyage* (1962). *Borrowed Wives* (1938). *Boy of the Streets* (1937). *The Buccaneer* (1937). *Bwana Devil* (1953). *The Cabinet of Dr. Caligari* (1921). *Captains Courageous* (1922). *The Chapman Report* (1962). *Charade* (1963). *Cleopatra* (1917). *College Swing* (1938). *Come and Get it* (1936). *Come Blow Your Horn* (1963). *Conquest* (1937). *The Crowd Roars* (1938). *Dark Journey* (1937). *A Day at the Races* (1937). *Desert Song* (1953). *Devil Song* (1927). *The Divorce of Lady X* (1938). *Double Wedding* (1939). *The Duke of West Point* (1938). *Easy Living* (1937). *The Emperor's Candlesticks* (1937). *Ensign Pulver* (1937). *Everybody Sing* (1938). *Father Goose* (1964). *The Firefly* (1937). *The Girl of the Golden West* (1938). *Give Her a Ring* (1934). *Great Day in the Morning* (1956). *The Great Ziegfeld* (1936). *Green Pastures* (1936). *The Guardsman* (1931). *The Guns of Navarrone* (1961). *The Happy Time* (1952). *Her Jungle Love* (1938). *Her Man* (1930). *Herod the Great* (1960). *High Lonesome* (1950). *Hotel Imperial* (1927 and 39). *I Am the Law* (1938). *I'm All Right Jack* (1960). *In Person* (1935). *The Incredible Journey* (1963). *Jalma* (1935). *Jeanne D'Arc* (1928). *Journey's End* (1930). *Jubal* (1956). *The Kid* (1921). *Kitten with a Whip* (1954). *Knock on Wood* (1954). *The L-shaped Room* (1962). *Libeled Lady* (1936). *Live, Love, and Learn* (1937). *Mad about Music* (1938). *Madison Avenue* (1961). *Mahogany* (1975). *A Man Alone* (1955). *Marco Polo* (1962). *Mariannne* (1929). *Marines Let's Go* (1961). *Maytime,* (1937). *A Message to Garcia* (1936). *Mr. Scoutmaster* (1953). *M'liss* (1931). *Moon Pilot* (1962). *My Pal Gus* (1952). *Navy Blue and Gold* (1937). *Never Wave at a WAC* (1953). *New Faces* (1954). *The Nibelungen* (1925-28). *Nine Hours to Rama* (1963). *Of Human Hearts* (1938). *The Old, Dark House* (1932). *Old Hutch* (1936). *Our Relations* (1936). *The Outcasts of Poker Flat* (1952). *Outside the Law* (1921). *Palm Spring Weekend* (1963). *Paradise for Three* (1938). *The Plough and the Stars* (1936). *Port of Seven Seas* (1938). *Portrait of a Mobster* (1961). *Pretty Ladies* (1925). *Prince of Players* (1954). *The Prince Who Was a Thief* (1951). *The Private Affairs of Bel Ami* (1947). *The Rack* (1954). *Rawhide* (1938). *Rebound* (1931). *Rich Man, Poor Man* (1918). *Rio Rita* (1929). *Roberta* (1935). *Rome Adventure* (1962). *Romeo and Juliet* (1936). *The Rose Tattoo* (1955). *Rough Riders* (1928). *Sail a Crooked Ship* (1961). *Sanctuary* (1960). *The Secret Ways* (1961). *Shady Lady* (1944). *Sin Takes a Holiday* (1930). *Slave Ship* (1937). *Slim* (1937). *The Solid Gold Cadillac* (1958). *The Song of the Soul* (1920). *The Southerner* (1945). *Speed Man* (1936). *The Square Jungle* (1955). *Stand In* (1939). *A Star is Born* (1936). *Stella Dallas*

(1936). Tabu (1931). Test Pilot (1938). They Gave Him a Gun (37). Three Comrades (1936). Three Young Texans (1954). Topper Takes a Trip (1938). Touchdown (1931). The Toy Wife (38). Treasure Island (1934). Uncle Tom's Cabin (1927). Up From the Beach (1965). The Victors (1965). We Went to College (1936). What a Way to Go (1964). Wings of the Hawk (1953). A Yank in Indo-China (1952). Yellow Jack (1938). Yellow Mountain (1954). The Young in Heart (1938). The Young Lovers (1964).

24 feet, silver gelatin prints; a small amount of nonphotographic material interfiled. Many additional production stills filed by performers' names in Movie Biography collection (vs). 1916 to present. [Dates are taken from the collection; they frequently vary by a year or two from *Halliwell's Film Guide* (4th ed., New York: Charles Scribner's Sons, 1985).]

A88.16 MUSICIANS COLLECTION. An artificial collection of studio publicity portraits of instrumentalists, singers, conductors, composers, and bands: Harold Bauer, Irving Berlin, Ben Bernie, Ole Bull, Russ Columbo, Mellie Dunham, Guy Lombardo, Vincent Lopez, Ignaz J. Padarewski, Ponce sisters, Moritz Rosenthal, and Paul Whiteman.

A88.17 OPERA COLLECTION. Artificial collection of libretti, programs, other nonphotographic materials, and photographs. Texas Opera Theater (Houston), New York Metropolitan Opera; 200 headings for portraits of many opera singers:

Lucretia Bori. Emma Calve. Enrico Caruso. Eleanor Di Cisneros. Emma Eames. Geraldine Farrar. Anna Fitziu. Olive Fremstad. Johanna Gladski. Amelita Galli-Curci. Louise Homer. Clara Jacobo. Mary Lewis. Grace Moore. Marguerite Namara. Lillian Nordica. Haru Onuki. Maria Rappold. Fritzi Scheff. Ernestine Schumann-Heink. Marcella Sembrick. Antonio Scotti. Marguerita Sylvia. John Charles Thomas. Reinhold Werrenrath. Alice Zeppelli.

8 feet photographs, including silver gelatin prints, cabinets, and cartes. 1860s to 1970s, most ca. 1900.

A88.18 SELZNICK (DAVID O.; 1902-1965) ARCHIVE. Predominantly an archive of master motion picture footage, outtakes, screen tests, and business records assembled by Selznick, noted for his productions *Gone with the Wind* and *Spellbound*. Production, makeup, and set stills for 34 Selznick International Pictures productions (virtually no photographic materials relating to productions done in conjunction with other studios); stills and portraits of performers and industry figures associated with Selznick, including Ingrid Bergman, Hazel Brooks, Anita Colby, Joseph Cotton, Alfred Hitchcock, Louis Jourdan, Gregory Peck, Joan Tetzel, Shirley Temple, and Alida Valli; Selznick family snapshots. 10,000 photographs, predominantly silver gelatin prints with many silver gelatin film negatives, and a few 8x10 Kodachromes. 1920s to 1965. See Bibliography—Wead.

A88.19 SWANSON (GLORIA; 1899-1983) ARCHIVE. Predominantly correspondence and memorabilia of the star of silent and sound motion pictures and Hollywood producer. Publicity and formal studio portraits; production stills from motion picture, stage, and television productions with performances by or produced by Swanson, with substantial coverage of *Sadie Thompson* and *Queen Kelly*; family photographs. 15,000 photographs, most silver gelatin prints. 1913 to 1983. See Bibliography—Swanson.

A88.20 THEATER BIOGRAPHY COLLECTION. An artificial collection of 5,000 performers and others associated with the theater; many production and publicity photographs; most from Europe and America; many noted studio photographers, including Sarony, Mora, and Van Vechten. Cartes, cabinets, and smaller mounted photographs divided by gender; prints to 10x12 of critics and authors interfiled; prints to 10x12 of actors and actresses interfiled; oversized prints to 18x18; and flat files.

A88.20.1 Theater Biography File—Actresses (cartes, cabinets, and small formats): Belle Archer. Mrs. Thomas Barry and family. Kate Bateman. Maud Branscombe. Marie Burroughs. Clark sisters (Mabel and Annie). Ida Conquest. Laura Hope Crews. Daly sisters (Lucy and Lizzie Derious). Ada Dyas. Isabelle Evesson. Pearl and Rose Eytinge. Nina Farrington. Maude Fealy. Mabel Fenton (Fenton and Ross). Cissy Fitzgerald. Katherine Florence. Mrs. W. J. Florence (Malvina Pray). Grace George. Marie George. Lulu Glaser. Amelia and Lillie Glover. Maude, Leila, and Lillian Granger. Katherine Grey. Pauline Hall. Marie Jansen. Verona and Nellie Jarbeau. Edith Kingdon. Jeffeys Lewis. Clara Lipman. Jeanette Lowry. Sadie Martinot. Margaret Mather. Julia Matthews. Melville sisters. Maggie Mitchell. Mip Ada and Adelaide Neilson. Nichols sisters (Mabel and Lulu). Mrs. James Brown Potter. Emily and Betty Rigl. Adelaide Ristori. Adele Ritchie. May Robson. Mrs. Rousby. Annie Russell. Josie Sadler. Mary Scott and Ida Siddons. Elizabeth and Bessie Tyree. Isabelle Urquinhart. Queenie Vassar. Theresa Vaughn. Lizzie Webster. 22 cubic feet, mostly albumen cartes, cabinets, and smaller formats. 1860s to 1900s, most 1880s.

A88.20.2 Theater Biography File—Actors (cartes, cabinets, and small formats): Pete Barker. Kyrle Bellew. C. J. Bell, E. M. Digby, and E. Hamilton. Robert Edeson. Mr. and Mrs. Charles T. Ellis and company. Billy Emerson family. James Fiske Jr. Foy family. Joseph Hayworth. Gus and Milnes Levick. James Lewis. Louis Mann. Harry J. Montague. Lewis Morrison. Chauncy Olcott. Charles Richman. George Rignold. Charles J. Ross [Ross and Fenton]. Tommy Russell. Napoleon Sarony [portraits of]. William J. Scanlan. Mark Smith. Osmond Tearle. Vokes family. 22 cubic feet, mostly albumen cartes, cabinets, and smaller formats. 1860s to 1900s, most 1880s.

A88.20.3 Theater Biography Files—Authors and Critics (prints to 11x14): Many individuals, none represented in quantity. 16 cubic feet, mostly silver gelatin prints; mostly newsclippings and nonphotographic imagery. 1910s to 1940s.

A88.20.4 Theater Biography Files—Actresses and Actors (prints to 11x14):

Actresses: Maude Adams. Viola Adams. Judith Anderson. Mary Anderson. Margaret Anglin. Belle Archer. Julia Arthur. Fay Bainter. Tallulah Bankhead. Ethel Barrymore and family. Blanche Bates. Edna Bennett. Sarah Bernhardt. Amelia Bingham. Mary Boland. Agnes Booth. Betty Bruce. Marie Cahill. Catherine Calvert. Mrs. Pat Campbell. Kitty Carlisle. Mrs. Leslie Carter. Georgia Cayran. Carol Channing. Ruth Chatterton. Ina Claire. Kate Claxton. Maggie Cline. Katherine Cornell. Jane Cowl. Lotta Crabtree. Henrietta Crossman. Adelaide, Charlotte, and Pauline Cushman. Fanny Davenport. Blanche Dayne (= Mrs. Will Cressy). Julia Dean. Emma Drew and family. Emma Dunn. Eleonora Duse. Dorothy Dwann. Jeanne Eagles. Maxine Elliot. Effie Ellsler. Maude Fealy. Minnie Maddern Fiske. Lynn Fontanne. Della Fox. Mary Garden. Grace George. Mrs. George Henry Gilbert. Mary Louise "Texas" Guinan. Virginia Harned. Anna Held. May Irwin. Fanny Janauschek. Elsie Janis. Bertha Kalich. Lillie Langtry. Eva La Galliene. Madge Lessing. Ethel Levey. Cecilia Loftus. Christi MacDonald. Mary Mannering. Julia Marlowe. Adah Isaacs Menken. Elsie Milliken. Maggie Mitchell. Mitzi. Ruth Mix. Helene Modjeska. Polly Moran. Clara Morris. Florence Nash. Alla Nazimova. Adalaid Neilsson. Olga Nethersole. Annie Pixley. Cora Urquhart Potter. Ada Rehan. Adelaide Ristori. Eleanor Robson. Annie Russell. Lillian Russell. Julia Sanderson. Effie Shannon. Cecil Spooner. Frances Starr. Marie Tempset. Ellen Terry. Sophie Tucker. Lenore Ulric. Marie Wainwright. Edna Wallace-Hopper. Blanche Walsh.

Actors: Fred Allen. Allen Lester. George Arliss. Lionel Atewill. Lawrence Barrett. Lionel Barrymore and family. David Belasco. Richard Bennett. Dion Boucicault. Edwin Booth. John Wilkes Booth. Edmund Breese. John Brougham. Buck and Bubbles [team]. John B. Buckstone. Charles and Rose Coghlan. George M. Cohan. William Collier. Joe Cook. William H. Crane. Will Cressy. Wellington Cross. Arnold Daly. Edward L. Davenport. Jefferson De Angelis. Carter De Haven and Co. Henry E. Dixey. Johnny Drew and family. Julian Eltinge. Joseph K. Emmet. Leon Errol. Maurice Evans. William Faversham Sr. Charles Fechter. Lew Fields. W. J. Fletcher. William J. Florence. Johnston Forbes-Robertson. Edwin Forrest. John G. Gilbert. William Gillette. Nat Goodwin. James K. Hackett. Walter Hampden. Edward Harrigan. Tony Hart. Raymond Hitchcock. De Wolf Hopper. Leslie Howard. Walter Huston. Sir Henry Irving. Louis James. Joseph Jefferson. Thomas Keene. Wilton Lackaye. Alfred Lunt. Richard Mansfield. Robert Mantell. John McCullough. Frank McIntyre. Henry Miller. James E. Murdock. Sir Lawrence Olivier. James O'Neill. Tony Pastor. John T. Raymond. Stuart Robson. Pat Rooney. Otis Skinner. E. H. Sothern. Fred I. Stone. Sir H. Beerbohm Tree. Lester Wallack. David Warfield. Joe Weber (Weber and Fields). Francis Wilson.

118 cubic feet, many loose and mounted silver gelatin prints and cabinets and cartes; some clippings and nonphotographic images interfiled; 63 prints of oversized prints; 15 flat file drawers. 1860s to 1950s, most ca. 1880s.

[End of Biography Files.]

A88.21 WARD (JOE) CIRCUS COLLECTION. Wichita Falls civil engineer who worked as a clown with the Ringling Brothers, Barnum, and Bailey Circus in the summers. Headings include acrobats and tumblers, aerialists, animals and animal acts, clowns, dancers, high wire, jugglers; portraits of John Philip Sousa. 3 feet unmounted silver gelatin prints, 10 feet framed silver gelatin prints; some non-photographic materials interfiled. 1900 to 1940.

A88.22 ZIEGFELD COLLECTION. Production photographs, portraits of performers, and various performances produced by Florenz Ziegfeld. 4 feet silver gelatin prints. 1920s.

Texas Memorial Museum (A92)

University of Texas at Austin
2400 Trinity
Austin, Texas 78705

512-471-3551. Contact: Anthropology/History Division.

PURPOSE: The museum is dedicated to the study and interpretation of the natural and social sciences, with emphasis on Texas, including the fields of geology, paleontology, zoology, botany, ecology, anthropology, and history. The museum holds internationally noted research collections of Amerind artifacts, guns, and fossils; many other materials are held by the museum, including photographs.

HOURS: Weekdays, 9:00-5:00; weekends, 1:00-5:00. Closed major holidays. Appointment required for use of reserve collections.

ASSISTANCE: Experienced, professional, specialized staff. Written inquiries accepted. Electrostatic copies available. Photoduplications may be made by the patron or ordered through the museum.

PUBLICATION: Publication fee charged. Collection credit required. Free copy of publication to the museum. Third-party permission required on some items (N. H. Rose and E. E. Smith).

FINDING AIDS: Card index; photographs arranged by subject.

BIBLIOGRAPHY:

Haley, J. Evetts; Erwin E. Smith, photog. *Life on the Texas range.* Austin: University of Texas Press, 1952. 2nd ed., 1973.

Kirkland, Forrest, and W. W. Newcomb. *The rock art of Texas Indians.* Austin: University of Texas Press, 1967.

SCOPE: 7,500 photographs, including cased images, silver gelatin glass negatives, and vintage and modern prints. Many photographic materials have related manuscripts documenting the images. 1860s to present.

Type of photo	Pre-1880	1880-1899	1900-1919	1920-1939	1940-1959	1960-1986
D/A/T-types	15					
Glass negs				200		
Vintage prints		100	1,000	2,000	2,000	1,000
Photo albums		5			1	

GEOGRAPHIC: Predominantly Texas, although many institutional photographs document ethnographic artifacts and cultures from the Americas and Africa.

SUBJECTS: Agriculture (cattle drives). Architecture (academic, courthouses, jails).

University of Texas Centennial. WW I veterans reunions.

PEOPLE: Many photographs of persons related to Texas history and southwestern Amerinds, including Cheyenne and Zuni. Cowboys. Texas Rangers.

PHOTOGRAPHERS: Few snapshot photographs, some amateur, many commercial.

Christen Barthelemess. Edward S. Curtis. N. H. Rose. Erwin E. Smith. William S. Soule.

RECORD GROUPS:

A92.1 BARTHELEMESS (CHRISTEN) COLLECTION. Cheyenne and Zuni Amerinds. 33 photographs. 1888 to 1897.

A92.2 Curtis, Edward S., photog. *The North American Indian: Being a series of volumes picturing and describing the Indians of the United States and Alaska.* Seattle WA: E. S. Curtis; [Cambridge: University Press], 1907-1930. 20 octavo and folio volumes containing photogravure plates.

A92.3 KIRKLAND (FORREST) COLLECTION. Art reproductions by Kirkland of Amerind pictographs made in Texas during the archaic and historic periods; snapshots of Kirkland and his wife Lula camping out at rock painting sites. 200 glass plate negatives. Late 1920s to 1942. See Bibliography.

A92.4 OLIVÁREZ (CARLOS) COLLECTION. 50 photographs.

A92.5 SMITH (ERWIN E.; 1886-1947) COLLECTION. Cowboys and cattle drives. 100 silver gelatin prints. 1890s to 1930s.

A92.6 SOULE (WILLIAM S.; 1836-1908) COLLECTION. Portraits and camp life of Amerinds. Copy prints, available for inspection only; originals at Barker Texas History Center, UT Austin (q.v.). 1890s.

Panhandle-Plains Historical Museum (C14)

Fourth Avenue at Twenty-fourth Street
P.O. Box 967, W.T. Station
Canyon, Texas 79016

806-655-7191. Contact: Archivist.

PURPOSE: A fine art, history, and natural history museum with an exhibition space and an extensive research center focusing on the Panhandle and the surrounding states. Holdings include books (incunabula to current titles), periodicals and newspapers, printed and recorded music, natural history, material culture of Amerind, Spanish Colonial, Texas Republic and statehood cultures, manuscripts, paintings, oral history, and vintage and copy photographs, and other artworks.

HOURS: Exhibit area—Monday through Saturday, 9:00-5:00; Sunday, 2:00-5:00. Research center—weekdays, 9:00-5:00; Saturday, 1:00-5:00; appointment recommended. Closed major holidays.

ASSISTANCE: Professional, experienced staff. Written and phone inquiries accepted. Electrostatic copies available. Photoduplications may be made by patron with prior arrangement or ordered through the museum.

PUBLICATION: Publication fee charged. Collection credit required. Free copy of publication to museum. Third-party permission required on a few items.

FINDING AIDS: Complete card index; access by location, proper name, general subject heading, major photographer. Photographs arranged by accession group.

BIBLIOGRAPHY:
> Robertson, Pauline Durrett, and R. L. Robertson. *Cowman's country: Fifty frontier ranches in the Texas Panhandle.* Amarillo: Paramount, 1981.
> Robertson, Pauline Durrett, and R. L. Robertson. *Panhandle pilgrimage: Illustrated tales tracing Texas history in the Panhandle.* Amarillo: Paramount, 1976.
> Warwick, Mrs. Clyde W. *The Randall County story, from 1541-1910.* Hereford: Pioneer Book Publishers, 1969.

SCOPE: 30,006 vintage photo prints, many large, framed portraits; 11,843 vintage photo negatives; 2,423 copy photo prints; 3,129 copy photo negatives; 1,113 stereographs; 68 panoramic prints and 10 negatives; 456 glass lantern slides; 2,863—35mm transparencies; and 550 reels of movie film. 1850 to the present, most 1900 to 1920.

Type of photo	Pre-1880	1880-1899	1900-1919	1920-1939	1940-1959	1960-1986
D/A/T-types	125					
Glass negs		370				
Film negs			704	4,500	6,500	525
Vintage prints		2,000	4,000	8,000	11,000	2,000
Copy prints		1,000	300	1,144		
Photo albums			167			

GEOGRAPHIC: Extensive coverage of the Panhandle; some coverage of surrounding states, including Colorado, New Mexico, Oklahoma, and Kansas. Many Panhandle locales represented in limited quantities.

Texas: Adobe Walls. Adrian. Alibates Flint Quarries/Monument. Amarillo. Antelope Creek Ruins. Armstrong County. Blanco Canyon. Bomarton. Borger. Bovina. Canadian. Canyon. Channing. Clarendon. Claude. Dalhart. Deaf Smith County. Farwell. Floyd County. Fort Davis. Fort Elliot. Friona. Goodnight. Hale County. Hemphill County. Hereford. Higgins. Llano. Lockney. Lubbock. Memphis. Miami. Mobeetie. Nazareth. Old Glory. Palo Duro Canyon. Pampa. Plainview. Randall County. Rhea. Saint Francis. Swisher County. Tascosa. Texline. Wellington.

Non-Texas: California. England. France. Mexico.

SUBJECTS: Rural and agribusiness topics predominate, documenting the economic and social development of the region.

Academia (schoolrooms). Agriculture (county fairs, farming—cotton, —farm machinery, —grain crops, —hay, —tractors, irrigation, ranching—branding, —chuckwagons, —corrals, —remudas, —roundups). Animals (buffalo, cattalo, cattle—hereford, hogs, horses, sheep). Architecture (barns, bridges, courthouses, domestic, dugouts, log cabins, railroad depots, windmills). Art reproductions (Bugbee murals, paintings). Artifacts (guns, plows). Economic and social development (emigration, immigration). Events (county fairs, dust storms, parades, reunions, weddings). Government (jails, Texas legislature). Industry (banks, general commerce, grocery stores, land companies, newspapers, offices, oil, saddlery, saloons). Landscape (Dust Bowl). Military (camps, forts). Religion (churches). Science (archaeology, paleontology). Services (hotels, surveying). Social life and customs (Amerind). Sport and amusement (buffalo hunters/hunting, recreation). Transportation (airplanes, bridges, automobiles, buggies, railroad—handcars, —locomotives, wagons).

Brazil Land, Cattle, and Packing Company. Frying Pan Ranch. Goodnight Ranch. Graham Plow Inc. Isaacs Ranch. JA Ranch. JJ Ranch. LS Ranch. LX Ranch. Landergin-Harrington House. Matador Land and Cattle Company (Brazil Division). Matador Ranch. Mill Iron Ranch. Morrow-Thomas Hardware Company. Mulberry Ranch. Old Home Ranch. Panhandle-Plains Museum (exhibits, building). Quaker settlement (Crosby County). Santa Fe Railroad. Shoe Bar Ranch. Smith-Walker and Company. T-Anchor Ranch. Texas Rangers. West Texas State University. XIT Ranch.

PEOPLE: Many family snapshots of Panhandle-area residents; few held in quantity. Ethnicities represented include Apache, Cheyenne, Comanche, Kiowa, and Seminole Amerinds, Blacks, and Hispanics; Caucasians of Czech, German, and Polish decent predominate.

Cornelius Adair. R. T. Alexander family. Hattie Mabel Anderson. G. W. Arrington family. Samuel and Elizabeth Axtell family. Baird family. J. Ernest "Pin" Batson. Alfred G. Boyce. Brace family. Charles Herbert Bugbee. Harold Dow Bugbee family. Sherrill Burks. William H. Bush family. Richard Bussell. B. C. D. Bynum. William A. "Jud" Campbell family. John Childress. J. T. Christian family. Wallace A. Clark family. Bill Clements. Frank Collinson. Lincoln Guy Conner family. F. T. Day family. Billy Dixon family. Olive King Dixon. J. Frank Dobie. Solon Dow family. Arthur B. Duncan family. Caroline Gentry Bush Emeny. Avis Baird Flesher. Gallmeier family. O. K. Gilvin family. Charles Goodnight family. Judge Lysius Gough. W. T. Graham family. J. Evetts Haley family. James D. Hamlin. Laura Hamner. Newton Harrell family. Don D. Harrington. Fred Hettler family. Joseph Abner Hill. Matthew "Bones" Hooks. William D. Howren family. Sam Isaacs. Clarence Hailey Long. O. H. Loyd family. C. Boone McClure. Crawford C. Martin. Mills family. O'Brien family. Georgia O'Keefe. Quanah Parker family. Frank Reaugh. Charles Roan family. Rogers family. Fred Scott. L. F. Sheffy. Max R. Sherman. Hank Smith. Studer family. Bob Wills.

PHOTOGRAPHERS: Extensive holdings of snapshot, commercial, and studio photography. The museum also holds some Pictorialist work made in Texas during the 1930s and business interiors made by itinerants.

E. S. Berry. Julius Born (Canadian). T. M. Caldwell. Edwards Studio (Amarillo). L. A. Huffman. Gray. Bob Kesterson. M. S. Lusby (Canyon). W. E. Perry (Perryton). Henry Douglas Smith. Floyd V. Studer.

RECORD GROUPS: Holdings are arranged by accession group; these groups are largely uniform in their nature, covering the Panhandle, including extensive coverage of Canyon and West Texas State University. They contain a balanced mixture of commerical and snapshot photography, portray the people, the land, and the economic development of the region, and span the 1890s to the present with an emphasis on the years 1900 to 1930. Listed below are unusual and extensive collections.

C14.1 ALEXANDER (R. T.) COLLECTION. Family portraits, scenes from Alexander's ranch. 150 silver gelatin prints. Ca. 1910. PPM# 1161.

C14.2 BECK (EUGENE T.) COLLECTION. Studio portraits of Amerinds photographed by W. P. Bliss (Fort Sill OK). 17 albumen cartes. 1870s. PPM# 1171.

C14.3 COX (MARY L.) COLLECTION. Plainview cityscapes and residents, especially early settlers; grain crops. 350 silver gelatin and collodio-chloride prints. 1890 to 1950s, most 1900 to 1920. PPM# 1612.

C14.4 HAMLIN (JAMES D.; 1871-1950) COLLECTION. Established Amarillo College, founded Farwell, and opened XIT Ranch to colonization. XIT Ranch and divisions, including a series tracing cattle from range to stockyards in Kansas City photographed by Davison (Kansas MO); cowboys; cattle and horses; feed crops; Plainview. 500 collodio-chloride and silver gelatin prints, many snapshots. Ca. 1900. PPM# 832.

C14.5 HILL (JOE, Jr.) COLLECTION. Snapshots of Byrd's second expedition to the Antarctic. 46 silver gelatin prints. 1934. PPM# 699.

C14.6 HOGGE FAMILY COLLECTION. Studio portraits by Teagarden (Minneola) and various Texas photographers; snapshots of cowboys. Photographs were collected in Claude. 32 photographs, mostly early albumen cartes. 1860s to 1900. PPM# 1786.

C14.7 LANTERN SLIDE COLLECTION. Hand-tinted, narrative slides, many with captions to accompany songs. Titles include *Ain't You Coming Back to Old New Hampshire Molly?*, *Farewell My Annabell*, *Not Because Your Hair is Curly*, *Oh! That Mezmerizing Mendelssohn Tune*, *A Prairie Song Bird*, *Spooning with Your Lady Love*, *Sweethearts and Wives*, *When I Woke Up This Morning*. Others are black-and-white lecture illustrations, including *Child Labor*. Publishers include Boswell (Chicago) and DeWitt C. Wheeler (New York). 500 lantern slides, many fractured. Ca. 1900.

C14.8 PERRY (W. E.) STUDIO ARCHIVES. Photographer in Perryton. Studio portraits of Texas and Oklahoma residents. 5,000 safety negatives; some with unfixed studio proof prints; itemized card inventory for first 1,000 images. 1940s.

C14.9 REAUGH (FRANK; 1860-1945) ESTATE. Texas artist of Western subjects who made amateur photographs as studies for his paintings. Cattle and landscape in the Panhandle and Cross Plains regions; some art reproductions of Reaugh's work. 348—4x5 glass negatives; 473 silver gelatin prints. Ca. 1900. PPM# 1865.

C14.10 SHAW (TRAVIS) COLLECTION. West Texas State University social life and customs, including football, students and faculty, and buildings. 500 silver gelatin prints. 1920s. PPM# 830.

C14.11 STEREOGRAPH COLLECTION. Arranged by location, mostly US, some foreign; narrative and genre subjects. Photographers and publishers include Keystone, E. and H. T. Anthony, Underwood and Underwood, D. J. Ryan (Savannah GA), and C. Pierre Havens (Savannah GA).

> *Telebinocular.* Meadville PA: Keystone View Company, [1920s]. 100 silver gelatin stereographs. 1920s. With companion volume, *A trip around the world through the telebinocular.* Burton Holmes, editor. Meadville PA: Keystone View Company, 1926, 1928, 1929.

> *Tour of the World.* Meadville PA: Keystone View Company, [1920s?]. 400 silver gelatin stereographs. 1920s. Two copies.

1,000 stereographs, mostly silver gelatin prints, including two boxed sets (v.s.). 1890s to 1900s.

C14.12 WARWICK (Mrs. CLYDE) COLLECTION. Development of Canyon; booster photographs of Canyon by Lusby 1900 to 1910; business interiors photographed by an unidentified, possibly itinerent photographer made ca. 1917; West Texas State University in the 1950s. 500 prints, silver gelatin and some collodio-chloride. 1890s to 1960s. PPM# 568.

Albums and published works:

C14.13 [*Crane family album 1508/79.*] Various Danville IL photographers, including Lawson and W. Boyce. Studio portraits. 64 cabinets dismounted. 1880s.

C14.14 [*Crane family album 1508/78.*] Various Danville IL photographers. Studio portraits. 41 gelatino-chloride and collodio-chloride cabinets. Ca. 1900.

C14.15 [*Demster Mill Manufacturing Company albums 1981-22/3 and 3b.*] Promotional album documenting the success of the Demster plow and seeding machines. 2 albums, 300 silver gelatin prints; captions. 1928 to 1930.

C14.16 Edmondon, G. W., photog. [*Carte album.*] Studio portraits by this Norwalk OH photographer. 18 cartes, 1 tintype. Early 1860s.

C14.17 [Hill, Joseph Abner, comp.?] *College days.* West Texas State Normal School (= West Texas State University) classes, students, buildings; military encampment at the school during WW I. 200 silver gelatin snapshot prints. Ca. 1918.

C14.18 [*Howren and Spivey families album 18-1978-127/62.*] Various Corsicana photographers. Studio portraits. 13 tintypes, 39 cartes. Early 1860s to 1870s.

C14.19 [*Sam Isaacs family cabinet album 227/26.*] Various Fort Worth photographers. Studio portraits. 51 snapshots and cabinet prints. 1900 to 1929.

C14.20 [*Leatherman family carte album 2558/3.*] Various photographers, many with Pennsylvania imprints. Studio portraits of unidentified sitters. 14 cartes, 32 tintypes in paper frames. Ca. 1876.

C14.21 *Scrapbook of photographs, WTSC campus.* Buildings, student social life and customs. 43 silver gelatin prints. Mid-1940s. PPM# 1974-168/1

C14.22 Tibbitts (San Francisco), H. C., photog. *Glimpses of California.* San Francisco: 1892. Commercial landscapes of California and Nevada, including Yellowstone and Lake Tahoe. 22 silver gelatin prints. Pre-1892. PPM# 18.1981-4/36.

Central Power and Light Company (C62)

120 North Chaparral Street
P.O. Box 2121
Corpus Christi, Texas 78403

512-881-5503. Contact: Information Specialist.

PURPOSE: A working collection of photographs gathered for use in the company news magazine, public relations efforts, and other projects. The photographs were and are used to show company operations, marketing and community relations programs, and employee activities. Central Power and Light is a privately owned utility.

HOURS: Weekdays; by appointment only to qualified researchers. Closed major holidays.

ASSISTANCE: Professional staff. Written inquiries accepted on a limited basis. Electrostatic copies available. Photoduplications must be ordered through the company.

PUBLICATION: No publication fee. Collection credit required. Free copy of publication to the company.

FINDING AIDS: Filed by subject or date.

BIBLIOGRAPHY:
CPL news. Corpus Christi: Central Power and Light.

SCOPE: 30,000 vintage silver gelatin prints, 20,000 copy photographs, 25,000—35mm color transparencies. A few copy prints from 1900, vintage prints from 1926 to the present; an open collection.

Type of photo	Pre-1880	1880-1899	1900-1919	1920-1939	1940-1959	1960-1986
Vintage prints			200	300	500	1,000
Copy prints			500	1,000	2,500	10,000

GEOGRAPHIC: Areas served by the company include the Valley and Gulf Coast plain (44 counties, 250 cities); divided into the Corpus Christi, Gulf Coast (Alice vicinity), Laredo, Mid-Coast (Victoria vicinity), Valley (McAllen vicinity), and Winter Garden (Uvalde vicinity) regions.

SUBJECTS: The company originally operated electrical utilities, mass transit, water utilities, gas utilities, and ice manufacturing; it now provides electrical service only. The collection documents various production and promotional aspects of these various enterprises, especially the effects of industrial design on material culture from the 1920s to the 1930s.

Agriculture (equipment; farming—citrus, —grain, —rice, —vegetables; ranching). Animals. Architecture (commercial, domestic, religious). Cityscapes. Exhibitions. Events (ceremonies, hurricanes, parades, storms, WW II). Government. Industry (ice, petroleum, shipping). Science. Services (electric utilities). Transportation (trucks).

PEOPLE: Domestic and personal activities. Social life and customs. Studio portraits. Black, Caucasian, and Hispanic ethnicities.

PHOTOGRAPHERS: Photographs were made by freelance, commercial photographers in the communities and later by photographers on the company's staff.

Edrington (Weslaco). Sammy Gold (= Regal Studios, Corpus Christi). The Hamiltons (Wharton). A. Holm. Lippe Studios (Del Rio). McCuiston Studio (Corpus Christi). John F. "Doc" McGregor (Corpus Christi). Harvey Patteson (San Antonio). Robert Runyon (Brownsville). Seranno (Laredo). Karl Swafford (Corpus Christi).

RECORD GROUPS: Photographs are arranged into inactive (or "historic") and active files.

C62.1 HISTORICAL READY-ACCESS FILE. Retail establishment, in-store and window displays of home appliances; power generation and distribution facilities, including interior and exterior views of power plants, generating equipment, and transmission lines at Mission, Victoria, La Palma, and Corpus Christi; ice distribution facilities, including delivery trucks; community relations photographs, including booster photographs of agriculture and domestic growth in South Texas, product demonstrations, and cooking schools. Most commercial views.

Industrial survey for the city of Del Rio, Val Verde County, Texas. Commercial, booster views of sheep and goat ranching, scenes around Del Rio, including Mexico, Southern Pacific Railroad, and civic refinements of the area. 33 silver gelatin prints with typescript commentary. 1927.

2,000 photo prints, most silver gelatin, a few color; some bound into albums (sample entry, v.s.). 1900 to 1976.

C62.2 HISTORICAL FILE. Subject headings (edited) include: Agriculture (citrus, cotton and grain, irrigation, livestock, ranching, vegetables). All-electric buildings (apartments, churches, commercial, medallion homes, schools). Atomic energy (Texas Atomic Energy Council). Awards (safety, service, scholarships, 4-H, Edision Electric Institute). Bridges (Corpus Christi Harbor Bridge). CPL district offices, local offices, service centers, substations. Cities. Customer service (commercial cooking; home economists; photographic meter reading, rural, street lighting). Dams (Falcon, Wesley Seale). Employees. Fairs and expositions (booths, floats, world's fair). Home office. Industry (metal refining, petroleum, canneries and packing houses, chemicals, corn products, grain elevators, Halliburton Portland Cement Company, Du Pont Company). Power plants (J. L. Bates, Devil's River, Eagle Pass Hydro, Lon C. Hill, La Palma, Victoria, Nueces Bay, Laredo, E. S. Joslin, Barney M. Davis). Servicemen and equipment (line crews, dispatching, meters, communications). Signs (office, outdoor, power plants). Transmission and distribution. Tourism (Padre Island, Coast Bend area). 48 feet (10,000 items) of silver gelatin prints. 1926 to 1976.

C62.3 ACTIVE FILES. Subject headings include: Aesthetics. Art and displays. Customer programs. Generation and distribution. Industry. Mariculture. Meetings and conferences (management seminars). Nuclear. Offices. Power stations (Coleto Creek, J. L. Bates, Barney Davis, Eagle Pass Hydro, Lon C. Hill, E. S. Joslin, La Palma, Nueces Bay, Victoria, and the South Texas Project Nuclear Plant). Tourism and scenics. 7.5 feet (5,000 images) photographs, most silver gelatin prints, many 35mm negatives with contact sheets; 25,000—35mm color transparencies. 1977 to present.

Corpus Christi Museum (C74)

1900 North Chaparral Street
Corpus Christi, Texas 78401

512-883-2862. Contact: Director.

PURPOSE: A regional history, natural history, anthropology, and marine science museum with exhibits and extensive reserve collections of fine art, historical and anthropological artifacts, natural specimens, and an extensive reference library. The museum's photographic collection is predominantly the archive of local studio, commercial, and journalistic photographer John F. "Doc" McGregor. The museum also holds for the state the Plutoro/Keennon/Purvis collection (see Record Groups).

HOURS: Tuesday through Saturday, 10:00-5:00; Sunday, 2:00-5:00.

ASSISTANCE: Professional, experienced staff. Written and phone inquiries accepted. Electrostatic copies available. Photoduplications must be ordered through the museum.

PUBLICATION: Publication fee charged. Collection credit required. Free copy of publication to the museum. Third-party permission required on a few items.

FINDING AIDS: Materials filed by subject; see note under Scope.

BIBLIOGRAPHY:
Walraven, Bill. *Corpus Christi: The history of a Texas seaport.* Woodland Hills CA: Windsor Publications, 1982. Includes samples of McGregor's work, although the images were not drawn from the museum's collection.

Zastrow, Steve. "Last Chance for the McGregor Collection." *Corpus Christi Monthly*. August, 1986: 44-51.

SCOPE: Approximately 500,000 negatives, including nitrate, diacetate, and safety-base supports; most 4x5, some 5x7, and a few cirkut panorama negatives. Approximately 10,000 silver gelatin prints, including a few cirkut panoramas. A few modern prints. Virtually all the material is black and white. Negatives are stored in McGregor's original envelopes, which usually have a date and subject information (a program to rehouse the materials is underway). Negatives are stored by subject and then by date. A few of McGregor's logs exist with identification information; these logs list photofinishing done by McGregor, portraits, and sittings. 1929 to the early 1970s, most mid-1930s to 1960. A substantial portion of McGregor's archive is housed at the University of Texas at Austin, HRHRC, Photography Collection (q.v.).

GEOGRAPHIC: Extensive coverage of Corpus Christi, with some coverage of the immediate vicinity. Some coverage of the northern US, the Rocky Mountains, and Mexico.

Texas: Alice. Aransas Pass. Cuero. Edinburg. Ingleside. Kingsville. Laredo. Port Aransas. Robstown. Rockport. Sinton. Taft.

SUBJECTS: McGregor's archive is arranged according to 237 categories, most of which are the photographer's (those marked with an asterisk are the museum's). Categories with more than 150 prints:

Air views (2,800). Airplanes (1,600). Animals (2,000). Apartments (300). Auto accidents, sales (1,600). Babies (11,200). Bakeries (150). Bands, orchestras (800). Baseball teams (800). Bathing beauties (800). Bathing beauties, kids (800). Bible classes (800). Birds (400). Birthdays (800). Boats (1,600). Buccaneer Days (1,600). Buildings (2,000). Caldwell Claim Service, wrecks (3,600). Catholic scenes (2,800) Centennial. Chamber of Commerce, West Texas trips (800). Children* (800). Churches (1,000). Circuses (200). Civil cases (800). Construction (1,600). Copies (5,600). Corpus Christi College (200). Cotton (800). Dancers (400). Events, dinners (3,000). Family groups (1,600). Farming activities (200). Filling stations (300). Fishing scenes (3,600). Flowers, plants (1,800). Football (2,400). Fruits and vegetables* (400). Funerals (800). Games, hunters (800). General views (1,600). Golf scenes, country club (800). Home loan (3,200). Homes (2,400). Horse riders (700). Hotels (400). Individuals (42,000). Kids at play* (100). Kingsville races (600). Knights of Pythias field trips (200). Legion (200). Machinery (800). Mug shots, criminals (800). Natives* (100). News photos (11,000). North Beach scenes (1,600). Oil (3,400). Other town views (150). Padre Island (400). Palms (150). Parades (800). Passports (400). Pathology, medical scenes* (800). Personalities (800). Pleasure Pier scenes (100). Police (800). Port scenes (1,600) Rodeo scenes (400). Senior high school portraits (7,200). Sheriff's Department (800). Ships (400). Sports (200). State highway police (200). Stereoscopic (88). Stores and windows (2,400). Storm scenes, 1933-1941 (150). Streets (200). Theaters (600). Trees (400). Weddings (2,400).

Bertha Lacey's Studio (800). Central Power and Light (200). Chester Heath School (200). Conway Violin Conservatory (200). Ritz Theater. Crossley School (400). David Hirsch School (400). Edward Furman School (800). Elizabeth Street School (150). George Evans School (200). Humble Oil Company (200). Marion Barnet School (200). McGregor family. Menger School (800). North Side Junior High School (150). Solomon Cole School (200). Southern Alkali employees* (2,400). Stearns and Rogers (800). Tower Theater, children's pictures (1,600). US Cavalry (150). Wright Studio (800). Wynn Seale School (200).

PEOPLE: Extensive coverage of Corpus Christi residents; studio and journalistic portraits, including individuals, family and social groups, and organizations. Most are Caucasian; McGregor places

Blacks under a separate heading, and the museum has maintained this separation for easier access. Subject headings used by McGregor and the museum are listed in Subjects (v.s.).

PHOTOGRAPHERS: John Frederick "Doc" McGregor (1892-1986) was a Corpus Christi studio and commercial photographer who also provided journalistic coverage of the city for the *Corpus Christi Caller-Times*. He was originally trained as a chiropractor, and practiced medicine when he first moved to Corpus in 1929. Newspaper clippings, oral interviews with McGregor, and other evidence point to the fact that several photographers' work is contained in the archive, although their identity remains unknown. The majority of the work, however, is assumed to be by McGregor.

RECORD GROUPS: The above description treats the archive of photographer John McGregor. The only other group of photographs at the museum:

C74.1 PLUTORO/KEENNON/PURVIS COLLECTION. Documention of the excavation of Spanish ships near North Padre Island. The museum holds the photographs as well as the artifacts for the Texas Historical Commission, Texas Antiquities Committee (q.v.), where the collection is described.

Corpus Christi Public Library (C78)

805 Comanche
Corpus Christi, Texas 78401

512-882-1937. Contact: Librarian, Local History Department.

PURPOSE: A local history collection in a public library collecting books and journals, manuscripts, genealogical materials, and photographs.

HOURS: Monday through Thursday, 9:00-9:00; Saturday, 9:00-6:00. Closed major holidays.

ASSISTANCE: Professional staff. Electrostatic copies available. Photoduplications may be made by the patron or ordered through the Library.

PUBLICATION: No publication fee. Collection credit required. A few photographs require third-party permission.

FINDING AIDS: Lists of subjects and individuals; material filed by subject.

BIBLIOGRAPHY:
Walraven, Bill. *Corpus Christi: The history of a Texas seaport.* Woodland Hills CA: Windsor Publications, 1982.

SCOPE: 13,000 photographs, most silver gelatin prints. The library also holds a few cirkut panoramas and scrapbooks with a few photographs. 1860s to present; most 1965 to 1966.

Type of photo	Pre-1880	1880-1899	1900-1919	1920-1939	1940-1959	1960-1986
Vintage prints	50	100	200	200	200	12,000
Photo albums				1		

GEOGRAPHIC: Nueces County, predominantly Corpus Christi and Padre Island.

SUBJECTS: Broad coverage of the economic and social development of the region.

Agriculture. Airplanes and airports. Apartments. Banks. Bayfront. Beaches. Boats. Boy Scouts. Bridges. Buildings. Businesses. Cattle. Cemeteries. Chamber of Commerce. Churches. Cotton. Clubs. Dams. Expressways. Festivals. Gas wells. Hospitals. Hotels. Homes. Hurricanes (1919, Carla, Celia). Industry (chemical, fishing, metal, petroleum). Fire department. Motor bus lines. Municipal buildings and city government. Oil wells. Organizations. Parks. Piers. Police department. Political parties. Railroads. Ranches. Schools. Sports. Street scenes. Transportation. Weather. Welfare.

Buccaneer Days. Bascule Bridge. Celanese Chemical Company. Coast Guard. Corpus Christi Port. Driscoll Junior High School. Du Pont. Harbor Bridge. Reynolds Metals Company. *USS Lexington* (ship). Wesley Seale Dam.

PEOPLE: Many area residents, none held in quantity.

PHOTOGRAPHERS: Most unidentified; few snapshooters. Corpus Christi photographers:

Louis de Planque. John F. "Doc" McGregor. Wheelus and Wheelus.

RECORD GROUPS: Photographs are sorted into two artificial collections, subjects and portraits. Many of the photographs fall into three categories:

C78.1 DE PLANQUE (LOUIS; 1842-1898) PHOTOGRAPHS. Studio photographer in Matamoros, Indianola, and Corpus Christi. Studio portraits made in Corpus Christi. 100 cartes and cabinet prints. Late 1880s to 1890s.

C78.2 KZTV TELEVISION PHOTOGRAPHS. Journalistic coverage of the city showing major events and important persons; possibly a photo morgue assembled by KZTV. 5,000 silver gelatin prints. 1965 to 1966.

C78.3 McGREGOR (JOHN F. "DOC"; 1892-1986) PHOTOGRAPHS. Commercial photographer, also made photographs for the *Corpus Christi Caller-Times*. Journalistic coverage of the city. Approximately 1,000 images. 1930s to 1960s.

Smaller significant groups include:

C78.4 *Dedication of the Bascule Bridge, Corpus Christi, Texas.* Snapshots of the opening of the bridge, ships in the Corpus Christi harbor, and a parade. 32 silver gelatin prints. 1926.

C78.5 OLIVARES (ANDRES) PHOTOGRAPHS. Snapshots of Olivares and his execution by hanging at the Nueces County Jail. 10 silver gelatin prints. 1902.

C78.6 SOIL CONSERVATION PHOTOGRAPHS. Agriculture as affected by dust bowl conditions, drought, and soil conservation in Texas and various midwestern states; produced by the US Department of Agriculture Soil Conservation Service. 34 silver gelatin prints. 1940s.

Dallas Historical Society (D18)

Texas Hall of State Building
Fair Park
Grand and Nimitz Street
P.O. Box 26038
Dallas, Texas 75226

214-421-5136. Contact: Archivist.

PURPOSE: A local history society and museum with extensive holdings of books, manuscripts, artifacts, and photographs.

HOURS: Exhibition area—Monday through Saturday, 9:00-5:00; Sunday, 1:00-5:00; closed Christmas. Reserve collections—weekdays, 9:00-5:00; appointment required; admission fee; closed major holidays.

ASSISTANCE: Professional staff. Written and phone inquiries accepted. Electrostatic copies available. Photoduplications must be ordered through the society.

PUBLICATION: Publication fee for commercial use. Collection credit required. Free copy of publication to the society. Third-party permission required on few items.

FINDING AIDS: Card-index inventory of holdings; a few collections have itemized lists; access by general subject heading, geographic location, photographer, personal name, and date.

BIBLIOGRAPHY:
Gambrell, Herbert, and Virginia Gambrell. *A pictorial history of Texas.* New York: E. P. Dutton, 1960.
McDonald, William. *Dallas rediscovered: A photographic chronicle of urban expansion, 1870-1925.* Dallas: Dallas Historical Society, 1978.
Payne, Darwin, et al. *Dallas: An illustrated history.* Woodland Hills CA: Windsor Publications, 1982.
Stark, Henry, photog.; commentary by A. C. Greene. *Views in Texas.* Austin: Encino Press, 1974.

SCOPE: 7,500 photographs, including vintage and copy prints, original negatives, glass lantern slides, and transparencies. Many photomechanical postcards. Some record groups have supporting manuscript materials. 1860s to present.

Type of photo	Pre-1880	1880-1899	1900-1919	1920-1939	1940-1959	1960-1986
D/A/T-types	20					
Glass negs				250		
Film negs			120	250		
Vintage prints	200	1,000	1,500	2,000	1,000	500
Copy prints	50	500	750	100		
Photo albums			3	2		

GEOGRAPHIC: Texas, including substantial coverage of Northeast Texas and extensive coverage of Dallas and Dallas County.

SUBJECTS: Academia. Agriculture. Architecture (domestic, public, industrial). Cityscapes (aerial views, street scene). Landscapes. Military (WW II domestic front). Organizations. Services. Sports and amusements (soldier shows—WW II). Transportation (light rail, public, railroad).

Texas Centennial Exposition. Texas State Fair.

PEOPLE: Many local individuals, few held in quantity. The society has made an effort to collect materials pertaining to Black and Hispanic ethnic history.

Dealey family. Gambrell family. Bishop Alexander P. Garrett.

PHOTOGRAPHERS: Predominantly Dallas photographers.

Church. Clogenson. J. R. Davis. Alfred Freeman. Squire Haskins. Lloyd M. Long. McClellan. Frank Rogers. Vorhee's. J. H. Webster.

RECORD GROUPS:

D18.1 ADAIR (WILLIAM WALTER) COLLECTION. Travel stereos of Eureka Springs AR photographed by Barker's Views and various other locations photographed by Webster Albee (Rochester NY); snapshots. 29 stereographs, 7 silver gelatin prints. 1890s. DHS# A5329.

D18.2 AMERICAN MAYFLOWER COLLECTION. Dallas branch of an American domestic and industrial transit and storage company. Commercial product shots of vans with loads, buildings; portraits and activities of company personnel. 74 silver gelatin prints; 80 nitrate negatives. 1910s to 1970s. DHS# V8527.

D18.3 ARNOLD (CHARLES ERWIN) COLLECTION. Dallas commercial photographer, operated a studio at 2902 Swiss Avenue. Domestic, retail, and industrial interiors; domestic and commercial architecture and construction; a few late-Pictorialist landscapes and cloudscapes; some family portraits. Photographed by Arnold, except early family portraits. 500 glass and film negatives with modern prints, some vintage prints. 1890s to 1930s, most ca. 1920. DHS# 6828.

D18.4 ARONSON (Mrs. HOWARD S.) COLLECTION. Snapshots of street scenes and a parade in Dallas; studio portraits of Wright family. 31 silver gelatin prints. Ca. 1900s. DHS# F807, V816.

D18.5 BAILEY (MOLLIE; 1841-1918) COLLECTION. Operated a traveling tent show. Studio and snapshot portraits of Bailey, her family, and associates; Mollie Bailey's tent show. 23 photo prints and 2 tintypes. 1900 to 1920. ACM# 39130.

D18.6 BARTLETT (RUTH C.) ESTATE COLLECTION. Commercial views of Greenville; vacation and family snapshots. 4 vintage silver gelatin prints; 256 negatives with modern contact prints. Ca. 1890. DHS# A6048.

D18.7 BESTERLING (Mrs. EDWARD A.) COLLECTION. Studio portraits of the Besterling family; by various Dallas photographers. 13 photo prints, including cabinets, cartes, tintypes, and silver gelatin prints. 1880s to 1900s. DHS# A44113.

D18.8 BIGBEE (NORTH) COLLECTION. Studio portraits, news photos, and a few snapshots of Bigbee and his associates. Many by Dallas, Georgetown, and Austin photographers. 135 photo prints, most silver gelatin, some color. 1880s to 1970s, most ca. 1940s. DHS# A7912.

D18.9 BYWATERS (Mr. and Mrs. JERRY) COLLECTION. Studio portraits and production stills of performers, including Paul van Katwijk; snapshots of travels in Texas, including Galveston, San Antonio, and Denison. 67 silver gelatin prints. 1900s to 1970s, most ca. 1910. DHS# A795.

D18.10 CALVERT (Mrs. N. C.) COLLECTION. Studio portraits of Thomas Volney "T. V." Munson (1843-1913) and family and commercial views of his home in Denison. 14 photo prints, 1 tintype. 1870s to 1890s. DHS# A4566.

D18.11 CARD (Mrs. L. HOLMAN) COLLECTION. Grape fields and packing plant at Comanche. 9 silver gelatin prints, 1 hand-colored. Ca. 1920. DHS# A4464.

D18.12 CARRUTH (Mrs. MARGARET SCRUGGS) COLLECTION. Snapshot vacation photos made in Texas; commercial retrospective views of historic sites in Texas; Carruth home in Turtle Creek; Southern Methodist University buildings. 500 silver gelatin prints and 250 film negatives, most snapshots; 1 ambrotype and 1 daguerreotype. 1910s. DHS# A6111, A6124, A6179, A6182.

D18.13 COBB (B. B.) COLLECTION. Cobb family photographs, including itinerant business interiors of the offices of Joseph L. Cobb; snapshot retrospective views of historic courthouses. 23 silver gelatin prints. Ca. 1910. DHS# A39148.

D18.14 COLQUITT (Mrs. O. B.) COLLECTION. Battlefield scenes in Luxembourg and France during WW I by US Army Signal Corps; Southern Pacific Railroad Pecos High Bridge. 21 photo prints, most silver gelatin. Early 1900s, most ca. 1918. DHS# A46146.

D18.15 CONNOR (Mrs. W. O.) COLLECTION. Snapshot views of Dallas street scenes, Guaranty and Republic banks in Dallas. 13 photo prints. Ca. 1890 to 1920. DHS# A4572.

D18.16 CRAIN (JOHN W.) COLLECTION. Franklin Delano Roosevelt, Winston Churchill, and other heads of state at the Yalta Conference; travel views in Texas and New Mexico; US Army in El Paso vicinity photographed by W. H. Horne. 41 silver gelatin prints; 26 silver gelatin snapshots and photo postcards. 1945. DHS# F805, V8116.

D18.17 CRETIN (CHARLES) COLLECTION. Commercial views of the Credit Foncier Colonists' settlement at Topolobampo (a socialist colony in Sinaloa, Mexico, founded by Albert K. Owen) photographed by I. D. Kneeland; 1 portrait of Cretin photographed by Freeman. 7 silver gelatin prints. 1860s, 1889. DHS# A37100.

D18.18 DALLAS ADVERTISING LEAGUE COLLECTION. League activities and members relating to the career of Richard Haughton; commercial product shots and commerce in Dallas. Many photographed by Frank Rogers. 18 silver gelatin prints. 1910s to 1920s. DHS# A5188.

D18.19 DALLAS (CITY OF) COLLECTION. Studio portraits of Dallas mayors formerly hanging in the city council chambers, some art reproductions. Various Dallas photographers. 40 silver gelatin prints, many copies. 1900 to 1956. DHS# A5643.

D18.20 DALLAS COUNTY HISTORICAL SOCIETY COLLECTION. Family photographs of Miss Jennie Bell Loughery, including snapshots, photo Christmas cards, and a few studio portraits. 100 photo prints, most silver gelatin snapshots, some color snapshots and hand-colored. 1910s to 1960s. DHS# A7885.

D18.21 DALLAS HISTORICAL SOCIETY COLLECTION. Studio portraits of Joseph Weldon Bailey by various photographers, including C. M. Bell (Washington DC). 7 photographs, including cabinets and imperials. 1870s to 1890s. DHS# A1073.

D18.22 DEALEY (TED) COLLECTION. A herd of bull elks taken from the Wichita Mountain Wild Refuge near Cache OK to a new home in the mountains of Mexico under the supervision of John A. Loomis, president of the Carmen Mountain Club. 20 silver gelatin prints. 1940. DHS# A41103.

D18.23 DENNIS (Mrs. A. L.) COLLECTION. Commercial views of a flood in Dallas, including damage to the Interurban and the Texas and Pacific Railroad tracks. 18 silver gelatin photo postcards. 1905 or 1908. DHS# A3617.

D18.24 DERFMAN (NAT) COLLECTION. Production stills from Irving Berlin's stage show, *This Is the Army.* Photographed by Vandamm Studio (New York). 12 silver gelatin prints. 1942. DHS# A42112.

D18.25 DOW (Captain L. J.) COLLECTION. Commercial views of a dinner at the Baker Hotel honoring Admiral Nimitz on the occasion of the presentation of his bronze likeness to the Hall of State; by an unidentified US Navy photographer. 26 silver gelatin prints. 1946. DHS# A46201.

D18.26 DOWNS (Dr. and Mrs. J. T., III) COLLECTION. Carte art reproductions of Civil War military figures; family snapshots.

[*Snapshot album.*] Snapshot portraits and outings. 49 silver gelatin prints. 1910s.

19 silver gelatin prints; 1 album (v.s.). 1910s. DHS# A7676.

D18.27 FOSCUE (EDWIN J.) COLLECTION. Commercial views of cotton farming, lumbering, petroleum in Northeast and East Texas; Dallas skyline. 21 silver gelatin prints. 1920s to 1930s. DHS# A5946.

D18.28 GAMBRELL (HERBERT) COLLECTION. Retrospective views of historic buildings, predominantly courthouses and the business section of Breckenridge. Many snapshot and many commercial views, including photographs by Aultmann (El Paso) and Frank Rogers (Dallas). 70 silver gelatin prints. 1910s to 1940s. DHS# A3795.

D18.29 GAMBRELL (HERBERT) COLLECTION. Exhibits of artifacts, manuscripts, maps, and other objects in cases at the Texas Centennial Exposition. Photographed by Paul R. Clegg (Dallas). 69 silver gelatin prints. 1936. DHS# A37118.

D18.30 GAMBRELL (HERBERT) COLLECTION. Commercial views of workers reconstructing La Villita in San Antonio as a National Youth Administration Project; construction of Denison Dam; various news photographs by the *Dallas Morning News* from Brownwood, El Paso, and Dallas. 100 silver gelatin prints. 1940s. DHS# A41148.

D18.31 GAMBRELL (Dr. and Mrs. HERBERT) COLLECTION. Illustrations used in their book of Texas history, including cityscapes of major Texas cities, art reproductions of Texas history subjects, series of cowboys working a roundup. Various and unidentified photographers. 175 silver gelatin prints, many copy prints and art reproductions. 1900s to late 1950s. DHS# A6195. See Bibliography.

D18.32 GARRETT (FREDRICK) COLLECTION. Commercial portraits of Bishop Alexander C. Garrett and associates; Saint Mary's College students, faculty, and facilities. 34 silver gelatin prints, possibly modern prints, some copy prints. 1920s. DHS# A4458.

D18.33 GERHART (Mrs. PAUL C.) COLLECTION. Studio portraits by various Dallas photographers. 18 cartes and cabinets. 1860s to 1880s. DHS# A4219.

D18.34 GILPIN (LAURA; 1891-1979) COLLECTION. Pictorial Postcards of the Southwest series (Colorado Springs CO: Gilpin Publishing Company): 1) *Navaho;* 2) *Acoma;* 3) *Mesa Verde;*

4) *Navaho;* 5) *Taos Pueblo;* 6) *San Idlefonso and Santa Clara Pueblos;* 7) *El Santuario de Chimayó;* 8) *Los Ranchos de Taos church.* Soft-focus Pictorialism. 48 photogravure postcards. Ca. 1930s. DHS# A4197.

D18.35 HALL (Mrs. ROBERT M.) COLLECTION. Interior and exterior views of the W. H. Abrams home, the Shingles. 5 gelatino-chloride and 2 collodio-chloride prints. 1890s. DHS# A41207.

D18.36 HAYES COLLECTION. Denny, Durwood, and Johnny Hays were contract photographers for the *Dallas Morning News.* Color material includes picturesque landscapes in West Texas, missions in San Antonio, and oil derricks in Kilgore. Black-and-white material includes retrospective views of Texas courthouses and other historic buildings; Texas Centennial Exposition buildings under construction. 360 color slides; 500 color prints, most badly color-shifted; 100 vintage silver gelatin prints; 500 film negatives, many nitrate, with modern prints. 1930s to 1950s. DHS# A5983, A6558.

D18.37 HENSLEY (Mrs. JULIA BEAUMONT) COLLECTION. Street scene in Port Lavaca dated "early 1850s"; Hensley home, statue of LaSalle, and snapshot views around Port Lavaca. 5 photo prints. 1850s to 1890s. DHS# A42176.

D18.38 HENSLEY (JULIA) HEIRS COLLECTION. Studio and snapshot portraits. Various photographers, many from Texas. 120 photo prints, most silver gelatin prints, many cabinets. 1880s to 1930s. DHS# A44118.

D18.39 HILDEBRAND (Miss HILDA) COLLECTION. Commercial travel views of Boston and Killarney Lakes, Ireland. Photographs by B. W. Kilburn, John P. Soule, and by King and Pearson. 15 albumen stereographs. 1880s. DHS# A42181.

D18.40 JOHNSON (JOHN J.) COLLECTION. Commercial Dallas photographer active 1890s to 1930s. Domestic and commercial architecture, architectural detail, and construction; retail and industrial interiors; theater interiors and façades; product illustration and window displays from the state fair; group portraits, many of school groups and social organizations; Camp Davis at the state fair grounds during WW I; Southwestern Telephone Company. Most photographed by Johnson. 1,051 glass and film negatives with modern prints; a few vintage prints. Ca. 1920s. DHS# 7787.

D18.41 LATTA (SMITH H.) COLLECTION. Cecil A. Keating, including portraits as King of the Carnival at the state fair, his home, and business. 9 silver gelatin prints. Ca. 1905. DHS# A3583.

D18.42 [LOWRY FIELD] PUBLIC RELATIONS OFFICER COLLECTION. Performance of "The Women" by an all-male cast at the Broadway Theater, possibly made at Fort Lowry CO. 16 silver gelatin prints. 1942. DHS# A42121.

D18.43 McCOY COLLECTION. Studio portraits by various American photographers. 82 photo prints, including albumen cartes, cabinets, and many silver gelatin prints. DHS# V82.24.

D18.44 McCOY FAMILY COLLECTION. Hester, Lee, Druley, and McCoy family members; some art reproductions, homesteads, and business interiors. Photographers include H. A. Doerr (San Antonio) and W. E. Douglas (Dallas). 12 photographs; most silver gelatin prints, many photomechanicals. 1860s to ca. 1900. DHS# A1082.

D18.45 McHALE COLLECTION. Street scenes, commercial and domestic buildings, and cityscapes representing the economic and social development of Dallas. Most by commercial photographers. 185 items, many copy prints, some photogravures and art reproductions. 1880s to 1930s. DHS# F802.

D18.46 MEXICO STEREOGRAPHS PURCHASE. Picturesque travel views of landscapes, city scenes, and buildings in Mexico. Photographers and publishers include A. Bríquet, Kilburn Brothers, and V. Contreras. 137 albumen stereographs. 1870s. DHS# A6254.

D18.47 MILAZZO (LEE) COLLECTION. Studio portraits and a few commercial and snapshot travel views. Various photographers, many from Texas. 34 photo prints, most albumen cabinets. 1880s. DHS# A7891.

D18.48 MILLER (Mrs. SETH) COLLECTION. Commercial views of cityscapes and buildings in Dallas by an unidentified photographer(s), early 1880s; aftermath of the 1900 Galveston hurricane photographed by F. E. Trube. 21 silver gelatin prints. 1880s to 1900. DHS# A4865.

D18.49 MORONEY (Colonel THOMAS J.) COLLECTION. Military engagements during WW I in Regnieville, France, vicinity photographed by US Army Signal Corps; Charles Lindbergh's visit to Dallas. 33 silver gelatin prints. Ca. 1916. DHS# A4664.

D18.50 MUSE (J. C.) ESTATE. Studio portraits including General W. L. Cabell; view of US Legation in Japan. 17 photo prints, most cartes. Mid-1850s to ca. 1890. DHS# A43115.

D18.51 PATTON (Dr. J. L., Jr.) COLLECTION. Principal of Booker T. Washington Technical High School, an all-Black school. Documents from Patton's career, including group portraits of students and faculty, activities at the school, and classroom interiors; many group photos of dinners and ceremonies associated with Patton's activities as a civic leader, including work with the Moorland Branch YMCA, United Negro College Fund, and March of Dimes fund raising; celebrities he met. Many by *Dallas Morning News* and other commercial photographers. 13 albums containing a total of 650 silver gelatin prints, 50 loose silver gelatin prints. 1930s to 1950s. DHS# 86.50.

D18.52 REAGAN (Mrs. JEFFERSON DAVIS) COLLECTION. Family photographs of Judge John H. Reagan. 21 photo prints, predominantly silver gelatin prints. 1890s to early 1900s. DHS# A4674.

D18.53 SAN ANTONIO STEREOGRAPHS PURCHASE. Picturesque scenes around San Antonio, the missions, and street life. From Doerr and Jacobson's Views in and around San Antonio series, others by F. Hardesty and unidentified photographer(s); picturesque views in Mexico by Kilburn Brothers. 24 albumen stereographs. 1870s. DHS# A6244.

D18.54 Stark, Henry, photog. *Views in Texas*. St. Louis MO photographer. Commercial, picturesque travel views made in Texas showing landscapes; cityscapes of Austin, Dallas, Houston, Galveston, Fort Worth, and other cities; agriculture and industry. 255 silver gelatin prints bound into a volume; itemized list and subject index. 1895 to 1896. DHS# A7878. See Bibliography.

D18.55 SUMMERS (HATTON WILLIAM; 1875-1962) COLLECTION. US Representative from Texas. Personal photographs from Summer's career; family and vacation snapshots; commercial travel views from Europe by various studios; cattle near Clarendon, possibly the Goodnight Ranch.

Photographed by Mulkey; some cancelled proof prints and studio portraits by Harris and Ewing (Washington DC). 216 silver gelatin photo prints; photogravure postcards. Ca. 1918. DHS# A46213.

D18.56 TOOMEY (Mrs. D. P.) COLLECTION. Predominantly studio portraits, a few of Harry Carrel; one home interior; photographers include Landy (Cincinnati OH), Deane (Dallas), Church (Dallas), Chalmers (Dallas), and E. Will Hays (Louisville KY). 11 albumen and silver gelatin photo prints, including some cabinets. 1880s to ca. 1900. DHS# A352.

D18.57 US ARMY CORPS OF ENGINEERS COLLECTION. Commercial views documenting the construction of locks and dams on various river projects in Texas, especially on the Trinity, Brazos, and Sabine rivers. 500 glass and nitrate negatives with modern prints. 1910 to 1918. DHS# A39118.

D18.58 WARE COLLECTION. *Texas Women's Press Association: Meeting at El Campo, Texas, June 20-21.* Cityscapes, rice and hay agriculture. Photographed by Louis Melcher (El Campo). 9 silver gelatin prints. 1906. DHS# A45195.

D18.59 WATKINS (ROBERT) COLLECTION. Studio portraits of theater performers. 18 silver gelatin prints. Ca. 1920s. DHS# A7894.

D18.60 ZAHRT (Mrs. PAT) COLLECTION. Portraits of T. E. Braniff; Braniff Airlines plane interiors and personnel. 17 modern silver gelatin prints with press release captions. Mid-1930s to 1954. DHS# A54112.

Fine Arts Division (D26)

Dallas Public Library
1515 Young Street, Fourth floor
Dallas, Texas 75201

214-670-1643   Contact: Theatre Librarian.

PURPOSE: A special-collection department within a public library emphasizing the fine arts, theater, television, motion pictures, music, fashion, dance, and architecture. Holdings include rare and recent books and journals; manuscripts, including music; business archives; press releases and newspaper clippings; costumes; sound recordings; ephemera; and photographs. The department concentrates on Dallas, but also collects much national and some international material. The Texas/Dallas History and Archives Divison (q.v.) holds the Margo Jones, John Rosenfield, and Interstate Theater collections.

HOURS: Monday through Thursday, 9:00-9:00; Friday and Saturday, 9:00-5:00; Sunday, 1:00-5:00. Closed major holidays. Appointments recommended.

ASSISTANCE: Professional, experienced, specialized staff. Written and phone inquiries accepted on a limited basis. Electrostatic copies available. Photoduplications may be made by the patron or ordered through the library.

PUBLICATION: No publication fee. Collection credit required. Free copy of publication to the library. Third-party permission required on some materials.

FINDING AIDS: Visual card index; registers for some record groups. Access by subject.

BIBLIOGRAPHY:

An exhibition of selected material from the W. E. Hill Collection: On the occasion of the opening of the collection April 28th and continuing through May 31, 1966 at the Dallas Public Library. [Dallas: Dallas Public Library, 1966.]

SCOPE: 100,000 vintage photographs, including some cartes, cabinets, and many mass-distribution, publicity, silver gelatin prints.

GEOGRAPHIC: Primary emphasis is on activities in Dallas and the immediate region, although the department collects materials pertaining to nationally distributed television and motion picture productions and has substantial files on the fine arts in major US cities, especially New York, and some coverage of international companies.

SUBJECTS: Extensive coverage of the arts and entertainment industry, including television, motion pictures, theater, dance, opera, and concerts.

Architecture. Clothing (designer fashions). Services (museums). Sports and entertainment (fine arts, music).

PEOPLE: Primarily performers; creative and interpretive artists in all media. See Record Groups for names, especially the W. E. Hill collection.

PHOTOGRAPHERS: Primarily commercial photography, including studio portraiture, production stills, and publicity photographs. Many local productions were photographed by *Dallas Morning News* staff photographers; many nineteenth-century studio portraits of theater personages by noted theater photographers such as Napoleon Sarony (New York), B. J. Falk (New York), and various other US East and West Coast photographers; a few European studio portrait photographers.

RECORD GROUPS: Materials in the department are arranged under the headings architecture, art, dance, fashion, motion picture, music, television, and theater. Most materials are treated as ephemera files, with large or valuable groups separated for easy access and preservation; collections are maintained separately by provenance but are described here under the appropriate heading.

Architecture collection:

D26.1 ARCHITECTURE COLLECTION. Newspaper clippings, articles, and a few photographs; predominantly Dallas. 100 photographs. 1960s to present.

D26.2 Baxter, Sylvester (1850-1927); Henry Greenwood Peabody, photographer. *Spanish colonial architecture in Mexico.* Boston: J. B. Millet, 1901. Commercial views of cityscapes and architecture. Text volume with halftone reproductions; portfolio of 150 silver gelatin prints.

Art collection:

D26.3 ART BIOGRAPHY FILE. Press clippings, exhibition catalogs, and other textual materials pertaining to creative artists working in all media (interpretive artists—for example, actors, musicians, and dancers—are filed under the appropriate medium). A small amount of photographic materials are interfiles, most are art reproductions of paintings. 60 feet, including 1,000 photographs. 1970s to present.

Dance collection:

D26.4 DANCE COLLECTION. An artificial collection of reviews, clippings, and photographs documenting national and international companies; all genres, especially folk, modern, and ballet. Companies include, among others

> Agnes de Mille Theater. American Ballet Theater. Ballet Russe de Monte Carlo. Devi Dja. Houston Contemporary Dance Theater. José Greco Spanish Ballet. The National Ballet of Canada. Sadler's Wells Ballet.

10 feet, including 1,500 photographs, most silver gelatin prints. 1960 to present.

D26.5 LÁBAN (JUANA DE) ARCHIVES. Dancer, instructor of dance, and daughter of the inventor of Lában-notation, Rudolph von Lában. Photographs document Lában's professional career, including dance performances and rehearsals; portraits of associates, including Ruth St. Denis and her father; some coverage of her private and family life. 500 photographs. 1910s to 1960s.

Fashion collection:

D26.6 BERGDORF-GOODMAN ARCHIVES. A *haute couture* clothing store in New York City noted for its designer furs. Photographs in the archive document activities of the firm; clothing styles, including fashions by Emric I. Partos, Leslie Morris, Mark Mooring, Bernard Newman, and Halston; runway shows; window displays. Most made in New York, some in Paris. At least one photograph each by Man Ray and Yosef Karsh. 2,500 photographs, most silver gelatin prints. 1920s to 1940s.

D26.7 Gaul, Franz; J. Löwy, photographer. *Österreichische-ungarische National Trachten.* Vienna: R. Lechner's K.K. Hof und Universitäts Buchhandlung, [n.d.] Studio portraits of folk costumes. 24 hand-colored plates. Ca. 1900.

Motion picture collection:

D26.8 BIOGRAPHY COLLECTION. An artificial collection of photographs, newspaper clippings, and press releases pertaining primarily to performing arts personalities containing some 68,000 names; none held in quantity. 275 feet, including 8,250 silver gelatin prints. 1950s to present.

D26.9 MOTION PICTURES COLLECTION. An artificial collection of movie stills, press kits, and reviews. A small amount of material on the Academy Awards and other award ceremonies, the collection consists primarily of materials relating to individual productions and includes some 37,500 titles (many without photographs). Extensive coverage of:

> *The Alamo* (1956). *Around the World in Eighty days* (1956). *Ben Hur* (1959). *The Cardinal* (1963). *Chitty-Chitty Bang Bang* (1968). *Cleopatra* (1963). *Doctor Zhivago* (1965). *The Great Race* (1965). *The Lion in Winter* (1968). *Papillon* (1973). *Ryan's Daughter* (1970).

Substantial coverage of:

> *Advise and Consent* (1962). *Anzio* (1968). *The Art of Love* (1965). *Baby, the Rain Must Fall* (1965). *Battle of Britain* (1969). *A Bedtime Story* (1964). *Billy Jack* (1971). *The Bird Man of Alcatraz* (1971). *Bus Riley's Back in Town* (1964). *Can Can* (1959). *Cast a Giant Shadow*

(1966). *The Dirty Dozen* (1967). *Duel at Diablo* (1965). *Fanny* (1960). *Father Goose* (1964). *Fitzwilly* (1967). *Genghis Khan* (1965). *Giant* (1965). *In Search of the Castaways* (1962). *Kitten with a Whip* (1964). *Les Liaisons Dangereuses* (1959). *The Longest Day* (1969). *Made in Paris* (1965). *Major Dundee* (1965). *Man of La Mancha* (1972). *Man's Favorite Sport* (1964). *Pinocchio* (1940). *Play Dirty* (1968). *The Pleasure Seekers* (1964). *Quackser Fortune Has a Cousin in the Bronx* (1970). *Ride Beyond Vengeance* (1965). *Royal Hunt of the Sun* (1969). *The Son of Flubber* (1962). *South Pacific* (1964). *Star!* (1968). *Those Magnificent Men in Their Flying Machines* (1965). *Topkapi* (1964). *2001: A Space Odyssey* (1968). *The Unforgiven* (1960). *Valdez is Coming* (1970). *Viva Maria!* (1965). *The War Lord* (1965). *A Warm December* (1972). *Will Penny* (1967).

250 feet, including 25,000 silver gelatin prints and a small amount of color transparency and color print material. Most 1960 to present, a few earlier.

D26.10 USA FILM FESTIVAL. Begun by Dr. G. William Jones in 1971 and continuing still, the festival honors US films and directors, often showing retrospectives of a director's work. Photographs include press kits with production stills of

Audrey Rose (1977). *The Bad News Bears* (1976). *Badlands* (1974). *Between the Lines* (1977). *Birch Interval* (1976). *Black Sunday* (1977). *Brothers* (1977). *Fraternity Row* (1977). *Islands in the Stream* (1977). *Leadbelly* (1976). *Love and Pain and the Whole Damn Thing* (1973). *The Sailor Who Fell from Grace with the Sea* (1976). *Sweet Revenge* (1977). *The Yakuza* (1975).

150 silver gelatin prints; associated programs, ephemera, and some records from the festival. 1970s.

Music collection:

D26.11 MUSIC COLLECTION. An artificial collection of newspaper clippings, reviews, photographs, and other materials pertaining to music, especially opera and symphonies; emphasis is on Dallas, although there is some coverage of Texas and the nation. Substantial coverage of the Dallas Opera, the Dallas Lyric Theater, the Dallas Symphony Orchestra, the Southern Methodist University, and the Metropolitan Opera of New York. 1,500 silver gelatin prints. 1950s to present.

Television collection:

D26.12 TELEVISION COLLECTION. An artificial collection primarily of press kits which contain photographs, news clippings, and reviews. Shows are almost exclusively from the three US commercial networks, although a small amount of material is from the Public Broadcasting System. Some 5,000 titles; shows with substantial coverage:

ABC's Wide World of Sports (ABC). *Adam-12* (NBC). *The Addams Family* (ABC). *The Adventures of Ozzie and Harriet* (ABC). *Alfred Hitchcock* (NBC). *Alumni Fun* (CBS). *American Sportsman* (ABC). *The Andy Griffith Show* (CBS). *Andy Williams* (NBC). *The Avengers* (CBS). *Batman* (ABC). *Bell Telephone Hour* (NBC). *Ben Casey* (ABC). *Beverly Hillbillies* (CBS). *Bewitched* (ABC). *The Bing Crosby Show* (ABC). *The Bob Cummings Show* (CBS). *Bob Hope Presents the Chrysler Theater* (NBC). *The Bold Ones* (NBC). *Bonanza* (NBC). *Branded* (NBC). *CBS Reports* (CBS). *Candid Camera* (CBS). *The Carol Burnett Show* (CBS). *The Cheyenne Show* (ABC). *Combat* (ABC). *The Courtship of Eddie's Father* (CBS). *The Danny Thomas Show* (CBS). *Days of Our Lives* (NBC). *The Dean Martin Show* (NBC). *Death Valley Days*. *Dr. Kildare* (NBC). *Du Pont Show of the Month* (NBC). *The Eleventh Hour* (NBC). *Empire* (NBC). *The F.B.I.* (ABC). *The Farmer's Daughter* (ABC). *Father Knows Best* (ABC). *The Felony Squad* (ABC). *The Flying Nun* (ABC). *For the People* (CBS). *The Fugitive*

(ABC). *General Electric Theater* (CBS). *Get Smart* (CBS). *Green Acres* (CBS). *The Guns of Will Sonnet* (ABC). *Gunsmoke* (CBS). *Hank* (NBC). *Hazel* (NBC). *Here Come the Brides* (ABC). *Here's Lucy* (CBS). *High Chaparral* (NBC). *Hogan's Heroes* (CBS). *Hollywood Palace* (ABC). *I Dream of Jeannie* (NBC). *I Spy* (NBC). *International Showtime* (NBC). *Ironside* (NBC). *The Jack Benny Program* (CBS). *The Jerry Lewis Show* (NBC). *The Joey Bishop Show* (NBC). *Judd for the Defense* (ABC). *The Judy Garland Show* (CBS). *Julia* (NBC). *Kentucky Jones* (NBC). *Kraft Suspense Theater* (NBC). *Land of the Giants* (ABC). *Little House on the Prairie* (NBC). *Look up and Live* (CBS). *Lost in Space* (CBS). *Love, American Style* (ABC). *Love Boat* (ABC). *The Lucy Show* (CBS). *The Man from U.N.C.L.E.* (NBC). *Marcus Welby M.D.* (ABC). *Mission Impossible* (CBS). *Mr. Novak* (ABC). *Mr. Roberts* (NBC). *Mod Squad* (ABC). *Moviola* (NBC). *The Munsters* (CBS). *My Three Sons* (CBS). *Nanny and the Professor* (ABC). *Ninety Bristol Court* (NBC). *The Odd Couple* (ABC). *The Outer Limits* (ABC). *The Partridge Family* (ABC). *Perry Mason* (CBS). *Petticoat Junction* (CBS). *Peyton Place* (ABC). *The Prisoner* (CBS). *Profiles in Courage* (NBC). *Rat Patrol* (NBC). *Rawhide* (CBS). *The Red Skelton Hour* (CBS). *Route 66* (CBS). *Rowan and Martin's Laugh-in* (NBC). *Run for Your Life* (NBC). *Slaterry's People* (CBS). *The Smothers Brothers Comedy Show* (CBS). *Star Trek* (NBC). *That Girl* (ABC). *To Tell the Truth* (CBS). *Trapper John M.D.* (CBS). *The Twilight Zone* (CBS). *US Steel Hour* (CBS). *The Untouchables* (ABC). *The Virginian* (NBC). *Wagon Train* (NBC). *The Wonderful World of Walt Disney* (NBC). *Westinghouse Presents* (CBS). *Wide Country* (NBC).

52 feet total, including 2,000 silver gelatin prints and a few color prints and color transparencies (badly color shifted). 1950s to present.

Theater collection:

D26.13 DALLAS LITTLE THEATER COLLECTION. Commercial portraits of performers and others associated with the theater, including Oliver Hinsdell, 500 names total; production stills and stage sets for some 2,000 productions including the world premier of George Bernard Shaw's *A Village Wooing*. 1,000 silver gelatin prints; extensive collection of business records and non-photographic materials. 1930 to 1950.

D26.14 DALLAS THEATRE CENTER COLLECTION. Portraits of performers and productions. 3,000 photographs; extensive supporting materials inclde directors' and stage managers' scripts, business records, graduate records, correspondence, motion picture and video tape, and blue-prints by Frank Lloyd Wright. 1960s.

D26.15 HILL (WILLIAM ELY "W. E."; 1886-1962) COLLECTION. Cartoonist for *Life* and the *New York Tribune*, and author of *Among Us Mortals*. Materials pertaining to the theater, primarily in New York, but also some British, French, and US coverage. A few production stills, but primarily studio portraits. More than 2,300 names total, with more than five images of:

Edwin Adams. Maude Adams. Emma Abani. Viola Allen. Mary Anderson. Julia Arthur. Henry Clay Barnabee. Ethel Barrymore. Jessi Batlett-Davis. Kyrle Bellew. Sarah Bernhardt. Edwin Booth. Hope Booth. Dion Boucicault. Maude Branscombe. Amy Busby. Carmencita. Georgia Cayvan. Albert Chevalier. Hilda Clark. Annie Clarke. Kate Claxton. Estelle Clayton. William F. Cody (= Buffalo Bill). Rose Coghlan. Lottie Collins. Corinne. Mathilde Cotrelly. William H. Crane. E. L. Davenport. Fanny Davenport. Jean de Reszke. Gaby Deslys. J. E. Dodson. John Drew. Virginia Earle. Maxine Elliot. J. K. Emmet. William Faversham. Cissy Fitzgerald. Katherine Florence. W. J. Florence. Edwin Forrest. Della Fox.

George L. Fox. Grace George. Etelka Gerster. Mrs. G. H. Gilbert. John Gilbert. N. C. Goodwin. Maud Granger. George Grossmith. Yvette Guilbert. James K. Hackett. Pauline Hall. Virginia Harned. Anna Held. DeWolfe Hopper. Edna Wallace Hopper. Henry Irving. Isabel Irving. Louis James. Elsie Janis. Marie Jansen. Joseph Jefferson. Tom Karl. Herbert Kelcey. Clara Louise Kellogg. Kathryn Kidder. Lillie Langtry. William J. Le Moyne. Madge Lessing. James Lewis. Clara Lipman. Cecilia Loftus. Lotta. John McCullough. Minnie Maddern. Louis Mann. Mary Mannering. Robert B. Mantel. Pauline Markham. Julia Marlowe. Sadie Martinot. Jno. B. Mason. Edna May. Adah Menken. Henry Miller. Caroline Miskel. Maggie Mitchell. Helena Modjeska. Clara Morris. Adelaide Neilson. Evelyn Nesbit. Alice Nielson. Christine Nillson. Chauncey Olcott. James O'Neill. Minnie Palmer. Adelinia Patti. Annie Pixley. James Powers. John T. Raymond. Ada Rehan. Mlle. Rhea. Fanny Rice. Charles Richman. Emily Rigle. George Righold. Marie Rose. Annie Russell. Lillian Russell. Zelda Seguin. Mary F. Scott Siddous. E. E. Sothern. E. H. Sothern. J. H. Stoddart. Annie Sutherland. Marie Tempest. Fay Templeton. Ellen Terry. Lydia Thompson. Emma C. Thursby. Vesta Tilley. Vokes family. Lester Wallack. David Warfield. William Warren. Joseph Wheelock Jr. Mrs. Barney Williams. Francis Wilson.

Many New York photographers with substantial amounts by B. J. Falk, Napoleon Sarony, Otto Sarony, and Schloss; various other US and European photographers, with a few woodburytypes withdrawn from *The Theater* magazine. 4,200 photographs, most cartes and cabinets; extensive associated theater ephemera, including programs, holograph letters, and other nonphotographic visual materials. 1860s to 1960s, most late 1870s to 1910.

D26.16 THEATER COLLECTION. Programs, reviews, and photographs, most collected by the department; broad subject coverage of live, stage performance including amusement parks (Disneyland, Six Flags Over Texas), circuses (Ringling Brothers, Barnum and Bailey; clowns), ice shows; some coverage of minstrelsy. Some national theater coverage, especially New York; some coverage of Texas, especially Fort Worth (Casa Mañana); extensive coverage of Dallas.

D26.16.1 Reviews. Newspaper clippings, production stills, and publicity photographs of performances, most in the Dallas area, arranged by title. 60 feet, including 1,000 silver gelatin prints. 1940s to present.

D26.16.2 Dallas. Productions and information pertaining to Dallas theatrical companies, including the Dallas Repertory Theater (300 photographs, 1970 to present), the Dallas Summer Musicals (2,000 photographs, 1958 to present), Southern Methodist University (200 photographs, 1968 to present), State Fair Musicals (500 photographs, 1951 to present), Theater 3 (750 photographs, 1961 to present), and inactive theatrical companies, including Arden Club of Southern Methodist University, the Cathedral Players, the Dallas Broadcast Theater League, the Great Play Series, Knox Street Theater, and the Round Up Theater.

40 feet of materials, total, including 4,500 silver gelatin prints. 1950s to present.

Texas/Dallas History and Archives Division (D30)

Dallas Public Library
1515 Young Street, Seventh floor
Dallas, Texas 75201

214-670-1435   Contact: Photographic Archivist.

PURPOSE: A local and state history archives collecting books and journals, manuscripts, maps, art works, and photographs.

HOURS: Monday through Thursday, 9:00-9:00; Friday and Saturday, 9:00-5:00; Sunday, 1:00-5:00. Closed major holidays. Appointments recommended.

ASSISTANCE: Professional, experienced, specialized staff. Written and phone inquiries accepted on a limited basis. Electrostatic copies available. Photoduplications may be made by the patron or ordered through the library.

PUBLICATION: No publication fee. Collection credit required. Free copy of publication to the library. Third-party permission required on some materials.

FINDING AIDS: Visual card index; registers for some record groups. Access by subject.

BIBLIOGRAPHY:

Boykin, Lucile. *Tent to towers*. Dallas: Dallas Public Library, 1982.

Callaway, Helen B. *A visitor's guide to Dallas*. Dallas: Dallas Chamber of Commerce, 1965.

Day, James M. *Captain Clint Peoples, Texas Ranger*. Waco: Texian Press, 1980.

Governor, Alan. *Living Texas blues*. Dallas: Dallas Museum of Art, 1985.

Green, A. C. *Dallas: The deciding years, a historical portrait*. Austin: Encino Press, 1974.

Grove, Larry. *Dallas Public Library: The first seventy-five years*. Dallas: Dallas Public Library, 1984.

Hinton, Ted. *Ambush*. Austin: Shoal Creek Publishers, 1979.

Kimball, Justin F. *Our city: Dallas today and tomorrow*. Dallas: Dallas Independent School District, 1978.

Lang, Pam, ed. *Family business in Dallas: A matter of values*. Dallas: Dallas Public Library, 1982.

McDonald, William. *Dallas rediscovered: A photographic chronicle of urban expansion, 1870-1925*. Dallas: Dallas Historical Society, 1978.

Meyers, Johnnie J. *Texas Electric Railway*. Chicago: Central Electric Railfan's Association, 1982.

Payne, Darwin, et al. *Dallas: An illustrated history*. Woodland Hills CA: Windsor Publications, 1982.

Rogers, Mary Beth. *We can fly: Stories of Katherine Stinson and other gutsy Texas women*. Austin: Ellen C. Temple, 1983.

Saxon, Gerald, ed. *Reminiscences: A glimpse of old East Dallas*. Dallas: Dallas Public Library, 1983.

Smith, Michael D. *Open Dallas: Getting to know your city*. Dallas: Dallas Public Library, 1984.

Sumner, Alan, ed. *Dallasights: An anthology of architecture and open spaces*. Dallas: American Institute of Architects, Dallas Chapter, 1978.

Treherne, John. *The strange history of Bonnie and Clyde*. New York: Stern and Day, 1985.

Wiley, Nancy. *The great State Fair of Texas: An illustrated history*. Dallas: Taylor Publishing, 1985.

Wise, Bob. *Oak Lawn 1880-1976: An historical study*. Arlington: University of Texas at Arlington, 1976.

SCOPE: 5,000 vintage photo prints and 100,000 original film negatives with modern prints, including panoramic prints and film transparencies.

Type of photo	Pre-1880	1880-1899	1900-1919	1920-1939	1940-1959	1960-1986
D/A/T-types		5	15			
Glass negs		100	400			
Film negs	20	400	1,500	32,500	32,000	2,000
Vintage prints	10	50	350	600	700	1,000
Copy prints	20	300	700	500	500	100

GEOGRAPHIC: Major emphasis is on local history with a secondary emphasis on the state.

Dallas County (Dallas, East Dallas, Oak Cliff). Fort Worth. Galveston.

SUBJECTS: Extensive coverage of economic and social development of the city.

Architecture (commercial). Events (Galveston Hurricane—1900, Texas Centennial Exposition). Industry (general commerce, radio stations). Sports. Cityscape (street scenes). Religion (churches). Transportation (aviation, railroad).

Braniff Airlines.

PEOPLE: Many local residents, celebrities, and newsworthy persons living in or visiting the Dallas vicinity; few held in quantity.

Bill Boyd. President Dwight Eisenhower. Fred Florence. W. R. Hatcher. H. L. Hunt and family. President Lyndon Johnson. Margo Jones. Douglas MacArthur. Chester Nimitz. President Franklin and First Lady Eleanor Roosevelt. John Rosenfield. Schepps family. Lew Sterrett. President Harry Truman. Henry Wade.

PHOTOGRAPHERS: Most photographers are local commercial or journalist professionals working in the twentieth century.

Charles E. Arnold. Harry Bennett. Biggs. Clifton Church. Henry Clogenson. James Crittenden. J. T. Flynn. Andrew "Andy" Hanson. Squire Haskins. Hayes family (Denny, Durwood, Johnny).* John J. Johnson. William Langley. Lloyd M. Long. George McAfee.* J. C. McClure. C. W. Maloney. John Mazziotta. Frank Rogers.* Frank Townsend.*

*See Record Groups.

RECORD GROUPS: Collections containing few photographs include: Baker Hotel (PA85-25). Barrow Gang (PA83-10). Mary Bywaters (PA84-4). Cowan (PA85-34). Dr. Ruth Guy (PA83-26). Jeffus (PA85-31). Santerre and Cretien families (MA63-2). Shamburger Business School (MA84-12). Trotter family (PA85-29).

D30.1 *Art work of Dallas, Texas.* [Chicago:] W. H. Parish Company, 1895. 104 photogravures. Architecture, street scenes, homes, and landscapes. DPL# PA83-34.

D30.2 *Art work of Dallas, Texas.* Chicago: Gravure Illustration Company, 1910. 136 photogravures. Architecture, street scenes, homes, and landscapes. DPL# R917.64.

D30.3 *Art work of Dallas, Texas.* 1925. Architecture, street scenes, homes, and landscapes. Copy prints.

D30.4 BAKER HOTEL COLLECTION. Commercial views of the exterior and interior, including banquet halls, suites, ballrooms, and staff. 50 silver gelatin prints. 1925 to 1975. DPL# MA79-5.

D30.5 BIGGS (BUD) COLLECTION. Commercial artist working in watercolor and oil. Photographs used as reference for artworks; Love Field, businesses and buildings, most in Dallas. Made by various and unidentified photographers. 400 silver gelatin prints. 1918 to 1960s. DPL# PA84-9.

D30.6 CHILDREN'S MEDICAL CENTER COLLECTION. Originally known as the Dallas Baby Camp and later known as the Freeman Memorial Clinic and Bradford Children's Hospital. Documents buildings and activities of the center. 30 silver gelatin prints. 1910 to 1980.

D30.7 CHISUM (JOHN AND ETHELYN M.) COLLECTION. Black teachers in the Dallas Independent School District and civic leaders. Studio and snapshot portraits of Chisum family members; Ethelyn Chisum's student days at Prairie View A&M College. 100 photographs, including cartes and silver gelatin prints. DPL# MA83-5.

D30.8 Church, Clifton, photog. [*Dallas Free Kindergarten.*] Commercial views of indoor and outdoor student activities. 10 cyanotype prints. 1903.

D30.9 CITY PHOTOGRAPHER COLLECTION. Dallas views compiled by city staff photographers. Little Mexico; City of Dallas flag; fire and police protection services; field work and activities of the city's planning and health departments; Dallas Public Library activities and buildings; park department and parks; legal department; court services and activities; cityscapes, including architectural views and street scenes; public utilities. Photographers include James Crittenden and others. 1,500 vintage and copy negatives; 314 black-and-white and color slides; list. 1880s to the present. DPL# PA85-46.

D30.10 CLARK (LEWIS W.) COLLECTION. Family portraits. 4 tintypes; 43 prints, including cartes and cabinets. 1880s to 1900. DPL# PA85-37.

D30.11 Clogenson and Franz, photogs. *Souvenir of consecration of Rt. Rev. Joseph P. Lynch, D.D.* 1911. 12 silver gelatin prints. Commercial views of ceremonies at Sacred Heart Cathedral in Dallas; portraits of clergy. DPL# PA82-1.

D30.12 CRAFT (JUANITA) COLLECTION. Black Dallas city council member. Commercial views of Craft's activities on the council and with the NAACP; a few family photographs. 20 photographs. 1920s to 1980s. DPL# MA79-1.

D30.13 CROW (AUSTIN) COLLECTION. Texas Centennial Exposition in Dallas. 24 silver gelatin prints; visual index. 1936. DPL# PA83-1.

D30.14 CRUTCHER FAMILY COLLECTION. Prominent East Dallas family. Studio portraits. 50 photographs, including tintypes, cabinets, cartes, and silver gelatin prints. 1860s to 1940s. DPL# MA67-1.

D30.15 DALLAS ADVERTISING LEAGUE COLLECTION. League members at conventions and meetings. 15 silver gelatin prints. 1940 to 1965. DPL# MA82-10.

D30.16 DALLAS AMERICAN REVOLUTION BICENTENNIAL CORPORATION. Dallas lifestyle at turn of the century and during the nation's bicentennial year. 32 copy and 57 vintage color slides; register available. 1900 to 1930, 1976. Removed from DPL# PA76-2.

D30.17 DALLAS INDEPENDENT SCHOOL DISTRICT COLLECTION. Schools, teachers, and administrators of the district; segregated Caucasian and Black schools; school activities, including shop, gym, band classes and drills, sports, cheerleaders, and spirit groups. 600 silver gelatin prints. 1885 to present. Visual index. DPL# PA85-30, PA85-12.

D30.18 DALLAS MAYORS COLLECTION. Portraits of Dallas mayors A. Starke Taylor, Jack Evans, Robert Folsom, and Wes Wise. Photographed by James Crittenden. 29 silver gelatin and 2 color prints. 1885 to present. Visual index. DPL# PA85-24.

D30.19 *DALLAS MORNING NEWS* PHOTO MORGUE. Journalistic coverage of Dallas by staff photographers; wire photos of national and international subjects. 10 cubic feet silver gelatin prints. 1940s to 1965. DPL# PA83-42.

D30.20 DALLAS POLICE ARCHIVES. Mug shots of the Barrow Gang men, one snapshot of Bonnie Parker; police personnel, activities, and equipment. 41 silver gelatin prints. 1885 to 1985. DPL# PA83-10.

D30.21 DALLAS POWER AND LIGHT COLLECTION. Commercial views of the library, including staff, buildings, and equipment; commercial, publicity views of home exteriors decorated with Christmas lights. 1930s to 1950s. 200 silver gelatin prints. DPL# PA86-15.

D30.22 *DALLAS TIMES HERALD* PHOTO MORGUE. Journalistic coverage of Dallas by staff photographers; wire service photos of national and international subjects. 10 cubic feet silver gelatin prints. 1940s to 1965. DPL# PA84-41.

D30.23 ERWIN (JOHN B.) COLLECTION. Snapshots, buildings, and street scenes in Dallas. 30 copy photographs. Ca. 1914. DPL# PA83-37.

D30.24 FAIRCHILD AERIAL PHOTOGRAPHY COLLECTION. Aerial surveys of Dallas and surrounding area into East and Central Texas and southern Oklahoma. 400 composite silver gelatin prints and negatives. 1950s. DPL# PA83-32.

D30.25 FUCUALS (DONALD) COLLECTION. Snapshot views of Dallas. 21 silver gelatin prints. 1910s to 1930s. DPL# PA86-6.

D30.26 GERSHATER-RUDNITZKY FAMILY COLLECTION. Studio portraits, Workmen's Circle, and business interiors. 19 photographs. Ca. 1910 to 1920s. Visual index. DPL# PA85-26.

D30.27 HANSON (ANDY) COLLECTION. Journalistic coverage of Dallas, especially the desegregation of the Dallas Independent School District. Made for the *Dallas Times Herald* by staff photographers, including Hanson, John Mazziotta, James Crittenden, and 15 others. 5,000—35mm negatives. 1973 to 1975.

D30.28 HATCHER (W. R.) COLLECTION. Building of Fair Park Coliseum in 1909 by Hatcher's construction company; moving Lake Cliff Casino in 1911; street scenes, political rallies, picnics, and the Grand Kaliph parade in 1902. 40 silver gelatin prints. 1880 to 1920. Visual index. DPL# PA56-1.

D30.29 HAYES FAMILY (DURWOOD, DENNY, AND JOHNNY) COLLECTION. Father and his sons who contracted with the *Dallas Times Herald* for news photograph services. State fairs (1929-1954); Texas Centennial architecture; mayors and civic officials; street scenes; Love Field and aviation; parades; sports; society; public transit (horse-drawn trolleys); Clyde Barrow and Bonnie Parker; businesses; conventions; disasters (fires); auto wrecks; police documents of murders and crimes; H. L. Hunt; polio epidemic. 75,000 negatives. 1929 to 1976; most 1930s to 1950s. Hayes' original card index; visual index. DPL# PA76-1.

D30.30 HUECK (JOHN F. AND ALBINA; 1903?-1963) FAMILY PHOTOGRAPHS. Czech-American residents of Dallas. Hueck family, including studio and snapshot portraits; vacations to the Artesia Hotel in Marlin. 87 prints. 1880s to 1940s. DPL# PA85-36.

D30.31 INTERSTATE THEATER COLLECTION. Exterior views, some aerial photographs of Interstate movie houses. 100 silver gelatin prints. 1940 to 1955. Extensive business records; most photographs and publicity stills from this archive are housed at the Theater Arts Collection, Harry Ransom Humanities Research Center, University of Texas at Austin (q.v.). DPL# MA77-1.

D30.32 JONES (MARGO; 1913-1955) COLLECTION. Dallas theater producer, pioneer of arena staging. Portraits of Jones, playwrights, and actors; production stills from the Margo Jones Theater (= Dallas Civic Theater). 200 silver gelatin prints. 1945 to 1960. DPL# MA61-2.

D30.33 LONGMORE (FRED) COLLECTION. Snapshots of Longmore family; downtown and East Dallas. 200 silver gelatin prints. 1900 to 1950s, most from 1920s to 1950s. DPL# PA83-24.

D30.34 McAFEE (GEORGE A.) COLLECTION. Commercial photographer and photojournalist for the *Dallas Morning News*. Aviation; cityscapes, including night scenes; architecture in Dallas, including domestic and office interiors; Dallas Power and Light Company employees, offices, plant, and equipment; state fair exhibits; churches. 1900 to 1950. 800 silver gelatin prints. Visual index, list. DPL# PA78-3.

D30.35 McCOY (MILLICENT) COLLECTION. Descendant of Colonel John C. McCoy, an early Dallas citizen. McCoy family; commercial views of Dallas businesses and the city. 20 copy photographs (open collection). 1872 to 1950s. DPL# PA86-5.

D30.36 MALONEY COLLECTION. Family portraits and activities; scenes of Lake Cliff Park and travel views in Louisiana, Arkansas, and Texas. 76 silver gelatin prints. 1900 to 1940s. DPL# PA74-1.

D30.37 MAXVILL (CHARLIE B.) COLLECTION. Operated concession stands at Fair Park. Fair Park, concession stands, marathon dances, and miniature golf course. 22 silver gelatin prints. 1925 to 1955. DPL# PA86-3.

D30.38 MAZZIOTTA (JOHN) COLLECTION. Chief photographer for the *Dallas Times Herald*. Dallas Cowboys and Dallas Texans football teams; Texas Stadium. 20,000 photographs, including transparencies, color and black-and-white negatives; oral history transcript. 1962 to 1976. DPL# PA85-5.

D30.39 MIZZELL (CHARLES) COLLECTION. Streetcars, most of the Dallas Railway and Terminal Company, in street scenes, photographed by Mizzell. 27 silver gelatin prints. Mid-1940s to 1956.

D30.40 NEIMAN-MARCUS ARCHIVES. Exterior and interior views of stores; fashion shows; visiting dignitaries; business activities. 100 silver gelatin and color prints; 50 color slides. 1910 to present, most before 1975. DPL# MA 82-5.

D30.41 PEOPLES (CLINT) COLLECTION. County sheriff, Texas Ranger, and US marshal. Biographical portraits of Peoples' law enforcement career. 100 photographs, a few copy prints. 1930 to 1985 (open collection). DPL# PA84-11.

D30.42 PUBLIC SCHOOL REPORT COLLECTION. Dallas Independent School District buildings. 35 prints. 1924 to 1925. DPL# PA85-30.

D30.43 PULTE (BRETT) COLLECTION. Views in Dallas, including modern and postmodern architecture, outdoor sculpture, and the Southern Methodist University campus. 136—4x5 original negatives, 90 contact prints. DPL# PA85-2.

D30.44 RICHARDS GROUP COLLECTION. Mercantile Bank (Dallas), interiors and exteriors, promotions, operations. By Squire Haskins and unidentified photographer(s). 41 prints. 1950s. Visual index. DPL# PA83-3.

D30.45 ROGERS (FRANK) COLLECTION. Commercial photographer and staff photographer for the *Dallas Times Herald*, 1917 to 1929. Dallas during WW I, the Roaring Twenties, and the Depression, including prohibition raids, stills, and speakeasies; parades; Liberty Bond drives; fire protection services; cityscapes; architecture and construction; chamber of commerce officials; flagpole sitters and marathon dancers; the development of aviation in Dallas and Braniff airways. 1,332 original photographs, including 340 glass and 879 nitrate negatives, 113 vintage prints; modern prints of all negatives. Visual index; "photo printing form" provides coarse list of subjects. 1917 to 1946. DPL# PA78-2.

D30.46 ROSENFIELD (JOHN) COLLECTION. Musicians, including Belá Bartók, Jan Sibelius, and Van Cliburn; Dallas Symphony Orchestra; portraits of Rosenfield and others. 90 photographs, most prints, some negatives and slides; related manuscripts. 1938 to 1967. DPL# PA85-2.

D30.47 SAINT MARY'S COLLEGE COLLECTION. Commercial views of student life at the college. 17 silver gelatin prints. Ca. 1922. DPL# PA86-8.

D30.48 SANGER-HARRIS COLLECTION. In-store and window displays in the A. Harris Company. 35 glass negatives and modern prints. Ca. 1903. DPL# PA84-10.

D30.49 SCHMUCKER FAMILY COLLECTION. Dallas families and businesses. 31 prints. Ca. 1890 to 1910. DPL# PA85-17.

D30.50 SPARROW (DOROTHY) COLLECTION. Galveston cityscapes including beach scenes, beachfront hotels, boarding houses and residents, domestic architecture, parades, shipping, and the Battleship Texas. 92 copy negatives. 1900. DPL# PA84-3.

D30.51 THOMPSON AERIAL PHOTOGRAPHY COLLECTION. Aerial survey photographs. 2 feet of safety negatives. 1950s. DPA# PA83-29.

D30.52 TOWNSEND (H. FRANK) COLLECTION. Fair Park, cityscapes, and residences in Dallas. Photographed by Townsend. 188 film and 13 glass slides. 1950s. DPL# PA78-1.

D30.53 Townshend, S. Nugent; J. G. Hyde, photog. *Our Indian summer in the Far West: An autumn tour of fifteen thousand miles in Kansas, Texas, and the Indian Territory.* London: printed by Charles Whittingham, 1880. Amateur travel views of landscapes, railroads, Fort Elliot, and Guyemos Canyon NM. 59 albumen prints on mounts bound into textblock.

D30.54 TRINITY RIVER IMPROVEMENT ASSOCIATION. Trinity River with ships. 59 prints. 1899. DPL# PA83-19.

D30.55 WOHLFELD (NATHAN) COLLECTION. Architect. Buildings designed by Wohlfeld, including the YMCA building in Dallas and the Southern Pacific passenger station in Houston, both now demolished. 146 copy photographs; visual index. Ca. 1930s. DPL# PA82-4.

D30.56 ZONTA CLUBS OF DALLAS COLLECTION. Professional women's organization. Commercial views of luncheons; members, including some studio portraits. 20 silver gelatin prints. 1930s to present. DPL# MA84-22.

DeGolyer Library (D42)

Southern Methodist University
P.O. Box 396
Dallas, Texas 75275

214-692-3231. Contact: Curator of Manuscripts.

PURPOSE: A research, rare books, and special-collections library concentrating on the western US, history, industry, and railroads.

HOURS: Weekdays, 8:30-5:00. Closed major and academic holidays. An appointment is recommended.

ASSISTANCE: Professional staff. Written and phone inquiries available. Electrostatic copies available. Photoduplications available.

PUBLICATION: Publication fee. Collection credit required. Free copy of publication to library. Library holds copyright on most items.

FINDING AIDS: Card catalog; in-house published guides (v.i.); computerized database under development. Access by general subject heading, geographic location, photographer, personal name.

BIBLIOGRAPHY:
DeGolyer, E. L., Jr. *The track going back*. Fort Worth: Amon Carter Museum. Exhibition catalog.
Donaldson, J. Charles, III. *Dallas Morning News photographs: A guide to the collection*. Dallas: DeGolyer Library, Southern Methodist University, 1985.
Letson, Dawn. *A catalog of photograph accessions in the DeGolyer Library*. Dallas: DeGolyer Library, Southern Methodist University, 1982.
Worley, E. Dale. *Iron horses of the Santa Fe Trail*. Southwest Railroad History Society.

SCOPE: 260,000 original and 30,000 copy photographs, including several hundred stereographs, microfilm copies of photographs, and transparencies.

Type of photo	Pre-1880	1880-1899	1900-1919	1920-1939	1940-1959	1960-1986
D/A/T-types	5					
Glass negs	500	1,000	20,000	20,000		
Film negs			25,000	25,000	25,000	25,000
Vintage prints	200	800	6,000	6,000	26,000	26,000
Photo albums	5	15	25	25		

GEOGRAPHIC: Substantial coverage of the western US; many locales represented by railroad subjects only.

Foreign: Brazil. England. Germany. India. Mexico (Juárez, Saltillo). Russia. Scotland.

US: Western US. Alaska. Arizona. California. Colorado (Denver). Florida (Key West). Kansas (Horton). Louisana (New Orleans.) New York (New York City). Pennsylvania. Utah. Wyoming (Yellowstone).

Texas: Aransas Pass. Dallas. El Paso. Houston. San Antonio.

SUBJECTS: Headings used in the library include the West, railroad and transportation, industrial photographs, miscellaneous, and portrait. Foreign photographs with substantial coverage in all but the last two categories.

Agriculture (ranching). Architecture (churches, missions). Cityscapes. Industry (mining—coal, oil, steel mills). Military (battles, encampments, Mexican Revolution). Transportation (airplanes, bridges, railroads, ships—ocean liners, tunnels).

American Locomotive Company. Baldwin Locomotive Works. Chicago, Rock Island, and Western. Kansas Pacific Railroad. Pennsylvania Railroad.

PEOPLE: Amerinds, including Acoma, Laguna, Moquir, Taos, Thlinket, Ute, and Zuni.

Theodore Roosevelt. Francisco "Pancho" Villa.

PHOTOGRAPHERS: Eugene Bourquin. Everett Lee DeGolyer Jr. Lee DeGolyer III. James L. Ehrenberger. Robert Foster. W. O. Gibson. F. Jay Haynes. John K. Hillers. William Henry Jackson. R. W. Jennings. Robert Yarnell Richie. C. R. Savage. Richard Steinheimer. Gary Yantis.

RECORD GROUPS:

D42.1 BOURQUIN (EUGENE) COLLECTION. Horton, Kansas, scenes of small-town life in the Midwest and the Chicago, Rock Island, and Pacific Railroad. Photographed by Bourquin. 8 boxes and 2 volumes photo prints, glass negatives, and post cards. Ca. 1910 to 1914. DL# AG82/213, 213X, 213l, others.

D42.2 BUDNER (LAWRENCE AND DORIS) COLLECTION. Views of Theodore Roosevelt's western trip, the 1904 campaign, the 1905 inaugural, the postpresidential trip to Africa, Egypt, and London, the Panama Canal, the Naval Reunion, on the Mayflower, and the Portsmouth NH Peace Conference. Photographs published by Underwood and Underwood. 1,110 silver gelatin prints (not stereographs). 1903 to 1908. DL# AG86/590.

D42.3 COLORADO SUBJECT COLLECTION. An artificial collection of Colorado, arranged by location. Garden of the Gods, Pike's Peak, Georgetown, Silverton, Denver. Photographs by William Henry Jackson, J. Collier, J. F. Haynes, and C. R. Savage. 6 boxes albumen prints and stereographs. Most nineteenth century.

D42.4 *DALLAS MORNING NEWS* COLLECTION. From the files of the paper's photo morgue. The collection is categorized into architecture, the Belo Corporation, city views, disasters, events, Fair Park, government, interiors, portraits, transportation, and miscellaneous. 1,200 copy negatives and copy prints taken from microfilm of Dallas scenes. Most of these images are the only surviving copies of the originals. 1853 to 1939. See Bibliography—Donaldson.

D42.5 DeGOLYER (EVERETT LEE, Jr.) RAILROAD COLLECTION. Railroad cars and locomotives; most US railroads are represented, as are many foreign lines. Photographs by DeGolyer and by Lee DeGolyer III, James L. Ehrenberger, Robert Foster, W. O. Gibson, R. W. Jennings, and Richard Steinheimer. 70,000 film negatives and several thousand prints. Most twentieth century.

D42.6 PENNSYLVANIA RAILROAD COLLECTION. Scenery along the route, photographed by Frederick Gutekunst; construction of a 6-8-6 type steam turbine; an album that is a "collection of photographs of locomotives typical of each class . . . Standard Wheels, Axles, Brake Hangers and Shoes, Brass Cocks"; Hudson River and East River tunnels, Penn Station, and Sunnyside Yards in New York, Board Street railway station during and after a fire. 25 albums and 3 boxes. 1868 to 1944. DL# AG82/54X, AG82/95, AG82/121l, AG82/47, AG82/39, AG82/62, AG82/25.

D42.7 RICHIE (ROBERT YARNELL) INDUSTRIAL PHOTOGRAPH COLLECTION. Richie's archive of commercial, industrial photographs, including oil, auto, railroad, and other industries, US and foreign. 80,000 items, mostly negatives, some prints and 35mm film. 1932 to 1975. DL# AG82/234, AG81/10.

D42.8 STEINHEIMER (RICHARD) RAILROAD COLLECTION. Steinheimer's photographs of railroads, especially the Union Pacific and western US railroads. Other Steinheimer items are interfiled with E. L. DeGolyer Jr. Collection (v.s.). 5,000 negatives. 1950 to 1970. DL# AG82/233.

D42.9 YANTIS (GARY) COLLECTION. Commercial, itinerant photographer who traveled the state photographing children. Photographs include views of small Texas towns photographed by Yantis as a hobby during his trips. 3 boxes. DL# AG82/194.

University Archives (D76)

North Texas State University
P.O. Box 5188, NT Station
Denton, Texas 76203

817-565-2766. Contact: University Archivist.

PURPOSE: A history archive collecting manuscripts, many with photographs.

HOURS: Weekdays, 8:00-5:00. Closed major holidays and spring break in March.

ASSISTANCE: Professional staff. Written and phone inquiries accepted. Electrostatic copies not available. Photoduplications must be ordered through the archive.

PUBLICATION: No publication fee. Collection credit required.

FINDING AIDS: Card index and descriptive lists; indices to separate collections; access by general subject heading, geographic location, personal name.

BIBLIOGRAPHY:

Jordan, Terry G. *Texas log buildings: A folk architecture.* Austin: University of Texas Press, 1978.

Lavender, Linda; Cirrus Bonneau, photog. *Dog trots and mud cats: The Texas log house.* Denton: NTSU, 1979.

Rogers, James. *The Story of North Texas from Texas Normal, 1890 to North Texas State University, 1965.* Denton: NTSU, 1965.

SCOPE: 610,000 photographs, including 3,000 lantern slides; 1,100 motion pictures, including home movies and athletics films. Many photographs have associated manuscript materials. 1860s to 1985.

Type of photo	Pre-1880	1880-1899	1900-1919	1920-1939	1940-1959	1960-1986
D/A/T-types		15				
Glass negs				15		
Film negs					5,000	600,000
Vintage prints	25	85	250	400	500	200
Copy prints				50	900	1,100
Photo albums		3	4	20	25	20

GEOGRAPHIC: Denmark (Copenhagen). France (Paris). Ireland (Dublin). Panama (Canal Zone). Philippine Islands. Rumania (Bucharest).

US: Indiana. Maine. Nebraska. New Mexico. Texas. Wyoming.

Texas: Austin. Carrollton. Dallas. Denton. Garland. Lewisville. Mesquite. Nocona. Richardson. San Benito. Cameron, Dallas, Denton, and Montague counties.

SUBJECTS: Substantial coverage of all subjects, with extensive coverage of the university.

Academia. Agriculture (cattle). Architecture (domestic). Cityscapes. Events. Industry (general commerce). Landscapes. Military. Organizations (fraternal). Politics. Sports and amusements (basketball).

PEOPLE: Extensive coverage of the social life and customs of the university, including portraits of students, faculty, and staff.

Frank Cuellar Sr. Thomas Whitfield Davidson. Lloyd Garrison family. Alba Heywood. Judge Sarah T. Hughes. T. Bullock Hyder. A. B. Jolley. Enid Justin. O. S. Levis family. Fred H. Minor. Alvin M. Owsley family. Ruth Roach Salmon.

Filipino, Guatemalan, and Mexican indigenous cultures. Amerind.

PHOTOGRAPHERS: Cirrus Bonneau (see Bibliography—Lavender). H. S. Goodall (New Hampton IA). G. F. Lewis (Carthage NY). S. S. Richards (Carthage NY).

RECORD GROUPS:

D76.1 CUELLAR (FRANK, Sr.) COLLECTION. Mexican restaurants, including El Chico in the Southwest; family portraits. 175 photographs.

D76.2 DAVIDSON (THOMAS WHITFIELD) COLLECTION. Portraits. 50 photographs.

D76.3 GARRISON (LLOYD) COLLECTION. Fort Bliss showing military drills and equestrian jumping; Philippines and Philippinos. 100 photographs. 1920s.

D76.4 HEYWOOD (ALBA) COLLECTION. Crops of the San Benito Tract in the Rio Grande Valley. 75 photographs. 1908 to 1909.

D76.5 HUGHES (SARAH T.) COLLECTION. Federal judge who swore in Lyndon Johnson as president aboard Air Force 1. Portraits of Hughes and family, photographs documenting her political and judicial career. 225 photographs.

D76.6 HYDER (T. BULLOCK) COLLECTION. Portraits of Hyder and family. 50 photographs.

D76.7 JOLLEY (A. B.) COLLECTION. Most farms and farming methods in Dallas County, some portraits of Jolley and family. 350 photographs. 1920s to 1950s.

D76.8 JORDAN (TERRY) TEXAS LOG CABIN REGISTRY. Retrospective views of log cabins. 100 photographs. Ca. 1978. See Bibliography.

D76.9 JUSTIN (ENID) COLLECTION. Bootmaker. Bootmaking industry (Nocona Boots), some portraits of Justin and family. 225 photographs.

D76.10 MINOR (FRED H.) COLLECTION. Portraits of Minor and family, some photographs of political career and inauguration of Governor Ross Sterling. 150 photographs. 1930s.

D76.11 OWSLEY (ALVIN M.) COLLECTION. Portraits of Owsley and family, American Legion activities, including his National Commandership, and documenting his career as a US minister to Rumania, Irish Free State, and Denmark. 700 photographs. 1919 to 1964, most 1920s to 1930s.

D76.12 NTSU PUBLIC AFFAIRS AND INFORMATION SERVICES. Photographs of the university assembled by this agency. 600,000 negatives.

D76.13 SALMON (RUTH ROACH) COLLECTION. Portraits of Salmon, friends, and rodeo performances. 350 photographs. 1914 to 1934.

Southwest Collection (E40)

El Paso Public Library
501 North Oregon
El Paso, Texas 79901

915-541-4869. Contact: Head, Southwest Collection.

PURPOSE: A special-collections division of the public library focusing on regional history. Holdings include rare and recent books and periodicals, manuscripts, and vintage and copy photographs.

HOURS: Monday through Thursday, 8:30-9:00; Friday and Saturday, 8:30-5:30. Closed major holidays. Appointment recommended.

ASSISTANCE: Professional, experienced staff. Written and phone inquiries accepted. Electrostatic copies available. Study photoduplications may be made by patron; reproduction photoduplications must be ordered through the library.

PUBLICATION: No publication fee. Collection credit required. Third-party permission required on little material.

FINDING AIDS: Card file for Aultman collection; access by subject and proper name. General collection arranged by subject.

BIBLIOGRAPHY:

Binon, Charles H. *An introduction to El Paso's scenic and historic landmarks.* El Paso: Texas Western Press, 1970.

Metz, Leon C.; picture research by Mary Sarber. *City at the pass: An illustrated history of El Paso.* Woodland CA: Windsor Publications, 1980.

Sarber, Mary A. *Photographs from the border: The Otis A. Aultman collection.* El Paso: El Paso Public Library, 1977.

Sarber, Mary A. W. H. Horne and the Mexican War Photo Postcard Company. *Password* 31(1):5-15 (Spring 1986).

SCOPE: 20,000 vintage negatives and prints; 5,000 copy prints. Associated manuscripts for some collections.

Type of photo	Pre-1880	1880-1899	1900-1919	1920-1939	1940-1959	1960-1986
Glass negs			2,000	1,000		
Film negs			2,000	3,000	1,000	1,000
Vintage prints	20	300	350	350	1,000	1,000
Copy prints						
Photo albums		1	2	2	5	

GEOGRAPHIC: Major emphasis is on the US Southwest and Northern Mexico, with extensive coverage of the El Paso and Juarez vicinity.

Mexico (Chihuahua, Cd Juárez). New Mexico. West Texas (El Paso, Hueco Tanks).

SUBJECTS: Extensive coverage of economic and social development of El Paso. See Record Groups—Aultman Archive for additional subjects.

Architecture (Henry C. Trost buildings, interiors). Landscape (arid). Military (Fort Bliss, Mexican Revolution, Pershing's Punitive Expedition). Plants (desert). Sports and amusements (rodeo).

PEOPLE: El Paso vicinity residents; most of Caucasian or Hispanic ethnicity, some Mescalero Apache Amerinds; few held in quantity.

PHOTOGRAPHERS: The collection attempts to obtain samples by all professional photographers who have worked in the El Paso vicinity. See Record Groups—Mexican Revolution Postcard Collection for additional photographers.

Jim Alexander (= LX and R). Alexander and Green. Otis A. Aultman.* Oscar C. Bernard. Charles H. Binon.* Harry Blumenthal.* J. C. Burge. Bushong. Bushong and Feldman. A. Casasola. Fred Feldman. Gerlach.* Karl Holm. Walter Henry Horne. Frank Hunter.* Earl Raymond McCracken.* Metcalfe. Francis Parker. E. S. Plumb.* W. D. Smithers. W. F. Stuart. Edgar Tobin.* James W. Ward.

*See Record Groups.

RECORD GROUPS: Frequently arranged under the headings El Paso, the Southwest, Mexico, and Portraits.

E40.1 *Alcazar de Velasco.* Snapshot portraits of Alcazar. 59 silver gelatin prints. 1930s?

E40.2 AULTMAN (OTIS A.; 1874-1943) ARCHIVE. El Paso commercial photographer. Photographs arranged under the headings El Paso, Mexico and the Mexican Revolution, the Southwest, and Portraits.

E40.2.1 Aultman—El Paso: Academia (public, private, Loretto School, Texas Western University). Agriculture (ranching, stockyards). Architecture (business exteriors—Herald Building, —Federal Building, —Southern Pacific buildings, —El Paso County Courthouse, —Masonic Building, —White House [department store], domestic, theaters—Alahambra). Cityscapes (land divisions, parks—San Jacinto Plaza, Pioneer Plaza, Smeltertown, street scenes). Events (parades, rodeos, Theodore Roosevelt in El Paso in 1911). Industry (banks—American National, —City National, —Commercial National, mills, saloons, smelting). Military (Fort Bliss, Mexican Revolution, military reviews, Pershing Expedition). Organizations (Masons, McGinty Club). Politics (Taft-Diaz meeting). Religion (by denomination, Loretto chapel). Services (fire protection, hotels—Grand Central, —Orndorff, —Sheldon, hospitals, law enforcement). Transportation (automobiles, aviation, railroads—Southern Pacific). Sports and amusements (baseball, cinemas). 1,500 images.

E40.2.2 Aultman—Mexico: Cd Chihuahua and cathedral; Cd Juarez, customs house, municipal building, commercial buildings, Mission Guadalupe, gambling, race trace; Mormon refugees. 250 images.

E40.2.3 Aultman—Mexican Revolution: Agua Prieta, artillery and explosives; battle scenes; rebel camps; Cd Chihuahua; dead and executions; Federales; Cd Juarez; machine guns; newsmen and photographers; Peace Commission of 1911; railroad and sabotage; Red Cross; refugees; women helpers; wounded. 250 images. Aultman—Portraits (v.i.) lists individuals.

E40.2.4 Aultman—Portraits: Many individuals; few held in quantity. General Emilio Campa. Delio Molina Canton. General Manuel Chao. Governor Oscar Branch Colquitt. Giuseppe Garibaldi. John S. Hart. Secretary Braulio Hernandez. General Victoriano Huerta. C. E. Henry Kelley. President Francisco I. Madera Jr. and family. General Pascual Orozco Jr. President Theodore Roosevelt. General José Inez Salazar. Major General Hugh L. Scott. Katherine Stinson. President Taft. General Venustiano. Francisco "Pancho" Villa. 3,000 images.

E40.2.5 Aultman—Southwest: Tucson AZ. Cloudcroft and Columbus NM. Elephant Butte. Agriculture (cattle, stockyards). Amerinds (Geronimo, Apache). Archaeology (petroglyphs). Architecture (Trost and Trost buildings). Military (camps, cavalry, forts, infantry, Pershing's Punitive Expedition, rail transport, WW I). Religion (missions).

6,000 film negatives, with modern prints. See Bibliography—Sarber.

E40.3 AUTOMOBILE COLLECTION. Compiled by Kopf. Automobiles from ca. 1900 to 1940s, including auto showrooms, product shots on the street, and engines; Lone Star Motor Company. Made in El Paso. 400 silver gelatin prints. 1920s to 1940s.

E40.4 BINION (CHARLES H.; b. 1937) COLLECTION. Fine art photographer working in a straight style trained at the New York School of Photography. Landscapes, including Hueco Tanks; architecture, including modern views of historical structures, the Brooklyn Bridge, and the Presidio County courthouse. 400—8x10 film negatives; 100—5x7 film negatives; 495—4x5 film negatives; 1,000 exhibition quality prints. See Bibliography.

E40.5 BLUMENTHAL (HARRY) COLLECTION. Commercial photographer in El Paso. Architecture and business exteriors; railroad insurance documents; speakeasy; product photographs and window displays; billboards; WW II domestic front; funerals, gravesites, and corpses in caskets; stockyards; wedding portraits; group portraits of organizations. 73—8x10 glass negatives, 1,081—8x10 film negatives, 47—5x7 film negatives, 63 copy negatives, 55 silver gelatin prints. 1920s to 1940s.

E40.6 DOUGLAS, ARIZONA COLLECTION. Amateur or commercial views; parade, military review, and auto race in Douglas AZ; Mexican Revolution in Agua Prieta. 100 silver gelatin prints. Ca. 1911.

E40.7 *El Paso photographic history: Volume one, public buildings, business blocks, churches, banks, hotels, and theaters.* El Paso: L. D. Hicks, 1909. Commercial cityscapes. 100 silver gelatin prints.

E40.8 *El Paso photographic history: Volume two, parks, street scenes, and Rio Grande views.* El Paso: L. D. Hicks, 1909. Commercial cityscapes. 85 silver gelatin prints.

E40.9 FIRST INFANTRY IN SAN ANTONIO. Camp scenes, personnel, and social life and customs. 25 silver gelatin prints. 1917.

E40.10 GENERAL COLLECTION—EL PASO. Economic and social development, 1880s to present, including academia, businesses, churches, city government, cityscapes, county sheriffs, fire protection, Fort Bliss, hospitals, and hotels; El Paso Public Library institutional photographs and Carnegie Library building; modern views of historical structures; police protection; ASARCO smelter; theaters; Harry Truman's visit; Ysleta Mission and Ysleta. 2 feet (500 leaves) silver gelatin prints; some color 35mm transparencies. 1870s to present.

E40.11 GENERAL COLLECTION—MEXICO. Catholic churches, Juarez, Mexican Revolution. 9 inches (200 leaves) silver gelatin prints. 1900 to 1940s.

E40.12 GENERAL COLLECTION—PORTRAITS. Many area residents; few held in quantity. 16 inches (350 leaves) silver gelatin prints. 1900 to present.

E40.13 GENERAL COLLECTION—SOUTHWEST. Christo Rey monument, Hueco Tanks, Tigua Amerinds, landscapes, Pershing's Punitive Expedition, and White Sands Missle Range. 1 foot (250 leaves) silver gelatin prints, some color material. 1900 to present.

E40.14 GERLACH COLLECTION. Commercial photographer. Cityscapes and business exteriors, group portraits, and landscapes in El Paso and vicinity photographed by Gerlach. 500—4x5 and 200—8x10 film negatives, many nitrate; envelopes with manuscript notes. Ca. 1945.

E40.15 HEWITT COLLECTION. Amateur travel views of China, Japan, and India, including Canton, the Forbidden City, Nikko, Yokohama, and Delhi. 175 silver gelatin prints. 1923.

E40.16 HOARD (L. ROY; b. 1887?) COLLECTION. Operated lumber company at Madera, Mexico, and later was president of the Mexico Northwestern Railroad. Snapshots and commercial views of train wrecks and sabotage along the Mexico Northwestern Railroad; Oriente Railroad.

> **E40.16.1** Hoard, L. Roy, comp. *Scenes along the Mexico Northwestern Railway and around the plants of the Madera Company Ltd.* "Practically all wrecks and destruction shown are directly or indirectly caused by Revolutionary or bandit activity." Madera lumber mill; Pearson lumber mill; train derailments and sabotage; some probably by Aultman. 139 silver gelatin prints. 1911 to 1919.

E40.16.2 *Juarez Mexico: Revolution led by Madero.* Juarez, including street scenes, bullfights, and troops. 65 silver gelatin snapshot prints. 1910 to 1920s.

E40.16.3 [*Pearson Mills album.*] Lumber mill physical plant, store, and company town, including school, hospital, hotel, and town social life and customs; at Pearson (possibly a Mormon settlement or mill operated by MNWRR in Chihuahua, Mexico). 65 silver gelatin prints. 1900 to 1910.

E40.16.4 *Views of F.C.N.O. de M. and adjacent territory: Mr. Walter Gow.* Commercial views of landscapes in the Black Canyon, Sahuaripa, and in the Rio Aros valley and of lumber mills and camps; some snapshots of Mexican Revolution. 233 silver gelatin prints. 1900 to 1910.

100 silver gelatin prints; 4 albums (v.s.); associated manuscripts. 1900 to 1920s.

E40.17 HORNE (WALTER HENRY) POSTCARD COLLECTION. Mexican Revolution, especially in Columbus NM, including refugees; Fort Bliss; US Army Camps, US Army parades, military reviews, portraits of military and political leaders, and Pershing's Punitive Expedition; El Paso cityscapes; Juarez street scenes; desert landscapes; Hueco Tanks; rodeos and Wild West shows. 400 silver gelatin postcard prints; associated manuscripts. 1910 to 1920.

E40.18 HUNTER (FRANK) COLLECTION. Panoramic views of El Paso's west side. 40 silver gelatin prints. 1981 to 1982.

E40.19 McCRAKEN (EARL RAYMOND) COLLECTION. Traffic manager for Western Union and amateur photographer. Street life in downtown El Paso; zoo; family portraits and vacations.

E40.19.1 McCraken, Earl Raymond, photog. [*El Paso scenes.*] Amateur views of El Paso street life. 71 silver gelatin prints, 13—35mm film negative strips. 1950s to 1960s.

E40.19.2 McCraken, Earl Raymond, photog. [*Vacation album I.*] Amateur travel views of Mexico, possibly Chihuahua. 70 silver gelatin prints. 1950s.

E40.19.3 McCraken, Earl Raymond, photog. [*Vacation album II.*] Amateur travel views of Mazatlán, Mexico. 43 silver gelatin prints, 9 color prints. 1969.

E40.19.4 McCraken, Earl Raymond, comp. [*Western Union album.*] History of McCraken's employment with Western Union; telegraph equipment, personnel, offices. 225 silver gelatin prints. 1918 to 1968.

1,000—120 film negatives, 1,500—35mm negative strips; 500 silver gelatin prints; some color; 4 albums (v.s.). 1918 to ca. 1970; most 1960s.

E40.20 McGAW COLLECTION. Commercial views of El Paso and vicinity, including street scenes, architecture, and some landscape; of Sacramento Mountains, Cloudcroft, Deming, and Tularosa NM; of lumber operations by Alamagordo Lumber Company; of landscapes in forested mountains, deserts and desert plants; of Southern Pacific and Sacramento Mountain and Alamagordo railroads; and of Mescalero Amerinds. Photographers include Jim A. Alexander (= LX and R), Karl Holm, Metcalfe, and unidentified others. 1,200 photo negatives, including 8x10 and whole-plate glass negatives, 4x5 film negatives, and 5 cirkut negatives. Ca. 1900 to 1930s.

E40.21 MEXICAN REVOLUTION POSTCARD COLLECTION. Arranged by photographer, including J. A. Alexander, H. J. Gutierrez, F. C. Hecox, Hill, D. W. Hoffman, Karl Holm, Lane, Morris, J. T. Neville, Cal Osborn, Osuna, W. F. Stuart, and unidentified photographer(s). 320 silver gelatin postcard prints. 1910 to 1920.

E40.22 Plumb, E. S., photog. *Pictures taken in and around Chihuahua Mexico.* Amateur views of cityscapes, religious festivals, and architecture. 72 gelatino-chloride prints. Winter, 1904.

E40.23 PONSFORD-TROST COLLECTION.   Commercial exterior and interior views of buildings designed by the architectural firm of Trost and Trost. 675 silver gelatin prints; some renderings and plans. 1920s to 1940s.

E40.24 SMITHERS (W. D.; 1895-1951) COLLECTION. Copy of Smithers' inventory for his archive located at the University of Texas at Austin, HRHRC, Photography Collection (q.v.). The library holds a number of Smithers' prints scattered throughout various collections as well as some of Smithers' manuscripts.

E40.25 TOBIN (EDGAR) AERIAL SURVEYS. San Antonio aerial photographer. Guadalupe Peak and McKittrick Canyon. 24 silver gelatin prints. 1940s.

E40.26 *Tour of the World.* Meadeville PA: Keystone Views Company, [1920s]. 200 stereographs.

E40.27 ZINGG (ROBERT) COLLECTION. Anthropologist at the University of Texas at El Paso noted for his studies of the Tarahumara Amerinds. Snapshot vacation views, including landscapes and city scenes, possibly Mexico; Tarahumara Amerinds; churches in New Mexico and southern Colorado. 1,000 film negatives, many nitrate. Ca. 1929.

El Paso Centennial Museum (E60)

University of Texas at El Paso
Wiggins Road and University Avenue
El Paso, Texas 79968

915-747-5565. Contact: Curator.

PURPOSE: A history and anthropology museum collecting books and journals, manuscripts, two- and three-dimensional art works, artifacts, natural history specimens, and photographs.

HOURS: Exhibits—Tuesday through Friday, 10:00-4:30, Sunday, 1:30-5:30.   Reserve collections—weekdays, 8:00-5:00; appointment required. Closed major and university holidays.

ASSISTANCE: Professional staff. Written and phone inquiries accepted. Electrostatic copies available. Photoduplications must be ordered through the museum.

PUBLICATION: Publication fee. Collection credit required. Free copy of publication to museum.

FINDING AIDS: Partial inventory and itemized listing; access by donor and acquisition.

SCOPE: 2,500 photo prints and negatives, 3,000 film transparencies, and other formats, including stereographs, panoramic prints, and lantern slides.

Type of photo	Pre-1880	1880-1899	1900-1919	1920-1939	1940-1959	1960-1986
D/A/T-types		5				
Glass negs		550				
Film negs			50	300	100	50
Vintage prints				600	200	100
Copy prints			100	100	50	
Photo albums			5	10		

GEOGRAPHIC: Substantial coverage of Mexico and the US Southwest, including Texas, New Mexico, and Arizona. Extensive coverage of El Paso; some coverage of Chihuahua and Juarez, Mexico, and Santa Fe NM.

SUBJECTS: Academia. Agriculture. Animals. Architecture. Artifacts (furniture). Cityscapes. Costumes. Events. Government. Industry (industrial relations). Landscapes. Military (personnel). Monuments. Organizations. Politics. Religion. Science (ethnographic, archaeological). Transportation. Weapons.

PEOPLE: Ethnic (Amerinds—Tarahumara, Huichol, Hispanic-Americans, Chinese). Domestic activities. Personal activities. Social life and customs.

PHOTOGRAPHERS: Ben Wittick. Robert Zingg.

RECORD GROUPS:

E60.1 WITTICK (GEORGE BEN; 1845-1903) COLLECTION. Photographs made by Wittick in southwestern and northern Mexico and New Mexico, including many portraits of Amerinds and soldiers. 600 vintage glass negatives and lantern slides. 1878 to 1898.

E60.2 ZINGG (ROBERT) COLLECTION. Tarahumara and Huichol Indians of Mexico and archaeological work in Mexico photographed by Zingg. 400 film negatives and 250 photo prints. 1920 to 1940.

Fort Davis National Historic Site (F14)

Highways 17 and 118
P.O. Box 1456
Fort Davis, Texas 79734

915-426-3225. Contact: Superintendent.

PURPOSE: Fort Davis was an active military post from 1854 to 1891. The site collects manuscripts, artifacts, and photographs pertinent to its history. A division of the US Department of the Interior, National Park Service.

HOURS: Daily 8:00-5:00; Memorial Day through Labor Day, until 6:00. Closed New Year's and Christmas. Appointment recommended for use of reserve collections. Admission fee.

ASSISTANCE: Experienced, specialized, professional staff. Written and phone inquiries accepted. Electrostatic copies available. Photoduplications may be made by patron or ordered through the site.

PUBLICATION: No publication fee. Collection credit required. Third-party permission required on a few items.

FINDING AIDS: Descriptive listing of photographs; access by general subject heading, geographic location, photographer, personal name, and date.

SCOPE: 2,200 vintage and 5,000 copy photographs. 1860s to the present.

Type of photo	Pre-1880	1880-1899	1900-1919	1920-1939	1940-1959	1960-1986
D/A/T-types	5	5				
Glass negs		15	100			
Film negs			50	50	2,000	2,000
Vintage prints	100	50	100	100	100	1,500
Copy prints	25	25	100	100	1,000	500
Photo albums	2	1	5			

GEOGRAPHIC: Fort Davis vicinity and the Davis Mountains.

SUBJECTS: Architecture (military). Events (Indian Wars). Military (cavalry, encampments, life and culture, personnel).

PEOPLE: Social life and customs around the fort. Studio portraits. Ethnic groups include Amerinds, Blacks, and Caucasians.

RECORD GROUPS:

F14.1 GRIERSON (BENJAMIN H.) FAMILY PAPERS. Commanding officer of the fort from 1882 to 1885. Family photographs, including studio portraits, although few, if any, were made during Grierson's tenure at the fort. 300 photographs, most prints, including cartes. 1840s to early twentieth century.

F14.2 NATIONAL PARK SERVICE PHOTOGRAPHS. Documents of the condition and restoration of the fort. 1,500 photographs. After 1960.

F14.3 OFFICERS AND ENLISTED MEN COLLECTION. Group portraits made outdoors of the military personnel of the fort and the fort itself; incorrectly ascribed to Mersfelder at one time. 12—8x10 glass negatives. Ca. 1884.

F14.4 VIEWS OF FORT DAVIS COLLECTION. Documents the period between the US Army occupation and ownership by the National Park Service. 300 photographs. 1891 to 1960.

First Cavalry Division Museum (F18)

United States Army
Building 2218, Headquarters Avenue
P.O. Box 5187
Fort Hood, Texas 76544

817-287-4198 or 287-3626. Contact: Museum Technician.

PURPOSE: An institutional museum documenting the history of the First Cavalry Division from 1921 to the present.

HOURS: Weekdays, 9:00-3:30; weekends, 12:00-3:30. Closed major and federal holidays. Appointment recommended for use of reserve collections.

ASSISTANCE: Professional staff. Written and phone inquiries accepted on a limited basis. Electrostatic copies available. Photoduplications must be ordered through the museum.

PUBLICATION: No publication fee. Collection credit required. Few items require third-party permission.

FINDING AIDS: Inventory, descriptive listing, and card index; access by personal and proper name, geographic location, date, and photographer.

SCOPE: 2,000 vintage and 19,000 copy photos, including panoramic prints, lantern slides, and film transparencies.

Type of photo	Pre-1880	1880-1899	1900-1919	1920-1939	1940-1959	1960-1986
D/A/T-types		3				
Glass negs			20			
Film negs				1,000	6,000	3,000
Vintage prints	75	75	450	375	600	900
Copy prints	75	375	1,500	4,000	2,000	1,500

GEOGRAPHIC: Areas where the First Cavalry Division has seen military action, including the Admiralty Islands, Australia, Japan, Korea, Mexico, Philippines, and Vietnam, and in the US, Louisiana, Oklahoma, South Dakota, and Wyoming. Texas locales include Central, South, and West Texas. El Paso (Fort Bliss). Fort Hood. Killeen. Marfa. San Antonio.

SUBJECTS: Activities of the First Cavalry Division with broad coverage of cavalry soldiers on maneuvers, training, and the social life and customs of military life; also included are a few combat scenes from the various wars in which the cavalry has seen action.

Military (cavalry, combat, maneuvers; Korean War, Pershing's Punitive Expedition, Vietnam, WW II). Social life and customs (military).

PEOPLE: Prominent military figures in the US Army, especially those connected with the First Cavalry Division; most other members of the division are represented but may not be identified.

Major General William C. Chase. General George A. Custer. Brigadier General Hugh F. T. Hoffman. General Douglas MacArthur.

PHOTOGRAPHERS: US Army Signal Corps.

RECORD GROUPS: Photographs are arranged as a single artificial collection as described above.

Amon Carter Museum (F34)

3501 Camp Bowie Boulevard
P.O. Box 2365
Fort Worth, Texas 76113

817-738-1933. Contact: Curator of Photographs.

PURPOSE: An exhibiting, fine art museum with a secondary emphasis on historical subjects, specializing in American and Western subjects. The museum holds extensive exhibition and reserve collections in all media and maintains a research library.

HOURS: Exhibition area—Tuesday through Saturday, 9:00-5:00; Sunday, 1:00-5:30. Reserve collections—weekdays, 9:00-5:00; appointment required. Closed major holidays.

ASSISTANCE: Professional, experienced staff. Staff assistance required. Written inquiries accepted; phone inquiries accepted as staff time permits. Electrostatic copies available.

PUBLICATION: Publication fee charged. Photoduplications must be ordered through the museum and must be placed in writing. Collection credit required. Free copy of publication to museum. Third-party permission required on some materials, especially twentieth-century images.

FINDING AIDS: Extensive, descriptive catalog by Carol Elaine Roark (forthcoming 1987); access by photographer. Mazzulla, Brininstool, Everhard, Struss, and Texas Architectural Survey collections have separate catalogs; complete in-house inventory; partial published catalog; computerized catalog under development.

BIBLIOGRAPHY:

Avedon, Richard. *In the American West.* New York: Abrams, 1985.

Benrimo, Dorothy, photog.; with commentary by Rebecca S. James. *Camposantos.* Fort Worth: Amon Carter Museum, 1966.

Bones, Jim, photog. *Texas west of the Pecos.* College Station: Texas A&M Press, 1981.

Clark, Ann. *Brave against the evening.* Lawrence KS: US Department of Interior BIA, 1943.

Current, William R., photog.; text by Vincent Scully. *Pueblo architecture of the Southwest: A photographic essay.* Austin: University of Texas Press for the Amon Carter Museum, 1971.

De Cock, Liliane, photog.; foreword by Ansel Adams. *Liliane De Cock, photographs.* Hastings-on-Hudson NY: Morgan and Morgan in cooperation with the Amon Carter Museum, 1973.

DeGolyer, Everett Lee, Jr. *The track going back: A century of transcontinental railroading.* Fort Worth: Amon Carter Museum, 1969.

Gardner, Alexander; new introduction by E. F. Bleiler. *Gardner's photographic sketch book of the Civil War.* New York: Dover, 1959 (1st reprint).

Gilpin, Laura, photog. *The enduring Navaho.* Austin: University of Texas Press, 1968.

Gilpin, Laura, photog. *The Pueblos: A camera chronicle.* New York: Hastings House, 1941.

Gilpin, Laura, photog. *The Rio Grande: River of destiny.* New York: Duell, Sloan and Pearce, 1949.

Gilpin, Laura, photog. *Temples in Yucatan: A camera chronicle of Chichén Itzá.* New York: Hastings House, 1948.

LaFarge, Oliver, photog. *As long as the grass shall grow.* New York: Alliance Book, 1940.

Lange, Dorothea, photog; introduction by Beaumont Newhall. *Dorothea Lange looks at the American country woman.* Fort Worth and Los Angeles: Amon Carter Museum and the Ward Ritchie Press, 1967.

Lemann, Nicholas. *Out of the forties.* Austin: Texas Monthly Press, 1984.

McQuaid, James, and Paulette Privitera Wilson, eds. *Index to American photographic collections.* Boston: G. K. Hall, 1981.

Mazzulla, Fred, and Jo Mazzulla. *Brass checks and red lights: Being a pictorial potpourri of historical prostitutes, parlor houses, professors, procuresses and pimps.* Denver: 1966.

Mazzulla, Fred, and Jo Mazzulla. *The first one hundred years: A photographic account of the rip-roaring, gold-plated days in world's greatest gold camp . . . in the Cripple Creek and Pike's Peak region.* Denver: A. B. Hirschfeld Press, 1964.

Muskat, Beth T. *An inventory of the Mazzulla collection.* Fort Worth: Amon Carter Museum, 1980. Typescript.

Mydans, Carl, photog., and Philip Kundhardt. *Carl Mydans: Photojournalist.* New York: Abrams, 1985.

Newhall, Beaumont, and Diana E. Edkins. *William H. Jackson.* Dobbs Ferry NY: Morgan and Morgan, in conjunction with the Amon Carter Museum, 1974.

Newhall, Beaumont, and Nancy Newhall. *T. H. O'Sullivan, photographer.* Rochester NY: George Eastman House and Amon Carter Museum, 1966.

Palmquist, Peter E.; introduction by Martha A. Sandweiss. *Carleton E. Watkins, photographer of the American West*. Albuquerque NM: University of New Mexico Press for the Amon Carter Museum, 1983.

Phillips, David R., ed. *The West: An American experience*. Chicago: A&W Visual Library by arrangement with Henry Regnery Company, 1973.

Phillips, David R., ed. *The West: A photographic perspective*. Chicago: Henry Regnery Company, 1973.

Sandweiss, Martha A. *Carlotta Corpron, designer with light*. Austin: University of Texas Press for the Amon Carter Museum, 1980.

Sandweiss, Martha A. *Laura Gilpin: An enduring grace*. Fort Worth: Amon Carter Museum, 1986.

Sandweiss, Martha A. *Masterworks of American photography, the Amon Carter Museum collection*. Birmingham AL: Oxmoor House, 1982.

Sandweiss, Martha A., Roy Flukinger, and Anne W. Tucker, eds.; introduction by Stephen Harrigan. *Contemporary Texas: A photographic portrait*. Austin: Texas Monthly Press, 1985.

Webb, Todd, photog.; text by Drury Blakeley Alexander. *Texas Homes of the nineteenth century*. Austin: University of Texas Press for the Amon Carter Museum, 1966.

Webb, Todd, photog.; text by Willard Robinson. *Texas public buildings of the nineteenth century*. Austin: University of Texas Press in cooperation with Amon Carter Museum, 1974.

Webb, Todd, photog.; introduction by Beaumont Newhall. *Todd Webb photographs: Early western trails and some ghost towns*. Fort Worth: Amon Carter Museum, 1965.

Weston, Brett, photog.; introduction by Nancy Newhall. *Brett Weston, photographs*. Fort Worth: Amon Carter Museum, 1966.

SCOPE: 250,000 photographs, including photographs in major processes as well as stereographs, published books with vintage photo prints tipped in, and portfolios. The research library holds facsimile editions of *Camera Works* and *Camera Notes* and microfilm copies of major nineteenth-century photographic journals, and maintains subscriptions to current photographic journals. 1840s to present.

Type of photo	Pre-1880	1880-1899	1900-1919	1920-1939	1940-1959	1960-1986
D/A/T-types	100	80	1			
Glass negs	7,500	12,500	10,000	3,000		
Film negs			5,000	10,000	7,500	7,500
Vintage prints	10,000	10,000	10,000	10,000	4,000	4,000
Copy prints	4,500	4,500	1,500	1,500		
Photo albums	10	30	20	20	3	

GEOGRAPHIC: Yucatan, Mexico. United States with extensive coverage of the western US, including Arizona, California, Colorado, eastern Kansas, New Mexico, and Oklahoma (including its organization as Indian Territory). Substantial coverage of Texas, including Buda, Clifton, Fort Worth, and Tomball.

SUBJECTS: Major emphasis is on fine art in all styles and the westward expansion and urban development of the US, with a secondary emphasis on documentary photography.

Architecture (retrospective views of historic structures). Cityscapes. Landscapes. Military (Civil War, Mexican War, Texas Rangers, US military). Photography (fine art, Pictorialism, Photo-Secession, survey). Sport and amusement (hunting). Surveying. Transportation (railroad).

PEOPLE: Many art portraits; few individuals held in quantity. Some coverage of Navaho and Southwest Plains Amerinds.

PHOTOGRAPHERS: Emphasis is on works by American photographers or American subjects, including US Geological Survey photographers, photographic artists, and women photographers. Quantities marked without a note symbol indicate loose prints not described in Record Groups. Absence of quantity or note indicates a single print. See also Record Groups—Fine Arts Photography—Stereographs for additional photographers.

Berenice Abbott (7/a). Ansel Adams (ac). Robert Adams (4). Manuel Alvarez Bravo (4/c). John A. Anderson (e). Paul Anderson. Lee Angle. Diane Arbus. Dick Arentz. Frank Armstrong (1/b). Francois Aubert. Richard Avedon (a). Morley Baer (2). Fred Baldwin/Wendy Watriss (b). George Barker. George N. Barnard (4). Bruce Barnbaum (7). Felix Beato (10). Lorenzo Becerril (d). John Beck (6). Charles Bell (e). William Bell (1/d). Dorothy Benrimo (a). Ruth Bernhard. Ronald Binks (b). Renny Blackstone. Gay Block (b). Ave Bonar (b). Howard Bond (2). Jim Bones (1/ab). W. Hanson Boorne. Alice Boughton (2). Margaret Bourke-White (2). Mathew Brady studio (2). Talbot M. Brewer. Annie Brigman. A. Bríquet (d). Esther Bubley (b). Clarence Sinclair Bull. John G. Bullock. Wynn Bullock (7). John Burris (5). Carol Cohen Burton (b).

J. E. Cakebread (3). Harry Callahan (4). Paul Caponigro (4/c). W. J. Carpenter (e). Keith Carter (3). Gary Cawood (b). Larry Clark. James Atkins Clayton. William Clift (4/c). Alvin Langdon Coburn (4). John Collier Jr. (b). Joseph Collier (e). Will Connell. Linda Connor. Carlotta M. Corpron (a). Harold Corsini (b). Imogene Cunningham (6). William R. Current (a). Edward S. Curtis (7/d). Dean Dablow (b). Bill Dane. C. M. Davis (e). Jim Day (2). Geri Della Rocca De Candal (5). Liliane De Cock (8). Adelaide De Menil (13). Detroit Publishing Company (41). Rita DeWitt (b). Rick Dingus. William Dinwiddie (e). Wesley Disney (2). Robert Disraeli. Nell Dorr. Henry B. DuPont (a).

Thomas Eakins. Michael Eastman. Tom Eckstrom. Harold Edgerton (4). John Paul Edwards (a). Morris Engel (a). C. W. Erdlen (e). Elliott Erwitt (c). Ron Evans. Walker Evans (9). G. R. Fardon. J. Fennemore (2). Phyllis Fenner. Peter Feresten (b). Jim Ferguson. George Fiske (13e). Steve Fitch. W. Grancel Fitz. Egbert Guy Fowx. Douglas Frank. Robert Frank (22).

Oliver Gagliani. Alexander Gardner (3/d). William Garnett (2). Rick Gast (b). Arnold Genthe (5). Henry Gilpin. Laura Gilpin (a). Frank Gohlke (b). John C. H. Grabill (5). Sid Grossman. Paul Grotz. John Gutmann (2). Philippe Halsman (1/c). Wanda Hammerbeck. Goodwin Harding. John Harkey (2). Frank Jay Haynes (28/d). Richard E. Haynes (b). E. E. Henry (e). Shel Hershorn. Paul Hester (b). [Andrew Putnam] Hill and [Mrs.] Watkins. Hill and Adamson. John K. Hillers (ae). H. B. Hillyer (2). Lewis W. Hine (a). Robert Hirsch (b). H. S. "Bert" Holmes Jr. (2). Diane Hopkins-Hughes (12/b). Laton Alton Huffman (26). Leopold Hugo. W. R. Humphries.

William E. Irwin (359/e). Robert L. "Bob" Isom. William Henry Jackson (ae). Frances B. Johnston. Charles Clifford Jones. Pirkle Jones (c). Peter A. Juley and Son (= Paul Juley, d).

John Kabel (e). Gertrude Käsebier (7). Arthur F. Kales. Consuelo Kanaga (2). Yousuf Karsh. Joseph T. Keily. Gibson Kennedy Jr. (3). Victor Keppler (c). André Kertész. Darius Kinsey. Charles D. Kirkland (22). Mark Klett. Stuart Klipper (5/b). Ernest Knee (2). Michael Kostiuk (a). George Krause (1/b). Kipton C. Kumler (c). Dorothea Lange (a). Robert B. Langham III (8). Clarence John Laughlin (2). Russell Lee (2/b). Nathan Lerner. Helen Levitt (4). Jerome Liebling. Robert Lewis. Edwin Hale Lincoln. O. Winston Link. Charles F. Lummis. George Platt Lynes. Danny Lyon (c).

Skeet McAuley (b). Lawrence McFarland. Alen MacWeeney (c). Fred E. Mang (2). Elli Marcus. Ira W. Martin (2). Ralph Eugene Meatyard. George F. Silas Melander (e). Mellen (9). Fred R. Meyer (e). Melissa Mial (b). Robert Mial (b). Tom Millea (2). Judy Miller (b). Richard Misrach. Eric H. Mitchell (15). Lisette Model. Tina Modotti. Fredrick Imman Monsen (6). Guy Monthan. Barbara Morgan (a). Willard D. Morgan (2). Moses and Piffet. Michael A. Murphy (b).

Eadweard Muybridge (a). Carl Mydans (a). Joan Myers (3/c). Beaumont Newhall (c). Nicholas Nixon (2). Anne Noggle. Dorothy Norman (4). William C. North (1 daguerreotype). Sonya Noskowiak. William Notman.

Arthur Ollman. Ted Orland (2). Timothy O'Sullivan (4/d). Paul Outerbridge Jr. William W. "Chip" Pankey (4). Robert Peary. Mary Peck (11/bc). Irving Penn. Michael Pevin (b). Brent Phelps (b). Bernard Plossu (14/c). Eliot Porter (7/c). Helen Post (a). Roger Prather (b). Winter Prather (33/a). Harrison Putney (e).

Edward Ranney (1/c). William H. Rau (5). Man Ray (3). Robert S. Redfield. Jane Reece. Ted Rice III (c). Frank A. Rinehart (4). Charles Rivers (4). H. F. Robeusne (e). Cervin Robinson (2). Byron Rogers. Ed Rosskam (b). Arthur Rothstein (c). Charles Rotkin (b). Meridel Rubenstein (c). Harry C. Rubincam. William Herman Rulofson. Hal Rumel. Andrew Joseph Russell (13/d). Charles R. Savage (2). David Scheinbaum (c). George H. Seeley. Ben Shahn (10). Charles Sheeler (4). Philip Shultz. Art Sinsabaugh (2). Clara E. Sipprell (a). Gail Skoff. Erwin E. Smith (607/e). Henry Holmes Smith. Michael Smith (10). Loyd Sneed. Southworth and Hawes. Peter Stackpole (7). George Stark (68/e). Susan Steffey (c). Edward Steichen. Ralph Steiner (3). Horace Stevenson (e). Richard Stevenson (e). Alfred Stieglitz (3). Seneca Ray Stoddard (3). Paul Strand (7/d). Karl Struss (ac). Nancy Sutor (c).

Isaiah West Taber (publisher; 6). Paul Schuster Taylor (2). George A. Tice (4/c). Richard Tichich (b). Ron Todd (b). George Trager (e). Charles Tremear (1 daguerreotype). Doris Ulmann (3). Willard Van Dyke (ac). Caroline Vaughn (a). David Vestal. Adam Clark Vroman (2).

E. O. Waite (4). Carleton E. Watkins (a). Margaret Watkins (4). Todd Webb (ae). Charles Leander Weed (5). Weegee (= Arthur Fellig; 2). Dan Weiner (2). Sandra Weiner. Brett Weston (13/c). Edward Weston (64a). Neil Weston. Minor White (6/c). Clarence H. White. Mitchell A. Wilder (20). Richard Wilder (c). Rick Williams (b). J. R. Willis (e). Garry Winogrand (c). Ben Wittick (3). Marion Post Wolcott (20). Myron Wood (8). Louise Deshong Woodbridge. Willard E. Worden (6). Max Yavno. Marilyn Zimmerman (b).

Notes:

a. See Record Groups—Fine Arts Photography, major subrecord groups.
b. See Record Groups—Fine Arts Photography, exhibitions.
c. See Record Groups—Fine Arts Photography, portfolios.
d. See Record Groups—Fine Arts Photography, published works and albums.
e. See Record Groups—Historical.

RECORD GROUPS: Divided roughly into three areas: Institutional record-groups created by the museum for in-house use, Fine Arts Photography, and Historical Photography; the latter two overlap to a considerable degree. Fine Arts Photography is an artificial collection of exhibition quality prints representing more than 325 photographers. This collection is described in terms of major subrecord groups, group exhibitions, published works and albums, including photographs, portfolios, and stereographs. Subrecord group title is photographer unless otherwise noted.

Institutional collections:

F34.1 EXHIBITION INSTALLATION RECEPTION FILE. Photographs of exhibitions as arranged in the galleries and opening of shows at the museum. 7 feet.

F34.2 EXHIBITION RESEARCH FILE. Copy prints of works in all media, including works in other institutions considered for inclusion in exhibitions organized by the museum. For in-house study use only. 69 feet.

Fine Arts Photography major subrecord groups :

F34.3 ABBOTT (BERENICE; b. 1898). Portraits of literary and art figures made in Paris and New York; Federal Arts project work to document the changing streetlife and buildings of New York; two portraits of Abbott by Man Ray. 505 modern prints. 1920 to 1930s. ACM# 84.35.

F34.4 ADAMS (ANSEL; 1902-1984). Commercial and fine art photographer noted for his landscapes and still lifes in the straight style; founding member of Group f/64; author of numerous books on Zone System photography. Landscapes and portraits. 30 silver gelatin prints, many modern prints by the photographer. 1938 to 1965.

F34.5 AVEDON (RICHARD; b. 1923). Large-format, posed portraits commissioned by the museum for the exhibition, "In the American West" (1985). 120 silver gelatin prints mounted on aluminum panels. 1979 to 1983. See Bibliography. ACM# 85.28.

F34.6 BENRIMO (DOROTHY; 1903-1977). *Camposantos* (grave markers) made by Spanish New Mexicans for the Amon Carter exhibition, "Camposantos: A Photographic Essay" (1966). Printed by Joel Baum. 75 silver gelatin prints mounted on plywood; 329 negatives. 1939 to 1965. See Bibliography. ACM# 77.35.

F34.7 BONES (JIM; b. 1943). Landscapes of West Texas for the Amon Carter Museum exhibit, "Texas West of the Pecos." 34 dye-transfer prints. 1981. See Bibliography. ACM# 82.17.

F34.8 CORPRON (CARLOTTA M.; b. 1901). Professor of design at Texas Woman's University, actively pursued photography mid-1930s to mid-1940s; influenced by Gyorgy Kepes. Design and pattern subjects drawn from natural forms. 44 silver gelatin prints, many modern prints by the photographer. 1938 to 1950. See Bibliography—Sandweiss.

F34.9 CURRENT (WILLIAM R.; b. 1923). Navaho dwellings and details, many from the Navaho National Monument for the Amon Carter Museum exhibit, "Pueblo Architecture of the Southwest" (1971). 80 silver gelatin prints. 1964. See Bibliography. ACM# 71.63.

F34.10 CURRENT (WILLIAM R.; b. 1923). Buildings and furniture designed by American architects used in the Amon Carter exhibit, "Greene and Greene, Architects in the Residential Style" (1974). 17 silver gelatin prints. 1969 to 1972. ACM# 76.94.

F34.11 DuPONT (HENRY B.; 1898-1970). Amateur views of a raft trip down Rio Grande through Big Bend. 138 images on 120 safety negatives, 12 vintage silver gelatin prints. 1946 to 1947. ACM# 75.153.

F34.12 EDWARDS (JOHN PAUL; 1883-1958). Pictorialist and later a member of Group f/64. Pictorialist scenes of California landscapes and towns in Germany; few prints from his f/64 work. 43 silver gelatin prints. ACM# 84.29.

F34.13 ENGEL (MORRIS; b. 1918). Documentary series on the Rylander family of Buda done for *Ladies Home Journal*. 20 silver gelatin prints. 1949. ACM# 83.32.

F34.14 GILPIN (LAURA; 1891-1979) ESTATE. Soft-focus, Pictorialist, fine art photographer. Commercial portraits, commissioned architectural studies; Pueblo and Navaho Indian life; landscapes in the Yucatan, the Rio Grande, and the southwestern US. Archive is maintained in two parts: material acquired before the photographer's death and her bequest to the museum of her estate. 233 silver gelatin, platinum, and color prints in the former; 27,000 negatives and 20,000 prints, slides, and autochromes in the latter; Gilpin's personal library of some 200 volumes plus exhibition and salon catalogs. Late 1900s to early 1970s. See Bibliography—Sandweiss.

F34.15 HILLERS (JOHN K.; 1843–1925). Survey photographer for the US Geological Survey and later for the Bureau of American Ethnology. Landscapes made for the second Powell survey in Utah and Arizona, many of Canyon de Chelly. 40 albumen prints. 1872 to 1885.

F34.16 HINE (LOUIS WICKES; 1874-1940). Social reformer known for work on non-English speaking immigrants and for the Child Labor Study Commission. Predominantly child laborers in Texas. 68 silver gelatin prints. Ca. 1913.

F34.17 JACKSON (WILLIAM HENRY; 1843-1942). Photographer for United States Geological Survey, Bureau of American Ethnology, various railroads. Landscapes, many for railroads, in the western US, especially Yellowstone National Park. 142 albumen and silver gelatin prints. 1871 to late 1880s.

F34.18 KOSTIUK (MICHAEL; b. 1944). Documentary photographs from the Big Thicket commissioned by the museum. 15 silver gelatin prints. 1970 to 1971. ACM# 75.91.

F34.19 LANGE (DOROTHEA; 1895-1965). Studied with Clarence White; studio photographer who later worked for the Farm Security Administration. Photographic essay on women of the agrarian US, *The American country women*. 28 silver gelatin prints. 1938 to 1956. Portraits of Charles M. Russell. 5 silver gelatin prints. 1924 to 1926. See Bibliography.

F34.20 MORGAN (BARBARA; b. 1900). Portraits, including Martha Graham; still lifes and nature subjects. 30 modern silver gelatin prints, photo montages, and photo murals. 1935 to 1968. ACM# 72.9, 74.21.

F34.21 MUYBRIDGE (EADWEARD; 1830-1904). Landscape and survey photographer. 23 motion-study sequences from his work *Animal Locomotion*; landscapes. 23 collotypes and 8 albumen prints. 1872 to 1887.

F34.22 MYDANS (CARL; b. 1907). Documentary photographs made for the Farm Security Administration and *Life* magazine; included in the exhibition, "Carl Mydans: A Photojournalist's Journey through War and Peace" (1985). 151 modern silver gelatin prints. 1935 to 1970.

F34.23 POST (HELEN; 1907-1979). Sister of Marion Post Wolcott; student of ceramics at Alfred University (New York), apprenticed with Trude Fleischmann, and later a freelance photographer in New York. Sioux, Navaho, Apache, Hopi, and Pueblo Amerinds and activities. 4,068 film negatives, most 120; 5,688 study prints, 235 exhibition prints; related papers. 1936 to 1941. See Bibliography—LaFarge, —Clark.

F34.24 PRATHER (WINTER; b. 1926). Architectural, industrial, and landscape photographer. Industrial and late Pictorialist, nature subjects in Texas and New Mexico. 33 silver gelatin prints, many negative prints. 1945 to 1971.

F34.25 SIPPRELL (CLARA E.; 1885-1975) ESTATE. Member of Pictorial Photographers of America and the Royal Photographic Society; ran portrait studios in New York City and Thetford VT. Unmanipulated, soft-focus, Pictorialist portraits, cityscapes, landscapes, and still lifes. Much from Europe (Sweden, and especially Yugoslavia), Mexico, Canada. 2,000 prints, most silver gelatin, some platinum. Ca. 1905 to mid-1960s, most 1926 to 1938.

F34.26 STRUSS (KARL; 1886-1981) ESTATE. Studied with Clarence White at Columbia University; published in *Camera Work*; advertising work for *Vogue*, *Vanity Fair*, and *Harper's Bazaar*;

later a cinematographer for Cecil B. deMille, who won the first Academy Award in cinematography for *Sunrise* (1927). Architecture, including cityscapes and public buildings in New York and some in California; portraits, including Struss family members and early American motion picture stars; landscapes in California, New York, Bermuda, and European cities; the Grand Canyon; beaches. 219 vintage prints and autochromes, including bromide, platinum, and silver gelatin prints; 500 silver gelatin movie stills; 5,058 glass plate, nitrate and safety negatives, many large format; card index. 1909 to 1920s.

F34.27 VAN DYKE (WILLARD; 1906-1986). Founding member of Group f/64; fine art photographer working in a straight style; later a film maker and director of the film department at the New York Metropolitan Museum of Modern Art. 1 vintage and 18 modern silver gelatin prints by the photographer, 2 dye-transfer prints. 1930 to 1937, 1979 to 1980.

F34.28 VAUGHAN (CAROLINE; b. 1949). Studied with John Menapace and Minor White. Ethereal landscapes and portraits. 49 silver gelatin prints. 1971 to 1978.

F34.29 WATKINS (CARLETON E.; 1829-1916). California landscape photographer who did commercial work for railroads. Landscapes. 6 mammoth and 6 smaller albumen prints. 1865 to 1876. See Bibliography—Sandweiss.

F34.30 WEBB (TODD; b. 1905). Studied with Ansel Adams in 1940; Navy combat photographer in WW II; participated in Stryker's Standard Oil Project; commissioned by Amon Carter Museum to document early Texas architecture. 7 silver gelatin prints. 1946 to 1964. See Bibliography.

F34.31 WESTON (EDWARD; 1886-1958). Commercial portrait and fine art photographer, noted for his aesthetic landscapes and his later work in the straight style; founding member of Group f/64. Landscape and portraits. 63 silver gelatin prints. 1915 to 1946.

F34.32 WILDER (MITCHELL A.; 1913-1979). Vacation views in Mexico by Wilder. 300—35mm safety negatives and vintage contact prints. 1941. ACM# 79.49.

Fine Arts Photography exhibitions:

F34.33 "CONTEMPORARY TEXAS: A PHOTOGRAPHIC PORTRAIT" (1986). Photographers include Frank Armstrong, Fred Baldwin/Wendy Watriss, Gay Block, Ave Bonar, Jim Bones, Carol Cohen Burton, Peter Feresten, Frank Gohlke, Paul Hester, Stuart Klipper, George Krause, Skeet McAuley, Michael A. Murphy, Mary Peck, and Rick Williams. 110 silver gelatin, 30 color, 10 dye-transfer exhibition prints; work prints and contact sheets. 1984 to 1985. Artistic interpretation of the state made for the sesquicentennial, commissioned by the Texas Historical Foundation under a grant from Conoco Inc. and E. I. du Pont de Nemours. See Bibliography—Sandweiss. ACM# 85.17.

F34.34 "OUT OF THE FORTIES: A PORTRAIT OF TEXAS FROM THE STANDARD OIL COLLECTION" (1983). Social documents made under the direction of Roy Stryker for the Standard Oil Company. Photographers include Esther Bubley (61), John Collier Jr. (3), Howard Corsini (7), Russell Lee (39), Ed Rosskam (1), and Charles Rotkin (1). 112 prints total, some color dye-transfer prints. 1940s. See Bibliography—Lemann. ACM# 84.37.

F34.35 "SOCIETY FOR PHOTOGRAPHIC EDUCATION, SOUTH CENTRAL REGIONAL PHOTOGRAPHY" (1981). Mounted by Richard Tichich. Photographers include Ronald Binks,

Gary Cawood, Dean Dablow, Rita DeWitt, Rick Gast, Richard E. Haynes, Robert Hirsch, Diane Hopkins-Hughs, Melissa Mial, Robert Mial, Judy Miller, Michael Peven, Brent Phelps, Roger Prather, Richard Tichich, Ron Todd, Marilyn Zimmerman, and one unidentified photographer. 18 prints. ACM# 83.31.

Fine Arts Photography in published works and albums:

F34.36 Curtis, Edward S. *The North American Indian: Being a series of volumes picturing and describing the Indians of the United States and Alaska.* [Seattle WA: E. S. Curtis; Cambridge University Press:] 1907-1930. Volumes 1, 2, 5, and 7 to 20; some plates wanting. ACM# 77.1.

F34.37 Gardner, Alexander, ed. *Gardner's sketchbook of the Civil War.* Washington DC: Philip and Solomons, 1865-1866. Photographers include Alexander Gardner, John Gardner, T. H. O'Sullivan, and various others. 100 albumen prints in 2 volumes. See Bibliography. ACM# 84.30.

F34.38 Hayden, F. V.; Russell, A. J., photog. *Sun pictures of Rocky Mountain scenery.* New York: Julius Bien, 1870. 30 albumen prints. Late 1860s. ACM# 79.63.

F34.39 Haynes, F. Jay. [*Yellowstone Park album.*] St. Paul MN: F. Jay Haynes, [1900?]. Landscapes of noted landforms in Yellowstone Park. 24 collodio-chloride prints. Ca. 1900. ACM #79.75.

F34.40 Juley, Peter A., and Son, photog. *The West.* Formal portraits, many of Taos artists, landscapes, and architecture made in the western US, especially along the California coast and in Taos NM; attributed to Juley's son Paul. 62 silver gelatin prints. Ca. 1930. ACM# 82.28.

F34.41 [*Mexican and island scenes.*] Mexican cities and railway; a Caribbean [?] island; and a few US scenes. Photographed by A. Bríquet, Lorenzo Becerril, Lilicorthal [?], and unidentified photographers. 88 albumen prints. Mid-1890s. ACM #81.45.

F34.42 Moran, John, and Timothy O'Sullivan. *Pictures of the Selfridge Darien expedition upon surveys for an interoceanic canal, 1870 and 1871.* Isthmus of Darien (= Panama), especially Limon Bay. 48 albumen prints. 1870 to 1871. ACM# 81.91, 82.1.

F34.43 Nordenskiold, Gustaf Nils Adolf. *Ruiner af Klippboninger 1, Mesa Verdes Canons.* Stockholm: P.A. Norstedt and Soners, 1893. Account of an expedition led by the archaeologist, Nordenskiold. 9 photogravures. 1891. ACM# 83.34.

F34.44 *Reise-Erinnerungen Amerika, 1890* [= Reminiscences of a journey in America, 1890.] Commercial travel views: 1) New York City, Niagara Falls, Philadelphia, Washington, Chicago, Denver, and Colorado Springs; 2) Prairie, cowboys, Clear Creek Canyon, Georgetown and Georgetown Loop, Colorado Springs, mines, Manitou, and Garden of the Gods; 3) Pike's Peak, Black Canyon, Cascade Falls, Silverton, Durango; 4) Toltec Tunnel, Animas Canyon, Royal Gorge, Iron Bridge, Marshall Pass, and Salt Lake City; 5) San Francisco, Monterey, Sequoias, Los Angeles, Santa Monica, Riverside, El Paso, Arizona Amerinds, Mexico City, Vera Cruz, Mexico, and native scenes. Photographers include Bagley, Johnston, William Laurence, Notman, Savage, and Taber. 600 photographs in 5 volumes, most albumen prints. Before 1890 ACM# 78.147.

F34.45 Russell, A. J., photog. *The great West illustrated: In a series of photographic views across the continent, taken along the line of the Union Pacific Railroad. West from Omaha, Nebraska. With an annotated table of contents, giving a brief description of each view; its peculiarities, characteristics and connections with the different points on the road.* New York: Union Pacific Railroad, 1869. 51 albumen prints. 1867 to 1869. ACM# 83.34.

F34.46 Stieglitz, Alfred, ed. *Camera notes.* Volumes 2-5 complete, and volume 6, numbers 1 and 2. From the Laura Gilpin estate.

F34.47 Stieglitz, Alfred, ed. *Camera work.* Numbers 1, 12, 16, 19, 21, 23-25, 28, 30-36, 38, 41-43, 45, 48-50; a few plates wanting. Many from the Laura Gilpin estate. ACM# 81.89.

F34.48 Watkins, Carleton, photog. *California views 1876.* Landscapes. 53 albumen prints. Ca. 1865 to 1876. ACM# 75.94.

F34.49 Wheeler, George M. *Geographical Explorations and Surveys West of the 100th Meridian—Wheeler Photographs.* Photographs by Timothy O'Sullivan (33) and William Bell (16). Documentation of Utah and Nevada from a military point of view. 48 albumen prints. 1871. ACM# 76.142, 82.27.

Fine Arts Photography portfolios:

F34.50 ADAMS (ANSEL; 1902-1984) PORTFOLIO. *What majestic word:* [*In memory of Russell Varien*]. [San Francisco: Sierra Club, 1963.] 15 silver gelatin prints. ACM# 66.11.

F34.51 ALVAREZ BRAVO (MANUEL; b. 1902) PORTFOLIO. *Photographs by Manuel Alvarez Bravo.* Geneva: Acorn Editions Ltd, 1977. 15 modern silver gelatin prints. 1920s to 1979. ACM# 80.63.

F34.52 ERWITT (ELLIOTT; b. 1928) PORTFOLIO. *Photographs: Elliott Erwitt.* Geneva: Acorn Editions, 1977. 14 silver gelatin prints. 1949 to 1968. ACM# 80.66.

F34.53 HALSMAN (PHILIPPE; 1906-1979) PORTFOLIO. *Halsman/Dali.* Neikrug Photographica Ltd, 1981. Printed by Stephen Gersch. 10 silver gelatin prints. 1948 to 1956. ACM# 84.32.

F34.54 HALSMAN (PHILIPPE; 1906-1979) PORTFOLIO. *Halsman/Marilyn.* Neikrug Photographica Ltd, 1981. Printed by Stephen Gersch. 10 silver gelatin prints. 1952, 1959. ACM# 84.31.

F34.55 JONES (PIRKLE; b. 1914) PORTFOLIO. *Portfolio two: Twelve photographs by Pirkle Jones.* Mill Valley CA, 1968. 12 silver gelatin prints. 1952 to 1958. ACM# 68.59.

F34.56 KEPPLER (VICTOR; b. 1905) PORTFOLIO. *Man and Camera I.* 10 modern silver gelatin prints. 1917 to 1969. ACM# 82.18.

F34.57 KUMLER (KIPTON C.; b. 1940) PORTFOLIO. *A portfolio of plants.* Lexington MA, 1977. 10 modern platinum and palladium prints. 1970 to 1974. ACM# 78.145.

F34.58 LYON (DANNY; b. 1942) PORTFOLIO. *Danny Lyon.* New York: Hyperion, 1979. 30 modern silver gelatin prints. 1962 to 1979. ACM# 80.67.

F34.59 MacWEENEY (ALEN; b. 1939) PORTFOLIO. *Alen MacWeeney.* New York: Hyperion, 1979. 12 silver gelatin prints. 1965 to 1972. ACM# 80.64.

F34.60 *NEW MEXICO LANDSCAPES* PORTFOLIO. Oklahoma City: Portfolio Editions, 1983. Photographers include Paul Caponigro, William Clift, Joan Myers, Bernard Plossu, Edward Ranney, Ted Rice III. 12 prints. ACM# 83.38.

F34.61 PLOSSU (BERNARD; b. 1945) PORTFOLIO. *Rancho de Taos Church.* 8 untoned silver gelatin prints. 1978 to 1979. ACM# 81.56.

F34.62 PORTER (ELIOT; b. 1901) PORTFOLIO. *Birds in flight.* Santa Fe: Bell Editions, 1978. 8 dye-transfer prints. 1959 to 1976. ACM# 79.5.

F34.63 PRATHER (WINTER) PORTFOLIO. *Portfolio I.* Architecture and nature subjects, one self-portrait. 16 silver gelatin prints. 1947 to 1968. ACM# 69.39.

F34.64 ROTHSTEIN (ARTHUR; b. 1915) PORTFOLIO. *Arthur Rothstein.* New Rochelle NY, 1976. Farm Security Administration photographs. 8 modern prints by the photographer. 1935 to 1939. ACM# 80.56.

F34.65 ROTHSTEIN (ARTHUR; b. 1915) PORTFOLIO. *Arthur Rothstein.* New York: Hyperion Press, 1981. Farm Security Administration subjects and photographs made around the world. 30 modern silver gelatin prints. 1935 to 1951. Long-term loan. L82.7.

F34.66 SANTA FE CENTER FOR PHOTOGRAPHY PORTFOLIO. *Portfolio I.* Santa Fe NM: Santa Fe Center for Photography, 1982. Photographs by Mary Peck, Bernard Plossu, Eliot Porter, David Scheinbaum, and Susan Steffy. 5 prints. ACM# 82.35.

F34.67 SANTA FE CENTER FOR PHOTOGRAPHY PORTFOLIO. *Portfolio II.* Santa Fe NM: Santa Fe Center for Photography, 1983. Photographs by Beaumont Newhall, Meridel Rubenstein, Nancy Sutor, Williard Van Dyke, and Richard Wilder. Produced by Janet Russek and Richard Wickstrom. 5 prints. ACM# 84.4.

F34.68 STRAND (PAUL; 1890-1976) PORTFOLIO. *Photographs of Mexico [= The Mexican portfolio.]* 2nd ed. DeCapo Press, 1967. Introductory essay by Leo Hurwitz. 20 photogravures. 1932 to 1933. ACM# 67.202.

F34.69 STRUSS (KARL; 1886-1981) PORTFOLIO. *Dawn of color.* Hamburg and Los Angeles: P.P.S. Galerie F. C. Grundlach and Stephen White Gallery, 1981. 8 modern dye-transfer prints from autochromes. 1910 to 1913. 82.23/186-193.

F34.70 STRUSS (KARL; 1886-1981) PORTFOLIO. *Karl Struss: A portfolio 1909/29.* Ann Arbor MI: Photofolio, 1979. Printed by Phil Davis. 15 modern platinum prints. 1909 to 1912. ACM# 80.3.

F34.71 TICE (GEORGE A.; b. 1938) PORTFOLIO. *Bodie.* Colonia: 1971. Cityscapes of Bodie CA, a ghost town. 12 modern silver gelatin prints by the photographer. 1965. ACM# 71.88.

F34.72 VAN DYKE (WILLARD; 1906-1986) PORTFOLIO. *Ten photographs.* New York: Van Tice Productions, 1977. 10 modern silver gelatin prints. 1930 to 1937. ACM# 80.2.

F34.73 WESTON (BRETT; b. 1911) PORTFOLIO. *Baja California.* Privately published, 1967. Landscapes. 15 silver gelatin prints. 1964 to 1967. ACM# 67.229.

F34.74 WESTON (BRETT; b. 1911) PORTFOLIO. *Ten photographs.* Carmel CA, 1958. 10 silver gelatin prints. 1945 to 1956. Landscapes in a straight style. ACM# 65.156.

F34.75 WHITE (MINOR; 1908-1976) AND BILL GRATWICK PORTFOLIO. *Peony portfolio.* Still life studies photographed by White of peonies grown by Gratwick. 11 silver gelatin prints. 1957 to 1960. ACM# 83.39.

F34.76 WINOGRAND (GARRY; 1928-1984) PORTFOLIO. *Garry Winogrand.* New York: Hyperion Press, 1978. Street scenes in Texas and New York City. 15 modern silver gelatin prints. 1960 to 1974. ACM# 80.65.

F34.77 Fine Arts Photography stereograph collection: An artificial collection, predominantly travel views of Western US subjects, including landscapes, cityscapes, and genre. Photographers and publishers include:

Charles Bierstadt (9). J. C. Burge (2). C. W. Carter (12). F. F. Childs (5). Continent Stereoscopic Company (3). Crater and Bill (4). John Moran (24). Doerr and Jacobson, H. A. Doerr (16). J. G. Evans (3). E. and H. T. Anthony Company (10). B. H. Gurnsey (2). Alfred A. Hart (3). F. Jay Haynes (19). Hayward and Mazzall (2). John K. Hillers (2). William Henry Jackson (150). J. F. Jarvis (10). N. P. Jones (6). Kilburn Brothers (17). A. V. Latourette (19). Leach and Hanna (1). Littleton View Company (8). Martin's Art Gallery (2). J. C. Macurdy (3). S. J. Morrow (2). J. Mueller (2). F. Parker (4). Parker and Parker (4). H. T. Payne (3). J. J. Reilly (22). P. H. Rose (5). C. R. Savage (5). W. H. Sherman (4). C. E. Watkins (42). C. L. Weed (attrib.; 55).

480 stereographs, most albumen. 1870s to 1900, most ca. 1880.

Historical record groups:

F34.78 BRININSTOOL (EARL A.; 1870-1954) COLLECTION. Nineteenth-century Indian wars; Plains Indians, US military, and Texas Rangers; aftermath of the Battle of Wounded Knee photographed by George Trager. Many portraits for the Bureau of American Ethnology photographed by Charles Bell, William Dinwiddie, John K. Hillers, William Henry Jackson, Mooney, and Shindler. 3,000 prints; inventory of prints. Late nineteenth century.

F34.79 CLARK (WILLIAM) COLLECTION. Eastern and southern American railroads. 345 stereographs, many albumen. Ca. 1890. ACM# 68.5998-6343.

F34.80 CAPPS COLLECTION. William Capps family photographs, mostly family portraits but including commercial and residential interiors in Fort Worth. 2 albums, 264 loose prints. 1880 to 1960, most 1900 to 1925. ACM# 74.119.

F34.81 CLIFTON, TEXAS COLLECTION. Amateur portraits, cityscapes, and rural scenes around Clifton, including the Lutheran school and the Scandinavian Evangelical Lutheran Church; possibly by Mr. Wiedemeyer, the pastor of the church. 175 silver gelatin glass negatives with modern prints. Ca. 1890. ACM# 79.41.

F34.82 DAVIS (ZOE) COLLECTION. Wyoming-Nebraska canal construction; family portraits; scenes in Wyoming, Colorado, and Arizona; buildings and scenes in Fort Worth and Dallas. Photographed by C. M. Davis. 236 nitrate negatives with modern prints, 43 vintage prints. 1904 to 1945. ACM# 80.18.

F34.83 EVERHARD (MARY) COLLECTION. Portraits and scenes of the army post in Leavenworth KS; western landscapes; Black community in eastern Kansas; 1898 Alaskan gold rush. Photographers include John Kabel, Silas Melander (Chicago); Leavenworth KS photographers include E. E. Henry, Harrison Putney, Horace Stevenson, and Richard Stevenson. 6,000 glass negatives. 1875 to 1918; inventory of prints. See Bibliography—Phillips.

F34.84 INDIAN PHOTOGRAPHS. Commercial portraits of Amerinds (mainly Plains tribes) and scenes of Amerind life; by John A. Anderson, Fred R. Meyer, and unidentified photographer(s). 25 photo prints, most albumen, some silver gelatin and photomechanical. 1893, 1900 to 1902. ACM# 68.6407-6432.

F34.85 IRWIN (WILLIAM E. "ED"; 1871-1935) COLLECTION. Studio photographer at Fort Sill OK. Studio portraits and genre images of Amerinds, including Kiowa, Comanche, and Cheyenne; bird and deer hunting scenes; landscapes in Texas, Colorado, and Oklahoma; portraits in domestic interiors. Photographed by Irwin in Oklahoma (Indian Territory), West Texas, and Arizona. 309 original glass negatives with modern prints; 50 vintage prints. 1894 to 1920. ACM# 67.3543-3901.

F34.86 KIRKLAND (CHARLES D.; 1857-1926). Cowboys, cattle industry, and ranch life in Wyoming. 19 albumen prints. 1877 to 1895.

F34.87 MAXIMILLIAN AND CARLOTTA IN MEXICO CARTES. Portraits of Ferdinand Maximillian Joseph, his consort, Carlotta, and associated people. Photographed by E. Neurdein (Paris), Agtin Peraire (Mexico), and various photographers. 34 cartes, many art reproductions. Early 1860s. ACM# 72.30.

F34.88 MAZZULLA (FRED; 1903-1981 AND JO; d. 1973) COLLECTION. Denver attorney and his wife. Extensive coverage of the western US with emphasis on early Denver and various Colorado mining towns; substantial coverage of railroads, prostitution, and Amerinds; by various early Colorado photographers, including William Henry Jackson, John K. Hillers, Joseph Collier, W. J. Carpenter, C. W. Erdlen, and George Fiske. Vintage travel views by various European photographers. 150,000 photographs, including cartes, stereographs, vintage and copy prints; 36 autochromes; glass and film negatives; arranged by subject with a listing of people, places, and photographers; extensive associated textual material; inventory of prints. 1860s to 1925. See Bibliography—Mazzulla, —Muskat.

F34.89 MEXICAN REVOLUTION PHOTOGRAPHS. Commercial views of soldiers, battle scenes, and casualties, photographed by W. H. Horne (El Paso) and distributed by the International News Service. 6 vintage silver gelatin prints, 29 silver gelatin photo postcards. Ca. 1914. ACM# 78.153.

F34.90 MEXICAN WAR DAGUERREOTYPES. Portraits of US military personnel stationed in Mexico, scenes of Mexican towns, other images indirectly related to the Mexican War. 50 daguerreotypes, and 8 blank daguerreotype plates. 1847 to 1849. ACM# 81.65, 83.9.

F34.91 SMITH (ERWIN E.; 1886-1947) COLLECTION. Texas cattle industry; scenes around Bonham; Smith home and family portraits; commercial portraits of Amerinds. Photographers include Smith, Frank Reeves, N. H. Rose, and Heyn. Compiled by Mary Alice Petties, Smith's half-sister. 287 glass negatives, 10 albums, 160 vintage prints. 1900 to 1930. ACM# 86.41-42.

F34.92 SOUTHWEST INDIAN PHOTOGRAPHS. Commercial portraits of Taos Pueblo, Hopi, Navaho, and Zuni Amerinds. Photographed by J. R. Willis, H. F. Robeusne, and various others. 20 silver gelatin prints. 1910 to 1930. ACM# 74.125.

F34.93 STARK (GEORGE; 1872?-1946). Lithographer for the St. Louis *Globe-Democrat* and photographer. Rural and sporting photographs in Arkansas, Oklahoma, and Missouri; stockyards in St. Louis MO. 68 prints. Ca. 1900. ACM# 85.37.

F34.94 TEXAS ARCHITECTURAL SURVEY COLLECTION. Retrospective views of more than 1,500 historical public and private structures in Texas; substantial coverage in Austin, Bastrop,

Brownsville, Burnet, Clarksville, Columbus, Cuero, Fort Stockton, Fort Worth, Fredericksburg, Galveston, Goliad, Granbury, Hillsboro, Houston, Hunstville, Jefferson, Lampasas, Llano, Marshall, Mason, Nacogdoches, New Braunfels, Paris, Round Top, San Antonio, San Augustine, Tyler, Victoria, and Waco; various forts. Photographed by Todd Webb. 3,500 safety negatives; card index arranged by city. Ca. 1964 to 1967. See Bibliography—Webb. ACM# 77.12.

F34.95 WOODWARD (EDWIN C.) COLLECTION. Vacation snapshots of the US Southwest, including the Grand Canyon, a Hopi house, mountain scenery, and fishing; road construction by the Texas Highway Department; El Morro National Monument; Yellowstone National Park and Cibola National Forest; Fort Caspar WY. Unidentified photographers. 495 items in 8 albums and 2 groups of loose prints; some photomechanical postcards included. Ca. 1940s. ACM# 74.16.

Fort Worth Public Library (F46)

300 Taylor Street
Fort Worth, Texas 76102

817-870-7740. Contact: Library Assistant.

PURPOSE: A local history collection in a public library with collections of books, genealogical references, and photographs.

HOURS: Monday through Thursday, 9:00-9:00; Friday and Saturday, 10:00-6:00. Closed major holidays.

ASSISTANCE: Specialized staff assistance. Written inquiries accepted. Photoduplications may be made by patron or ordered through the library. Electrostatic copies not available.

PUBLICATION: No publication fee. Collection credit required. Free copy of publication to library. No publication for commercial purposes. Third-party permission required on some photographs.

FINDING AIDS: Visual index; access by subject headings.

BIBLIOGRAPHY:
Sanders, Leonard. *How Fort Worth became the Texasmost city.* Fort Worth: Amon Carter Museum, 1973.
Schmetzer, Janet L. *Where the West begins: Fort Worth and Tarrant County.* Northridge CA: Windsor Publications, 1985.

SCOPE: 2,500 vintage and 500 copy photographs. 1880s to present.

Type of photo	Pre-1880	1880-1899	1900-1919	1920-1939	1940-1959	1960-1986
D/A/T-types	20					
Vintage prints	200	200	700	400	100	50
Photo albums		2				

GEOGRAPHIC: The library collects only Fort Worth, North Fort Worth, and Tarrant County, including the Trinity River; other locales are represented only incidentally and in no great quantity.

SUBJECTS: Economic and social development of the region. Subject headings used in the library:

Animals. Blacks. Businesses. Churches. Fort Worth Public Library. General views [cityscapes]. Groups. Houses. Meeting halls. Monuments. Non-Fort Worth. North Fort Worth. Parks. Portraits. Public Buildings. Schools. Street scenes.

Architecture (academic, domestic, public, retrospective views of historic structures). Events (flood—1949). Industry (general commerce—interiors). Landscape (aerials). Organizations (civic, social). Religion (churches).

Tarrant County Courthouse—1873, —1893. Texas Christian University. Texas Wesleyan College. Union Pacific Depot.

PEOPLE: Residents of Fort Worth, none held in quantity, representing domestic and personal activities; some family snapshots; a small collection of Blacks.

PHOTOGRAPHERS: W. L. French. C. L. Schwarz.

RECORD GROUPS: The collection is maintained as a single, artificial collection arranged by subject heading. Significant groups of related photographs include:

F46.1 BUSINESS INTERIORS. Commercial interiors with calligraphic captions, in an itinerant style possibly by W. L. French. 73 silver gelatin prints mounted 4 to a sheet recto and verso. 1912.

F46.2 FORT WORTH PUBLIC LIBRARY. Previous structures of the library, including the original Carnegie building, showing interior, exterior, and exhibits and the replacement building erected in 1940. 51 silver gelatin prints. Ca. 1900 to 1950s.

F46.3 PUBLIC BUILDINGS. Vintage photographs of major buildings in Fort Worth, including the 1876 and 1895 Tarrant County courthouse, the Fort Worth City Hall, and the Union Pacific depot and its burning. 42 photo prints. 1870s to 1910s.

Texas Baptist Historical Collection (F70)

Southwestern Baptist Theological Seminary
Archives Department
A. Webb Roberts Library
4500 Stanley
Fort Worth, Texas 76115

817-923-1921, extension 333. Contact: Archivist.

PURPOSE: The collection has been the official repository of the executive board of the Baptist General Convention since 1933, collecting records of the General Convention and member congregations, oral histories, Baptist newspapers, manuscripts, mission artifacts, and books. A museum exhibits materials from the reserve collections.

HOURS: Weekdays, 8:00-5:00. Closed major holidays and week between Christmas and New Year's. Appointment preferred.

ASSISTANCE: Professional staff. Written inquiries accepted on a limited basis (genealogical inquiries not accepted). Electrostatic copies available. Photoduplications may be made by patron or ordered through the collection.

PUBLICATION: No publication fee. Collection credit required. Free copy of publication to the collection. Third-party permission required on some photographs; required before photoduplications are released.

FINDING AIDS: Card index and guide; access by personal name. Photographs arranged by collection and by subject.

SCOPE: 10,000 vintage and 1,000 copy photographs; 10 panoramic prints, 1,000 lantern slides, 500 motion pictures. Many photographs are associated with manuscript collections. 1879 to present.

GEOGRAPHIC: Photographs made by Texas missionaries around the world. Many photographs from Texas.

Argentina. Brazil. China. Nigeria.

SUBJECTS: Academia (seminaries). Religion (congregations, seminaries).

PEOPLE: Many students and faculty of Southwestern Seminary; many peoples served by Texas Baptist missionaries, especially Southeast Asians and Chinese.

W. B. Bagby. J. M. Carroll. M. E. Dodd. Billy Graham. Blanch Groves. T. B. Maston. Alpha Melton. James M. Price. L. R. Scarborough. Ann Swenson. George W. Truett.

Amerinds. Ministers (Baptist).

PHOTOGRAPHERS: Staff photographers David Bell, Phil Copeland, and Roger Kettering. Louise Treadwell. Wire services.

RECORD GROUPS:

F70.1 ALL CHURCH PRESS COLLECTION. News photographs used to illustrate publications of the *All Church Press*, edited by Lambuth Thomlinson; many wire service photographs. 5,000 photographs; arranged by topics or personal name. 1950s to 1970s.

F70.2 SOUTHWESTERN SEMINARY COLLECTION. Faculty, students, and buildings of the seminary. 15,000 photographs. 1910 to present, most 1960s to present.

F70.3 TEXAS BAPTIST HISTORICAL COLLECTION. Portraits of Texas Baptist pastors and churches. 1,000 photographs. 1879 to present.

Texas and Southwestern Cattle Raisers Association (F74)

1301 West Seventh Street
Fort Worth, Texas 76102

817-332-7064. Contact: Photo Archivist or Editorial Assistant.

PURPOSE: The Texas and Southwestern Cattle Raisers Association (TSCRA) was formed to protect independent cattlemen from rustlers and still maintains an active force of inspectors. The TSCRA archive includes the records and photo morgue of its publication, *The Cattleman*. The Texas and Southwestern Cattle Raisers Foundation (TSCRF) maintains a small exhibiting museum with display photographs drawn from the magazine, images copied from other collections, paintings, and artifacts.

HOURS: Weekdays, 8:00-5:00. Closed major holidays. Appointment required to use the reserve collections.

ASSISTANCE: Professional staff. Written and phone inquiries accepted. Electrostatic copies available. Photoduplications may be made by patron or ordered through the foundation.

PUBLICATION: Nominal publication fee. Collection credit required. Free copy of publication to foundation. Third-party permission required for a few images.

FINDING AIDS: Card index, inventory, and itemized, descriptive listing of photographs; access by general subject heading, geographic location, photographer, personal name, and date.

BIBLIOGRAPHY:

The cattleman. Fort Worth: Texas and Southwestern Cattle Raisers Association, 1914 and following.

A century of photographs, 1846-1946. Washington DC: Library of Congress, 1980.

Clarke, Mary Whatley. *A century of cow business: A history of the Texas and Southwestern Cattle Raisers Association.* Fort Worth: TSCRA, 1976.

Foreman, Monte, and Patrick Wyse. *Monte Foreman's horse training science.* Norman OK: University of Oklahoma Press, 1984.

Perkins, Doug, and Nancy Ward. *Brave men and cold steel: A history of range detectives and their peacemakers.* Fort Worth: TSCRF, 1984.

Smith, Erwin E., photog.; text by J. Evetts Haley. *Life on the Texas range.* Austin: University of Texas Press, 1952.

SCOPE: 25,000 photographs, most vintage silver gelatin prints; many were made by staff writers and photographers for the magazine. 1900 to present.

Type of photo	Pre-1880	1880-1899	1900-1919	1920-1939	1940-1959	1960-1986
Film negs					200	5,000
Vintage prints			500	750	5,000	12,000
Copy prints			50	100	200	200

GEOGRAPHIC: Predominantly Texas, including Austin, Corpus Christi, Dallas, Fort Worth, Houston, San Antonio, and Waco. Minor representation of Austria, Canada, England, Germany, Italy, and Mexico.

SUBJECTS: Agriculture (cattle ranching). Animals (cattle, horses). Architecture (historic structures). Cityscapes. Exhibitions (livestock shows). Landscapes. Sports and amusements (rodeo).

Armour and Company. Burnett (= 6666), King, Matador, Pitchfork, Swenson, and Waggoner ranches.

PEOPLE: Persons associated with Burnett (= 6666), King, Matador, Pitchfork, Swenson, and Waggoner ranches. See Record Groups—Portrait file for additional names.

Cowboys. Ethnic (Amerinds, Black, Hispanic).

PHOTOGRAPHERS: Predominantly commercial photography, although some images were made by the magazine staff while on assignment. Fort Worth photographers unless noted.

James Cathey. Frank Reeves. Erwin E. Smith (Bonham). W. D. Smithers (Alpine). John D. Stryker. Elna Wilkinson.

RECORD GROUPS:

F74.1 CATEGORY FILE. An artificial collection arranged by generic subjects, generally pertaining to cattle raising or cattle breed. Cattle breeds:

> Afrikaner. Angus. Beefmaster. Blonde d'Aquitaine. Braford. Brahman. Brangus. Charolais. Chianina. Crossbreeds. Dairy cattle. Devon. Hereford. Limousin. Longhorn. Maine Anjou. Murray Grey. Polled Hereford. Red Angus. Red Brangus. Red Poll. Santa Gertrudis. Shorthorn. Simbrah. Simmental.

Other subject headings include (subjects with substantial historical coverage marked with an asterisk):

> Artwork. Auction. Barbed wire. Branding.* Briggs Ranch. Brush and brush control. Burnet (= 6666) Ranch. Cattle hides. Chuckwagon. Cities. Cowboy equipment. Diseases and parasites (foot and mouth, screwworm). Dogs. Entertainment. Farm and ranch animals, miscellaneous. Farm and ranch equipment. Feedlot. Fish and game wildlife. Grasses and grains. Health and preventive medicine. Horses, general.* Indians. Insects. Irrigation. Jacks, jennets, and mules. Judgings and shows. King Ranch. Matador Ranch. Landscapes. Meat, nutrition, and packing houses. Pitchfork Ranch. Plants, trees, and flowers. Portraits.* Predators. Ranch operations. Ranch and range scenes.* Range management. Reunions, trail drives, and round-ups. Rodeo. Roping.* Schools. Stock exchanges. Stockyards and market shipping. Structures.* Swenson SMS Ranch. TSCRA. TSCRF. Texas Rangers. Waggoner Ranch. Weather and environment. Windmills.

1,300 photographs in the active file; 3,900 photographs in the inactive file; most vintage silver gelatin prints, a few color transparencies. A few copy photographs date from the 1870s; most are vintage images from late 1890s to 1980s.

F74.2 HORSE FILE. Commercial views of horses, many with a person (breeder, trainer, or owner) adjacent; 925 names (few with six or more images):

> Bill Cody. Booger Bear. Brady Lady. Dee Gee. Jesse James. Jole Blon. King's Pistol. LH Quarter Moon. Little Peggy H. Major King. Marion's Girl. Monsieur Joe. Poco Bueno. Poco Dell. Poco Stampede. Snipper W. Town Crier.

Breeds and classes represented include appaloosa, Arabian, Belgian, cutting, paint, palomino, thoroughbred, and racing. 3 feet silver gelatin prints; arranged by horse. 1940s to 1960s.

F74.3 ISSUE FILE. Editorial and advertising photographs used as illustrations for *The Cattleman*. 16 linear feet; arranged by issue. 1960s to present.

F74.4 PAST BREED WINNERS (CATTLE) FILE. Breed winners at various shows. 1 foot silver gelatin prints; arranged by breed. 1930s to 1970s.

F74.5 PAST INSPECTORS FILE. Journalistic and commercial portraits of TSCRA inspectors individually and in groups, including market and auction ring, inspectors' meetings, school, guns and badges, inspectors on the job, and cattle thefts and brand alterings; 71 names, each represented by about 3 images. 300 silver gelatin prints; arranged by name. Ca. 1930s to 1970s.

F74.6 PORTRAIT FILE. Individual and group portraits of TSCRA directors, officials, and employees, breed association officials, and others associated with the cattle and agriculture industry

1,102 names (none represented by more than eight images) including:

> Don C. Collins. Kirby Cunningham. Dr. Herrell De Graff. Wray Finney. Monte Foreman. Clifford Hardin. Judge Joe Montague. William Ruckleshaus. James Watt. John Wayne. John C. White. Jackie Worthington.

2 feet silver gelatin prints; arranged by name. 1950s to 1970s.

Morton Museum of Cooke County (G10)

Cooke County Heritage Society
210 South Dixon Street at Pecan
P.O. Box 150
Gainesville, Texas 76240

817-668-8900. Contact: Director.

PURPOSE: A local history museum operated by the local history society collecting artworks, artifacts, books and journals, manuscripts, government records, newspapers, and photographs.

HOURS: Exhibition area—Tuesday to Saturday, 12:00-5:00. Reserve collections—weekdays, 8:00-5:00. Closed major holidays. An appointment is recommended.

ASSISTANCE: Professional, specialized, experienced staff. Written and phone inquiries accepted. Electrostatic copies available. Photoduplications may be made by the patron with advance arrangement or ordered through the museum.

PUBLICATION: Publication fee. Collection credit required. Free copy of publication to the museum.

FINDING AIDS: Card index and inventory of uncataloged material.

BIBLIOGRAPHY:
Collins, Michael. *Cooke County, Texas: Where the South and the West meet.* [Gainesville:] Cooke County Heritage Society, 1981.
Parker, Frank and James Smallwood. *History of Cooke County: A pictorial essay.* Gainesville: Gainesville American Revolution Bicentennial Committee, 1975.

SCOPE: 10,000 vintage and 500 copy photographs, including stereographs, panoramic prints, and postcards. Majority of collection is the archive of Boyd and Breeding Studio (v.i.). 1860s to present.

Type of photo	Pre-1880	1880-1899	1900-1919	1920-1939	1940-1959	1960-1986
D/A/T-types	25					
Film negs				3,000	3,000	3,000
Vintage prints		200	300	3,000	3,000	3,000
Copy prints						250

GEOGRAPHIC: Cooke County, especially Gainesville.

SUBJECTS: Economic and social development (academia, cotton, cattle, events, government, industry, oil, politics, fire protection). Military (WW II). Sports and amusements (Circus).

Camp Howze. Fort Fitzhugh. Gainesville Community Circus.

PEOPLE: Area residents, none held in quantity.

PHOTOGRAPHERS: Boyd and Breeding Studio (Gainesville). Goben. Manderfield.

RECORD GROUPS:

G10.1 BOYD AND BREEDING STUDIO (GAINESVILLE) ARCHIVE. Local photography studio. Weddings and individual studio portraits; Gainesville Community Circus; journalistic coverage of the community for the *Gainesville Daily Register*, including numerous car wrecks. 8,000 negatives; arranged by year, then alphabetically. 1935 to 1960.

Rosenberg Library (G40)

2310 Sealy Avenue
Galveston, Texas 77550

409-763-8854. Contact: Archivist.

PURPOSE: An archive and exhibit space concentrating on local and state history within a community library. The archive has extensive holdings of rare and recent books, journals, and newspapers; manuscripts and business records; city and county records and directories; maps, paintings, and art works in all media; extensive three-dimensional artifacts, including ship models; and photographs.

HOURS: Tuesday through Saturday, 10:00-5:00. Closed major holidays.

ASSISTANCE: Professional staff. Written and phone inquiries accepted on a limited basis; patrons are encouraged to visit the collection in person. Electrostatic copies available. Photoduplications must be ordered through the library.

PUBLICATION: Publication fee. Collection credit required. Free copy of publication to library. Few items require third-party permission.

FINDING AIDS: Descriptive lists by subject, location, proper name, and collection; access by general and proper subjects. Some collections have itemized lists.

BIBLIOGRAPHY:

Barnstone, Howard; Henri Cartier-Bresson and Ezra Stoller, photogs. *The Galveston that was.* New York: Macmillan, 1965.

Eisenhour, Virginia. *Galveston, a different place: A history and guide.* Galveston: V. Eisenhour, 1983.

Green, Nathan C., ed. *Story of the Galveston flood.* Baltimore MD: R. H. Woodward, 1900.

Kenamore, Jane, and Michael E. Wilson, ed. *Manuscript sources in the Rosenberg Library: A selective guide.* College Station: Texas A&M Press for the Rosenberg Library, 1983.

Lester, Paul. *The great Galveston disaster: Containing a full and thrilling account of the most appalling calamity of modern times. . . .* Chicago: A. B. Kuhlman, 1900.

McComb, David G. *Galveston: A history.* Austin: University of Texas Press, 1986.

McQuaid, James, and Paulette Privitera Wilson. *An index to American photographic collections.* Boston: G. K. Hall, 1981.

Mason, Herbert Molloy. *Death from the sea: Our greatest nature disaster, the Galveston hurricane of 1900.* New York: Dial Press, 1972.

Miller, Ray. *Ray Miller's Galveston.* Houston: Cordovan Corporation, 1983.

Ousely, Clarence, ed. *Galveston in nineteen hundred.* Atlanta GA: William C. Chase, 1900.

Weems, John Edward. *A weekend in September.* New York: Henry Holt and Company, 1957. College Station: Texas A&M University Press, 1980, 1984.

SCOPE: 20,000 vintage photographs, including daguerreotypes and ambrotypes, glass and film negatives, stereographs, and prints. Late 1850s to present.

Type of photo	Pre-1880	1880-1899	1900-1919	1920-1939	1940-1959	1960-1986
D/A/T-types	35	10				
Glass negs		250	700	700		
Film negs			1,100	2,100		11,000
Vintage prints	500	1,500	2,500	2,000	1,500	2,000
Copy images						
Photo albums	12	9	25	23	9	7

GEOGRAPHIC: Extensive coverage of Galveston and Galveston Bay, with a secondary emphasis on the Southeast Texas coast.

Texas: Alvin. Arcadia. Austin. Bay City. Beaumont. Bessmay. Brazoria. Browndell. Brownsville. Call. Corpus Christi. Cuero. Dallas. Dickinson. El Paso. Fort Stockton. Fort Worth. Fredericksburg. Gonzales. Houston. Huntsville. Indianola. La Grange. New Braunfels. Palestine. Port Aransas. Port Arthur. Port Isabel. Port Lavaca. Rio Grande Valley. Sabine Pass. San Antonio. Seabrook. Sour Lake. Stamford. Texas City. Tyler. Victoria. Waco. Weatherford.

Non-Texas: Arizona. Germany (Bremen). California. Canada (Saint John, New Brunswick). Japan (Niigata). England (London, Manchester). Louisiana (Abbeville, New Iberia). Massachusetts (Worcester). Mexico. Oklahoma (Oklahoma City). Pennsylvania (Philadelphia). Puerto Rico. South Pacific Theater (WW II).

SUBJECTS: Most photographs maintained in an artificial collection arranged by subject. Extensive coverage of all subjects; Galveston subjects separated from other locations. 8,000 photo prints. Street scenes are separated and arranged by building. 600 photo prints. Headings (edited) used in the collection include:

Galveston as background (aerial, construction at wharves, harbor, parks, skylines). Homes and living conditions (exteriors, gardens, interiors). Intellectual and creative activities (museums, newspapers, photography). Land (accidents at the wharf, bay improvements, causeway, historic sites, hurricanes, lighthouses, plants, railroad bridges, seashore and open sea, wharf areas). Medicine (hospitals, infirmary, nurses, pediatrics, quarantine station). Organized society (courts, elections, festivals, fraternal organizations, government and agencies, patriotism, police, politics, veterans' organizations). People (class reunions, organizations, public buildings, schools, scouts, studio portraits, youth). Processing and manufacturing (bagging, cotton mills, flour mills, food production, leather, steel, sugar mills). Recreation (amusement parks, bands, bathing beauty pageants, carhop queen contest, clubs, dancing, fishing, hay fever contest, gambling, hotels, parades, restaurants, sailing, saloons, singing, swimming, theater). Religion (ceremonies, churches, clergy, lay activities, services). Selling and distribution (drugstores, food stores, grain elevators, stores, warehouses, wholesale exchanges). Service (auto sales, communications, fire fighting, fireboats, markets, personal, postal, municipal, street cleaning, water supply). Social and personal activity (funerals, holidays, practical jokes). Transportation (aircraft, airports, autos, emigration and immigration, horse and buggy, railroads, ships—captains, —cargo, —deck activities, —dry dock, —maintainence, —ferryboats, —tugboats, —warships, space travel, street railroad, wharf scenes). War and military affairs (armed forces, civilian participation, combat, military camps, naval vessels, veterans of San Jacinto, women's groups, parades, WW I, WW II). Work (banking, building trades, business, civil engineering projects, fishing—commercial, grade raising, insurance, jetties, laboratories, oil, orchards, roadbuilding, seawall).

Red Cross. Beach Hotel. Buccaneer Hotel. Concrete ship experiment. Garten Verein. Hotel Galvez. International Longshoremen's Association. The Little Theater of Galveston. Paris Exposition—1867. The Pavilion. Pier 19 controversy. Rosenberg Fountain. Rosenberg Library. San Luis Pass Bridge. Texas City Explosion. Texas Heroes Monument. Tremont Hotel. US Army Corps of Engineers. UT Medical Branch. YMCA and YWCA.

PEOPLE: Predominantly Galveston residents; many civic leaders, post-Republic settlers, and Civil War soldiers. Headings represent both portraits and nonpersonal imagery related to the individual. Some nonphotographic imagery, mostly engravings, interfiled. 750 names (3,000 photographs), many represented by only a few images. 1850s to the present, most from the nineteenth century.

Badgett quadruplets.* Gail Borden. Henry Y. Cartwright. Marius S. Chataigon. Cherry family. John L. Darrough family. Milo P. Fox family. Ed J. Harris. John Woods Harris. Daniel W. Kempner. Harris Kempner. James M. Kirwin. Thomas Jefferson League. Chauncey Leake. Benjamin W. LeCompte. Jack Mankey. Ballinger Mills. Mary Moody Northen. Frank D. Patten. Thomas Geale Rice. Henry Rosenberg family.* Henry Sampson family. William Schadt family. Aaron Robert "Babe" Schwartz.* William Willis Sealey family. Theodore Stubbs. Clark W. Thompson. Libby Moody Thompson. Phillip Crosby Tucker and family. Lewis Valentine Ulrey. Aaron Waag family. Samuel May Williams.

*Extensive coverage.

PHOTOGRAPHERS: Most are Galveston studio photographers from the nineteenth or early twentieth centuries; few snapshooters.

Duncan Caldwell Crooks.* Deane. John Hanna.* Susan King. Joseph M. Maurer.* H. H. Morris.* Paul H. Naschke. P. H. Rose. Traube. Paul Verkin.* Witwer Studios. Justus Zahn.

*See Record Groups and Record Groups—Albums.

RECORD GROUPS:

G40.1 AFRO-AMERICAN FAMILY COLLECTION. Most snapshots, a few studio portraits. Possibly belonging to [illegible first name] Mae Gerard, possibly made while at attendance at a girls' school, possibly Howard University.

> **G40.1.1** Simms, Lionel. *Vietta.* Snapshot portraits, possibly from Straight College. 16 silver gelatin prints in a handmade album. Ca. 1920. RL# 72.1.

> **G40.1.2** [*(Illegible) Mae Gerard album.*] Snapshot portraits. 18 silver gelatin prints. Ca. 1920. RL# 72.2.18.

70 silver gelatin prints; 2 albums (v.s.). 1920s. RL# 72.

G40.2 BLACK HISTORY COLLECTION. Copy photographs used in an exhibit on Galveston Black history. 100 silver gelatin prints. 1880 to 1980. RL# 60.

G40.3 CAMPBELL-FULLER FAMILY COLLECTION. Studio and snapshot portraits of the family and their friends; most from Galveston, a few from Augusta ME showing landscapes, studio portraits from New York and other cities; interior view of a lounge on the SS *Lusitania*.

> [*Campbell-Fuller family snapshot album.*] Snapshot portraits, vacation views along the East Coast, and Black sharecroppers. 167 silver gelatin prints, 1 tintype. Mid-1900s to ca. 1915.

1,000 photographs, including ambrotypes, cartes, cabinets, and silver gelatin prints; 1 album (v.i.). 1860 to 1935. RL# 62.

G40.4 DOW (DOROTHY) COLLECTION. Buildings, including Sacred Heart Church and the Texas Heroes Monument, El Mina Shrine Temple parade, boats, and city scenes. 141 photographs, including color snapshots. 1900 to 1985. RL# 70.

G40.5 HANNA (JOHN; 1863-1943) COLLECTION. Amateur views of the Hanna family, including Joseph Clark residence, Griffin family, Pearl Burck, L. J. Selby, Bolivar Bay, Bain family, Gengler residence, Saint Mary's Orphan Asylum; domestic interiors. 220 glass negatives with modern prints. 1895 to 1901. RL# 12.

G40.6 HISTORIC AMERICAN BUILDINGS SURVEY COLLECTION. Retrospective views of Galveston-area historic structures included in this register. 1,000 negatives and modern prints. 1966 to 1967. RL# 48.

G40.7 KANE SHIPBUILDING COMPANY COLLECTION. Commercial views of ships constructed by the company and activities of the firm. 1950s. 200 silver gelatin prints. RL# 75.

G40.8 KING (SUZANNE) COLLECTION. Part of the Town versus Metropolis: The Galveston Story project sponsored by the Texas Committee for the Humanities and the Moody Foundation; includes some copy photographs from the Black and Hispanic communities in Galveston. Photographed by King. 10,000 photographs, including 35mm and 4x5 negatives and prints. 1979 to 1980. RL# 58.

G40.9 MANKEY (FRANK) COLLECTION. Publicity agent for the Galveston Beach Association. In situ portraits of Mankey and publicity photographs of Galveston events. 12 silver gelatin prints. 1940s. RL# 73.

G40.10 MAURER (JOSEPH I.) COLLECTION. Cityscapes and buildings, including Saint Mary's University, beauty contests, portraits, boats and wharves, Beth Jacob Synagogue, Murdoch's Bath House, churches, and residences. 60 negatives, many glass, many with modern prints. 1927 to 1935. RL# 56.

G40.11 MAURER (JOSEPH M.; 1876-1953) ARCHIVES. Galveston commercial photographer. Galveston residents and their activities; churches; buildings and street scenes, including views of palm trees and residences along Broadway; ships. 3,000 nitrate and glass negatives, many with modern prints; partial, itemized list. 1920s to 1946. RL# 34, 47.

G40.12 MILITARY CAMP COLLECTION. Unidentified camp showing soldiers; Texas 1884 Capitol. 7 silver gelatin glass negatives. Ca. 1900. RL# 54.

G40.13 MORGAN FAMILY COLLECTION. Portraits of Morgan, Thomas, Burrows, and Scrimgeour families; family friends; Galveston Public Health Nursing Service, Knights Templar, residences, and ships; vacations.

G40.13.1 [*Morgan album I.*] Snapshots of Morgan family; Galveston cityscapes; travel photographs to New York. 64 gelatino-chloride prints. 1899 to 1902.

G40.13.2 [*Morgan album II.*] Commercial travel views of Seattle WA; snapshots of Texas City, of Highways 6 and 35, and of Galveston city scenes. 86 silver gelatin prints; withdrawn from album. 1928 to 1932.

G40.13.3 [*Morgan album III.*] Snapshots, including seaplanes, Kemah-Seabrook and Lynchburg ferrys, Galveston cityscapes, pilot boat *Texas*, auto travel trip scenes through West Texas to the Grand Canyon. 96 silver gelatin prints; withdrawn from album. 1927 to 1928.

G40.13.4 [*Morgan album IV.*] Snapshots of road construction near Alvin. 65 silver gelatin prints; withdrawn from album. 1933.

G40.13.5 [*Morgan album V.*] Snapshots of Virginia Point causeway construction. 157 silver gelatin prints; withdrawn from album. 1935 to 1938.

G40.13.6 [*Morgan album VI.*] Snapshots of Highway 35, road construction, tugboat *Sea King*. 74 silver gelatin prints; withdrawn from album. 1934.

G40.13.7 [*Morgan album VII.*] Snapshots of Highway 35; road construction; Galveston-Bolivar ferry; causeway. 77 silver gelatin prints; withdrawn from album. 1934 to 1937.

G40.13.8 [*Morgan album VIII.*] Snapshots of YMCA camp at Dickinson; Galveston-Bolivar ferry; Fort Crockett; Morgan's Point; pilot boat Texas; 1915 and 1919 hurricanes; commercial souvenir views of Hoover Dam. 71 silver gelatin prints, postcards; withdrawn from album. 1915 to 1934.

G40.13.9 [*Morgan album IX.*] Snapshots of Highway 75, road construction, 1909 hurricane, and causeway. 267 silver gelatin prints. 1937 to 1938.

5 boxes of photo prints and 9 albums (v.s.); postcards; descriptive inventory. 1845 to 1938. RL# 65.

G40.14 NASCHKE (PAUL; 1872-1932) COLLECTION. Galveston commercial photographer. Photographs of the Naschke family and pertaining to his career. 17 silver gelatin vintage and modern prints. 1890s to 1950s. RL# 74.

G40.15 1900 HURRICANE COLLECTION. Aftermath of storm, including salvage workers, storm survivors, First Methodist Church, Sacred Heart Church. 40 stereographs. 1900. RL# 31.

G40.16 PORTRAITS COLLECTION. Studio portraits by an unidentified photographer. 12 silver gelatin glass negatives. 1880s. RL# 55.

G40.17 ROLLFING (A. O.) COLLECTION. Aftermath of the 1900 hurricane. 36 modern prints. 1900. RL# 63.

G40.18 ROSE (PHILLIP H.; b. 1829?) COLLECTION. Galveston cityscapes and street scenes, showing businesses and residences; entertainment, including the Opera House and beach scenes. 24 stereographs. 1880. RL# 66.

G40.19 ROSENBERG LIBRARY COLLECTION. Construction of the Moody Memorial Wing. 6 slide trays of 35mm color slides. 1969 to 1970. RL# 46.

G40.20 SCHULDT 1915 HURRICANE COLLECTION. Snapshots of storm damage, many showing houses upturned. 50 silver gelatin prints. 1915. RL# 13.

G40.21 SEA WALL AREA COLLECTION. Amusement park on the seawall, Crystal Palace diving board, 1915 hurricane. 17 glass negatives and photo prints. Ca. 1915. RL# 43.

G40.22 STORM AND FIRE DEPARTMENT COLLECTION. Horse-drawn fire engine, old city hall rebuilt as a fire station, and aftermath of 1900 hurricane. 7 silver gelatin glass negatives. Ca. 1900. RL# 53.

G40.23 THOMPSON (LIBBY MOODY) COLLECTION. Commercial studio portraits of women wearing Mardi Gras costumes. 46 nitrate negatives. 1920s to 1930s. RL# 68.

G40.24 TURN OF THE CENTURY COLLECTION. Amateur views of cityscapes and buildings by an unidentified photographer(s). 270 glass negatives, many with modern prints; itemized list. 1890 to 1900. RL# 52.

G40.25 WORLD WAR I COLLECTION. Commercial, probably military staff photographs, views of the French fronts at Marne, Aisne, Flanders, and others; French troops in the trenches and in encampments; American and Russian troops; wounded soldiers; equipment; aftermath showing terrain and damage to buildings. 170 silver gelatin prints; most with printed or calligraphic captions. 1914 to 1918. RL# 59.

G40.26 WORLD WAR I COLLECTION. Official military journalistic photographs of British troups in battle scenes, including trenches, aftermath of conflicts, and domestic front. 35 silver gelatin prints. 1914 to 1918. RL# 64.

Albums and published works illustrated with photographs (see Record Groups—Afro-American collection and —Morgan collection for additional albums):

G40.27 [*Album 38.*] Snapshots made in Galveston and San Antonio; includes Lasker residence, Seeligson family; possibly a girls' college. 105 silver gelatin and cyanotype prints. Ca. 1905. RL# 38.

G40.28 [*Album 39.*] Snapshots, predominantly portraits, some vacation views; made in Galveston, Boerne, Pinehurst NC, and the Giant Forest Park. 320 silver gelatin prints. 1927 to 1936. RL# 39.

G40.29 *Art work of Galveston.* Chicago: W. H. Parish, 1894. Residences and buildings. 70 photogravures. RL# F394.G2H/A7.

G40.30 *Children's Department of the Rosenberg Library.* Amateur views of children and exhibits in the department showing the interior; antique dolls and doll houses; staff portraits. 75 silver gelatin prints. 1924 to 1930. RL# 15.

G40.31 Crooks, Duncan Calwell, photog. [*Duncan Calwell Crooks album.*] Amateur views of construction and workers on the causeway and other sites in the area, including cityscapes, domestic interiors, fishing fleet and harbor views, the Rosenberg Library, and Grace Episcopal Church; Frisco Railroad construction at Choctaw; powerhouse construction at McKinney. 532 silver gelatin prints and cyanotypes in 5 volumes. 1907 to 1915. RL# 22; Mss 77-0026.

G40.32 [*Pauline Dyer.*] Scenes of San Antonio, including missions, plazas scenes, and Fort Sam Houston; Austin scenes include the 1884 Capitol, powerhouse, and dam. 71 gelatino-chloride Kodak and silver gelatin prints. Ca. 1890. RL# 5.

G40.33 Dyer, J. O., ed. *Pageant of progress*. History of Galveston, including art reproductions and structures to accompany a lecture by Dyer. 150 lantern slides. 1923. RL# 50.

G40.34 [*European landscape album.*] Commercial travel views of landscapes in Germany, Switzerland, and Italy, many mountain scenes, some showing railroads; art reproductions of statuary. Most photographed by Giorgio Sommer (Naples, Italy). 41 albumen prints. Ca. 1890. RL# 76.

G40.35 *Galveston scenes*. Amateur views of cityscapes and residences. 127 silver gelatin and color prints. 1940 to 1950. RL# 33.

G40.36 *Galveston: The sea wall city*. Galveston: Charles Daferner, [ca. 1910.] Commercial city scenes, including churches, schools, and commercial and residential architecture. 25 Albertypes, including 1 panorama; 2 copies. RL# F394.G2GF/G357; RL# 7.

G40.37 *Galveston: The treasure island of America, port and playground*. Galveston: Daferner's Book Store, [ca. 1913.] Commercial cityscapes, including Hotel Galvez, Interurban railway. 11 Albertypes. RL# 8.

G40.38 *Galveston Wharf Company: Views along Galveston's waterfront*. Chicago: Process Photo Studio, [ca. 1920s]. Commercial souvenir photographs of the company's grain elevator, warehouse interiors, and activities. 12 silver gelatin prints. RL# 71.

G40.39 *Glimpses of Texas*. Austin, Galveston, and Houston views. Ca. 1873. 16 items. RL# 28.

G40.40 *Have a look at our city*. Postcard views of Galveston and area businesses with letterheads. 2 volumes; 24+24 pp, includes 3 silver gelatin prints, most nonphotographic photomechanical postcards. Ca. 1920. RL# 2.

G40.41 [*Loeff family album.*] Cityscapes during the raising of the island grade and seawall, including panoramas photographed by Edworthy; Loeff family, including Black servants and domestic interiors; landscapes and natives in the Dutch East Indies (= Indonesia). 327 silver gelatin prints and collodio-chloride prints. 1904 to 1915. RL# 27.

G40.42 [*Mallory Docks pier construction.*] Snapshots of construction workers and equipment. 46 silver gelatin prints, handwritten captions. 1926. RL# 4.

G40.43 Maurer, Joseph M., photog. [*City hall and auditorium.*] Exterior and interior showing various painted stage background scenes. 10 silver gelatin prints. Ca. 1920. RL# 9.

G40.44 *El Mina Shrine Temple*. San Francisco: Imperial Council, 1922. Amateur travel views of a Shriner train trip to and from San Francisco via Winnipeg and Vancouver, Canada. 49 silver gelatin postcards. RL# 6.

G40.45 [Morris, H. H., attrib. photog.] [*Galveston album.*] [Galveston: H. H. Morris, ca. 1909.] Commercial views of harbor and skylines including 1895 snowstorm. 12 silver gelatin copy prints; 3 copies. 1860 to 1895. RL# 11.

G40.46 [Morris, H. H., attrib. photog.] *Galveston: The sea wall city.* Cityscapes, including a fold-out panorama of the skyline; residences, churches, and commercial buildings; skyline. 18 photo-collotypes. Late 1910s. RL #3.

G40.47 Morris, H. H., photog. [*Morris album.*] Construction of the Galveston causeway, the La Porte drawbridge, Hotel Galvez, and beaches. 53 silver gelatin prints. 1892 to 1915. RL# 18.

G40.48 Naschke, Paul H. and Della B., photog. *City of Galveston.* Storm damage by the 1900 hurricane, including general views of the city showing debris, damage to brick structures, and the harbor. 51 silver gelatin prints. 1900. RL# 14.

G40.49 [*1915 storm.*] Commercial views of aftermath, including wrecked homes and industry, beached ships, damage to the Interurban and restoration of rail service, and scenes along the water-front. 79 silver gelatin prints. 1915. RL# 67.

G40.50 Ovies, Raimundo de. *American art.* Art reproductions of civic art, murals, and sculpture photographed by Albert Kirk to accompany lecture by Ovies. 35 lantern slides. 1924. RL# 51.

G40.51 *Photographs of the Texas City Disaster.* Galveston: US Army Corps of Engineers, 1947. "Explosion area prior to blast; aerial views of fires and damage; ground views of fires and damage; Corps of Engineers, sweeping operations for submerged obstructions in turning basin; obstructions in, and removed from, the Texas City harbor; missiles and damage. 116 images on 14 leaves of silver gelatin paper.

G40.52 [*Norman Ricker album.*] Snapshots of damage from the 1915 hurricane; snapshots of Austin, Rice Institute, Texas Heroes monument, Battleship Texas, Cotton Carnival. 55 silver gelatin prints. 1915.

G40.53 *Seventy-fifth anniversary of the opening of the Rosenberg Library.* Activities commemorating the 75th anniversary of the library. 47 silver gelatin prints, 4 contact sheets with 8 images each. 1979. RL# 29.

G40.54 Talfor, R. B., photog. *Photographic views illustrating the experimental work undertaken by the United States for improvement of the entrance to Galveston Harbor, Texas.* Documents of experiment to construct jetties of woven cane for the harbor entrance; steam tug. 18 albumen prints; typescript captions. 1875. RL# 23.

G40.55 Thomson, Cecil, photog. [*Imperial Sugar Company.*] Presentation album stamped "I. H. Kempner." Commercial aerial views of the sugar plant and Sugarland; interiors of plant showing workers; city scenes showing residential and commercial structures. 67 silver gelatin prints; typescript captions. Ca. 1930. RL# 16.

G40.56 Townshend, S. Nugent; Hyde, John George, photog. *Our Indian summer in the Far West: An autumn tour of fifteen thousand miles in Kansas, Texas, New Mexico, and the Indian Territory.* London: printed by C. Whittingham, 1880. RL# F391.H895-ov. 59 albumen prints bound into the text block. Amateur travel views of landscapes, railroads, Fort Elliot, and Guyemos Canyon NM.

G40.57 *Tropical hurricane of August 16, 1915.* Commercial souvenir views of aftermath of storm in Galveston, Seabrook, Texas City, and surrounding communities, including damage to buildings and the causeway, beached boats, and Interurban cars off tracks. 49 silver gelatin prints. 1915. RL# 69.

G40.58 Verkin, Paul, photog. [*Paul Verkin album.*] Commercial views of wharf scenes loading cargo onto ships, including aerial views; interiors of warehouses; and harbor scenes. 55 silver gelatin prints. Ca. 1925. RL# 17.

G40.59 Viewfinders Camera Club (Galveston), ed. *Life in Galveston County—today and yesterday.* Program prepared for the US Bicentennial. 3 slide trays with audio tape. 1976. RL# 19.

US Army Corps of Engineers, Galveston District (G50)

444 Barracuda Street
P.O. Box 1224
Galveston, Texas 77550

409-766-3004. Contact: Public Affairs Office.

PURPOSE: A working collection created to document the activities of the corps and for reference by the corps.

HOURS: Weekdays, 7:30-4:15. Closed major holidays. Appointment recommended.

ASSISTANCE: Specialized, experienced staff. Written and phone inquiries accepted. Electrostatic copies available. Photoduplications must be ordered through the agency.

PUBLICATION: No publication fee. Collection credit required. Third-party permission required on a few items.

FINDING AIDS: Access by general subject heading, geographic location, and date.

BIBLIOGRAPHY:
Alperin, Lynn M. *Custodians of the coast.* Galveston: US Army Corps of Engineers, Galveston District, 1977.

SCOPE: 51,000 original photographs, most 35mm color transparencies. A few copy transparencies from the late nineteenth century, vintage transparencies from the 1960s; an open collection.

Type of photo	Pre-1880	1880-1899	1900-1919	1920-1939	1940-1959	1960-1986
Glass negs				20		
Film negs				350	350	350

GEOGRAPHIC: Texas Gulf coast and roughly 50 miles inland.

Beaumont. Brownsville. Corpus Christi. Freeport. Galveston. Houston. Orange. Port Arthur. Texas City.

SUBJECTS: Documents the corps' activities to ensure and facilitate safe navigation and to provide protection from floods and hurricanes.

Architecture (coastal engineering projects). Events (floods, hurricanes). Government. Landscapes (seashore). Military (Galveston forts). Transportation (boats, causeways, waterways).

Texas City Explosion.

PEOPLE: Staff of the corps, working on projects and portraits.

RECORD GROUPS: A working collection arranged by subject.

G50.1 BROWNSVILLE AREA. South Padre Island and Port Isabel. 540—35mm color transparencies. 1960s to 1980s.

G50.2 CORPUS CHRISTI AREA. Corpus Christi ship channel, Alice, Baker's Port, Harbor Island, Aransas Pass, Port Ingleside; includes a few satellite aerial photographs. 600—35mm color transparencies. 1970s to 1980s.

G50.3 DREDGING. Dredging ships *Manhattan Island, McFarland, Fritz Jahnke,* and *MacKenzie* in operation along Galveston Island, Sabine-Netches, Corpus Christi, and Matagorda Bay; other, smaller launches. 700—35mm color transparencies. 1960s to 1970s.

G50.4 ENVIRONMENT. Landscapes documenting the flora and fauna of the Bolivar Habitat, shrimp mariculture at Freeport, and Texas City habitat. 640—35mm color transparencies. 1982 to 1984.

G50.5 FREEPORT. Brazos River diversion channel and floodgate, Bryan Mound Strategic Petroleum Reserve Site, Chocolate Bayou, Colorado River locks, Freeport harbor, Freeport Hurricane Flood Protection Project and guillotine gate, Freeport jetties, Guadalupe River, Lower Colorado River, Oyster Creek, Peyton Creek, San Bernard River and Channel, and Surfside. 3,000—35mm color transparencies. 1960s to 1980s.

G50.6 GALVESTON. Galveston Harbor, Bay, Ship Channel, jetties, beach; bayous, Big Reef, Bolivar Peninsula, Essayons Building, ferry landing, Fort Point, Henderson Hole, Hendly Building, North Jetty, Pelican Island, Rollover Pass, San Louis Pass, Santa Fe Building, Scholes Field, and South Jetty. 4,500—35mm color transparencies. 1950 to 1980s.

G50.7 GULF INTRACOASTAL WATER WAY. Ships and corps projects in the water way 770—35mm color transparencies. 1950s to 1985.

G50.8 HOUSTON FLOOD CONTROL. Barker and Addicks dams; White Oak, Sims, Buffalo, Brays, Vince, Little Vince, Greens, and Halls bayous; Seabrook; Caney, Peach, Cole, Lake, Sugar, Cypress, Spring, and Clear creeks; Clear Lake. 5,000—35mm color transparencies. 1960s to 1980s.

G50.9 HOUSTON NAVIGATION. Houston skyline, Hobby Airport, San Jacinto River, Houston Ship Channel, Barbour's Cut, Baytown, Wallisville, Channel to Liberty, Bayport. 2,500—35mm color transparencies. 1960s to 1980s.

G50.10 HURRICANE AND FLOOD DAMAGE. Aftermath of hurricanes Carla (1961), Beulah (1967), Camille (1969), Celia (1970), Alicia (1983), and tropical storm Claudette (1979) showing damage to property emphasizing storm effects on public works and roadways; many aerial views; most along the coast. 2,000—35mm color transparencies. 1961 to 1983.

G50.11 PEOPLE. Staff of the corps. 1,000—35mm color transparencies. 1970s to 1980s.

G50.12 PORT ARTHUR AREA. Port Arthur Area Office, Pleasure Island, disposal areas, Kirbyville, Orange, bridges, Pine Island Bayou, Port Arthur Hurricane Flood Protection Project, Sabine-Neches Water Way, Taylor's Bayou, Taylor's Bayou Salt Water Barrier, Sabine Pass, Big Hill Strategic Petroleum Reserve, mothball fleet. 2,500—35mm color transparencies. 1960s to 1980s.

G50.13 SALVAGE OF THE A. MacKENZIE. Operations to remove the wreckage of the sunken ship from Galveston Bay. 50–35mm color transparencies. 1974.

G50.14 SHIPS AND CONSTRUCTION. 500–35mm color transparencies. 1970s to 1980s.

G50.15 TEXAS CITY. Texas City Dyke, Dickinson Bayou, Moses Lake Gate, Texas City Hurricane Flood Protection Project, Texas City Ship Channel, Highland Bayou and Diversion Channel, Snake Island. 2,500–35mm color transparencies. 1960 to 1980s.

Truman G. Blocker Jr.
History of Medicine Collections (G60)

University of Texas Medical Branch
Moody Medical Library
Ninth and Market Street
Galveston, Texas 77550-2782

409-761-2397. Contact: Curator.

PURPOSE: An academic library supporting teaching, patient care, and research at the Medical Center and including a photographic collection that relates to the history of the institution and to the history of occupational therapy. Historical collections include artifacts, rare and recent books and journals, manuscripts, microscopes, postage stamps, postcards, prints, and photographs.

HOURS: Exhibition space—weekdays, 7:30 a.m.-midnight; Saturday, 10:00-7:00; Sunday, noon to midnight. Historical collections—weekdays, 1:00-5:00; appointments preferred. Closed major holidays.

ASSISTANCE: Professional, experienced, specialized staff. Written and phone inquries accepted. Electrostatic copies available. Photoduplications must be ordered through the library.

PUBLICATION: No publication fee. Collection credit required. Some material requires third-party permission.

FINDING AIDS: Itemized listing, computer database. Access by general subject, geographic location, personal name, and date. Photographs are arranged by subject.

SCOPE: 3,000 vintage and copy photo prints. 1890 to 1980.

GEOGRAPHIC: Galveston (campus area only). See Subjects—Non-UTMB headings for additional locations.

SUBJECTS: Extensive coverage of the UTMB, including the activities of the students and faculty, facilities, and patients. Subject headings used in the collection (edited) include:

UTMB: Alumni activities and reunions. Ambulances. American Cancer Society. Auxiliary services. Blood bank. Campus (aerial views, general views). Celebrations (fiftieth anniversary). Classrooms and laboratories (anatomy, bacteriology, biochemistry, clinical, histological—embryology, parasitology, pathology, pediatrics, pharmacology, physiology, surgery, tissue culture). Dietary. Ear, nose, and throat. Graduation ceremonies. Groups meetings. Heart Career Day. Hospital nursery. Hospital wards. Interns. Libraries. Long-term employees recognition. Medical records. Medicine. Meetings and conference groups (Sigma Xi, pediatric, internal medicine, clinical war session). Mental Health Week. Miscellaneous. National Hospital Week. Nurses. Occupational therapy. Operation Knot Hole. Operating room. Ophthamology. Orientation. Patient care. Pediatrics. Pharmacy. Physician Assistants. Psychiatry. Quarantine station. Radiology. Rehabilitation clinic. Resident staff. Residents. Sterile supply. Storms (1900, 1943, 1961, 1983). Student groups. Student housing (fraternities, Sealy Smith apartments). Student life (Alpha Mu Phi Omega, Alpha Omega Alpha, Catus staff, Jolly Bone Jugglers, Phi Alpha Sigma, social activities). US Army. Valentine Blood Club. Visitors.

UTMB Buildings: Bethel Hall. Gail Borden Building. Children's Hospital. Graves Hospital. John W. McCullough Negro hospital. Outpatient Clinic. Randall Pavilion. Jennie Sealy Hospital. John Sealy hospitals (1889, 1947, 1978). Shriner's Burn Hospital. Ashbel Smith Building ("Old Red"). Zeigler Hospital.

Non-UTMB: Base Hospital, France. Brooklyn State Hospital. Camp Custer, Battle Creek MI. Camp Gordon, German prisoner of war camp, Atlanta GA. Camp Taylor KY. Clifton Springs Sanatorium NY. Fort McPherson GA. Fort Sheridan IL. New York State Tuberculosis Hospital, Mount Morris NY. Niagara Sanatorium, Lockport NY. Pennsylvania State Sanitorium for Tuberculosis, Mount Alto PA. Psychiatric Hospital, Rio Piedras PR. Queen's Hospital, Honolulu HI. US Marine Hospital, Louisville KY.

PEOPLE: Many portraits of students, faculty, and staff of UTMB, especially class groups; few held in quantity, with the exception of Dr. Truman G. Blocker Jr. Members of the American Occupational Therapists Association.

Harris County Heritage Society (H37)

5400 Mitchelldale, Suite A1
Houston, Texas 77092

713-956-0480. Contact: Photography Curator.

PURPOSE: A local history society operating a park with historical buildings and an exhibiting museum with reserve collections of manuscripts, three-dimensional artifacts, including the decorative arts, and photographs.

HOURS: Reserve collections—by appointment only. Closed major holidays.

ASSISTANCE: Staff assistance. Written and phone inquiries accepted. Electrostatic copies available. Photoduplications may be made by the patron or ordered through the society.

PUBLICATION: No publication fee. Collection credit required. Free copy of publication to society. Third-party permission required on few items.

FINDING AIDS: Card index; access by subject and personal name.

BIBLIOGRAPHY:
Siegel, Stanley E., et al. *Houston: A chronicle of the supercity on Buffalo Bayou.* Woodland Hills CA: Windsor Publications in cooperation with the Harris County Heritage Society, 1983.

SCOPE: Photographs in major processes, including cirkut panorama prints and negatives and professional photographer's ephemera. 1857 to present.

Type of photo	Pre-1880	1880-1899	1900-1919	1920-1939	1940-1959	1960-1986
D/A/T-types	20					
Glass negs	2,165					
Film negs				2,800		50,000
Vintage prints	80	335	295	1,500	240	
Copy prints						
Photo albums	1	4	1	7		

GEOGRAPHIC: Emphasis is on Harris County, with extensive coverage of Houston, including the Ship Channel and Buffalo Bayou. A few other Texas locales are represented, including Beaumont, Texarkana, Freeport, Morgan's Point, and Galveston.

SUBJECTS: Emphasis is on architecture, with some emphasis on buildings designed by Alfred Finn. Major headings used in the collection include:

Aerial, general views. Advertisement. Agricultural machinery. Agricultural products. Agriculture (cotton). Airplanes. Ambulance. Amusement. Animals. Apartment buildings. Appliances. Architecture (domestic). Art, decorative. Associations. Athletics. Automobile. Automobile showroom and building. Bakery building. Bank buildings (State National). Banquets. Bayou. Boats. Brewery building. Bridges. Business and professions, general. Cattle. Cemetery. Christmas. Churches and religious affairs. Cities (not Houston). Cleaners and laundry. Clothing and dress. Clubs. College and university buildings. Commerce. Construction. Conventions. Department stores. Disaster. Downtown views (Houston). Drugstores. Electrical apparatus. Electric power plant. Farm produce. Fire fighting. Florist. Fountains. Funeral homes. Funerals. Government (county, federal, state). Grocery stores. Horses. Hospitals. Hotels and motels (exteriors, interiors). Houses. Ice company. Industrial landscapes. Library. Lumber. Machinery. Manufacturers. Military buildings. Office buildings. Office interiors. Parks. People. Performing arts. Petroleum industry (derricks). Portraits (individual, group). Public buildings. Railroads. Recreation. Resturants. Retail trade buildings. School buildings. Shipping (water vessels). Small business. Social functions. Sports. Street railroads. Street scenes. Transportation (trucks). Turning Basin. Warehouse (interiors). Wells (water). Zoo.

Lamar Hotel. Plaza Hotel. Rice Hotel. Texas State Hotel. *USS Houston*. William D. Cleveland and Sons. Electric Building. Houston Light and Power. Humble Oil Company (= Exxon). Loew's State Theater. Magnolia Brewery. Texaco service stations. Weingarten's grocery stores. Westheimer Transfer Company.

PEOPLE: Area residents, few held in common.

PHOTOGRAPHERS: Predominantly studio photographers, most from Houston. Barr and Wright.* George Beach. Robert D. Dixon.* Fred A. Gildersleeve (Waco). Harper and Company. Litterst.* Miller (Tulsa OK). Milstead. Schlueter. Story Sloan. Cecil Thomson. Chas. J. Wright.

*See Record Groups.

RECORD GROUPS:

H37.1 BARR AND WRIGHT ARCHIVES. Studio portraits photographed by Barr and Wright. 2,165 collodion negatives used to print cartes; a few developed as ambrotypes. Late 1860s to 1880s

The original owner of this collection gave a group of negatives from this collection to the Smithsonian Institution. HCHS# 984.81.

H37.2 BENZIGER (J. C.) FAMILY COLLECTION. Snapshot portraits of the Benziger family. 90 silver gelatin prints. 1910s to 1920s. HCHS# 984.19.

H37.3 HOPKINS (T.) COLLECTION. Portraits of firemen in uniforms. 5 tintypes and ambrotypes in cases. 1870s. HCHS# 978.99.

H37.4 KERNS COLLECTION. Studio portraits and snapshot portraits of individuals and groups, most individuals are not from Texas. Photographed by various studio and unidentified snapshot photographers. 170 photographs, many cabinets. 1890s to 1920s. HCHS# 984.60.

H37.5 LITTERST-DIXON ARCHIVES. Commercial photography firm founded by Joseph D. Litterst (1896-1949) in 1903; Litterst's son, Joseph Jr. (d. 1940) took over the company in 1927, leaving it to his wife, Joy, on his death; Robert D. Dixon joined the firm in 1949 and acquired it from Mrs. Litterst in 1954.

> **H37.5.1** Litterst Commercial Photo Company archive. Documents the economic development of the city, especially in terms of the petroleum and shipping industries. Much architecture, including commercial interiors and storefronts, religious, academic, residential; cityscapes, including aerials, street scenes, and skylines; petroleum industry, including oil fields, derricks, tank farms, laying pipeline, refineries, and workers from Houston area east to Liberty County; Port of Houston and Galveston Bay shipping industry, including ships, wharves, warehouses, and dock workers; industrial, commercial, and retail businesses, especially grocery interiors; some commercial product photography; and some group portraits, most sports teams. Subjects with substantial treatment include:
>
> > Battleship Texas. Brazos River Diversion Channel and Levees. Freeport sulphur refinery. Galena Signal Oil Company. Humble Oil rail and truck tankers. Madding's Drug Store. Majestic Theater (Houston, designed by John Eberson). Seaport Bag Company, Houston Terminal Warehouse and Cold Storage Company, and Lykes Brothers Steamship Company. Shriner's convention. Southwest Automotive Show—1938 (a dealers' and mechanics' exhibition), including product displays and general views of the exhibition floor. Staiti home and interiors with family members, some hand-colored. Studio portraits of Amerinds and vaqueros. Sylvan Beach. YMCA, including indoor sports and facilities. York Refrigeration and Air Conditioning Company. 2,000 film negatives; 2,000 prints, most modern, a few vintage silver gelatin; 800 circkut negatives. 1903 to 1950s.
>
> **H37.5.2** Robert Dixon archives. Commercial photography in Houston by Dixon. 25 feet 4x5 safety negatives with assignment information on storage envelope; arranged chronologically; unprocessed. 1960 to mid-1970s.

The Litterst-Dixon archives contain more than 10,000 photographs, total. 1857 to mid-1970s. HCHS# 977.72.

H37.6 SEIBERT (FRED C.) COLLECTION. Chief of Houston Fire Department. Houston Fire Department firefighters, station houses, including interiors, group portraits with fire trucks and fire boat, and parades. 42 photo prints. 1890s to 1920s. HCHS# 980.51.

H37.7 SHAMROCK HOTEL COLLECTION. Documentation of the opening of the hotel; actors, singers, musicians, and prominent individuals; Glenn McCarthy, John Carroll, Dorothy Lamour, Fred Nahas; ceremonies. 240 silver gelatin prints. HCHS# 978.103.

H37.8 STUDIO PORTRAITS COLLECTION. Various Houston studio photographers, many by Charles J. Wright. 54 prints, most cabinets. 1870s to ca. 1900. HCHS# 984.66.

Albums:

H37.9 [*Amateur album 983.58.02.*] Informal portraits, travel photographs, street scenes in unidentified locales, bullfights in Mexico, Mexican Revolution. 205 silver gelatin prints. 1910s.

H37.10 [*Cabinet album.*] Studio portraits by various Houston photographers. 21 photo prints, most cabinets. 1870s to 1890s.

H37.11 [*Cabinet album 976.90.*] Studio portraits. Various US Midwest photographers, including E. Decker (Cleveland OH), and North and Oswald (Toledo KS). 37 albumen cabinet prints. 1880s.

H37.12 [*Cabinet album 979.8.1.*] Studio portraits by various Central Texas photographers, including Walker (Brenham). 21 photo prints, most cabinets. 1880s.

H37.13 [*Cabinet album 985.38.01.*] Unidentified studio portraits by various photographers, including C. J. Ostberg (Bridgeport CT) and Bronson (Bridgeport CT). 4 cartes and 27 cabinet prints. 1880s.

H37.14 [*Carte album 976.15.*] Studio portraits, some identified by various Illinois photographers, including B. A. Ford (Braidwood IL) and W. H. Mitchell (Wilmington IL). 26 albumen cartes and tintypes. 1860s.

H37.15 [*Family album 973.103.1.*] Vacation and portrait snapshots made in the vicinity of Houston, Rockport, and Beaumont. 239 silver gelatin prints. 1914 to 1924.

H37.16 [*Family album 974.103.2.*] Vacation and portrait snapshots made in Houston, Rockport, and Beaumont vicinity; many beach scenes. 149 silver gelatin prints. 1920s.

H37.17 [*Family album 974.103.3.*] Vacation and portrait snapshots, many made in Houston vicinity, others made on trip(s) to Niagara Falls and through the Midwest. 346 silver gelatin prints. 1918 to 1924.

H37.18 [*Family album 974.103.4.*] Vacation and portrait snapshots; a few commercial views of Rockport buildings with hurricane damage in 1919. 325 silver gelatin prints. 1916 to 1925.

H37.19 [*Family album 974.103.5.*] Vacation and portrait snapshots. 127 silver gelatin prints. 1918 to 1927.

H37.20 [*Family album 974.103.6.*] Vacation and portrait snapshots, including many beach and ranch scenes. 154 silver gelatin prints. 1918 to 1924.

H37.21 [*Snapshot album 984.59.20.*] Corps men and female visitors at Texas A&M. 90 silver gelatin prints. 1920s.

Historical Research Center (H40)

Houston Academy of Medicine-Texas Medical Center Library
1133 M. D. Anderson Boulevard
Houston, Texas 77030

713-797-1230, extension 139. Contact: Director.

PURPOSE: A library collecting books and journals, manuscripts, artifacts, and photographs.

HOURS: Weekdays, 8:00-5:00; weekends and evenings by appointment. Closed major holidays.

ASSISTANCE: Professional staff. Written and phone inquiries accepted. Electrostatic copies not available. Photoduplications may be made by patron or ordered through the library.

PUBLICATION: No publication fee. Collection credit required. Free copy of publication to library. Third-party permission required on some materials.

FINDING AIDS: Card index and descriptive listing; access by general subject heading, personal name, and photographer.

SCOPE: 50,000 vintage prints and negatives, 100 copy photographs; other formats include 700 stereographs, 100 lantern slides, 12 motion picture, 20 videotapes, and some photographic postcards. 1870s to present, most after 1940.

Type of photo	Pre-1880	1880-1899	1900-1919	1920-1939	1940-1959	1960-1986
D/A/T-types	3	3		-		
Film negs					5,000	45,000
Vintage prints					10,000	40,000
Photo albums			1	1		

GEOGRAPHIC: Predominantly Harris County and Houston, although many portraits were made in other parts of the US.

SUBJECTS: Photographs document Houston and Harris County physicians, nurses, hospitals, medical schools, and other medical facilities in the area; all are in some way connected to health care; major emphasis is on the Texas Medical Center. The center also holds the photographic archives for the journal, *Medical World News,* documenting changes in American medicine from 1960 to the present.

Academia (medical, nursing; students, faculty). Animals (laboratory monkeys, rats). Architecture (hospitals). Interiors (hospitals). Government (city). Landscape (aerial). Military (Veterans Administration). Science (biological, medical). Services (medical, nursing).

PEOPLE: Many studio portraits of physicians.

Dr. Ernst Bertner. Dr. Lee D. Cady. Richard Eastwood. Dr. Ruth Hartgraves. Dr. H. Grant Taylor.

PHOTOGRAPHERS: Joseph I. Maurer.

RECORD GROUPS: Photographs are arranged by accession group.

H40.1 ATOMIC BOMB CASUALTY COMMISSION COLLECTION. Commission members, their families, their work, and some views of Japan. 1949 to 1960.

H40.2 *MEDICAL WORLD NEWS* PHOTOGRAPH MORGUE. Medicine and physicians from throughout the US. 1960 to 1980.

H40.3 MEMORIAL HOSPITAL COLLECTION. Development of this Baptist hospital. 1907 to 1960.

H40.4 POSTCARD COLLECTION. Predominantly hospitals with some coverage of medical schools and physicians' homes in Texas. 1895 to 1940.

H40.5 TEXAS MEDICAL CENTER COLLECTION. Schools, hospitals, and institutions in Houston. 1949 to 1975.

Houston Metropolitan Research Center (H52)

Houston Public Library
Julia Ideson Building, Third floor
500 McKinney
Houston, Texas 77002

713-222-4900. Contact: Archivist.

PURPOSE: A special-collection division of the main branch of the public library with collections of rare and recent books, periodicals, manuscripts, business and government records, ephemera, and photographs. The library's Texas and Local History Division documents the economic and social development of the community with an exceptional emphasis on ethnic minorities. The library serves as the repository for the noncurrent records of the City of Houston, Houston Independent School District, and Harris County.

HOURS: Monday through Saturday, 9:00-6:00. Closed major holidays. Appointment required to view unprocessed collections.

ASSISTANCE: Professional, specialized staff. Written and phone inquiries accepted. Electrostatic copies available. Photoduplications must be ordered through the library.

PUBLICATION: No publication fee. Collection credit required. Free copy of publication to the library. Few photographs require third-party permission.

FINDING AIDS: Card index, access by general and proper subject; visual index, access by record group; inventory of record groups.

BIBLIOGRAPHY:
Fuermann, George Melvin; Bert Brandt, photog. *Houston: The once and future city*. New York: Doubleday, 1971.
Hutton, Jim, et al. *Houston: A history of a giant*. Tulsa OK: Continental Heritage, 1976.
Kreneck, Thomas H. Camp Logan and the photography of Fred L. Vermillion. *The Houston Review* 7(3): 143-156 (July 1985).
Kreneck, Thomas H. Documenting a Mexican American community: A Houston example. *The American Archivist* 48(3): 272-285 (Summer 1985).

Miller, Ray. *Ray Miller's Houston*. Houston: Cordovan Press, 1982.

Moutoussamy-Ashe, Jeanne. *Viewfinders: Black women photographers*. New York: Dodd, Mead, and Company, 1986.

Nahas, Fred, ed. *Houston: City of destiny*. New York: Macmillan, 1980.

Siegel, Stanley E., et al. *Houston: A chronicle of the supercity on Buffalo Bayou*. Woodland Hills CA: Windsor Publications in cooperation with the Harris County Heritage Society, 1983.

Twomey, Dannehl. Into the mainstream: Early Black photography in Houston. *The Houston Review*. Forthcoming.

Wilson, Ann Quin. *Native Houstonian: A collective portrait*. Norfolk VA: Donning Company, 1982.

Wilson, Michael E. *Alfred C. Finn, builder of Houston: A catalogue of drawings of the firm in the Houston Public Library/Houston Metropolitan Research Center*. Houston: Houston Public Library, 1983. Describes nonphotographic materials.

SCOPE: 1,500,000 photographs, most vintage prints and original negatives. Many record groups have associated, nonphotographic materials; a few photographers' archives have associated business records and ephemera. 1866 to the present.

Type of photo	Pre-1880	1880-1899	1900-1919	1920-1939	1940-1959	1960-1986
D/A/T-types	4					
Glass negs		50	10,200			
Film negs			10,000	10,000	100,000	400,000
Vintage prints	1,000	4,000	30,000	70,000	250,000	300,000
Copy prints	100	100	150	150	150	
Photo albums		2	3		5	8

GEOGRAPHIC: Extensive coverage of Houston and Harris County; some coverage of other Texas locales, especially historical sites. A few non-Texas areas are represented in minor quantities.

Texas locations: Abilene. Alpine. Amarillo. Angleton. Austin. Barker. Bastrop. Batson. Bay City. Baytown. Beaumont. Beeville. Benbrook. Blue Ridge. Boerne. Bolivar. Bonham. Brazoria. Brenham. Brownsville. Brownwood. Burkburnett. Camp Verde. Canyon. Castroville. Chenango. Clarksville. Cleburne. College Station. Columbus. Conroe. Corpus Christi. Dallas. Dayton. Desdemona. Eagle Pass. Edinburg. El Paso. Fort Bend County. Fort Worth. Fredericksburg. Freeport. Galveston. Goliad. Gonzales. Goose Creek. Hallettsville. Harlingen. Harrisburg. Hoskins Mounds. Houston (Heights, Buffalo Bayou). Hull. Humble. Huntsville. Jefferson. Junction. Kemah. Kerrville. La Grange. La Porte. Lake Jackson. Langtry. League City. Liberty County. Livingston. Llano. Longview. Lubbock. Lynchburg. Manchester. Marlin. Marshall. Mexia. Mineral Wells. Mission. Moody. Morgan's Point. Mount Pleasant. Nacogdoches. Navasota. New Braunfels. Orange. Paducah. Palacios. Palestine. Pasadena. Pecos. Pierce Junction. Port Arthur. Quintana. Ranger. Raymondville. Richmond. Round Rock. Rosenberg. Sabine Pass. Salado. San Angelo. San Antonio. San Augustine. San Benito. San Felipe. San Juan. San Marcos. Saratoga. Sherman. Sierra Blanca. Somerset. Sour Lake. Spindletop. Sugarland. Temple. Terrell. Texarkana. Texas City. Tomball. Tyler. Velasco. Victoria. Waco. Waxahachie. Webster. West Columbia. Wichita Falls. Woodville.

Non-Texas regions: Cuba (Havana). Philippines (Apalit, Caloocan, Cavite, Dagupan, Harrisburg, Malibon, Malolas, Manila, Paranque, San Roche).

SUBJECTS: Major emphasis on the economic and social development of the community, with emphasis on the various ethnic divisions in Houston. Extensive coverage of churches and religious organizations, civic organizations, including women's clubs, and of political activities, including civil rights organizations, party politics, and special-interest groups.

Major headings with subdivisions in the card file: Animals and plants. Architecture (bank buildings, bridges, domestic, factories, farm buildings, hospitals, hotels and taverns, library, miscellaneous, monuments, office, petroleum derricks and refineries, public buildings, religious, restaurants, schools—private, stores—retails, theaters). Artifacts. Cityscapes. Dress. Events (academic, agricultural, athletic, civic, cultural, disasters—fire, —floods, —hurricanes, festivals, military, miscellaneous, religious, scientific). Government. Industry and business (by location; mining, sulphur). Landscape (bayou, cemetery, field, forest, garden, marine, miscellaneous, orchard, park, port, river, shoreline, swamps, winter). People (by ethnicity, by name, by occupation). Street scenes. Transportation (air, land—animals, land—highways, land—railroad, water—port).

Astrodome. Gulf Building. Houston Ship Channel. Metropolitan Theater (Houston). National Association for the Advancement of Colored People (= NAACP). Niels Esperson Building. Rice Hotel. Rice University. San Jacinto Monument at Lynchburg. University of Houston.

PEOPLE: Area residents, many individuals held in small quantities. Extensive coverage of Black, Hispanic, and other ethnicities in Houston. See Record Groups for additional names.

Vanita E. Crawford. Fonsworth family. Gay family. Hicks family. Oscar Holcombe. Ideson family. Johnson family. Jesse Jones. Robert Kneebone. Ligons family. Leopold Meyer family. Roos family. Louis Welch.

Athletes. Bands. Baseball clubs. Fishermen. Football clubs. Petroleum workers. Police.

PHOTOGRAPHERS: Mostly local commercial and studio photographers; some snapshot material.

Barr and Wright. George Beach. Edward Bourdon. Bert Brandt.* Nicholas Broussard. Dixon-Litterst.* William Fritz. Harper and Company. Lucius Harper. Charles G. Harris. Paul Hester. Early Hudnall. Charles Hutchcraft. Harper Leiper.* Matthew L. Lilly. Joseph D. Litterst.* Louise Martin. Joseph I. Maurer.* Alfred Menn. John D. Moore. W. D. Murdy.* Louis de Planque. Herbert J. Provost. Frank J. Schlueter.* Yolita Schmidt. Jack Stiles. Arthur C. and Elnora Teal. Jim Thomas.* Cecil M. Thomson.* Gregorio Torres Valerio. Alfonso Vasquez. Calvin Wheat. C. J. Wright.

*See Record Groups.

RECORD GROUPS: All materials are accessed in the Texas and Local History Division, with the exception of the Milsaps collection (H52.88) which is accessed in Special Collections. Archives collections are received from or pertain to organizations and government agencies; manuscript collections are obtained from individuals or families. Most archival and manuscript collections have substantial associated nonphotographic material.

Archives collections with photographs include:

H52.1 ANDERSON CLAYTON AND COMPANY COLLECTION. Agriculture. 1,000 prints and negatives. 1940s to 1950s. HMRC# D-65.

H52.2 CHRIST CHURCH CATHEDRAL. Houston's first Episcopal parish. Pastors, building, and the Gray family. 53 photo prints. 1900 to 1950s. HMRC# I—1.

H52.3 COLONIAL DAMES OF THE XVII CENTURY, HOUSTON CHAPTER. Caucasian women's organization interested in historical and social matters. Commercial views of the club's activities. 50 prints. 1950s. HMRC# E-52.

H52.4 COLORED TRAINMEN OF AMERICA COLLECTION. Black labor union for railroad workers in Texas and Louisiana Gulf Coast area. Commercial portraits of members. 10 photo prints. 1920s to 1980s. HMRC# R-3.

H52.5 DAUGHTERS OF THE AMERICAN COLONISTS, HOUSTON CHAPTER COLLECTION. Caucasian women's organization interested in historical and social matters. Commercial views of the club's activities. 50 photo prints. 1950s. HMRC# SE-54.

H52.6 FRANKLIN BEAUTY SCHOOL COLLECTION. Black-owned enterprise operating three establishments. Commercial views of operation of the school, including manicures, hair styling, fashion shows; many fashion portraits of Black women modeling hairstyles, some clothing; graduates; career of J. H. Jemison, president of the school, and activities in Houston civic and political affairs. 3,500 photo prints. 1920s to 1980s. HMRC# D-44.

H52.7 FRANKLIN PRINTING HOUSE. Firm of A. Franklin Setting. 1900 to 1906. HMRC# D-29.

H52.8 HESTER HOUSE COLLECTION. Black community center in Houston. Commercial and snapshot views of activities at Hester House. 50 prints. 1943 to present. HMRC# F-22.

H52.9 HOUSTON CENTER FOR THE HUMANITIES COLLECTION. Unprocessed collection. 5 boxes of photographs. HMRC# F-15.

H52.10 *HOUSTON CHRONICLE* COLLECTION. Photo morgue of this daily paper. Journalistic coverage of Houston by staff photographers; does not include wire service photos. 400,000 silver gelatin negatives, most 35mm. 1950s to 1980; an open collection. HMRC# D-13.

H52.11 HOUSTON COTTON EXCHANGE COLLECTION. 1 album of photo prints. HMRC# D-16: v90.

H52.12 HOUSTON JUNIOR CHAMBER OF COMMERCE COLLECTION. Activities of the chamber. 150 glossy photo prints. 1931 to 1981. HMRC# E-45.

H52.13 HOUSTON LIGHT GUARD COLLECTION. Founded in 1873 serving in the Spanish-American War, WW I, and WW II; a prominent social organization in Houston around the turn of the century. Portraits of groups and individuals in the guard; Spanish-American War. 1870s to 1900. HMRC# F-4.

H52.14 *HOUSTON POST* COLLECTION. Photo morgue of this daily paper. Journalistic coverage of Houston by staff photographers; does not include wire-service photos. 100,000 silver gelatin negatives, most 35mm. 1950s to 1980; an open collection. Published index to stories. HMRC# D-6.

H52.15 *HOUSTON PRESS* COLLECTION. A Scripps-Howard newspaper published daily between 1911 and 1964; a booster and a sensationalist paper targeted to the "common man." Journalistic coverage of Houston and Galveston, including substantial coverage of the Astrodome and its proposed use as a fallout shelter; disasters, including Hurricane Carla and the Texas City Explosion; politicians and elections; city and county government; business and civic leaders, including banks, industry; the "common man" of the city, including housewives, students, and career women; Blacks are represented almost exclusively in the sports section, although Hispanics received more coverage, including LULAC; gambling; hospitals; organizations; police; promotions; radio and television stations; Rice University; school board; traffic and accidents; sports, including professional, college, and local high school; outdoor recreation; press releases of network television series and stars. 7,400 folders in 155 boxes (50,000 images) includes negatives, wire service telephotos, printing mats, and prints; clippings file. 1920 to 1964. Card index and list of subject headings. HMRC# D-5.

H52.16 HOUSTON PUBLIC LIBRARY COLLECTION. Activities and buildings of the library, including its branches. 500 photo prints. 1950s to 1970s.

H52.17 HOUSTON WATER DEPARTMENT COLLECTION. Snapshots and commercial views of flood waters and aftermath along Buffalo Bayou. 65 silver gelatin prints. May 1929. HMRC# A-21a.

H52.18 INTERFAITH WORKSHOP COLLECTION. Ecumenical study organization. Twelfth through eighteenth annual workshops. 7 photo albums. 1970 to 1976. HMRC# I-2.

H52.19 JOHNSON (ELIZA) HOME FOR AGED NEGROES COLLECTION. Founded by Anna Dupree in 1952. 58 photo prints. 1950s to 1970s. HMRC# E-47.

H52.20 KU KLUX KLAN COLLECTION. Public activities of the KKK in Houston. Photographed by Howard Beeth. 50 snapshots. 1980s. HMRC# E-58.

H52.21 THE MARRIED LADIES SOCIAL, ART, AND CHARITY CLUB COLLECTION. Black women's social organization founded in 1902. 3 photo prints. HMRC# E-46.

H52.22 NATIONAL COUNCIL OF JEWISH WOMEN COLLECTION. Jewish community service organization. 2 folders of photo prints. HMRC# E-23.

H52.23 PAN AFRICAN ORTHODOX CHRISTIAN CHURCH COLLECTION. "Separatist, apocalyptic, apostolic, pentecostal, and messianic" church. Ceremonies and social activities of the church. 25 photo prints. Ca. 1981. HMRC# I-12.

H52.24 PLEASANT GROVE MISSIONARY BAPTIST CHURCH AND TAPSCOTT FAMILY COLLECTION. Black church in Houston's Fifth Ward. Successive buildings, leading church officials and members of the congregation, including the Tapscott family. 22 photo prints. 1905 to 1965. HMRC# I-13.

H52.25 PORT OF HOUSTON COLLECTION. Port facilities, shipping activities, and downtown Houston. Two albums and loose prints. Late 1910s to 1930s. HMRC# J-1.

H52.26 SAINT JOHN BAPTIST CHURCH and Reverend N. C. CRAIN (1886-1974) COLLECTION. Black Houston church. Portraits of church members and Crain. 25 photo prints. HMRC# I-15.

H52.27 TYPOGRAPHICAL UNION COLLECTION. Labor union, Houston Local #87 AFL-CIO. Union members and activities. 100 glossy prints. 1930s to 1970s. HMRC# R-4.

H52.28 YWCA COLLECTION. Houston YWCA. 150 prints. 1904 to 1980s. HMRC# F-17.

H52.29 ZETA AMICAE COLLECTION. A Black women's educational sorority established in Houston in 1948. Club activities. 2 scrapbooks with photo prints. 1973 to 1978. HMRC# E-50.

Manuscript collections with photographs include:

H52.30 ACKERLY (GERTRUDE) COLLECTION. La Porte cityscapes and people. 100 photo prints. 1910s to 1920s. HMRC# Mss 273.

H52.31 ADAIR (CHRISTIA V.) COLLECTION. Houston civil rights activist, 1920 to present; Secretary of NAACP Houston branch and Democratic party leader. Democratic party and civil rights. 50 photo prints. 1940s to 1960s. HMRC# Mss 109.

H52.32 ALONZO (FRANCISCO "FRANK" AND VENTURA) COLLECTION. Commercial group portraits of the Hispanic dance orchestra, Alonso y sus Rancheros con la Famosa Acordeonista Sra Ventura Alonzo, including Alonzo H., Frank, Frank Jr., and Ventura Alonzo. 36 silver gelatin prints. 1940s to 1950s. HMRC# Mss 202.

H52.33 ALVAREZ (J. A. "TONY") COLLECTION. Mexican-American political affairs. 100 photo prints. 1960s to 1970s. HMRC# Mss 228.

H52.34 ARROYOS (ALEX)—JOHN F. KENNEDY COLLECTION. Reception for Kennedy. 50 photo prints. November 21, 1963. HMRC# Mss 255.

H52.35 BANK OF THE SOUTHWEST—FRANK J. SCHLUETER COLLECTION. Archive of Houston commercial photographer. Architectural photography, predominantly commercial and industrial; product photography; freelance work, including groups and events; booster photographs of agriculture, especially citrus and figs, including fields, workers, and harvesting in Fort Bend County and League City, or possibly West Texas; landscapes; petroleum industry showing derricks, oil fields, tanks between Houston and Liberty County; a few studio portraits of individuals, many in situ group portraits; Texas Gulf Sulphur Company; railroad; Prest-O-Lite Company; Houston Ship Channel. 1,070 silver gelatin prints, including cirkut panoramas; many negatives. 1910s to 1940s. Itemized list of cirkut panoramas. HMRC# Mss 100; see also Mss 223.

H52.36 BEARD (CHESTER A.) COLLECTION. Ellington Air Force Base. 50 photo prints. 1910s to 1920s. HMRC# Mss 275.

H52.37 BRANDT (BERT) ARCHIVES. Commercial photographer, worked with Acme in Europe during WW II. Industrial and commercial photography in Houston; extensive coverage of petroleum industry. 200,000—120 silver gelatin negatives; a few vintage prints. 1953 to 1975. See Bibliography—Fuermann. HMRC# Mss 87.

H52.38 BRODE (FRED AND LAURA) COLLECTION. Founding members of the Socialist Workers Party in the US; moved to Houston in 1939 where Fred Brode worked on the railroad until the 1970s; both were outspoken Marxists, prominent in the civil rights and anti-Vietnam War movements. Snapshots of the Brodes, political associates, political activities, including marches and rallies. 200 photo prints. 1960s to 1980s. HMRC# Mss 225.

H52.39 BUSINESS ALBUMS OF HOUSTON. Retail, commercial, and industrial interiors, and businesses (exteriors) of Houston. Possibly by an itinerant photographer. 160 silver gelatin prints; handwritten captions. 1911. HMRC# Mss 145.

H52.40 CAMP LOGAN—HEGAR COLLECTION. Camp Logan. 50 glass negatives. 1910s. HMRC# Mss 286.

H52.41 CARLETON (A. T.) COLLECTION. Civic and women's affairs in Houston. 100 photo prints. 1930s to 1950s. HMRC# Mss 52.

H52.42 CASTRO (TEODORO) FAMILY HISTORY COLLECTION. Castro family. 20 photo prints. 1905 to 1930s. HMRC# Mss 133.

H52.43 CHAIREZ FAMILY COLLECTION. Chairez family. 40 photo prints. 1919 to 1970s. HMRC# Mss 94.

H52.44 CLEVELAND-KIRKLAND FAMILY COLLECTION. Cleveland and Kirkland families. 50 photo prints. 1890s to 1930s. HMRC# Mss 295.

H52.45 COLLINS (JEFF) FAMILY COLLECTION.   Studio and snapshot portraits of the Collins and Gay families; in Houston County, Willard, Trinity, and Houston. 58 photographs, including a few tintypes and silver gelatin prints. 1880s to 1979. HMRC# Mss 184.

H52.46 COMBS (W. ARTHUR) COLLECTION. Athletic games, agricultural workers, soldiers, casualties, and diplomats in Madrid during the Spanish Civil War. 132 silver gelatin prints. 1937. HMRC# Mss 59.

H52.47 COVINGTON (BENJAMIN) FAMILY PAPERS. Black Houston physician and local politician, affiliated with Booker T. Washington's Tuskegee Institute. Covington family, area residents, and associates. 30 copy photo prints. 1900 to 1925. HMRC# Mss 170.

H52.48 CRAWFORD (VANITA E.)—ANTIOCH BAPTIST CHURCH COLLECTION. Black church in Houston. Studio and snapshot portraits of individuals associated with the church and activities of the church. 73 silver gelatin prints. 1940s to 1960s. HMRC# Mss 192.

H52.49 CULLINAN (JOSEPH S.) COLLECTION. Oil drilling near Price UT and the Utah Oil Refining Company; landscapes with mine sites identified in manuscript; family photographs, including the ruins of a house after a flood and snapshot portraits; art reproductions of paintings by Remington; oil drilling bits; skylines in Houston and Mexia; Houston Ship Channel; Nira Park subdivision of Houston; dedication of the Houston Negro Hospital. Photographers include Schlueter and Thomson. 277 silver gelatin prints. 1920s to 1930s. HMRC# Mss 69.

H52.50 CUTRER (LEWIS and CATHERINE) COLLECTION. Political and civic events in Houston. 100 photo prints. 1950s to 1960s. HMRC# Mss 45.

H52.51 DIXON-LITTERST COLLECTION. Commerical photography in Houston. 22 boxes photographs (40,000 items), including negatives and prints. 1940s to 1950s. HMRC# Mss 89.

H52.52 DUPREE (ANNA) COLLECTION. Black businessperson who operated hair-styling salons and a philanthropic millionaire; founded Eliza Johnson Home for Aged Negroes. Dedication of the Anna Dupree Cottage of the Negro Child Center in Houston; portraits of Blacks, including Dupree. 36 silver gelatin prints. Ca. 1950. HMRC# Mss 110.

H52.53 FARRIOR (A. D.) COLLECTION. Caucasian active in American Legion, YMCA, and Boy Scouts of America. Commercial views of Farrior's activities with those organizations. 350 photo prints. 1920s to 1970s. HMRC# Mss 261.

H52.54 FINN (ALFRED CHARLES; 1883-1964) COLLECTION. Houston architect. Commercial architectural photography (furnished interiors and exteriors), art reproduction of plans, renderings, and models of projects designed by Finn's firm, including many buildings at the University of Houston, the San Jacinto Monument, US Naval Hospital (Houston), and commercial office buildings, including the City National Bank, Commerce Building, Gulf Building, Loew's Metropolitan Theater (most interiors), Rice Hotel, Sakowitz department store; portraits of Finn and associates; artists' studies of female nudes. Many photographed by Schlueter and Litterst. 1,300 silver gelatin prints. 1920s to 1950s. HMRC# Mss 19. See Bibliography—Wilson.

H52.55 FORMER SLAVES COLLECTION. Portraits of men and women outside their homes who were formerly slaves in the US; made for the Texas Works Progress Administration. 54 silver gelatin prints. 1930s. HMRC# Mss 154.

H52.56 FRUCHT (SIG) COLLECTION. Jewish Houston distributor of fruits and vegetables from the Valley. Portraits of Frucht and associates; Sig Frucht Gamblers basketball team; personal and family photographs, including snapshots of service during WW II. 546 silver gelatin photo prints; printed ephemera. 1930s to 1950s. HMRC# Mss 136.

H52.57 GOMEZ (MELECIO) FAMILY COLLECTION. Gomez family and civic and social affairs. 65 photo prints. 1919 to 1950s. HMRC# Mss 135.

H52.58 GRAY STUDIOS-ARLA BINTLIFF STUDIOS. Operated by various photographers, including Charles Hutchcraft, from 1913 to 1917. Studio portraits, possibly by Hutchcraft. 8,000—5x7 silver gelatin glass negatives. 1913 to 1920. HMRC# Mss 215. Restricted access.

H52.59 GREEK COMMUNITY COLLECTION. Portraits of members of the Greek community in Houston. 200 copy photo prints. 1920s to 1970s. HMRC# Mss 199.

H52.60 GRIFFITH (JAMES S.) COLLECTION. Postmaster of Houston, member of the Houston City Council. Commercial views documenting Griffith's public career. 150 photo prints. 1920s to 1950. HMRC# Mss 296.

H52.61 HARD (CHARLES C.) COLLECTION. Caucasian pioneer radio evangelist and an executive in Houston and Galveston YMCAs. Hard's career in the YMCA and as an evangelist. 100 photo prints. Late 1920s to mid-1950s. HMRC# Mss 181.

H52.62 HARRISON (Reverend EDWARD S.) FAMILY COLLECTION. Black pastor at a United Methodist Church in Houston and also executive in the Boy Scouts of America. Many studio and some snapshot portraits of Blacks; some identified, including the Fonsworth and Constant families, Harrison is a central figure, photographs pertain to his church and scout activities. Many from Houston, some from other Texas cities and from Louisiana. Many photographed by Harper and Company (Houston). 11 tintypes; 91 prints, including cabinets and cartes. 1870s to 1920s. HMRC# Mss 182.

H52.63 HERNANDEZ (ALFRED J.) COLLECTION. Mexican-American civic, social, and political activities. 100 photo prints. 1940s to 1980s. HMRC# Mss 159.

H52.64 HERRERA (JOHN H.) COLLECTION. Mexican-American civil rights lawyer. Mexican-American political, civic, and social affairs. 150 photo prints. 1930s to 1970s. HMRC# Mss 160. See Bibliography—Kreneck, "Documenting . . ."

H52.65 HEWES (SAMUEL D.) COLLECTION. Street scenes of Houston. 5 albumen prints and 7 albumen cartes. Ca. 1866. HMRC# Mss 102.

H52.66 HICKS FAMILY COLLECTION. Black Houston family, many of whom were teachers and worked for the Southern Pacific Railroad. Family photographs focusing on those occupations. 241 photo prints. 1890s to 1960s. HMRC# Mss 190.

H52.67 HITLER (ADOLPH) COLLECTION. 1940s. HMRC# Mss 217.

H52.68 HOUEY (WILLARD) COLLECTION. La Porte cityscapes and people. 100 photo prints. 1910s to 1920s. HMRC# Mss 274.

H52.69 HMRC COLLECTION. Artificial collection of unrelated images documenting the economic and social development of the city; predominantly commercial views, including businesses, street scenes, and people.

H52.69.1 Beach, George, photog. *Views of Houston*. Houston: George Beach, 1916. Commercial views of street scenes, skylines, and buildings in Houston; a few non-Houston images of a historical nature, including the capitols at Austin, art reproductions of Sam Houston, and Roy Bean's court at Langtry. 50 silver gelatin prints; typescript index. Early 1910s. HMRC# 114:655-704.

H52.69.2 Fritz, William, photog. *Album of Houston, Texas*. Commercial views of Houston, including skylines, street scenes, and buildings. 24 albumen prints. Ca. 1890. HMRC# 144:705-728.

H52.69.3 *Art work of Houston, 1894*. [Chicago: Gravure Illustration Company,] 1894. Commercial cityscapes, including street scenes, commercial and domestic architecture. 87 photogravures. HMRC# 114:729-823.

H52.69.4 *Art work of Houston, 1904*. [Chicago: Gravure Illustration Company,] 1904. Commercial cityscapes, including street scenes, commercial and domestic architecture. 108 photogravures. HMRC# 114:824-932.

1,700 photographs, most silver gelatin prints, including 2 albums and 2 photogravure books (v.s.). 1890s to 1950s. HMRC# Mss 114.

H52.70 HOUSTON COLLECTION. Aerial views of downtown skyline; commercial and snapshot landscapes; in situ portraits of residents; commercial views of commercial and domestic architecture; President Eisenhower's visit to Houston; fire department and fires; news photos of Mayor Louis Welch in public ceremonies; Shamrock Hilton and other hotels; freeways; the Astrodome; aftermath of fire of 1912; flood of 1929; cotton baling and grading; studio portraits of various and unidentified persons, including Sam Houston (daguerreotype and albumen print by Barr and Wright). Various Houston, Texas, and other photographers, many of which were done for newspapers. 2,000 photo prints, most silver gelatin prints and a few cabinets and cartes. 1860s to 1970s, most ca. 1960. HMRC# Mss 157.

H52.71 *Houston mayors*. Album of portraits of Houston mayors, most black-and-white art reproductions of paintings. 45 photo prints, most silver gelatin prints and a few color prints. 1980s. HMRC# T976.41M.

H52.72 *Houston Public Library, views 1921-1925*. [Houston: Houston Public Library, 1925?] Old Carnegie Library building; preparation of site and construction of the Julia Ideson Building by the Southwestern Construction Company; Heights and all branches for Blacks. Most photographed by F. J. Schlueter. 64 silver gelatin prints; art reproductions of building plans.

H52.73 "ICONS AND EYE-CONS: SIGNS IN THE HOUSTON LANDSCAPE" EXHIBITION. Commercial photographs made as documentation of "modern icons," including domestic and commercial architecture in revival styles, billboards, and storefronts. Photographed by Paul Hester for an exhibition commissioned by the Houston Public Library. 118 silver gelatin prints. Ca. 1980. HMRC# Mss 155.

H52.74 IDESON (JULIA) COLLECTION. Offices of the US Food Administration's Texas Division in Houston and food conservation exhibits. 93 silver gelatin prints. Ca. 1918. HMRC# Mss 32.

H52.75 *Julia Ideson, Librarian, Houston Public Library, 1903-1945*. Studio, in situ, and snapshot portraits of Ideson; many from her personal and professional life. 37 silver gelatin prints. 1920s to 1945.

H52.76 JACKSON (B. M.) COLLECTION. Black editor and publisher of *Galveston Examiner*; founder and self-annointed head of his own religious denomination, First Universal Church of Christ Astrology; president of National Association of Industrial Labor for Colored People (Houston); president of the Goldsound Recording Studio and Dance Band; author. Commercial views pertaining to Jackson in his various careers. 50 photo prints. 1930 to 1965. HMRC# Mss 285.

H52.77 JONES (JESSE H.) FAMILY COLLECTION. Jones family. 30 photo prints. 1900 to 1950s. HMRC# Mss 254.

H52.78 KNEEBONE (ROBERT) COLLECTION. United Fund campaign led by Kneebone, including portraits of United Fund beneficiaries, victory banquet; National Bank of Commerce staff. 96 silver gelatin prints. 1955. HMRC# Mss 22.

H52.79 LARKIN (MILTON) COLLECTION. Internationally noted Black musician recording with his own band. Commercial portraits of Larkin and associates in the musical world, mostly Blacks, including many of the great Black instrumentalists. 120 photo prints. 1930s to 1970s. HMRC# Mss 252.

H52.80 LEIPER (HARPER) ARCHIVES. Houston commercial and industrial photography. 200,000—4x5 silver gelatin safety negatives; business records and job books; unprocessed. 1945 to 1974. HMRC# Mss 287.

H52.81 MARLO-TERRY FAMILY COLLECTION. Caucasian working-class family who operated a vegetable stall, shrimp boat, and vegetable farm in Harris County. Business and family life. 300 photo prints, many snapshots. 1920 to 1975. HMRC# Mss 180.

H52.82 MATTESON-SOUTHWEST COLLECTION. Snapshots of street scenes, most in Houston, emphasizing billboard advertisements and other forms of outdoor display advertising, most of which were rented by the Matteson-Southwest Company. 707 silver gelatin prints. 1940s to 1950s. HMRC# Mss 227.

H52.83 MAURER (JOSEPH I.) COLLECTION. Commercial photography with an emphasis on Catholic religious ceremonies. 2,000 negatives; unprocessed. 1940s to 1960s. HMRC# Mss 188.

H52.84 MENDOZA (LYDIA) COLLECTION. Folk musician. Mendoza's career, other Mexican-American entertainers. 150 photo prints. 1920s to 1960s. HMRC# Mss 123.

H52.85 MEXICAN-AMERICAN PHOTOGRAPH AND FAMILY COLLECTION. Artificial collection pertaining to Mexican-American political, social, and civic affairs. 200 photo prints. 1920s to 1970s. HMRC# Mss 282.

H52.86 MEYER (LEOPOLD) COLLECTION. Civic and business affairs of Houston; family photographs; Houston Fat Stock Show. 2,000 photo prints. 1892 to 1960s. HMRC# Mss 67.

H52.87 MILROY (JOHN A.) COLLECTION. Milroy family and Houston Heights residences. 50 photo prints. 1910s to 1920s. HMRC# Mss 169.

H52.88 MILSAPS COLLECTION. Studio portraits of officers in the Salvation Army, most from San Francisco; California landscapes from "Watkin's new boudoir series"; commercial travel views of the Philippines; photographers include Brewster and Carleton Watkins. 200 photographs, many cabinet prints; diaries also contain photo prints tipped in. Ca. 1890 to 1910. HMRC# Mss 33.

H52.89 MORALES (FELIX H.) COLLECTION. Mexican-American business and civic leader. Civic affairs. 50 photo prints; unprocessed. 1940s to 1970s. HMRC# Mss 122.

H52.90 MURDY (W. D.) COLLECTION. Commercial photographer. Industrial and architectural views, including Cameron Iron Works. 5,000 photo prints, most silver gelatin prints and a few color prints; unprocessed. Late 1950s to 1960s. HMRC# Mss 243.

H52.91 NELSON-ABBOTT FAMILY COLLECTION. Black women who served in the Armed Forces during WW II, most in Army post offices as mail clerks, and sorters, including portraits of the Nelson-Abbott family. 50 photo prints. 1940 to 1945. HMRC# Mss 206.

H52.92 PEREZ (ELOY) FAMILY COLLECTION. Mexican-American big band directed by Perez. 50 photo prints. Late 1940s to 1960s. HMRC# Mss 191.

H52.93 PERRY (HELEN G.) FAMILY COLLECTION. Black Houstonian active in civic affairs. Snapshot interiors of Black nightclubs. 100 photo prints. 1930s to 1980s. HMRC# Mss 276.

H52.94 PICKETT (C. A. NEAL) COLLECTION. Pickett's tenure as mayor. 100 photo prints. HMRC# Mss 3.

H52.95 POSTCARD COLLECTION. Predominantly architecture and cityscapes of Houston.

> *Greater Houston: Its leading firms.* Commercial views of commercial establishments. 48 photomechanical postcards; letterheads. 1913.

1,800 postcards, most photomechanical and many silver gelatin prints; 1 album (v.s.). 1900s to 1950s; most 1920s. HMRC# Mss 187.

H52.96 PRICE (Reverend M. L.) COLLECTION. Black Baptist clergyman. Commercial portraits of Price, his family, and his professional associates. 50 photo prints. 1920s to 1980s. HMRC# Mss 277.

H52.97 REYNA (MARIA) COLLECTION. Mexican-American civic affairs. 15 photo prints. 1940s to 1950s. HMRC# Mss 256.

H52.98 RICE (C. W.) FAMILY AND *NEGRO LABOR NEWS* COLLECTION. Black businessperson and editor of this paper; proprietor and founder of a Black employment agency; controversial figure regarded as an Uncle Tom and an accommodationist, militantly anti-union, anti-civil rights, and anticommunist. Commercial portraits of Rice, family members, business establishments. 20 photo prints. 1950s to 1970s. HMRC# Mss 242.

H52.99 RODRIGUES (ERNEST) COLLECTION. Rodrigues family. 25 photographs, including negatives, prints, and slides. 1920s to 1940s. HMRC# Mss 107.

H52.100 RODRIGUEZ FAMILY COLLECTION. Rodriguez family. 50 photo prints. 1920s to 1960s. HMRC# Mss 99.

H52.101 *Roos family album.* Snapshot portraits of various individuals and family pictures; buildings and skylines; shipyards; in the Houston and Heights subdivision. 1,024 silver gelatin prints. 1920s to 1950s. HMRC# Mss 156.

H52.102 SCHACHTEL (Rabbi HYMAN JUDAH) COLLECTION. Pertaining to his rabbinate. 30 photo prints. 1950s to 1960s. HMRC# Mss 172.

H52.103 SCHLUETER (FRANK J.) COLLECTION. Commercial photographer. See H52.35 for description of typical subjects. 450 glass and film negatives, including 8x10 and cirkut panoramas. 1910s to 1920s. HMRC# Mss 223.

H52.104 SCHMIDT (YOLITA) COLLECTION. Mexican-American commercial photographer. Commercial buildings and a few homes photographed by Schmidt. 103 silver gelatin prints. Ca. 1970. HMRC# Mss 97.

H52.105 SHEELER (Dr. JOHN REUBEN) COLLECTION. Black professor of history at Texas Southern University; president of the Association for the Study of Negro Life and Culture; editor in chief of the *Journal of Negro History*, performed various services for the UN abroad. Many commercial and some snapshot portraits of Sheeler, his family, academic associates, and professional activities. 100 photo prints. 1930s to 1970s. HMRC# Mss 268.

H52.106 SIMPSON (A. D.) PAPERS. Houston banker. Simpson, family, and business associates; leading financiers of Houston. 500 silver gelatin prints. 1920 to 1925. HMRC# Mss 41.

H52.107 SIMPSON (Reverend L. H.) COLLECTION. Black Baptist pastor in Houston from 1920s to 1960s; president of the Houston Colored Baptist Ministers Association for more than thirty years; president of the Houston NAACP for more than ten years. Simpson, family, the Pleasant Hill Baptist Church; most are commercial-journalistic portraits. 400 photo prints. 1920s to 1960s. HMRC# Mss 239.

H52.108 SMITH (C. F.) FAMILY COLLECTION. Smith was the first licensed Black electrical contractor in Houston, and possibly in Texas. Smith and family; his business. 50 photo prints. Mid-1950s to Mid 1970s. HMRC# Mss 249.

H52.109 SNEED FAMILY COLLECTION. Black Houston residents. Studio and snapshot portraits, chronicling the life and career of two sisters, Ruth Sneed (Mrs. Andrew) Jefferson and Martha Sneed (Mrs. Judson) Robinson, teachers in the Houston Independent School District. Portraits of the sisters and their teaching activities; a few images of the husbands. 50 photo prints. 1900 to 1950. HMRC# Mss 293.

H52.110 STILES (JACK) COLLECTION. Commercial photographer. Architecture photographed by Stiles. 2,000 negatives. 1950s to 1960s. HMRC# Mss 288.

H52.111 SULLIVAN (MAURICE) COLLECTION. Prominent Houston architect. Architecture designed by Sullivan. 800 photo prints. 1920s to 1950s. HMRC# Mss 54.

H52.112 TAPSCOTT FAMILY COLLECTION. Black Houston residents. Tapscott family, particularly their membership in the Pleasant Grove Missionary Baptist Church. 30 photo prints. 1890s to 1960s. HMRC# Mss 263.

H52.113 TAYLOR FAMILY COLLECTION. Black family from Houston and vicinity. Taylor family, most studio portraits. 200 photo prints. 1880s to 1920s. HMRC# Mss 222.

H52.114 TERRY (ELBERT) FAMILY COLLECTION. Developer of first all-Black suburban community, Sunnyside; civic leader; active in Houston NAACP, Black Chamber of Commerce. Snapshots of Terry, associates, and family. 50 photo prints. 1950s to 1960s. HMRC# Mss 266.

H52.115 TEXAS COLLECTION. Galveston hurricane of 1900; Port Arthur street scenes photographed about 1940; booster photographs of agriculture and commercial views of United Irrigation Company's river plant in the Valley photographed by Eskildsen; commercial views and snapshots of surveyors, camp life, and trench digging machinery of railroad track crew; "Louis de Planque's photo views of the ruins of Indianola; after the flood, storm, and fire of August 20, 1886"; Fort Sam Houston Eighth Corps Area Communications station WVR; San Antonio, especially retrospective views of the Spanish missions, many photographed or published by Brack; exhibits at the Texas Museum.

> **H52.115.1** Menn, Alfred. *The Texas album.* Snapshot travel views, including art reproductions, retrospective views of historic structures, and historical personages. 35 photo and photomechanical prints; handwritten captions. After 1951.

> **H52.115.2** Menn, Alfred. *The Texas album [II].* Snapshot travel views including art reproductions, retrospective views of historic structures, and historical personages. 25 photo and photomechanical prints. After 1951.

424 items, some nonphotographic images; two albums (v.s.). 1860s to 1970s. HMRC# Mss 151.

H52.116 THOMAS (JIM) ARCHIVES. Commercial photographer. Commercial and industrial photography by Thomas. 10,000—4x5 silver gelatin negatives; a few vintage silver gelatin prints. 1940s to 1970s. HMRC# Mss 84.

H52.117 THOMPSON (CHESTER AND EXVELMA) FAMILY COLLECTION. Black residents of Houston. Many studio portraits and some snapshots of the Thompson-Wilson family. 112 silver gelatin prints. Ca. 1906 to 1940s. HMRC# Mss 232.

H52.118 THOMSON (CECIL M.) COLLECTION. Commercial photographer working in Houston and Galveston. Houston and Galveston ports showing docks, dock workers loading freight onto ships, passenger, freight, and military ships, freight, including cotton and grain, aerial views of the docks; fat stock show; movie theaters, including the Isis, Granada, Kirby, and Loew's State; promotions for movies; oil fields; street scenes with trolleys and cars; architectural photography, including construction; group portraits, including hunters with their catch; bathing beauty contestants; Houston Aerial Transport Company staff and others posed with planes. 344 modern prints. 1910s to 1940s. HMRC# Mss 200. Restricted access; originals at San Jacinto Museum of History Association (q.v.).

H52.119 TIJERINA SENIOR FAMILY. Mexican-American business and civic affairs; Tijerina Senior family. 150 photo prints. 1920s to 1960s. HMRC# Mss 108.

H52.120 TORRES VALERIO (GREGORIO) COLLECTION. Commercial photographer in Houston serving the Hispanic community. Latin dance bands, most performing on stage; audience and dancers; studio portraits, especially of soldiers; groups, including schools and organizations; weddings. Photographed by Torres Valerio. 338—4x5 negatives with modern prints. 1950s. HMRC# Mss 101.

H52.121 VASQUEZ (ALFONZO) COLLECTION. Commercial photographer. Mexican-American political and civic affairs photographed by Vasquez. 100 photo prints. 1950s to 1970s. HMRC# Mss 93.

H52.122 VERMILLION (FREDERICK L.) COLLECTION. Camp life and portraits of soldiers at Camp Logan. 2,000—4x5, 5x7, and 8x10 silver gelatin glass negatives. 1910s to 1920s. HMRC# Mss 224.

H52.123 WALKER (LESLEY LEWIS) COLLECTION. Early aviation in Houston. 50 photo prints. 1910s to 1920s. HMRC# Mss 253.

H52.124 WARD (PAUL E.) COLLECTION. Studio portraits of C. V. Buster Kern and in groups; people posed next to airplanes. 24 silver gelatin prints. 1930s to 1951. HMRC# Mss 11.

H52.125 WARNER (A. E.) COLLECTION. Black millionaire businessperson and car dealer; president of the Houston Colored Chamber of Commerce. Commercial portraits of Warner and his associates. 50 photoprints. Mid-1950s to mid-1970s. HMRC# Mss 251.

H52.126 WHEAT (CALVIN) COLLECTION. Photographer. Cityscapes and Camp Logan. 1910s to 1920s. HMRC# Mss 64.

H52.127 YATES (Reverend JACK) FAMILY COLLECTION. Black founder of Antioch Baptist Church and Bethel Baptist Church in Houston; civic leader; many family members are teachers. Studio and snapshot portraits document family members and their professional life, principally in the church and education. 200 photo prints. 1890s to 1970s. HMRC# Mss 281.

H52.128 YIPIÑA (MARIANO ROZALES) COLLECTION. Mexican-American social and civic affairs. 15 photo prints. 1940s to 1950s. HMRC# Mss 130.

Menil Collection (H58)

Menil Foundation
1515 Sul Ross
Houston, Texas 77006

713-525-9400. Contact: Curator.

PURPOSE: An exhibiting museum housing a private collection of fine art ranging from Neolithic artifacts to contemporary art including paintings, drawings, prints, rare books, film and video, and photographs. The materials were collected by Dominiques de Menil and her late husband, John de Menil.

HOURS: Exhibition area—hours not set at time of publication. Reserve collections—by appointment only.

ASSISTANCE: Professional, specialized, experienced staff. Written requests only. Electrostatic copies available. Photoduplications available through the collection.

PUBLICATION: Written request required. Publication fee charged. Collection credit required. Free copy of publication to the collection. Third-party permission required on most items.

FINDING AIDS: Complete descriptive list and card index; complete computerized database. Access by artist, personal and proper name, geographic location, date, photographer, and general subject heading.

BIBLIOGRAPHY:

Davidson, Kathryn, and Elizabeth Glassman. *Transfixed by light: Photographs from the Menil Collection.* Houston: Menil Foundation, 1980.

La rime et la raison: Les collections Menil. Paris: Galeries Nationales du Grand Palais, 1984.

Gombrich, Ernst, and Mark Haworth-Booth. *Henri Cartier-Bresson.* Edinburgh, Scotland: Scottish Arts Council, 1978.

SCOPE: 2,500 photographs, including 187 stereographs. Type-C, dye-transfer, Ektacolor, Cibachrome, and Polaroid color processes; silver gelatin, platinum, Rayogram, solarized, and hand-gravure black-and-white processes. Predominantly mid-twentieth century; a few nineteenth century.

Type of photo	Pre-1880	1880-1899	1900-1919	1920-1939	1940-1959	1960-1986
D/A/T-types	10	29				
Vintage prints			300	90	202	1,849

GEOGRAPHIC: Broad coverage of Asia, Europe, Central America; in the US of New England and the Northeast, the Far West, and the South.

Foreign: Africa. England. France. Guatemala. India. Mexico.

US: California. Louisiana. New Mexico. New York. Texas. Washington DC.

SUBJECTS: A fine art collection with broad subject coverage.

PEOPLE: Famous artists, writers, poets, scientists, actors, and Blacks; few individuals held in quantity.

Yves Klein. Abraham Lincoln.

PHOTOGRAPHERS: More than 170 photographers, including many European and American art photographers; the collection concentrates on photographers working in journalistic and surrealistic styles. Photographers with no quantity indicated have only one print in the collection.

Ansel Adams (8). Eugène Atget (7). Frederick Baldwin. Gertrude Duby Blom (15).* Félix Bonfils (8). Edouard Boubat (15).* Mathew B. Brady (17). Brassaï (= Gyula Halász; 28).* John Brathwaite (4). Peter Brown (7). Larry Burrows (18). Emil Cadoo (33).* Harry Callahan (5). Paul Caponigro (2). Mario Carrieri (65).* Ovie Carter (2). Henri Cartier-Bresson (848).* William Christenberry (212).* Alain Clement (8). Scott Michael Coburn (28).* David Crossley. Edward S. Curtis (35).* Roy DeCarava (4). Joe Dugan (20). William Eggleston (47).* Frederick Henry Evans (4).* Walker Evans (204). Ira Friedlander (12).* John Gossage (55).* Sidney Grossman (2). Blaine Hickey (2). Lewis Hine (5). Gertrude Käsebier. André Kertész (5). Balthazer Korab (27).* George Krause (10).* Jacques-Henri Lartigue (5). Clarence John Laughlin (42). Helen Levitt (3). Danny Lyon (70).* Walter De Maria. Richard Misrach. Lisette Model (7). Ruth Morgan (8).* George Francois Mugnier. Eadweard Muybridge. Nadar (= Gaspard Félix Tournachon, 12*). Hans Namuth (3). Beaumont Newhall (4). Arnold Newman (4). Joshua Mann Pailet (69).* Gordon Parks (2). J. Pinderhughes (5). Charles Pratt (5). Man Ray (14).* Ogden Robertson. H. Roger-Viollet (58).* George Rousse (2). Addison N. Scurlock. Harry Shunk (406).* Charles Simonds (24).* Clara Sipprell. Aaron Siskind. Moneta Sleet Jr. (2). Michael A. Smith (7).* W. Eugene Smith (6). Eve Sonneman (5). Edward Steichen (3). Paul Strand (2). James Van Der Zee (19).* Carl Van Vechten (50).* Shawn Walker (2). Thomas Weir (2).

*See Record Groups.

RECORD GROUPS: Descriptions provided by Kathryn Davidson, Curator of the Menil Collection. Record Group title is photographer unless otherwise noted.

H58.1 BLOM (GERTRUDE DUBY; b. 1901) PORTFOLIO. *Chiapas: Mayas.* Centro de Estudios Científicos: San Cristóbal de las Casas, Chiapas, Mexico, 1982. 15 modern silver gelatin prints. 1982.

H58.2 BOUBAT (EDOUARD; b. 1923) PORTFOLIO. *Boubat.* New York: Hyperion, 1981. 15 modern silver gelatin prints. 1947 to 1981.

H58.3 BRASSAÏ (= Gyula Halász; b. 1899) PORTFOLIO. *Brassaï.* New York: Witkin Berely, 1973. 10 silver gelatin prints.

H58.4 BRASSAÏ (= Gyula Halász; b. 1899) COLLECTION. Graffiti in Paris. 19 silver gelatin prints. Ca. 1950.

H58.5 BURROWS (LARRY; 1926-1971) PORTFOLIO. *Vietnam: The American intervention, 1962-1968.* New York: Laurence Miller Gallery, 1986. 18 dye-transfer prints. 1962 to 1968.

H58.6 CADOO (EMIL) PORTFOLIO. *Harlem photographs.* 33 silver gelatin prints. 1966.

H58.7 CARRIERI (MARIO) PORTFOLIO. *Pore.* Art reproductions of African sculptures in the collection of Carlo Monzino in Venice, Italy. 65 silver gelatin prints. 1976.

H58.8 CARTIER-BRESSON (HENRI; b. 1908) COLLECTION. At the request of the Menil Foundation, Cartier-Bresson spent two years selecting 385 photographs from thousands of contact sheets that were printed and processed by Pictorial Services of Paris, France, between 1972 and 1973. One set was acquired by the Menil Foundation, the Bibliothèque National in Paris, France, Osaka University of Arts in Japan, and the Victoria and Albert Museum in England. Cartier-Bresson has grouped the photographs by country and by type so to give an insight into his methods of pictorial construction. He has promised to add new subjects to the collection as time permits. The full archive is over 450 photographs and now spans 1929 to 1985. See Bibliography—Gombrich.

H58.9 CHRISTENBERRY (WILLIAM; b. 1936) PORTFOLIO. *Southern photographs.* 140 type-C prints. 1982.

H58.10 CHRISTENBERRY (WILLIAM; b. 1936) COLLECTION. 72 type-C prints. 1982.

H58.11 COBURN (SCOTT MICHAEL; b. 1950) COLLECTION. Mardi Gras celebrations in New Orleans LA. 28 silver gelatin prints. 1972.

H58.12 Curtis, Edward Sheriff, photog. *The North American Indian.* [Seattle WA: E. S. Curtis; Cambridge: University Press], 1915 and 1916. 30 loose photogravures plus volumes IX and X from this series.

H58.13 EGGLESTON (WILLIAM; b. 1937) PORTFOLIO. *Troubled waters.* New York: Caldecot Chubb, 1980. 15 dye-transfer prints.

H58.14 EGGLESTON (WILLIAM; b. 1937) PORTFOLIO. *Graceland.* Washington DC: Middendorf Gallery, 1984. Elvis Presley's mansion at Graceland. 11 dye-transfer prints.

H58.15 EGGLESTON (WILLIAM; b. 1937) COLLECTION. 6 dye-transfer prints.

H58.16 EVANS (WALKER; 1903-1975) COLLECTION. Work from the Farm Security Administration period made in Illinois, New York, Louisiana, Pennsylvania, Virginia, Alabama, Georgia, California, Mississippi, and Ohio. 204 vintage prints. 1928 to 1970.

H58.17 FRIEDLANDER (IRA) PORTFOLIO. *The ecstasy of the dervishes.* 12 silver gelatin prints. 1979.

H58.18 GOSSAGE (JOHN; b. 1946) PORTFOLIO. *Views of the Far West.* Washington DC, 1970. 55 silver gelatin prints.

H58.19 KLEIN (YVES; 1928-1962) PHOTOGRAPH ARCHIVE. Images documenting the life of French artist Klein, made by French photographer Harry Shunk. 408 silver gelatin prints.

H58.20 KORAB (BALTHAZAR; b. 1926) COLLECTION. Hungarian photographer. Rothko Chapel. 27 silver gelatin prints. 1976.

H58.21 KRAUSE (GEORGE; b. 1937) COLLECTION. Three prints from the portfolio *George Krause, 1960-1970* and other work. 10 silver gelatin prints. 1958 to 1984.

H58.22 LYON (DANNY; b. 1942) PORTFOLIO. *Danny Lyon.* New York: Hyperion, 1979. 30 silver gelatin prints. 1965 to 1979.

H58.23 LYON (DANNY; b. 1942) PORTFOLIO. *Southwestern portfolio.* 25 silver gelatin prints, 5 color prints. 1962 to 1973.

H58.24 MORGAN (RUTH; b. 1946) COLLECTION. Prints from the portfolio, *Maximum security*, made in San Quentin CA. 8 silver gelatin prints. 1981 to 1984.

H58.25 NADAR (= GASPARD FÉLIX TOURNACHON; 1820-1910) PORTFOLIO. Paris, 1979. Twelve modern prints from Nadar's collodion negatives by Claudine Sudre, from the series *Collections of the great masters.*

H58.26 PAILET (JOSHUA MANN; b. 1950) COLLECTION. 70 silver gelatin prints. 1972 to 1985.

H58.27 RAY (MAN; 1890-1976) PORTFOLIO. *Electricité.* Paris: La Compagnie de Distribution d'Electricité, 1931. 10 Rayograms.

H58.28 ROGER-VIOLLET (H.) COLLECTION. French, twentieth-century photographer. Portraits of Africans. 58 silver gelatin prints.

H58.29 SIMONS (CHARLES; b. 1945) COLLECTION. *Birth.* New York: 1970. 24 color photographs.

H58.30 SMITH (MICHAEL; b. 1943) PORTFOLIO. *Landscapes.* 7 silver gelatin prints from a portfolio of 35. 1975 to 1979.

H58.31 VAN DER ZEE (JAMES; 1886-1983) PORTFOLIO. *James Van Der Zee.* Washington DC: Lunn Graphics, 1974. 19 silver gelatin prints.

H58.32 VAN VECHTEN (CARL; 1880-1964) PORTFOLIO. *O write my name.* New York: Eakins Press, 1983. American portraits, Harlem heroes. 50 modern handgravures by Richard Benson.

Museum of Fine Arts, Houston (H64)

1001 Bissonnet
P.O. Box 6826
Houston, Texas 77265

Photography—713-526-1361. Contact: Curator of Photographs.
Archives—713-526-6197. Contact: Museum Archivist.

Bayou Bend

1 Westcott
P.O. Box 13157
Houston, Texas 77219

713-529-8773, extension 25. Contact: Associate Curator.

PURPOSE: An exhibiting art museum encompassing the Glassell School of Art and the Bayou Bend Collection holding extensive reserve collections in all media, including photography. The museum maintains an institutional archive, including correspondence with Mies van der Rohe, the designer of the expansion wings.

HOURS: Exhibit space—Tuesday through Saturday, 10:00-5:00; Sunday, 1:00-6:00. Reserve collections and archive—weekdays, 10:00-4:00, by appointment. Closed major holidays. Bayou Bend open by advanced reservation only.

ASSISTANCE: Professional, specialized staff. Written inquiries accepted. Electrostatic copies available. Photoduplications may be made by patrons for research purposes only; photoduplications for publication must be ordered through the museum.

PUBLICATION: Publication fee charged. Collection credit required. Free copy of publication to museum. Third-party permission required on about half of the materials.

FINDING AIDS: Inventory and descriptive list; artist index.

BIBLIOGRAPHY:
Agee, William C. *The Museum of Fine Arts, Houston: A guide to the collection.* Houston: Museum of Fine Arts, Houston, 1981.

Baltz, Louis, ed. *Contemporary American photographic works.* Houston: Museum of Fine Arts, Houston, 1977.

Baltz, Lewis, photog. *The new industrial parks near Irvine, California.* New York: Castelli Graphics, 1974.

Barnstone, Harold; Henri Cartier-Bresson and Ezra Stoller, photogs. *The Galveston that was.* New York: Macmillan, 1966.

Bauhaus Fotographie. Edition Marzona, 1982.

Carmean, E. E. *Geoff Winningham, photographs.* Houston: Museum of Fine Arts, Houston, 1974.

Danese, Renato. *American images: New work by twenty contemporary photographers*. New York: McGraw-Hill, 1979.

Edward Steichen: The Condé Nast years. Houston: Houston Museum of Fine Arts, Houston, 1984.

Frank, Robert, photog.; introduction by Jack Kerouac. *The Americans*. 2nd ed., Millerton NY: Aperture, 1978 and 1986.

Herzfeld, Wieland. *John Heartfield: Leben und Werk*. Dresden: Verlag der Kunst, 1962.

McQuaid, James, and Paulette Privitera Wilson. *An index to American photographic collections*. Boston: G. K. Hall, 1982.

Porter, Eliot, photog. *Intimate landscapes*. New York: Metropolitan Museum of Art and E. P. Dutton, 1979.

Porter, Eliot, photog. *Intimate landscapes*. Houston: Museum of Fine Arts, Houston, 1984

Sandweiss, Martha A., Roy Flukinger, and Anne Tucker. *Contemporary Texas: A photographic portrait*. Austin: Texas Monthly Press, 1986.

Tucker, Anne. *Target II, 5 American photographers: De Meyer, White, Stieglitz, Strand, Weston*. Houston: Museum of Fine Arts, Houston, 1981.

Tucker, Anne Wilkes, and William C. Agee. *The Target Collection of American photography*. Houston: Museum of Fine Arts, Houston, 1976.

Tucker, Anne, and Philip Brookman. *Robert Frank: New York to Nova Scotia*. Houston: Museum of Fine Arts, Houston.

Tucker, Anne Wilkes, and Maggie Olvey. *The Sonia and Kaye Marvins portrait collection*. Houston: Museum of Fine Arts, Houston, 1986.

Tucker, Anne Wilkes, and Leroy Searle. *Target III, in sequence: Photographic sequences from the Target Collection of American photography*. Houston: Museum of Fine Arts, Houston, 1982.

SCOPE: Reserve collections—3,000 photographs, two-thirds of which is American and one-fifth of which is avant-garde European. 1877 to present, most 1945 to present. Archives—18,000 original and 12,000 copy photographs, predominantly prints. 1900 to present.

Type of photo	Pre-1880	1880-1899	1900-1919	1920-1939	1940-1959	1960-1986
D/A/T-types	19					
Film negs				8		
Vintage prints	4	91	173	600	750	1,350
Photo albums	1	2				

GEOGRAPHIC: Some coverage of the US and Japan.

SUBJECTS: Predominantly a fine art collection with many abstract images.

Landscape. Photography (art).

PEOPLE: Some studio and art portraits, no individuals held in quantity.

PHOTOGRAPHERS:

American, 19th century: E. and H. T. Anthony (2). George N. Barnard. Mathew B. Brady. Cole's Studio. A. P. Critchlow and Company. Donaldson. Doolittle. Thomas Eakins (4/b). Evans. William Henry Jackson (2). Journeay. Littlefield, Parsons and Company (2). H. R. Marks. Millard. Eadweard Muybridge (7/bc). Timothy O'Sullivan. Powelson and Company. D. A. Sander. Scoville. J. D. Tooker. Tupper. Warwick. Carleton Watkins. J. E. Watson.

European, 19th century: J. Craig Annan. Francis Bedford. Bertall. Samuel Bourne. Adolphe Braun et Cie (2). Lady Caroline Bridgeman. Julia Margaret Cameron (2/a). Etienne Carjat (4).

Charles Clifford. F. C. Curry. Dean. Debenham. W. and D. Downey. Peter Henry Emerson (4). Roger Fenton. Franck. Francis Frith (b). H. Hallier. Maull and Polyblank. Nadar (= Gaspard Félix Tournachon, 10). Charles Nègre (b). Ferdinand Ongania (pub., 12). Charles Reutlinger. Horatio Ross. Lang Sims (4). Giorgio Sommer. John Thomson (b). James Valentine. George Washington Wilson.

American, 1900-1945: Berenice Abbott (3). Ansel Adams (3). Herbert Bayer. E. J. Bellocq. Louis Bernstein. Margaret Bourke-White (2). Alice Boughton. Francis Bruguière. Rudolph Burckhardt. Paul Carter (2). John Collier (2). Alvin Langdon Coburn (5/a). Carlotta Corpron. Ralston Crawford (2). Imogen Cunningham (3). Edward Curtis (42/b). Jack Delano (4). Baron Adolphe de Meyer (47/abc). Mike Disfarmer. Harold E. Edgerton. Rudolph Eickemeyer. Morris Engel. Frank Eugene (2/a). Walker Evans (15). Louis Faurer. Farraud. Arnold Genthe. Laura Gilpin (3). Sidney Grossman (14). Paul Grotz. John Gutmann. Florence Henri (4). Lewis Hine (16/b). George Hurrell. Lotte Jacobi (3). Theodore Jung (2). Consuelo Kanaga. Gertrude Käsebier. Sidney Kerner. André Kertész (21/b). Lloyd Koenig. Dorothea Lange (10). Clarence John Laughlin. Alma Lavenson. Russell Lee (12). Helen Levitt (2). Sol Libsohn. George Platt Lynes (2). Richard Lyon. Jack Manning. Man Ray (5). Margrethe Mather. Lisette Model (9). László Moholy-Nagy (46/b). Barbara Morgan (2). William Mortensen (2). Carl Mydans. Paul Outerbridge. Dorothy Norman. Gordon Parks (2). Diane Petteys. P. H. Polk. Walter Rosenblum. Theodore Roszak. Henry Rothman. Arthur Rothstein (32). Harry Rubincam. Ben Shahn (7). Charles Sheeler. Aaron Siskind (30). Edward Steichen (90/ab). Alfred Stieglitz (17/ac). Paul Strand (31/b). Karl Struss. Doris Ulmann. John Vachon. James Van Der Zee. Willard Van Dyke (3). Adam Clark Vroman (2). Eva Watson-Schütze (2). Weegee (= Arthur Fellig). Edward Weston (25). Clarence Hudson White (15/a). Marion Post Wolcott (15).

European, 1900-1945: Franz Aichinger (4). Eugène Atget (3). Bauhaus (unattrib., 16). Lotte Beese (2). Hans Bellmer. Karl Blossfeldt (12/b). Katt Both. Pierre Boucher. Bill Brandt (3). Brassaï (= Gyula Halász, 3). Marianne Breslauer. Henri Cartier-Bresson (2). Erich Consemuller. Robert Demachy. Zoltan Deucht. František Drtikol (3; with Spol, 1). Lux Feininger (3). Gisèle Freund (2). Ernst Fuhrmann (5). Jaromir Funke (7). Edward Hartwig. John Heartfield (77/b). Heinrich Heidersberger. Irene Hoffman. Vaclav Jiru. Germaine Krull. Heinrich Kühn (2/a). Jacques-Henri Lartigue (2). Adolf Lazi (2). Helmar Lerski. Mandel. Werner Mantz. Wera Meyer-Waldeck (attrib.). Lucia Moholy (4). Johan Niegemann. Albert Renger-Patzsch. Franz Roh (4). Werner Rohde. Jaroslav Rössler (28/b). Rubinstein or Bohm. Charlotte Rudolph (attrib.). Erich Salomon. August Sander (2). Fritz Scheifer. Joost Schmidt (4). Adolf Schneeberger. Herbert Schurmann (3). Jindrich Stryrsky. Maurice Tabard. Umbo (= Otto Umbehr, 4). Piet Zwart.

American, 1945 to present: Ansel Adams. Robert Adams (17/c). Shelby Lee Adams. James Alinder (2). Diane Arbus. Frank Armstrong (10/c). Neil Armstrong. Eve Arnold (12/b). Richard Avedon (4/c). James Baker. John Baldessari. Fred Baldwin and Wendy Watriss (15/c). Lewis Baltz (67/c). Tina Barney. Richard Baron (2). Thomas F. Barrow (3). Daniel Barsotti. David Batchelder. Michael Becotte. Louis Bernstein (65/c). Paul E. Berger (c). Sandra Binion and Dirk Bakker (c). Michael Bishop. Melinda Blauvelt (2). Gay Block (16/c). Barbara Blondeau (c). Erwin Blumenfeld. Ave Bonar (5/c). Harry Bowers. Marilyn Bridges. Ken Brown. Laurie Brown (c). Marion Brown. Peter Brown (22/b). Dan Budnik. Wynn Bullock (2/c). Jerry Burchard (2). Marsha Lynn Burns. Michael John Burns. Carol Cohen Burton (10/c). Debbie Caffery. Andrew Cahan (2). Harry Callahan (20/c). Paul Caponigro (5). Keith Carter. James Casebere. Walter Chappell. Carl Chiarenza (2). William Christenberry. Robert Clemons. William Clift (15/c). Alan Cohen (4). Bernard Cole. Linda Connor (18/c). Bob Covington. Konrad Cramer. Arnold Crane (57/b). Barbara Crane. Ralston Crawford (9/b). Anthony G. Cronin. Robin Zimmerman Cronin. Robert Cumming (38/bc). Bill Dane. Bruce Davidson. Bevan Davies (16/c). Joe Deal (3). Roy

DeCarava (19/c). William DeLappa (c). Paul Diamond. John Divola (2). William Eggleston (17/c). Alfred Eisenstaedt. Elliott Erwitt (35/bc). Rodney Evans. Marion Faller and Hollis Frampton (c). John Spencer Fay. Gary Faye (2). Jo Alison Feiler (8). Peter Helms Feresten (11). Robert Fichter. Larry Fink (15/c). Linda Fennell. Judy Fiskin. Steve Fitch (2). Frederic Fleming. Robert Flick. Robert Frank (280/bc). William Frazier. David Freund. Gisèle Freund. Lee Friedlander (9/b). Benno Friedman. Sally Gall (4). Rick Gardner (2). Morgan Garwood. Ralph Gibson (15/b). Arnold Gilbert (3). Paul Linwood Gittings (35). Frank Gohlke (24/c). Leo Goldstein. John Gossage (20/c). Emmet Gowin (1). David Graham. Edward Grazda (4). Jonathan Green (15/c). Paul Greenberg (2). Jan Groover (17/c). Sidney Grossman (26/c). Gary Hallman. Wanda Hammerbeck (2). Robert Heinecken (4/c). Jan Henle. Anthony Hernandez (12). Paul Hester (12). Lewis Hodnett. Evelyn Hofer (10). Horst P. Horst. Douglas Huebler (c). Dale Hueppchen (2). Debora Hunter. Terry Husebye. Gerald Incandela (c). Doug Ischar. Joseph Jachna. Lotte Jacobi (2). Christopher James. Harold Jones. Kenneth Josephson. Steve Kahn (2/c). Douglas Peter Keats. André Kertész (13). Joseph Kinnibrew (3). E. F. Kitchen. William Klein (5). Mark Klett. Stuart Klipper (12). Grace Knowlton (10/b). George Krause (8). Les Krims (8). Kipton Kumler. Philip Lamb. Victor Landweber (2). William Larson. Annie Leibovitz. Arthur Leipzig. Lynn Lennon. Vincent Leo (2). Nathan Lerner (2). Helen Levitt (3). Sol LeWitt (c). Nathaniel Lieberman. Jerome Liebling. Peter de Lory. Lynn Lown. George Platt Lynes. Danny Lyon (31/b). Joan Lyons (2/c). Nathan Lyons (6/c). Skeet McAuley (10/c). Kenneth McGowan (22). Gregory McGregor. Larry McPherson. Mike Mandel (134). MANUAL (= Suzanne Bloom and Ed Hill, c). Robert Mapplethorpe. Mary Ellen Mark (15/c). Louise Martin. Kaye Marvins. Elaine Mayes. Ralph Eugene Meatyard. Lawrence Merrill (2). Roger Mertin (7). Ray K. Metzker (18/c). Sheila Metzner. Joel Meyerowitz (15/c). Chester Michalik (4). Duane Michals (c). Judy Miller. Roger Minick (26/c). Richard Misrach (17). Lisette Model (3). Jeannette Montgomery. Wright Morris. NASA (25). Bea Nettles. Beaumont Newhall. Arnold Newman (4). Nic Nicosia (2). Nicholas Nixon (16/c). Anne Noggle. Nancy O'Connor. Arthur Ollman (6). Dennis Oppenheim. Ruth Orkin. Robert Page (2). Marion Palfi. Tod Papageorge (18/c). Esther Parada (c). Bart Parker (c). Susie Paul. Richard Payne (26). Mary Elizabeth Peck (8). Irving Penn (2). John Pfahl. Eliot Porter (55/b). Winter Prather. Charles Pratt (21). Michael Putnam. Carmen Quesada-Burke. Penny Rakoff. Glenn Rand. Christopher Ransom. Marcia Resnick (c). Barbara Jo Revelle. Nancy Rexroth. Milton Rogovin. Charles Roitz. Walter Rosenblum. Arthur Rothstein (13/b). Janice Rubin. Ed Ruscha (c). Robert Joel Sagerman (2). Laurence Salzmann. Lucas Samaras. Danny Samuels (4). Douglas Sandhage. Margaret Sass. Naomi Savage (9/b). Sherie Scheer. Charles Schorre (6). John Schutze. Joseph Schwartz. John Sebert. Cindy Sherman (2). Stephen Shore (17/c). Arthur Siegel (2). Brent Sikkema. Larry Silver. Laurie Simmons. Art Sinsabaugh. Aaron Siskind (16/b). Henry Holmes Smith. Keith Smith (2). Sharon Smith (2). W. Eugene Smith (12). Rosalind Solomon. Frederick Sommer. Eve Sonneman (4/c). Al Souza (2/c). Jan Staller. David Stark. Ron Starr (5). Robert von Sternberg (2). Joel Sternfeld (13). Craig Stevens. Ezra Stoller (48/c). Jim Stone (2). Lou Stoumen. Paul Strand (20/bc). John Szarkowski. Athena Tacha (c). Arthur Taussig. Val Telberg. Edmund Teske. Lew Thomas (c). Ruth Thorne-Thomsen (2). George Tice. Alex Traube (3). Jerry Uelsmann (5). Willard Van Dyke. David Vestal. Catherine Wagner (2). Todd Walker. Marke Daryl Webb (2). Todd Webb (2/c). Weegee (= Arthur Fellig). William Wegman. Dan Weiner. Alice Andrews Wells (2/c). Jack Welpott. Henry Wessell Jr. (2). Brett Weston (4). Cole Weston (2). Edward Weston (c). Minor White (13/bc). Robert Widdicombe. Terry Wild. Casey Williams. Rick Williams (10/c). Geoff Winningham (36/b). Garry Winogrand (14/b). K. Kelly Wise (2). Joel Peter Witkin (2). John Wood (c). Max Yavno. Tom Zetterstrom.

European, 1945 to present: Bernhard and Hilla Becher. Ferenc Berko. Edouard Boubat (14/b). Bill Brandt (2). Brassaï (= Gyula Halász). Larry Burrows. Henri Cartier-Bresson (49/c). Vaclau Chochola (3). Alain Clement. Lucien Clergue (5). Jan Dibbets. Robert Doisneau (15/b). Franco

Fontana (25). Mario Giacomelli. Serge Hambourg. Robert Hausser. Beatrice Helg. Keld Helmer-Petersen. Pierre Jahan. Bill Jay. Peter Keetman. Art Klein. Jacques-Henri Lartigue. Alen MacWeeney (12/b). Andre Ostier. Neil Selkirk. Josef Sudek (2). Karin Székessy. George Tatge. Wim Wenders (3).

Non-Amerian, non-European, 1945 to present (Mexican unless otherwise noted): Manuel Alvarez Bravo (17/b). Micha Bar-Am (Israeli). Ricardo Block (3). Manuel Carrillo (15/b). Rafael Doniz (2). Hector García (2). Flor de María Garduno Yanez (2). Eikoh Hosoe (Japanese). Graham Howe (Australian). Graciela Itúrbide (2). Yousuf Karsh (Canadian). Pedro Meyer (2). Pablo Ortiz Monasterio (2). Grant Mudford (Australian). Kenji Nakahashi (Japanese, 2). Ikko Narahara (Japanese, 29). Eduardo Obregón Lavin (2). Antonio Reynoso Castañeda (2). Jesús Sanchez Uribe (2). Pedro A. Valtierra Ruvalcaba (2).

Notes:

a. Includes photogravures from *Camera Works*.
b. See Record groups—works by a single photographer.
c. See Record groups—works by more than one photographer.

RECORD GROUPS: Described as institutional archives, the Bayou Bend collection, and reserve collections.

Institutional archives:

H64.1 MUSEUM OF FINE ARTS, HOUSTON INSTITUTIONAL ARCHIVES. A center for research on the museum (as opposed to its holdings), the Glassell School of Art, and the Bayou Bend Collection of American Decorative Arts. The archives is the repository for all museum papers. These records include policies, activities, and persons associated with the museum. Of special note are documents relating to Houston Public School Art League/Houston Art League (1900 to 1929); exhibiting artists, including Forrest Bess, Alexander Calder, Anthony Caro, Helen Frankenthaler, Robert Motherwell, and Charles Umlauf; architectural records associated with museum designers William Ward Watkin and Ludwig Mies van der Rohe; photographic records of the museum buildings, exhibitions, special events, and works of art.

Bayou Bend collection:

H64.2 BAYOU BEND COLLECTION. Overall and detail views of American gravestones photographed by Daniel and Jessie Lie Farber. 50 silver gelatin prints. 1973 to 1983. Part of a larger Farber collection located at the American Antiquarian Society in Worcester MA.

Reserve collections: Described in terms of work by more than one photographer (exhibitions, portfolios, and team and unidentified photographers) and groups of work by a single photographer (published works, portfolios, and books).

Record groups containing work by more than one photographer, photographers working as a team, and collections of unidentified photography, including portfolios, books, and exhibitions:

H64.3 "AMERICAN IMAGES: THE AMERICAN TELEPHONE AND TELEGRAPH COMPANY COLLECTION." Work commissioned by ATT, including landscape, cityscapes, some social commentary, and some highly stylized imagery; 15 works each by photographers Robert Adams, Lewis Baltz, Harry Callahan, William Clift, Linda Connor, Bevan Davies, Roy DeCarava,

William Eggleston, Elliott Erwitt, Larry Fink, Frank Gohlke, John Gossage, Jonathan Green, Jan Groover, Mary Ellen Mark, Joel Meyerowitz, Richard Misrach, Nicholas Nixon, Tod Papageorge, and Stephen Shore. 300 photo prints, many in color. 1977 to 1978. See Bibliography—Danese.

H64.4 *AMERICAN ROADS* PORTFOLIO. Los Angeles: Landweber/Artists, 1982. Photographs by 20 American photographers. 20 photographs in various media. 1969 to 1981.

H64.5 BAUHAUS PHOTOGRAPHS. Mostly from the Dessau period, including the photographs of T. Lux Feininger, Franz Roh, Lucia Moholy, and others. 40 photo prints. 1920s.

H64.6 BINION (SANDRA) AND DIRK BAKKER PORTFOLIO. *The green dress: A Chicago story*. Chicago: Interiors and Fine Art International Inc., 1980. Contrived photography by Binion and Bakker. 21 Ektacolor prints.

H64.7 CRONIN (ANTHONY G.) MEMORIAL COLLECTION. An artificial collection of works by 49 photographers donated to the museum as a memorial to Cronin. 125 photographs. 1979 to 1985.

H64.8 CZECH AVANT-GARDE COLLECTION. Movement, fine art/abstracted photographs including some portraits 32 photographs. 1918 to 1940.

H64.9 *THE GALVESTON THAT WAS* COLLECTION. Commissioned photographs of Galveston by Ezra Stoller (48) and Henri Cartier-Bresson (46). 94 silver gelatin prints. 1965. See Bibliography—Barnstone.

H64.10 [*George M. Tuttle album.*] Yokohama: Farsari and Company, [after 1886.] Predominantly Japanese temples and a few landscapes by an unidentified photographer. 72 hand-tinted albumen prints.

H64.11 INCANDELA (GERALD) PORTFOLIO. *Pictures/Stories*. Oakhurst Press, 1981. 11 platinum prints with text by Brad Gooch, printed by Sal Lopez. 1977 to 1980.

H64.12 [*Japanese travel album*]. Studio genre photographs, landscapes, and temples made for tourists by an unidentified photographer. 18 albumen prints, some hand-tinted. 1880s?

H64.13 MARVINS (SONIA AND KAYE) PORTRAIT COLLECTION. Art portraits in a wide range of styles of noteworthy personages by prominent photographers. 35 photo prints. 1857 to 1986. See Bibliography—Tucker and Olvey.

H64.14 *NEW CALIFORNIA VIEWS* PORTFOLIO. Los Angeles: Landweber/Artists, 1979. 20 photographers. 20 photographs in various media. 1964 to 1979.

H64.15 NEW YORK PHOTO LEAGUE COLLECTION. Sociodocumentary photographs by Sid Grossman and Lou Bernstein, with representative pieces by 23 other photographers. 150 photographs. 1940s to 1950s.

H64.16 TARGET COLLECTION OF AMERICAN PHOTOGRAPHY. Target I includes work by 68 major American photographers from 1945 to the present. Target II includes substantial coverage of Baron Adolphe de Meyer, Minor White, Alfred Stieglitz, Paul Strand, and Edward Weston. Target III includes sequences by the following photographers (quantities represent different sequences, each sequence containing several images): Richard Avedon, Paul Berger, Barbara Blondeau, Laurie Brown, Wynn Bullock, Harry Callahan, Robert Cumming, William DeLappa, Thomas Eakins, William Eggleston, Hollis Frampton and Marion Faller, Robert Frank, Sidney Grossman, Robert Heinecken, Douglas Huebler, T. W. Ingersoll (publisher), Steve Kahn, Sol LeWitt, Joan Lyons, Nathan Lyons, MANUAL (Suzanne Bloom and Ed Hill), Ray K. Metzger, Duane Michals, Eadweard Muybridge, Esther Parada, Bart Parker, Marcia Resnick, Edward Ruscha, Eve Sonneman, Al Souza, Athena Tacha, Lew Thomas, Todd Webb, Alice Wells, Minor White, and John Wood. 235 photographs. 1877 to 1984. See Bibliography—Tucker, —Tucker and Searle, —Tucker and Agee.

H64.17 *TEN PHOTOGRAPHS: AN ALLEN STREET GALLERY COMMEMORATIVE* PORT-FOLIO. Dallas: Allen Street Gallery, 1982. 10 photographers. 10 photographs in various media.

H64.18 TEXAS HISTORICAL FOUNDATION COLLECTION. Work commissioned by the foundation under a grant from Conoco and E. I. du Pont de Nemours for the Texas Sesquicentennial including landscape and social documentary; photographers held by the museum include Frank Armstrong, Fred Baldwin/Wendy Watriss, Gay Block, Ave Bonar, Skeet McAuley, and Rick Williams. Silver gelatin and color prints. 1978 to 1979. See Bibliography—Sandweiss, et al.

Record groups of work by a single photographer, including portfolios and published works (record group title is photographer unless otherwise noted):

H64.19 ALVAREZ BRAVO (MANUEL; b. 1902) PORTFOLIO. *Manuel Alvarez Bravo.* Geneva: Acorn Editions, 1977. 15 modern silver gelatin prints. 1930 to 1977.

H64.20 ARNOLD (EVE) PORTFOLIO. *In China.* Self-published, 1982. 12 dye-transfer prints. 1979.

H64.21 BALTZ (LEWIS; b. 1945) PORTFOLIO. *The new industrial parks near Irvine, California.* 51 silver gelatin prints. 1974. See Bibliography.

H64.22 BLOSSFELDT (KARL; 1865-1932) PORTFOLIO. *Karl Blossfeldt.* Köln: Galerie Wilde, 1975. 12 modern silver gelatin prints. 1927 to 1929.

H64.23 BOUBAT (EDOUARD; b. 1923) PORTFOLIO. *Boubat.* New York: Hyperion, 1981. 15 modern silver gelatin prints. 1947 to 1981.

H64.24 BROWN (PETER) PORTFOLIO. *Seasons of Light.* Self-published, 1982. 20 dye-transfer prints; text block legends. Interior still lifes. 1979 to 1981.

H64.25 CARRILLO (MANUEL) PORTFOLIO. *Manuel Carrillo.* Chicago: Gilbert Gallery Ltd, 1981. 15 silver gelatin prints. 1960 to 1975.

H64.26 CRANE (ARNOLD) COLLECTION. Portraits of famous photographers. 57 silver gelatin prints. 1960s.

H64.27 CRAWFORD (RALSTON) COLLECTION. American painter. 9 silver gelatin prints. 1938 to 1972.

H64.28 CUMMING (ROBERT; b. 1943) COLLECTION. Conceptual, contrived photography. 34 photo prints, a few color. 1970 to 1976.

H64.29 CURTIS (EDWARD S.; 1868-1952) COLLECTION. Formal portraits of Amerinds from *North American Indians.* 40 photogravures. 1903 to 1927.

H64.30 DE MEYER (BARON ADOLPHE; 1868-1946) PORTFOLIO. *Nijinsky, L'après-midi d'un faune.* New York: Eakins Press, 1977. Theatrical portraits of the dancer, Nijinsky. 33 modern palladium prints; printed by Richard Benson. 1912.

H64.31 DOISNEAU (ROBERT; b. 1912) PORTFOLIO. *Robert Doisneau.* New York: Hyperion, 1979. 15 silver gelatin prints. 1945 to 1972.

H64.32 ERWITT (ELLIOTT; b. 1928) PORTFOLIO. *Elliott Erwitt: The Alchan edition.* New York: Alchan Editions. 15 silver gelatin prints. 1952 to 1976.

H64.33 ERWITT (ELLIOTT; b. 1928) PORTFOLIO. *Recent developments.* Geneva: Acorn Editions. 10 modern silver gelatin prints.

H64.34 FRANK (ROBERT; b. 1924) COLLECTION. Documents of the American social landscape noted for not reinforcing the positive image of the country during the Eisenhower Administration made under a Guggenheim Fellowship for *The Americans.* 80 silver gelatin prints. 1958 to 1959. See Bibliography—Frank, —Tucker and Brookman.

H64.35 FRANK (ROBERT; b. 1924) COLLECTION. From his early New York, Paris, Spain, London, and Wales periods in a similar style to *The Americans.* Made before and immediately after *The Americans.* 201 photo prints. Late 1950s, early 1960s.

H64.36 FRIEDLANDER (LEE; b. 1934) AND JIM DINE PORTFOLIO. *Work from the same house.* Etchings and silver gelatin prints on single sheets. 1962 and later. See Bibliography.

H64.37 Frith, Francis, photog.; Joseph Bonomi and Samuel Sharpe. *Egypt, Nubia, and Ethiopia.* London: Smith, Elder, and Company, 1857. Ancient Egyptian ruins. 100 albumen stereo prints.

H64.38 GIBSON (RALPH; b. 1939) PORTFOLIO. *Chiaroscuro.* New York: Hyperion, 1982. 15 silver gelatin prints. 1972 to 1981.

H64.39 HEARTFIELD (JOHN; 1891-1968) COLLECTION. Sociopolitical, reform photo montages. 74 rotogravure montages reproduced in *AIZ* magazine; additional issues without Heartfield's work. 1929 to 1936. See Bibliography—Herzfeld.

H64.40 HINE (LEWIS WICKS; 1874-1940) COLLECTION. Portraits of child workers in Texas and one print of the Empire State Building. 12 silver gelatin prints. 1913 to 1932.

H64.41 KERTÉSZ (ANDRÉ; b. 1894) PORTFOLIO. *André Kertész, volume I, 1913-1919.* New York: Light, 1973. 10 modern silver gelatin prints.

H64.42 KERTÉSZ (ANDRÉ; b. 1894) PORTFOLIO. *André Kertész, volume II, 1930-1972.* New York: Light, 1973. 10 modern silver gelatin prints.

H64.43 KNOWLTON (GRACE) PORTFOLIO. *Adobe.* Self-published, 1983. 10 platinum prints. Ca. 1983.

H64.44 LYON (DANNY; b. 1942) PORTFOLIO. *Danny Lyon.* New York: Hyperion, 1979. 30 silver gelatin prints. 1965 to 1979.

H64.45 MacWEENEY (ALEN) PORTFOLIO. *Alen MacWeeney.* New York: Hyperion, 1979. 12 silver gelatin prints. 1968 to 1972.

H64.46 MOHOLY-NAGY (LÁSZLÓ; 1895-1946) COLLECTION. Photograms and cityscape abstractions; a few made while at the Chicago Institute of Design. 29 vintage and 16 modern prints; 8 rolls of film negatives; typescript materials. Late 1920s to 1940s.

H64.47 MINICK (ROGER) PORTFOLIO. *Delta portfolio.* Self-published, 1976. 12 silver gelatin prints. 1966 to 1969.

H64.48 MINICK (ROGER) PORTFOLIO. *Ozark portfolio.* Self-published, 1976. 12 silver gelatin prints. 1968 to 1973.

H64.49 Muybridge, Eadweard, photog. *Panorama of San Francisco from California Street Hill.* 1877. 11 albumen prints mounted as an accordion-folding panorama.

H64.50 Nègre, Charles, photog.; André Jammes. *Charles Nègre: Photographe 1820-1880.* Paris: L'Imprimerie de France à Choisy-le-Roi, 1963. 31 modern phototypies.

H64.51 PORTER (ELIOT; b. 1901) PORTFOLIO. *Intimate landscapes.* Fine print landscape photography made in the US. 55 dye-transfer prints. 1954 to 1974. See Bibliography.

H64.52 RÖSSLER (JAROSLAV) PORTFOLIO. *Jaroslav Rössler, 10 photographs, 1923-1930.* Köln: Rudolph Kicken Gallery, 1982. 1923 to 1930. 10 modern silver gelatin prints.

H64.53 ROTHSTEIN (ARTHUR; b. 1915) PORTFOLIO. *Arthur Rothstein.* New York: Hyperion, 1981. 30 modern silver gelatin prints. 1935 to 1951.

H64.54 SAVAGE (NAOMI; b. 1927) PORTFOLIO. *Portfolio IV.* Self-published, 1981. 8 mixed media. 1969 to 1980.

H64.55 SISKIND (AARON; b. 1903) PORTFOLIO. *Harlem document.* 30 silver gelatin prints. 1932 to 1939.

H64.56 STEICHEN (EDWARD; 1879-1973) BEQUEST. Studio and in situ portraits; fashion photography made for Condé Nast's magazine *Vanity Fair.* 75 silver gelatin prints. 1923 to 1937.

H64.57 STEICHEN (EDWARD; 1879-1973) PORTFOLIO. *The Early years.* Millerton NY: Aperture, 1981. 12 photogravures. 1900 to 1925.

H64.58 STRAND (PAUL; 1890-1976) PORTFOLIO. *Paul Strand: The formative years.* Millerton NY: Silver Mountain Foundation, 1983. 10 photogravures. 1914 to 1917.

H64.59 STRAND (PAUL; 1890-1976) PORTFOLIO. *Paul Strand: Portfolio three.* Millerton NY: Paul Strand Foundation, 1980. 10 silver gelatin prints. 1916 to 1963.

H64.60 STRAND (PAUL; 1890-1976) PORTFOLIO. *Paul Strand: Portfolio four.* Millerton NY: Paul Strand Foundation, 1980. 10 silver gelatin prints. 1950 to 1973.

H64.61 Thomson, John, photog. *Illustrations of China and her people.* London: S. Low, Marston, Low, and Searle, 1873-1874. 4 volumes, 222 autotype prints.

H64.62 WHITE (MINOR; 1908-1976) PORTFOLIO. *Jupiter portfolio.* Self-published, 1975. 12 silver gelatin prints. 1947 to 1971.

H64.63 WINNINGHAM (GEOFF; b. 1943) PORTFOLIO. *Texas Dozen.* Houston: Cronin Gallery, 1976. Houston culture, including cheerleaders, wrestling, rodeo, and cityscapes. With an introduction by Robert Adams. 15 silver gelatin prints. 1971 to 1974. Itemized list.

H64.64 WINNINGHAM (GEOFF; b. 1943) PORTFOLIO. *Wrestling in Houston.* 35 photographs. 1975 to 1984. See Bibliography—Carmean.

H64.65 WINOGRAND (GARRY; 1928-1984) PORTFOLIO. *Garry Winogrand.* New York: Hyperion, 1978. 15 silver gelatin prints. 1960s to 1970s.

National Aeronautics and Space Administration
Lyndon B. Johnson Space Center (H67)

Film Repository
Building 424
Johnson Space Center
Houston, Texas 77058

History Office
Building 420, Room 105B
Mail Code BY4
Johnson Space Center
Houston, Texas 77058

713-483-2838. Contact: History Office Coordinator.

Public Affairs Office – Film/Video Distribution Library
1020 Bay Area Drive
Houston, Texas 77058

713-486-9606. Contact: Film Librarian.

Public Affairs Office – Still Photo Library
Building 2, Room 187
Media Services Branch/AP3
Johnson Space Center
Houston, Texas 77058

713-483-4231. Contact: Public Affairs Officer.

Public Affairs Office – Stock Film Library
Building 2
Media Service Branch/AP3
Johnson Space Center
Houston, Texas 77058

713-483-5111. Contact: Audiovisual Manager.

Television Office
Building 8
Johnson Space Center
Houston, Texas 77058

PURPOSE: A government agency collecting photographs in the course of its activities; these photographs have been assembled into an archive at the Film Repository, which houses extensive files of photographs made during and pertaining to space missions. The divisions within the Johnson Space Center provide access to different portions of the Film Repository. NASA/Ames High-Altitude Survey photographs are located at the Technology Application Center, University of New Mexico, Albuquerque NM. Many of the NASA/Ames Survey photographs and other earth surface views made during the various space missions are at the Texas Natural Resources Information System Central in Austin (q.v.).

HOURS: Weekdays, 8:00-5:00. Closed federal holidays. Appointment required for History Office. Appointment made well in advance required to use materials in the Film Repository (generally restricted access).

ASSISTANCE: Professional, specialized, experienced staff. Written and phone inquiries accepted on a limited basis; researchers should plan to visit the collection in person. Electrostatic copies available. Photoduplications must be ordered through the Public Affairs Office; delivery takes three weeks. When possible, orders should be accompanied by a photograph ID number. The Teacher's Resource Center provides three-quarter-inch video cassette reproducers and half-inch Beta and VHS recorders that allow teachers to copy NASA educational and historical presentations.

PUBLICATION: No publication fee. Photographs are government documents in the public domain.

FINDING AIDS: Archival guides for material in the History Office; Film Repository photographs stored by number. Extensive, complete finding aids available.

BIBLIOGRAPHY: Extensive list of special publications produced by NASA includes more than 100 titles. NASA Special Publications (SP) may be ordered from the US Government Printing Office, Washington DC.

Brooks, Courtney G., James M. Grimwood, and Loyd S. Swenson. *Chariots for Apollo: A history of manned lunar spacecraft.* 1979. NASA SP# 4205.
Earth photographs from Gemini III, IV, and V. NASA SP# 129.
Earth photographs from Gemini VI through XII. NASA SP# 171.
Ezell, Edward Clinton, and Linda Neuman Ezell. *The partnership: A history of the Apollo-Soyuz test project.* 1978. NASA SP# 4209.
Johnson Space Center Film Catalog. [Produced by the Film/Video Distribution Library.]
Newkirk, Roland W., and Ivan D. Ertel, with Courtney G. Brooks. *Skylab: A chronology.* 1977. NASA SP# 4011.
Swensen, Loyd S., James Grimwood, and Charles Alexander. *This new ocean: A history of Project Mercury.* 1966. NASA SP# 4201.

SCOPE: History Office contains 4,000 photo prints, many art reproductions, with related papers; Public Affairs Still Photo Library holds 10,000 photographs, including prints and transparencies; the Film Repository holds 200,000 negatives and transparencies, most color, and 6,000,000 feet of stock motion picture and film footage.

GEOGRAPHIC: Extremely high altitude views of earth and space shots.

SUBJECTS: All aspects of NASA manned space flight programs, including Mercury, Gemini, Apollo, Skylab, Space Shuttle, and the Space Station under development. In addition to subjects shot in space, the collection documents training, engineering development, and associated programs such as the development of space food.

PEOPLE: Astronauts, some views of ground staff.

PHOTOGRAPHERS: Many images are machine-generated, others were made by the crews of space missions.

RECORD GROUPS: Each subdivision represents a different division within the Johnson Space Center; addresses are noted below.

H67.1 Film Repository: Houses the original film of Johnson Space Center ground based photography and printing masters (transparencies) of all of the film exposed in space during the Manned Spaceflight Program. The repository is not established as a research library, but as an archival facility for material for reproduction. Proof books in the Public Affairs Still Photo Library (v.i.) contain reproductions of basically the same material stored in this facility. Upon special written requests to the Audiovisual Manager in the Public Affairs Office, arrangements can be made to perform research in this facility for material that may not be available in the Public Affairs Library.

History Office: Maintains files generated by historians in the production of NASA-generated histories and chronologies of the space program. The files for the Mercury, Gemini, Skylab, and Apollo-Soyuz programs described here are stored and accessed at the Houston, Rice University, Woodson Research Center (q.v.).

H67.2 HISTORY OFFICE—APOLLO FILES. Development of the Apollo project and many photographs made in space by astronauts, including many images of the lunar surface. 2,000 photographs. 1963 to 1972.

H67.3 HISTORY OFFICE—SPACE SHUTTLE FILES. NASA- and contractor-generated photographs of the development of the Space Shuttle; many are art reproductions of artist renderings. 2,000 photographs. 1969 to 1983.

History files stored and accessed at the Woodson Research Center (q.v.):

H67.4 APOLLO-SOYUZ TEST PROGRAM. Docking module, meetings in Houston and Moscow. 100 photographs. 1971 to 1975.

H67.5 GEMINI FILE. Gemini flights, not all covered, including launches, astronauts, landings, and earth/sky photographs. 1 box. 1960s.

H67.6 MERCURY FILE. Photographs used in publication *This New Ocean*; capsule, capsule assembly and test; exhibits; aerial of launch pad; launch and Launch Operations Directorate; astronauts press meeting at Lewis Research Center. Generated by Space Task Group, McDonell Aircraft Corporation, the Langley Research Center, Goddard (Beltsville), Marshall, and Kennedy space flight centers, NASA, and NACA. 350 photographs. 1960s. See Bibliography—Swenson.

H67.7 NASA PHOTOGRAPH FILE. Subjects include the Gemini, Skylab, Apollo-Soyuz, and Space Shuttle programs with some coverage of the Mercury and Apollo missions, including the NASA S series (generated by the Space Task Group), aerials of the Earth and Moon surfaces made on Apollo missions 6 through 13, Moon surface made on missions 15 through 17, and photographs from the series 64-H to 75-H. Most are copies from other areas in the collection. 7 boxes of photographs, including prints and transparencies. 1960 to 1981.

H67.8 SKYLAB PHOTOGRAPH ALBUMS. Originally stored in three-ring binders, now stored in original order, loose in folders. Arranged under the headings Systems, including MDA (multiple docking adapter); AM (airlock module); OWS (orbital work shop); ATM (Apollo telescope mount); EVA (extra vehicular activity), including vehicle EVA equipment; EREP (earth resources experiments package) experiments; ATM experiments including, quad 1 through quad 4 experiments, EVA activities, and MDA/AM/OWS/CSM; Bio-Med experiments; corollary experiments; and communications, including communications equipment. 8 boxes of photo prints. Early 1970s.

Public Affairs Office: Provides support for the general public, including civic organizations, schools, academics, contractors, the media, and other governmental agencies.

H67.9 PUBLIC AFFAIRS OFFICE—FILM/VIDEO DISTRIBUTION LIBRARY. Lends NASA motion picture programs. 2,000 titles; catalog available.

H67.10 PUBLIC AFFAIRS OFFICE—STILL PHOTO LIBRARY. Proofs of all still photographs made in space in the course of the US Manned Spaceflight Program, including the Mercury, Gemini, Apollo, Skylab, Apollo-Soyuz, and Space Shuttle projects, as well as photographs of astronaut training, spacecraft manufacturing, selected launches, engineerings and development activities at the Johnson Space Center, and selected views from deep-space probes, including Voyager, Viking, and Mariner. 17,000 photographs.

H67.11 PUBLIC AFFAIRS OFFICE—STOCK FILM LIBRARY. All motion picture footage exposed during manned spaceflights, including all television from Apollo and Skylab, which has been transferred to film for archival purposes. In addition, it contains a broad selection of television from the Space Shuttle program. Six million feet of 16mm motion picture footage.

H67.12 Television Office: Operates all the television systems at the Johnson Space Center. Maintains a repository of spaceflight television; much material is housed at the Film Repository.

University Art Collection (H73)

Rice University
Department of Art and Art History
6100 South Main Street
Houston, Texas 77251

713-527-8101, extension 3470. Contact: Curator.

PURPOSE: An academic, fine art collection with an exhibition space collecting painting, sculpture, and photographs.

HOURS: Exhibition space—Monday through Saturday, 12:00 to 5:00. Reserve collections—by appointment only. Closed major and university holidays, and in the summer.

ASSISTANCE: Professional, specialized staff. Written and phone inquiries accepted. Electrostatic copies available. Photoduplications must be ordered through the collection.

PUBLICATION: No publication fee. Requests must be in writing. Collection credit required. Free copy of publication to collection. Third-party permission required on some photographs.

FINDING AIDS: Card index; access by photographer. Published catalog forthcoming.

SCOPE: 200 vintage photographs; most silver gelatin prints, some color prints. 1908 to 1982.

GEOGRAPHIC: France (Paris). Mexico. US (New York City).

SUBJECTS: A fine art collection with no specific subject concentration.

PHOTOGRAPHERS: The collection holds works by established fine art photographers, including a number who worked for the Farm Security Administration (marked with an asterisk).

John Albok (48). Manuel Alvarez Bravo (12). Sheldon Dick (1).* Robert Doisneau (13). Elliott Erwitt (14). Joseph B. Englander (2). Walker Evans (4).* Lewis W. Hine (5). Richard Johnson (27).* André Kertész (15). Dorothea Lange (11).* Russell Lee (8).* Walter de Maria (1). Carl Mydans (2).* Gordon Parks (1).* Richard Pipes (5). Arthur Rothstein (3).* Stephen Shore (1). John Vachon (6).* Garry Winogrand (15). Geoff Winningham (4). M. Post Wolcott.*

RECORD GROUPS:

H73.1 ALBOK (JOHN; 1894-1985) COLLECTION. Hungarian-born, immigrated to America in 1921, worked as a tailor, exhibited at Museum of City of New York in 1937 and 1982. New York City urban scene, including the 1939 World's Fair, Central Park, and street life. 48 vintage prints. 1928 to 1982, most from the Depression Era.

H73.2 ALVAREZ BRAVO (MANUEL; b. 1902) PORTFOLIO. *Manuel Alvarez Bravo.* Geneva: Acorn Editions, 1977. 15 modern silver gelatin prints. Ca. 1930 to 1970s.

H73.3 DOISNEAU (ROBERT; b. 1912) PORTFOLIO. *Robert Doisneau.* New York: Hyperion, 1979. 15 modern silver gelatin prints. 1945 to 1972.

H73.4 ERWITT (ELLIOTT; b. 1928) PORTFOLIO. *Elliott Erwitt.* New York: Alchan Editions. 15 silver gelatin prints. 1952 to 1976.

H73.5 JOHNSON (RICHARD) COLLECTION. High-contrast, near-abstract compositions apparently from a montage of Houston's elevated freeways. 27 silver gelatin prints.

H73.6 WINOGRAND (GARRY; 1928-1984) PORTFOLIO. *Garry Winogrand.* New York: Hyperion, 1978. 15 modern silver gelatin prints. 1960s to 1970s.

Woodson Research Center (H76)

Rice University
Fondren Library
6100 South Main Street
P.O. Box 1892
Houston, Texas 77251

713-527-8101, extension 2586. Contact: Director.

PURPOSE: A special-collections division within a university library collecting rare books and journals, fine bindings, manuscripts, maps, some realia, and photographs; the center also serves as the university's archive. The materials frequently relate to the university or the careers of its alumni.

HOURS: Weekdays, 9:00-5:00. Closed major and academic holidays. Appointment recommended. A few record groups require advance application for permission to view.

ASSISTANCE: Professional, experienced staff. Written inquiries accepted. Electrostatic copies available. Photoduplications must be ordered through the center.

PUBLICATION: No publication fee. Collection credit required. Free copy of publication to center. Third-party permission required on some material.

FINDING AIDS: Collection-level card index notes photographs, collection file frequently contains inventory. Participates in NUCMC.

SCOPE: 7,000 photographs, most vintage prints, many transparencies. Most collections have supporting manuscript materials. 1860s to present.

Type of photo	Pre-1880	1880-1899	1900-1919	1920-1939	1940-1959	1960-1986
Film negs						
Vintage prints	350	300	1,000	1,000	1,250	2,000
Copy prints						
Photo albums	3	2	5	3	8	5

GEOGRAPHIC: Most photographs represent Texas, especially the Houston region.

Houston. Japan. Mexico. Space (Moon).

SUBJECTS: Extensive coverage of Rice University; other subjects receive less than substantial coverage.

Academia (graduation, university). Architecture (academic, construction). Industry (petroleum). Landscape (snapshot, survey). Military (Civil War, WW II). Social life and customs (university). Transportation (space, water).

PEOPLE: Many portraits of faculty and students of the university, although few are held in quantity. See Record Groups—Institutional Archives—Portraits for specific names.

PHOTOGRAPHERS: E. W. Irish. Kaiden Kazanjian (New York). F. J. Schlueter.

RECORD GROUPS: Described in terms of the university archives, manuscript record groups, and albums and published works containing photographs.

University Archives: Arranged by headings portraits, geographic, events, sports, and miscellaneous. The archive reflects in subject matter the technological bias of the university's academic programs, especially in engineering and the space sciences. See also Albums and Published Works for additional institutional archive photographs.

H76.1 Portrait group depicts faculty, students, and prominent alumni of the university, most journalistic, in situ or studio portraits, including W. W. Akers, Franz Brotzen, Alexander J. Dessler, William Vermillion Houston, J. Dennis Huston, Harold M. Hyman, Samuel Jones, Oswald Joseph Lassig, Edgar Odell Lovett, John L. Margrave, William H. Masterson, Kenneth Sanborn Pitzer, Harold E. Rorschach Jr.; campus organizations represented include the Marching Owl Band (= MOB) and depict student social life and customs. 4.5 feet photo prints, most vintage, a few color. 1910s to present (open collection).

H76.2 Geographic group depicts the campus grounds and buildings; groundbreaking ceremonies and later construction well represented; some aerials and general views. 4 feet silver gelatin prints. 1911 to present.

H76.3 Events group depicts campus social life and customs, including baccalaureate and commencement exercises, garden parties, the General Electric College Bowl, Hiroshima Scientific Advisory Group inspection tour—1947, homecomings, laying of cornerstones, and the university's opening ceremonies—1912. 3.5 feet, most silver gelatin prints, a few color prints. 1910s to present.

H76.4 Sports group depicts the university's athletics department and the Rice Owls. 6 inches silver gelatin prints. 1940s to 1970s.

H76.5 Manuscript record groups: The following record groups contain a small number of photographs: James L. Autry papers, William Lockhart Clayton papers, William Goyen papers, Rienzi Melville Johnston papers, and Frankie Carter Randolph papers.

H76.6 ALLEN (LUDWIG) COLLECTION. New England gravestones dating from 1653-1810.

H76.7 BROWN (CAMILLE WAGGAMAN; b. 1895) AND WAGGAMAN FAMILY COLLECTION. Radio talk-show hostess and socialite in Montgomery AL. Documents the career of Brown; life with her husband in the military while stationed in the Philippine Islands; the Waggaman Family. 150 photo prints. Ca. 1890 to 1970s. WRC# 394. See Albums and Published Works—Waggaman.

H76.8 CHARLOTTE (1840-1927) AND MAXIMILLIAN (1832-1867) COLLECTION. Emperor of Mexico and his consort. Art reproductions, travel views of Mexico and Europe, and portraits.

> **H76.8.1** [*Charlotte and Maximillian carte album.*] Studio portraits, many art reproductions of painted portraits of Charlotte, Maximillian, and military leaders; a few photographed by Aubert y Cíe (Cd México) and Cruces y Campa. 33 albumen cartes. 1860s.

> **H76.8.2** [*Mexico album I.*] Travel views of landscape, picturesque views of city life; commercial or amateur photographs. 48 silver gelatin prints. Ca. 1890.

> **H76.8.3** [*Mexico album II.*] Many views duplicate those in *Mexico album I.* 26 silver gelatin prints. Ca. 1890.

38 photo prints, most albumen; 3 albums (v.s.). 1860s to 1890s. WRC# 356.

H76.9 CHILLMAN (JAMES H., Jr.; 1891-1972) PAPERS. Professor of art, fellow emeritus of the American Institute of Architects, and first director of the Museum of Fine Arts, Houston. American Academy in Rome, Europe, family, and Rice University. 150 photo prints. 1915 to 1920s, 1960s.

H76.10 CIVIL WAR COLLECTION. Landscapes, cityscapes and ruins, military encampments, battle aftermath with corpses, government buildings in Appomatox VA and Richmond VA; photographed by Mathew Brady and Alexander Gardner. 90 albumen prints. 1860s.

H76.11 DAVIES (JOSPEPH I.) PAPERS. Rice University history. 15 glass lantern slides; 220—35mm slides. Ca. 1912 to 1980. WRC# 286.

H76.12 DILLINGHAM (MARY PAULINE) COLLECTION. Dillingham family portraits, including Paul, governor of Vermont; William Paul, US senator; and Charles K., founder of Texas Commerce Bank. 25 photo prints. 1863 to 1890. WRC# 257.

H76.13 FONDREN (ELLA F. C.; 1880-1982) FAMILY COLLECTION. Houston civic leader, wife of Walter William Fondren, founder of Humble Oil and Refining Company (= Exxon); member of the board of directors of Methodist Hospital (Houston) and Southern Methodist University. Journalistic portraits of Fondren and her activities; Methodist Hospital; Scarritt College; Southern Methodist University; studio portraits of the Fondren family, including Walter William, Catherine, Sue, Walter Jr., and grandchildren; National Conference of Christians and Jews; Kinkaid School (Houston). 300 photo prints, most silver gelatin, some color. Ca. 1900 to 1982. WRC# 340. Additional Fondren family material in WRC# 390, an unprocessed, restricted collection.

H76.14 FREEMAN (JOHN W., Jr.) PAPERS. Assistant professor of space science at Rice. NASA photographs of Apollo missions 12, 14, and 15, including the lunar surface; acquired during research on a NASA suprathermal ion detector (SID) experiment, a part of the Apollo lunar surface experimental package (ALSEP). 7 rolls 70mm black-and-white transparencies; 12 rolls 70mm color transparencies; 1 foot color and silver gelatin prints. 1965 to 1979. WRC# 344.

H76.15 NASA FILES. The Woodson Research Center holds many files received from the National Space and Aeronautics Administration, Lyndon B. Johnson Spacecraft Center (q.v.).

H76.16 RICKER (NORMAN HURD; 1896-1985?) PAPERS. Physicist in oil industry, then Western Electric.

>   **H76.16.1** Ricker, Norman Hurd. *The autobiography of Norman Hurd Ricker.* 1966. Life of Ricker as student at Rice and school of military aeronautics during WW I; seismographic research for Humble Oil. 19 silver gelatin prints tipped into a bound typescript. 1916 to 1928.

>   **H76.16.2** Ricker, Norman Hurd, photog. *Plunger lift.* "Installation of oil well pumps for Gulf Productions Co. and Standard Oil, Pampa Texas." 41 silver gelatin prints, handwritten captions. 1930 to 1931.

>   **H76.16.3** Ricker, Norman Hurd, photog. *The Rice Institute.* Amateur views of campus including interiors. 40 silver gelatin prints. Ca. 1916.

>   **H76.16.4** Ricker, Norman Hurd, comp. [*Rice University album I.*] Mechanics students and faculty; dorm life, including pranks; campus buildings. A few commercial views, most snapshots, probably by Ricker. 82 silver gelatin prints. Ca. 1915.

>   **H76.16.5** Ricker, Norman Hurd, photog. *Seismic exploration.* "Humble camp on John Jackson Ranch; first seismic survey of Humble Oil and Refining Co; Chambers County Texas." 35 silver gelatin prints. 1920s.

>   **H76.16.6** Ricker, Norman Hurd, photog. *West Texas.* Amateur views of Fort Davis and Crane landscapes. 13 silver gelatin prints. 1920s.

5 albums (v.s.). 1896 to 1930s. WRC# 284.

H76.17 WAIT (J. RUSSELL) PAPERS. Director of the Port of Houston from 1930 to 1947. Houston wharves and docks, ship channel.

>   [*Brazos River Harbor Navigation District.*] Aerial views of the construction of the harbor; ships in harbor after its completion; dock workers. Many photographed by Glen Heath. 206 silver gelatin prints in 4 ring binders. 1952 to 1954.

10 silver gelatin prints, 4 albums (v.s.). Mid-1950s. WRC# 346.

Albums and Published Works (Many entries in Manuscript (v.s.) include albums):

H76.18 [*Adele Waggaman album.*] Snapshots of Rice campus, student social life. 247 silver gelatin prints. 1911 to 1918.

H76.19 *Allen Center open house.* 23 silver gelatin prints. 1967.

H76.20 *Cleveland Sewall Hall.* Dedication ceremonies, architectural detail and interior views of the hall; portraits of Mrs. Sewall. 27 color photo prints. 1971.

H76.21 *Cleveland Sewall Hall groundbreaking ceremony.* Ceremonies, portraits of Mrs. Sewall. 28 silver gelatin and color photo prints. 1969.

H76.22 Cram and Ferguson, Architects, and James Stewart and Company Inc., Contractors, comp. *Dormitory number two for the William M. Rice Institute.* Commercial views of building construction. 21 silver gelatin prints. 1912.

H76.23 Cram, Goodhue, and Ferguson, Architects, and James Stewart and Company, Contractors, comp. *Residential hall for men.* Commercial views of building construction. 55 silver gelatin prints. 1912.

H76.24 Embree, E. D., and Thomas B. Eaton. *The Flying Owls: Rice Institute from the air.* Aerial views of the Rice campus. 12 silver gelatin prints; 7 copies. 1921.

H76.25 Hayden, F. V.; A. J. Russell, photog. *Sun pictures of Rocky Mountain scenery: With a description of the geographical and geological features, and some accounts of the resources of the great West; containing thirty photographic views along the line of the Pacific railroad from Omaha to Sacramento.* New York: Julius Bien, 1870. 30 albumen prints.

H76.26 Heartsill, W. W. *Fourteen hundred and ninety-one days in the Confederate Army: Camp life day by day of the W. P. Lane Rangers from April 19th 1861 to May 20th 1865.* Marshall: W. W. Heartsill, 1874-1876. Studio portraits of Heartsill and military associates. 61 albumen prints tipped into the textblock. WRC# Masterson E580.6/M84.

H76.27 *Inauguration of Norman Hackerman as fourth president of William Marsh Rice University.* Ceremony and reception. 36 color photo prints. 1971.

H76.28 Leiper, Harper, photog. *Semi-centennial.* Ceremonies commemorating the first fifty years of the University. 84 silver gelatin prints. 1952.

H76.29 *Rice Institute: Photographs of special occassions.* 1960. Visiting dignitaries and campus ceremonies; many photographed by F. J. Schlueter. 272 silver gelatin prints in 3 volumes. 1912 to 1946.

H76.30 [*US occupation of Japan I.*] Snapshot portraits of soldiers, possibly of the Eleventh Airborne. 59 silver gelatin prints. Ca. 1945.

H76.31 [*US occupation of Japan II.*] Snapshot portraits of soldiers, possibly of the Eleventh Airborne, including snapshot travel views on homeward journey of Grand Canyon and unidentified locales. 50 silver gelatin prints. Ca. 1945.

H76.32 [*US occupation of Japan III.*] Snapshot travel views and portraits of soldiers, possibly of the Eleventh Airborne. 50 silver gelatin prints. Ca. 1945.

H76.33 Walter, Herbert J. *Photographic exhibits used in the Rice-Patrick will case.* [Chicago]: American Society of Questioned Documents Examiners, 1952. Reproductions of documents and William Marsh Rice's signature used as evidence of a forged will created by Rice's murderers, Patrick and Jones.

University of Houston Library (H82)

University of Houston
Special Collections
M. D. Anderson Library, Eighth floor
Houston, Texas 77004

713-749-2726. Contact: Special Collections Librarian.

PURPOSE: The special-collections division of a university library collecting rare books, manuscripts, and photographs. The library also houses the university's archives.

ASSISTANCE: Professional assistance. Written inquiries accepted. Electrostatic copies available. Photoduplications must be ordered through the library.

PUBLICATION: No publication fee. Collection credit required. Free copy of publication to library. Third-party permission required on few items.

FINDING AIDS: None.

BIBLIOGRAPHY:
Fuermann, George Melvin; Bert Brandt, photog. *Houston: The once and future city.* New York: Doubleday, 1971.

SCOPE: 3,000 photographs. 1860s to present.

Type of photo	Pre-1880	1880-1899	1900-1919	1920-1939	1940-1959	1960-1986
Glass negs		42				
Film negs			500			
Vintage prints			200	1,000	2,000	1,000
Copy prints	25	50				
Photo albums			4			

GEOGRAPHIC: Houston. China. Japan. Philippine Islands.

SUBJECTS: Academia (university). Cityscape. Economic and social development. Military (*USS Houston*). Sports.

PEOPLE: Many portraits of faculty and students of the University; seamen of the *USS Houston*. Few held in quantity.

PHOTOGRAPHERS: George Beach.

RECORD GROUPS:

H82.1 FUERMANN (GEORGE) COLLECTION. Author and historian of Houston. Economic and social development, including aerial photographs, street scenes, storefronts, and cityscapes; petroleum industry; snapshot travel views, including Salt Lake City UT; some art reproduction. Many photographed by Beach, many copy prints and snapshots. Maintained as two collections totaling 250 modern, copy, and vintage silver gelatin prints, 750 nitrate negatives. 1869 to 1950s. See Bibliography.

H82.2 HEITZMANN (F. W.) AND COMPANY COLLECTION. Hardware company in Houston established in the 1860s. Photographs of the store interior, exterior, warehouse, stock, and offices; Heitzmann family. Many photographed by George Beach. 42 gelatin glass negatives with modern prints; 3 vintage panoramic prints. 1899 to 1909. Associated manuscript material at Houston Metropolitan Research Center, Mss 42.

H82.3 KIRKSEY (GEORGE) PAPERS. Sportswriter. Commercial portraits of Kirksey alone and in groups; commercial portraits of athletes and sports figures, many inscribed; Colt .45s (baseball team); Kirksey's military service and paratroopers during WW II. 350 photographs, most silver gelatin prints, a few negatives. 1940s to 1960s.

H82.4 UNIVERSITY OF HOUSTON ARCHIVE PHOTOGRAPHS. Documentation of campus activities. Major subjects include campus buildings, Hugh Roy Cullen, Delphians, UH Band, Board of Governors, General A. D. Bruce, student activities, library exhibits, and academic departments, including the School of Technology, Music and Drama, Journalism, and Nursing. 3 feet of silver gelatin prints. Most 1950s to 1970s, most ca. 1960.

H82.5 *USS HOUSTON* COLLECTION. A CA-30 battleship launched in 1929 and sunk by the Japanese in 1942; known as Franklin Roosevelt's Floating Whitehouse. Replaced by a CL-81. Primary focus of the collection is on the first ship. Officers and crew of the ship on board and survivors of its sinking as prisoners of war in Japan; events surrounding the history of the ship.

> **H82.5.1** DuRose, Arthur Floyd, comp. *Photo album; USS Houston.* Snapshot portraits of shipmates; Neptune's Court; shore visits in Manila, Philippines, and Key West FL. 99 silver gelatin prints. 1930.

> **H82.5.2** Layne, Gutherie F., Jr., comp. *US Navy Log Album.* Record of 30 months in the Philippine Islands. Amateur views of shipmates and officers; ship activities, including boxing, USS Houston, and other ships; social and economic life of the Philippines, including city, rural, and agricultural scenes; Igorot tribe; fishing; cathedral. 395 silver gelatin prints with handwritten captions. 1941.

> **H82.5.3** Lima, F. E., comp. [*My Oriental album II.*] Snapshot views made while on tour in the Orient. Junks; Neptune's Court; travel scenes in China include "Jap and China trouble in 1932," Peking, Shanghai, Hangchow, Amoy, Great Wall, temples and floods in villages; Moro Village, Philippines; Yangtze Gorge; Guam; dry dock repairs in Manila, Philippines; torpedo practice; Japan. 704 silver gelatin prints. 1933.

> **H82.5.4** [*My Oriental album I.*] Snapshots of seaplanes (biplanes catapult-launched from deck of ship), including accidents; China, including Shanghai and the Ming Tombs. 319 silver gelatin prints. Ca. 1937.

350 silver gelatin prints; 4 albums (v.s.). 1920s to 1980s.

John E. Conner Museum (K30)

Texas A&I University
Baugh Hall
820 West Santa Gertrudis
Campus Box 134
Kingsville, Texas 78363

512-595-2777. Contact: Archivist.

PURPOSE: A regional history and natural history museum with extensive reserve collections, including manuscripts, books and journals, artifacts, natural specimens, and photographs.

HOURS: Exhibition area—weekdays, 10:00-5:00; Sunday, 2:30-5:00. Reserve collections—by appointment only. Closed major holidays and Christmas through New Year's.

ASSISTANCE: Professional, specialized, experienced staff. Written and phone inquiries accepted. Electrostatic copies available. Photoduplications must be ordered through the museum.

PUBLICATION: No publication fee. Collection credit required. Free copy of publication to museum. Third-party permission required on some items.

FINDING AIDS: Descriptive, itemized lists, card index, computer database; access by general subject heading, geographic location, date. Photographs stored by accession group.

BIBLIOGRAPHY:
Kleberg County Historical Commission. *Kleberg County, Texas: A collection of historical sketches and family histories.* Kingsville: Kleberg County Historical Commission, 1979.
Parker, A. Leland. *A pictorial history of the Coastal Bend.* Corpus Christi: South Coast Publishing, 1983.

SCOPE: 3,000 vintage and 3,000 copy photographs, both with negatives and prints. 1850s to the present.

Type of photo	Pre-1880	1880-1899	1900-1919	1920-1939	1940-1959	1960-1986
D/A/T-types	22	45				
Film negs			15	1,000	4,000	5,000
Vintage prints	108	10	270	206	37	10
Copy images	50	300	700	850	400	
Photo albums	5		1		1	

GEOGRAPHIC: Major emphasis is on the Coastal Bend region including Bee, Brooks, Duval, Jim Wells, Kleberg, Nueces, and San Patricio counties; secondary emphasis is on the Valley, between the San Antonio River and the Rio Grande.

Texas cities: Alice. Beeville. Bishop. Falfurrias. Flowella. Kingsville. Premont. Taft.

SUBJECTS: Economic and social development of the region.

Academia. Agriculture (ranching). Animals (cattle, horses, sheep). Architecture. Events. Industry. Military (personnel). Sports and amusement. Transportation.

King Ranch (Norias Division).

PEOPLE: Area residents, documenting the bi-cultural, Caucasian-Hispanic heritage of the region and the ranching industry.

R. B. Cousins family. King-Kleberg family. Meek family. M. K. Simons family.

PHOTOGRAPHERS: Jimmie Dodd (Kingsville). Carol Dryden (Falfurrias). Billy Newton (Bishop). C. L. Sult and Sons (Corpus Christi).

RECORD GROUPS:

Manuscript collections and record groups of vintage photographs:

Manuscript collections with small amounts of photographic material include Carrie Northway Coleman papers, John E. Conner papers, Cousins family collection, Walter W. Meek Jr. papers, and J. K. Northway papers.

K30.1 ARMSTRONG (TOBIN) COLLECTION. Snapshots of ranch scenes, hunting party; snapshot and studio portraits of the Armstrong family. 90 film negatives with modern prints; 8 copy prints. 1890s to 1910s. JECM# 1985-3.

K30.2 FLATO (C. H.) COLLECTION. Studio portraits of members of the Kingsville Rotary Club, King Ranch historical marker dedication, and street scenes of early Kingsville.

> [*C. H. Flato scrapbook.*] Cattle operations on the King Ranch Norias Division, including many corral and branding scenes, hunting, and early scenes of Kingsville. Amateur photographs, possibly by Flato. 209 silver gelatin prints, many panoramas. 1913 to 1915.

80 photographs, most silver gelatin prints; 1 album (v.s.). 1896 to 1950s.

K30.3 GIBSON (CLIFFORD L.) COLLECTION. Commercial panoramas of Kingsville cityscapes. 13 silver gelatin prints. 1912. JECM# 1984-22.

K30.4 GILLIAM (NANCY) COLLECTION. Snapshots of aftermath of 1916 hurricane in Corpus Christi and Kingsville; city scenes in Corpus Christi. 37 silver gelatin prints. 1916 to 1929. JECM# 1984-20.

K30.5 JACOBS (Mrs. W. W.) COLLECTION. Lantana celebration showing parade floats and beauty queens. 49—35mm Kodachrome color transparencies. 1960. JECM# 1982-105.

K30.6 KLEBERG COUNTY COLLECTION. An artificial collection of Kingsville vicinity scenes, including school groups and residences. 36 photographs, including cartes, most silver gelatin prints. 1860s to 1970s, most ca. 1930. JECM# 83-3.

K30.7 KOCH (THEODORE F.) PAPERS. Dutch Consul in Minneapolis MN and land developer in the Coastal Bend. Booster photographs of Koch's developments at Riviera and Riviera Beach showing homes, agriculture, ocean front, and electric railroad running between the two communities; a few views of the Koch family. Commercial views, many by C. L. Sult and Sons (Corpus Christi), a few by George Beach (Houston). JECM# 1973-33. 67 vintage silver gelatin prints, many hand tinted; 15 nitrate negatives with modern prints.

K30.8 LOS OJUELOS COLLECTION. Snapshot retrospective views of ruins of family home of Genoveva Barrera Leach. 18 color prints. Ca. 1984.

K30.9 TEXAS A&I UNIVERSITY ARCHIVES. Documentation of the development of the university, including faculty, staff, and students, buildings, and yearbook photographs; photographs from the Texas A&I News and Information Department of campus events, including athletics, dances, rallies, museums. 10,000 negatives. 1930s to 1970s. Unprocessed collection.

Albums:

K30.10 [*Carte album 1978-6-3.*] Unidentified studio portraits by unidentified and various photographers from Pecatonia IL. 7 albumen cartes, 17 tintypes. Ca. 1870.

K30.11 [*Carte album 1980-27-12.*] Studio portraits of McKinnon family and others, including published portraits of men and women with physiological anomalies. Many photographed by Barr and Wright (Houston). 15 tintypes, 21 albumen cartes. Ca. 1880.

K30.12 [*Robert Driscoll presentation album 1983-3-26.*] Commercial aerial views of Corpus Christi harbor showing the Bascule Drawbridge and ships at dock. Stamped on cover: "Robert Driscoll, esq., chairman Nueces Navigation Committee, port of Corpus Christi, Texas: compliments of Lorine James Spoonts, Chairman Bayfront Improvement Committee, Corpus Christi, Texas." 26 silver gelatin prints. Ca. 1926.

K30.13 [*Hatcher family Carte album PA 3059.*] Studio portraits of the Hatcher family and others. Various photographers from Missouri, Tennessee, and Illinois. 23 albumen cartes, 4 tintypes. Ca. 1870.

K30.14 [*Japanese military album 65-17.*] Japanese soldiers in military camps; other in situ portraits of Korean or Japanese individuals. 17 silver gelatin prints. Ca. 1940s.

K30.15 [*Simons family carte album.*] Studio portraits of La Forge, Simons, and Hatcher families; published photographs of Civil War military figures. By various photographers from Missouri and Texas. 57 albumen cartes, 9 tintypes. Ca. 1870.

K30.16 [*Simons family carte album 3074.*] Studio portraits of the Simons family. Photographs by Fey and Braunig (Cuero) and by L. Rice and Company (Victoria). 5 tintypes, 18 cartes. Ca. 1880.

K30.17 Sult, C. L. and Sons, photog. [*Coastal Bend views album A-31-1.*] Booster album of commercial views of farming in the Coastal Bend, including scenes in Corpus Christi and Kingsville; residences. 40 silver gelatin prints, many hand-tinted; typed captions. Ca. 1919.

Copy prints:

K30.18 HISTORICAL PHOTOGRAPH COLLECTION. An artificial collection, most copy prints from originals held by families in the community and a few vintage prints. Subjects include:

Agriculture. Animals (cattle, draft). Architecture. Businesses. Cowboys. Homes. Hunting. King Ranch. Parades. Petroleum industry. Railroads. Ranching; ranch life and customs. Schools. Stores. Transportation. Water.

Major groups within this collection include:

K30.18.1 BISHOP CHAMBER OF COMMERCE COLLECTION. Commercial and snapshot views showing economic and social development of the community. 105—35mm copy negatives and prints. 1910s. JECM# A1985-66.

K30.18.2 DODD (JIMMIE A.; 1917-1984) COLLECTION. Commercial photographer in Kingsville who had unrestricted access to the King Ranch. Businesses and events in Kingsville; in situ portraits. 425 copy photographs. 1940s to 1950s. JECM# 1985-18, 1985-64.

K30.18.3 ELLING (Mrs. HULDA JESSE BOLTING) COLLECTION. Snapshots of family members in Corpus Christi and Kingsville; 1916 hurricane damage. 228—35mm copy negatives and prints. 1900s to 1920s.

K30.18.4 KING RANCH COLLECTION. King and Kleberg families; ranching activities; thoroughbred horses. 293 copy photographs. 1880s to 1920s. JECM# 1980-30; 1981-41; A1984-11. Restricted access.

K30.18.5 KOPP (DAVID) COLLECTION. Humble Oil (= Exxon) exploration and development of oil fields in the Valley. 100—35mm copy negatives and prints. 1940s.

K30.18.6 SMITH (Dr. JULIA A.) COLLECTION. Studio portraits of Garcia and Gonzales families in the Valley, San Antonio, and Mexico. 71—35mm copy negatives and prints. 1870s to 1920s. JECM# 85-68.

2,500 copy negatives, many with modern prints. 1860s to 1960s, most 1900 to 1940s.

Fayette Heritage Museum and Archives (L10)

Fayette Public Library
855 South Jefferson
La Grange, Texas 78945

409-968-6418. Contact: Curator.

PURPOSE: A local history museum with exhibits and reserve collections of manuscripts, artifacts, books and journals, and photographs. Part of the local library.

HOURS: Tuesday, 10:00-6:30; Wednesday through Friday, 10:00-5:00; Saturday, 10:00-1:00; Sunday, 1:00-5:00. Closed major holidays.

ASSISTANCE: Experienced staff. Written and phone inquiries accepted on a limited basis. Electrostatic copies available. Photoduplications must be ordered through the museum.

PUBLICATION: No publication fee. Collection credit required. Free copy of publication to museum.

FINDING AIDS: Card index and inventory; access by general subject and personal name.

SCOPE: 3,000 vintage and 50 copy photographs, including stereographs and panoramic prints. 1865 to present.

Type of photo	Pre-1880	1880-1899	1900-1919	1920-1939	1940-1959	1960-1986
D/A/T-types	10	15				
Film negs					1,500	
Vintage prints	75	125	200	200		
Copy prints			25	25		
Photo albums	1	6				

GEOGRAPHIC: Primarily Fayette County, with substantial coverage of La Grange; some coverage of other Texas locales and Colorado.

SUBJECTS: Economic and social development of the community, including the Kreische Brewery.

PEOPLE: Area residents; substantial coverage of Czech and German, minor coverage of Black, Hispanic, and Jewish ethnicities. See Record Groups—Crayton for additional names.

Luck-Loessin, Reichert, and Tauch families.

PHOTOGRAPHERS: C. C. Crayton Studio (La Grange and Giddings). C. Luck. Louis Melcher (O'Quinn). A. A. Nichols (Industry). Pannewitz. Conradt Peterson (La Grange). Henry Tauch (traveling and Fayetteville). William Tauch (Schulenburg). F. C. Winklemann (Brenham).

RECORD GROUPS: The collection contains a small number of photographs arranged into an artificial collection, described above, the archive of C. C. Crayton, and albums.

L10.1 CRAYTON (C. C.) ARCHIVES. Studio photographer in La Grange and Giddings. Some commercial photography, most studio portraits. Approximately 1,000 individuals, including the families:

> Baca. Blume. Chovanec. Dippel. Fritsch. Giese. Janda. Janssen. Kana. Kovar. Krenek. Kulhanek. Opperman. Pietsch. Polasek. Svrcek. Teinert. Tiemann. Tietjen. Urban. Vitek. Von Minden. Weishuhn. Wessels. Zapalac. Zbranek.

5,000 film negatives. Late 1940s to 1964.

L10.2 [*Cabinet album 76.4.1.*] Studio portraits, possibly the Willenburg family. Various photographers, most by C. Peterson (La Grange), some German photographers, including Julius Stiffel (Liegnitz, Germany). 14 cabinets, 1 albumen print, 80 albumen cartes, 4 tintypes. 1880s.

L10.3 [*Cabinet album 80.106.58.*] Studio portraits of the Tauch family, most photographed by William Tauch (Schulenburg). 37 cabinets, 8 cartes. Ca. 1885.

L10.4 [*Carte album 81.24.9.*] Studio portraits by various Lüneberg, Germany, photographers, including Johannes Saltan, Lühr Gebrüder, and Julius Rathje. Ca. 1870.

L10.5 [*Cabinet album 81.59.21.*] Studio portraits, many by Nichols (Industry). 2 albumen cartes, 6 gelatino-chloride prints, 14 cabinets. 1870s to 1890s.

L10.6 [*Cabinet album 81.59.23.*] Studio portraits, many by C. Peterson (La Grange). 11 cabinets, 11 gelatino-chloride prints, 3 silver gelatin prints. 1890s.

L10.7 [*Cabinet album 83.1.2.*] Studio portraits of wedding couples; portraits of children. Many photographed by C. Peterson (La Grange). 10 cabinets and 13 cartes. 1890s.

L10.8 [*Emily Dornhoefer cabinet album.*] Studio portraits of Dornhoefer and others; many photographed by Nichols (Industry). 15 collodio-chloride cabinets, 15 photo prints. Ca. 1890. FHMA# 81.59.18.

San Jacinto Museum of History Association (L20)

3800 Park Road 1836
La Porte, Texas 77571

713-479-2421. Contact: Librarian.

PURPOSE: A museum located in the San Jacinto Monument concentrating on Texas history with an emphasis on the Texas Revolution. The museum has an exhibit space and holds extensive reserve collections, including manuscripts, rare and recent books and journals, paintings and other visual media, three-dimensional artifacts, and photographs.

HOURS: Museum and observation tower—daily, 10:00-6:00; admission charge for observation tower only. Reserve collections—weekdays, 10:00-4:30; appointment required; closed major holdiays.

ASSISTANCE: Professional, specialized staff. Written inquiries accepted. Electrostatic copies available. Photoduplications must be ordered through the museum.

PUBLICATION: Publication fee. Collection credit required. Free copy of publication to museum. Third-party permission required on a few items.

FINDING AIDS: Complete card index for photographs and other visual media interfiled; access by subject and proper name.

SCOPE: 7,000 photographs, including a substantial collection of daguerreotypes and ambrotypes, many vintage prints and negatives, some copy photographs. 1850s to present, with a substantial number of early photographs.

Type of photo	Pre-1880	1880-1899	1900-1919	1920-1939	1940-1959	1960-1986
D/A/T-types	150					
Film negs				2,000	200	
Vintage prints	50	150		3,800	200	200
Copy prints	100	100	20			
Photo albums	4	2	1			

GEOGRAPHIC: Texas, including substantial coverage of southeastern Houston and some coverage of Galveston and southeastern Texas.

SUBJECTS: Some coverage of the development of Texas after the revolution.

Art reproductions. Cityscapes. Events (reunions). Industry (drug stores, shipping). Landscape (graves). Military (Civil War soldiers, federal occupation of Brownsville—1866). Organizations (veterans). Transportation (water).

San Jacinto Monument—dedication, —building and grounds, —interior, —exhibits. Texas capitols. Texas Veterans Association. USS *Houston*. USS *San Jacinto*. USS *Texas*.

PEOPLE: Veterans of the Texas Revolution and the Mier Expedition, early Texas politicians, and early Texas settlers' families; some coverage of Civil War military figures. In addition to photographs, most subjects are represented by photographic art reproductions, copy photographs, and artworks from photographs. Some important figures not listed here are represented only by nonphotographic media.

A. C. Allen family. Stephen F. Austin descendants. John R. Baylor family. Birdsall family. Marvin Delano family. William Delmas Givens. Governor James S. Hogg. T. W. House family. Sam Houston. Con Kirtland and Etti Estelle (née White) Lockhart family. Labadie family. Mirabeau B. Lamar. Francis Richard Lubbock family. William and Mary McDowall family. James Nicholson family. R. B. Russell family. General López de Santa Anna. Washam family.

Single daguerreotypes of: Julia Batchelor. Abbie Chubb (Mrs. Thomas Jefferson) Chambers. Stella Chambers. Thomas Jefferson Chambers. Joseph Alvey Clayton. Marvin Delano. Sarah Jane Dunton. Sidney L. Dunton. Robert Hall. Dr. Nicholas D. Labadie. Mrs. Bettie Washam Miller. Charles Schadt. Alice Grey Goodwin Smith. Ann Margaret Lucas Dickson Sutherland. Mr. Jordan Sweeny. Mrs. Jordan Sweeny. Edward M. Tanner (photographed by Sam Brasher of Jonesboro, Coryell County). Captain Amasa Turner. Mrs. Amasa Turner. George T. Turner. Julia and Marcellus G. Turner. Mary Cunningham Van den Berge. William Bradley Washam Jr. William Bradley Washam Sr.

PHOTOGRAPHERS: Some coverage of nineteenth-century Texas studio photographers, most from Houston; other photographers of note held in limited quantity include Charles Fredricks (New York, 1 print) and Mathew Brady (New York, 2 daguerreotypes), Edward Weston (2 prints), and Margaret Bourke-White (1 print).

Barr and Wright. P. H. Rose (Galveston). F. W. Seiders. Cecil Thomson. Charles J. Wright.

RECORD GROUPS: Photographs are stored by accession group; most accession groups contain fewer than 25 photographs. The Hill, Looscan, and Campbell collections were received over a period of time and have been described as single groups.

Major collections and subject groups:

L20.1 CAMPBELL (H. H.) COLLECTION. Robert Benedict Russell family and others; many from Houston and from Lexington KY. 54 photographs. 1860s to 1890s. SJMH# 8182.

L20.2 HILL (Mr. and Mrs. GEORGE A., Jr.) COLLECTION. George Hill (1892-1949) was the founder and first president of the San Jacinto Museum of History. Studio portraits of the Hill family, descendants of James Monroe Hill, a veteran of the Battle of San Jacinto; Briscoe family; Texas Revolutionary figures, including Sam Houston. 35 photographs. 1850s to 1910s. SJMH# 1736.

L20.3 KEMP (LOUIS WILTZ) COLLECTION. Snapshots of graves of notable Texans for whom counties have been named; retrospective views of historic sites. 100 silver gelatin prints. Ca. 1950. SJMH# 15372c.

L20.4 LOOSCAN COLLECTION. Studio portraits of Andrew and Mary Jane Briscoe family. 33 photographs. 1890s to 1910s. SJMH# 3616.

L20.5 KUYKENDALL (Reverend RHEA) COLLECTION. Terry Caruthers family. 23 photographs. 1860s to 1940s. SJMH# 11831.

L20.6 ROCKWELL (JAMES W.) COLLECTION. Rockwell's service during WW I in France and England. 8 silver gelatin prints. 1917 to 1918. SJMH# 3336.

L20.7 TEXAS WORKS PROGRESS ADMINISTRATION COLLECTION. Views of construction of the San Jacinto Monument, a Works Progress Administration project. 15 silver gelatin prints. 1938. SJMH# 8760c.

L20.8 THOMSON (CECIL M.) ARHIVES. Commercial/industrial photographer in southeastern Houston. Aerial views from 1920 to 1930; skylines, architectural views and street scenes showing commercial and public buildings in Houston, including the Niels Esperson Building; churches; Mayor Oscar Holcombe; beauty contestants (Bathing Girl Review); Houston Fat Stock Show and cattle; oil fields, fires, and gushers; copy photographs of historical subjects; Houston Ship Channel and shipping. 2,000 silver gelatin film negatives, many 8x10; modern prints. 1900s to early 1940s, most 1920s to 1930s. SJMH# 14885c.

Albums:

L20.9 [*Cabinet album 14360c.*] Studio portraits of the Cora and Edith House and others, including Joseph D. Sayers and wife. Many photographed by C. J. Wright (Houston); a few by Deane (Galveston). 29 cabinet, 2 silver gelatin prints. 1890s.

L20.10 [*Carte album 12413*] Portraits of Napoleon Bonaparte and his consort, Eugénie, of Maximillian, Emperor of Mexico, and of Mexican generals that supported him. 21 albumen cartes. 1860s.

L20.11 [*Carte album 14360c I.*] Studio portraits of the Nicholson, T. W. House, and McDowall families. 34 cartes, 1 tintype, 1 silver gelatin print. 1860s.

L20.12 [*Carte album 16095c.*] Most studio portraits and portrait composites of Civil War military figures published by Brady and by E. and H. T. Anthony; art reproductions of Civil War memorials and European statues; studio portraits by Marks (Houston), Louis de Planque (Matamoros), and from England by various photographers; General Land Office and Governor's Mansion in Austin photographed by G. H. Joslyn and Company (Galveston). 97 albumen cartes, many with tax stamps; 5 loose cartes, cabinets, and print. 1860s.

L20.13 *Mrs. W. L. Lubbock from W. Arthur Jenkins, St. Louis, Mo., arranged by JAPE Peddicord.* Snapshots, including the Saint Louis flood of 1903, the Saint Louis Transit Company powerhouse explosion of January 1904, and the Galveston storm of 1901. 53 gelatino-chloride prints. Early 1900s. SJMH# 14262c.

L20.14 *Mr. Wm. McDowall's album* [= *Carte album 14360c II.*] Most studio portraits, including some group portraits, of the Nicholson, House, and McDowall families and others; landscapes of a flood in Bastrop; travel views from Bath, England; photographed by various European photographers, including Disderi, and various Texas photographers, including Blessing and Company (Galveston), Marks (Houston), and Jas. Nicholson (Bastrop). 75 cartes, 8 tintypes. 1870s.

Sam Houston Regional Library and Research Center (L50)

Texas State Library Local Records Division
Farm Road 1011
P.O. Box 989
Liberty, Texas 77575

409-336-7097. Contact: Director-Archivist.

PURPOSE: A regional branch of the Texas State Library collecting local government records, books and journals, manuscripts, maps, artworks, artifacts, music, sound recordings and oral history tapes, and photographs. The library concentrates on materials that document the history of Southeast Texas.

HOURS: Weekdays, 8:00 to 5:00 and by appointment. Closed major holidays.

ASSISTANCE: Professional, specialized staff. Written and phone inquiries accepted. Electrostatic copies available. Photoduplications may be made by the patron or ordered through the library.

PUBLICATION: No publication fee. Collection credit required. Third-party permission required on no materials.

FINDING AIDS: Itemized, descriptive inventory for photographs in manuscript collections; descriptive lists and card index for other photographs. Access by general subject, geographic location, and personal name. Photographs are stored by record group.

BIBLIOGRAPHY:
Partlow, Miriam. *Liberty, Liberty County, and the Atascosito District*. Pemberton Press: Jenkins Publishing Company, 1974.

Trammell, Camilla D. *Seven pines*. Dallas: SMU Press, 1986.

Wright, Mildred S. *Jasper County cemeteries*. Decorah IA: Anundsen Publishing Company, 1976.

Wright, Mildred S. *Newton County cemeteries*. Decorah IA: Anundsen Publishing Company, 1975. 2nd ed., Beaumont: Southeast Texas Genealogical and Historical Society, 1979.

Wright, Mildred S., and Zelma W. Wright Jr. *Chambers County, Texas cemeteries*. Decorah IA: Anundsen Publishing Company, 1975. 2nd ed., Beaumont: Southeast Texas Genealogical and Historical Society, 1979.

SCOPE: 12,296 vintage and 283 copy photographs and negatives; 400 halftone blocks for newspaper printing. 1848 to 1986.

Type of photo	Pre-1880	1880-1899	1900-1919	1920-1939	1940-1959	1960-1986
D/A/T-types	63	40	17			
Glass negs		5			14	
Film negs			13	374	699	307
Vintage prints	164	338	1,863	2,935	1,738	1,619
Copy prints	60	117	98	34	35	18
Photo albums	3	1	2	1	5	

GEOGRAPHIC: Primarily coverage of Southeast Texas, including Chambers, Hardin, Jasper, Jefferson, Liberty, Newton, Orange, Polk, San Jacinto, and Tyler counties.

Foreign countries and cities: Australia. Cambodia. Canada. Cuba (Havana). Egypt. England. Fiji Islands. France (Paris). Germany. Greece. Guam. India. Indochina. Indonesia (Bali, Java). Iran. Ireland. Italy (Rome, Venice). Mexico. Morocco (Casablanca). Panama. Puerto Rico. New Zealand. Scotland. Singapore. Switzerland. Thailand. Vietnam. Wales.

US: Alabama. Arizona. Arkansas. California. Colorado. Connecticut. District of Columbia. Florida. Georgia. Illinois. Iowa. Louisiana. Maine. Maryland. Massachusetts. Michigan. Minnesota. Mississippi. Missouri. Nebraska. New Mexico. New York. North Carolina. Ohio. Oklahoma. Oregon. Pennsylvania. Tennessee. Texas. Virginia. Washington. West Virginia.

Texas: Alpine. Ames. Anahuac. Austin. Barbers Hill. Batson. Bay City. Beaumont. Beeville. Bevilport. Cedar Bayou. Cleveland. Coldspring. College Station. Cove. Daisetta. Dallas. Dayton. Dublin. Fort Davis. Galveston. Hardin. Hightower. Holly Springs. Hondo. Houston. Hull. Huntsville. Independence. Jasper. Kilgore. Kirbyville. Kountze. Lamb. Liberty. Livingston. Mineola. Mineral Wells. Moscow. Moulton. Navasota. New Caney. Orange. Point Blank. Port Arthur. Romayor. Rye. San Antonio. San Marcos. Schulenburg. Shepherd. Splendora. Sour Lake. Stowell. Tarkington Prairie. Taylor. Trinity River. Waco. Wallisville. Winnie. Woodville.

SUBJECTS: Economic and social development of the region, with an emphasis on historical subjects.

Academia (students). Agriculture. Animals (farm, wild, zoo). Architecture (churches, commercial, domestic, interiors). Cityscapes. Events (parades). Industry (lumber, oil). Landscape (rural). Military (personnel). Monuments and memorials (tombstones). Organizations. Services. Sports and amusements.

PEOPLE: Area residents, predominantly of English, German, and French extraction, with significant numbers of Blacks. Many snapshot shots and studio portraits.

Individuals: Chief Fulton Battise. Governor Bill Daniel. Judge Price Daniel. US congressman Martin Dies. General Sam Houston. Robert W. Humphreys. Jean Laffite. J. H. Manthey Jr. Adah Isaacs Menken. Watson Neyland. President Franklin Delano Roosevelt. President William H. Taft.

Families: Avenell. Baldwin. Bond. Burson. Conroy. Crow. Dailey. Daniel. Davis. DeBat. Duncan. Gay. Gillard. Hardin. Houston. Humphries. Johnston. Jones. Kountz. Kubenka. Laffite. Manthey. Neyland. Partlow. Perkins. Reid. Roberts. Sloan. Stubbs. Waldo. Wallace. Welder. Woods. Woodland.

PHOTOGRAPHERS: Lone Star Studios. Moon Young Photography (Cleveland).

RECORD GROUPS: Descriptions provided by Robert L. Schaadt, Director-Archivist of the center. "Photographs" may include art reproductions.

L50.1 Record groups with fewer than 10 photographs: Atascosito Camellia Club. W. F. Blair. John V. Clay. Carey H. Currey. Harry G. Daves Jr. General James Davis. John and Marie Dutt. Charles W. Fisher Sr. Charles W. Fisher Jr. Girls Haven. Green Thumb Garden Club. Eliza Strickland Griffith. Jewell Wilcox Key. William M. Kirkland. Liberty Bicentennial. Liberty Women's Club. Jesse D. Lumm. Mrs. Clyde McCreight. Madeleine Martin. Lester J. Moore. Oak Shade Baptist Church. Pam Lowe O'Quinn. Elnett Browning Partlow. Jewell Patton. Bradford Pickett. Mrs. Jimmy R. Roper. Troy Robert Sherman Sr. Samual Max Smith. Swinney family. Texaco Inc. C. C. Thornton. Trivium collection. Agnes Ward collection. Jesse Adolph Ziegler.

Record groups with more than 10 photographs:

L50.2 AMERICAN FIELD SERVICE COLLECTION. Foreign-exchange students and group activities of the society in Liberty. 30 photographs. 1962 to 1971.

L50.3 ATASCOSITO HISTORICAL SOCIETY COLLECTION. Early citizens, buildings, transportation, social activities, and cityscapes in Southeast Texas. 13 photographs. 1865 to 1925.

L50.4 AVENELL (GLORIA WALLACE) COLLECTION. WW I, social events, students, boats, and the Wallace, Conroy, Stubbs, and Avenell families in Liberty and Chambers counties, San Antonio, Mineola, and Taylor. 114 photographs. 1916 to 1985.

L50.5 BALDWIN (JEAN HOUSTON) COLLECTION. Great-granddaughter of Sam Houston. Portraits of Sam Houston, Margret Lea Houston, and descendants; related historical markers, homes, grave markers, artifacts, and historical sites. 51 vintage and 550 copy photographs. 1850 to 1964.

L50.6 BALDWIN (THOMAS EDWIN) COLLECTION. Baldwin family, WW I, Knights of Columbus, Frisca General Committee, and military scenes in Southeast Texas and various central and northeastern states. 103 photographs. 1884 to 1967.

L50.7 CANNAN (E. B.) COLLECTION. Liberty High School Band members and activities under Cannan's directorship. 25 photographs. 1937 to 1948.

L50.8 COLONIAL FLOWER SHOP COLLECTION. Floats entered in the 1956 Bicentennial Baby Parade and cityscapes in Liberty. 43 color slides. 1956.

L50.9 DANIEL (ELLEN VIRGINIA) COLLECTION. Daniel and Partlow families, family trips, group activities, and boating on the Trinity River; in Liberty, Anahuac, and Galveston, some in California and Arkansas. 3 photographs and 13—8mm films. Ca. 1890 to 1939.

L50.10 DANIEL (PRICE) PAPERS. Texas attorney general, US senator, and governor of Texas. Family members, campaign events, political figures, interior office scenes, cityscapes, social activities, and state government activities. 149 photographs. 1952 to 1962.

L50.11 DAUGHTERS OF THE AMERICAN REVOLUTION—LIBERTAD CHAPTER COLLECTION. Society activities, Plantation Ranch, Historical Homes Tour, and members; in Liberty and Romayer. 40 photographs. 1963 to 1979.

L50.12 DAVIS (Dr. T. O.) COLLECTION. Rotary Clubs, buildings, railroads, and group activities; Liberty and Southeast Texas. 28 photographs. 1913 to 1975.

L50.13 DeBAT FAMILY COLLECTION. DeBat, Legett, and Palmer families, transportation, railroad construction, buildings, cityscapes, county fairs, and Liberty citizens; most in Liberty, some in Michigan and Massachusetts. 157 photographs. Ca. 1850 to 1919.

L50.14 DEVINE (FAY BALLIO) COLLECTION. Confederate Civil War album; students and faculty at Washington College in Lexington VA, Civil War military personnel, including General Robert E. Lee and staff, President Jefferson Davis, General Stonewall Jackson; the Devine, Hardeman, DeBlanc, and Ballio families. 51 photographs. Ca. 1850 to 1866.

L50.15 DIES (MARTIN) COLLECTION. US congressman from the Second District (Southeast Texas) from 1931 to 1945, and US congressman-at-large from Texas from 1952 to 1959. Press photographs, congressmen, congressional hearings, social activities, family members, and the 1918 Beaumont football team; documenting Dies's political career; many from Texas, others from Washington DC, New York, and Florida. 32 photographs. 1918, 1931 to ca. 1960.

L50.16 DISCOVER DAYTON COLLECTION. Buildings, businesses, rice farming, lumber and oil industry, churches, historical sites, and students; in Dayton. 65 photographs, 25 color slides. Ca. 1930 to 1984.

L50.17 FREGIA (MARIE PATTERSON) COLLECTION. Lumber industry, homes, rural scenes, oil industry, and transportation in Southeast Texas, including Batson, Saratoga, Silsbee, and the Port of Beaumont. 161 photographs. Ca. 1870 to 1925.

L50.18 HARDIN PAPERS. Hardin, Davis, and Humphreys families, slaves, homes, buildings, social activities, travel, US presidents Franklin D. Roosevelt, William H. Taft, Warren G. Harding, and Calvin Coolidge, the Republican party of Texas, animals, cityscapes and rural scenes, military personnel, sports, theater, transportation, the oil industry, and the Galveston customshouse; Texas, including Galveston and Liberty, and various other states. 3,061 photographs. 1852 to 1956.

L50.19 HOUSTON (SAM) REGIONAL LIBRARY AND RESEARCH CENTER COLLECTION. Exhibits and activities held at the center. 39 photographs (open collection). 1977 to present.

L50.20 JONES (JESSE M., Jr.) COLLECTION. Tombstones, graves, and cemeteries pertaining to the Adams, Blount, Jones, Pugh, Smith, Stanly, Watkins, and Worthey families in Shelby and Jasper counties and in Louisiana. 57 photographs. 1976.

L50.21 KOUNTZ (JOHN H.) COLLECTION. Oil industry, rural scenes, transportation, cityscapes, social activities, buildings, citizens, and the Kountz and Perkins families. Locations include Hardin County, Missouri, New York, Oklahoma, Pennsylvania, and West Virginia. 431 photographs. 1892 to 1925.

L50.22 LaCOUR (ANNIE CAMPBELL) COLLECTION. Students, church groups, and the LaCour family; in Liberty. 23 photographs. 1892 to 1925.

L50.23 LADD (KEVIN) COLLECTION. Area residents and the Brasher, DeBlanc, Robinson, and Stubbs families; in Chambers and Liberty counties. 13 photographs. Ca. 1860 to 1960.

L50.24 LAFFITE (FOCH, Sr.) COLLECTION. The Pierre Laffite, Bouet Laffite, and Jean Laffite families in Louisiana. 11 photographs. 1858 to 1977.

L50.25 LAFFITE (JEAN) COLLECTION. Gulf Coast pirate. Subjects include Laffite, his family, and descendants; locations include Iowa, Nebraska, Missouri, and Pennsylvania. 60 photographs. 1848 to 1901.

L50.26 LIBERTY ART LEAGUE COLLECTION. League members, social activities, artwork, and art shows; in Liberty. 106 photographs. 1969 to 1980.

L50.27 LIBERTY COUNTY A&M MOTHER'S CLUB COLLECTION. Members, social activities, and Texas A&M students; in Liberty. 37 photographs. 1967 to 1975.

L50.28 LIBERTY GARDEN CLUB COLLECTION. Flower shows, social activities, seasonal flower arrangements, and members; in Liberty and Beaumont. 72 photographs. 1969 to 1978.

L50.29 LIBERTY ROTARY CLUB COLLECTION. An album of portraits of club members. 35 photographs. 1938.

L50.30 *LIBERTY VINDICATOR* COLLECTION. Businesses, Sam Houston Regional Library and Research Center, cityscapes, advertising materials; in Liberty County. 32 photographs, 400 photographic printing plates. Ca. 1950 to 1977.

L50.31 McCLENNY (LENA) COLLECTION. Colonial Flower Shop and Baby Parade floats in Liberty. 11 photographs. Ca. 1930 to 1960.

L50.32 MANTHY (J. H., Jr.) *CLEVELAND ADVOCATE* COLLECTION. Students, schools, cityscapes, Trinity River, transportation, churches, sports, businesses, industry, and leading citizens; locales include Cleveland and the surrounding counties of Polk, Liberty, Hardin, San Jacinto, and Montgomery. 619 photographs. 1901 to 1967.

L50.33 MAULDIN (SUSAN WRIGHT) COLLECTION. Schools, businesses, homes, railroad, and portraits of the Mauldin family and friends; in Cleveland, Hightower, and Lamb. 21 photographs. Ca. 1900 to 1919.

L50.34 MEACHAM (MILO FITCH) COLLECTION. A Union Civil War album with portraits of military personnel, the Meacham family and friends. Locales include Texas and Illinois. 40 photographs. 1856 to 1862.

L50.35 NEYLAND (ALLEN and WATSON) COLLECTION. Civil War, WW I, cityscapes, social events, buildings, homes, leading Texas citizens, animals, bridges, parades, transportation, and the Neyland and Bryan (= O'Brian) families. Locales include Texas, Arkansas, Pennsylvania, Virginia, and travel views to Cuba. 383 photographs. 1856 to 1940.

L50.36 O'BRIEN-REID COLLECTION. Students, buildings, and the Bond, Crow, Goosebee, O'Brien, Reid, and Roberts families. Locales include Texas, Missouri, Georgia, and Tennessee. 125 photographs. 1885 to 1909.

L50.37 PARKER (C. SCOTT) COLLECTION. Restoration of the 1848 Gillard-Duncan house and construction of the Price Daniel home in Liberty. 473 photographs. 1982 to 1983.

L50.38 PARKER-VENABLE COLLECTION. WW I, homes, sports, and the Parker and Venable families. 48 photographs. 1891 to 1918.

L50.39 PARTLOW (MIRIAM) COLLECTION. Historical figures and markers, buildings, city and rural scenes, oil industry, lumber industry, transportation, social events, family trips, churches, animals, homes, sports, group activities, and the Partlow, Daniel, and Johnston families. Locales include Southeast Texas, Maine, Oregon, and Washington. 708 photographs. Ca. 1860 to 1974. See Bibliography.

L50.40 PARTLOW (WILLIAM) COLLECTION. Partlow family and friends, WW II, travel views from foreign countries, and group activities. Locales include Liberty and College Station, the Middle East and North Africa. 213 photographs. 1930 to 1945.

L50.41 PARTLOW (WILLIAM D.) COLLECTION. Travel, ranching, students, animals, sports, social activities, transportation, and the Partlow, Johnston, Daniel, Kubenka, Harris, Dailey, and Waldo families. Locales include Liberty and San Marcos; non-Texas locales include Virginia, Colorado, Illinois, Washington, and Connecticut. 490 photographs. 1860s to 1977.

L50.42 SANDERS (DUB) COLLECTION. Retrospective views of historical buildings, homes, and sites in Liberty County. 37 color transparencies. 1966 to 1970.

L50.43 SHORT (LOIS) COLLECTION. Black community in Ames and Liberty, including individuals, homes, businesses, churches, and schools. 78 photographs. 1931 to 1932.

L50.44 SLOAN (TENNIE BELL) COLLECTION. Agriculture, ranching, buildings, city and rural scenes, transportation, social activities, and the Sloan family in Liberty County. 31 photographs. 1900 to 1940.

L50.45 STEUSOFF (HENRY) COLLECTION. Animals, buildings, city scenes, oil industry, military, transportation, social activities, and the Steusoff family in Liberty and Hull. 75 photographs. 1887 to ca. 1930.

L50.46 WATSON (H. V.) COLLECTION. Businesses, homes, oil industry, and transportation in Batson, Hull-Daisetta, and Galveston. 32 photographs. 1917 to 1920.

L50.47 WELDER (JULIA DUNCAN) COLLECTION. Lumber industry, rural scenes, homes, and the Gillard, Duncan, Welder, and Gay families in Southeast Texas. 46 photographs. Ca. 1860 to ca. 1950.

L50.48 WOODLAND (MARY BALDWIN AND NAAMON J., Jr.) COLLECTION. Costumes, stage sets, musicians, and actors pertaining to the Beaumont Symphony Orchestra and Civic Opera; social activities, students, travel, and the Woodland and Coe families. Locales include Southeast Texas, New York, Ohio, and Louisiana. 250 photographs. 1926 to 1981.

L50.49 WOODS (SALLIE AND NADINE) COLLECTION. Liberty Muscular Dystrophy Research Foundation, including Foundation board members, activities, and local events news releases, many including portraits of celebrities. 13 photographs, 33—16mm films. Ca. 1950 to 1963.

L50.50 WRIGHT (MILDRED S. AND Z. H.) COLLECTION. Tombstones dating from 1846 to 1972, graves, and cemeteries in Jasper, Chambers, and Newton counties. 84 photographs. 1975. See Bibliography.

L50.51 YOUNG (Sergeant JAMES H.) COLLECTION. French and German scenes in WW I;

family and friends in Hardin. 15 photographs. 1917 to 1918.

Southwest Collection (L65)

Texas Tech University
106 Mathematics Building (on the Circle)
P.O. Box 4090
Lubbock, Texas 79409

806-742-3749. Contact: University Archivist.

PURPOSE: A special-collections library concentrating on the Southwestern US. Holdings include books, periodicals, newspapers, manuscripts, photographs, oral history, and ephemera.

HOURS: Monday, Wednesday to Friday, 8:00-5:00; Tuesday, 8:00-7:00. Saturday and summer hours vary. Closed major, academic holidays.

ASSISTANCE: Professional, experienced staff. Written inquiries accepted. Electrostatic copies available. Photoduplications may be ordered through the collection or made by the patron.

PUBLICATION: No publication fee. Collection credit required. Free copy of publication to collection. Third-party permission required on some materials.

FINDING AIDS: Item-level inventories for some collections.

BIBLIOGRAPHY:

Andrews, Ruth Horn. *The first thirty years: A history of Texas Technological College, 1925-1955.* Lubbock: Texas Tech Press, 1956.

Bronwell, Nancy Brooker. *Lubbock: A pictorial history.* Virginia Beach VA: The Donning Company, 1980.

Graves, Lawrence L. *A history of Lubbock.* Lubbock: West Texas Museum Association, 1962. Revised edition forthcoming.

Griggs, William C., et al, ed. *A pictorial history of Lubbock, 1880-1950.* Lubbock: Lubbock County Historical Commission, 1976.

Rister, Carl Coke. *Oil! Titan of the Southwest.* Norman OK: University of Oklahoma Press, 1949.

Sellmeyer, Ralph and James E. Davidson. *The Red Raiders: Texas Tech football.* Huntsville AL: Strode, 1978.

SCOPE: 300,000 photographs in major processes, most collections with associated manuscript and printed materials. 1870s to the present.

Type of photo	Pre-1880	1880-1899	1900-1919	1920-1939	1940-1959	1960-1986
D/A/T-types	100					
Glass negs			750	750		
Film negs		300	30,000	60,000	33,000	33,000
Copy prints		5,000	8,000	8,000	8,000	1,000
Vintage prints	100	500	15,000	15,000	10,000	10,000

GEOGRAPHIC: Emphasis on the US Southwest with extensive coverage of Texas, especially Lubbock, and some coverage of New Mexico, especially Roswell. See Record Groups—Southwest Collection Photograph Collection—Copyprint Project for list of Texas counties. See Record Groups—Grover Elmer Murray for list of foreign countries.

SUBJECTS: Extensive coverage documenting the economic and social development of the US Southwest with an emphasis on the petroleum industry and tent shows.

Subject headings (with examples of subdivisions) used in the collection are: Adornment. Advertising. Aerial view. Agricultural activity (butchering, plowing, harvesting). Agricultural tools and equipment (horse plow, silo, garden hoe, thresher, gang plow). Animals (domestic, fauna). Architecture (activity, commercial, private, public, rural, types/style, utility). Archival materials. Armament tools and equipment (rifle, cannon, hunting, military). Art. Associations and organizations. Automobiles. Bands and orchestras (Boy Scouts, dance, high school). Bridges. Building accessories (lightning rods, weathervanes). Buildings—interior. Celebrations. Cemeteries. Ceremonies and ceremonial artifacts. Certificates. Cityscapes. Clothing and dress (accessories, everyday, formal, semiformal, types, uniforms, work). Commemorative artifact. Construction. Construction equipment. Cotton industry. Cowboys. Dental instruments and apparatus. Documents. Emblems and insignia. Entertainment (circus, movie, opera, rodeo). Events (July 4th, train wrecks, community dinners). Farm scenes. Fencing. Flags. Flora. Floor coverings. Food and food preparation. Forest industry. Forestry tools and equipment. Forts. Furniture. Harness and saddle equipment. Home appliances and housekeeping. Household accessories (soap dish, spittoon, vase, wastebasket, window covering). Illumination devices. Indians. Insects. Land companies. Landscape. Medical instruments and apparatus. Medicine. Metalworking industry. Metalworking tools and equipment. Mining industry (administrators, coal mines, camps, company towns). Mining tools and equipment. Money. Musical instruments. Oil and gas industry. Panoramic view. Personal gear. Portraits (male, female, child, couples, dead bodies, groups). Railroad industry (car, locomotive, trains). Ranching (activity—branding, —breaking horse, —campfire, architecture—barn, —corrals, tools and equipment—brands, —cooking utensils). Recreational devices (carousel, pinball machine). Sound communication equipment (record player, microphone). Sound communication industry. Sports. Sports equipment. Stagecoach lines. Street scenes. Telecommunication equipment. Telecommunication industry. Toilet article. Toys (dolls, stuffed animals, cast iron). Transportation (aerospace, land, water). US Air Force (bases, Army life, uniforms, soldiers). US Army. Weather (flood, hurricane). Windmills. Woodworking tools and equipment. Wool and mohair industry.

Fort Worth and Denver Railroad. Matador Land and Cattle Company. Quanah, Acme, and Pacific Railroad. Texas Technological University.

PEOPLE: Predominantly residents of the US Southwest. See Record Groups—Southwest Collection Photograph Collection—Copyprint project and —Manuscript Collections for additional names.

PHOTOGRAPHERS: Alpine Studio. Julius C. Born (Canadian TX). Brown Studio.* Jim Dallas Studio.* W. L. Daniel Studio.* Fritz Henle. Jack Nolan (Odessa and itinerant). M. C. Ragsdale (San Angelo and itinerant). C. W. Ratliff.* Bert P. Willis.

*Lubbock photographer.

RECORD GROUPS: The collection's holdings are arranged into five major areas: Heritage Club, Museum photographs, Southwest Collection Photograph collection, and Manuscript collections.

L65.1 Heritage Club: Photographs of Texas Tech, arranged into categories of campus, people, and events; includes photographs from the Texas Tech Student Publications annual, *La Ventana,* and the paper, *Toreador* (= *University Daily*); some motion picture material photographed for the University Information Service by Jim Childress. 60 cubic feet, silver gelatin print and safety negatives. 1923 to present.

Manuscript collections with photographs: Most manuscript collections have extensive associated materials.

L65.2 ADAMS (H. F.) FAMILY PAPERS. First settlers of Terry County; worked as farmer, carpenter, and Certified Public Weigher. Two albums (v.i.).

L65.2.1 [*Adams album I.*] Family portraits, both studio and snapshot by various Texas photographers. 46 photographs, many collodio-chloride cabinets and silver gelatin snapshots in a commercial, music-box cabinet album. 1880s to 1920s.

L65.2.1 [*Adams album II.*] Family portraits. 23 snapshot photographs, many silver gelatin photo postcards. 1910s.

[End of Adams papers.]

L65.3 ARMSTRONG (MARY ELIZABETH "MOLLIE"; b. 1875) PAPERS. First woman optometrist in Texas; resident of Brownwood. Studio and snapshot portraits of Armstrong family. 149 silver gelatin prints and 1 tintype. 1880s to 1940s.

L65.4 BIGGS (GLENN) PAPERS. Commercial views of landscape and hunting in McKittrick Canyon and the Guadalupe Mountains; photographers include Don Hutchinson (Abilene). 145 silver gelatin prints; 65 color prints; 10—35mm color transparencies; 16mm motion picture film. 1950s.

L65.5 BOTSFORD (E. M.) COLLECTION. Commercial views and snapshots of Wild West show performers, cowboys and cowgirls, and Amerinds, predominantly portraits; rodeos; many made in Oklahoma. 69 silver gelatin prints, many photo postcards. 1910s to 1920s.

L65.6 BREEDLOVE (WILLIAM CLENT; 1900-1953) PAPERS. Pioneer aviator and manager of the Lubbock airport. Portraits of associates of Breedlove; Lubbock airfield and aviation in the South Plains region.

[*Breedlove album.*] Snapshots of biplanes on the ground and flying in formation, crashes, early aviators, and aerial views. Kelly Field (San Antonio), March Field, and West Virginia locations. 281 silver gelatin prints. 1920s to 1930s.

410 silver gelatin prints and 1 album (v.s.). Late 1920s to 1940s.

L65.7 BURSON (KATHERINE LUCILLE HEARNE) PAPERS. Studio and snapshot portraits of Burson and friends, most from her high-school period in Stephenville.

L65.7.1 [*Small Burson album.*] Snapshot portraits of friends. 28 silver gelatin prints. 1920s.

L65.7.2 [*Large Burson album.*] Snapshot portraits of Burson's family and friends. 95 silver gelatin prints. Early 1920s.

37 silver gelatin prints and two albums (v.s.). 1920s.

L65.8 CARD (LOTTIE HOLMAN; 1882-1964) PAPERS. Studio and snapshot portraits of various family and friends, including Nancy Burnam and George Holman; Civil War soldiers; Comanche TX. Photographers include Brodie (Comanche) and J. L. Wright (Comanche). Unidentified photographer(s). 260 photographs, most silver gelatin prints; a few cartes, cabinets, and tintypes; some negatives. 1860 to 1958.

L65.9 CARR (WAGGONER) PAPERS. Member of the Texas House of Representatives from 1951 to 1967, Texas Speaker of the House from 1961 to 1963, and Texas Attorney General from 1963 to 1967. Images relating to the assassination of President John F. Kennedy, including Oswald's murder, Edwin Walker, and J. D. Tippitt; campaign photographs. 150 silver gelatin prints; 16mm motion pictures and video tapes. 1960s.

L65.10 CATTLE KINGS OF TEXAS. Studio portraits of Texas cattle barons. 57 copy negatives and prints. Itemized list. 1890 to 1900s.

L65.11 CHENOWETH (DEAN) PAPERS. Editor of San Angelo *Standard-Times* and amateur historian. Commercial and news photographs, including many portraits from the San Angelo and West Texas region; many by Hunter (Alpine). 103 silver gelatin prints. 1950s.

L65.12 CORNICK (BOYD) FAMILY PAPERS. San Angelo physician. Arranged by family member, with substantial numbers of photographs in the Boyd and Louis Cornick, Philip and Freida Cornick, and Aime Cornick materials. Landscapes and ranch scenes, possibly near San Angelo; cartes of Civil War leaders, buildings, and scenes, many published by Selden and Company (Richmond VA); Aime Cornick at college, including many portraits of friends and family; snapshots in USSR made by George Cornick while working with American Relief Administration from 1921 to 1922. 886 photographs, most silver gelatin prints, some nitrate negatives. 1860s to 1960s, most 1910s to 1930s.

L65.13 CORYELL (HENRY CLAY; 1880-1962) PAPERS. Born in Galveston, a resident of San Saba from 1903 to 1962; postal clerk, real estate agent, and served on the Board of Regents for Southwestern University and on the Texas Good Roads Association. Economic and social development of San Saba, including residents and fairs; studio portraits of Coryell and family. Photographers include Morris (Galveston), Zahn (Galveston), and Detwiler (Canton MO).

    L65.13.1 [*Coryell album.*] Construction of the seawall at Galveston and raising the grade of the island. 29 silver gelatin prints. Ca. 1904.

    L65.13.2 [*Coryell portrait wallet.*] Portraits of Coryell family members. Photoduplications by Morris (Galveston) of originals by Rose and various other photographers. 10 silver gelatin copy prints. 1903.

196 photographs, including silver gelatin prints, albumen cartes, cabinets, a few hand-colored lantern slides; 2 albums (v.s.). 1860s to 1960s, most ca. 1920s.

L65.14 DICKERSON (TESSIE FRANK) PAPERS. Manuscript notes "All of these of (me) Tessie Frank Dickerson made in Shreveport, Louisiana in studio where I started my training and worked. Early 1900s." Studio portraits of Dickerson, her sister and mother. 49—5x7 silver gelatin glass negatives. 1905 to 1918.

L65.15 DUNCAN (ARTHUR B.; 1862-1931) COLLECTION. First Caucasian settler in Floyd County; served as local justice, public school official, and land agent and abstractor for the Arthur B. Duncan Abstract Company. Duncan family photographs, including studio and snapshot portraits; vacation snapshots; economic and social development of Floydada, including the railroad, street scenes and businesses, farming and homesteads, and early settlers. 200 photo prints, most silver gelatin, few cabinets; 20 safety negatives. 1890s to 1950s, most ca. 1915.

L65.16 DYCHES (JOE A.; 1883-1970) FAMILY PAPERS. Early settler in San Angelo; rancher and Texas Ranger. Predominantly portraits of family and friends, many snapshots and some studio portraits; early settlers and scenes on the range.

    [*Roff family* (?) *album*] Snapshots of ranch life in Oklahoma, including many in situ portraits and early automobiles; soldiers in WW I camp. 187 silver gelatin prints. 1910s.

600 photographs, most silver gelatin prints, including a few cartes, cabinets, and color prints; 20 tintypes; 1 album (v.s.). 1870s to 1970; most ca. 1900 and 1950s to 1960s.

L65.17 ELLWOOD (ISAAC L.; d. 1910) PAPERS. Co-inventor and developer of barbed wire and owner of the Spade Ranch. Ellwood Farms physical plant, crops, and farming activities; photographers include Daniel (Lubbock) and Brown Photo (Lubbock). 168 silver gelatin prints and nitrate negatives. Most ca. 1930, a few to 1950.

L65.18 FARRIS (Mrs. IRA J.) COLLECTION. Studio portraits by various Midwest and Colorado photographers; Camp Pike AR; Big Wells TX. 257 items, many photomechanical and silver gelatin postcards, some cabinets and cartes. 1870s to 1931, most 1909 to 1920s.

L65.19 FORD (HENRY; 1845-1910) PAPERS. Brownwood business leader, banker, and civic worker. Predominantly studio portraits; some snapshot portraits on outings; a few scenes of Brownwood and Brady. Various Texas and other photographers.

> [*Texas Sanatorium album.*] Buildings of the sanatorium. 23 silver gelatin prints. 1920s.

275 photographs, including many cabinet prints and 1 album (v.s.). 1880s to 1930s.

L65.20 FORT CONCHO ONE-HUNDREDTH ANNIVERSARY PAPERS. Centennial celebration parade and festivities. Photographed by Jack Hughes. 32 silver gelatin prints. 1962.

L65.21 GETZENDANER (W. H.; b. 1834) PAPERS. Resident of Ellis County. Children of Getzendaner and their families; trip to Egypt. 131 copy negatives with modern prints. 1880s to 1920s.

L65.22 GODWIN (KENNETH EUGENE) ESTATE. Essayist, Church of Christ minister, farmer, and political critic. Vacation snapshots, some from Boston, most unidentified locales; military ships and submarines. 157 silver gelatin prints. 1950s.

L65.23 GREEN (DONALD E.) PAPERS. History professor. Cattle and ranching scenes. 191 photographs. 1960s to 1970s.

L65.24 Hayden, F. V.; A. J. Russell, photog. *Sun pictures of Rocky Mountain scenery: With a description of the geographical and geological features, and some account of the resources of the great West, containing thirty photographic views along the line of the Pacific Railroad from Omaha to Sacramento.* New York: Julius Bien, 1870. 30 albumen prints. SWC# 20/H414.

L65.25 HART (JULIA DUGGAN; 1873-1970) PAPERS. Studio portraits of the Hart, Duggan, and Webb families. 98 photographs. 1860s to 1930s.

L65.26 HAVERSTOCK (HARVEY) PAPERS. Tent show comedian. Studio portraits of Haverstock, his wife, Lotta, their son, Roland, and Roland's wife, Peggy; studio portraits of his troupe, Harvey's Comedians, and other tent show troupes.

> **L65.26.1** [*Lotta Haverstock album I.*] Snapshot, in situ portraits of Harvey's Comedians, many in costume, traveling companions, and friends; social life and customs of tent show performers includes traveling by car, pets, and recreation; Texas Panhandle, Oklahoma, and St. Louis MO. 430 silver gelatin prints. Ca. 1921.

> **L65.26.2** [*Haverstock scrapbook II.*] Studio and snapshot portraits of Harvey's Comedians, the Haverstock family, Paul and Ed Thardo, and other performers; travels by auto, truck, and train; tent blow-downs. 460 silver gelatin prints; typescript identifications. 1920s to 1940s.

> **L65.26.3** [*Haverstock album III.*] Snapshot, in situ portraits of Harvey's Comedians, many in costume, traveling companions, and friends; other troupes, including Bobby Warren's Comedians; raising the big top and interior. 264 silver gelatin prints. Ca. 1919.

> **L65.26.4** [*Haverstock album IV.*] Mostly snapshot and a few studio portraits of Harvey's Comedians and the Haverstock family; tent shows, including jazz musicians. 193 silver gelatin prints. Ca. 1925.

L65.26.5 [*Roland Haverstock WW II scrapbook.*] Snapshots from Roland Haverstock's service in Germany during WW II, a few battle scenes and aftermath, landscape and buildings, civilian casualties, and portraits of other members of his battalion. 198 silver gelatin prints; manuscript captions; newsclippings. 1940s.

241 silver gelatin prints; 3 albums (v.s.); 4 scrapbooks, 2 with a few photographs. 1910s to 1960s, most ca. 1920s.

L65.27 HILL (JIM DAN; b. 1897) PAPERS. Major General in the US National Guard, author, and president of Wisconsin State College (Superior). Hill's activities with the guard and a few from his academic career.

L65.27.1 *Thirty-second Division FCI* [Field Camp of Instruction]. Personnel, training maneuvers, and social life and customs at Camp McCoy WI; photographers include Bernard Benson, Arthur La Fountain, William March, Neal Thorkildsen, Howard Nieman, and John Bentz. 34 silver gelatin prints; typescript commentary. 1950.

L65.27.2 *Thirty-second Infantry Division training report.* Personnel, artillery training, activities at Camp Riley MN. 38 silver gelatin prints; typescript. 1953.

L65.27.3 *Thirty-second Infantry Division training report.* Personnel, artillery training, activities at Camp McCoy and Camp Haven WI. 38 silver gelatin prints; typescript. 1954.

380 silver gelatin prints; 3 reports illustrated with photographs (v.s.). 1930s to 1960s.

L65.28 HILL (Dr. KATE ADELE; 1902?-1983) PAPERS. Author who worked with Texas Agricultural Extension Service. Snapshots and some studio portraits of Hill and family; ranch scenes. Various Austin photographers. 90 photographs, including snapshots and cabinet prints. 1880s to 1930s.

L65.29 HUGHES (JOHN SAMUEL "JACK"; b. 1902) PHOTOS AND NEGATIVES. Commercial photographer who began as a freelancer in 1936 and later worked with the British Army during WW II; settled in San Angelo in 1954. Architecture, business exteriors, interior of studio, horses and horse racing, studio portraits, and landscape. Most in San Angelo area. 138 photographs, including 7x11 film and 5x7 film and glass negatives and silver gelatin prints. 1930s to 1950s.

L65.30 JONES (Dr. CLIFFORD BARTLETT; 1885-1972) COLLECTION. Manager of Spur Ranch and president of Texas Technological College. Commercial travel views of Fairbanks AK and Alaskan landscapes; vacation snapshots of outings in Alaska and Yellowstone. 607 color transparencies. Freeport TX, Hawaii, sulfur mining, and ranch scenes. 100 "French" silver gelatin glass stereographs (1-5/8" x 4-1/4"). Studio portraits. 30 silver gelatin prints. 1920s to 1960s.

L65.31 JONES (OTTO F.; 1889-1975) PAPERS. Manager of Renderbrook-Spade Ranch from 1912 to 1969. Studio and snapshot family portraits; cowhands working cattle; economic and social development of Colorado City TX. 2,301 photographs. 1859 to 1975.

L65.32 KNAPP (BRADFORD; 1870-1938) PAPERS. Agriculture instructor at University of Arkansas and at Alabama Polytech (= Auburn) and later President of Texas Technological College. Studio and in situ portraits of Knapp and family; photographs from his career. 87 photo prints, most silver gelatin and a few cyanotypes. 1910s to 1930s.

L65.33 KNIGHT (CECIL) PAPERS. Brownwood family. Studio and in situ portraits by various Brownwood photographers, including Weatherington; snapshot portraits; social life in Brownwood. 172 photographs, most silver gelatin prints, some cabinets. 1904 to 1916.

L65.34 McKEE (Mrs. A. W.; 1882?-1973) PERSONAL PAPERS. McKee family and relatives, family friends, home and store in Honey Grove; many Bonham photographers, including Will S. Thompson and Foster, and J. R. Keasler (Honey Grove). 174 photographs. 1880s to 1912.

L65.35 McKEOWN (FRANK "HAPPY") PAPERS. Lost both forearms in WW I and became an entertainer known as the Armless Wonder. Two albums:

> **L65.35.1** McKeown, Frank, comp. [*Sideshow performers.*] Entertainers, most with physiological anomalies, including giants, dwarfs, contortionists, siamese twins, hermaphrodites. 130 gelatino-chloride and silver gelatin prints. 1910s.

> **L65.35.2** McKeown, Frank, comp. [*Career of Frank McKeown.*] Side shows in which McKeown worked as the Armless Wonder; his work with others in their adjusting to the recent loss of limb or other handicap by demonstrating how he could live an independent life-style. 325 silver gelatin prints. Ca. 1960.

[End of McKeown papers.]

L65.36 McKNIGHT STATE TUBERCULOSIS HOSPITAL RECORDS. Formerly the Texas State Tuberculosis Sanatorium, located in Sanatorium TX. Physicians, staffs, patients, and physical plant, including medical facilities and dormitories; treatment; Christmas publicity; Kerrville State Sanatorium. 2,598 photographs. 1925 to 1959.

L65.37 MAHON (GEORGE) PAPERS. US representative from the Nineteenth Congressional District from 1935 to 1979. Portraits of Mahon; Appropriations Committee; awards; banquets and celebrations; members of Congress and important figures; constituents; dedications and christenings; press and speeches; trips; White House; presidents Truman through Carter; personal photographs. 6,164 photographs. 1918 to 1978.

L65.38 MAIZE (NANCY STALLINGS LEE; b. 1944) COLLECTION. Educator at Texas A&M University. Lee, Ray, Edmonds, and Curtis families.

> [*Maize carte album.*] Studio portraits of various individuals. Various and unidentified photographers, many from Louisville KY, including Brown and Stowe, and a few by F. P. Cooper (Belton). 33 cartes and 2 tintypes. Early 1860s to ca. 1875.

112 photographs and 1 album (v.s.). 1884 to 1920s.

L65.39 METHODIST HOSPITAL (LUBBOCK) RECORDS. Commercial views of physical plant and construction of the new eastern wing; various departments of the hospital; staff and volunteers.

> Methodist Hospital (Lubbock). *A pictorial study of cardiovascular and cancer care.* Facilities for patient care and staff performing various treatments, including radiation therapy and surgery. 15 color prints with typescript captions. 1965.

713 photo silver gelatin prints, 710 color slides; 1 album (v.s.). 1960 to 1975.

L65.40 MOHAIR COUNCIL OF AMERICA RECORDS. Headquartered in San Angelo. Four albums (v.i.).

> **L65.40.1** *Miss Wool and Mohair of Texas scrapbook.* Contestants in a beauty competition, won by Jonni Kay Johnson; portraits and fashion shots of Johnson. 141 photographs, many silver gelatin and color prints; newsclippings. 1968 to 1969.

> **L65.40.2** *Miss Wool and Mohair of Texas scrapbook.* Contestants and runway competition won by Jan Ellen Green; portraits of Green. 55 photographs, most silver gelatin, some color prints; newsclippings. 1969 to 1970.

L65.40.3 *Miss Wool and Mohair of Texas scrapbook.* Contestants and competition won by Judy Womack, portraits and fashion shots of Womack, and Womack doing publicity activities. 68 photographs, most silver gelatin, some color; newsclippings. 1970 to 1971.

L65.40.4 *Miss Wool and Mohair of Texas scrapbook.* Contestants in a beauty competition won by Sandi Tomczak; fashion photographs of Tomczak. 59 photographs, most silver gelatin, some color; newsclippings. 1971 to 1972.

[End of Mohair Council records.]

L65.41 MULLICAN (CLARK MARION; 1887-1950) PAPERS. Lubbock justice, colonel in US Army Infantry. Landscapes along country road, possibly insurance documents; studio portraits of Mullican in military uniform, many by Montgomery (Dallas); studio and snapshot portraits of Mullican and family; trip to Hawaii in 1926. 437 silver gelatin prints. 1910 to 1948.

L65.42 MURPHY (JOHN JOSEPH "PAT"; 1879-1957) PAPERS. Operated J. J. Murphy Lumberyards. Family and friends, including many studio portraits; Murphy's lumberyards in Crosbyton, Lorenzo, Idalou, and Lubbock. 255 silver gelatin prints, including a few cabinet prints. 1890 to 1945.

L65.43 MURRAY (GROVER ELMER; b. 1916) PAPERS. Geologist, Director of Ashland Oil Global Exploration, president of Texas Technological University. Photographs document Murray's professional activities, including Ashland Oil and the National Science Foundation; some family photographs. Major headings used by Murray on slide collections include:

Alaska. Algeria. Antarctica. Africa. Arizona. Ashland Coal and Oil. Australia. Baja. Cacti. California. Chile. China. Colorado. Durango. Europe. Greenland. Hawaii. Hong Kong and Malaysia. India. Iran. Italy. Louisiana. Mexico. New Zealand. Niger. Northern Canada. Norway. Peru. Russia. Spain. Switzerland. Texas. Turkey. Utah. Vegetation.

1,524 photo prints, most silver gelatin, some color; 21,568—35mm color transparencies. 1917 to 1973, most slides date from the 1970s.

L65.44 MYERS (S. D.) SADDLE COMPANY AND ESTATE. Samuel Dale Myers (1871-1953) began making saddles in Sweetwater in 1898 and moved the company to El Paso in 1920. Leatherwork produced by the company, predominantly saddles, but including belts, holsters, and western wear; snapshot and studio portrait of the Myers family; Western entertainers; movie stills with Pauline Fredrick.

[*Myers album.*] Unidentified snapshots of people probably on vacation; beachfront at a city resort. 128 silver gelatin prints. Ca. 1920.

1,034 photographs; 1 album (v.s.). 1890s to 1950s; most 1950s.

L65.45 PATTON (JOSEPH T.) ALBUM. *Photographs taken by the first field geology class on the trip in New Mexico.* Snapshots of landscape, class members; Roswell and New Mexico Military Institute; in the Sierra Blanca Mountains and Lincoln National Forest; White Sands. 142 silver gelatin prints; handwritten captions. 1927.

L65.46 RIORDAN (J. E.) FAMILY PAPERS. Residents of Colorado City TX. Studio portraits and some snapshots of J. S. Douglas, Fred F. Stocking, and the Riordan family, including Frances "Frank," Mr. and Mrs. J. E., Mrs. J. E. Sr., J. G., Jerold, Mamie, and Nellie; Riordan home; Tucson and Amerinds. Photographers include Chapman (Colorado City TX), W. F. Hughes (Colorado City TX), A. G. Gaige (AZ), C. W. Carter (Salt Lake UT), Charles Gentile (Chicago), and various photographers from Texas, Chicago, Milwaukee WI, and Toronto, Canada. 869 photographs, including many cartes and cabinets, some silver gelatin prints, a few cased images, and a few negatives. 1850s to 1920s, most ca. 1870s.

L65.47 RISTER (CARL COKE; 1889-1955) COLLECTION. Author of Southwestern US historical subjects and the petroleum industry. Refining, storage, laboratory, marketing, oil fields, offshore operations, exploration, drilling, production, boom towns, and pipelines. Obtained from Kerr-McGee, including photographs by Robert Yarnell Richie; Humble Oil; Standard Oil, including photographs by Lee, Bubley, and Corsini; and Cities Service, including photographs by Fritz Henle.

L65.47.1 Rister, Carl Coke, comp. *Arkansas to Oklahoma (N).* Commercial views of oil industry, arranged by state, including Carter Oil Company and Standard Oil Company. Many photographs from Stryker's Standard Oil Project by Corsini, Bubley; some snapshots by Rister. 150 silver gelatin prints, some copy prints. 1915 to 1946.

L65.47.2 Rister, Carl Coke, comp. *Illustrations used in "Oil! Titan of the Southwest."* Oil industry. Some photographs from Stryker's Standard Oil Project by Corsini and Bubley. 71 silver gelatin prints, come copy prints; itemized list. 1898 to 1946.

L65.47.3 Rister, Carl Coke, comp. *Miscellaneous photographs from National Archives.* Commercial views of oil industry, arranged by state. Many photographs from Stryker's Standard Oil Project by Collier and Corsini; some snapshots by Rister. 200 silver gelatin prints, some copy prints. 1940s.

L65.47.4 Rister, Carl Coke, comp. *Oklahoma (O) to Texas (Br).* Commercial views of oil industry, arranged by state. Many photographs from Stryker's Standard Oil Project by Corsini and Bubley; the "Big Inch" (pipeline) from the Library of Congress; some snapshots by Rister. 160 silver gelatin prints. 1940s.

L65.47.5 Rister, Carl Coke, comp. *Refineries.* Oil refineries in Louisiana, Oklahoma, and especially Texas. Some photographs from Stryker's Standard Oil Project by Corsini and Rosskam. 43 silver gelatin prints, some copies. 1917 to 1948.

L65.47.6 Rister, Carl Coke, comp. *Texas (Bu) to Texas (Va).* Commercial views of oil industry in Texas, arranged by town; some snapshots by Rister. 120 silver gelatin prints, some copy prints. 1918 to 1946.

1.5 cubic feet silver gelatin prints, some copies, including 6 albums (v.s.). 1910s to 1948.

L65.48 SHERIDAN (JACK WALRATH; b. 1916) PAPERS. Author and former arts editor for the Lubbock *Avalanche-Journal*. News and snapshot portraits of Sheridan and associates from his career; a parade; unidentified movie stills. 145 photo prints, many color. 1920s to 1970s, most ca. 1960s.

L65.49 TEXAS TECH PARK ADMINISTRATION AND HORTICULTURE DEPARTMENT. Guadalupe Mountains National Park, Lubbock, internal documents. 150 photo prints; 2,283—35mm color slides. 1970s.

L65.50 WAGNER (CHARLES JOHN) PAPERS. Lubbock physician and cofounder of West Texas Hospital. Studio and snapshot portraits of patients and nurses associated with Wagner, most identified; many photographs from Texas Technological College's first scientific expedition to the Yaqui Indians of Mexico. 771 photographs, including prints, negatives, and photo postcards. 1915 to 1932.

L65.51 WALLACE (ERNEST) PAPERS. Amerinds, a few from the Bureau of American Ethnology; Amerind artifacts, many from museum exhibitions. 100 silver gelatin prints. 1870s to 1950s.

L65.52 WARREN (E. K.) PAPERS. Warren and his son Charles operated cattle ranches in Texas, New Mexico, and Mexico from their home base in Three Oaks MI. One album (v.i.).

> *Mr. Edward K. Warren.* Three Oaks MI, 1913. Presentation album of commercial views of farming on the YL Ranch; grain and forage crops; irrigation. 63 silver gelatin prints; typescript captions.

[End of Warren papers.]

L65.53 WEBSTER AND HARRIS ADVERTISING AGENCY RECORDS. Publicity photographs for Children's Television Workshop's program "Feeling Good"; aerials of Lubbock; Methodist Hospital; farming equipment. 225—35mm slides; 8 silver gelatin prints. 1967 to early 1969.

L65.54 WILEY (D. O.; 1899?-1980) PAPERS. Director of the Hardin-Simmons College Cowboy Band from 1922 to 1934 and Texas Tech Band from 1934 to 1959. Commercial photographs from Wiley's career; snapshots and some studio portraits of family.

> [*Wiley album.*] Wiley conducting various bands and classroom instruction; Texas Tech band performing in concerts, at football games; various scenes from his career. 67 silver gelatin prints. Ca. 1946.

200 photo prints, most silver gelatin, some color; one album (v.s.). 1920s to 1970s, most ca. 1950s.

[End of Manuscript collections.]

L65.55 Museum collection: Materials transferred from the museum at Texas Tech. Regional subjects from the Panhandle, including portraits of Amerinds, Blacks, and Caucasians; locations, including Dickens, Donley, Ector, Floyd, Gaines, Garza, Hale, Hockley, Lubbock, Lynn, and Mitchell counties; businesses, churches, homes, animals, civic events, buildings, ethnic groups, farming, government, schools, transportation, recreation, religion, and weddings; ethnological expedition from Tech to study the Yaqui Indians in Mexico; 127 glass negatives of temporary soldiers colony in Gibbon, New Brunswick in the 1890s. Most vintage photographs, including some tintypes, daguerreotypes, and ambrotypes. 20 cubic feet, all processes. 1860s to 1960s.

Southwest Collection Photo Collection:

L65.56 ALPINE STUDIO COLLECTION. Unidentified commercial and studio portraits; oil-field operations; Sul Ross State Teacher's College; Alpine and Brewster County, Marfa and Presidio County; photographs by Frank Duncan (Marfa) and J. C. Thain (Alpine). 321—5x7 glass negatives, all have been water damaged. 1900 to 1920.

L65.57 AVIATION COLLECTION. Randolph Field in San Antonio; most by US Army Air Corps, some snapshots. 92 silver gelatin prints. 1929. SWCPC# 395.

L65.58 BAXTER (PHIL) COLLECTION. Studio portraits of musical celebrities, many autographed. 130 copy negative with copy prints. 1920s. SWCPC# 11.

L65.59 BLEDSOE (WILLIAM H.; 1869-1936) PAPERS. Texas representative from 1915 to 1919 and Texas senator from 1919 to 1927. Snapshot and studio portraits of family and associates; V. L.

Shurtleff home interiors in Hillsboro. 280 silver gelatin prints, 8 negatives. 1910s to 1930s. SWCPC# 409.

L65.60 Brenner, C. Louis, photog. *Anacacho Ranch.* Grounds, building, and interior of the ranch house. 28 silver gelatin prints. 1940s.

L65.61 BROWN STUDIO COLLECTION. Located at 2123 Twenty-third Street in Lubbock, operated by Arthur L. Brown. Studio portraits, most of Lubbock residents; 5,000 names represented; some photofinishing. 18 linear feet containing 22,000 items, most 5x7 film negatives, many nitrate, with two images per sheet; some with unfixed studio proofs; modern prints of many; in original envelopes with Brown's price and manuscript notes. 1920s to 1940. Itemized inventory available. SWCPC# 412.

L65.62 CALIFORNIA COLLECTION. Commercial photographs of California missions, especially Mission San Diego de Alcala; published by Frashers Quality Photos. 20 silver gelatin prints. 1940s. SWCPC# 391-E1.

L65.63 COPY PRINT PROJECT. Arranged as non-Texas subjects, Texas by county, subject headings, personal headings, Texas ranches, tent shows, and miscellaneous collections, with quantity and collection number indicated in parentheses. Record groups with some vintage material interfiled are marked with an asterisk.

L65.63.1 Non-Texas subjects: Arizona (1, #297). Arizona Chemical Company (2, #226). California, tourist views of missions and stars' homes (40, #391*). Colorado, modern views of Chivington massacre site (8, #387). Mexico (2, #372). New Mexico (28, #93). New Mexico, Cloudcroft (36, #126). New Mexico, Elizabethtown (1, #248). New Mexico, Lincoln County (1, #298). New Mexico, Roswell (325, #125). New Mexico, Tucumcari (4, #163). Oklahoma (1, #339). Oklahoma, Grove, Morris Sellers family and business (11, #142).

L65.63.2 Texas by county (grouped alphabetically):

Anderson County (5, #336). Archer County: Archer City, Holliday, Scotland, Winthorst (81, #10).

Bailey County: Muleshoe, YL Ranch, E. K. Warren (409, #107). Bandera County: Bandera (1, #208). Bell County: Temple, Fletcher family (21, #23). Bexar County: San Antonio (54, #148); San Antonio Musicians Local #23 (65, #91); San Antonio, Stanley family (25, #169):earch q Mrs. Millard Cope collection (17, #363). Borden County (117, #17). Brazos County: College Station, Texas A&M University (23, #215). Brewster County: (300+, #41); Big Bend National Park (69, #184); Bill Stokes Big Bend wanderings (113, #105). Briscoe County: Silverton (40, #14). Brown County (130, #22*); *Brownwood Bulletin* "As We Were" series (140, #25); Brownwood, Howard Payne College (64, #21); Brownwood, Mitcham family (16, #164); Brownwood, Weatherby family (45, #20); Camp Bowie (47, #18); McGaugh family (36, #162); water district (44, #19*). Callahan County: Baird (129, #1).

Castro County: Dimmitt (61, #242). Cherokee County: Colliton Discovery Well (5, #270*). Childress County (11, #243*). Clay County (5, #327). Cochran County: Bledsoe family (16, #263). Coke County: Bronte (94, #29); Clark family (14, #28); Knierim family (36, #27). Coleman County: Morris family and ranch (35, #35); Santa Anna (98, #80); Santa Anna, Elgen Shield family (50, #30). Collingsworth County: Wellington, Templeton family (96, #260). Comanche County (113, #124). Concho County: Paint Rock (9, #205). Cooke County: Gainesville (16, #139). Cottle County (100, #31). Crockett County: Coates family (37, #261); Ozona (50, #75); West family (38, #241). Crosby County (200, #291*). Culberson County: Guadalupe Peak (7, #160).

Dallam County: Dalhart (32, #210). Dallas County: Dallas, Adolphus Hotel (44, #40); Dallas, Southern Mills Company (1, #286*). Dawson County (44, #233). Deaf Smith County (10, #182); Hereford (300+, #38); Mercer family (10, #189); Witherspoon family (16, #183); Worton family (18, #188). Delta County (11, #338). Dickens County: Spur (32, #202); Pitchfork Ranch (#284). Donley County (31, #203): Clarendon, Bairfield family (19, #234*).

Eastland County: Cisco (6, #156); Desdemona (105, #43*); Gorman (90, #16); Gorman, Higginbotham Brothers (60, #42*); Pioneer (6, #362); Ranger (147, #147); Rising Star (26, #257). Ector County: Odessa (5, #217); Odessa, J. Parker Ranch (38, #46). Edwards County: Rocksprings (399, #49). El Paso County (65, #320). Ellis County (3, #292). Erath County: Dublin, Bowden family (34, #136); Neel family (12, #278); Stephenville Museum collection (341, #383); Thurber (50, #209*).

Fisher County: Roby (6, #200). Floyd County (286, #211). Foard County (31, #190): Crowell, John Ray family (53, #34); Crowell, N. J. Roberts family (38, #33); Grady Halbert family (22, #37).

Gaines County: Seagraves (15, #223*). Galveston County: Galveston (1, #249). Garza County: Post (18, #344*). Gillespie County: Fredericksburg (8, #230). Gray County (23, #174). Grayson County: Sherman (87, #94).

Hale County (146, #222*). Hall County (31, #331). Hamilton County (163, #52). Hansford County (10, #325). Hardeman County (2, #201). Hardin County* (1, #303). Harris County: Allen family (60, #252); Houston, Camp Logan (3, #228). Hartley County (130, #355). Haskell County (2, #306). Hays County: San Marcos (12, #258). Hemphill County: Canadian, Born photographs (288, #253*); Lake Marvin (7, #187). Henderson County (16, #232). Hill County: Itasca (37, #130). Hockley County (40, #181); Ropesville Rural Resettlement Colony (28, #61). Howard County: Big Spring (31, #12); Soash (1, #381). Hudspeth County: Dell (116, #370). Hutchinson County (7, #315).

Irion County (194, #55). Jack County (59, #328*): Williams family (22, #231). Jeff Davis County: Davis Mountains (15, #159); Kent, Reynolds X Ranch (55, #113). Jones County: Stamford (68, #132).

Kent County: Clairemont (1, #385*). Kerr County (102, #63): Kerrville, Schreiner family (29, #114). Kimbell County: Junction (2, #213). King County, Pitchfork Ranch (47, #284). Knox County (64, #70).

Lamar County: Paris (4, #140*). Lamb County (4, #316): Amherst, Mashed O Ranch (27, #115); Littlefield (28, #186). Lampasas County (29, #62*): Huling family (17, #271). Leon County: Normangee, Hill family (55, #97); Normangee, Rogers Prairie (1, #216). Llano County: Kingsland (3, #219); Sam Wallis Ranch (3, #218*). Loving County: Goodrich family (53, #69). Lubbock County (72, #299*): Bledsoe family (74, #237); Lubbock, KFYO Radio (100, #287); Lubbock, Pre-1909 (35, #197*); Lubbock (142, #57b; 207, #57a; 72, #57k*); Lubbock agriculture (182, #60); Lubbock Army Air School (28, #58); Lubbock aviation (53, #388); Lubbock, Texas Technological University (201, #59*); Lubbock, Underwood family and business (47, #109); Shallowater (2, #259). Lynn County (64, #273).

Martin County (18, #337). Mason County (82, #247): Hugo Schulze family (62, #67); Pontotoc, John McLeod family (93, #77). Maverick County: Eagle Pass, Eagle Pass Army Camp (13, #131). McCulloch County (123, #68): Engdahl family (68, #177); Johnson family (12, #176); McLennan County: Elk City, Paul E. Peeler homestead (1, #262); Waco (1, #290). Menard County (48, #71): Black family (57, #72); Los Moras Ranch, Runge family (42, #32). Midland County (16, #149). Milam County: Cameron (48, #137); Cameron, Henderson family (24, #172); Homer Nabors family (44, #65). Mills County: Goldthwaite (131, #98). Mitchell County (94, #296): Colorado City TX (100, #39*). Montague County: Nocona (3, #212). Morris County: Daingerfield (6, #134). Motley County: Matador, Luckett family (15, #254*); Matador, oil spill (42, #207*).

Nolan County: Roscoe, Whorton (22, #129); Sweetwater (140, #146). Nueces County: Corpus Christi (12, #170); Corpus Christi, Stanley family (25, #169).

Ochiltree County: Perryton (6, #198). Oldham County (18, #334).

Palo Pinto County (121, #301): Mineral Wells (270, #111). Parmer County (161, #341): Farwell (34, #360). Pecos County: Fort Stockton (250, #79); Fort Stockton, Hadden family (17, #53). Potter County: St. Francis (82, #295); Amarillo (20, #229). Presidio County: Marfa (5, #66); Shafter (27, #76).

Randall County: Canyon (4, #204). Real County: Campwood (48, #150); Leakey (256, #153); Godbald family (10, #193); Auld family (12, #194); Rio Frio (35, #152); Vance (15, #151). Reeves County (88, #351). Roberts County (50, #85). Robertson County: Ledrick family (12, #2*). Rockwall County (6, #166). Runnels County: Ballinger (69, #15); Miles (48, #73); Miles, Cunningham family (9, #178); Theile family (68, #83).

San Saba County (49, #88). Schleicher County: Eldorado (37, #50). Scurry County: Snyder (61, #101*). Shackleford County (371, #74): Albany, Hill family (12, #128); Albany, Reynolds and Matthews families (15, #371); Fort Griffin (40, #185). Spiller County (37, #173). Stephens County: Breckenridge (115, #13); Breckenridge, Judge Floyd Jones Family (1, #92). Sterling County: Sterling (2, #214). Stonewall County (6, #269*): LBJ Ranch (4, #224). Sutton County: Senora (140, #95).

Tarrant County: Fort Worth (1, #396). Taylor County: Abilene (465+, #9); Abilene 1904, *Our Homes and Country Illustrated* (445, #8); Abilene, Cannon family (14, #4); Abilene, Cunningham family (18, #135); Abilene, Dyess Air Force Base (52, #6); Abilene, Merchant family and Old Texas Trail Drivers Association (14, #5). Terry County: Brownfield (12, #236*). Tom Green County: Christoval, William Anson: Head-of-the-River Ranch (33, #106); Fort Concho (86, #144); Fort Concho, Noelke family (82, #51); San Angelo (428, #143); San Angelo Pioneers (89, #191); San Angelo, Emmanuel Episcopal Church (157, #48); San Angelo, Goodfellow Air Force Base (91, #96); San Angelo, M. C. Ragsdale family (21, #100); San Angelo, Tankersley family (21, #102); San Angelo, Ted Harris family and ranch (79, #89); San Angelo, Dyche family (106, #44*). Travis County: Austin (7, #244*); Austin, University of Texas (29, #225); Mrs. Millard Cope collection (17, #363).

Upton County: Rankin (52, #82); Rankin (9, #389). Val Verde County: Del Rio (100, #36*); Del Rio, Cadena family (11, #239); Del Rio, De La Garza family (40, #45); Del Rio, Hunnicutt family (19, #276); Pandale and Del Rio, Henry Mills family (40, #108).

Ward County: Barstow (199, #375); Monahans (15, #161). Webb County: Callaghan Ranch (54, #240). Wheeler County (14, #199). Wichita County: Burkeburnett (84, #26); Electra (190, #47); Wichita Falls (326, #112). Willbarger County: Vernon (10, #175). Yoakum County: Denver TX (12, #376). Young County (90, #168).

L65.63.3 Subject headings: Agriculture (115, #196*). Band photographs, Bynum collection (102, #358*). Banks (4, #272). Buffalo (4, #274). Cattle (33, #195). Cotton Industry (323, #104). County Courthouses (371, #122). Churches, E. L. Yeats collection (7, #354). Educational Laboratories, Inc. (9, #56*). Farming miscellany (13, #340*). Fort Worth and Denver Railroad (306, #121*). Irrigation (21, #343). Lake Whitney (5, #171). Land documents (6, #133). Longhorn trail drive (1, #368). McMurry-LCC football game 1979 (19, #279). Military leaders, 19th century (1, #308). Musicians (6, #380). Oil geologists and equipment (21, #145). Oil and gas industry (24, #349*). Parramore sketches [art reproductions by D. P. Parramore] (80, #78). Postcards (572, #167). Prostitution (2, #304). Quanah, Acme, and Pacific Railroad, #81). Railroad collection (11, #314). Texas Tech football team, Ralph Sellmeyer, comp. (202, #310). Ranching Heritage Center collection (16, #335*). Rodeos (15, #158). Santa Fe Railway (36, #119*). Southern Pacific Railway (9, #157). State Representatives (24, #402). Ross Sutherland, Ten Sheep, Wyoming Rodeo (11, #141). Texas and Pacific

Railway (63, #120). Texas Cottonseed Crushers Association (100, #103). Texas Sheep and Goat Raisers Association (500, #90). Texas writers (2, #302). Universalists (1, #289). Weather (3, #397). West Texas Chamber of Commerce (111, #155). Whipple-Sellers horseback trip (58, #405). Winkler (199, #110).

L65.63.4 Personal subjects: Alexander family (4, #359). Amerinds (35, #280). Blaschke, Glumper, Jungman families (47, #283). Boren family (11, #245). Brillhart family (8, #246). Brunk family (38, #268). Buie family (66, #378*). Burnett family (27, #238, #293). Burns family (16, #24). Butcher family (5, #307). Cooper family (6, #267). Cornick family (5, #221). Craft, Huffman, Larrimore families (3, #318). DeCaughey, Stevens, Stone, and Inman (11, #275*). DeVitt family (1, #319). Dwight Eisenhower (1, #277). Farr family (8, #323). Bennett Freeman collection (221, #353*). Haverstock family and theater company (501, #250). Hereford, Black, English, Stanford families (91, #294). Hollingsworth family (24, #377). Jowell family (29, #179). Klattenhoff family (65, #305). Lambert family (11, #192). Lynn family (17, #255). Murdo Mackenzie (11, #116). McVickers family collection (162, #342). Masterson family (20, #390*). Francisco "Pancho" Villa (8, #206). Quanah Parker family reunion (4, #282). Ratliff family (6, #369). Reed family (26, #256). Harley Sadler family (96, #365*). Slaughter family and ranch (336, #154). Lon Smith family (11, #116). Hagler Sparks family (14, #7). Traweek family (47, #288). Waggoner family (49, #138). Westerman family portraits (11, #54). K. M. Van Zandt family (7, #399*). Bob Wills and his Texas Playboys (183, #356*).

L65.63.5 Texas Ranches: Bridwell Hereford Ranch (44, #118). Callaghan Ranch (54, #240). 6666 Ranch (108, #264). Ted Harris Ranch (79, #89). Head-of-the-River Ranch (33, #106). Hiley Boyd Ranch (28, #373). JA Ranch (3, #165). Lambshed Ranch (21, #220). Mashed O Ranch (27, #115). Matador Ranch (519, #64 a,b,c). Maverick Boy's Ranch (4, #227). Los Moras Ranch (42, #32). Morris family ranch (35, #35). J. Parker Ranch (38, #46). Parramore family and ranch (35, #3). Pitchfork Ranch (#284). Ranches (71, #265). Ranches, Don Ray comp. (184, #382*). Reynolds Ranch (55, #113). Slaughter Ranch (336, #154). Spur Ranch (18, #285*). Swenson Land and Cattle Company (198, #123*). Triangle R Ranch (8, #293*). Sam Wallis Ranch (9, #218*). XIT Ranch (222, #117). YL Ranch (409, #107). Zollners—Hobo Ranch (8, #180).

L65.63.6 Tent show collections include: Harley Sadler tent show (300, #87). Lew Henderson tent show (7, #352). Jenning's tent show (94, #367*). Kalmbacher tent shows (11, #251). Russell Snow tent show collection (#403). Tent shows (131, #366).

L65.63.7 Miscellaneous copy print collections: C. P. Laughlin collection (45, #361). De Loach collection (20, #398). Dorothy Rylander collection (65, #332*). Ewing Hasell collection (12, #347). Fred Carpentar photos (97, #127). George Mahon collection (#394). Huffman-Raines (#404). I. W. Ayres Jr. (4, #235). Inez Morrison collection (197, #311). Jack Hayworth collection (1, #324). John D. Alexander collection (44, #384). Judge Allan Stovall (53, #400*). Leavelle/Sadler collection (52, #364*). Mosslyn Gammill collection (191, #322). Mrs. A. Lee Henderson collection (66, #348). Mrs. G. L. Everett collection (39, #321). Mrs. John Walker collection (62, #357). Pete Peterman collection (155, #329). Rex Pries collection (17, #379). Robert F. Nail Foundation (306, #312). Sallie Brittingham (6, #266). Stephen Schmidt collection (17, #333*). Struve and Hoffman collection (37, #350). T. Lindsay Baker collection (43, #317). Weston Pettey collection (18, #330).

[End of copy print project.]

L65.64 CROP EXPERIMENTS. Agriculture experiments at Texas Tech. 592—35mm color slides. 1960s. Slide collection.

L65.65 DALLAS (JIM) STUDIO COLLECTION. Member of South Plains Professional Photographers Association, located at 2207 Thirty-fourth Street in Lubbock. Studio portraits; commerical product and business photographs; Lubbock cityscapes and aerial views; exhibition of work by the association; historical photographs copied by Dallas; photofinishing. 54 cubic feet containing 162,994 photographs, most 4x5 silver gelatin safety negatives, some silver gelatin contacts, color transparency, and color print materials; in original envelopes with Dallas' manuscript notes; arranged chronologically. 1946 to 1972.

L65.66 GILDERSLEEVE (FRED A.) COLLECTION. Commercial views of Waco buildings, street scenes, and events photographed by Gildersleeve. Originals at the Texas Collection, Baylor University (q.v.). 635 modern prints; copy of Gildersleeve's studio register. 1900s to 1920s. SWCPC# 408.

L65.67 HARRIS (Mrs. T. J.) COLLECTION. Commercial views and snapshots of Lubbock; studio portraits and snapshots of the Studer family. 1.5 cubic feet silver gelatin prints; 1 cubic foot film negatives. 1900 to 1970s. SWCPC# 410.

L65.68 HERALD (ROLLIN) COLLECTION. Commercial photographer in Lubbock, retired in 1985. Commercial product photography, weddings, architecture, aerials and cityscapes of Lubbock, studio portraits. 4,000 film negatives ranging from 4x5 to 8x10 many with silver gelatin contact prints. 1945 to mid-1960s.

L65.69 HIATT (DEAN B.) COLLECTION. Texas surveyor. Survey crew during resurvey of XIT Ranch, 1914 to 1917; crew on NT&SF Railway construction from Shatlock OK to Spearman, including trestle bridges; Texas and Pacific Coal and Oil Company in Thurber. 122 snapshot silver gelatin prints. 1914 to 1917. SWCPC# 300.

L65.70 HURD (PETER) MURAL SLIDE SHOW. Hurd working on the mural and close-ups of the mural itself. 97 color and black-and-white slides. Slide collection.

L65.71 JACK COUNTY COLLECTION. Fort Richardson and Jacksboro; civic groups; individuals. Withdrawn from the Mrs. Laura Peacock manuscript collection. 54 silver gelatin prints, some copy. 1900s, 1950s. SWCPC# 382-E3.

L65.72 KARDOS (MICHAEL) COLLECTION. Midland newspaper photographer. 1970s. SWCPC# 411.

L65.73 LARKAM (PAUL E.) COLLECTION. Professional photographer who moved to Roswell in 1935. Studio portraits of Roswell NM citizens.

> **L65.73.1** Larkam, Paul E., comp. [*Roswell NM scrapbook.*] 1978. Street scenes, buildings, and some rephotography. 143 silver gelatin copy prints with typescript captions. 1893 to 1975.

> **L65.73.2** Larkam, Paul E., comp. *Book 5: Cover Cloudcroft and places near there....* [1975?] Landscape, people, railroad, timber industry; many by Alexander and Lusk. 253 silver gelatin copy prints. 1910s to 1920s.

38,640—4x5 film negatives and contact prints in envelopes with Larkam's manuscript notes; a few items of color material; 3 albums (v.s.). 1893 to 1980, most 1948 to 1980. Arranged alphabetically.

L65.74 LEIDIGH COLLECTION. Milo and grain farming activities and views in Lubbock vicinity; snapshot closeups of plants and fields. 218 silver gelatin prints. Ca. 1920. SWCPC# 374.

L65.75 LUBBOCK COLLECTION—GERALD FORD'S VISIT. President Ford's visit to Lubbock, including a reception and scenes at the airport. 200 color prints. 1976. SWCPC 57h-1.

L65.76 LUBBOCK—RATLIFF COLLECTION. Photographs made by Ratliff while working for the Lubbock *Avalanche-Journal*. People, aerial views, flood. 890—4x5 safety negatives with modern prints. 1938 to 1936. SWCPC# 57c.

L65.77 LUBBOCK—RATLIFF PRINTS. Commercial views of Lubbock, possibly made while Ratliff was working for the *Avalanche-Journal*. 79 silver gelatin prints. 1940s. SWCPC# 57n.

L65.78 LUBBOCK HERITAGE SOCIETY COLLECTION. Modern views of historical architecture in Lubbock. 180 images on 120 film negatives, 15 silver gelatin contact sheets. 1980s. SWCPC# 401.

L65.79 LUBBOCK PICTORIAL HISTORY COLLECTION. Copy negatives and slides used in the production of *A Pictorial History of Lubbock*. Arranged by people, buildings, and miscellaneous; Blacks segregated for access. 910 copy transparencies, 50 copy prints, 1,000 copy negatives; itemized list. 1880s to 1970s. SWCPC# 417. See Bibliography—Griggs.

L65.80 LUBBOCK TORNADO DAMAGE. Aftermath, including aerial views. 126—35mm color slides. 1983. Slide collection.

L65.81 MATADOR RANCH COLLECTION. Commercial and snapshot views of cattle, horses, ranching activities, landscapes, Brazil division, sheep and goat raisers.

> [*Matador Ranch album.*] Commercial and snapshot views of life on Matador Ranch; Campbell family and house; Tee-Pee Creek and City. 44 albumen and gelatino-chloride prints. 1883 to 1890s.

750 silver gelatin prints, 1 album (v.s.). 1930s to 1960s. SWCPC# 64.

L65.82 MATERSON (Dr. and Mrs. ROBERT) FAMILY PHOTOGRAPHS. Materson home in Amarillo, including interiors; family members. 20 silver gelatin prints. 1920s. SWCPC# 390.

L65.83 MINNIS (MHYRA S.) COLLECTION. Travel and vacation views of Alaska, Asia, France, Mexico, the Orient, Russia, Scandinavia, and South America. 840—120 color transparencies; 100—35mm transparencies. 1940s to 1970s. SWCPC# 407.

L65.84 PATULLO (GEORGE) COLLECTION. Modern prints (made ca. 1949) by Erwin E. Smith of ranching activities, cowboy social life and customs in the Panhandle. 17 vintage silver gelatin prints, 12 modern prints from the Library of Congress. Ca. 1906; most captioned. SWCPC# 346.

L65.85 PRESIDIO COUNTY, MARFA COLLECTION. US military operations against Francisco "Pancho" Villa on the Texas-Mexico border photographed by Frank Duncan. 12 silver gelatin prints, with copy negatives and prints. 1910 to 1920. SWCPC# 66 E1.

L65.86 REEVES (FRANK; b. 1884) COLLECTION. Secretary on SMS Ranch, photographer active from 1900 to 1972, and farm editor for the *Fort Worth Star-Telegram*. Ranches, including

6666, Spurs, Spade, Ellwood-Renderbrook, Hereford-Hills, Kimball, Hickory Hills, SMS, T Bone, 9 Bar, JY, King, and Waggoner; cowboy social life and customs; ranching activities; livestock; landscape and flora; personal vacation and family. 330 glass and 13,896 film negatives; 16,886 silver gelatin prints, many duplicates; 1,260 slides. 1900 to 1972.

L65.87 SLAUGHTER (CHRISTOPHER COLUMBUS; 1837-1919) FAMILY AND RANCH COLLECTION. Banker, philanthropist, and cattleman. Snapshots and commercial views of Colonel C. C. Slaughter and family; cattle, including prime bull, Sir Bredwell; ranching activities in Big Spring vicinity.

> **L65.87.1** Kennedy Photo Company (Fort Worth). *Exterior and interior views of the home of Mrs. C. C. Slaughter, Sr., Dallas, Texas.* Fort Worth, 1925. 22 silver gelatin prints. 1925.

> **L65.87.2** Haddix, photog. [*Slaughter Ranch album.*] Views on Slaughter Ranch, including landscape of White Mountains, North Spring, land and development; cattle and ranching activities; Roswell NM. 24 silver gelatin prints. Ca. 1907.

84 photographs, including silver gelatin, gelatino-chloride, and copy prints; two albums (v.s.). Ca. 1900 to 1920s.

L65.88 *SOUTHWESTERN CROP AND STOCK* MAGAZINE. Morgue files. Agriculture activities. SWCPC# 413.

L65.89 SPADE RANCH COLLECTION. Ranching activities, cowboy social life and customs, cotton ginning, farming, wheat harvesting at Spade Ranch and Ellwood Estates. 63 silver gelatin prints; some copies included. 1920s to 1930s. SWCPC# 393.

L65.90 TARBOX (ELMER) COLLECTION. Texas Tech football player and Texas representative from Lubbock. Family photographs; Tarbox at Tech and in US Air Force; political career and associates. 1,000 photographs, most silver gelatin prints; 260—35mm color slides. 1922 to 1971. SWCPC# 406.

L65.91 TEXAS ASSOCIATION OF ACCREDITED BEAUTY CULTURISTS. Beautician contest won by Walter Lang, who styled Mrs. Lang's hair; various photographers. 26 silver gelatin, 8 color prints. 1960s. SWCPC# 392-E1.

The Museum of East Texas (L70)

503 North Second Street
Lufkin, Texas 75901

409-639-4434. Contact: Photographic Curator.

PURPOSE: A museum with exhibits of art, science, and history.

HOURS: Exhibit space—Tuesday through Friday, 10:00-5:00; weekends, 1:00-5:00. Reserve collections—weekdays, 8:00-5:00; appointment required. Closed major and federal holidays.

ASSISTANCE: Limited staff. Written inquiries will be forwarded to individuals who can be contracted to do research. Electrostatic copies available. Photoduplications must be ordered through the museum.

PUBLICATION: Publication fee. Collection credit required. Museum holds copyright on most items.

FINDING AIDS: Card index, descriptive list, and inventories; access by general subject heading, geographic location, date, personal name, and photographer.

SCOPE: 25,000 photographs, predominantly film negatives, a few cased photographs, and some vintage and copy prints. 1880s to present, most from early 1930s to the late 1970s.

GEOGRAPHIC: Extensive coverage of Lufkin.

SUBJECTS: Economic and social development of the community.

Animals. Arts and crafts. Advertising. Buildings (interior and exterior; auto sales and repair supply, bakery, bank, cafe, candy company, church, Coca Cola, depot, funeral home, house, ice company, lumber, machinery, news stand, printing office, variety store). Celebrity (political, special event, personality). Documents. Evidence (damage, injury, scene). Funeral. Furniture. Groups (businesses, churches, clubs and fraternities, official, school, sports). Insects. Lumbering. Parade. Portraits (fashion, costume). Special occasions. Uniform. Vehicle (airplane, auto, machine, train, truck, wagon). View (street scenes, landscape, Lufkin). Wedding.

PEOPLE: Studio portraiture of area residents.

PHOTOGRAPHERS: Keith Carter (Beaumont). Heifner (Lufkin). C. N. Merrill (Lufkin).

RECORD GROUPS:

L70.1 MERRILL (C. N.) ARCHIVE. A local studio and commercial photographer. Studio portraits; insurance adjustment documents, including damage, injury, and evidence; special occasions, including weddings, funerals, reunions and family groups, clubs, and athletic team members; business advertising, including theater marquees and Abram's Department store. 25,000 negatives. Early 1930s to late 1970s.

L70.2 LUFKIN COLLECTION. A photographic survey of the city documenting the economic and social development of Lufkin; interior and exterior views of businesses, including hotels and rooming houses, drugstores, cafes, gasoline stations, theaters, grocery stores, department stores, laundries and cleaners, beauty and barber shops, flower shops, and retirement homes; street scenes. Many of the images contain people within the frame. 1940.

Permian Basin Petroleum Museum (M82)

1500 Interstate 20 West
Midland, Texas 79701

915-683-4403. Contact: Archivist.

PURPOSE: An exhibiting history museum with an extensive archive devoted primarily to the oil and gas industry.

HOURS: Exhibit area—weekdays and Saturday, 9:00-5:00; Sunday, 2:00-5:00. Reserve collections—weekdays, 8:00-5:00. Closed Thanksgiving and Christmas.

ASSISTANCE: Professional, specialized, experienced staff. Written and phone inquiries accepted. Electrostatic copies available. Photoduplications must be ordered through the museum.

PUBLICATION: Publication fee charged for commercial use. Collection credit required. Third-party permission required on few items.

FINDING AIDS: Partial card index and inventory, complete itemized accession records; access by general subject heading, geographic location, photographer, and personal name.

BIBLIOGRAPHY:

Clemens, Gus. *Legacy: The story of the Permian Basin region of West Texas and Southeast New Mexico.* Midland: Mulberry Avenue Books, 1983.

Myres, Samuel D. *The Permian Basin, petroleum empire of the Southwest: Era of discovery* (volume 1); *Era of advancement* (volume 2). Midland: Permian Press, 1973 and 1977.

Olien, Roger M., and Diana Olien. *Life in the oil fields.* Austin: Texas Monthly Press, 1986.

Olien, Roger M., and Diana Davids Olien. *Oil booms: Social change in five Texas towns.* Austin: Texas Monthly Press, 1982.

Olien, Roger M., and Diana Davids Olien. *Wildcatters: Texas independent oilmen.* Austin: Texas Monthly Press, 1984.

Rundell, Walter, Jr. *Early Texas oil: A photographic history, 1866-1936.* College Station: Texas A&M Press, 1977.

Rundell, Walter, Jr. *Oil in West Texas and New Mexico, a pictorial history of the Permian Basin.* College Station: Texas A&M Press, 1982.

SCOPE: 6,000 photographs; a few copy prints, most vintage prints, including 25 cirkut panoramas and 160—9" high-altitude survey films. 1880 to the present, most after 1920.

GEOGRAPHIC: The museum's holdings are almost entirely from the 100,000 square miles in the Permian Basin region especially Andrews, Borden, Crane, Crockett, Culberson, Dawson, Ector, Glasscock, Hale, Hockley, Howard, Loving, Lubbock, Martin, Midland, Mitchell, Pecos, Reeves, Scurry, Tom Green, Ward, Winkler, and Yoakum counties. All county seats and many boom towns and oil camps are represented, including Best, Santa Rita, and Texon. Other states include California, Kansas, Oklahoma and New Mexico, including Eddy, Lea, and Chavez counties.

SUBJECTS: Subject headings used at the museum for petroleum include:

Biographical. Cattle industry and trade. Commerce. Conservation and proration. Drilling. Education. Equipment and supplies. Exploration. Fine arts. Geology. Geophysics. Government and politics. Housing and economic conditions. Law and legislation. Lease and land records. Marketing. Military affairs. Pipelining. Production. Refining and petrochemicals. Religion. Science. Social (cultural affairs). Transportation. Travel and exploration.

Agriculture (ranching). Animals (horses, oxen, mules). Architecture (churches, commercial, domestic, oil camp housing). Cityscapes. Events (parades, parties—oil company, WW II, oil wells blowing in). Industry (oil, gas, general commerce). Landscape. Military (personnel, forts). Organizations (Abell-Hanger Foundation). Sports and amusements (baseball, football, movies, picnics and barbecues, theater, McCamey's Rattlesnake Derby). Transportation (auto, railroad, airplane).

Big Lake Oil Company. West Texas Geological Society.

PEOPLE: The museum holds numerous portraits of persons connected with the petroleum industry in Texas and the Southwest, with special emphasis on honorees in the museum's Petroleum Hall of Fame.

Hall of Fame Honorees: George T. Abell. Robert O. Anderson. Jesse C. Barnes Sr. Horace M. "Rusty" Bayer. Ben C. Belt. Michael Late Bendedum. Charles E. Beyer. Claude W. Brown. Prentice F. Brown. Raiford H. Burton. Jno P. Butler. Dr. Jim Camp. N. Ford Champman Jr.

Carl G. Cromwell. Caven J. "Red" Davidson. Morgan J. Davis. Ronald K. DeFord. Floyd C. Dodson. Hiram M. Dow. Herbert B. Fuqua. Lovic Pierce Garrett. Arthur M. "Jack" Hagan. Berte R. Haigh. Erle P. Halliburton. Oliver C. "Kip" Harper. Houston Harte. Ray V. Hennen. Thomas Stephen Hogan. Eugene Holman. Howard R. Hughes Sr. Herbert C. Irwin. Paul Kayser. Frank H. Kelley. Haymon Krupp. Edward A. Landreth. E. Russell Lloyd. Arthur M. Lockhart. Dean E. "Cap" Lounsbery. Ralph Frank Lowe. Charles V. "Cap" Lyman. George B. McCamey. Ernest W. Marland. Joseph C. Maxwell. Stanley C. Moore. William D. Noel. Robert W. Patterson. Neville G. Penrose. Frank T. Pickrell. Wallace E. Pratt. Sid W. Richardson. James Thomas Robison. Earl G. Rodman Sr. Arch H. Rowan. Charles H. Rowan. Robert W. Russell. William G. Skelley. Hazen P. "Cap" Slagel. Samuel A. Sloan. Levi Smith. Joseph C. Trees. Fred Turner Jr. Charles D. Vertress. Van Stratton Welch. Wilbur Arthur Yeager Sr.

Charles E. Beyer. J. D. Bonner. William L. Buckley. James "Blondie" Flowers. Berte R. Haigh. Lee and Nona Jones Jr. Samuel D. Myres. Betty Orbeck. Charles Rogers. Paul O. Sill. Word "Tex" Thornton.

PHOTOGRAPHERS: E. J. Banks (Kansas). George Black (Colorado City TX). Bradshaw Studio (Big Spring). Doubleday (Wyoming). Arthur C. Flores (Texon). Howard's Studio (Pecos). Jack Nolan (Wink, Odessa, Monahans). Pinkerton Studio (Monahans). Paul Roberts (Odessa). Randolph Rubin (Midland). Bill Shoopman (Odessa).

RECORD GROUPS:

M82.1 ABELL-HANGER FOUNDATION COLLECTION. Assembled by George T. and Gladys Hanger Abell. Texas petroleum industry, including prominent individuals, equipment, pipelining, cattle and cowboys, railroads and subjects arranged by counties from the Permian Basin and West, East, and Central Texas; portraits of George Abell and immediate family; many photographs from collections of American Petroleum Institute, H. L. Lock, and Eleanor Wheeler. 275 silver gelatin prints, most copy prints. 1876 to 1979, most 1900 to 1930. PBPM # 76-93.

M82.2 ADVERTISING ARTS OF DALLAS COLLECTION. Exhibit designers contracted by the museum. Unidentified views of oil production, pipelining, and rigs used in consideration of exhibit. 75 copy prints. 1900s to 1980s. PBPM #76-76.

M82.3 ANDREWS (MIMI) COLLECTION. Aerial views; grids from West Texas and New Mexico; series of prints of Midland; made by Muldrow Aerial Survey Company. 160 cans of 9" continuous film (36,000 images); indices available. 1943 to 1952. PBPM #76-15.

M82.4 *BIG LAKE WILDCAT* COLLECTION. Newspaper. City scenes in Big Lake and Stiles; Johnny Kovach; photographs by Quinn. 15 copy prints. 1920s.

M82.5 BONNER (Mrs. J. D.) COLLECTION. Views associated with career of Mr. J. D. Bonner (d. 1955), pipeline foreman for Gulf Oil. Commercial views of pipelining and production in Breckenridge, Desdemona, and Eastland photographed by Texas Studio. 66 silver gelatin prints, many photo postcards. 1920s. PBPM #72-17.

M82.6 BUCKLEY (LIONEL) COLLECTION. Seismographic crews for Roxana (= Shell Oil); in Texas Gulf Coast and Dawson County, interiors of camps; oil camp social life and customs. 56 silver gelatin prints, some snapshots and copy prints. 1928 to 1929. PBPM #74-38.

M82.7 CARR WELL SERVICE COLLECTION. Odessa-based company. Montgomery Transportation Company, Kermit vicinity. 5 copy prints. 1930s.

M82.8 CHAPMAN (FORD) COLLECTION. Independent oil producer starting in 1929. West Texas production, cable-tool drilling crews and rigs. 18 vintage and copy prints, some color; 1—8mm film. 1930s. PBPM #76-42.

M82.9 CONTINENTAL SUPPLY COMPANY. Second-supply (equipment and materials) company in the Permian Basin, also known as the LTV Energy Company (v.i.), beginning in 1924. 5 copy prints. Ca. 1930s. PBPM #76-70.

M82.10 DONNELLEY (RICHARD) COLLECTION. Oil industry subjects and rodeos photographed by Jack Nolan. 6 copy prints. 1930s. PBPM #69-29.

M82.11 FLOWERS (Mrs. JAMES "BLONDIE") COLLECTION. Burkburnett boom days, Bartlesville OK drilling operations; various photographers. 24 silver gelatin photo postcards. 1905 to 1918.

M82.12 FORSYTHE (FRANK) COLLECTION. Early Permian Basin oil fields and derricks; nitro shooters; equipment; housing; Hendrick field Winkler County; Artesia field, Eddy County NM; Powell field and World Pool, Crockett County; JAL field, Lea County; conservation. 71 silver gelatin snapshot prints. 1929 to 1934. PBPM #76-85.

M82.13 FRAME (PAUL) COLLECTION. Texas and Pacific Railroad depot in Metz and Monahans, office operations, train derailments in West Texas. 19 copy prints. 1888 to 1938.

M82.14 GARDNER (Mrs. ROY F.) COLLECTION. Big Lake Oil Company; oil camps, including Texon and camp social life and customs. Photographed by company photographer, Arthur C. Flores. 24 silver gelatin prints, some copy prints. 1924 to 1960s. PBPM #78-12.

M82.15 GREGORY (Mrs. JOSEPH T.) COLLECTION. Snapshots and commercial views associated with the career of Texas geologist H. A. Everest. Snapshots of Rodessa-McAfuel venture; commercial views, including panoramas of Trans-Pecos. 30 silver gelatin prints. 1930s. PBPM #70-12.

M82.16 HUMBLE PIPELINE COMPANY COLLECTION. Oil camps in the Wink and Ector area, Kemper Station and Yates field, including family housing, early pipelines, offices, and equipment. 17 silver gelatin prints. Ca. 1940. PBPM #70-20.

M82.17 IRBY (BETTY) COLLECTION. Santa Rita camp social life and customs, schools. 5 silver gelatin snapshots. 1928 to 1929.

M82.18 IVY (ROBERT L.) COLLECTION. Oil-field activities in Pecos and Winkler counties; Yates and Wink fields; Frick-Reid Company; sheep ranching and Mexican laborers. Photographed by Lois G. Ivy. 18 copy prints. 1927 to 1936. PBPM #82-2.

M82.19 JOHNSON (CHARLES E.) COLLECTION. Snapshots of construction of West Texas Gulf pipeline (= the "Big Inch") from Colorado City TX to Beaumont; commercial views of construction of the Trans-Mountain pipeline in Canada. 18 silver gelatin prints. 1940s. PBPM #77-65.

M82.20 LAKE (FRANK W.) COLLECTION. Wilshire Oil Company; dinner party in Austin; opening of Wilshire-Lone Star McElroy Gasoline Plant (Crane or Upton county). Photographed by Neal Douglass (Austin). 23 silver gelatin prints. 1949. PBPM A69-10.

M82.21 LECHNER (W. W.) COLLECTION. Independent oilman. Drilling operations in Scurry and Mitchell counties. 16 silver gelatin prints, some copy prints. 1920s. PBPM #72-16.

M82.22 LTV ENERGY CORPORATION COLLECTION. Also known as Continental Supply (v.s.). Plant operations in Houston photographed by W. D. Murdy; dinner honoring Billy Morris. 35 silver gelatin prints. 1959.

M82.23 McVEAN (Mrs. J. A.) COLLECTION. Pipelining, trench digging equipment, workers, by Frank Miller (Midland) and unidentified photographer(s). 69 silver gelatin prints, many snapshots. 1920s to 1940s. PBPM #74-46.

M82.24 MYERS (SAMUEL D.) COLLECTION. Images used in researching his books. All aspects of US petroleum industry, especially Texas. 400 silver gelatin prints, most copy prints. 1880s to 1976, most 1900 to 1930. See Bibliography.

M82.25 NOLAN (JACK) COLLECTION. Oil production, rodeos, and West Texas social life and customs. PBPM #76-94.

M82.26 NOLAN (JACK) ESTATE. Predominantly studio portraits made in Odessa; some architectural views, insurance record documents, and cattle industry. 1,065 envelopes containing 4,000 film and glass negatives, many with proofs. 1942 to 1953. Itemized card file of subjects.

M82.27 ORBECK (BETTY) COLLECTION. Archivist for Permian Historical Society, who compiled this collection for the museum. Individuals and groups, cattle industry, railroad, steel and timber derricks, mule and truck freighting. Subjects arranged by county, covering Eastland County and the Permian Basin area in Texas and New Mexico. 212 silver gelatin prints, most copy prints. 1876 to present. 31 copy prints. 1920 to 1930s. PBPM #76-94.

M82.28 RADFORD (W. T.) COLLECTION. Commercial views and snapshots of Rio Bravo Gusher, fire at Spindletop Field and aftermath, November 4th 1926. Many photographed by L. L. Allen. 20 silver gelatin prints. 1926.

M82.29 RAPP (JACK) COLLECTION. Texas Torpedo Company (= Specialty Shooting Company) operated by Jack Rapp and based at Ranger; nitro shooting, mostly in Texas; camps; Rapp family in field. 38 copy prints. 1920s.

M82.30 ROGERS (CURTIS) COLLECTION. W. Lee "Pappy" O'Daniel performing in Odessa; National Tank Farm Company; oilwell fire fighting; construction of bomber base during WW II. Photographed by Jack Nolan and unidentified other(s). 95 silver gelatin prints and film negatives, many snapshots. 1920s to 1940s.

M82.31 RUNDELL (WALTER, Jr.) COLLECTION. Images used in researching his books. All aspects of US petroleum industry, especially West Texas and New Mexico. 171 prints in book, 122 additional prints; most copy prints. 1880s to 1979, most 1900 to 1940s. See Bibliography.

M82.32 SALMON (JOE) COLLECTION. News reporter on oil topics for the *Midland Reporter-Telegram*. Prominent oilmen, Yates Field in Pecos County, crews, Ohio Oil Company, and tank farms. 14 silver gelatin prints. 1960s to 1970s.

M82.33 *SAN ANGELO STANDARD TIMES* COLLECTION. Big Lake Oil Company, Santa Rita #1, #2, and #3; Texon; University of Texas lands; associated people. 8 modern prints, 7 copy prints. 1923 to 1925.

M82.34 SILL (PAUL O.; 1883-1977) COLLECTION. Timber-rig construction and crews in Humble TX and Spindletop. 13 silver gelatin prints. Ca. 1908. PBPM #75-107.

M82.35 SURVEYORS COLLECTION. Commercial views of surveyors in Texas, field shots and meetings; surveying equipment. 75 silver gelatin copy prints. 1880s to 1950s. PBPM #75-113.

M82.36 TEXACO COLLECTION. Snapshot views of oil-field production for Texas Company (= Texaco) in East Texas or Arkansas. 26 modern prints. Ca. 1920s. PBPM #75-112.

M82.37 WEBER (JOHN) COLLECTION. Oil boom towns, including Borger, Burkburnett, Desdemona, New Town, Kilgore; cityscapes and oil fields; by Gale Baker and various photographers. 99 silver gelatin prints, most photo postcards; additional photomechanical postcards. 1901 to 1920s.

M82.38 WRIGHT (Mrs. GEORGE L.) COLLECTION. Production, nitro shooters, gushers; Stephens County. 10 copy prints. 1920s. PBPM #76-40.

Albums:

M82.39 *Desk and Derrick Club of Midland, Texas.* Organization of secretaries in oil-related companies; social affairs and activities; persons; Midkiff and Midland vicinity. 72 silver gelatin prints, many associated newspaper clippings and ephemera. 1951 to 1952.

M82.40 Donnelly, A. S., comp. *Fishing trip to Great Slave Lake, Yellowknife NWT; McCullough Tool Company.* Fishing and landscapes. 15 snapshot silver gelatin prints. 1955.

M82.41 Donnelly, A. S., comp. [*Oil company parties scrapbook.*] Party scenes, unidentified people. 25 leaves containing 200 silver gelatin snapshot prints. 1953 to 1959.

M82.42 Donnelly, A. S., comp. *Scrapbook: Business activities and associates . . .* Geologist for and later vice-president of the Honolulu Company; record of the company. 100 photographs, silver gelatin and color snapshot prints, captions and newsclippings. 1928 to 1978.

M82.43 Graybeal, Joe T., comp. *Scrapbook.* Commercial views of oil fields, equipment closeups, some personnel in Andrews, Ector, Gaines, Howard, Ward, Winkler, and Upton counties, and in Lea County NM; made for Humble Oil and Refining Company (= Exxon). 137 leaves with 613 silver gelatin prints with extensive captions. 1936 to 1942.

M82.44 *Midland Oil Scouts Wives Association.* Women's auxiliary of the Oil Scouts Association; portraits of members. 12 silver gelatin prints, many associated newspaper clippings. 1951 to 1961.

Ralph W. Steen Library (N10)

Stephen F. Austin University
Special Collections Department
P.O. Box 13055
Nacogdoches, Texas 75962

409-569-4104. Contact: Special Collections Librarian.

PURPOSE: Institutional and regional history archive in an academic library collecting books and journals, manuscripts, and photographs.

HOURS: Weekdays, 8:00-5:00; Saturday, 10:00-12:30 and 1:00-6:00. Appointment recommended. Closed major and university holidays.

ASSISTANCE: Professional staff. Written and phone inquiries accepted. Electrostatic copies available. Photoduplications must be made by patron.

PUBLICATION: No publication fee. Collection credit required. Free copy of publication to library. Third-party permission required on some materials.

FINDING AIDS: Complete card index; access by general subject heading, geographic location, personal name, date.

BIBLIOGRAPHY:
The Bicentennial commemorative history of Nacogdoches. Nacogdoches: Nacogdoches Jaycees, 1976.
Ericson, Carolyn. *Nacogdoches: Gateway to Texas.* Arrow/Curtis, 1974.
MacDonald, Archie P. *Nacogdoches: Wilderness outpost to modern city, 1779-1979.* Austin: Eakin Press, 1980.
MacDonald, Archie P. *The Old Stone Fort.* Austin: Texas State Historical Association, 1981.
Maxwell, R. S., and R. D. Baker. *Sawdust empire: The Texas lumber industry, 1830-1940.* College Station: Texas A&M University Press, 1983.

SCOPE: 2,000 vintage and 1,000 copy photographs, including 10 panoramas and 70 glass lantern slides.

Type of photo	Pre-1880	1880-1899	1900-1919	1920-1939	1940-1959	1960-1986
D/A/T-types	25	30				
Film negs						100
Vintage prints	100	100	100	200	300	400
Photo albums		2	4		2	

GEOGRAPHIC: East Texas, predominantly Nacogdoches County and Nacogdoches.

SUBJECTS: Major concentration is on social life and customs at the university and the lumbering industry in East Texas.

Academia (university). Agriculture. Architecture (academic). Cityscapes. Costume. Events (disaster). Industry (lumber). Landscape (forests). Organizations. Sports and amusements.

Old Stone Fort. Stephen F. Austin University. Thompson Lumber Company.

PEOPLE: Faculty, staff, and students of the university.

Paul L. Boynton. Durst family. Legg family. Ralph W. Steen.

PHOTOGRAPHERS: Elliot A. P. Evans. Albert L. Long. Milton Turner.

RECORD GROUPS: Record groups with photographs: Thompson Lumber Company Albums, East Texas Architecture Collection, East Texas Schools Collection, and the Milton Turner Collection.

Sophienberg Memorial Museum and Archives (N20)

401 West Coll
New Braunfels, Texas 78130

Archives—512-629-1900. Museum—629-1572. Contact: Archivist.

PURPOSE: An exhibiting museum concentrating on local history and the community's original settlers led by Prince Carl Solms-Braunfels from Germany in 1845, with extensive reserve collections of manuscripts, oral history, rare books and journals, costumes, artifacts, and photographs.

HOURS: Museum—Monday through Saturday, 10:00-5:00. Archives—Tuesday and Thursday, 9:00-4:00. Appointment recommended for research in archives. Admission fee to museum and archives. Closed major holidays.

ASSISTANCE: Experienced staff. Written inquiries accepted on a limited basis; response takes roughly six weeks. Phone inquiries not accepted. Electrostatic copies available. Photoduplications must be ordered through the museum.

PUBLICATION: Publication fee charged. Collection credit required. Free copy of publication to museum. Third-party permission required on few items.

FINDING AIDS: Card index; access by subject and proper name.

BIBLIOGRAPHY:

Haas, Oscar. *The history of New Braunfels and Comal County.* New Braunfels: Sophienberg Memorial Association, 1968.

SCOPE: 10,000 photographs from various sources and 40,000 photographs in the Seidel archive (v.i.). 1860s to present.

Type of photo	Pre-1880	1880-1899	1900-1919	1920-1939	1940-1959	1960-1986
D/A/T-types	5					
Glass negs	2					
Film negs				20,000	15,000	5,000
Vintage prints	200	300	300	200		
Copy prints						
Photo albums	5	10	5			

GEOGRAPHIC: Substantial coverage of New Braunfels and of Comal County. A few photographs from Germany and communities in Comal and surrounding counties that do not represent the landscape.

Boerne. Braunfels, Germany. Buda. Bulverde. Comfort. Cranes Mill. Dale. Dripping Springs. Fischer Store. Honey Creek. Indianola. Kreuslerville. Luxello. New Braunfels. San Antonio. San Marcos. Seguin. Wimberley.

SUBJECTS: Economic and social development of the community. Seidel archives (v.i.) lists additional subjects.

Academia (class portraits, retrospective views of historic sites, student portraits). Agriculture (cotton). Architecture (commercial, domestic). Cityscapes (storefronts, street scenes, town square). Economic and social development. Events (funerals, parades, weddings). Industry (cotton mill, grocery, mills, photography studio, restaurants). Landscape. Organizations. Sports and amusements (horse racing, movies).

Dittlinger Flour Mills. Faust Hotel. Landa Park. New Braunfels Volunteer Fire Department. New Braunfels *Zeitung.*

PEOPLE: Extensive coverage of area residents in Seidel archives (v.i.), predominantly of German and Hispanic ethnicities. Servicemen from Gary AFB and Randolph AFB; few held in quantity.

Families: Baermann. Coreth. Dittlinger. Faust. Gruene. Hoffmann. Krause. Landa. Liebscher. Rennert. Scherff. Schuenemann. Staatz.

PHOTOGRAPHERS: Many Central Texas studio photographers and a few nineteenth-century German studio photographers. Texas photographers (not all held in quantity) include:

Aggieland Studio. Ankenman and Company. R. R. Ansley and S. M. Alester (OK). D. P. Barr (San Antonio). Blumel. Bolton and Mitchell (San Antonio). Brack and Raba. Callaway (San

Antonio). H. Celiax (New Braunfels). Cones (San Antonio). Oliver Cozby. Deane (Houston). Henry A. Doerr. Doerr and Jacobson (San Antonio). Doerr and Jesse (San Antonio). Doerr and Winther (San Antonio). John Dornaus (New York). Eckerskorn (San Antonio). Elliotts (Austin). Gustafson (San Antonio). Karl Halm (Seguin). Harper and Company (Galveston and Houston). O. Hegemann (San Antonio). H. Heyland (Fredericksburg). C. L. Hickson (Seguin). Hildebrandt (New Braunfels). S. B. Hill (Austin). Franz Carl Hoffmann (New Braunfels). Holland (Brenham). [H. Y.] Klenke (New Braunfels). Louvre Studios (New York). Lungkwitz and Iwonski (San Antonio). Martins Gallery (Austin). John Martinez (Johnson City). Morris Studio (San Antonio). G. Moses (New Orleans). B. Nauschuetz (San Antonio). Oiler (Denver CO). Harvey Patteson (San Antonio). Paris and Rothwell (San Antonio). Peyton's (New Orleans). Purcell (AL). Ernst Raba (San Antonio). N. Rabor (San Antonio). L. Rice (Seguin). A. Richter (Maxwell). R. C. Saur (New Braunfels). J. B. Scholl (Chicago). George Schuwirth (Austin). Schwarz and Burgert (New Braunfels). F. W. Schwarz. Otto Seidel (New Braunfels). J. Serdinko (New Braunfels). E. Simon (New Braunfels). G. W. Smith (Fredericksburg). G. W. Stepp (Fredericksburg). Hugo Summerville (San Antonio). Emil C. Thiele (Fredericksburg). [Frank] Townsend (Austin). W. T. Walker (Seguin). Weiss. R. D. Wilde (New Braunfels). N. Winther (San Antonio). Woodworth (Kenosha WI). C. J. Wright (Houston).

RECORD GROUPS:

N20.1 SEIDEL (OTTO; 1892-1972) ARCHIVES. Commercial and studio photographer in New Braunfels. Studio portraits and weddings, including many Hispanics and residents from New Braunfels and surrounding communities; approximately 10,000 names many with several sittings. Some industrial photography. Subjects include:

> American Legion. Bock Motor Company. Boy Scouts. Brauntex Theater. Churches. Commette Hoisery Mill. Elks. Gemischter Chor (Clear Spring). Gesängverein "Echo." Gode Realty Company. Landa Park. Mission Valley Mills. Missouri Pacific Railroad. New Braunfels—Chamber of Commerce, —Lions Club, —Rotary Club, —*Zeitung,* Singer Sewing Machine Company. Structural Metals Incorporated (Seguin). US Gypsum Company. United Gas Company.

1,000 vintage prints; 20,000 film negatives, most nitrate; positive microfilm copies for research; original studio card index by name. 1927 to 1968.

University of Texas of the Permian Basin (O50)

Special Collections Library
4901 East University Avenue
Odessa, Texas 79762

915-367-2318. Contact: Special Services Librarian.

PURPOSE: A special-collections library holding books and journals, manuscripts, two-dimensional art works, three-dimensional artifacts, printed ephemera, and photographs. The collection serves as the university's archive.

HOURS: Weekdays, 8:00-5:00. Closed major and university holidays.

ASSISTANCE: Professional staff. Written and phone inquiries accepted. Electrostatic copies available. Photoduplications must be ordered through the collection.

PUBLICATION: No publication fee. Collection credit must appear in publication. Free copy of publication to collection. Third-party permission required on some items.

FINDING AIDS: Inventory and descriptive list.

BIBLIOGRAPHY:

Greene, A. C. *Dallas: The deciding years, a historical portrait.* Austin: Encino Press, 1974.

SCOPE: 6,000 vintage photographs, including prints and negatives. 1900s to present.

Type of photo	Pre-1880	1880-1899	1900-1919	1920-1939	1940-1959	1960-1986
Glass negs			400			
Film negs			200			1,000
Vintage prints				5,000		1,000
Photo albums						3

GEOGRAPHIC: Predominantly the Permian Basin region, including Odessa, Midland, and Ector County. Other cities include Dallas and Fort Worth.

SUBJECTS: Economic and social development of the Permian Basin region.

PHOTOGRAPHERS: Ellen Quillan. James A. Stryker.

RECORD GROUPS:

O50.1 DALLAS PLATES COLLECTION. Street scenes, businesses, and events in the Dallas vicinity. 200 glass plates and 75 safety negatives with modern prints. See Bibliography—Greene.

O50.2 QUILLAN (ELLEN DOROTHY SCHULTZ) BOTANICAL COLLECTION. Director of the Witte Museum (San Antonio) from 1926 to 1960 and author of a number of nature study pamphlets and books. Desert plants, primarily cacti, native to the San Antonio and West Texas regions. Photographed by Quillan. 300 prints and negatives. 1917 to 1928.

O50.3 STRYKER (JOHN A.) RODEO COLLECTION. Early Texas rodeo depicting all events sanctioned by the Rodeo Cowboys Association, including bareback bronc riding, saddle bronc riding, calf roping, steer wrestling, and bull riding; also included are team roping, cutting horse competition, girl's barrel racing, and parades. 1,000 vintage glass plate negatives with modern prints. 1939 to 1945.

University Archives and Special Collections (P82)

Prairie View A&M University
W. R. Banks Library
Prairie View, Texas 77446

409-857-3119. Contact: University Archivist.

PURPOSE: Repository for university records and materials pertaining to the history, development, traditions, and activities of the university, founded in 1878 as the state's first institution of higher learning for Blacks. Materials include manuscripts, rare books, pamphlets, audio recordings, reports, minutes, memoranda, yearbooks, memorabilia, and photographs. Emphasis is on the university, local history as it relates to the university, and Black studies.

HOURS: Weekdays, 8:00-12:00 and 1:00-5:00. Closed major holidays. Appointments recommended.

ASSISTANCE: Professional staff. Written and phone inquiries accepted on a limited basis. Electrostatic copies available. Photoduplications not available at this time.

PUBLICATION: Policies under development; permissions granted on case-by-case basis.

FINDING AIDS: Preliminary inventory; access by proper name and subject.

SCOPE: 1,300 vintage and 400 copy prints, 56 negatives. 1880s to present, most 1920s to 1960s.

GEOGRAPHIC: Predominantly Prairie View, especially the campus area, and Waller County.

> **Texas counties:** Bowie. Brazos. Dallas. Falls. Fayette. Fort Bend. Freestone. Guadalupe. Harris. Jefferson. Kaufman. Madison. McLennan. Navarro. Rusk. Smith. Travis. Victoria. Washington.

SUBJECTS: History and development of Prairie View A&M University.

> Academia (university; segregated). Agriculture (Extension Service).

PEOPLE: Extensive coverage of Prairie View staff, faculty, principals, presidents, students, and visitors. Extensive coverage of Negro Agricultural Extension Service staff and of farm families.

PHOTOGRAPHERS: Ellison Photo Service (Austin). Fox Studio (San Antonio). E. C. Hunton (US Department of Agriculture Extension Service). Leon Studio (Seguin). Teal Studio (Houston). Weiss Studio (Seguin).

RECORD GROUPS:

> **P82.1** NEGRO AGRICULTURAL EXTENSION SERVICE COLLECTION. Butchering, canning, conference and workshop delegations, demonstrations, exhibits, extension agents, state leaders and employees, fairs and shows, home scenes and some domestic interiors, judging, masonry, mattress making, recreation, sanitary improvements, saw mills, and leather making, including tanning. 1919 to 1961.
>
> **P82.2** PRAIRIE VIEW CAMPUS COLLECTION. Campus, staff, faculty, activities, ROTC, and classes. 1884 to present, most 1930s to 1960s.

History of Aviation Collection (R30)

University of Texas at Dallas
McDermott Library
Floyd Road at Lookout
P.O. Box 830643
Richardson, Texas 75083

Archives—214-690-2931; Special Collections—214-690-2570. Contact: Assistant Library Director for Special Collections.

PURPOSE: A special-collections library specializing in philatelic and aviation materials collecting rare and recent books and journals, three-dimensional artifacts, paintings and prints, and photographs, including the personal library of photographer Arthur Siegel (1,500 volumes).

HOURS: Monday through Thursday, 9:00-6:00; Friday, 9:00-5:00. Closed on major and university holidays. Appointment recommended.

ASSISTANCE: Professional, specialized staff. Written inquiries accepted. Electrostatic copies available. Photoduplications may be made by patrons or ordered through the collection.

PUBLICATION: No publication fee. Collection credit required. Third-party permission required on much material.

FINDING AIDS: Complete inventory of all holdings by record groups; photographs usually indicated in collection findings guides; access by general subject heading and personal name.

BIBLIOGRAPHY:

Cleveland, Carl M. *"Upside-down" Pangborn: King of the barnstormers.* Glendale CA: Aviation Book Company, 1978.

Grooch, Stephen. *From crate to clipper: With Captain Musick, pioneer pilot.* New York: Longman's, 1939.

Ronnie, Art. *Locklear: The man who walked on wings.* South Brunswick and New York: A. S. Barnes and Company, 1973.

Rosendahl, Charles E. *Up ship.* New York: Dodd, Mead, and Company, 1931.

Rosendahl, Charles E. *What about the airship?* New York: Scribner's Sons, 1938.

Rowe, Basil L. *Under my wing: The adventurous autobiography of a great airline pilot from crates to clippers.* New York: Bobbs-Merrill Company, 1956.

SCOPE: 120,000 photographs, most vintage material, including panoramic prints, glass lantern slides, film transparencies, motion pictures, and video. Most record groups have supporting, associated manuscript and other materials.

Type of photo	Pre-1880	1880-1899	1900-1919	1920-1939	1940-1959	1960-1986
Glass negs			50			
Vintage prints			15,000	40,000	40,000	25,000

GEOGRAPHIC: Europe. South America. US. All WW II theaters.

SUBJECTS: The collection concentrates on materials relating to all aspects of aviation.

Architecture (airport). Cityscapes. Events (disaster). Exhibitions. Industry. Landscapes. Military (aircraft, WW I, WW II). Monuments. Organizations. Science. Sports and amusements. Transportation (balloons, dirigibles, helicopters, lighter-than-air craft, planes). Weapons.

Benoist Aviation. Curtiss Aviation. Major US air carriers (TWA, Pan American, Braniff). OX-5 Club.

PEOPLE: Many early aviators and pilots.

Braniff family. Dr. Hugo Eckener. Wright Brothers. Count Ferdinand von Zeppelin.

RECORD GROUPS: The collection holds more than 217 separate record groups. Many contain only a few photographs.

R30.1 ADAMS (CLARA GRABAU = Mrs. GEORGE L. ADAMS; 1884-1971) COLLECTION. Pioneer pilot. Snapshots of Adams; aircraft, many of Pan American Airlines; aviation personalities, including Zeppelin, Augustus Post, Dr. Hugo Eckener. 1920s to 1940s. 100 photographs.

R30.2 BAUCOM (BYRNE VIRCHOW; 1892-1928) COLLECTION. Aerial observer in France during WW I. Pilot training in WW I, social life and customs at Kelly Field. 200 photographs. 1917 to 1920.

R30.3 BLAKEMORE (THOMAS L.) COLLECTION. Famous US, Italian, and German lighter-than-air airships. 250 photo prints, lantern slides, and negatives; a small quantity of motion picture stock. 1919 to 1960.

R30.4 BRANIFF INTERNATIONAL AIRLINES COLLECTION. Texas-based airline, records cover period before reorganization. Pilots, crew, staff, and others associated with the airline, including Captain R. V. Carleton, Mrs. Charles E. Beard, Judge Thurman, T. E. Braniff and family; planes taking off, in flight, and details of interiors, including the Concorde, 1011, 727, and 747; Alexander Calder working on and executing designs for Braniff's Flying Colors (planes painted with his designs); airport facilities and equipment; uniforms designed by Pucci; commercial and product photography produced by Braniff's in-house photographic lab. Subject headings used in the collection include:

Ed Acker. Aircraft. Boutique. Braniff facilities. Braniff personnel. Calder. Canada. Cargo. Celebrities. Charts. Domestic points. Engineering, maintenance, operations. Equipment. European countries. Executives. Far East. Flight attendants, hostesses. Flying Colors, US. Food, in-flight service. Groups, tour agents, military, etc. Halston. Hotel division, resort property. Hong Kong. Hunting and fishing. History. Internal relations. Harding L. Lawrence. Maps. Miscellany. Miss Teenage America. Promotion, advertising. Public relations. Sales, interline tours. Slide file. Slide presentations. South American countries. Special events. Sports. Snow skiing. Training. Uniforms.

150,000 photographs including 35mm, 120, and 4x5 negatives; 35mm, 120, and 4x5 transparencies; many vintage prints; some copy prints; some motion pictures. 1940s to 1980.

R30.5 BURNS (ARTHUR C.; 1892-1970) COLLECTION. Pilot, served with the Civilian Aviation Board. Portraits of Burns, aircraft, and associates. 27 photographs. 1912 to 1963.

R30.6 CAMPBELL (MARK M.; 1897-1963) COLLECTION. Pioneer aircraft manufacturer and stuntman, later worked with Lockheed. Campbell barnstorming, planes, and portraits of associates. 34 slides, 73 silver gelatin prints. 1917 to 1961.

R30.7 CLEVELAND (CARL M.) COLLECTION. Barnstorming, used in Cleveland's biography of Clyde Pangborn. 32 photographs. 1920s to 1940s. See Bibliography.

R30.8 DOLE RACE PHOTOGRAPHIC COLLECTION. Dole Race of 1927 from Wheeler Field near Oakland CA to Honolulu HI. Planes; pilots and navigators. 32 photographs. August to November 1927.

R30.9 FANCIULLI (JEROME) COLLECTION. President of Curtiss Exhibition Company, arranged barnstorming exhibitions. Aircraft flying and on the ground, portraits of Glenn H. Curtiss and Fanciulli. 100 silver gelatin prints. 1909 to 1912.

R30.10 FULLER (WILLIAM G.; 1895-1978) COLLECTION. Founded and managed Meacham Field, managed Amon Carter Airport in Fort Worth. Portraits of Fuller and associates; governmental regulatory agencies, including the Civil Aeronautics Board, the Federal Aviation Agency, and the Civil Aeronautics Administration; Charles Lindberg; Fuller's US Army career; his family; Fort Worth Municipal Airport; Love Field; air carriers; aircraft manufacturers; domestic and military aircraft; helicopters; accidents, including news photos from Associated Press. 33 archive boxes of photographs; some motion picture stock. 1914 to 1968.

R30.11 JOHNSON (PHILLIP) COLLECTION. Foreign and domestic military aircraft used by the US Air Force for training and recognition. 211 slides. 1956 to 1961.

R30.12 LOCKLEAR (ORMER LESLIE; 1891-1920) COLLECTION. Stunt pilot who flew with William H. Pickens' International Flying Circus, later a Hollywood air stuntman. Portraits of Locklear, Pickens, W. H. Howard, and Viola Dana; barnstorming and stunts; early aircraft; US Army Air Corps; publicity stills from *The Great Air Robbery* and other films. Locklear's funeral. 390 photographs. 1910 to 1920. See Bibliography—Ronnie.

R30.13 MOORE (WYLE V.; 1898-1969) COLLECTION. Pioneer pilot and later an air traffic controller at Albuquerque NM, Meacham Field, and Love Field. Early Dallas aviation, including Love Field; military and commercial airplanes. 232 photographs. 1918 to 1960.

R30.14 MUSICK (Captain EDWIN C.; 1894-1938) COLLECTION. Chief pilot in Pan American Airlines Caribbean Division. Musick and his career as an early Pan American Airlines Clipper pilot; launching of the Liberty ship USS *Edwin C. Musick*. 23 silver gelatin prints. 1935 to 1938. See Bibliography—Grooch.

R30.15 ROSENDAHL (Admiral CHARLES EMORY; 1892-1977) COLLECTION. Pioneer US Navy aviator of lighter-than-air (LTA) craft. All aspects of LTA and some heavier-than-air (HTA) planes. Personal photographs documenting Rosendahl's career from the US Naval Academy before 1920, WW II, Goodyear Zeppelin Corporation, his Norwegian elkhounds, and friends; trips to Germany in 1938, 1955, and the 1960s; rigid airships, many of which he commanded, including the USS *Shenandoah* and its wreck, the USS *Los Angeles*, the USS *Akron*, and the USS *Macon*; German rigid airships, including the *Graf Zeppelin* and its circumnavigation of the globe in 1929, and the *Hindenberg* and its crash; rigid and semirigid airships from Great Britain and other countries; blimps, hangars, mooring masts, and accidents; Naval Air Stations, landing fields, and installations at Lakehurst NJ and other sites; Works Progress Administration projects at Lakehurst Naval Air Station; ships, submarines, and HTA, including the USS *Minneapolis*; photographs Rosendahl obtained from other collections, including the Royal Airship *R-101* in Cardington, England, Mrs. Henry Breckenridge, Herr Zaschka, Henri Farman. Additional photographs are scattered throughout the nonphotographic materials in this collection. About 100,000 photographs, mostly silver gelatin prints; some film and a few glass negatives; an extensive, complete inventory describes the collection. 1900s to 1960s. See Bibliography.

R30.16 ROWE (Captain BASIL L.; 1896-1973) COLLECTION. Pioneer pilot, founded West Indian Airline, later acquired by Pan American Airlines. Early aviation, including barnstorming and commercial passenger service, especially Pan American Airlines Clipper flights. 43 photographs. 1911 to 1956. See Bibliography.

R30.17 TIBBS (BURRELL; 1896-1965) COLLECTION. Apprenticed to Tom Benoist and graduate of the Curtiss School; a barnstormer, military pilot in WW I and instructor during WW II, and operated a flying service at Grand Prairie. Burrell Tibbs and Associates (company), personal and business airplanes, racing planes and pilots, famous aviators. 265 photographs. 1907 to 1960.

R30.18 VOUGHT AERONAUTICS COLLECTION. Member of the Ling-Temco-Vought (= LTV) complex and the second oldest aircraft company in existence today. Chance Vought (1888-1930); planes he produced, including the Vought VE-7, 8, and 9, the OS2U-3 King Fisher, the F4U-1 and A-7B, N, and E Corsair, and the F8D Crusader; the Vought plant. 200 photo prints, 77—35mm and 4x5 negatives. 1914 to 1971.

R30.19 WEDDINGTON (Colonel HARRY; 1893-1963) COLLECTION. Began his military career as instructor at Kelly Field and Payne Field MS, retired as commanding officer of Avenger Field in 1945. Personal and career portraits of Weddington and his associates; aircraft, airports, and military bases. 150 photographs. 1921 to 1964.

R30.20 YANCEY (LEWIS A.) FLIGHT TO ROME (1929) COLLECTION. Yancey was navigator and copilot on this flight from New York City to Rome. Takeoff and landing ceremonies, including portraits of Benito Mussolini; celebrations in Paris, France; return celebrations in New York; additional flights to Bermuda and Havana, Cuba. 247 photographs. 1927 to 1932.

Portfolios and books with photographs tipped in include:

R30.21 Haynes, F. Jay, photog. *Yellowstone Park: Color photogravures.* Picturesque landscapes in Yellowstone with color added. 20 photogravure plates. 1910.

R30.22 HERON (REGINALD) PORTFOLIO. *Student independent 5.* Chicago: Chicago Institute of Design, 1965. Photographs by Heron of an experimental nursery at the University of Chicago Psychology Department. 12 silver gelatin prints. 1965.

R30.23 *INSTITUTE OF DESIGN, STUDENT INDEPENDENT* PORTFOLIO. Chicago: Chicago Institute of Design, 1971. Fine art photography by various photographers associated with the institute and by Arthur Siegel. 18 silver gelatin prints. 1971.

R30.24 LANGMORE (BANK) PORTFOLIO. Cowboys working and the cowboy life in Texas, New Mexico, Montana, and Wyoming, especially at the Bell Ranch in New Mexico and the 6666 Ranch in Guthrie. 24 silver gelatin prints. 1974.

R30.25 *PHOTOGRAPHS, RHODE ISLAND SCHOOL OF DESIGN* PORTFOLIO. Providence RI: Photographic Education Society, 1963. Various photographers. 24 silver gelatin prints. 1963.

R30.26 R.S.O. *Cruise of the Lucy.* 1872. Travel album with typeset text illustrated with some art reproductions and commercial travel views of a trip up the Nile, including Karnack and Philae by Pascal Sebah and unidentified photographers. 45 albumen prints. Ca. 1870.

Fort Concho Museum (S13)

Building OQ7
213 East Avenue D
San Angelo, Texas 76901

915-657-4441. Contact: Librarian.

PURPOSE: A historic site museum with local history exhibits and holding artifacts, manuscripts, and photographs with an emphasis on the fort, which was active 1867 to 1889. Owned and operated by the City of San Angelo.

HOURS: Museum hours—Monday through Saturday, 9:00-5:00, Sunday, 1:00-5:00. Offices—weekdays, 8:00-12:00 and 1:00-5:00. Closed major holidays.

ASSISTANCE: Professional, experienced staff. Written inquiries accepted on a limited basis. Electrostatic copies available. Photoduplications may be ordered through the museum or made by the patron.

PUBLICATION: No publication fee. Collection credit required. Free copy of publication to museum. Third-party permission required on few items.

FINDING AIDS: Itemized, descriptive list of Ragsdale collection; lists for other collections under development. Access by accession number and subject.

BIBLIOGRAPHY:

Fort Concho report. San Angelo: Fort Concho National Historic Landmark, beginning 1972.

SCOPE: 5,000 vintage and copy photographs, including 16 cirkut panoramic prints and numerous framed photographs, especially charcoal-reinforced prints. 1870s to present.

Type of photo	Pre-1880	1880-1899	1900-1919	1920-1939	1940-1959	1960-1986
D/A/T-types	50					
Glass negs		30	40			
Film negs			75			
Vintage prints	200	750	1,000	1,000	100	1,000
Copy prints	240	1,320	1,320	800	240	
Photo albums	4	2	5	3	1	

GEOGRAPHIC: West Texas, especially Tom Green County, Benficklin, Fort Concho, and San Angelo.

SUBJECTS: Extensive coverage of the fort and activities there since its restoration; broad coverage of the economic and social development of the region.

Agriculture (ranching). Architecture (academic, commercial, domestic, industrial). Cityscapes. Industry (barber, ice, insurance). Landscape. Military (cavalry, encampments, personnel). Ranching (sheep). Transportation (railroad).

PEOPLE: Many area residents, including cowboys and San Angelo servicemen killed in WW II; few held in quantity.

John Colbert. Dr. Boyd Cornick. John A. Drennan. Lieutenant Charles Cooper family. Nasworthy family. M. C. Ragsdale family. Tweedy family.

PHOTOGRAPHERS: Cravey (San Angelo). Miller (Marlin). Henry Ragsdale.* McArthur Cullen Ragsdale.* William George Wedemeyer.

*See Record Groups.

RECORD GROUPS:

S13.1 COPY PRINT COLLECTION. Copy photographs gathered from the community by the museum. Economic and social development from the 1880s to the 1920s; portraits of area residents; Fort Concho social life and customs. Some duplicate vintage prints held by the museum. 1870s to present, most 1880s to 1920.

S13.2 EXHIBITION PRINTS COLLECTION. Copy prints mounted for exhibition at the museum. Views of the fort. 175 silver gelatin copy prints. 1870s to 1900.

S13.3 FORT CONCHO SLIDE COLLECTION. Modern views of activities at the fort arranged by activities, archaeology and building details, buildings and grounds, collections, property, staff, and San Angelo. 2,800—35mm color transparencies. 1976 to present.

S13.4 RAGSDALE (McARTHUR CULLEN; 1849-1945) COLLECTION. Worked with Chas. T. Vanriper in Belton before becoming an itinerant photographer in Texas during the 1870s, settled in Fort Concho in 1875 as a commercial and studio photographer until about 1910; Ragsdale's son, Henry, continued in the business. Family photographs; trick photography; Fort Concho architecture, social life and customs, and personnel; interiors; cityscapes; commercial studio photography; narrative; two picturesque landscape series, Views of the Concho Country and Views around San Angelo. Subjects in the collection:

Agriculture (ranching—wool trade). Cityscapes (street scenes). Industry (banking). Photography (trick). Services (fire protection, hotel). Transportation (streetcars).

Landon Hotel. Nimitz House Hotel.

Ragsdale albums and albums attributed to Ragsdale:

S13.4.1 [*Carte album 00.435.4.*] Studio portraits of unidentified infants, some children and adults. Most photographed by M. C. Ragsdale 37 cartes, 9 tintypes. Pre-1875 to 1880s.

S13.4.2 [*Carte album of infant portraits 00.435.6.*] Unidentified studio portraits of infants, possibly used by M. C. Ragsdale as examples of his work. 21 albumen cartes. 1870s.

S13.4.3 [*Carte album 00.435.8.*] Unidentified studio portraits and outdoor scenes of what is likely M. C. Ragsdale's traveling photographic tent; imprints of J. Serdinko, Charles T. Vanriper (Belton), and M. C. Ragsdale; probably used by Ragsdale as sample work. 40 cartes, most albumen. 1870s.

S13.4.4 [*Tintype portrait album 00.435.5.*] Unidentified studio portraits, possibly used by M. C. Ragsdale during his itinerant period to show samples of his work. 31 tintypes. 1870s.

S13.4.5 [*Ragsdale album I.*] Ragsdale family auto tours including landscapes of Grand Canyon and Davis Mountains, Nimitz Hotel, camping with a Model T Ford; flood in San Antonio, 1911; family pets. 203 silver gelatin prints. 1920s.

S13.4.6 [*Ragsdale album II.*] Ragsdale family and friends, outings, motorcycle trip. 391 photographs, most silver gelatin prints. 1920s.

S13.4.7 *Henry Ragsdale's book* [= *Album III*]. Boating on Lake Nasworthy; Boy Scout trips in West Texas, Colorado, and Michigan; houseboat. 93 silver gelatin prints; photomechanical postcards. 1937 to 1939.

S13.4.8 [*Ragsdale postcard album IV.*] Hunting, cityscapes, cattle and sheep ranching, flood around San Angelo. Most photographed by M. C. Ragsdale. 101 silver gelatin postcard prints; some photomechanical postcards. 1900 to 1910.

S13.4.9 [*Ragsdale vacation snapshot album V.*] Commercial landscapes, including 2 by J. P. Alexander; vacation snapshots, many camping scenes, made in Yellowstone WY, Ruidoso NM, Grand Canyon AZ, and Garden of the Gods CO; family snapshots made around San Angelo; water skiing. 128 silver gelatin prints, some commercial views, most snapshots. 1920s to 1940s.

2,200 photographs, including cartes, cabinets, silver gelatin prints, some stereographs; 9 albums (v.s.). 1870s to 1920s. Itemized inventory.

S13.5 RUFFINI (OSCAR) COLLECTION. Unidentified studio portraits; daguerreotypes by Pollack (Baltimore MD) and F. Dritton. 3 daguerreotypes, 2 ambrotype, 18 tintypes. 1850s to 1860s.

S13.6 WEDEMEYER (WILLIAM GEORGE) COLLECTION. Captain and commanding officer of Company F, Sixteenth Infantry Regiment at Fort Concho. Photographs by Wedemeyer. Cityscapes, military subjects, and informal portraits from Austin, Fort Concho and San Angelo, Fort Stockton, Kickapoo Springs, San Antonio, Fort Duchesne UT, Fort Huachuca AZ, Hot Springs AR, Watertown WI. 112 varnished silver gelatin glass, silver gelatin paper, and nitrate negatives. 1884 to 1890. Itemized description.

Albums: The Ragsdale collection (v.s.) also contains albums.

S13.7 [*Angelo Furniture and Undertaking Company album 75.2.*] Parade floats; storefront and interiors; San Angelo street scenes. 59 silver gelatin snapshot prints. Some manuscript captions. Ca. 1914.

S13.8 [*Angelo Furniture and Undertaking Company album II.*] Interior of stores showing products, including Victrolas, caskets, and a cooking demonstration; parade with company floats; Fort Concho before restoration; building of causeway over Concho River; San Angelo cityscapes; landscapes near Alpine and San Angelo. 74 silver gelatin snapshot prints. 1910s.

S13.9 [*Family album 00.435.9.*] Vacation portraits, possibly from Roanoake VA; scenes in San Angelo, possibly including Bismark farm; family portraits. 100 silver gelatin snapshot prints, some photomechanical postcards. 1910s.

S13.10 [*Heald family album 79.34.5.*] Commercial carte album with identified studio portraits, some by G. H. Scripture (Petersboro NH) and Stephen Piper (Manchester NH). 35 cartes, 1 tintype. 1860s to 1870s.

S13.11 [*Heald family album 79.34.5a.*] Commercial cabinet and carte album containing studio portraits. Various photographers, many from Indiana and Missouri, including E. B. Radabaugh (Huntington IN), and Ragsdale (San Angelo). 30 cartes; 28 cabinets, many collodio-chloride. 1870s to 1900s.

S13.12 [*Heald/Wood family album 79.34.4.*] Studio portaits of Heald and Wood families, various photographers from the northeastern US. 35 albumen cartes, 5 tintypes; many with tax stamps. 1860s.

Daughters of the Republic of Texas Library (S24)

Alamo Plaza at Crockett
On the Alamo Grounds
P.O. Box 2599
San Antonio, Texas 78299

512-225-1071. Contact: Director.

PURPOSE: A special-collections library holding books and journals, documents, clippings files, manuscripts, maps, architectural drawings, artworks, and photographs. Emphasis is on Texas history and the Alamo. Maintained by the Daughters of the Republic of Texas.

HOURS: Weekdays and Saturday, 9:00-5:00. Closed major holidays. Appointment preferred.

ASSISTANCE: Professional, experienced, specialized staff. Written and phone inquiries accepted. Electrostatic copies available. Photoduplications may be made by patron with advance notice and under restricted circumstances or may be ordered through the library.

PUBLICATION: No publication fee. Collection credit required. Free copy of publication to the library. Third-party permission required on some items.

FINDING AIDS: Card index, some collections have inventories; access by collection, general subject, geographic location, photographer, and proper or personal name.

BIBLIOGRAPHY:
> *One hundredth anniversary, Pioneer Flour Mills, San Antonio, Texas, 1851-1951.* San Antonio: Naylor, 1951.
> Ramsdell, Charles. *San Antonio: A historical and pictorial guide.* Austin: University of Texas Press, 1959.

SCOPE: 5,000 vintage and 7,000 copy photographs; most prints, some stereographs, panoramic prints, glass negatives, lantern slides, film transparencies, and motion pictures. 1860s to present.

Type of photo	Pre-1880	1880-1899	1900-1919	1920-1939	1940-1959	1960-1986
D/A/T-types	25	10				
Glass negs		600				
Film negs				700	800	
Vintage prints	100	300	600	1,000	1,000	400
Photo albums		1	7	1		

GEOGRAPHIC: Extensive coverage of San Antonio with some general coverage of Texas.

SUBJECTS: Substantial coverage of the Alamo, area architecture, and area military.

Architecture (commercial, domestic, domestic interiors, missions). Cityscapes. Military (personnel, encampments). Social life and customs.

PEOPLE: Limited coverage of area residents, most of Amerind, Caucasian, and Hispanic ethnicity; some early and prominent Texas individuals.

Families: Carleton. Cassiano-Perez. Gentilz-Frétellière (limited access). Houston. Tengg (limited access).

PHOTOGRAPHERS: Primarily San Antonio commercial and studio photographers.

Claude B. Aniol. D. P. Barr. H. L. Bingham. A. A. Brack. H. A. Doerr. C. J. Ekmark. Joe Elicson. Sue Flanagan. E. O. Goldbeck. Frank Hardesty. Mary Jacobson. Charles Long. A. S. Masterson. Harvey Patteson. N. H. Rose. Fred Schmidt. John M. Steinfeldt. E. K. Sturdevant. H. L. Summerville. Zintgraff Studios.

RECORD GROUPS: Descriptions provided by Martha Utterback. The library maintains both artificial collections and provenance groups.

Artificial collections:

S24.1 ALBUM FILE. Primarily family albums with photographs depicting Texas and San Antonio scenes and domestic subjects. 9 albums. 1880s to 1930s.

S24.2 GENERAL PICTURE FILE. Broad subject coverage, most relate to San Antonio. 3,000 photographs, including albumen and silver gelatin prints, stereographs, and glass plate negatives; some nonphotographic illustrations interfiled. Card index. 1860s to the present.

S24.3 PANORAMIC VIEWS FILE. San Antonio scenes and civic groups. 40 silver gelatin prints. 1910s to 1970s.

Provenance groups:

S24.4 ANIOL (CLAUDE B.) COLLECTION. Photographer and collector. San Antonio street scenes, commercial and domestic architecture, missions, and local customs. 800 photographs, including stereographs. 1870s to 1950s. Inventory available.

S24.5 DIELMANN (LEO) COLLECTION. Architect. Texas architecture, including his own work during construction and completed, historic Texas and San Antonio domestic and commercial buildings, churches, schools; many interior scenes, including domestic interiors; elevating buildings when raising the grade of Galveston Island after the 1900 hurricane. 300 photographs, including silver gelatin prints, cyanotypes, panoramic prints, and glass negatives; associated plans, drawings, records, and scrapbooks. Early 1880s to 1930s. Inventory available.

S24.6 EICKENROHT (MARVIN) COLLECTION. Architect. Texas and San Antonio architecture, including historic commercial and domestic buildings, churches, and his own work. Retrospective views from the Historic American Buildings Survey. 100 photographs; associated records and papers. 1930s to 1960s.

S24.7 EKMARK (C. J.) COLLECTION. Military photographer. Primarily military bases in Texas showing personnel, equipment, encampments, maneuvers, military parade units, buildings on army posts, horse shows, parades in downtown San Antonio; other subjects include China, Panama, and the Philippines. 1,200 vintage negatives with modern prints. 1930s to 1940s. Limited access.

S24.8 ELICSON (JOE) COLLECTION. San Antonio photographer. San Antonio scenes, local civic and patriotic events, and personalities. 2,000 photo prints. 1940s to 1970s. Unprocessed, not accessible at time of publication.

S24.9 GRANDJEAN (EDWARD) COLLECTION. Collector. Primarily San Antonio scenes, including streets, missions, customs, early illustrations, churches, domestic and commercial architecture. Photographs include lantern slides, glass plate negatives, and 1,000 prints in albums (originals not accessible, copy prints are available). 1870s to ca. 1910.

S24.10 RAMSDELL (CHARLES) COLLECTION. Historian. San Antonio scenes, buildings, customs. 50 photographs. 1870s to 1960s. See Bibliography.

S24.11 SCHMIDT (FRED) COLLECTION. Photographer. San Antonio and the missions. 500 photographs. 1930s to 1960s. Unprocessed, not accessible at time of publication.

S24.12 SCHUCHARD (ERNST) COLLECTION. Engineer. Primarily San Antonio scenes, including missions, mills, and milling. 400 photo prints, including stereographs, 100 negatives; associated scrapbook and manuscript materials. 1880s to 1950s. Limited access. See Bibliography—*One hundredth anniversary.* . . .

Fort Sam Houston Museum (S27)

US Army
Building 123, S-4 Road
San Antonio, Texas 78234

512-221-6117. Contact: Museum Director.

PURPOSE: A historic site housing an interpretive museum that identifies, collects, preserves, and exhibits materials that depict the history of the fort, the activities of the US Army in Texas, and the activities of the US Army that were influenced by Fort Sam Houston. The museum maintains the institutional archives for the fort and selected archival records on Army headquarters in Texas. Collections include artifacts, artworks, manuscripts, and books and journals.

HOURS: Wednesday through Sunday, 10:00-4:00. Closed major holidays. Appointment preferred for reserve collections.

ASSISTANCE: Professional staff. Written and phone inquiries accepted. Electrostatic copies available. Photoduplications must be ordered through the museum for educational or research purposes.

PUBLICATION: No publication fee. Collection credit required. Free copy of publication to museum. Publication permission must be obtained from Army Public Affairs Officer; museum holds reproduction rights on most materials.

FINDING AIDS: Guide to holdings; access by general subject, location, personal name, and date.

SCOPE: 5,000 vintage and 10,000 copy photographs, including 200 stereographs, 300 panoramic prints, 4,000 film transparencies, 200 postcards, and 25 motion pictures. 1855 to 1986.

Type of photo	Pre-1880	1880-1899	1900-1919	1920-1939	1940-1959	1960-1986
D/A/T-types	50	100				
Glass negs						
Film negs				500	500	2,000
Vintage prints		200	1,000	1,000	1,000	2,000
Copy prints	100	500	1,000	1,000	1,000	1,000
Photo albums	1			3	2	5

GEOGRAPHIC: Many locations represented were photographed during WW I and WW II.

Foreign countries: Northern Africa. Bataan. France. Germany. Italy. Korea. Mexico (northern provinces, 1916-1917). Pacific Islands. Philippines. Corregidor.

Texas: Southern Central Texas, including Bexar County and San Antonio, especially locations with abandoned military posts. Brackettville. Brownsville. Christine. Eagle Pass. Fredericksburg. Laredo. San Angelo.

SUBJECTS: Academia. Architecture (barracks, headquarters, military, stables). Artifacts (military uniforms, weapons). Documents. Landscape (aerial). Military (Civil War, drills, Korean War, personnel, prisoners of war, training, WW I, WW II). Monuments/memorials. Organizations. Sports and amusements. Transportation (military vehicles).

PEOPLE: Various US Army officials stationed at Fort Sam Houston and visiting dignitaries.

Benjamin F. Bowen. Gustave Dittmar. President Dwight Eisenhower. Walter Krueger. General John J. Pershing.

PHOTOGRAPHERS: Ekmark. E. O. Goldbeck. [William D.] Hornaday. C. O. Lee. E. K. Sturtevant. Nic Tengg. US Army Signal Corps.

RECORD GROUPS: Arranged into broad categories of the real estate files, including the buildings and regions of the post; the organizations and agencies files, including military units; the personality files including individuals who served at the post; and the event/chronological files, and the uniforms and equipment files.

San Antonio Museum Association (S51)

San Antonio Museum of Art
200 West Jones Avenue

Texas Science Center
HemisFair Plaza

Witte Memorial Museum
3801 Broadway

P.O. Box 2601
San Antonio, Texas 78299

512-226-5544. Contact: Registrar; for rights and photoduplications, Librarian.

PURPOSE: A consortium of three museums under one administration. The San Antonio Art Museum collects fine arts in all media, including photography. The Witte focuses on natural and regional history, including anthropology, material culture, ecology, and wildlife. The Science Center, formerly the San Antonio Museum of Transportation, collects specimens of antiquarian vehicles and science exhibits. The Witte houses the administrative offices and the reserve collections for all three museums.

HOURS: Exhibition space—Tuesday through Sunday, June 1-August 31, 9:00-6:00; September 1-May 31, 10:00 to 5:00; closed major holidays; admission fee. Administrative offices—weekdays, 9:00-5:00; appointment required.

ASSISTANCE: Professional, experienced staff. Written and phone inquiries accepted. Electrostatic copies available. Photoduplications must be ordered through the museum.

PUBLICATION: Publication fee charged. Collection credit required. Third-party permission required on a few items.

FINDING AIDS: Card index; photographs arranged by subject. Photographer index.

BIBLIOGRAPHY:
Henle, Fritz. *Casals*. Garden City NY: American Photographic Books Publishing Company, 1975. 2nd ed., 1975.

McQuaid, James, and Paulette Privitera Wilson. *An index to American photographic collections*. Boston: G. K. Hall, 1982.

Steinfeldt, Cecilia. *San Antonio was: Seen through a magic lantern, views from the slide collection of Albert Steves Sr*. San Antonio: San Antonio Museum Association, 1978.

SCOPE: 25,000 photographs, including vintage and copy prints, stereographs, cirkut panoramas, lantern slides, autochromes, and photomechanical postcards. 1860s to present.

Type of photo	Pre-1880	1880-1899	1900-1919	1920-1939	1940-1959	1960-1986
D/A/T-types	200	25				
Glass negs		100	100			
Film negs					100	
Vintage prints	1,500	5,000	5,000	7,000	1,000	1,000
Copy prints	150	150				
Photo albums	8	25				

GEOGRAPHIC: Extensive coverage of San Antonio; substantial coverage of Texas; some coverage of Mexico, Africa, and the Philippines. Photographs arranged by location.

Alaska. California (earthquake—1906). South Dakota. San Antonio River. Argentina. Cuba. Brazil. Mexico (Cd México, Monterrey, Morelia, Torreón). Nepal. Philippines. Turkey.

SUBJECTS: Primarily economic and social development of San Antonio with some coverage of Texas.

Academia (military). Animals (war dogs). Architecture (domestic, domestic interiors, governmental, jacales, missions, religious). Artifacts (Amerind). Events (events, floods). Industry (breweries, cotton mills, grain mills, saloons). Landscapes (aerial views, parks). Military (encampments, Mexican Revolution, Pershing's Punitive Expedition, WW I, WW II). Organizations (music societies, shooting clubs). Photography (picturesque, Pictorialism). Religion (churches). Services (hotels). Street scenes (Commerce Street, Houston Street). Transportation (railroad).

Alamo Mission. Alamo Plaza. Belknap Rifles Drill Team. Bluebonnet Hotel. Brackenridge Park. Brackenridge Zoo. Brooks Air Force Base. Brooks Army Medical Center. G. S. Chabot home. Chicago Columbian Exposition—1893. Concepción Mission. Espada Mission. Fort Sam Houston. Lone Star Brewery. Lone Star Cotton Mills. Menger Hotel. Henry Michelsen home. Main Plaza. Military Plaza. Mutual Life Insurance of New York (San Antonio offices). Pearl Brewery. Pioneer Mills (= Guenther Mills). San Antonio Gun Club. San Antonio Post Office (main). San Juan Capistrano Mission. San José Mission. San Pedro Springs. Scientific Shoer (E. H. Vollrath blacksmith). W. P. Stevens home (Cuba NY). Texas Military Institute. Turnverein.

PEOPLE: Many San Antonio residents, some Texas residents; few held in quantity.

Colonel Augustus Belknap family. Cassiano family. Edwin Chamberlain family. General John Lincoln Clem. H. Diess family. Gentilz-Frétellière family. Hadra-Weisselberg family. Hirschfeld family. Florence Eager Roberts. Elizabeth Sperry Roberts. Will Rogers. John M. Steinfeldt family. Vollrath family. General William Worth family.

Actors. Amerinds (Aleuts, Eskimo, Northwest Coast, Plains, Southwest). Artists. Cowboys. Hispanics (Mexican Americans, Mexicans). Filipinos. Turks.

PHOTOGRAPHERS: Most are nineteenth-century studio portraitists, especially from Texas, and commercial travel photographers making picturesque views. Some twentieth-century art photographers, including Pictorialists. Some amateur, but a few snapshot photographers. San Antonio photographers are marked with an asterisk.

Historical collection photographers: Gordon C. Abbott. D. P. Barr.* H. L. Bingham.* A. A. Brack.* A. N. Callaway.* Cones.* Cockrell (= Mexican National Railway Views). Louis de Planque (Brownsville, Matamoros, Corpus Christi). A. L. Delfraisse.* William DeRyee.* Henry

Doerr.* Frank Duncan (Marfa). Eckerskorn.* Albert Fahrenberg.* P. Fey and H. J. Braunig. E. O. Goldbeck.* E. Goodman.* Ford Green.* F. Hardesty.* Otto Hegemann.* S. B. Hill (Austin). H. B. Hillyer (Austin). M. E. Jacobson.* A. V. Latourette (Texas Scenery series). Virgil E. Lundell.* Bruno Nauschuetz. Carl D. Newton. A. C. Paris.* Paris and Rothwell.* Harvey Patteson.* L. T. Powell. Ernst Raba.* I. B. Rotherwell. C. H. Savage.* Serdinko. Jack Specht.* H. R. Stein. E. P. Steinmann.* Stillings.* E. K. Sturdevant.* H. L. Summerville.* W. C. A. Thielepape.* N. Winther.*

Art collection photographers (single print unless otherwise indicated): Berenice Abbott (2). Ansel Adams (9). Diane Arbus. Richard Avedon. Judy Bankhead (4). Lorenzo Becerril (29). Louis Carlos Bernal (8). Ron Binks. Erwin Blumenfeld. Sally Boothe. Margaret Bourke-White. Hugo Brehme (100). Dean Brown. Harry Callahan (2). David Caardenas (2*). Paul Caponigro (6). Keith Carter (2). [Augustin] Casasola and [Hugo] Brehme (78). Imogen Cunningham (11). Swain Edens. Eliot Elisofon. Morris Engle (4). Walker Evans (34). Robert Frank (2). Laura Gilpin (2). George Goodenow. Roy Hamric (68). Fritz Henle (38). Tina Henle. John Henry (2). Jim Hicks (3). Lewis Hine. André Kertész. Michael Kostiuk. George Krause (2). Dorothea Lange (2). Bank Langmore (13). Clarence John Laughlin (3). Russell Lee (5). Neil Maurer (2). John A. McConkey (2). Ray K. Metzker (2). Robert Mial. Gjon Milli. Barbara Morgan. Nicholas Nixon. Paul Outerbridge (2). Patricia Park. Irving Penn. Jack Puryear. Key Bell Reynal. Zade Rosenthal (2). Thurman Rotan (5). Steven Sellers (3). Ben Shahn. W. Eugene Smith (7). Edward Steichen. Ralph Steiner (2). Paul Strand (21). George Tice. Richard Tichich (2). Frank Tilley (12). Tim Tilton. Doris Ulman. James Van Der Zee (3). Kathy Vargas (2). Hap Veltman. Brett Weston (2). Edward Weston (6). Minor White (12). Casey Williams. Geoff Winningham (15). John A. Yatteau (2).

RECORD GROUPS: Most photographs are arranged in an artificial collection under the geographic headings of foreign countries, Mexico, San Antonio, Texas, and US; additional record groups follow.

Artificial collection:

S51.1 FOREIGN COUNTRIES COLLECTION. Argentina, Cuba, Brazil, and the Philippines; Turkey, including carte studio portraits and cityscapes by Abdullah Frères, Pascal Sebah, D.I.B.Z. (= D. Iskender and B. Zirbdji), and Rubellin. 10 inches of photoprints. 1860s to 1960s.

S51.2 MEXICO COLLECTION. Travel views by Waite, Scott, M. Lopez, and Lorenzo Becerril (Puebla); Cd México; photo postcards of Mexican Revolution; Monterrey; Morelia; Mexican Centennial and International Exposition, many photographed by Lee; Pershing's Punitive Expedition; Mexican International Railway Views photographed by Cockrell (Laredo); Torreón. 1.5 feet, many photomechanicals. 1890s to 1930s.

S51.3 SAN ANTONIO COLLECTION. Extensive coverage of economic and social life of San Antonio, especially between 1870s and 1900. Academia (German-English School). Architecture (commercial, domestic—jacales, —G. S. Choat residence, —Henry Michelson residence; La Villita reconstruction, missions—Alamo, —Concepción, —Espada, —San José, —San Juan Capistrano; Post Office; religious—Saint Mark's, —San Fernando Cathedral). Cityscapes (parks—Brackenridge Park and Zoo, —San Pedro Springs; plazas—Alamo, —Main, —Military; San Antonio River; streets—Commerce, —Houston; Cowboys in San Antonio. Economic and social life (Mexican-American). Events (floods). Industry (blacksmith, general commerce, hotels—Bluebonnet, —Menger, Lone Star Brewery, Lone Star Cotton Mill, Mutual Life of New York offices, Pearl Brewery, Pioneer Mills, saloons). Landscape (aerial views). Military (Brooks AFB, Brooks Army

Medical Center, Fort Sam Houston, US Army war dogs). Organizations (Belknap Rifles, Beethoven Männerchor, San Antonio Gun Club, San Antonio Zouaves, Turnverein). Transportation (railroad). 6.5 feet of photo prints. 1860s to 1970s.

S51.4 SAN ANTONIO (FIESTA) COLLECTION. Parades, floats, officials, and Fiesta queens and members of her court. Many photographed by Ernst Raba, Powell, Cones, and Crown Art Studio.

> *Her Majesty Katherine of the House of McGown, queen of the court of the fairies: From Prime Minister Robert R. Witt Jr.* Portraits of McGown and her attendents. 31 silver gelatin prints; newspaper clippings. 1916.

1,000 silver gelatin prints; 1 album (v.s.). 1898 to 1978.

S51.5 TEXAS COLLECTION. Broad coverage, including cattle; Fredericksburg; Galveston, including views, shipping, and the 1900 hurricane; New Braunfels, including views and hunting camp; Marfa refugee camp, Medina Dam construction, US Army, and rivers. Of note is a carte series of cityscapes photographed by R. H. Wallis and albumen prints of the 1867 hurricane photographed by Louis de Planque from Brownsville. 3 feet of photo prints, many cartes and cabinets, few snapshots. 1860s to 1940s.

S51.6 US COLLECTION. Actors, some photographed by Sarony, Mora, and Falk; Alaska, including landscapes, Eskimos, Aleuts; California, including the 1906 earthquake; the 1893 Chicago Columbian Exposition, including stereographs by Kilburn and by Underwood and Underwood; Amerinds, including Northwest coast, Southwest, Plains, baskets and totems; Spanish American War, WW I, WW II, and South Dakota. 2 feet of prints, most silver gelatin, few snapshots. 1880s to 1940s.

Additional Record Groups:

S51.7 BENNETT-GOLDTHORP COLLECTION. Civil engineer. Amateur views, mostly informal portraits. Possibly photographed by R. Lee Goldthorp. 120 glass negatives. 1897 to ca. 1907.

S51.8 BROOKS (LEONA GILBRETH) COLLECTION. Pictorialist portraits. 9 autochromes. Ca. 1910.

S51.9 CLEM (E. SULLIVAN) ESTATE. Studio portraits of the Dan Sullivan family. Various photographers, many from San Antonio. 93 photo prints, including cartes and cabinets. 1860s to 1910s.

S51.10 EVANS (WALKER; 1903-1975) COLLECTION. Photographs by Evans for the Farm Security Administration. 35 modern prints. 1930s. SAMA# 75-143-35.

S51.11 GREEN (F.) COLLECTION. WW II airplane identification slides. 540—35mm black-and-white transparencies. Ca. 1940. SAMA# 51-51-47.

S51.12 HAMRICH (ROY) COLLECTION. Landscapes in the Big Thicket. Photographed by Hamrich. 68 photographs. SAMA# 81-127-249.

S51.13 HENLE (FRITZ; b. 1909) COLLECTION. Portraits of cellist Pablo Casals. Photographed by Henle. 25 photographs. 1970s. See Bibliography. SAMA# 82-16-274.

S51.14 LANGMORE (BANK) COLLECTION. Photographs by Langmore from his series, *The Cowboy Collection*. 13 photographs. 1970s. SAMA# 80-39-177.

S51.15 MUSEUM COLLECTION. Copy photographs and art reproductions of the museum's holdings arranged by collection. 2,000 photo negatives and transparencies. Ca. 1926 to present.

S51.16 NUERNBERG COLLECTION. Landscapes and portraits of natives in Africa; Zulu tribe. 68 silver gelatin prints. Ca. 1950.

S51.17 RABA (ERNST; 1874-1951) COLLECTION. Exhibition prints, including, Pictorialist portraits, landscapes, contrived images such as *Judas Iscariot* and *St. Peter*. Photographed by Raba and submitted to various Pictorialist salons during the 1930s. 40 photo prints in various art processes; most mammoth. 1930s.

S51.18 SPECHT (JACK; b. 1896) COLLECTION. Photojournalist for the *San Antonio Light*. Missions, courthouses, wildlife, and aviation in San Antonio and Texas. 1,170 negatives, including glass, nitrate, and safety; 325 vintage prints; film transparencies and motion picture stock. 1910s to 1950s. SAMA# 81-135.

S51.19 STEVES (ALBERT, Sr.) COLLECTION. Street scenes in San Antonio. 200 copy prints from lantern slides. 1890s. See Bibliography—Steinfeldt.

S51.20 STREZISHAR COLLECTION. Strezishar family, his real estate business, including properties he sold and his employees in Chicago and Texas. 1900 to 1920s. 319 glass transparencies with viewer.

Albums and portfolios:

S51.21 [Chabot, Fred, comp.?] [*Chabot family album I.*] Commercial or amateur views of the Chabot and other families' homes, San Antonio views, including picturesque San Antonio River, Guenther's Mill, and Chabot family members. 52 albumen prints. 1889.

S51.22 [Chabot, Fred, comp.?] [*Chabot family album II.*] San Antonio River; homes, including interiors. 49 albumen prints. 1889.

S51.23 [Chabot, Fred, comp.?] [*Chabot family album III.*] Scenes in San Antonio, including the Lewis Mill Bridge, Galveston wharfs, and domestic interiors. 54 albumen prints. 1890.

S51.24 [Chabot, Fred, comp.?] [*Chabot family album IV.*] San Antonio homes and orphanage. 9 silver gelatin prints. 1890.

S51.25 [Chabot, Fred, comp.?] [*Chabot family album V.*] Commercial travel views of Yosemite National Park. Photographers include Haynes and Fiske. 12 silver gelatin prints. 1890.

S51.26 [Chabot, Fred, comp.?] [*Chabot family album VI.*] Commercial travel views in Great Britain, Germany, and France. Photographs by Frith Series, George Washington Wilson, and X Phot. 1880s.

S51.27 Cooke, Lieutenant Fred. *Manila*. Cityscapes, landscapes, and natives in the Philippine Islands; camp life of the 39th US Infantry. 63 gelatino-chloride prints, 1 tintype. 1898 to 1902. SAMA# 77-15-4.

S51.28 *Dem Jubelpaare John C. Dielmann und Frau zur silbernen Hochzeit: Gewidmet von den Activen des S. A. Liederkranz.* San Antonio, 1902. Members of the San Antonio Liederkranz photographed by Ernst Raba. 30 silver gelatin prints.

S51.29 [*Pat Jones album.*] Commercial views of damage to buildings in San Francisco after the 1906 earthquake and a few general views of the city. 83 silver gelatin prints. 1906.

S51.30 Strand, Paul, photog. *Photographs of Mexico* [= *The Mexican portfolio*]. 2nd ed., DeCapo, 1964. 20 photogravures. 1940s.

S51.31 *Views of Fort Sam Houston and vicinity.* Picturesque views of San Antonio missions, landscapes, and Fort Sam Houston buildings and parade grounds. 13 cyanotypes. Ca. 1890. SAMA# 79-91-141.

S51.32 *Visit of general officers of the Republic of Mexico to the Fourth US Army area.* Commercial group portraits and views of receptions and military reviews. 24 silver gelatin prints, typescript captions. 1953. SAMA# 66-127-39.

S51.33 White, Minor, photog. *The Jupiter portfolio.* Self-published, 1975. 12 silver gelatin prints. 1947 to 1971. SAMA#76-107-28.

S51.34 Winningham, Geoff. *Portfolio two.* 15 silver gelatin prints. SAMA# 78-779-104ff.

Institute of Texan Cultures (S63)

University of Texas
801 South Bowie
P.O. Box 1226
San Antonio, Texas 78294

512-226-7651. Contact: Photo Librarian.

PURPOSE: The institute is committed to the preservation and interpretation of Texas' diverse cultural heritage through its collection of original historical artifacts, vintage and copy photographs, museum exhibits, publications, and audiovisual programs.

HOURS: Exhibit space—Tuesday through Sunday, 9:00-5:00; closed Christmas. Research library—weekdays, 8:00-5:00; appointment recommended for use of the research library, closed major holidays.

ASSISTANCE: Professional, experienced staff. Written inquiries accepted. Electrostatic copies available. Photoduplications must be ordered through the institute.

PUBLICATION: No publication fee. Credit line requested. Third-party permission required on some material.

FINDING AIDS: Card index; access by ethnicity, date, general subject, and photographer. Visual access file arranged by date of acquisition, except *San Antonio Light* collection maintained in provenential order. Files connected through accession number.

BIBLIOGRAPHY:

Institute of Texan Cultures, pub. *Catalog of products and services.* San Antonio. Updated annually.

Institute of Texan Cultures, pub. *A teacher's guide to the Institute of Texan Cultures.* San Antonio.

Institute of Texan Cultures, pub.; various authors. The Texians and the Texans series. San Antonio, beginning in 1972. A series of pamphlets, each oriented around a single ethnic group: *The Afro-American Texans. The Anglo-American Texans. The Belgian Texans. The Chinese Texans. The Czech Texans. The Danish Texans. The English Texans. The German Texans. The Greek Texans. The Indian Texans. The Irish Texans. The Italian Texans. The Jewish Texans. The Japanese Texans. The Mexican Texans. Los Mexicanos Texanos. The Norwegian Texans. The Polish Texans. The Spanish Texans. The Swiss Texans. The Syrian and Lebanese Texans. The Wendish Texans.*

SCOPE: 35,000 copy negative/print pairs; 28,000 vintage glass negatives with modern prints; 28,000 vintage safety negatives with modern prints. Many of the copy photographs are copies of nonphotographic processes such as paintings, manuscripts, or printed materials. Quantities listed for date and ethnicity include both photographic and nonphotographic materials; quantities for subject description have been limited as much as possible to photographic images.

Type of photo	Pre-1880	1880-1899	1900-1919	1920-1939	1940-1959	1960-1986
Glass negs				25,000		
Film negs				5,000	13,000	
Vintage prints						5,000
Copy neg/print	7,500	9,000	14,000	55,000	1,500	3,500
Photo albums					3	3

GEOGRAPHIC: Extensive coverage of Texas; although many locales represented by few images. Extensive coverage of San Antonio, arranged by street and building.

Texas cities (with more than 10 entries): Alice. Amarillo. Austin. Ballinger. Bandera. Bastrop. Beaumont. Beeville. Belton. Boerne. Brackettville. Brady. Bremond. Brenham. Brownsville. Camden. Castroville. Cat Springs. Comfort. Corpus Christi. Cotulla. Crystal City. Cuero. Dallas. Danevang. Denison. Dickinson. Eagle Pass. El Campo. El Paso. Fayetteville. Floresville. Fort Bliss. Fort Sam Houston. Fort Worth. Fredericksburg. Galveston. George West. Goliad. Granger. Hallettsville. Harlingen. Hempstead. Houston. Johnson City. Karnes City. Kenedy. Kerrville. La Grange. Laredo. Louise. Nederland. New Braunfels. Norse. Panna Maria. Port Aransas. Port Arthur. Raymondville. Rockport. Refugio. Riviera. Round Top. San Angelo. San Antonio. San Benito. San Marcos. Schulenburg. Seguin. Serbin. Shiner. Simmons. Sisterdale. Terry. Thurber. Victoria. Waco. Wesley. Wharton. Wichita Falls. Wortham. Ysleta.

Texas counties (with more than 10 entries): Austin. Bee. Bexar. Bosque. Brazos. Brewster. Cameron. Comal. Crosby. Dimmit. El Paso. Fayette. Gillespie. Kendall. Kenedy. Kerr. La Salle. Lee. Live Oak. McCulloch. Medina. Menard. Nueces. Refugio. Victoria. Webb. Wharton.

Texas regions: Big Bend. Guadalupe River. Hill Country. Red River Valley. Rio Grande and Rio Grande Valley.

Non-Texas locales: Mexico (Juarez, Matamoros). Minor coverage of European countries from which Texans emigrated.

SUBJECTS: The institute collects images that help to explain the development of Texas as a state. Many pictures collected are art reproductions of prephotographic imagery. Hence, the institute's copy files make it an excellent source for the study of nonphotographic imagery pertaining to Texas, gathering in one place reproductions from many sources of the work of McArdle, Huddle, Gentilz, Lungkwitz, Remington, and Russell, and the Texas imagery of other artists who worked largely outside the state. The institute also holds many reproductions from *Harper's* and *Frank Leslie's Illustrated* magazines.

The institute's photographic images include extensive coverage of famous and anonymous Texans, their occupations, the environment they fashioned, and the events in their lives that have defined a life that is characteristically Texan. Because of the large *San Antonio Light* collection, many of the subjects are biased towards San Antonio.

Academia (schools, schoolrooms, students—by locale, teachers, universities). Agriculture (cotton, farms, gardens, irrigation, ranches, rice). Animals (cattle, chickens, dogs, donkeys, horses, longhorns, mules, sheep). Architecture (by locale or structural composition; banks—by locale, barns, cabins, churches, city halls, construction, courthouses—by county, domestic—by locale, fencing and gates, forts, harbors and docks, jacales, kitchens, synagogues, water towers, water wells, windmills). Art reproductions (paintings). Cemeteries and gravestones. Cityscapes (street scenes). Costume (by ethnicity and date; bathing suits, hats, shoes, uniforms). Domestic activities (cooking, home economics, tea parties). Events (accidents, fires, parades and floats, floods, HemisFair—1968, hurricanes, Mexican Revolution, murders, publicity stunts, religious pageants, shootings, tornados, wedding and anniversaries). Government (city, courts, fire department, law enforcement, legislatures, police, post office). Historic sites (monuments, Spanish missions). Industry (advertising, bakeries, banks—by locale, bars and saloons, factories, laundries, markets, mills, newspapers, offices, oil, street merchants, restaurants, retail stores). Labor relations (Auditorium Riot—1939, communists, Depression—1930s, strikes). Landscape (aerial views, rivers, trees). Military (bases, concentration and internment camps in Texas, personnel—by country, USAF, US Army, US Navy). Organizations (Boy Scouts, choirs and choral societies, clubs, conventions, fraternal organizations, Freemasons, Girl Scouts, YMCA, YWCA). Personal activities. Politics (campaigns, conventions, elections, politicians). Religion (altars, churches, convents, synagogues). Services (hospitals—by locale, hotels—by locale, medical, orphanages, telephone, water utilities). Social life and customs (debutantes, dining, drinking, Prohibition). Sports and amusements (baseball, basketball, boxing, circuses, contests, concerts, dancers—by ethnicity, dolls, entertainers, festivals, fishing, football, golf, hunting, movies, opera, picnics, radio, swimming, tennis, theater, toys). Transportation (automobiles, airplanes, bicycles, boats, bridges, carriages, carts, railroads, street cars, wagons).

San Antonio subjects: Alamo and the missions. Alamo Downs Race Track. Battle of the Flowers parade. Brackenridge High School. Brackenridge Park. Bright Shawl Tea Room. Brooks AFB and Medical Center. Curtiss Aeroplane and Motor Company. Fiesta San Jacinto. Gunter Hall. Incarnate Word College. Kelly AFB. Menger Hotel. Military Plaza. Municipal Auditorium. Plaza Hotel. Residences designed by the Ayres Brothers. San Antonio River. San Fernando Cathedral. Tower Life Building. Veramendi Palace. Union Stockyards. Witte Memorial Museum.

Texas subjects: Denison Dam. King Ranch. Love Field (Dallas). Medina Dam. La Mota Ranch. Los Pastores (religious pageant). Pershing Expedition. Southern Pacific Railroad. Texas A&M University. Texas capitols.

PEOPLE: The institute holds thousands of images of Texas individuals and families; few held in quanity. Emphasis is on major figures in Texas history, community leaders, and politicians. This area can also be approached through generic headings, ethnic groups, and proper names.

Generic headings: Aged. Artists. Artisans (all media, fine arts and handicrafts). Authors. Bakers. Bank robbers. Blacksmiths. Businessmen. Cattlemen. Children. Cowboys. Clergymen. Criminals. Debutantes. Emmigrants and immigrants. Family portraits. Firemen. Governors. Infants. Journalists. Judges. Laborers. Lawyers. Mayors. Musicians. Nuns. Nurses. Photographers. Physicians. Pilots. Politicians. Presidents—US. Sheriffs. Texas Rangers. Women. Youth.

Ethnicities (photographic and nonphotographic): Afro-American (1,300). Amerind (Alabama-Coushatta, Apache, Kiowa, Tigua; 1,100). Anglo-American (21,500). Austrian (25). Arab (25). Belgian (400). Canadian (25). Central American (25). Chinese (300). Cuban (25). Czech (600). Danish (350). Dutch (250). English (400). French (800). German (35,500). Greek (400). Gypsy (25). Hungarian (40). Irish (350). Italian (450). Japanese (250). Jewish (550). Korean (25). Lebanese (300). Mexican (2,300). Norwegian (300). Philippine (100). Polish (650). Portuguese (25). Prussian (25). Russian (100). Scottish (200). Spanish (1,100). South American (25). Swedish (250). Swiss (100). Welsh (25). Wendish (200). Yugoslav (100).

Individuals and families: Akagi family. Governor James Allred. Atlee B. Ayres. Robert M. Ayres. Gutzon Borglum. Pompeo Coppini. Douglas "Wrong Way" Corrigan. Archbishop Arthur Drossaerts. Governor Miriam Ferguson. John Nance Garner. Guenther family. Daisy and Violet Hilton. Hooge family. Janic Jarrett. President Lyndon Johnson. Hermann Lungkwitz. Maury Maverick. Elisabet Ney. Nimitz family. Governor W. Lee O'Daniel. Persyn family. Dan Quill. Charles K. Quin. Franklin and Eleanor Roosevelt. Theodore Roosevelt. George Saunders. Steves family. Emma Tenayuca.

PHOTOGRAPHERS: Photographic styles include snapshooters, newspaper photographers, art photographers, commercial studio portraitists, and trick photographers. Many Texas photographers, though few are held in quantity.

Texas photographers: Barr (Barr and Wright, 21). George Bartholomew (15,000 for the *Light*). George Beach (15). Art Bennack. H. L. Bingham (13). Birdsong and Potchernick (5). A. A. Brack (7). Herbert Brandt (16). Alonso N. Callaway (20). Cones (5). Court Studio (7). Louis de Planque (29). William DeRyee (6). Dickinson Photo (8). Doerr (Doerr and Jacobson, Jacobson; 62). Elicson (31). A. M. Fielder (6). Sue Flanagan (50). William Fritz (8). Fred A. Gildersleeve (14). Gustafson (50). Frank Hardesty (50). H. Heyland (12). S. B. Hill (8). H. B. Hillyer (50). F. C. Hoffmann (12). Peter Hooge (18). W. D. Hornaday (30). Ray Howell (15). Jordan's (6). H. D. Klenke (7). Jean Lange (12). Alexis V. LaTourette (9). C. O. Lee (5). Lewison Studio (8). J. D. Litterst (5). Lungkwitz and Iwonski (17). Harvey R. Marks (12). A. S. Masterson (6). Louis Melcher (24). C. A. Meyer (5). Joseph Daniel Mitchell (50). Bruno Nauschuetz (11). William J. Oliphant (10). Pack Brothers (6). A. C. Paris (Paris and Rothwell, 12). Parks (11). Harvey Patteson (80). Charles Petter (19). John Poindexter (12). Mose L. Potash (14). Ernst Raba (35). McArthur Cullen Ragsdale (12). Friederike Rechnagel (25). P. H. Rose (Rose and Zahn, Zahn; 11). N H. Rose (4). Rothwell (9). Robert Runyan (9). Rust Studio (6). C. H. Savage (7). Frank J. Schlueter (22). F. W. Schwarz (6). [Otto and J.] Seidel (24). J. Serdinko (72). Erwin E. Smith (9). W. D. Smithers (19). Jack Specht (15,000 for the *Light*). Steinle (8). Studer's (12). Studio Graphics (6). C. L. Sull [Sult?] and Sons (6). Hugo L. Summerville (7). John R. Swanton (7). Odd Magar Syverson (12). Tauch (Tauch and Pannewitz, 5). Jno P. Trlica (15). R. H. Wallis (6). S. C. Wilson (9). Nicholas Winter (9).

Non-Texas photographers: Mathew Brady. Fredricks (NY). Alexander Gardner. William S. Soule.

RECORD GROUPS:

S63.1 FOLKLIFE FESTIVAL PHOTOGRAPHS. Documents made by the institute of its annual summer folklife festival. 5,000—35mm negatives and contact prints. 1968 to present.

S63.2 INSTITUTE OF TEXAN CULTURES COLLECTION. Documents of institute exhibitions and functions. 1,000—35mm negatives and contact prints. 1968 to present.

S63.3 *SAN ANTONIO LIGHT* COLLECTION. Photomorgue of this San Antonio paper. Cityscapes, events, and persons. 24,000 glass plate negatives with modern prints. 1924 to 1940. The institute also holds a complete run of bound volumes of the *Light* for the same period.

Texarkana Historical Society and Museum (T58)

219 State Line Boulevard
Texarkana, Arkansas/Texas 75501

214-793-4831. Contact: Registrar.

PURPOSE: A historical society with an exhibition space collecting book and manuscript materials, photographs, and other material culture artifacts pertaining to local history.

HOURS: Weekdays, 10:00-4:00. Closed federal holidays.

ASSISTANCE: Experienced staff. Written inquiries accepted. Electrostatic copies not available. Photoduplications may be made by patron or ordered through the museum.

PUBLICATION: No publication fee. Collection credit required. Free copy to museum. Third-party permission required on a few items.

FINDING AIDS: Card index and inventory.

SCOPE: 7,000 photographs, most vintage prints. Late nineteenth century to present, most ca. 1900.

Type of photo	Pre-1880	1880-1899	1900-1919	1920-1939	1940-1959	1960-1986
Glass negs		700	800			
Film negs				100		
Vintage prints		2,000	3,000	2,000	1,000	1,000
Copy images						5,000
Photo albums				5	5	

GEOGRAPHIC: Extensive coverage of Texarkana and some coverage of the surrounding area, including Bowie County and Miller County AR.

SUBJECTS: Photographs document the economic and social development of the region with an emphasis on the cotton industry.

Agriculture. Albums. Amusement and entertainment. Archaeology. Black history. Beauty in Texarkana. Bridges and highways. Business. Cemeteries. Climatic. Communications. Clubs and organizations. Documents. Drawings and sketches. Education (medicine, law, banking). Farm life. Fire Department. Flora and fauna. Folk artists. Furniture. Governmental. Homes. Homesteads. Hotels. Industry. Miscellaneous landscape. Main Street, Texarkana. Military. Monuments. Moore House (Ace of Clubs). Postcards. Parks and recreation. Portraits. Prints. Quadrangle. Religion. Schools. Texarkana. Texarkana Historical Museum. Transportation. Unknown residences. Visiting politicians and celebrities.

PEOPLE: Many local residents; few held in quantity, with the exception of Scott Joplin. Substantial coverage of Black ethnicity; Amerinds represented through documents of the archaeological excavation of Caddoan Indian mounds in the area.

PHOTOGRAPHERS: Bob Burns. Cyril Casteel. Owen English. Gus Ghio. Don Hale. Meg McKinney. James Tennison.

Smith County Historical Society Archives (T82)

125 South College
Tyler, Texas 75702

214-592-5993. Contact: Chairman of Archives.

PURPOSE: A local history society with an archive of local history photographs, manuscripts, and books.

HOURS: Wednesday, 1:00-4:30; first Saturday, 1:00-4:30; or by appointment. Closed major holidays.

ASSISTANCE: Volunteer staff. Written inquiries accepted. Electrostatic copies available. Photoduplications may be made by patrons or ordered through the society.

PUBLICATION: No publication fee. Collection credit and accession number required in publication. Free copy of publication to the society. Society holds reproduction rights on all materials.

FINDING AIDS: Card index inventory. Some images arranged by subject.

BIBLIOGRAPHY:

Chronicles of Smith County, Texas. Tyler: Smith County Historical Society and Historical Commission. Beginning 1961.

SCOPE: 4,500 photographs, many postcard prints. 1850s to 1940s.

Type of photo	Pre-1880	1880-1899	1900-1919	1920-1939	1940-1959	1960-1986
D/A/T-types	8					
Glass negs						
Film negs						
Vintage prints	20	400	1,750	1,750		

GEOGRAPHIC: Substantial coverage of Smith County, including Grand Saline and Tyler.

SUBJECTS: Economic and social development of the region with an emphasis on agriculture and the cotton industry.

Agriculture (cotton). Architecture. Cityscapes. Industry (general commerce). Sports and amusements (baseball).

PEOPLE: Many postcard portraits made of area residents posed outdoors; substantial coverage of the William J. Goodman family.

PHOTOGRAPHERS: Most photographs in the archives are by the local commercial photographer, Henry York. Other photographers include:

Alonzo N. Callaway. C. A. Davis. Alfred Freeman. Harper and Company (Dallas). Edwin W. Mims.

RECORD GROUPS:

T82.1 YORK (HENRY) COLLECTION. Mostly portraits of area residents which document the social life, customs, and people of Tyler and Smith County. 3,500 silver gelatin postcard prints. 1907 to 1915.

Armstrong Browning Library (W10)

Baylor University
700 Speight Avenue
P.O. Box 6336
Waco, Texas 76706

817-755-3566. Contact: Librarian.

PURPOSE: A research center housing the "world's largest" literary archive of Robert and Elizabeth Barrett Browning materials, Browning ephemera, and scholarship about the poets. The library holds 4,751 manuscripts and letters, 12,465 books and journals, 149 two- and three-dimensional artifacts, and 2,500 photographs.

HOURS: Weekdays, 9:00-12:00 and 2:00 to 4:00; Saturday, 9:00-12:00. Closed major holidays. Appointments preferred.

ASSISTANCE: Professional staff. Written and phone inquiries accepted. Electrostatic copies not available. Photoduplications must be ordered through the library.

PUBLICATION: No publication fee. Collection credit required. Free copy of publication to library. Third-party permission required on some materials.

FINDING AIDS: Partial card index and descriptive listing of photographs; access by photographer and personal name.

BIBLIOGRAPHY:

Kelley, Philip, and Betty Coley. *The Browning collections: A reconstruction.* [Waco]: Armstrong Browning Library and the Wedgestone Press, 1984.

Thomas, Charles Flint. *Robert Browning's poetic art objects: An illustrated compendium.* Doctoral dissertation, Baylor University, 1979.

SCOPE: 2,000 vintage and 400 copy photographs, including lantern slides and film transparencies. 1800s to present

Type of photo	Pre-1880	1880-1899	1900-1919	1920-1939	1940-1959	1960-1986
D/A/T-types	1					
Vintage prints	35	200	300	300	300	300
Copy prints	60	200	200			
Photo albums	80					

GEOGRAPHIC: England. Italy.

SUBJECTS: Most materials pertain to the Brownings, their work, and the Armstrong Browning Library. Many of the images reproduce the landscape or art object that inspired one of the Brownings' poems.

Academia (library). Art reproduction (paintings, sculpture). Architecture (domestic interiors, European). Landscape. Organizations (literary societies). Photography (travel).

Armstrong Browning Library (building, events). Palazzo Rezzonico (Robert Wiedeman Barrett Browning's home).

PEOPLE: Elizabeth Barrett Browning (1806-1861). Robert Browning (1812-1889). Browning family. Andrew Joseph Armstrong.

PHOTOGRAPHERS: Alessandri. Alinari Fratelli. Herbert Barraud. Alexander Bassano. Julia Margaret Cameron. Elliot and Fry (London). William H. Grove. P. A. Hood. C. Naya.

RECORD GROUPS:

W10.1 BROWNING PHOTOGRAPHS. A collection of photographs owned by the Brownings and sold at Sotheby's in 1911. Studio portraits of Browning family, including Robert W. B. Browning, Sarianna Browning, Elizabeth Barrett Browning, Robert Browning; associates, including Samuel Taylor Coleridge, Blanche Roosevelt, and others; residences and cities where the Brownings lived; photo prints by Julia Margaret Cameron inscribed to the Brownings: *"Stella"*, *(Mrs. Herbert Duckworth)*, *Friar Lawrence and Juliet, La Madonna Aspettante, Annie Thackeray, Lady Ritchie*, and two portraits of Robert Browning. Various photographers from England and Italy. 74 photographs, including cartes, cabinets, mostly albumen prints; many art reproductions. Early 1860s to 1890s.

W10.2 Browning, Robert, comp. [*Album.*] 1 volume with 31 albumen prints. [1880?] Art reproductions of classical Mediterranean vases, one photographed by Giorgio Sommer.

W10.3 INSTITUTIONAL FILE. An artificial collection of photographs gathered by the library. Library activities and famous visitors; the building; record photographs of the library's holdings; images of places and objects that inspired the Browning's poetry; nineteenth century travel photographs of Italy by Alinari and unidentified photographer(s); art reproductions; one group of performance stills from the Oxford Playhouse production of *Pippa Passes*, 1968; 1930s travel views of Italy, places, and objects associated with the Brownings by P. A. Hood. 6 feet (3,000 photoprints), some nonphotographic materials interfiled. 1880s to present.

W10.4 LANTERN SLIDE COLLECTION. Slide presentation on Browning and the Browning collection at Baylor. 50 lantern slides with modern prints. 1930s.

Texas Collection (W20)

Baylor University
Fifth and Speight Street
P.O. Box 6396
Waco, Texas 76706

817-755-1268. Contact: Head, Historical Manuscripts and Archives.

PURPOSE: A special collection, university library concentrating on materials that record the ways in which life, in all its aspects, is lived and has been lived within Texas. The library collects books (80,000 volumes), periodicals (950 titles), newspapers, maps and charts, theses and dissertations, directories, governmental records, personal manuscripts, oral history, genealogical materials, photographs, and other artifacts.

HOURS: Weekdays, 9:00-5:00. Closed major, academic holidays. Appointment recommended.

ASSISTANCE: Professional, experienced staff. Written inquiries accepted. Electrostatic copies available. Photoduplications may be made by the patron or ordered through collection.

PUBLICATION: No publication fee. Collection credit and identification number required. Free copy to collection. Third-party permission required on some material.

FINDING AIDS: Inventories for collections indicate photographs. Card index for photographs; access by proper name, geographic location, general subject.

BIBLIOGRAPHY:
Conger, Roger N. Gildy Remembered. *The Baylor Line* (April 1976).
Conger, Roger N. Photographs tell the story: Gildersleeve, Waco. *The Baylor Line* (April 1976).

SCOPE: More than 100,000 photographs in every major format, most with supporting manuscripts or other materials. 1870s to present.

Type of photo	Pre-1880	1880-1899	1900-1919	1920-1939	1940-1959	1960-1986
D/A/T-types	100	20				
Glass negs			1,000+	1,000		
Film negs			500	1,000	2,000	2,000
Vintage prints	1,000	5,000	20,000	30,000	20,000	10,000
Photo albums		5	10	5	5	3

GEOGRAPHIC: Extensive coverage of Texas, especially Central Texas, Waco, and McLennan County. Many Texas locales held in limited quantity.

Texas: Austin (40). Beeville (6). Bellmead (15). Belton (22). Big Bend National Park (16). Bosqueville (6). Brazos River. Bruceville (7). Comfort (21). Corsicana (12). Crush (6). Dallas (18). Decatur (6). El Paso (15). Fort Worth (12). Fredericksburg (12). Galveston (44). Gatesville (18). Glen Rose (9). Hillsboro (18). Independence (80). Kimball (8). Kountze (10). La Grange (19). Lubbock (21). McGregor (8). McLennan County (17). Marlin (19). Mexia (7). Moody (6). Paisano Baptist Encampment (21). Pluto (7). Rising Star (7). Round Rock (15). Salado (12). San Antonio (100). Sour Lake (24). Sparta (7). Vaughn (18). West (7). Wichita Falls (49). Waco (3,480).

Non-Texas: New Mexico (25). Mexico (Carmen, Campeche; 25).

SUBJECTS: Extensive coverage of Texas history and Baylor University.

General subjects: Academia (primary, secondary, university). Agriculture (cotton). Animals (dinosaur fossils). Architecture (academic, churches, courthouses, dams, general commerce, religious). Cityscapes (street scenes). Events (fires, flood, natural disasters, parades, Wichita Falls tornado—1979). Industry (banks, general commerce, publishing). Landscape (rural). Military (encampments). Organizations. Plants (flowers). Religion. Services (communication— telegraphy, fire protection, hotels). Sports and amusements (baseball, church socials, football, picnics). Transportation (auto, interurban, rail, streetcar).

Waco subjects: Agriculture. Architecture. Businesses. Churches. Cityscapes (bird's eye view, street scenes). Events (floods, tornado—1953). Homes. Military (encampments, VA hospital). Organizations (Freemasons). Parks, playgrounds. Public servants (fire, police). Schools, colleges. Street scenes. Theaters and halls. Transportation (railroads, auto accidents). Urban renewal.

Baylor University subjects: Art collection. Athletics (baseball, basketball, football—by year, intramurals, track and field). Departments (physics, School of Law, College of Dentistry, College of

Medicine, School of Nursing, University Medical Center). Beauty nominees. Buildings (aerial views). Events (American Ideals Conference, best dressed contest, centennial celebration, commencements—by year, Founder's Day, homecoming). Organizations (fraternities, clubs, Board of Trustees). Students.

ALICO (Amicable Life Insurance Company Building). Artesian Manufacturing and Bottling Company (= Dr. Pepper Company). Benevolent and Protective Order of Elks. Camp MacArthur. Cotton Palace. Hippodrome Theater. H. O. T. Fair. Missouri, Kansas, and Pacific Railroad. Paul Quinn College. Rich Field. Southern Traction Company. Texas Christian University. *Waco Examiner. Waco Tribune-Herald.* Young Men's Business League.

PEOPLE: Many individuals, especially Baylor faculty, staff, and students; few held in quantity. Minor coverage of Huaco Amerinds.

Andrew Joseph Armstrong. Rufus Columbus Burleson. Vice President George Bush. President Dwight Eisenhower. F. A. Gildersleeve family. Wilby T. Gooch. Leon Jaworski. Abner Vernon McCall. Audie Leon Murphy. Governor Pat Neff. Thomas Zaner Parrish. President Harry Truman. W. J. Wimpee.

PHOTOGRAPHERS: Many snapshooters; some commercial photographers, most from Waco.

Brookshire Banks. C. R. Bullock. Paul Currier. Jervis C. Deane. Windy Drum. Ruth Frank. Fred A. Gildersleeve. Chris Hansen. W. D. Jackson. Fred Marlar. Thompson.

RECORD GROUPS: Virtually all record groups have some supporting materials. Processed collections have an inventory outline.

W20.1 Collections with a small amount of photographs: Frank Elisha Burkhalter items. Janie Pender (= Mrs. Jack C.) Castellaw papers. Madison Cooper papers. Duer-Harn family items. Kate Harrison Friend papers. Emma Louise McDonald (Mrs. Jesse) Harrison papers. Hicks-Hall-Harmon family papers. William J. and Hattie Green Hill papers. Joseph Moritz Maedgen papers. Ann Oldham papers. Edward and Kate (née McCall) Rotan papers. Speight-McKenney family items. Winchester family items.

W20.2 ACREE (FRED; 1878-1947) PAPERS. Poultry farmer, rancher, real estate developer and politician. Snapshots, studio portraits of individuals and groups, many informally posed, humorous scenes; A&M Kountry Store, businesses and scenes in Galveston, South Bosque, Waco, McGregor, and Coryell County. Photographers, most unidentified, include Justus Zahn (Galveston), Deane (Waco), Jackson (Waco), and various Texas others. 137 glass negatives with modern prints; 19 folders containing 600 items, predominantly silver gelatin snapshot prints, some tintypes, cartes, cabinets, and silver gelatin photo postcards. 1876 to 1941, most ca. 1900.

W20.3 ALEXANDER (JAMES PATTERSON; 1883-1948) PAPERS. Chief Justice, Texas Supreme Court. Snapshots and studio portraits pertaining to Alexander's career. 15 silver gelatin prints. Ca. 1900 to 1948.

W20.4 ARBON (LEE) ITEMS. Early aviation at Rich Field. 50 silver gelatin copy prints. Ca. 1907 to 1912. Unprocessed.

W20.5 AYNESWORTH (JOSEPH HICKMAN; 1874-1940) COLLECTION. Studio and snapshots portraits of Aynesworth and family. 14 silver gelatin prints. 1900 to 1920. Unprocessed.

W20.6 AYNESWORTH (KENNETH HAZEN; 1873-1944) PAPERS. Waco physician and archaeologist. Studio portraits, including many cartes and cabinets from Louisville KY and Waco vicinity. Various photographers. 100 photo prints, including tintypes, albumen cartes, and silver gelatin snapshots. 1870s to 1920s. English military buildings. 6 color prints. 1948. Unprocessed.

W20.7 BANKS (BROOKSHER) COLLECTION. Baylor student. Retrospective views of historical buildings and architectural details in Waco with captions. Photographed by Banks. 75 silver gelatin prints. 1971 to 1972. Unprocessed.

W20.8 BARNARD (GEORGE; 1818-1883) PAPERS. Early Texas settler and merchant. Portraits, including Charles Barnard, Lawrence Sullivan Ross, Harvey Barnard Jr., and Annie Ross. 7 photo prints, 4 daguerreotypes, 1 ambrotype.

W20.9 BAYLOR-CARRINGTON FAMILY PAPERS. Studio and snapshot family portraits, including Addie Hamer Baylor, George Wythe Baylor, Henry Weidner Baylor, John Robert Baylor, John Roy Baylor, Sue Adams Baylor Illg, Jessie Kelso; pioneer homesteads. 200 prints, many cartes and cabinets, silver gelatin prints; 1 commercial cabinet album with 12 prints, most loose; draft of register. 1860s to 1910s.

W20.10 BAYLOR PUBLIC RELATIONS OFFICE FILES. Prints made by this office documenting university departments, student life, and campus events. Index at the Texas Collection, photographs on file at the Public Relations Office.

W20.11 BEATON (ALEXANDER; 1820-1895) PAPERS. Corsicana lawyer, partner with R. Q. Mills. Snapshot and studio portraits. 75 silver gelatin prints, some cabinets; most severely water damaged; register. Ca. 1890 to 1920.

W20.12 BLEDSOE (JULES; 1898-1943) COLLECTION. Waco-born Black baritone and composer. Publicity portraits of Bledsoe, productions of various musicals and operas, snapshots, and studio portraits by Rodriguez (Paris). 150 silver gelatin prints; register. Ca. 1940.

W20.13 BRANN (WILLIAM COWPER; 1855-1898) COLLECTION. Publisher of *The Iconoclast* (Waco, 1894-1898) and essayist. Brann, his funeral, his home; modern reenactment of the Gerald-Harris duel. 27 silver gelatin prints. Late 1890s, 1960s.

W20.14 BROWN (OWEN) PAPERS. Studio and snapshot portraits of Brown, including childhood and military; Beulah Brown; Tom Brown; Trice family; aviation. 1,500 photo prints, most silver gelatin, many copy prints, some cartes, cabinets, and photo Christmas cards; register. 1860 to 1950s, most ca. 1900.

W20.15 BURLESON (RUFUS COLUMBUS; 1823-1901) PAPERS. President of Baylor University. Studio portraits of Burleson and family. 1 commercial carte album with 24 albumen cartes and tintypes; register. Late 1860s.

W20.16 CAMP MacARTHUR PHOTOGRAPHS. Military personnel, including officers at their desks and social life and customs at the base; Rich Field; airplanes in flight. Most photographed by Gildersleeve. 43 silver gelatin prints; register. Ca. 1918.

W20.17 CHILTON (FRANK BOWDEN; 1845-1926) COLLECTION. Member of Hood's Texas Brigade; lawyer who lived in Marlin and Houston. Snapshots, movie still and publicity prints; travel views in Wyoming and Mexico; military portraits. 4 cabinets, 1 mammoth tintype, 75 silver gelatin prints and photo postcards; draft of register. 1870s to 1950s.

W20.18 COKE (RICHARD; 1829-1897) PAPERS. Governor of Texas. McCelvey family album containing snapshot and studio portraits; interiors; Jack McCelvey. 1 commercial cabinet album with snapshots pasted in, 80 silver gelatin prints, 1 tintype. 1860s to 1940s, most ca. 1900.

W20.19 CONNER (GEORGE S. AND JEFFIE O. A.) PAPERS. Portraits of Blacks; Black education in Texas, including the Paris TX public school. 33 albumen and silver gelatin prints; register. Early 1880s to 1940.

W20.20 COPPINI (POMPEO; 1870-1951) ITEMS. Italian-born sculptor, noted for his Littlefield Fountain. Art reproductions of Coppini's sculpture, some with Coppini; Littlefield Fountain with Old Main in background at the University of Texas at Austin. 74 silver gelatin prints; 1 album with 88 silver gelatin prints. 1920s. Unprocessed.

W20.21 COTTON PALACE PAPERS. Cotton Palace buildings, parades, and associated people. Many photographed by Gildersleeve. 65 vintage and modern silver gelatin prints. 1912. Unprocessed.

W20.22 CROW (CECIL H. "CAPPY") COLLECTION. Aerial views of Baylor stadium and a dam; copy slides of artworks. 73 film negatives, 5 silver gelatin prints, 100 color copy transparencies. Unprocessed.

W20.23 DAWSON (GEOFFREY SAMUEL) PHOTOGRAPHS. Snapshots of steam and electromotive locomotives, rolling stock, cabooses, derailments. Arranged by line, including Missouri, Kansas, and Texas, Burlington-Rock Island, Santa Fe, Texas and Pacific, Southern Pacific, Ringling Brothers, Barnum and Bailey Circus, various small Texas lines. 500 photo prints, most silver gelatin snapshots, some color snapshots; some negative material. 1950s to present (open collection). Unprocessed.

W20.24 EBY (FREDRICK) COLLECTION. Educator and author of articles and books on Texas pedagogy. Copy photographs and retrospective views of historical educational buildings in Texas, including ruins of Baylor College (for women) at Independence and Texas Military Institute. Arranged by county. 100 silver gelatin prints. Ca. 1940s. Unprocessed.

W20.25 EDMOND (KATHERINE "KATE" McKINNON) PAPERS. Unidentified portraits. 5 folders. Ca. 1945.

W20.26 GRAVES-EARLE FAMILY PAPERS. Studio portraits by various Texas photographers, upper New York, San Jose CA, and one by Taber (San Francisco CA); snapshot portraits and family scenes; WW I soldiers returning to Waco. 36 prints, including cartes, cabinets, and albumen and silver gelatin prints; 1 snapshot album with 100 silver gelatin prints; 1 commercial carte album; 1 daguerreotype; 1 ambrotype. 1860s to 1920s.

W20.27 EDWARDS (MARGARET ROYALTY; 1895-1969) COLLECTION. Baylor alumna and author. Snapshot and studio portraits, many tipped into her wedding and baby memory books; WW I and Red Cross uniforms. 100 silver gelatin prints. Ca. 1918. Unprocessed.

W20.28 EMMONS (MARTHA LENA) COLLECTION. Snapshot and studio portraits of Emmons and family; B. F. Goodnight family; Mansfield TX. 100 photo prints, including cabinets, tintypes, and silver gelatin prints. 1880s to late 1960s. Unprocessed.

W20.29 GEOLOGY AUDIO-TUTORIAL COLLECTION. Student papers for a geology course illustrated with photographs; papers describe the relation of the locale to the land. Snapshots generally include portraits of citizens, landscape, and architecture. 759 papers containing 5,000 photographs, including type-C prints and color slides. Mid-1970s to present (open collection). Arranged by city.

W20.30 GROVE (ROXY HARRIET; 1889-1952) PAPERS. Missionary, professor of music at Payne College, Baylor, and Hardin-Simmons. Portraits of Grove and others. 12 silver gelatin prints. Ca. 1940.

W20.31 GUITTARD (FRANCIS GEVRIER; 1867-1950) PAPERS. History professor at Baylor. Studio portraits of Ewing family; Arthur, Claude, Francis, Victor, and Virgil Guittard and the Guittard family; most from Ohio, especially New Bedford OH. 1 daguerreotype, 1 ambrotype, 300 silver gelatin prints; 1 commercial cabinet albumen with 100 cabinets, 30 cartes. 1860s to 1910s, most ca. 1900. Unprocessed.

W20.32 HAASS (HERMAN E.) PAPERS. County official and businessman in Castroville. Portraits, cityscape of Castroville. 12 photographs, including 3 cartes, 1 stereo.

W20.33 HARRINGTON (JOHN THOMAS; 1858-1947) PAPERS. Physician and founder of Simmons University (= Hardin-Simmons) at Abilene. Studio portraits, many by various Texas photographers. 75 silver gelatin prints. 1900 to 1930s.

W20.34 HUCKLEBERRY (E. R.) PHOTOGRAPHS. Snapshots from Waco, Mount Calm, and Palacios. 100 silver gelatin prints. Ca. 1910s. Unprocessed.

W20.35 JOHNSON (F. ARTHUR; 1874-1971) ITEMS. Music instructor. Portraits of Johnson, his wife, students, teachers, and recital programs. 14 silver gelatin prints; 1 album of 19 silver gelatin snapshot prints with handwritten notes. 1920-1971.

W20.36 JOHNSON (JOHN OSCAR BIRGEN "SWEDE") ITEMS. Railroad machinists and locomotives. 12 silver gelatin prints. Ca. 1930s. Unprocessed.

W20.37 JONES (CLITUS) PAPERS. Snapshots of military personnel, trenches, ambulances, aerial reconnaissance, armaments, ruins of buildings, maneuvers in France during WW I; snapshot album, *My Memory Book*, with family and scenes from Austin and the University of Texas at Austin. 1,000 silver gelatin prints, some stereo pairs; 200 film negatives; 1 album containing 400 silver gelatin prints. 1916 to 1920. Unprocessed.

W20.38 LANE (ROY ELLSWORTH) PAPERS. Architectural studies of buildings in the Waco vicinity; some portraits. 20 silver gelatin prints; 1 album with 100 silver gelatin prints. 1910s to 1920s. Unprocessed.

W20.39 McLENNAN COUNTY TUBERCULOSIS ASSOCIATION COLLECTION. Portraits of physicians and staff members. 19 silver gelatin prints, some color. 1930s to 1940s. Unprocessed.

W20.40 MURPHY (AUDIE LEON; 1924-1971) COLLECTION. Actor in movie Westerns. Portraits, military service, awarding of Legion of Honor; continuity and dialogue with stills from Murphy's acting career with Universal Pictures. 100 silver gelatin copy and publicity photographs; 200 silver gelatin stills. 1930s to early 1970s, most 1950s.

W20.41 NEY (ELISABET; 1833-1907) COLLECTION. German-born sculptor. Ney, her family, and her home in Austin; art reproductions of her sculpture. 25 photographs, most albumen and some silver gelatin, 1 salted-paper print. 1853 to 1900. Unprocessed.

W20.42 PARKER FAMILY AND FORT PARKER COLLECTION. Snapshots of the restored Fort Parker in Groesbeck; Cynthia Anne Parker and family members, many art reproductions; Amerinds. Many copy prints from the Western History Collection at University of Oklahoma. 100 silver gelatin prints, some negatives. 1900 to 1940. Unprocessed.

W20.43 PERRIN FAMILY COLLECTION. San Antonio family photographs, portraits, and homestead; early Texas braggadocio humor photo postcards. Photographers include H. L. Bingham (San Antonio). 150 photo prints; 2 albums containing 200 prints. 1860s to 1940s. Unprocessed.

W20.44 REAGAN-PETTIGREW FAMILY PAPERS. Portraits of men, including Civil War leaders and others identified. Many photographed by Bankes (Little Rock AR) and by McCabe (Little Rock AR). 52 albumen cartes, 1 tintype, 1 cabinet. Ca. 1865.

W20.45 REAVES (MARTHA REBECCA "MART"; 1894-1922) COLLECTION. Snapshot portraits and family outings. 75 silver gelatin prints. 1910s. Unprocessed.

W20.46 ROSS FAMILY PAPERS. Studio portraits of the Harrington family. Photographers include Carter (Bryan) and various others. 15 photo prints, including albumen and collodio-chloride cabinets. 1860s to 1910s.

W20.47 *ROUND-UP* COLLECTION. Staff and student life gathered for Baylor student annual. Interfiled with general picture collection.

W20.48 SALLEE (ANNIE JENKINS; 1877-1967) PAPERS. Missionary of the Southern Baptist Convention to China. Snapshots and commercial views; interiors of the Sallee home in China; William Eugene and Annie Jenkins; cattle; China; family albums. 200 prints, mostly silver gelatin snapshots, some color; 2 albums containing 100 prints. 1897 to 1967.

W20.49 SCHLEICHER FAMILY COLLECTION. Studio portraits, including Sarah Williams. Various Texas and Massachusetts photographers. 500 photo prints, many cartes and cabinets. 1880s to 1910s. Unprocessed.

W20.50 STASNY FAMILY PAPERS. Studio and snapshot portraits, largely from Texas. 250 photographs, including albumen prints, cartes, and cabinets. 1870s to 1900s. Unprocessed.

W20.51 SWAN (MARGARET) PAPERS. Swim team coach. Commercial and snapshot images of the Cygnets of San Antonio, a synchronized swimming team. 500 photographs, most silver gelatin prints, some color negatives. 1960s to 1970s. Unprocessed.

W20.52 TEGENER FAMILY COLLECTION. Studio portraits from Germany and Austin. Photographers include H. B. Hillyer's Art Rooms (Austin) and the Austin Photograph Company (W. D. Stone and William T. Waggoner). 9 albumen cartes and cabinets. 1866 to 1880. Unprocessed.

W20.53 VETERANS ADMINISTRATION MEDICAL CENTER COLLECTION. Buildings and physical plant of the hospital, including some aerials; services; publicity photographs; events. 1,000 silver gelatin prints; 200 film negatives. 1947 to 1970s. Unprocessed.

W20.54 WALKER (JAMES) PHOTOGRAPHS. Studio photographer in Waco. Studio portraits by Walker, Deane, and W. D. Jackson. 23 photo prints, most albumen, many cabinets. 1870s to 1910s. Unprocessed.

W20.55 WILKES (WILLIAM ORVILLE) ITEMS. Portraits of medical men tipped into a type-script, *History of the Waco Medical Association*. 12 silver gelatin prints. Ca. 1880 to 1920.

W20.56 WILLIS (JIMMIE) NEGATIVES. Professional photographer in Waco. Baylor University, including Football team, Homecoming parade, PALs club, Pat Neff, baseball players, graduation, Daps club, campus, and buildings. 2,290—4x5 film negatives. Ca. 1920s. Unprocessed.

W20.57 ZAHORIK (GORDON) COLLECTION. Texas Electric Railway, the Interurban trolley service operating in Waco, Dallas, and Fort Worth; cars and tracks. 40 silver gelatin prints. 1947. Unprocessed.

Albums:

W20.58 Anderson, Nan Allene. *Baylor via the Kodak.* Snapshots of Baylor University architecture, classroom and dormitory interiors, students (many female), outings, sports. 639 collodio-chloride and silver gelatin prints. 1900 to 1909.

W20.59 [*Chamberlin family album.*] Family lived in the Evergreen Community; snapshot family portraits, servicemen from Rich Field, aerial views of Waco, Baylor University, and Rich Field. 100 silver gelatin prints. 1914.

W20.60 Conger, Mrs. Robert E., comp. *Cavalcade of Texas.* Texas Centennial Exposition album containing peformance photographs and behind the scenes portraits of actors in and out of costume for this production of reenacted Texas history. Conger was a member of the cast. 200 silver gelatin snapshot prints. 1936.

W20.61 Durkee, Ralph Henry. [*Durkee albums.*] Colonel in US Army; training camp for US Army Infantry at University of Michigan during WW I; Durkee family; snapshot portraits of acquaintences of Durkee with associated letters and official documents. 3 albums containing 750 silver gelatin snapshots. 1898 to 1960s. Unprocessed.

W20.62 Edwards, Elmer J., Jr. *Texas and Southwestern Localism.* Amateur photographs from around Texas, including Dallas and Fort Worth. 1 bound term theme with 25 silver gelatin prints tipped in, additional halftone images. 1943.

W20.63 Embree, E. D., and Thomas B. Eaton, photog. *The Flying Owls: Rice Institute from the air.* Houston: Rice Institute, 1921. Aerial photographs of Rice University buildings. 12 silver gelatin prints.

W20.64 Eubank, Champe Carter. [*Album.*] Snapshot portraits, landscapes, water scenes, Victorian architecture and interior scenes with people; in Waco and at the New England resort home of Mr. and Mrs. Edward Rotan. 546 silver gelatin and cyanotype prints. Ca. 1890 to 1910.

W20.65 Evangelia Settlement, comp. [*Albums.*] Day care center in Waco for children from low-income, often single-parent families. Center buildings, faculty, children, classroom scenes, and activities at the center. Many photographed by Gildersleeve and Boyd. 2 albums containing 250 photographs. 1920 to 1970s.

W20.66 Gildersleeve, Fred A. [*Personal albums.*] Personal photographs belonging to photographer Fred A. Gildersleeve. Many informal snapshots of Gildersleeve's life, including outings, friends, and vacations; self-portraits; domestic interiors; Railroad YMCA; early professional work, including still lifes of flowers, animals, and landscapes. Most from Texas, some from the East Coast, including New York and Rhode Island, and from the West, including Yellowstone and California. 3 albums containing 600 silver gelatin prints. 1903 to 1907.

W20.67 *Bonnie MacLeary Scrapbook.* A presentation album given to Governor Pat Neff containing art reproductions of works by Texas-born sculptor, Bonnie MacLeary, and one portrait of MacLeary; assembled by the Texas Centennial Club of New York. 21 silver gelatin prints. 1936.

W20.68 Pickett, Harold Lord, Sr. *Four years of Baylor life: Seen and told by the Kodak.* Snapshots of Baylor University architecture, interiors of classrooms, faculty, students, student activities, and medical school labs; Columbia University. 440 silver gelatin prints, most captioned. 1906 to 1910.

W20.69 Shelton, Horace H. [*Albums.*] Major in US Army, later an educator in the Philippines, lawyer in Austin. Military service at Camp Bowie and Europe during WW I, figure studies, Hawaii; schools, Manila cityscapes, landscapes, and farming in the Philippines; China. 5 albums with 1,000 silver gelatin snapshot and amateur photographs; 40 loose prints. Most 1901 to 1902, some to 1960s.

W20.70 Stribling, Davis. [*Albums.*] Baylor University, architecture, students and faculty, student life and customs; Gurley family; Amicable Building. 750 silver gelatin prints in 2 albums. 1907 to 1910.

W20.71 Sutton, Roy F. *The saga of the bloody Barrows with Bonnie Parker.* 1943. Post-mortem closeups of Bonnie Parker and Clyde Barrow showing wounds. Typescript term paper with 6 silver gelatin prints, additional half-tone prints. 1934.

W20.72 Willis, Louise. *Baylor* [and] *Chinese missionary experience.* Amateur photographs of student life and customs, students and faculty, commencement at Baylor University; vacation photographs; landscape, architecture and architectural detail, including the Great Wall, Ming tombs, shrines and temples, people, and cityscapes in China. 250 silver gelatin prints, some amateur panoramas, some hand-colored. Early 1920s to 1940s.

Wallisville Heritage Park (W35)

Interstate 10, Exit 807
P.O. Box 16
Wallisville, Texas 77597

409-389-2252. Contact: Executive Director.

PURPOSE: A complex of restored historic structures which houses historical exhibits and collections of artifacts, artworks, manuscripts, books and journals, and photographs.

HOURS: Weekdays and Saturday, 8:00-5:00. Closed major holidays. Appointment preferred.

ASSISTANCE: Experienced staff. Written and phone inquiries accepted. Electrostatic copies available. Photoduplications may be made by the patron or ordered through the center.

PUBLICATION: No publication fee. Collection credit required. Third-party permission required on few items.

FINDING AIDS: Card index and descriptive item listing; access by general subject, location, photographer, personal name, and date. Photographs arranged by accession group.

SCOPE: 40,000 vintage photographs, 9,000 copy photographs. 1870s to 1960s.

Type of photo	Pre-1880	1880-1899	1900-1919	1920-1939	1940-1959	1960-1986
D/A/T-types	4					
Film negs					40,000	
Vintage prints		500	500	500	200	
Copy images		2,000	4,000	2,000		

GEOGRAPHIC: The Atascocita region of southeastern Texas, including Chambers, Harris, and Liberty counties.

Anahuac. Baytown. Cove. Dayton. Double Bayou. Galveston. Hankamer. Houston. Liberty. Moss Bluff. Mont Belvieu. Old River-Winfree. Smith Point. Wallisville. Winnie-Stowell.

SUBJECTS: Architecture (academic, domestic, general commerce, religious). Historic sites (retrospective views). Domestic activities. Industry (ship building).

PEOPLE: The majority of the collection's holdings is studio portraiture. Virtually all families in Chambers County are represented; many families from surrounding counties are represented. Few individuals held in quantity.

Families: Barber. Barrow. Davis. Dugat. Dunman. Eley. Fisher. Jackson. Kilgore. Lawrence. Mayes. Middleton. Morgan. Moss. Scherer. Shepard. Silva. Stubbs. Van Pradelles. Wallis. White. Whitehead. Wiggins. Wilcox. Williams. Wooten. Wothy.

PHOTOGRAPHERS: Curley Atkinson (= Crystal Studios, Liberty).* Gus Bedler (Liberty). Thomas Brady (Raywood). John V. Clay.* Donaldson Studios. Figley (La Porte). Gustafson (Beaumont). Harper and Company (Houston). Herbter Studio. Montgomery Joseph.* Robertson and Donaldson. P. H. Rose (Galveston). Rose and Zahn (Galveston). G. R. Yancey (Beaumont).

*See Record Groups.

RECORD GROUPS:

W35.1 CLAY (JOHN V.) COLLECTION. Retrospective views of historic structures in the region photographed by Clay. 1960 to the present.

W35.2 CRYSTAL STUDIO COLLECTION. Archives of studio photographer Curley Atkinson (Liberty). 40,000 film negatives. 1940s to 1960s.

W35.3 JOSEPH (MONTGOMERY) COLLECTION. Chambers and Harris counties. Photographs by Joseph. Vintage photographs. 1914 and 1970.

W35.4 LA FOUR (TAVIA KILGORE) COLLECTION. Wallisville and area families. Vintage photo prints.

W35.5 SILVA (LORRAINE BARROW) COLLECTION. Area families, buildings, events. Copy negatives and prints.

Star of the Republic Museum (W40)

Park Road 12 (Off FM 1155)
P.O. Box 317
Washington, Texas 77880

409-878-2461. Contact: Curator of Education.

PURPOSE: An exhibiting, history museum specializing in the period of the Texas Republic (1836-1846) and to a small extent local history; collecting rare and recent books and journals, manuscripts, paintings, costumes, artifacts, and photographs. Administered by Blinn College on the grounds of Washington-on-the-Brazos State Historical Park which is operated by Texas State Parks and Wildlife Department.

HOURS: March 1 to Labor Day, 10:00-5:00; September through February, closed Mondays and Tuesdays. Appointments to view reserve collections recommended.

ASSISTANCE: Professional staff. Written and phone inquiries accepted. Electrostatic copies available. Photoduplications are handled on a case by case basis.

PUBLICATION: No publication fee. Collection credit required. Free copy of publication to museum. Third-party permission required on few items.

FINDING AIDS: Card index, itemized inventory of holdings by collection.

SCOPE: 400 photographs in major formats, most prints. 1860s to 1910s, most 1860s to 1870s.

Type of photo	Pre-1880	1880-1899	1900-1919	1920-1939	1940-1959	1960-1986
D/A/T-types	10					
Film negs			5			
Vintage prints	100	75	25			
Copy prints	5	10	10	10		
Photo albums	3		1			

GEOGRAPHIC: Central Texas, including Anderson, Brenham, Gay Hill, Independence, Plainview, and Washington-on-the-Brazos.

SUBJECTS: Predominantly portraiture.

Academia (women's college). Architecture (retrospective views of historic structures). Artifact (pottery). Landscape (aerial).

PEOPLE: Predominantly early settlers of the area, their families, some coverage of veterans of the Texas Revolution.

S. S. Ashe family. Brockman-Meador families. Cooper-Mayer families. Jaquith family. E. E. Groce family. Anson Jones family. Sullivan-Miles family.

PHOTOGRAPHERS: Most unidentified, some Texas photographers.

Lone Star Gallery (Fred W. Bartlett, Bartlett and Hooker; Galveston). Marks (Houston).

RECORD GROUPS:

W40.1 ANDERSON HOMES COLLECTION. Retrospective views of historic homes and buildings built between the 1840s and 1870s in Anderson. 50 photographs. 1970s. SRM# C149.

W40.2 [*Captain S. S. Ashe family carte album.*] Ashe family, including members of the Anson Jones family. 18 albumen cartes, 10 tintypes. Ca. 1870. SRM# 72-164.

W40.3 BROCKMAN COLLECTION. Pearl Lance Meader, Theron Lance Meador, and other family members. 16 photographs. Ca. 1900. SRM# 79-184.

W40.4 COOPER-MAYER COLLECTION. Eugene Bibb Wallace family portraits, including Eugene Bibb Wallace, Catherine Veazey Wallace, Eugenia Wallace, Leon Blum Wallace, John Basil Gossard, and others.

> *Eugenia Wallace album.* Snapshot portraits of the Wallace family of Gay Hill and the burning of the girls' dormitory in Plainview. 254 silver gelatin prints with handwritten captions; inscribed "To Gene from Pat." 1917. SRM# 83-82.

45 photographs, including prints and negatives; 1 album (v.s.). Ca. 1915. SRM# 83-82, 84-37.

W40.5 *P. and S. Diller.* Album includes Jaquith family and Roland Diller. 57 photographs. 1863.

W40.6 *Eliza Ellen Groce carte album.* Portraits of various Groce family members and unidentified sitters. Many Texas photographers, including Lone Star Gallery (Fred W. Bartlett, Bartlett and Hooker; Galveston) and Marks (Houston). 34 albumen cartes, 1 tintype. 1864 to 1870. SRM# 81-36.

W40.7 HISTORICAL TEXAS POTTERY COMPANIES COLLECTION. Art reproductions of pottery made by various, noted pottery manufacturers of the nineteenth century. 12 photographs. 1970s. SRM# 498.

W40.8 LONG COLLECTION. Studio portraits of the Sullivan family, including Mary Ann Miles, Sara Jane, Rebecca, and James L.; the Miles family, including J. W. and Sullivan; and the Charles N. Smith family. 2 daguerreotypes, 1 ambrotype, 4 tintypes, and 1 photo print. 1860s. SRM# 566.

W40.9 MARCUS MALLARD COLLECTION. Copy photographs and a few retrospective views of buildings and notable persons in Washington TX and Navasota. 35 silver gelatin photographs. 1870s to 1910s, 1950s. SRM# 77-70.

W40.10 NAVASOTA COLLECTION. Navasota street scenes. 12 copy photographs. 1890s. SRM# C145.

W40.11 WASHINGTON-ON-THE-BRAZOS STATE PARK COLLECTION. Aerial views of the park site. 16 silver gelatin prints. Ca. 1965. SRM# C-500.

Wichita Falls Museum and Art Center (W85)

Two Eureka Circle
Wichita Falls, Texas 76308

817-692-0923. Contact: Registrar.

PURPOSE: An art, science, and regional history museum. The history collections relate primarily to North Texas.

HOURS: Exhibit space—Tuesday through Friday, 9:00-4:30; Saturday, 10:00-4:00; Sundays, 1:00-5:00. Reserve collections—Tuesday through Friday, 8:30-4:30; appointment required. Closed major holidays.

ASSISTANCE: Professional staff. Written and phone inquiries accepted. Electrostatic copies available. Photoduplications must be ordered through the museum.

PUBLICATION: No publication fee. Collection credit required. Free copy to museum. Third party permission required on many items.

FINDING AIDS: Card index; access by general subject headings.

BIBLIOGRAPHY:

Duty, Michael. *Wichita Falls: A century in photographs.* Wichita Falls: Midwestern State University Press.

SCOPE: 3,000 photographs, including lass and film negatives and vintage and copy prints). Pre-1880 to 1960s.

Type of photo	Pre-1880	1880-1899	1900-1919	1920-1939	1940-1959	1960-1986
D/A/T-types	10					
Glass negs			300	15		
Film negs			100	300	50	50
Vintage prints		25	1,000		200	100
Copy images			500	100	100	

GEOGRAPHIC: Wichita Falls. Brazil.

SUBJECTS: Economic and social development of the region, with special emphasis on the oil industry.

Academia. Agriculture. Cityscapes. Events (natural disaster—1979 tornado). Exhibitions. Events (parades). Industry. Landscape. Military. Organizations. Personal activities. Politics. Sports and amusement. Transportation.

PEOPLE: Many area residents with some coverage of Amerind and Black ethnicities.

Fulcher Armstrong. Lester Jones.

PHOTOGRAPHERS: Edward S. Curtis. Charles A. Fuhs. Frank Gohlke.

RECORD GROUPS: Record groups containing some photographs:

W85.1 ARMSTRONG (FULCHER) COLLECTION. Aviation in Wichita Falls. 325 photographs. 1920 to 1950.

W85.2 CRAWFORD (Captain JAMES) COLLECTION. Native scenes in Brazil and shots of Rio de Janeiro. 27 photographs.

W85.3 CURTIS (EDWARD S.) COLLECTION. Portraits from *The North American Indian.* 47 photogravures, disbound. Ca. 1910.

W85.4 FUHS (CHARLES A.) COLLECTION. Candid photographs of unidentified people outdoors. 500 photographs. 1915 to 1920.

W85.5 GOHLKE (FRANK) COLLECTION. Aftermath of the 1979 tornado in Wichita Falls and rephotographs of the same scenes one year later; scenes in Wichita Falls. 1979 to 1982.

W85.6 JONES (LESTER) COLLECTION. Economic and social development of Wichita Falls. 500 photographs. 1890s to 1940s.

W85.7 KIDWELL (JOHN) COLLECTION. Wichita Truck. 22 glass and nitrate negatives. 1920s.

W85.8 ROGERS (L. C.) COLLECTION. Early Wichita Falls and eastern Oklahoma. 10 photographs; postcards.

W85.9 TANKERSLEY (ERMA) COLLECTION. Scenes from Newcastle and Mineral Wells and from Dewar OK. 40 photo postcards and a few tintypes.

W85.10 WICHITA FALLS CHAMBER OF COMMERCE. Early Wichita Falls and portraits of chamber directors. 190 photographs. 1930s.

UNABSTRACTED COLLECTIONS

Abilene State School (a10)
Maple and South Twenty-fourth Street
P.O. Box 451
Abilene, Texas 79604

915-692-4053, extension 437. Contact: Librarian.

An institutional collection documenting the history of the Abilene State School. 250 photographs. 1901 to present.

**Hardin-Simmons University,
Abilene Photograph Collection (a12)**
Rupert Richardson Research Center for the Southwest
P.O. Box 1172
Abilene, Texas 79698

915-677-7281, extension 239. Contact: Director.

A regional history collection in an academic library documenting the economic and social development of Abilene and of Taylor County, including the Abilene Chamber of Commerce, the First State Bank of Abilene, Hardin-Simmons University, and the J. D. Moore Transfer and Storage Company. Area residents in the collection include the families of Wally Akin, James Aneff, Matilda Baker, Bill Barton, William O. Beazley, Raymund Bynum, Ms. Tomie Clack, Mrs. J. W. Cole, Mrs. Don St. Cyr, Lawrence Clayton, Mrs. D. R. Derusha, Mrs. H. A. Daniel, Ms. Deborah Dennis, Ed George, Patricia Louise McDaniel Garren, Earl Hardt, Mrs. D. P. James, Alan Lindley, Mrs. Kirk McKinnon, Mrs. Wanda McVea, Mrs. Maxine Perini, Mrs. Mary Paxton Pender, Leo Rynders, Reynolds family, Ms. Harral Steel, Mrs. Menivil Mae Seastrunk, Merle Stevens, and Mrs. William Walker. 7,100 copy negatives and prints, 500 vintage prints. 1880s to 1960s, most 1920 to 1940.
Bibliography: Fane Downs and Roy Flukin-ger, *Abilene: An American centennial* (Abilene: Rupert N. Richardson Press, 1982).

**Robert E. Nail Foundation,
Shackelford County Archives (a14)**
Old Jail Art Center
314 Ledbetter
RR 1, Box 1
Albany, Texas 76430

915-762-2269. Contact: Archivist. Research fee charged.

A local history archive housed in an art and history museum. Photographs depict area residents, including Berta Harte Nance, poet laureate of Texas, and the economic and social development of Albany and of Shackelford County. Photographers include Jim George. Many photographs collected by Robert E. Nail and Joan Farmer. 1,000 vintage and 400 copy photographs. 1860s to the present.
Bibliography: Sallie Reynolds Matthews, *Interwoven: A pioneer chronicle* (1st ed., Houston: Anson Press, 1936; 4th ed., College Station: Texas A&M University Press, 1982.

Amarillo Art Center (a20)
2200 South Van Buren
P.O. Box 447
Amarillo, Texas 79109

806-372-8356. Contact: Curator of Art.

A local art museum concentrating on American art since 1900. Photographs in the reserve collections include work from the Farm Security Administration project by Russell Lee and Dorothea Lange documenting the economic and social development of Amarillo and the Panhandle. 123 copy prints, 275 modern prints. 1920s to 1960s.

Brazoria County Historical Museum (a22)
100 East Cedar
P.O. Box 1222
Angleton, Texas 77515

409-849-5711, extension 1208. Contact: Director.

A local history museum located in the county courthouse. Photographs document the economic and social development of Brazoria County, including Alvin, Angleton, Brazoria, Columbia, Lake Jackson, and Sweeney. Copy prints.

Archer County Historical Committee and Museum (a24)
Old Jail
101 North Sycamore
Archer City, Texas 76351

No phone. Contact: Chairman.

A local history museum with photographs documenting the economic and social development of the Archer County area, including Archer City, Dundee, Holliday, Megargel, Scotland, and Windthorst; portraits of area residents, most of English or German ethnicity and Amerinds, including James Branch, O. V. Hampton, and Jack Loftin. 2,000 copy photographs. Nineteenth century to present.

Bibliography: Jack Loftin, *Trails through Archer: A centennial history* (Austin: Eakin Press, 1979).

Austin Chamber of Commerce (a30)
901 West Riverside Drive
P.O. Box 1967
Austin, Texas 78767

512-478-0098. Contact: Director of Tourism Development.

The collection consists of many cityscapes and tourist attractions documenting the recent and contemporary economic and social life in Austin; a portion has been assembled into a slide presentation. 460—35mm color transparencies. 1960s to present.

Elisabet Ney Museum (a36)
Austin Parks and Recreation Department
304 East Forty-fourth Street
Austin, Texas 78751

512-458-2255. Contact: Administrator.

Devoted to the German-Texan sculptress Elisabet Ney (1833-1907) and exhibiting her work in the building that served as her home and studio, the museum holds photographs of the Ney family, including snapshots and formal portraits, art reproductions of sculpture, architecture, and monuments. Many photographs made in Germany and Austin. Photographers include Ernst Raba (San Antonio). 400 photographs, including vintage prints and negatives. 1880s to 1950s.

French Legation Museum (a38)
802 San Marcos
Austin, Texas 78736

512-472-8180. Contact: Director.

A historic structure with a collection of photographs pertaining to the site and the museum, including its buildings, grounds, furnishings, former occupants, and its current custodians, the Daughters of the Republic of Texas. 300 vintage and 50 copy negatives. 1880s (copy prints) to present.

Laguna Gloria Art Museum (a40)
3809 West Thirty-fifth Street
P.O. Box 5568
Austin, Texas 78763

512-458-8191. Contact: Registrar.

Cirkut, panoramic photography of E. O. Goldbeck; 65 modern silver gelatin prints (originals at the University of Texas at Austin, HRHRC, Photography Collection, q.v.). Portfolio by Manuel Alvarez Bravo (Geneva, Switzerland: Acorn Editions, 1977); 15 silver gelatin prints; 1930 to 1977. Portfolio by Lee Friedlander; 15 prints.

Saint Edward's University Archives (a44)
3001 South Congress
P.O. Box 685
Austin, Texas 78704

512-444-2621, extension 216. Contact: Archivist.

An institutional archive documenting the history of the university, its faculty, students, and staff, and its physical facilities, including the Mary Moody Northen Theater. 500 silver gelatin prints. 1900 to present.

Texas Air Control Board (a46)
6330 Highway 290 East
Austin, Texas 78723

512-451-5711, extension 209. Contact: Public Information Officer.

A working photo file gathered by the agency as evidence in the course of its operations in Texas documenting sources monitored by the board and geographical sites around the state. Many made by staff photographers. 1,000 photo prints, many with original negatives. 1972 to present.

Texas Attorney General's Office (a48)
Texas Supreme Court Building
Fourth and Lavaca
P.O. Box 12548
Austin, Texas 78711

512-463-2182. Contact: Photographer.

A working collection gathered by the office documenting the activities of the agency in Abilene, Amarillo, Austin, Beaumont, Corpus Christi, Dallas, El Paso, Fort Worth, Galveston, Houston, Lubbock, McAllen, Rockdale, San Antonio, San Angelo, Texarkana, and Waco; Texas Attorney General Jim Maddox and his staff; and a few national politicians, including Edward Kennedy and Joan and Walter Mondale. Most photographed by staff photographer Steve Oleson. 11,000 vintage and 200 copy photographs, most negatives and some film transparencies. December 1983 to present.

Texas Commission on Jail Standards (a50)
Texas Jails Collection
611 South Congress, Suite 200
Austin, Texas 78701

512-463-5505. Contact: Executive Director.

An institutional collection documenting Texas county jails, including the openings of many new facilities; all Texas counties are represented. Polaroid photographs. 1977 to present.

Texas Comptroller of Public Accounts (a52)
111 West Sixth Street (collection location)
111 East Seventh Street (mailing address)
Austin, Texas 78774

512-463-4735. Contact: Photographer.

A working collection created to illustrate publications distributed by the comptroller's office and in-house training programs. Coverage of broad subject areas, including academia, agriculture, architecture, cityscapes, documents, events, government, industry, landscape, services, and transportation. Most made in Texas, which is divided into six economic regions: Plains, Border, Gulf Coast, Central Corridor, East Texas, and the Metroplex; substantial coverage of Austin, Dallas, Houston, and San Antonio. Photographers include Keith Dannemiller, Mitchell Elliot, Michael P. Flahive, Jack Greider, Russell Penn, and Robert White. 12,500 vintage and 12,500 copy photographs; about half of the photographs are color transparencies. 1975 to present.

Texas Department of Human Resources (a56)
Media Services Division Archives
701 West Fifty-first Street
P.O. Box 2960, mail code 206-E
Austin, Texas 78769

512-450-4282. Contact: Photographer. Public use of the collection is restricted.

An in-house, working archive for use in agency publications and media productions. The archive concentrates on domestic and personal activities, but contains other subjects including ceremonies, children and the elderly, state government, and auto transportation; most were made in Texas. Photographers include Chuck Greffen, Teresina Guerra, and Jack Storey. 10,000 film negatives and color transparencies. 1973 to present.

Texas Department on Aging (a58)
1949 South Interstate 35
P.O. Box 12786
Austin, Texas 78711

512-444-2727. Contact: Chief, Public Affairs/ Public Information.

An institutional collection documenting services for the elderly and state activities; many reproduced in *The Older Texan* magazine. 1,000 vintage photo prints. 1960 to present.

Texas Planning Council for Developmental Disabilities (a64)
118 East Riverside Drive, Room 163
Austin, Texas 78704

512-445-8867. Contact: Public Information Specialist.

A federally funded program administered by the Texas Rehabilitation Commission with an institutional collection of photographs documenting the domestic and personal activities of Texans with disabilities living outside of institutions and the activities of the council; many used as illustrations in the agency's newsletter, *Highlights*. Photographers include Chris Burroughs and Judy DeDonato. 500 images, most 35mm photo negative strips with contact sheets; some prints and film transparencies. 1982 to present.

Texas Railroad Commission and Surface Mining and Reclamation Division (a66)
1701 North Congress
William Travis Building
P.O. Drawer 12967
Austin, Texas 78711

Commission—512-463-6710. Contact: Director, Office of Information Services.
Surface Mining and Reclamation Division— 512-463-6900. Contact: Director.

The commission's photographs were made for an employees' newsletter and to document personnel making field inspections. The Surface Mining and Reclamation Division's photographs were gathered by staff members to document mining activities, predominantly of East Texas mines. 100 vintage transparencies; 150 vintage and 50 copy photographs; some color material. 1970s to present.

Texas Tourist Development Agency (a70)
Capitol Square II
611 South Congress
P.O. Box 12008
Austin, Texas 78711

512-463-7400. Contact: Photographer.

A working collection gathered by the agency emphasizing the natural and cultural resources of the state, depicting them in a light that would make the state attractive to tourists. Extensive coverage of Texas arranged by region. Although photographs often include figures, they are depicted as anonymous parts of the scenery; few portraits. Photographers include Michael A. Murphy and Richard Reynolds; free-lance work by Harry Seawell. Photographs are arranged by geographic region and general subject headings. 25,000 photographs, predominantly 35mm color transparencies with some 4x5 color transparencies, black-and-white negatives, and silver gelatin prints. 1965 to present.

Trammell Crow Company (a72)
301 Congress Avenue
Austin, Texas 78701

512-320-4143. Contact: Tenant Services.

A development corporation with photographs documenting the discovery and excavation of prehistoric mastodon and mammoth bones and teeth and of other artifacts at the construction site of one of the company's buildings in Austin. Photographs emphasize the public tour of the site in January 1985. 100 photographs, including prints and 35mm color transparencies in public files. 1985. A separate in-house file relates to the company's activities; restricted access.

University of Texas, Perry-Castañeda Library (a90)
Microfilm Department
Twenty-first and Speedway
Austin, Texas 78712

512-471-3813. Contact: Microfilm Librarian.

The library holds a complete microfiche copy of the photographs in the Farm Security Administration collection at the Library of Congress. 180,000 images represented on 3,000 microfiche. 1930s to 1940s.
Bibliography: *America, 1935-1946: Guide and subject index to the photographs of the Farm Security Administration and the Office of War Information* (Teaneck NJ: Somerset House, n.d.).

University of Texas, Todd-McLean Sports History Collection (a94)
Department of Physical Education
Twenty-first and Speedway
217 Gregory Gym
Austin, Texas 78712

512-471-4890. Contact: Archivist.

A research archive devoted to sports and physical fitness. Photographs include weight training, boxing, wrestling, and other sports. Record groups include the Ottley Coulter Strength and Physical Fitness collection; the archive of David Willoughby, strength historian and physical anthropolgist; the George Hackenschmidt Wrestling collection; the Bill Ward Sports collection, containing commercial photographs of sports events, including baseball, boxing, and other sports; the Albert Davis Boxing collection; and the Todd collection of contemporary strength athletes. 5,000 photographs, including vintage and copy prints, a few cased images and glass negatives; an extensive collection of magazines and books supporting

research in sports and physical fitness. 1860s to present, most 1900 to present.
Bibliography: *Strength* magazine (Alan Calvert Publishing, 1914-1918). Jan and Terry Todd, *Lift your way to youthful fitness* (Boston: Little, Brown and Company, 1985). Terry Todd, *Inside powerlifting* (Chicago: Contemporary Books, 1978). erry Todd and Dick Hoover, *Fitness for athletes* (Chicago: Contemporary Books, 1978). Terry Todd and Herschel Walker, *Herschel Walker's basic training* (Garden City NJ: Doubleday, 1985).

Callahan County Pioneer Museum (b10)
Fourth and Market Street
Baird, Texas 79504

915-854-1718. Contact: Librarian.

A local history museum with photographs that include many unidentified portraits, the economic and social development of Baird and of Callahan County, and Belle Plain College. 1,000 photographs.

Beaumont Public Library System, Tyrrell Historical Library (b16)
695 Pearl Street
P.O. Box 3827
Beaumont, Texas 77704

409-838-0780. Contact: Director.

A public library with a local history and genealogy department collecting photographs documenting the economic and social development of southeastern Texas, including Beaumont and early Sabine Pass; many area residents with substantial coverage of Blacks. Photographers include Robert J. Keith and the Young Men's Business Studio. An extensive collection of stereographs published by Keystone and by Underwood and Underwood. 500 vintage and 100 copy photographs; 2,000 stereographs. 1860s to 1950s.

Lamar University, Mary and John Gray Library (b22)
P.O. Box 10021
Beaumont, Texas 77710

409-838-8261.   Contact: Head, Documents Department.

Lamar University; landscapes of the Big Thicket photographed by Larry Jene Fisher; the Sproule School of Dance; biographical materials pertaining to Babe Didrikson Zaharias. Many manuscript record groups have a few photographs interfiled. 1,500 photographs. 1930s to 1960s.

Lamar University, Spindletop Museum (b28)
950 East Florida Street
P.O. Box 19982
Beaumont, Texas 77710

409-838-8896. Contact: Operations Director.

A local history museum concentrating on the development of the petroleum industry in Beaumont and southeastern Texas, including the Gladys City boom town, Batson, Beaumont, and Sour Lake. Some photographed by F. J. Trost (Beaumont).   10,000 photographs, including vintage prints and negatives. Ca. 1900 to 1940s.
Bibliography: Walter E. Rundell, *Early Texas oil: A photographic history, 1866-1936* (College Station: Texas A&M Press, 1977).

University of Mary Hardin-Baylor, Sid Richardson Museum (b34)
Tenth and College
Belton, Texas 76513

817-939-5811, extension 272. Contact: Curator.

An institutional museum with photographs documenting the history of the university, prominent alumni, and the economic and social development of Belton and of Bell and Washington counties. Photographers include Runelle Baker. 200 vintage photographs. 1890s to present.

Big Bend National Park (b40)
Visitor Center
Panther Junction
Big Bend National Park, Texas 79834

915-477-2251. Contact: Park Superintendent.

Photographs pertaining to the region, including work by Bank Langmore and W. D. Smithers. 129 copy photographs. 1880 to 1920.

Bishop Chamber of Commerce (b46)
115 South Ash
Bishop, Texas 78343

512-584-2214. Contact: Manager.

Photographs document the residents of Bishop (founded 1910) and Nueces County, predominantly of English, German, and Mexican ethnicities; town founder F. Z. Bishop; and the economic and social development of the community, including the Bishop Hotel, the Celanese Plant, and agriculture. Photographers include John F. "Doc" McGregor (Corpus Christi) and Lawrence Guess. 3,000 vintage and 10,000 copy photographs. 1910 to present.

Boerne Area Historical Society (b52)
Behind 402 East Blanco
P.O. Box 178
Boerne, Texas 78006

512-249-2030. Contact: Historical Preservation Chairman.

An archive maintained by a local history society documenting the economic and social development of Boerne and of Kendall County and area residents, many of whom are of German ethnic orgins. Photographers include Fred Hillman and Garland Perry. 500 original and 1,500 copy photographs, including panoramic prints. 1840s [sic] to present.
Bibliography: Kendall County Historical Commission, *Rivers, ranches, railroads, and recreation* (Dallas: Taylor Publishing, 1984). Garland Perry, *Historic images of Boerne, Texas* (Boerne: Perry Enterprises, 1982).

Sam Rayburn Library (b58)
Sam Rayburn Foundation
800 West Sam Rayburn Drive
Bonham, Texas 75418

214-583-2455. Contact: Director.

An archival library housing the papers and

memorabilia of the former US representative and Speaker of the House. Photographs document Rayburn's career, political colleagues, and family; many made in Texas, especially the Fourth Congressional District, and in Washington DC. Many wire service photographs, including United Press International and Associated Press. 2,000 vintage and 500 copy photographs. 1900 to present, most 1920 to 1962.

Swenson Memorial Museum of Stephens County (b64)
116 West Walker Street
P.O. Box 350
Breckenridge, Texas 76204

817-559-8471. Contact: Museum Curator.

A private, local history museum collecting artworks, manuscripts, books and journals, artifacts, and photographs. Economic and social development of Stephens County, especially Breckenridge, Necessity, and Caddo; studio portraits and family snapshots of area residents; a few photographs from France made during WW I. Photographers include Basil Clemons and Walton's Studio. 1,000 vintage and 200 copy photographs, most prints and a few negatives. 1895 to 1985, most 1920 to 1940.

Bibliography: Betty Elliot Hanna, *Doodle bugs and cactus berries* (Nortex Press; distributed by Austin: Eakin Press, 1975).

Texas Baptist Historical Center and Museum (b70)
Baptist General Convention of Texas
Route 5, Box 222
Brenham, Texas 77833

409-836-5117. Contact: Director.

History of the Baptist church in Texas; many portraits of members of the Independence Baptist Church; Baylor University and Baylor Female College at Independence, 1845-1886. 374 photographs on exhibit. 1880s.

Waller County Historical Museum (b76)
906 Cooper Street
P.O. Box 235ESS
Brookshire, Texas 77423

713-934-2826. Contact: Administrator.

A local history museum with photographs documenting the economic and social development of Brookshire and of Waller County. 75 photographs. 1900 to present.

Gladys Porter Zoo (b82)
500 Ringgold
Brownsville, Texas 78520

512-546-7187. Contact: Education Coordinator.

A zoological garden with a photographic collection used for exhibits and education programs. Many photographs of animals were made at the zoo by staff photographers. 18,000 original photographs, including negatives, vintage prints, and transparencies; a few copy photos. 1960s to the present.

Bibliography: *Gladys Porter Zoo animal album* (Brownsville: Gladys Porter Zoo); available from the zoo.

Bryan Public Library (b88)
201 East Twenty-sixth Street
Bryan, Texas 77803

409-779-1736. Contact: City Librarian.

Economic and social development of Brazos County, including Bryan and College Station; Ana Ludmila Gee Ballet collection, containing studio portraits of ballet personalities from Europe and Panama, including Pavlova and Margot Fonteyn. 285 vintage photographs. 1920s to 1970s.

Hemphill County Library (c10)
Fifth and Main streets
Canadian, Texas 79014

806-323-5282. Contact: Librarian.

Studio portraits and some commercial work photographed by Canadian TX commercial photographer, Julius C. Born, including landscapes documenting local residents and the economic and social development of Hemphill County and of Canadian, Miami, and Higgins; additional work photographed by G. A. Addison. 1,000 glass plate and 500 nitrate negatives; a few modern prints. 1900 to 1960s.

Northwood Institute Library (c18)
P.O. Box 58
Cedar Hill, Texas 75104

214-291-1541.

A campus library not generally collecting photographs, but holding an album of photographs of Volk's Shoe Store of Dallas. 100 photographs. 1950s.

Hartley County Historical Commission (c22)
P.O. Box 77
Channing, Texas 79018

806-235-3749. Contact: County Historian.

A local historical commission with no permanent facility that is beginning a collection of photographs. The collection documents the economic and social development of the Panhandle with emphasis on the ranching community of Channing. 175 photographs. 1898 to the present.

Childress County Heritage Museum (c26)
210 Third Street Northwest
Childress, Texas 79201

817-937-2261. Contact: Director. Appointment preferred.

A local history museum with photographs documenting the economic and social development of Childress and of Childress County. 600 vintage and 150 copy photographs.

Layland Museum (c30)
201 North Caddo
Cleburne, Texas 76031

817-641-3321, extension 375. Contact: Curator.

A local history museum documenting the economic and social development of Cleburne and of Johnson County. Photographers include Davis' Studio, Lindgren Studio, and Shaw's. 500 vintage and 1,500 copy prints; 20 silver gelatin Keystone stereographs; some equipment and ephemera. 1860 to present, most 1880 to 1920.

Bosque Memorial Museum (c34)
South Avenue Q
Clifton, Texas 76634

817-675-3845. Contact: President.

A local history museum with a collection of photographs documenting the economic and social development of Bosque County, including Clifton, Cranfill Gaps, and Norse, primarily farming communities; area residents, many of whom are of Norwegian ethnicity; an album assembled by the museum of all the schools in Bosque County, many with group portraits of students, made between the 1920s and the 1940s. Many photographs made by local photographer S. F. Larsen (1850-1925). 350 vintage and 250 copy photographs, most prints. 1880s to 1940s.

Texas A&M University Archives (c38)
Sterling C. Evans Library
College Station, Texas 77843

409-845-1815. Contact: University Archivist.

An institutional archive collecting artworks, artifacts, books and journals, manuscripts, and photographs. Materials pertain to Texas A&M University and other divisions within the Texas A&M University System, especially the Texas Agricultural Extension Service. Subjects cover all aspects of agriculture, including farming and ranching; university ceremonies; aerial landscapes; libraries; and sports, including baseball, basketball, and football. Substantial geographic coverage of College Station and Brazos County, with some coverage of El Paso, the state of Texas, China, and Juarez, Mexico. 5,000 vintage and 3,000 copy photo prints, including panoramic prints; 25 glass negatives; 200 film transparencies; 1,000 motion pictures. 1880 to present, most after 1960.

Bibliography: John A. Adams Jr., *We are the Aggies* (College Station: Texas A&M Press, 1979). Henry C. Dethloff, *Pictorial History of Texas A&M University, 1876-1976* (College Station: Texas A&M Press, 1975). John D.

Fovsy, *Aggies and 'Horns: Eighty-six years of bad blood* (Austin: Texas Monthly Press, 1981).

Texas A&M University, Texas Forest Service Headquarters Library (c42)
300 System Adminstration Building
College Station, Texas 77843

409-845-2641. Contact: Head, Information and Education Section.

A state agency serving as depository of government records. Photographs depict forestry activities in East Texas. Photographers include Hal Harris and Malcolm Moore. 1,500 original photographs, including prints and transparencies. 1940 to present; a few from the 1920s.

Texas A&M University, University Art Exhibits (c46)
Memorial Student Center
Joe Routt Boulevard
P.O. Box 5718
College Station, Texas 77844

409-845-845-8501. Contact: Registrar.

An exhibition space with a small reserve collection of primarily fine art photographs, including the Danny Lyon portfolio *Pictures from the New World* (Millerton NY: Aperture) and work by contemporary, regional photographers. 30 silver gelatin prints. Early 1960s to late 1970s.

East Texas State University, University Archives and Oral History Center (c50)
University Library
Commerce, Texas 75428

214-886-5737. Contact: Archivist.

An archive devoted to the history of the university and oral history. The collection documents the social life and customs of area residents, with a special concentration on ethnic minorities, from Northeast Texas, including Bonham, Commerce, Greenville, Honey Grove, and Sulphur Springs. 100,000 photographs, most copy negatives and prints. 1880s to present.

Delta County Patterson Memorial Museum (c54)
700 West Dallas Avenue
Cooper, Texas 75432

214-395-2934. Contact: Vice-Chairman.

A local history museum operated by a local history society with photographs documenting the economic and social development of Cooper and of Delta County, including courthouses, churches, schools, gins, a sorghum mill, doctors, lawyers, early lawmen, and family groups. 60 photographs, many copy prints. 1876 to present.

Art Museum of South Texas (c58)
1902 North Shoreline Drive
Corpus Christi, Texas 78401

512-884-3844. Contact: Curator/Registrar.

A fine art museum with a collection of photocollages by Dale Eldred which deal with the structure and appearance of the museum building. 65 photocollages. Ca. 1980.

Coastal Bend Council of Governments (c66)
2910 Leopard Street
P.O. Box 9909
Corpus Christi, Texas 78469

512-883-5743. Contact: Information Director.

A state agency coordinating local governmental agencies and services with an institutional collection gathered to illustrate newsletters and annual reports of the council. Photographs depict recent and current economic and social development of the region, including elected officials, civic leaders, committee meetings, historic homes, public buildings, landscape, health planning, emergency medical services, environmental quality, alcohol abuse, technical assistance to local governments, criminal justice, fire protection, and aging. 1,000—4x5 and 35mm silver gelatin negatives and some prints. 1975 to present.

Corpus Christi Area Convention and Tourist Bureau (c70)
1201 North Shoreline Drive
P.O. Box 2664
Corpus Christi, Texas 78403

512-882-5603. Contact: Tourism Assistant.

A local promotional organization with photographs documenting the recent economic and social development of Corpus Christi, Port Aransas, and Rockport, with an emphasis on the tourist industry; subjects include cityscapes, festivals, fishing, and hotel/inn services. Photographers include Michael Murphy, Richard Reynolds, Ron Randolph, and Ray Scott. 500—35mm copy color transparencies and 60 copy photographs. 1970s to present.

Padre Island National Seashore (c82)
Interpretive Division Collection
US National Park Service
Malaquite Beach Visitor Center
9405 South Padre Island
Corpus Christi, Texas 78418

512-949-8173. Contact: Chief Naturalist/ Interpreter. The collection is primarily for use by the park staff; open to qualified researchers by appointment only; requests must be made in writing.

A natural history exhibit and reserve collections concentrating on the various ecosystems of the seashore, including the identification of native flora and fauna, the interaction of that wildlife, and the seashore's recreational visitors and their impact on the ecosystem. A small collection of historical copy prints pertaining to the seashore is under development. Most photographed by the National Seashore staff. 2,000 silver gelatin prints, 6,000—35mm color transparencies; some copy prints. Most after 1960.

Brush Country Museum (c86)
La Salle County Historical Commission
North Front Street
Cotulla, Texas 78014

512-879-2326. Contact: Chairperson.

A local history museum with an exhibition of photographs documenting area residents; the economic and social development of the region, including Cotulla, Fowlerton, Gardendale, and Millett; the La Motta, La Salle County, and Dull ranches. Photographers include I. N. Hall. 283 photo prints. 1870 to 1925.

Discover Houston County Visitors and Learning Center and Museum (c90)
Historical Projects of Houston County
303 South First Street (street address)
629 North Fourth Street (mailing address)
Crockett, Texas 75835

409-544-5304. Contact: Commission Chairman.

A local history museum operated jointly by a nonprofit organization and the local historical commission. Photographs in the collection document the economic and social development of Houston County, including Augusta, Crockett, Grapeland, Kennard, Latexo, Lovelady, and Ratcliff. Many photographed by Eliza H. Bishop. 370 photographs, most copy prints; some film transparencies. 1890 to 1984.
Bibliography: Eliza H. Bishop, *Houston County history* (Tulsa OK: Heritage Publishing, 1980).

Crosby County Pioneer Memorial Museum (c94)
101 Main Street
P.O. Box 386
Crosbyton, Texas 79322

806-675-2331. Contact: Executive Director.

A local history museum with photographs documenting the economic and social development of the Crosby County area, including Crosbyton, Ralls, Lorenzo, Snyder and the Llano Estacado, especially ranching and farming agriculture. A 1912 album includes views in the region with photographs by E. H. Higginbotham (Snyder). 5,000 photographs, roughly half are copy photographs. 1900 to 1940.

Catholic Diocese of Dallas (d10)

Diocesan Archives
3915 Lemmon Avenue
P.O. Box 19507
Dallas, Texas 75219

214-528-2240. Contact: Diocesan Archivist.

An institutional archive documenting the history of the Catholic Diocese of Dallas and the Catholic church in Northeast Texas, including church schools, churches and congregations, religious ceremonies and events, and religious organizations. Photographers include Johnny Hayes and Frank Rogers. 400 vintage photo prints and 5,000 negatives. 1940s to present; a few nineteenth-century images.

Dallas County Heritage Society, Old City Park (d14)

1717 Gano
Dallas, Texas 75215

214-421-5141. Contact: Curator of Collections.

A museum of architectural and cultural history with photographs of the Frankie Bodeker, Bonner, and Mixon families and, to a lesser extent, documenting the economic and social development of Dallas. 300 photographs. 1870s to 1920s.

Dallas Museum of Natural History (d22)

Fair Park
Second and Grand Streets
P.O. Box 26193
Dallas, Texas 75226

214-421-2169. Contact: Curator.

A natural history museum interpreting native flora, fauna, and geology of Texas, including the Trans-Pecos and Gulf Coast through natural specimens. Photographs include wildlife and plants of the region. Photographers include Walter R. Davis. 20,000 photographs, primarily 35mm color transparencies. 1965 to present.

International Museum of Cultures (d34)

7500 Camp Wisdom Road
Dallas, Texas 75236

214-298-9446. Contact: Director.

An exhibiting museum focusing on contemporary cultures of living peoples with reserve collections of artifacts and a library. The museum serves as the repository for materials gathered by the Summer Institute of Linguistics over the past forty years. Photographs depict societal artifacts and activities, including costumes, weapons, and ceremonies from more than 600 living, indigenous cultures worldwide, many from Africa, Mexico, Vietnam, and including US Amerinds. 2,000 vintage transparencies, 2,000 original negatives, 1,000 copy photographs, 5 motion pictures. 1960 to present, a few from the 1940s.

Saint Paul Medical Center (d38)

5909 Harry Hines Boulevard
Dallas, Texas 75235

214-879-2496.   Contact: Public Relations Specialist.

A hospital, operated by the Daughters of the Charity, with an institutional collection of photographs documenting the current hospital and older facility, including the pharmacy, patient ward, dietary, surgery, laundry, and central service departments; most views are interiors which give views of period surgical instruments. Additional photographs depict many of the religious staff workers, secular staff, and patients. 200 photographs. 1918 to 1928.

Southern Methodist University, Meadows Museum (d46)

Dallas, Texas 75275

214-692-2740. Contact: Curator.

A fine art museum. Two portraits from *The North American Indian* photographed by Edward S. Curtis and seven portfolios (v.i.). 100 photographs. 1920s to present.

Portfolios: Manuel Alvarez Bravo, *Manuel Alvarez Bravo* (Geneva: Acorn Editions, 1977); 15 modern silver gelatin prints, ca. 1930 to ca. 1970. J. A. Coderch de Sentmenit, Luis Gardeta, José Bergamín, and Antoni Tápies, *Del Toreo* (Barcelona: 1977); 23 black-and-white photographs. Robert Doisneau, *Robert Doisneau* (New York: Hyperion, 1979); 15 silver gelatin prints, 1945 to 1972. Elliott Erwitt, *Photographs: Elliott Erwitt* (Geneva: Acorn Editions, 1980); 15 silver gelatin prints, 1949 to 1969. Ralph Gibson, *Chiraoscuro* (New York: Hyperion, 1982); 15 silver gelatin prints, 1972 to 1981. Michael Peel, *The camera never lies . . .* (New York: Circle Press, 1979); a bound book of type-C and silver gelatin prints. Garry Winogrand, *Garry Winogrand* (New York: Hyperion, 1978); 15 silver gelatin prints, 1960s to 1970s.

Southland Corporation (d50)
2828 North Haskell Avenue
P.O. Box 719
Dallas, Texas 75221

214-828-7385. Contact: Assistant to the Vice-President for Public Relations.

A corporate archive documenting the activities of the company in retailing (especially 7-Eleven convenience stores) in Canada, Japan, the United Kingdom, and in the US, including the East and West coasts, Colorado, Utah, and the Texas cities of Austin, Dallas, Fort Worth, and Houston. The archive also contains documentation of various community and public relations programs of the corporation, including work with the Muscular Dystrophy Association, the March of Dimes, and the 1984 Summer Olympics. 4,000 photographs, most color and black-and-white prints. 1927 to 1985.
Bibliography: Allen Liles, *Oh thank heaven! The story of the Southland Corporation* (Dallas: Southland Corporation, 1977).

Temple Emanu-El (d54)
8500 Hillcrest
Dallas, Texas 75225

214-368-3613. Contact: Archivist.

History of Temple Emanu-El, including group and individual portraits of the congregation, the temple and services, and a few photographs from WW I and WW II. 275 vintage photographs, including 150 stereographs; 30 copy photographs. 1860s to present, most after 1940.

University of Texas Health Science Center at Dallas (d58)
History of the Health Sciences Collection
Library
5323 Harry Hines Boulevard
Dallas, Texas 75235

214-688-3368. Contact: Head, Information Services Department.

The university's archive, with photographs documenting the UTHSCD Campus, Parkland and Children's Hospitals; and the students, faculty, and staff of UTHSCD. 800 vintage photographs, including 150 stereographs. 1943 to present.

Wise County Heritage Museum (d61)
1602 South Trinity
Decatur, Texas 76234

817-627-5586. Contact: Executive Director.

A local history museum with a collection of photographs documenting the economic and social development and area residents of Wise County and Decatur. 60 photographs, including stereographs and panoramic prints. 1880s to 1940s.

Deer Park Independent School District Historical School Museum (d64)
204 Ivy Street
Deer Park, Texas 77536

713-479-2831. Contact: Chairperson.

An institutional collection documenting the history of the school district, including students, faculty, staff, activities, and buildings. 1,000 vintage and 1,000 copy photographs. 1920s to present.

Val Verde County
Historical Commission (d67)
308 Orbit Circle
Del Rio, Texas 78840

512-775-5203. Contact: Chairman.

A local history collection documenting the economic and social development of Val Verde County and West Texas. Many photographs are copies from the N. H. Rose Collection housed at the University of Oklahoma in Norman. 15,000 photographs. 1880s to present.

Grayson County
Frontier Village (d70)
Route 5, Box 169
Loy Park
R5 Box 112
Denison, Texas 75020

214-465-5647. Contact: Executive Director.

A museum with a collection of historically significant buildings and photographs documenting the economic and social development of Grayson County. 200 photographs. 1880s to the present.

Denton Public Library (d73)
502 Oakland
Denton, Texas 76201

817-566-8478. Contact: Reference Librarian.

A public library with a local history file containing photographs that document the area residents in family snapshots and the economic and social development of Denton County. 1,818 vintage photographs. 1893 to 1965.

Bibliography: F. Bates, ed., *History and reminiscences of Denton County* (Denton: McNitzky Printing Company, 1918); reprint available. C. A. Bridges, *History of Denton, Texas, from its beginning to 1960* (Waco: Texian Press, 1978).

Texas Woman's University,
Blagg-Huey Library (d79)
P.O. Box 23715
Denton, Texas 76204

817-898-3751. Contact: Special Collections Librarian.

An archive documenting the history of the university and the history of women in Texas, with collections of artworks, artifacts, books and journals, manuscripts, and photographs. The institutional archive documents faculty, students, and university social life and customs, many photographed by Charles Carruth. 10,000 photographs, most negatives and some vintage prints, 1910s to present, most after 1950. The Texas Women's History Project collection contains photographs gathered for the exhibit, "Texas Women: A Celebration of History," depicting individual women and women's activities from Texas history. 150 photo prints and negatives, late 1880s to present. Texas Women's Hall of Fame collection contains studio portraits of all the women who have been inducted into that group.

T. L. L. Temple
Memorial Library (d82)
300 Park
P.O. Box 597
Diboll, Texas 75941

409-829-5497. Contact: Librarian.

An academic library with a collection of photographs documenting the economic and social development of Diboll. 100 photographs.

Moore County
Historical Museum (d85)
Dumas Avenue and West Eighth
Dumas, Texas 79029

806-935-3113. Contact: Director.

A local history museum with a collection of photographs documenting the economic and social development of Moore County and Dumas, emphasizing farming; many area residents are represented in the collection. 400 copy photographs. 1880s to 1960s.

Duncanville Public Library (d88)
103 East Wheatland Road
Duncanville, Texas 75116

214-298-5400. Contact: Librarian.

A public library with a local history collection containing photographs that document the economic and social development of Duncanville; other photographs include an album belonging to Minnie Rader Crews, one of the first registered nurses in Texas, which includes views of her nursing class at Saint Joseph's Hospital in Houston, cityscapes, and early residents of Port Arthur. 300 photographs. 1940s to present.

Hidalgo County Historical Museum (e10)
121 East McIntyre
P.O. Box 482
Edinburg, Texas 78539

512-383-6911. Contact: Director.

A regional history museum with photographs documenting the economic and social development of the Lower Rio Grande Valley, including Edinburg and Hidalgo County, particularly the period of its boom growth between 1900 and 1940; some coverage of the Mexican Revolution in the region, including bandit raids and occupation by US troops, 1915 to 1916. Other major subjects include agriculture, land excursions and development, irrigation, lawmen, and city and town growth. 3,000 photographs, including copy photographs; some film negatives. 1853 to present, most before 1945.

El Paso Museum of Art (e20)
1211 Montana
El Paso, Texas 79902

915-541-4040. Contact: Curator.

A history, art, and science museum documenting the economic and social development of El Paso and of Juarez, Mexico. Photographers include Manuel Carillo. 1,500 photographs, most vintage prints and some transparencies. 1880s to present; most after 1960.

El Paso Museum of History (e30)
12901 Gateway West
El Paso, Texas 79927

915-858-1928. Contact: Curator.

A regional history museum with a collection of photographs documenting the area residents and the economic and social development of El Paso and West Texas. Photographers include Vaughn and Bushnell. 150 vintage and 100 copy photographs. 1870s to 1940s.

Fort Bliss, Museum of the Non-Commissioned Officer (e50)
Building 11331
Fifth and Barksdale streets
El Paso, Texas 79918

915-568-8646. Contact: Director.

A history museum collecting books and periodicals, two-dimensional artworks, artifacts, and photographs. The museum focuses on military personnel, predominantly studio portraits; some coverage of Vietnam. Photographers include Sergeant Major William Elazer. 1,167 vintage and 274 copy photographs. 1850s to present.

University of Texas at El Paso, Special Collections Department (e70)
El Paso, Texas 79968

915-747-5697. Contact: Curator of Manuscripts.

The manuscript library of the University of Texas at El Paso. Photographs in the library are reproduced from the Otis A. Aultmann Collection at the Southwest Collection, El Paso Public Library (q.v.).

West Texas Council of Governments (e80)
Two Civic Center Plaza
El Paso, Texas 79999

915-541-4681. Contact: Executive Director.

A state agency coordinating local governmental agencies and services with a collection of institutional photographs documenting the recent economic and social development of West Texas, including Brewster, Culberson, El Paso, Jeff Davis, Hudspeth, and Presidio counties; cities represented include Alpine, Anthony, Clint, Dell City, Fort Davis, El Paso, Marfa, Presidio, Sierra Blanca, and Van Horn. 200 vintage photographs. 1965 to present.

Heritage Museum (f10)
North Saint Mary Street
P.O. Box 86
Falfurrias, Texas 78355

512-325-2907. Contact: Museum Director.

A local history museum with a collection of photographs containing the archives of Falfurrias studio and commercial photographer Carol Dryden (1918-1972); most photographs are studio portraits of area residents with some work for the newspaper and some commercial photographs for local businesses, including Falfurrias Dairies. The collection also contains portraits of area residents and their families by various studio photographers. 65,000 film negatives, 1,000 vintage prints; Dryden's name index. 1890s to present, most late 1940s to 1960s.

Fort Hood, Second Armored Division Museum (f22)
Battalion Avenue, Building 418
P.O. Box 5009
Fort Hood, Texas 76546

817-287-8811. Contact: Director.

An institutional history museum documenting the history of the Second Armored Division, formed in 1940 and later commanded by General George S. Patton Jr. Photographs document the military actions of the division in Belgium, France, Germany, Morocco, Vietnam, their base at Fort Hood, and members of the division, including General Patton. Photographs are contained in the papers of General John Hulen (1913 to 1920) and General James King (1930 to 1960). Many photographs by the US Army Signal Corps. 2,000 vintage and 500 copy

photographs, including panoramic prints and film transparencies. 1913 to present, most 1940s to present.

Fort McKavett
State Historic Site (f26)
Texas Parks and Wildlife Department
23 miles West of Menard on US 190 and FR 864
P.O. Box 867
Fort McKavett, Texas 76841

A nineteenth-century fort with many of its buildings restored. The site maintains a collection of photographs of the fort and the Menard area. 70 vintage and copy photographs. 1890 to ca. 1940.

Annie Riggs Museum (f30)
Fort Stockton Historical Society
301 South Main
Fort Stockton, Texas 79735

915-336-2167. Contact: Curator.

A local history museum with photographs documenting the economic and social development of Fort Stockton and of Pecos County; area residents, including the families of Fred Achterberg, Francis Rooney, and H. H. Butz. Photographers include C. C. Howard, W. W. Monteith, and Pittaway. 1,000 copy and vintage photographs, including 100 stereographs. 1900 to 1959.

Bibliography: Marsha Daggett, ed., *Pecos County History* (Canyon: Staked Plains Press, 1984).

Amon G. Carter Archives (f38)
c/o Amon Carter Museum
P.O. Box 2365
Fort Worth, Texas 76113

817-738-1933. Contact: Administrative Assistant. Access is heavily restricted and limited to scholarly projects; all requests must be made in writing.

Activities of Amon G. Carter, publisher of the *Fort Worth Star-Telegram* and civic leader. Photographs include portraits of Carter with business acquaintances, various US presidents, sport figures, military heros, and entertainers; aviation; Fort Worth; and WW II. Photographers include staff of the *Star-Telegram*. 15 linear feet of photographs, including silver gelatin prints and film negatives; extensive associated archival materials. 1900 to 1955.

Fort Worth Parks and Recreation Department, Log Cabin Village Historical Complex (f42)

University Drive at Log Cabin Village Lane
2301 Rogers Road
Fort Worth, Texas 76109

817-926-5881. Contact: Historical Curator.

A collection of restored log structures with a collection of photographs of the early economic and social development of Fort Worth and portraits of the city's founders. 300 vintage and 300 copy photographs. 1870s to 1920s.

Fort Worth Transportation and Public Works Department (f50)

1000 Throckmorton
Fort Worth, Texas 76102

817-870-7902. Contact: Administrative Assistant.

An institutional collection of photographs documenting major construction projects, predominantly the Fort Worth Stockyards restoration. Many photographed by Wilford Saxton and Keith Smith. 10,000 photographs. 1970 to 1981.

Fort Worth Water Department (f54)

P.O. Box 870
Fort Worth, Texas 76101

817-870-8208. Contact: Public Information Specialist.

An institutional collection with photographs documenting the activities of the department, including construction of water and wastewater treatment plants, reservoirs, storage tanks, and the installation and repair of water lines. 5,000 vintage photographs. 1900 to present.

Fort Worth Zoological Park (f58)

2727 Zoological Park Drive
Fort Worth, Texas 76110

817-870-7055. Contact: Supervisor of Education.

A zoological garden with an institutional collection documenting the grounds, animals, scenery, and activities of the zoo. 1,500 photographs, most negatives. 1920 to present.

Gearhart Industries (f62)

Publications Department
9100-B Forum Way
Fort Worth, Texas 76140

817-293-1300, extension 5386. Contact: Publications Department. Research fee charged.

Corporate collection documenting the company's products and activities; Gearhart specializes in oilfield wireline services and manufacturing. 2,000 original photographs, including film transparencies. 1958 to present.

Southwest Aerospace Museum (f66)

300 North Spur 341
Fort Worth, Texas 76108

817-735-4143. Contact: Director.

A museum concentrating on the history of aviation collecting photographs with emphasis on military aviation, including accidents and weaponry; many are duplicates from the General Dynamics archives; many made in Fort Worth, San Antonio, and San Diego CA. 5,000 vintage and 300 copy photographs. 1920s to present, most after 1940.

Texas Christian University, Mary Couts Burnett Library (f78)

South University Drive
P.O. Box 32904
Fort Worth, Texas 76129

817-921-7106. Contact: Special Collections Librarian.

Most photographs pertain to the university, documenting the students, faculty, and staff, university buildings, ceremonies, sports, and the Clark family (founders of TCU). Photographs were made in the North Central Texas region, including Waco and Fort Worth. 2,500 photographs. 1880s to 1973.

Texas College of Osteopathic Medicine (f82)

Camp Bowie at Montgomery
Fort Worth, Texas 76107

817-735-2000. Contact: Curator, Special Collections.

An academic library containing a collection of photographs. Subjects include the Texas Osteopathic Medical Association and the Texas College of Osteopathic Medicine. 1,000 photographs, including film negatives and vintage prints. 1940s to the present.

Admiral Nimitz State Historical Park (f86)

Texas Department of Parks and Wildlife
328 East Main
P.O. Box 777
Fredericksburg, Texas 78624

512-997-4379. Contact: Director of Research and Collections.

A state historical park commemorating Chester William Nimitz, US Navy Fleet Admiral, and those who served in WW II. Photographs relate predominantly to WW II; a few turn-of-the-century and contemporary photos from Fredericksburg, Japan, and the Pacific Theater. 100 original photographs; 2,500 copy prints and slides. 1880s to 1960s.

Pioneer Memorial Museum (f90)

Gillespie County Historical Society
309 West Main Street
P.O. Box 765
Fredericksburg, Texas 78624

512-997-2835. Contact: Executive Secretary.

A local history museum with a collection of nineteenth-century structures. Photographs held by the museum document the economic and social development of Fredericksburg.

Center for Transportation and Commerce (g20)

123 Rosenberg
Galveston, Texas 77550

409-765-5700. Contact: Executive Director.

A museum concentrating on railroad history with a collection of restored railroad cars and photographs. Photographs document various aspects of railroad history. 300 vintage photographs. 1920s to 1960s.

Galveston County Historical Museum (g30)

Galveston Historical Foundation
2219 Market Street
P.O. Drawer 539
Galveston, Texas 77553

409-765-7834. Contact: Curator.

A local history museum with a photograph collection documenting the economic and social development of Galveston County, including Galveston and Texas City, with some coverage of southeastern Texas, and a few items from Michigan. Record groups include the Felix Stella collection documenting Stella's career with various musical organizations, including Stella's Band, the Galveston Melody Orchestra, the Galveston Municipal Band, and the Shrine Temple Band between 1914 and 1960; the Ken Pagan collection contains vacation snapshots made by Pagan in Michigan about 1900; the Davis collection documents the aftermath of the 1915 hurricane in Galveston, including damage to buildings, grounded ships, harbor damage, and the destruction of the causeway bridge; the Paul Naschke collection contains work by this Galveston commercial and studio photographer, including portraits of civic leaders and businessmen, most of whom were from Galveston and some from Texas City, made in the 1920s. 565 photographs, including a few stereographs and panoramic prints. 1880s to present, most 1900 to 1939.

Southwestern University, Mood Heritage Museum (g70)

Mood-Bridwell Hall
East University Avenue
SU Box 6371
Georgetown, Texas 78626

512-863-6511.

A local and institutional history museum with photographs depicting the students, faculty, and staff of the university, including Dr. Durwood Fleming. 100 vintage photographs.

W. Walworth Harrison Public Library (g80)

3716 Lee
Greenville, Texas 75401

214-455-2205. Contact: Genealogy Librarian.

A public library with a local history collection containing photographs that document the economic and social development of Greenville and of Hunt County.

Lavaca County Historical Commission (h10)

P.O. Box 45
Hallettsville, Texas 77964

512-798-3322. Contact: Chairman.

A local history society with a collection of photographs documenting the economic and social development of Hallettsville and of Lavaca County, including the work of local studio photographer H. J. Braunig. 500 photographs, some copy prints. 1895 to the present.

Confederate Air Force Museum (h13)

Rebel Drive
Valley International Airport
P.O. Box CAF
Harlingen, Texas 78551

512-425-1057. Contact: Museum Director.

An aviation history museum emphasizing military subjects and WW II. Many photographs from the US and Texas, with some coverage of all WW II theaters. 1,000 vintage and 2,000 copy photographs; 3,000 transparencies; 25 albums. Ca. 1900 to present, most after 1940.

Howard-Dickinson House (h16)

Rusk County Heritage Association
501 South Main Street
Henderson, Texas 75652

214-657-6925. Contact: Secretary.

A restored, nineteenth-century house museum with a collection of photographs documenting the economic and social development of Henderson and of Rusk County; the Alexander Institute; portraits of Captain J. H. Henson and the Arnold, Chamberlain, Dickinson-Graham, Howard-Lavendar, and Novell-Hendricks families. Photographers include Bailey (Henderson), Bernard (Quincy IL), The Globe Studio, Hollopeter (Red Oak IA), Madame Magehee (Ophelia AL), Morast (Clinton MO), Myers Studio (Henderson), Miss Punch (Jacksonville), Ragsdale (San Angelo), Railroad Photo Car, and various others, many from New Orleans LA. 200 vintage photographs, including daguerreotypes and tintypes. 1850s to present.

Rusk County Depot Museum Complex (h19)

Rusk County Commissioner's Court and Rusk County Historical Commission
302 Waskom
Henderson, Texas 75652

214-657-4303. Contact: Depot Director.

A local history museum with photographs documenting the economic and social development of Rusk County. 75 vintage and 150 copy photographs. 1880s to present.

Deaf Smith County Museum (h22)

400 Sampson Street
P.O. Box 1007
Hereford, Texas 79045

806-364-6847 or 806-364-4338. Contact: Executive Director.

A local history museum emphasizing the settlement period of the county with a collection of photographs documenting the economic and social development of the community, including 150 glass negatives of Hereford businesses made in 1912. Photographers include Bill Bradley, Elmer Patterson, W. H. Patton, and Alex O. Thompson. 500 photo prints and 150 glass negatives. 1900 to 1940.

Hill College, Confederate Research Center and Audie L. Murphy Gun Museum (h25)
P.O. Box 619
Hillsboro, Texas 76645

817-582-2555. Contact: Curator.

A special collection in an academic library with photographs of Hood's Texas Brigade, the Civil War, and the Confederacy. 200 copy prints, many with halftone screens. Ca. 1860s.

Hillsboro Heritage League (h28)
Hillsboro Public Library
P.O. Box 2
Hillsboro, Texas 76645

817-582-3434. Contact: Historian.

A local history society. Photographs include restrospective views of historic structures in Hillsboro and photographs from the local paper, *The Hillsboro Mirror*. 500 photographs. 1900 to present, most after 1960.

American Brahman Breeders Association (h31)
1313 La Concha Lane
Houston, Texas 77054

713-795-4444. Contact: Director of Communications.

An institutional collection with photographs of Brahman cattle ranching in the southern United States. 150 photographs. 1940s to the present.

Counsulate General of the Republic of Korea (h34)
1990 Post Oak Boulevard, Suite 745
Houston, Texas 77056

713-961-0186. Contact: Vice-Consul.

A diplomatic post of the government of Korea with an exhibition of photographs, "President Chun Doo Hwan and President Ronald Reagan's Washington summit, April, 1985." The exhibition chronicles President and Mrs. Chun's state visit to Washington DC, Los Angeles, and Hawaii. 40 color prints.

Houston Chamber of Commerce (h43)
1100 Milam, Twenty-fifth floor
Houston, Texas 77002

713-651-1313, extension 425. Contact: Photography and Audio/Visual Staff Associate.

Publicity photographs and photo files for *Houston* magazine, documenting the economic and social development of Houston and Harris County with extensive coverage of architecture, some coverage of local events and government. Area residents, none held in quantity; many figures represented in the landscape. Broad coverage of all ethnicities. Photographers include James Lacombe and Carl D. Miller. Vintage and copy photographs, most film negatives and transparencies. 1920 to present, most 1960 to present.

Houston Museum of Natural Science (h46)
1 Hermann Circle Drive
Houston, Texas 77030

713-526-4273. Contact: Registrar.

A natural history museum. Photographs include the Paul Dorsey collection of commercial views of the Texas oil industry and the Gulf

Coast, photographed by Dorsey, 10,000—4x5 negatives and 6,000 vintage prints, 1948 to 1963; and the Harvard African Expedition collection made in Liberia and the Rift Valley area of East Africa, 1,000—4x5 negatives identified by location, 1925 to 1926.

Bibliography: Richard P. Strong, ed., *The African Republic of Liberia and the Belgian Congo: Based on the observations made and material collected during the Harvard African Expedition, 1926-1927* (Cambridge MA: Harvard University Press, 1930).

Houston Police Museum (h49)
Houston Police Department
17000 Aldine Westfield Road
Houston, Texas 77073

713-230-2300, extension 360 or 361.   Contact: Director.

A museum documenting the Houston Police Department and serving as a community outreach facility.   Photographs relate to law enforcement in general and to the Houston Police Department in particular.   1,000 vintage and 1,500 copy prints; a few film negatives. 1890s to the present.

Menil Foundation, Image of the Black (h55)
1519 Branard
Houston, Texas 77006

713-528-1345. Contact: Project Director.

Photographs are art reproductions of paintings, sculpture, manuscript pages, stained-glass windows, decorative arts, and other media that depict the Black African or Afro-American in Western art from antiquity to the present; from works in museums, galleries, private collections, public and private institutions, and auction houses throughout the world.   10,000 photographs, most black-and-white prints.

Methodist Hospital, Department of Medical Photography and Television (h61)
6565 Fannin M.S. B-102
Houston, Texas 77030

713-790-3171. Contact: Manager. Requests for nontechnical, public information photographs should be directed to the Public Affairs Department.

A working collection providing documentation of clinical studies, pathology specimens, significant medical procedures, and institutional photographic services, including public relations and construction documentation. Photographs document the activities of Methodist Hospital, including clinical research and medical services. Many portraits of the hospital staff and of the Alkek, Bowen, Fondren, Mathis, and Scurlock families. Many were used in the hospital publications *Journal*, *Happenings*, and *Medical Staff News*. Photographers include Ron Ferguson, Tim Gee, Bill Pittman, Mel Reingold, Chris Saho, Bob Simmons, Gordon W. Stanley, and Peter Traylor. 500,000 vintage and 5,000 copy photographs, including prints, negatives, and transparencies; some motion picture footage. 1924 to present; many from the 1940s, most from the 1960s to 1970s.

Oceaneering International (h70)
16001 Park 10 Place, Suite 600
P.O. Box 218130
Houston, Texas 77218

713-578-8868.   Contact: Communications Manager.

A corporate collection intended for inhouse use. The collection consists almost entirely of underwater photography documenting the company's underwater petroleum support services; some effort has been made to collect photographs of the history of diving. Underwater photography from the North Sea, Asian Pacific, and Gulf of Mexico; topside shots from Alaska, offshore California, Louisiana, and Texas. Photographers include Hank Fannin, Frank Palm, Mungo Ross, and various others. 10,000 original photographs, predominantly 35mm transparencies. 1965 to present.

Sisters of Charity of the Incarnate Word, Villa de Matel (h79)
6510 Lawndale
Houston, Texas 77023

713-928-6053. Contact: Curator of photographs.

An institutional archive. Photographs document the activities of the Sisters of Charity of the Incarnate Word at Saint Mary's Infirmary and Saint Mary's Orphanage in Galveston; Saint Joseph's Infirmary, Saint Anthony's Home, and Villa de Matel in Houston; and Hotel Dieu Hospital in Beaumont. Many photographed by Frank J. Schlueter and Joseph Maurer. 2,000 photographs. 1920s to 1950s.

Huntsville Arts Commission, "Times and Places Gone By" (h85)
Hunstville Public Library
1216 Fourteenth Street
Huntsville, Texas 77340

409-291-5422. Contact: Program Coordinator.

A collection of photographs maintained in the public library depicting the economic and social development of Huntsville and of Walker County, including Sam Houston State University and the Texas Department of Corrections Huntsville Unit. 450 copy prints. 1890s to present.

Bell Helicopter Textron (h88)
600 East Hurst Boulevard
P.O. Box 482
Hurst, Texas 76101

817-280-8565. Contact: Staff Assistant—Public Affairs.

A corporate public relations file documenting Bell Helicopter products, including exhibitions and accidents; many made in Dallas, Fort Worth, Houston, and Vietnam. 70,000 vintage and 70,000 copy photographs, including panoramic prints, film transparencies, and motion pictures. 1951 to present.

Hurst Public Library (h91)
901 Precinct Line Road
Hurst, Texas 76053

817-485-5320. Contact: Technical Services Librarian.

A public library with a local history collec-tion with photographs of early settlers of Hurst, including William Letchworth Hurst. 100 photographs. Ca. 1900.

Tarrant County Junior College, Heritage Room (h94)
Northeast Campus Library
828 Harwood Road
Hurst, Texas 76053

817-282-7860, extension 477. Contact: Manager of Heritage Room.

An academic library with a collection of photographs depicting the economic and social development of northeastern Tarrant County, including Bedford, Euless, Fort Worth, and Hurst; portraits of Judge Benjamin Franklin Barkley. 75 vintage photographs, 1,500 copy prints. 1880s to 1900.

Irving Municipal Photographic Archives (i10)
City Secretary's Office
825 West Irving Boulevard
Irving, Texas 75060

214-721-2512. Contact: Records Manager/ Archivist.

A photographic collection maintained by the city documenting the economic and social development of the Dallas County and Irving vicinity, and area residents, including the Otis Brown, C. P. Schulze, J. O. Schulze, and William Smith families. 150 vintage and 500 copy photographs; 23 glass lantern slides. 1880s to present.

Lyndon B. Johnson National Historical Park (j10)
National Park Service
Nugent Street and US 290
P.O. Box 329
Johnson City, Texas 78636

512-868-7128. Contact: Park Ranger (Historian).

A national park located in Stonewall at the site of President Lyndon Johnson's boyhood home and the LBJ Ranch which served as the

Texas White House. Photographs, stored at the administrative offices in Johnson City, document Johnson's boyhood and political career. 650 copy photographs. 1920s to present.

Cowboy Artists of America Museum (k10)
1550 Bandera Highway
P.O. Box 1716
Kerrville, Texas 78029

512-896-2553. Contact: Librarian.

A museum dedicated to the works and history of the Cowboy Artists of America, a group of Western artists focusing on the US frontier. Arizona and New Mexico locales, including Shiprock, the Navajo Reservation in Taos, and desert landscapes. Portraits of Navajo Amerinds and family photographs by amateur photographer Judge William Searcy. 150 silver gelatin prints, some hand-tinted. 1910s to 1930s.

Kilgore College, Rangerette Showcase (k20)
1100 Broadway
Kilgore, Texas 75662

214-983-8265. Contact: Showcase Attendant.

An institutional museum documenting with photographs and artifacts the activities of the Kilgore Rangerettes drill team, their travels around the country and abroad, and the college. 2,000 vintage prints on permanent exhibit. 1940s to present.

Battleship Texas State Historic Site (l15)
Texas Parks and Wildlife Department
3527 Battleground Road
La Porte, Texas 77571

713-479-2411. Contact: Curator.

A dreadnought-class battleship in service from 1914 to 1948 and preserved as a military memorial with museum exhibits and collections. Photographic subjects include British, German,

and US navies during WW I and WW II, with a major emphasis on the Battleship Texas. 400 vintage and 100 copy photographs. 1880 to present, most 1900 to 1940.

Brazosport Museum of Natural Science (l25)
400 College Drive
Lake Jackson, Texas 77566

713-265-7831.

Four scrapbooks collected by Dr. A. P. Bentel, the first general manager of Dow Chemical Company, Texas Division. 30 photographs. 1940 to present.

Laredo Public Library (l30)
Bruni Plaza
1000 San Bernardo
Laredo, Texas 78040

512-722-2435. Contact: Librarian.

A public library with a local history room. Photographs in the collection document the economic and social development of Laredo and Nuevo Laredo. 300 vintage and 300 copy photographs. 1880s to 1960s, most 1900 to 1940.

Webb County Heritage Foundation (l35)
518 Pappas Street
Laredo, Texas 78041

512-727-0977. Contact: Exective Director.

A private, local history and preservation organization with a collection of photographs documenting the historical, economic, social, and cultural development of South Texas, including Cotulla, Laredo, San Ygnacio, and Zapata; some coverage of Nuevo Laredo and Tamaulipas, Mexico. Collections include those of Mark Cook, John Keck, the Laredo Public Library, and Ursuline Convent of Laredo. Photographers include T. R. Esquivel Sr., Sam N. Johnson Jr., Lyle C. Perkins, and Nick Sanchez. 30 vintage and 2,000 copy photographs. 1860s to present.

Real County
Historical Commission (140)
P.O. Box 74
Leakey, Texas 78873

512-232-6931.

A local history commission collecting photographs which document the economic and social development of Real County and landscapes of the Frio and Nueces canyons. 300 copy photographs. Nineteenth century to present.

Liberty County
Historical Commission (145)
1710 Sam Houston
P.O. Box 23
Liberty, Texas 77575

409-336-5397. Contact: Chairman.

A local history commission actively collecting copies of photographs in the community. Subjects include the economic and social development of Liberty with an emphasis on the local oil industry. 1,500—35mm copy negatives with contact sheets. 1880s to present.

Gregg County
Historical Museum (155)
Gregg County Historical Foundation
214 North Fredonia Street
P.O. Box 3342
Longview, Texas 75606

214-753-5840. Contact: Museum Director.

A local history museum with photographs documenting the economic and social development and area residents, of Gregg County, including Longview, Kilgore, Gladewater, and other, smaller communities. Many of the photographers were made by Cody Culpepper, a local studio and commercial photographer (1,500 negatives with some modern prints, 1910s to 1940s); various other photographers, including Mims. 450 vintage and 300 copy prints; 1,600 glass and nitrate negatives with a few modern prints. 1880s to 1950s.

Bibliography: *Longview, Texas Centennial, 1870-1970* (Longview: Longview Centennial Committee, 1970).

R. G. LeTourneau Archives (160)
LeTourneau College
2100 South Mobberly Avenue
P.O. Box 7001
Longview, Texas 75602

214-753-0231. Contact: Director of Library Services.

An academic library and museum housing the archives of the R. G. LeTourneau Corporation (now Marathon LeTourneau), a manufacturer of large-scale earth-moving equipment. The archive covers the operations of the R. G. LeTourneau Corporation, its philanthropic ventures, its missions in South America and West Africa, and its various government contracts throughout the world, including Africa, Libya, Peru, South America, and in the US, including Alaska, California, Pennsylvania, Texas. The archives also holds family snapshots of the LeTourneau family and photographs documenting the college. Many photographs by R. G. LeTourneau. Richard H. LeTourneau. 7,000 vintage and 2,000 copy photo prints, and 20 lantern slides. 1926 to present.

Texas Forestry Museum (175)
Texas Forestry Association
1905 Atkinson Drive
P.O. Box 1488
Lufkin, Texas 75901

409-632-8733. Contact: Trustee.

An industrial history museum with exhibits and collections of artifacts, books and journals, and photographs. Photographs document the development of the forest products industry in East Texas, especially Sour Lake, Trinity, and Willard; photographs depict logging, sawmills, and CCC camps. The Thompson collection contains images of Thompson lumber interests made by John Cress for *The American Lumberman* between 1907 and 1908. The aeria photographs collection contains 2,000—9" x 9" glass negatives. 2,700 photographs, total, including panoramic prints and motion picture stock. 1900 to 1920.

United States Forest Service (l80)
US Department of Agriculture
701 North First
Lufkin, Texas 75901

409-639-8573. Contact: Visual Information Specialist.

An institutional archive documenting the activities of the service in East Texas. 10,000—35mm color transparencies. 1950s to the present.

First Baptist Church (l85)
218 North Magnolia
P.O. Box 90
Luling, Texas 78648

512-875-2227. Contact: Church Secretary.

An institutional collection documenting the history of the church, including the building, Sunday schools, and other church groups. 100 photographs. Nineteenth century to present.

Lower Rio Grande Valley Development Council (m10)
707 Texas Commerce Bank Building
1701 West Business Highway 83
McAllen, Texas 78501

512-682-3481. Contact: Director of Regional Planning and Services.

A state agency coordinating the local governments of Cameron, Hidalgo, and Willacy counties. Photographs gathered by the council include retrospective views of historical sites, buildings, structures, and objects in the region used in the council's historical preservation plan. 100 photographs. 1978.

McAllen International Museum (m18)
1900 Nolana
McAllen, Texas 78501

512-682-1564. Contact: Curator of Collections.

An art and science museum with a collection of photographs documenting the economic and social development of McAllen, the Valley, and to a lesser extent, nearby Mexican cities; a few images pertain to the New York National Guard stationed in the area in response to border bandits. 200 vintage photographs. 1900 to 1940.

Marfa-Presidio County Museum (m26)
221 North Mesa
Marfa, Texas 79843

915-729-4942. Contact: Director.

A regional history museum holding the archive of Marfa studio and commercial photographer Francis King "Frank" Duncan (1878-1970), including picturesque views of landscapes and ranch scenes in the Davis Mountains, Big Bend, Alpine, Fort Davis, and Marfa, studio portraits of area residents, and local events. 10,000 nitrate and glass negatives, most 4x5, many 5x7; 200 nitrate, cirkut panorama negatives; 2,000 vintage silver gelatin prints, including a few panoramas; 500 modern prints. 1920s to 1950s.

Harrison County Historical Museum (m34)
Harrison County Historical Society
Old Courthouse
Marshall, Texas 75670

214-938-2680. Contact: Director.

A local history museum with a collection of photographs documenting the economic and social development of Harrison County. 250 vintage and 250 copy photographs. Nineteenth century to present.

Menardville Museum (m42)
Menard Historical Society
Frisco and Highway 83
P.O. Box 663
Menard, Texas 76859

915-396-4318. Contact: Vice-President.

Photographs document the economic and social development of Menard, including schools, businesses, churches, and homes; portraits of Menard veterans of WW I and WW II. Photographers include N. H. Rose and F. L. Wilkinson. 680 vintage and 60 copy photographs. 1880s to present, most 1940s.

Bosque County Historical Commission (m50)
Bosque County Courthouse, Third floor
P.O. Box 534
Meridian, Texas 76665

Contact: Chairman.

A local history commission collecting photographs that document the economic and social development of the urban and rural communities of Bosque County, including the towns Clifton, Cranfills Gap, Meridian, Morgan, Laguna Park, Kopperl, Valley Mills, Walnut Springs, and Iredell, and the rural communities Coon Creek, Rock Church on Hog Creek, Kimball, Norway Mills, Footout, Cayote, Womack, Norse, Harmony, Searsville, Boggy, and others; area residents, including Hugh Combs, Knowles family, George Lewis, Lowry Scrutchfield, Iva Pool Torrence, and many others; subjects include interiors of grocery stores, barber shops, and railroads shops; farming; street scenes; rural school houses; doctors, teachers, county officials, and lawyers. The commission is currently assembling photographs of cemetery markers in the county. 1,500 copy photographs, 250 vintage silver gelatin prints, 100 vintage color prints, and some transparencies. Early 1860s to present.

Nita Stewart Haley Memorial Library, Erwin E. Smith Photographic Collection (m58)
1805 West Indiana
Midland, Texas 79701

915-682-5785. Contact: Librarian.

Ranching in the Panhandle and West Texas photographed by Erwin E. Smith and J. Evetts Haley. Negatives, modern prints. 1900 to 1920.

Midland County Historical Museum (m66)
301 West Missouri
Midland, Texas 79701

915-683-2708. Contact: President.

A local history society collecting photographs which document the economic and social development of Midland and of Midland County. Photographers include Miller, Prothro, Muldrow's, and Rosenbaum. 1,500 vintage photographs. 1882 to present, most 1920s to 1940s.

Bibliography: Midland County Historical Society, *The pioneer history of Midland County, 1880-1926* (Dallas: Taylor Publishing Company).

Museum of the Southwest (m74)
1705 West Missouri
Midland, Texas 79701

915-683-2882. Contact: Director or Curatorial Assistant.

A museum specializing in fine art, archaeology, and anthropology with photographs pertaining to the Taos School of painters, especially the Holstron, Johnson, and Nilson families; some portraits of Amerinds from Edward S. Curtis' *North American Indian*. Locations include Arizona, Illinois, and New Mexico. Other photographers include Master's and Skold (Princeton IL). 300 vintage prints. 1900 to 1920.

Muleshoe Area Public Library (m90)
322 West Second Street
Muleshoe, Texas 79347

806-272-4707. Contact: Librarian.

A public library with a collection of photographs documenting the economic and social development of Muleshoe and of Bailey County, with an emphasis on ranching and the use of mules as draft animals.

Ector County Library (o10)
321 West Fifth Street
Odessa, Texas 79761

915-332-0634. Contact: Southwest History and
Genealogy Department Head.

A public library with a collection of photographs documenting the economic and social
development of Odessa and of Ector County.
100 vintage photographs, copy photographs and
copy slides. 1900 to 1960.

Odessa Chamber of Commerce (o20)
400 West Fourth Street
P.O. Box 3626
Odessa, Texas 79761

915-332-8189. Contact: Director.

An association promoting local industry,
business, history, and special events with photographs documenting the economic and social
environment of West Texas with major emphasis
on Odessa and Ector County, some coverage of
the Big Bend. 1,500 film negatives, 2,500 slides,
150 vintage prints, and 250 copy negatives.
1930s to present.

Second Baptist Church (o30)
711 East Seventeenth
Odessa, Texas 79761

915-337-8381. Contact: Media Center Director.

A church with an institutional collection
documenting its history and congregation. 450
photo prints and 50 photo negatives. 1951 to
present.

Texas State Library and Archives
Local Records Division, Permian
Historical Archives (o40)
University of Texas of the Permian Basin
4901 East University
Odessa, Texas 79762

915-367-2128. Contact: Archivist.

A government archive preserving regional
history with collections of photographs

documenting the economic and social development of the Permian Basin region with an
emphasis on Odessa and Ector County. Area
residents include the Cooper (Jal NM) and B. C.
Hendricks families. Photographers include
commercial photographer Bill Shoopman
(Odessa) and itinerant photographer Jack
Nolan. 450 vintage and 500 copy prints, 900
negatives, and some transparencies. 1880s to
1950s.

White-Pool House (o60)
112 East Murphy
Ector County Historical Commission
1705 East Forty-sixth Street
Odessa, Texas 79762.

915-333-0472. Contact: Chairman, Ector County
Historical Commission.

A restored historic structure with holdings
pertinent to the families who lived there. 400
vintage and copy photographs. 1880s to present,
most after 1960.

Sabine River Authority (o70)
P.O. Box 579
Orange, Texas 77630

409-883-9334. Contact: Administrative
Assistant.

A government agency collecting photographs of its activities and projects along the
Sabine River Basin. 200 photo prints, loose and
in albums. 1949 to present.

Palacios Area
Historical Association (p10)
403 Commerce Street
P.O. Box 1050
Palacios, Texas 77465

512-972-5241. Contact: Chairman.

A local history society with a collection of
photographs that document the economic and
social development of Palacios, Blessing, and
Collegeport and of Matagorda County, including
Camp Hulen and the fishing industry. Area resi-

dents included in the collection are predominantly Caucasian with some coverage of Hispanic, Black, and Vietnamese ethnicities, and include the families of Guy and Blanche Claybourn, Ruel B. Foley, and Jake Wilkerson. Photographers include Colleen Claybourn, E. O. Goldbeck, Hill Photos, J. P. McDonald, D. L. Stump, and Nick West. 500 vintage and 200 copy photographs. 1836 [sic] to present, most after 1960.

Carson County
Square House Museum (p18)
Fifth and Elsie Streets
P.O. Box 276
Panhandle, Texas 79068

806-537-3118. Contact: Director.

A local history museum with a collection of photographs documenting the economic and social development of the Panhandle region with an emphasis on Carson County, including ranching and the oil industry. 3,000 vintage and 1,000 copy photographs. 1880s to present.

Paris Junior College,
A. M. and Welma Aikin Regional Archives (p26)
Paris, Texas 75460

214-785-7661, extension 411. Contact: Librarian.

An academic library with collections containing photographs that document the economic and social development of Lamar, Delta, Fannin, and Red River counties, including the college, the career of Senator A. M. Aikin and his wife's involvement with the state garden club, and the career of Judge A. W. Neville. 1,000 photographs. 1900 to the present.

S. B. Maxey House (p34)
Texas Parks and Wildlife Department
812 Church
Paris, Texas 75460

214-785-5716. Contact: Superintendent.

A restored historic structure with photographs of the Maxey, Lightfoot, Long, and Williams families. Many photographed by Hudson (Paris TX) and S. Lynn (Paris TX). 600 vintage prints. 1880s to 1940.

Pasadena Public Library (p42)
1201 Minerva
Pasadena, Texas 77506

713-477-0276. Contact: Chief of Public Services.

A public library with a collection of local history photographs, most of area residents and some of preeminent buildings and businesses. 300 photographs. 1900 to 1930, a few later.

Bibliography: *A pictorial history of Pasadena* (Pasadena: Pasadena Historical Society and the City of Pasadena, [1976]).

Texas Chiropractic College (p50)
5912 Spencer Highway
Pasadena, Texas 77505

713-487-1170. Contact: Director, Library Services.

An academic library with a collection of photographs documenting the history of the school and chiropractic services; Oklahoma, Texas, and San Antonio are represented. 100 photographs. 1900 to present.

Hale County Historical Commission (p58)
Plainview, Texas 79072

A local history commission collecting photographs that document the economic and social development of Hale County. 200 photographs. 1900 to present.

Longhorn Museum (p66)
222 North Main (Highway 97E)
Pleasanton, Texas 78064

512-569-3219. Contact: President.

A local history museum with photographs documenting the economic and social development of the area and area residents. 100 photographs. Nineteenth century to present.

Bell Public Library (p74)
Eighth and Austin Street
Portland, Texas 78374

512-643-6527.

A public library with a local history collection documenting the Portland and San Patricio County area. 100 photographs. 1900 to present.

Princeton Independent School
District Museum (p90)
304 Panther Parkway
P.O. Drawer B
Princeton, Texas 75077

214-736-3741.   Contact: Director Community Education.

A collection gathered by the school district with subjects that document the economic and social development of Princeton and of northeastern Collin County, including the communities of Branch, Clear Lake, Climax, Culleoka, Lake Lavon, Lowry Crossing, and Ticky Creek; a German prisoner of war camp and a migrant-labor camp. 200 vintage and 500 copy photographs. 1880 to present.

Governor Hogg Shrine
State Historical Park (q10)
Texas Parks and Wildlife Department
518 South Main
Route 3, Park Road 45
Quitman, Texas 75783

214-763-2701. Contact: Park Superintendent.

A state park with photographs pertaining to the life and career of Governor James Hogg, and the Hogg and Stinson families. 62 copy photographs. Pre-1900.

Ralls Historical Museum (r10)
801 Main Street
P.O. Box 384
Ralls, Texas 79357

806-253-2425. Contact: Deputy Director.

A local history museum with photographs depicting the economic and social development of Ralls and of Crosby County. 1,000 vintage prints. 1880s to present.

Rankin Museum (r20)
Sixth and Main Streets
P.O. Box 82
Rankin, Texas 79778

915-693-2770. Contact: Museum.

A local history museum and archive documenting area residents and the economic and social development of Upton County, including Rankin and Upland. Photographs are contained in the papers of Ann M. Clark, Gena Johnson, Opal Nix, Grace Roach, Gertrude Smith, and Maggie Taylor.   Photographers include J. B. Hutchens, Ann M. Clark, and Mickey Reece.

Subject headings used in the collection include bank, baseball, celebrations, churches, courthouse, graves, historical society, hospital, hotels, houses, library, museum, organizations, personages, petroleum, post office, ranches, Rankin newspaper, schools and students, street scenes, weather, and weddings and parties.

1,600 vintage prints. 1900 to present, most after 1960.

Fort Bend County Museum (r40)
500 Houston Street
P.O. Box 251
Richmond, Texas 77469

409-342-6478. Contact: Director.

A local history museum documenting the economic and social development of Richmond, Rosenberg, and Sugarland and of Fort Bend County, especially the sugar industry. The collection includes many photographic postcards by Frank J. Schlueter. 2,500 photographs, most prints. 1860s to 1960s, most ca. 1900.

Round Rock Public Library (r50)
216 East Main
Round Rock, Texas 78664

512-255-3939. Contact: Director.

A public library with a local history collection containing photographs of public schools, architecture, cityscapes, documents, natural disasters, city government, aerial photographs, organizations, fire protection services, libraries, and railroads. 50 vintage and 100 copy photographs. 1900 to present.

University of Texas, Winedale Historical Center (r60)

FM Road 2714
P.O. Box 11
Round Top, Texas 78954

409-278-3530. Contact: Administrator or Registration Clerk.

A collection of restored historical structures dating from the Texas colonial period collecting photographs that document the economic and social development of the farming communities in Fayette County. Many photographs by Round Top amateur photographer Friederike Recknagel. 500 vintage and 7,000 copy photographs. 1900 to 1960s.

Rusk State Hospital (r70)

Highway 69 North
P.O. Box 318
Rusk, Texas 76785

An institutional collection documenting the history of the hospital and the state penitentiary, including many farm scenes. 80 slides. 1884 to present.

Sea Rim State Park and Sabine Pass Battleground State Historic Park (s10)

Texas Parks and Wildlife Department
Highway 87, 10 miles West of Sabine Pass
P.O. Box 1066
Sabine Pass, Texas 77655

713-971-2559. Contact: Park Superintendent.

An institutional collection documenting the flora and fauna of the park. 2,000—35mm color transparencies. 1977 to present.

Alamo Area Council of Governments (s16)

118 Broadway, Suite 400
San Antonio, Texas 78205

512-225-5201. Contact: Director, Intergovernmental and Community Relations.

A regional council coordinating local governmental entities and services with an institutional collection documenting the council's education, water conservation, criminal justice, aging, economic development, and substance-abuse programs in Atascosa, Bandera, Bexar, Comal, Frio, Gillespie, Guadalupe, Karnes, Kendall, Kerr, Medina, and Wilson counties. 1,000 original and 500 copy photo negatives. 1969 to present.

Brooks Air Force Base, Hangar 9, Edward H. White II Memorial Museum (s19)

6570th ABG/HOM
San Antonio, Texas 78235

512-536-2203. Contact: Director.

A restored historic structure now housing a museum of flight medicine. Photographs in the collection document the history of flight medicine, including doctors and nurses, especially in the US Air Force; some coverage of WW I. 2,500 photographs, including vintage and copy photo prints, negatives, panoramic prints, and glass lantern slides. 1917 to present.

Catholic Archdiocese of San Antonio, Catholic Archives of Texas (s21)

9123 Lorene Lane
P.O. Box 32648
San Antonio, Texas 78284

512-344-2331, extension 70. Contact: Archivist.

An institutional archive with a collection of photographs that includes portraits of the Catholic clergy, churches and religious activities, restoration of the missions, and the Fiesta celebration. 500 vintage and 250 copy photographs. 1890s to present.

Fort Sam Houston, US Army Medical Museum (s30)

Academy of Health Science
Health Service Command
San Antonio, Texas 78234

512-221-2358. Contact: Curator.

An institutional museum concentrating on the history of the US Army Medical Department. Photographs document military medicine as practiced during the Civil War, WW I, WW II, and the Korean War. 224 processed photographs; additional unprocessed photographic materials include stereographs and film transparencies. 1860s to 1970s.

Lackland Air Force Base, Air Force Military Training Center (s33)

AFMTC/HO
San Antonio, Texas 78236

512-671-2211. Contact: Assistant Historian.

An institutional collection of military subjects, including the cryptographic school, encampments, language center, personnel, and Police Technical Training School. 1,000 photographs. 1940 to present.

Lackland Air Force Base, History and Traditions Museum (s36)

Orville Wright Drive
San Antonio, Texas 78236

512-671-3444. Contact: Curator.

A museum interpreting the evolution of aviation and the operation of the US Air Force and its predecessor organization. Photographs depict aircraft and missiles in combat during WW II, the Korean War, and the Vietnam conflict. Several thousand photographs, mostly copy prints, some vintage prints, film transparencies, and 16mm motion picture stock. 1900 to present.

Museum of American Aviation (s39)

American Aviation Research Association
3119 Growndon Road
San Antonio, Texas 78227

512-828-6862 or 512-436-9299. Contact: Director.

A history museum focusing on aviation in the United States. Record groups include the Jacob Brodbeck collection; the Barton Neal Jr. Aviation collection, containing Kelly AFB in San Antonio; the Fernando Cortez collection of aviation history. 14,000 vintage photographs, including stereographs and transparencies. 1880s to present, most after 1960.

Saint Mary's University, Anita C. Saxine Special Collections Library (s42)

One Camino Santa Maria
San Antonio, Texas 78284

512-436-1323 or 512-436-3441. Contact: Librarian.

An academic library with a collection of photographs. Subjects include the campus facility and the faculty, staff, and students, including Ann Armstrong, Dr. Michael DeBakey, President Dwight D. Eisenhower as a football coach in 1916, and William F. Quinn. Photographers include Ed Gaida, Fr. Herbert Kramer, and Mario C. Ramirez. 2,100 photographs. 1892 to present.

San Antonio Conservation Society (s45)

107 King Williams
San Antonio, Texas 78204

512-224-6163. Contact: Librarian.

A historical society preserving "historic buildings, objects, and places, relating to this history of Texas, its natural beauty, and all that is admirably distinctive of [the] state." The society collects books and journals, manuscripts, architectural plans, artifacts, and photographs relating to Texas with an emphasis on San Antonio and architecture. Area residents in the collection include the Edward Steves family, including stereographs of the interior of their Victorian home from about 1880, and the Anton Wulff family. The society also holds studio portraits of its presidents and members, and its activities. Photographers include Louis Hoffman, Barbara Jones, and Ernst Raba (San Antonio). 700 vintage and 1,000 copy prints; 250 glass and a few film negatives. 1870s to present.

Record Groups: Ernst Raba (1874-1951) collection of landmarks, structures, and street scenes in San Antonio photographed by Raba; 250 vintage glass negatives with modern copy negatives and prints, 1890s to early 1900s.

Dorothy Matthies postcard collection of landmarks, structures, and street scenes in early San Antonio, Houston, and Galveston; 767 postcards, ca. 1906.

San Antonio Public Library (s48)
203 South Saint Mary's
San Antonio, Texas 78205

512-299-7790. Contact: Librarian.

A public library with a local history collection documenting the economic and social development of San Antonio. 50 photographs.

Sisters of Charity of the Incarnate Word Generalate Archives (s54)
4503 Broadway
San Antonio, Texas 78209

512-826-7142. Not open to the public.

A private, institutional archive of the Sisters of Charity of the Incarnate Word documenting their activities and members. Geographic coverage in areas where the sisters have served, including Ireland, Mexico, Peru, and the US, including Mississippi and Texas. Subjects cover activities and members of the congregation, including academia, hospitals and health care, congregation, and ministry. Institutions represented (San Antonio unless otherwise noted) include Brackenridge Villa, Santa Rosa Medical Center, Motherhouse of the Sisters of Charity of Incarnate Word, Saint Joseph's Hospital (Fort Worth), Saint Jospeh's Hospital (Paris TX), Saint Anthony's Hospital (Amarillo), Spohn Hospital (Corpus Christi), Incarnate Word Hospital (St. Louis MO), Incarnate Word College, and Incarnate Word High School. People in the collections are predominantly members of the congregation, including co-founders of the order, Mother Pierre Cinquin and Mother Madeleine Chollet, Bishop Claude M. Dubuis, Bishop John Marie Odin, Bishop A. Dominic Pellicer, Bishop John C. Nerez, and Bishop Arthur J. Drossaerts. Many snapshots by members of the congregation; commercial, San Antonio photorgaphers include Joe Bacon, Harvey Patteson, Powell Studio,

Charles A. Stread, and Summerville. 3,200 photographs. 1870s to the present, most after 1940.

Sisters of the Sacred Heart of Jesus of St. Jacut (s57)
5922 Blanco Road
San Antonio, Texas 78216

512-344-4805. Contact: Archivist.

Archives of the Sisters of the Sacred Heart of Jesus documenting their activities and members of the order in South Central Texas and the foreign countries Africa, Canada (Quebec, Ontario, and Great North), France (Brittany), Great Britain, and Peru. 750 photographs.

University of Texas Health Sciences Center, Library and Special Collections (s60)
7703 Floyd Curl Drive
San Antonio, Texas 78284

512-691-6271. Contact: Special Collections Librarian.

An institutional collection of photographs documenting the history of the center and local hospitals; portraits of members of the Bexar County Medical Society; some manuscript collections have photographs of local health care practitioners. 1,000 vintage photographs. 1895 to present.

San Marcos Public Library, Tula Townsend Watt Collection of Local History (s66)
310 West Hutchinson
San Marcos, Texas 78666

512-392-8124. Contact: Library Director.

Subjects include area residents, predominantly Caucasian, with substantial coverage of Black and Hispanic ethnicities; the economic and social development of San Marcos and of Hays County, including vintage and restrospective views of houses, public buildings, scenes, and events. Photographers include Anita Miller. 1,000 vintage and 1,000 copy photographs, including a few cased images and glass negatives. 1880s to 1960s.

San Saba County Historical Museum (s68)
Mill Pond Park
P.O. Box 242
San Saba, Texas 76877

No phone. Contact: Chairman.

A local history museum with photographs that document the economic and social development of San Saba and of San Saba County. 300 vintage and 60 copy photographs. Ca. 1895.

Canadian River Municipal Water Authority (s70)
(One mile west of Sanford)
P.O. Box 99
Sanford, Texas 79078

806-865-3325. Contact: General Manager.

A state agency with an institutional collection of photographs documenting the maintainence, repair operation, and condition of the projects; made during inspection of facilities of the dam, reservoir, and aqueduct. 5,000—35mm color transparencies. 1971 to present.

Seguin-Guadalupe County Public Library (s72)
707 East College
Seguin, Texas 78155

512-379-1531. Contact: Library Director.

A private, community library with a local history division holding artworks, manuscripts, books and journals, land records, and photographs. Many photographs from foreign countries, none held in quantity. Major emphasis is on Guadalupe County, especially Geronimo, Schwartz, and Seguin. 1,000 vintage and 100 copy photographs, including 600 film transparencies and 45 stereographs. 1925 to present.

Sherman Historical Museum (s74)
301 South Walnut
Sherman, Texas 75090

214-893-7623. Contact: Director.

A local history museum. Photographs in the collection document area residents and the economic and social development of Sherman and Denison in Grayson County, including modern rephotographic surveys of historic sites; other subjects include Carr-Burdette and Kidd-Key colleges, and camp scenes from the Spanish-American War. Many photographed by Wears Studio (Sherman); rephotography by Bebe Armstrong and Joan Huseman Ball. 1,000 vintage photographs, including cased images, prints, and stereographs. 1850s to present, most 1880 to 1900 and 1930 to 1950.

Bibliography: *Lost Sherman* (Sherman: Sherman Historical Museum, 1981).

Sherman Public Library (s76)
421 North Travis
Sherman, Texas 75090

214-892-4545, extension 240. Contact: Librarian.

A public library with a local history collection. Photographs document the economic and social development of Grayson County, including Denison, Mormon Grove, Rockport, Sherman, Tioga, Whitemound, and Whitesboro. 500 negatives and prints. 1969 to 1973.

Scurry County Library (s78)
1916 Twenty-third Street
Snyder, Texas 79549

915-573-5572. Contact: Head Librarian.

A public library with a local history collection. Photographs document the economic and social development of Scurry County, including the communities of Camp Springs, Dunn, Fluvanna, Green Springs, Hermleigh, Ira, Knapp, Snyder. 100 vintage and 100 copy photographs.

Scurry County Museum (s80)
Western Texas College
College Avenue
P.O. Box 696
Snyder, Texas 79549

915-573-6107. Contact: Curator.

An academic library with a local history collection. Photographs document the economic and social development of Scurry County, including Fluvanna, Hermleigh, Ira, Post, and Snyder, with an emphasis on the oil industry and farming; area businesses, including interiors. Portraits of area residents, including Judy Hayes, Edith McKanna, J. Wright Mooar family, Allan Shivers, and Pete Snyder. Photographers include Delbert Hirst and Joe Dave Scott. 450 vintage photographs, including 150 stereographs; 200 copy photographs. 1920s to the present.

Bibliography: Charles G. Anderson, *Deep creek merchant: The story of William Henry "Pete" Snyder* (Snyder: Snyder Publishing Company, 1984). Charles G. Anderson, *In search of the buffalo* (Seagraves: Pioneer Book Publishers, 1974). Wayland G. Holt, *The first one hundred years* (Scurry County Historical Commission, Scurry County Museum, and the Friends of Judge Holt, 1985). Shelton Hooper, *From buffalo to oil: The history of Scurry County, Texas.* (Feather Press, 1973). Ranch Headquarters Association, Snyder Unit, *Early ranching in West Texas* (Ann Arbor MI: Braun-Brumfield, 1986).

Splendora City Library (s82)
300 FM 2090 East
P.O. Drawer C
Splendora, Texas 77372

713-689-1818. Contact: Librarian.

A public library with a local history collection. Photographs document the economic and social development of Splendora. 100 copy photographs. Ca. 1900.

Cowboy Country Museum (s84)
Stamford Chamber of Commerce
113 Wetherbee
P.O. Box 1206
Stamford, Texas 79553

915-773-2411. Contact: Cowboy Country Museum.

A local history museum focusing on the farm and ranching aspects of the community. Photographs in the collection document the economic and social development of Stamford and vicinity with an emphasis on ranching. 5 albums; loose prints. 1920s to present.

Stephenville
Historical House Museum (s86)
525 East Washington
Stephenville, Texas 76401

No phone. Contact: President of the Board.

A group of restored historic structures with a local history archive. Photographs document the economic and social development of Stephenville and the Cross Timbers region; other Texas locales represented include Austin, Boerne, Houston, Nacogdoches, New Braunfels, San Antonio, and Waco; vacation photographs gathered by travelers from the Stephenville area taken in Austria, Denmark, England, France, Germany, India, Ireland, Italy, Luxembourg, Mexico, Norway, Peru, Portugal, and Sweden, as well as in states of Arizona, Hawaii, Missouri, Oklahoma, New Mexico, and Wyoming; area residents, predominantly of English, Italian, and Polish ethnicities, including the Clinkscales, Frey, King, Neill, and Reil families and Leonard Roberts. Photographers include K. N. Baxley, W. Baxley, Birdie Hartsough Frey, C. Richard King, and Lenox. 8,000 photographs, including copy slides. 1880s to present, most 1900 to 1980.

Sunset Trading Post and
Old West Museum (s88)
Highway 287
Sunset, Texas 76270

817-872-2027. Contact: Proprietor.

A regional history museum with photographs of Comanche, Creek, Crow, Kiowa, and Sioux Amerinds, including Geronimo and Quanah Parker, made in Texas, Oklahoma, and Montana. 330 glass and 100 film negatives; 100 vintage and 100 copy prints. 1880s to 1920s.

Pioneer City/County Museum (s90)
610 East Third
Sweetwater, Texas 79556

915-235-8547. Contact: Director.

A restored historic structure housing a local history museum. Photographs in the collection document the pioneers and the economic and social development of Nolan County. Photographers include R. C. Crane, Mike Graves, and Willis Art Gallery. 700 vintage photographs. 1880 to 1920.

Taylor Public Library (t10)
721 Vance
Taylor, Texas 76574

512-352-3434. Contact: Librarian.

A public library with a local history collection. Photographs document the economic and social development of Taylor and of Williamson County. 250 vintage and 200 copy prints. 1876 to present.

Burlington-Rock Island Railroad Museum (t18)
208 South Third Avenue
Teague, Texas 75860

817-739-2645. Contact: Curator.

A local history museum collecting photographs that document the economic and social development of Teague and of Freestone County with an emphasis on railroads, including the Burlington-Rock Island and the Trinity and Brazos Valley ("Boll Weevil") railroads. Area residents include the Teague, Headlee, W. R. Boyd, and Notley families. Many photographed by Harry Glenn Hippel. 2,000 vintage and copy prints, 100 stereographs, and 25 cased images. 1880s to present, most ca. 1900.

Railroad and Pioneer Museum (t26)
710 Jack Baskin Street
P.O. Box 5126
Temple, Texas 76501

817-778-6873. Contact: President.

A local history museum with an emphasis on railroads in Central Texas. Photographs in the collection document the various ethnic groups in Bell County and in Temple, and railroads. 350 photographs, including vintage and copy prints, cased images, and film negatives. 1850s to 1940s.

SPJST Archives, Library, and Museum (t34)
SPJST Fraternal Life Insurance
520 North Main
P.O. Box 100
Temple, Texas 76503

817-773-1575. Contact: Curator.

An institutional collection containing photographs of the organization's activities and of members of the organization and Czech ethnic groups. 100 copy photographs. 1880 to present.

Temple Public Library (t42)
101 North Main
Temple, Texas 76501

817-778-5555. Contact: Librarian.

A local history collection in a public library with photographs documenting the economic and social development of the Temple area, and area residents. 600 photographs. 1880s to present.

Silent Wings Museum (t50)
Military Glider Pilots Association
Municipal Airport
P.O. Box 775
Terrell, Texas 75160

214-563-0402. Contact: President, Board of Directors.

An aviation history museum. Photographs in the collection depict the training of glider pilots of WW II and various landings in combat in the European Theater, as well as glider aviation in China, Burma, and India. Various military photographers; some photographs made by the pilots. 700 photographs. 1940s.

Trinity Historical Society (t66)
Blanche K. Werner Library
Highway 19 North
P.O. Box 1168
Trinity, Texas 75862

409-594-2087. Contact: Librarian.

A local history collection documenting the economic and social development of the Trinity County area, and area residents. 1,000 vintage and 60 copy photographs, including daguerreotypes and prints. Ca. 1860 to present.

Bob Wills Museum (t74)
Bob Wills Foundation
Sixth and Lyles Street
Turkey, Texas 79261

806-423-1033. Contact: Secretary.

A collection of memorabilia, including photographs, pertaining to Bob Wills, donated by his widow, Betty Wills. 100 photographs.

Tyler Museum of Art (t90)
1300 South Mahon
Tyler, Texas 75701

214-5955-1001. Contact: Curator of Exhibitions.

An art museum with a limited reserve collection. Photographs depict cityscapes, domestic activities, landscapes, and social life and customs in California and Texas. Photographs by Judy Bankhead and others. 64 photographs. 1960s to 1980s.

El Progresso Public Library (u10)
129 West Nopal
Uvalde, Texas 78801

512-278-2017. Contact: Librarian.

A public library with a local history collection containing photographs that document the economic and social development of the Uvalde

vicinity. 200 copy photographs and negatives. 1900 to 1940.

John Nance Garner Museum (u20)
333 North Park
Uvalde, Texas 78802

512-278-3315. Contact: Curator.

A memorial to former US vice-president John Nance Garner located in his restored home. Photographs in the collection include biographical portraits of Garner. 40 vintage and 180 copy photographs. 1900s to 1980s, most 1920s to 1940s.

Bosque Valley Heritage Society (v10)
Fifth Street and Avenue E
P.O. Box 168
Valley Mills, Texas 76689

817-932-5277. Contact: Chairperson.

A local history society collecting photographs that document the economic and social development of Valley Mills. 175 photographs. 1880 to 1940.

Victoria College, Local History Collection (v20)
2200 East Red River Street
Victoria, Texas 77901

512-573-3291, extension 265. Contact: Director.

An academic library with a local history collection. Photographs document the economic and social development of Victoria County, including Rockport and Victoria, with emphasis on cattle ranching; the papers of biologist James Daniel Mitchell document the marine culture and his life. Photographers include Miss Crew, Louis de Planque, and S. R. Weisiger. 2,000 copy slides and 1,000 vintage photo prints. Late 1870s to present; most 1900s to 1920s.

Bibliography: Roy Grimes, *Three hundred years in Victoria* (Victoria Advocate Publishing Company, 1968; 2nd ed., 1986). Robert W. Shook and Charles Spurlin, *Victoria: A pictorial history* (Norfolk VA: Donning, 1986).

Victoria County Historical Commission (v30)

210 East Forrest
Victoria, Texas 77901

512-575-5210. Contact: Chairman.

A local history commission collecting photographs, many of which are on permanent exhibit in the mayor's and sheriff's offices and at the county jail. Subjects include local officials and the economic and social development of Victoria, with an emphasis on cattle ranching. Photographers include M. L. Potash. 40 vintage and 500 copy photographs. 1855 to present.

Baylor University, Strecker Museum (w10)

Sid Richardson Science Building
South Fourth Street
Waco, Texas 76798

817-755-1110. Contact: Director.

A natural history museum. 500 vintage photographs.

Brazos River Authority (w25)

4400 Cobbs Drive
P.O. Box 7555
Waco, Texas 76714

817-776-1441. Contact: Administrative Assistant.

A government agency collecting photographs documenting its activities; subjects include the public works of the authority, the Morris Sheppard Dam in the Brazos River Valley and Lake Possum Kingdom, Lake Granbury, Lake Limestone, Brazoria and Fort Bend counties, Waco, Temple-Belton, and Sugarland. 2,000 vintage prints and 35mm color transparencies. 1930s to present.

Texas Old Missions and Forts Restoration Association (w30)

524 North Twenty-second Street
Waco, Texas 76707

817-753-7503. Contact: Archivist.

An institutional collection with photographs made by the search committee when looking for sites of Spanish missions and forts, including retrospective views of historic structures and sites. 100 photographs.

Ellis County Museum (w45)

201 South College
P.O. Box 706
Waxahachie, Texas 75165

214-937-0681. Contact: Curator.

A local history museum. Photographs in the collection document the economic and social development of Waxahachie and Ellis County, and the area residents, including Alemeda Griggs, John Prince, and Clemons Ragsdale. Photographers include Dawson and Pitts, Davenport, Moreland Herring, Hudson, and Montgomery Middleton. 1,000 vintage photographs, most prints. 1880s to present.

N. P. Sims Public Library (w50)

515 West Main
Waxahachie, Texas 75165.

214-937-2671. Contact: Reference Librarian.

A public library with a local history collection. Photographs in the collection document the economic and social development of the region, including Marvin College and the USS Waxahachie. 300 photographs. Ca. 1900.

Weatherford Public Library (w55)

1214 Charles
Weatherford, Texas 76086

817-594-2767.

A public library with a local history collection. Photographs in the collection depict the economic and social development of Weatherford. 50 photographs.

Wharton County Museum (w60)

231 South Fulton
P.O. Box 349
Wharton, Texas 77488

409-532-2600. Contact: Curator.

An exhibiting local history museum. Photographs documenting the economic and social development of the area, including Bay City, Eagle Lake, Egypt, Houston, and Wharton; substantial coverage of rice farming. Area residents include Albert Clinton Horton, and Abel Head "Shanghai" Pierce. Photographers include Blessing and Brothers, Louis de Planque, Eagle Lake Studios, Hamilton Studios, H. B. Hillyer, Hillyer and Son, Louis Melcher, and Rooker and Frasier. 3,000 vintage and 1,000 copy photographs, most prints. Late nineteenth century to present.

Whitesboro Public Library (w65)
308 West Main
P.O. Drawer B
Whitesboro, Texas 76273

214-564-5432.

A public library with a local history collection documenting area residents and the economic and social development of Whitesboro. 100 photographs. Nineteenth century to present.

Whitewright Public Library (w70)
300 Grand
P.O. Box 128
Whitewright, Texas 75491

214-364-2955. Contact: Librarian.

A library with a local history collection containing photographs documenting Whitewright, especially family snapshots of area residents and local architecture. Photographers include Brenda Wilson. 100 photographs, including panoramic prints. 1880s to present.

Kell House (w75)
Wichita County Heritage Society
900 Bluff Street
Wichita Falls, Texas 76301

817-723-0623.

A house museum with photographs pertaining to the Kell and Kemp families, former residents. 900 vintage prints, 300 negatives. 1880s to 1980, most after 1920.

Midwestern State University (w80)
Wichita Falls, Texas 76308

817-692-6611. Contact: History Department.

An institutional collection with photographs of the university. 100 photographs. 1940 to present.

Allan Shivers
Library and Museum (w90)
302 North Charlton
Woodville, Texas 75979

409-283-3709. Contact: Director.

A Victorian house-museum housing memorabilia from Governor Shivers' tenure as governor, including photographs from his career and the Shivers family. 115 photographs. 1905 to 1984.

COLLECTIONS

BELTON (Bell County)
   University of Mary Hardin-Baylor, Sid Richardson Museum, b34

BIG BEND NATIONAL PARK (Brewster County)
   Big Bend National Park, b40

BISHOP (Nueces County)
   Bishop Chamber of Commerce, b46

BOERNE (Kendall County)
   Boerne Area Historical Society, b52

BONHAM (Fannin County)
   Sam Rayburn Library, b58

BRECKENRIDGE (Stephens County)
   Swenson Memorial Museum of Stephens County, b64

BRENHAM (Washington County)
   Texas Baptist Historical Center and Museum, b70

BROOKSHIRE (Waller County)
   Waller County Historical Museum, b76

BROWNSVILLE (Cameron County)
   Gladys Porter Zoo, b82

BRYAN (Brazos County)
   Bryan Public Library, b88

CANADIAN (Hemphill County)
   Hemphill County Library, c10

CANYON (Randall County)
   Panhandle-Plains Historical Museum, C14

CEDAR HILL (Dallas County)
   Northwood Institute Library, c18

CHANNING (Hartley County)
   Hartley County Historical Commission, c22

CHILDRESS (Childress County)
   Childress County Heritage Museum, c26

CLEBURNE (Johnson County)
   Layland Museum, c30

CLIFTON (Bosque County)
   Bosque Memorial Museum, c34

COLLEGE STATION (Brazos County)
   Texas A&M University
      Archives, c38
      Texas Forest Service Headquarters Library, c42
      University Art Exhibits, c46

COMMERCE (Hunt County)
   East Texas State University, University Archives and Oral History Center, c50

COOPER (Delta County)
   Delta County Patterson Memorial Museum, c54

CORPUS CHRISTI (Nueces County)
   Art Museum of South Texas, c58
   Central Power and Light, C62
   Coastal Bend Council of Governments, c66
   Corpus Christi Area Convention and Tourist Bureau, c70
   Corpus Christi Museum, C74
   Corpus Christi Public Library, C78
   Padre Island National Seashore, c82

COTULLA (La Salle County)
   Brush Country Museum, c86

CROCKETT (Houston County)
   Discover Houston County Visitors and Learning Center and Museum, c90

CROSBYTON (Crosby County)
   Crosby County Pioneer Memorial Museum, c94

DALLAS (Dallas County)
   Catholic Diocese of Dallas, Diocesan Archives, d10
   Dallas County Heritage Society, Old City Park, d14
   Dallas Historical Society, D18
   Dallas Museum of Natural History, d22
   Dallas Public Library
      Fine Arts Division, D26
      Texas/Dallas History and Archives Division, D30
   International Museum of Cultures, d34
   Saint Paul Medical Center, d38
   Southern Methodist University
      DeGolyer Library, D42
      Meadows Museum, d46
   Southland Corporation, d50
   Temple Emanu-El, d54
   University of Texas Health Science Center at Dallas, d58

DECATUR (Wise County)
   Wise County Heritage Museum, d61

DEER PARK (Harris County)
   Deer Park Independent School District Historical School Museum, d64

DEL RIO (Val Verde County)
Val Verde County Historical Commission, d67

DENISON (Grayson County)
Grayson County Frontier Village, d70

DENTON (Denton County)
Denton Public Library, d73
North Texas State University, University
Archives, D76
Texas Woman's University, Blagg-Huey
Library, d79

DIBOLL (Angelina County)
T. L. L. Temple Memorial Library, d82

DUMAS (Moore County)
Moore County Historical Museum, d85

DUNCANVILLE (Dallas County)
Duncanville Public Library, d88

EDINBURG (Hidalgo County)
Hidalgo County Historical Museum, e10

EL PASO (El Paso County)
El Paso Museum of Art, e20
El Paso Museum of History, e30
El Paso Public Library, Southwest Collection,
E40
Fort Bliss, Museum of the Non-Commissioned
Officer, e50
University of Texas at El Paso
El Paso Centennial Museum, E60
Special Collections Department, e70
West Texas Council of Governments, e80

FALFURRIAS (Brooks County)
Heritage Museum, f10

FORT DAVIS (Jeff Davis County)
Fort Davis National Historic Site, F14

FORT HOOD (Bell County)
First Cavalry Division Museum, F18
Second Armored Division Museum, f22

FORT McKAVETT (Menard County)
Fort McKavett State Historic Site, f26

FORT STOCKTON (Pecos County)
Annie Riggs Museum, f30

FORT WORTH (Tarrant County)
Amon Carter Museum, F34
Amon G. Carter Archives, f38

Fort Worth (City of)
Parks and Recreation Department, Log
Cabin Village Historical Complex, f42
Public Library, F46
Transporation and Public Works Depart-
ment, f50
Water Department, f54
Zoological Park, f58
Gearhart Industries, f62
Southwest Aerospace Museum, f66
Southwestern Baptist Theological Seminary,
Texas Baptist Historical Collection, F70
Texas and Southwestern Cattle Raisers Associ-
ation, F74
Texas Christian University, Mary Couts
Burnett Library, f78
Texas College of Osteopathic Medicine, f82

FREDERICKSBURG (Gillespie County)
Admiral Nimitz State Historical Park, f86
Pioneer Memorial Museum, f90

GAINESVILLE (Cooke County)
Morton Museum of Cooke County, G10

GALVESTON (Galveston County)
Center for Transportation and Commerce, g20
Galveston County Historical Museum, g30
Rosenberg Library, G40
US Army Corps of Engineers, Galveston
District, G50
University of Texas Medical Branch, Truman
G. Blocker, Jr. History of Medicine Collec-
tion, G60

GEORGETOWN (Williamson County)
Southwestern University, Mood-Heritage
Museum, g70

GREENVILLE (Hunt County)
W. Walworth Harrison Public Library, g80

HALLETTSVILLE (Lavaca County)
Lavaca County Historical Commission, h10

HARLINGEN (Cameron County)
Confederate Air Force Museum, h13

HENDERSON (Rusk County)
Howard-Dickinson House, h16
Rusk County Depot Museum Complex, h19

HEREFORD (Deaf Smith County)
Deaf Smith County Museum, h22

HILLSBORO (Hill County)
Hill College, Confederate Research Center and Audie L. Murphy Gun Museum, h25
Hillsboro Heritage League, h28

HOUSTON (Harris County)
American Brahman Breeders Association, h31
Counsulate General of the Republic of Korea, h34
Harris County Heritage Society, H37
Houston Academy of Medicine-Texas Medical Center Library, Historical Research Center, H40
Houston Chamber of Commerce, h43
Houston Museum of Natural Science, h46
Houston Police Museum, h49
Houston Public Library, Houston Metropolitan Research Center, H52
Menil Foundation
  Image of the Black, h55
  Menil Collection, H58
Methodist Hospital, Department of Medical Photography, h61
Museum of Fine Art, Houston, H64
National Aeronautics and Space Administration (NASA), Johnson Spacecraft Center, H67
Oceaneering International, Inc., h70
Rice University
  University Art Collection, H73
  Woodson Research Center, H76
Sisters of Charity of the Incarnate Word, Villa de Matel, h79
University of Houston, University Library, Special Collections, H82

HUNSTVILLE (Walker County)
Huntsville Public Library, Times and Places Gone By, h85

HURST (Tarrant County)
Bell Helicopter Textron, h88
Hurst Public Library, h91
Tarrant County Junior College, Heritage Room, h94

IRVING (Dallas County)
Irving Municipal Photographic Archives, i10

JOHNSON CITY (Blanco County)
Lyndon B. Johnson National Historical Park, j10

KERRVILLE (Kerr County)
Cowboy Artists of America Museum, k10

KILGORE (Gregg County)
Kilgore College, Rangerette Showcase, k20

KINGSVILLE (Kleberg County)
Texas A&I University, John E. Conner Museum, K30

LA GRANGE (Fayette County)
Fayette Heritage Museum and Archives, L10

LA PORTE (Harris County)
Battleship Texas State Historic Site, l15
San Jacinto Museum of History Association, L20

LAKE JACKSON (Brazoria County)
Brazosport Museum of Natural Science, l25

LAREDO (Webb County)
Laredo Public Library, l30
Webb County Heritage Foundation, l35

LEAKEY (Real County)
Real County Historical Commission, l40

LIBERTY (Liberty County)
Liberty County Historical Commission, l45
Sam Houston Regional Library and Research Center, L50

LONGVIEW (Gregg County)
Gregg County Historical Museum, l55
LeTourneau College, R. G. LeTourneau Archives, l60

LUBBOCK (Lubbock County)
Texas Tech University, Southwest Collection, L65

LUFKIN (Angelina County)
The Museum of East Texas, L70
Texas Forestry Museum, l75
United States Forest Service, l80

LULING (Caldwell County)
First Baptist Church, l85

McALLEN (Hidalgo County)
Lower Rio Grande Valley Development Council, m10
McAllen International Museum, m18

MARFA (Presidio County)
Marfa-Presidio County Museum, m26

MARSHALL (Harrison County)
Harrison County Historical Museum, m34

MENARD (Menard County)
Menardville Museum, m42

MERIDIAN (Bosque County)
Bosque County Historical Commission, m50

MIDLAND (Midland County)
Nita Stewart Haley Memorial Library, Erwin E.
Smith Photographic Collection, m58
Midland County Historical Museum, m66
Museum of the Southwest, m74
Permian Basin Petroleum Museum, M82

MULESHOE (Bailey County)
Muleshoe Area Public Library, m90

NACOGDOCHES (Nacogdoches County)
Stephen F. Austin University, Ralph W. Steen
Library, N10

NEW BRAUNFELS (Comal County)
Sophienberg Memorial Association Archives,
N20

ODESSA (Ector County)
Ector County Library, o10
Odessa Chamber of Commerce, o20
Second Baptist Church, o30
Texas State Library and Archives Local
Records Division, Permian Historical
Archives, o40
University of Texas of the Permian Basin,
Special Collections, O50
White-Pool House, o60

ORANGE (Orange County)
Sabine River Authority, o70

PALACIOS (Matagorda County)
Palacios Area Historical Association, p10

PANHANDLE (Carson County)
Carson County Square House Museum, p18

PARIS (Lamar County)
Paris Junior College, A. M. and Welma Aikin
Regional Archives, p26
S. B. Maxey House, p34

PASADENA (Harris County)
Pasadena Public Library, p42
Texas Chiropractic College, p50

PLAINVIEW (Hale County)
Hale County Historical Commission, p58

PLEASANTON (Atascosa County)
Longhorn Museum, p66

PORTLAND (San Patricio County)
Bell Public Library, p74

PRAIRIE VIEW (Waller County)
Prairie View A&M University, University
Archives and Special Collections, P82

PRINCETON (Collin County)
Princeton Independent School District
Museum, p90

QUITMAN (Wood County)
Governor Hogg Shrine State Historical Park,
q10

RALLS (Crosby County)
Ralls Historical Museum, r10

RANKIN (Upton County)
Rankin Museum, r20

RICHARDSON (Dallas County)
University of Texas at Dallas, History of Aviation Collection, R30

RICHMOND (Fort Bend County)
Fort Bend County Museum, r40

ROUND ROCK (Williamson County)
Round Rock Public Library, r50

ROUND TOP (Fayette County)
University of Texas, Winedale Historical
Center, r60

RUSK (Cherokee County)
Rusk State Hospital, r70

SABINE PASS (Jefferson County)
Sea Rim State Park and Sabine Pass
Battleground State Historic Park, s10

SAN ANGELO (Tom Green County)
Fort Concho Museum, S13

SAN ANTONIO (Bexar County)
Alamo Area Council of Governments, s16
Brooks Air Force Base, Hangar 9—Edward H.
White II Memorial Museum, s19
Catholic Archdiocese of San Antonio, Catholic
Archives of Texas, s21
Daughters of the Republic of Texas Library,
S24
Fort Sam Houston,
Fort Sam Houston Museum, S27
US Army Medical Museum, s30
Lackland Air Force Base
Air Force Military Training Center, s33
History and Traditions Museum, s36
Museum of American Aviation, s39

WHITESBORO (Grayson County)
Whitesboro Public Library, w65

WHITEWRIGHT (Grayson County)
Whitewright Public Library, w70

WICHITA FALLS (Wichita County)
Kell House, w75
Midwestern State University, w80
Wichita Falls Museum and Art Center, W85

WOODVILLE (Tyler County)
Allan Shivers Library and Museum, w90

GEOGRAPHIC INDEX

Most collections provide extensive coverage of the region in which they are located. The Collections List orders collections by location. Entries are grouped by country, and in the United States, by state as well; for example, for Austin, see US, Texas, Austin. An asterisk indicates extensive coverage.

PERSONAL NAME INDEX

Entries in this index generally reflect the form in which a name was recorded in the collection. Variant forms of a name were consolidated only when the different forms were known to represent the same person or family; e.g., Fred Chabot and Frederick Chabot. Identical forms of a name were consolidated, although it is not to be assumed that only one person or family is represented by that name; e.g., more than one family may be represented by Williams family. One the other hand, separate entries should not be assumed to be different individuals; e.g., E. K. Warren and Earl Warren may be the same person. An asterisk (*) indicates extensive coverage.

For additional names of theater and motion picture personalities, most represented by production stills, see Theatre Arts Collection, Harry Ransom Humanities Research Center, University of Texas, Austin (A88) and Fine Arts Department, Dallas Public Library, Dallas (D26).

Winfrey, Dorman H., A78.1*
Winkler, Ernst William, A78.1*
Wirtz, Willard, A42/Pe
Wise, Wes, D30.18
Wismann, Elizabeth Wilder, A80.34*
Wister, Owen, A68.82*
Witt, Robert R., Jr., S51.4
Wohlfeld, Nathan, D30.55*
Womack, Judy, L65.40.3
Wood, Robert, A42/Pe
Wood, Sam, A42.7*
Woodland, Mary and Naamon J., Jr.,
    L50.48*
Woodman, Charles, A86.105*
Woods, Sallie and Adine, L50.49*
Woodward, Dudley Kezer, Jr.,
    A78.150*
Woodward, Edwin C., F34.95*
Wooten family, W35/Pe
Worth, William family, S51/Pe
Worthey family, L50.20
Worthington, Jackie, F74.6
Worton family, L65.63.2
Wothy family, W35/Pe
Wright Brothers, A86.66, R30/Pe
Wright family, D18.4
Wright, Arvilla, A68.84*
Wright, Frank Lloyd, A76.1
Wright, George L., Mrs., M82.38*
Wright, Josepha "Jodie", A78.1*
Wright, Mildred S. and Z. H., L50.50*
Wulff, Anton family, S45
Wykoff, Roy A., A68.85*

Yamasaki, M., A76.1
Yancey, Lewis A., R30.20*
Yarboro family, A16.18
Yarborough, Ralph, A26.5, A42/Pe,
    A78.92
Yates, Jack, Rev., H52.127*
Yeager, Wilbur Arthur, Sr., M82/Pe
Yipiñia, Mariano Rozales, H52.128*
Young, Andrew, A78.58
Young, James H., L50.51*
Young, Whitney, A42/Pe
Youngblood, Rufus, A42/Pe

Zablocki, Clement, A42/Pe
Zaharias, Babe Didrikson, b22
Zahorik, Gordon, W20.57*
Zahrt, Pat, Mrs., D18.60*
Zapalac family, L10.1
Zbranek family, L10.1
Zeppelin, Ferdinand von, R30/Pe
Ziegeld, Florenz, A88.22*
Ziegler, Jesse Adolph, L50.1
Ziegler, Jessie D., A78.152*
Ziller, Michael, A32/Pe
Zingg, Robert, E40.26
Zucker, Alfred, A74.4
Zukovsky, Louis, A86.5
Zwick, Charles, A42/Pe

PHOTOGRAPHER INDEX

Entries in this index generally reflect the form in which the photographer's name was recorded in the collection. Variant forms of a name were consolidated only when the different forms were known to represent a single photographer; for example, Nicolas Winter and Nicolas Winther. Identical forms of a name were consolidated, although it is not to be assumed that only one individual was responsible for all the photographs; for example, some work by Otto Sarony may be listed with his brother under Sarony. On the other hand, separate entries should not be assumed to be different photographers; for example, Evans may be Rodney, Ron, or Walker Evans. An asterisk (*) indicates extensive coverage.

Diamond, Paul, H64/Ph
Dibbets, Jan, H64/Ph
Dick, Sheldon., H73/Ph
Dickerson, Tessie Frank, L65.14*
Dickinson Photo, S63/Ph
Dingus, Rick, A86.88, F34/Ph
Dinwiddie, William, F34.78
Disderi, André Adolphe, A80.12.4,
    A86.201, L20.14
Disfarmer, Mike, H64/Ph
Disney, Wesley, F34/Ph
Disraeli, Robert, F34/Ph
Divola, John, H64/Ph
Dixon, Henry and T. J., A86.110*
Dixon, Robert D. (Houston), H37.5.2*,
    H52.51*
Dixon-Litterst Studios (Houston),
    H52/Ph
Dodd, Jimmie A., A78.55*, K30.18.2
Dodgson, Charles Lutwidge A86.2.19*,
    177-181*
Doerr and Jacobson (San Antonio),
    D18.53, F34.77, N20/Ph, S63/Ph
Doerr and Jesse (San Antonio),
    N20/Ph
Doerr and Winther (San Antonio),
    N20/Ph
Doerr, Henry A. (San Antonio),
    A78.67, D18.44, F34.77, N20/Ph,
    S24/Ph, S51/Ph, S63/Ph
Doherty, Brad, A32/Ph
Doisneau, Robert, A86.210*, d46,
    H64.31*, H73.3*
Dolan, John, D30/Ph
Donaldson, H64/Ph
Donaldson Studios, W35/Ph
Doniz, Rafael, H64/Ph
Doolittle, H64/Ph
Dornaus, John (New York), N20/Ph
Dorr, Nell, F34/Ph
Dorsey, Paul, h46
Doubleday (Wyoming), M82/Ph
Dougherty, Jim, A32/Ph
Douglas, W. E. (Dallas), D18.44
Douglass, Neal (Austin), A32.10*,
    M82.20
Downey, W. and D., A86/Ph, H64/Ph
Drecker, E. (Cleveland OH), H37.11
Dritton, F., S13.5
Drtikol, František, H64/Ph
Drum, Windy, W20/Ph
Dryden, Carol (Falfurrias), f10*, K30
Du Camp, Maxime, A86.115*
Duchenne, C. B., A86/Ph
Dudley Studio (Alpine), A16/Ph
Dugan, Joe, H58/Ph
DuHauron, Ducos, A86/Ph
Duncan, Francis King "Frank"
    (Marfa), A16/Ph, A86.8, L65.56,
    85; m26*, S51/Ph
Duncan, Kenn, A88.8
Dupont, Aimé, A86.82, A88/Ph
Dupont, Henry B., F34.11*

Eagle Lake Studios, w60
Eakins, Thomas, F34/Ph, H64/Ph
Eastman, Michael, F34/Ph
Eastman, Robert, A86.97

Eaton, Thomas B., H76.24*, W20.63*
Eckerskorn (San Antonio), N20/Ph,
    S51/Ph
Eckstrom, Tom, F34/Ph
Edens, Swain, S51/Ph
Edgerton, Harold, F34/Ph, H64/Ph
Edizioni Brogi, A86.85
Edmondon, G. W. (Norwalk OH),
    C14.16*
Edrington (Weslaco), C62/Ph
Edwards Studio (Amarillo), C14/Ph
Edwards, John Paul, F34.12*
Edworthy, G40.41
Egerton, Philip Henry, A86.116*
Eggleston, William, H58.13-15*,
    H64/Ph
Ehrenberger, James L., D42/Ph
Eickemeyer, Rudolph, H64/Ph
Eisenstaedt, Alfred, H64/Ph
Ekmark, C. J., S27.7*
Elazer, William, e50
Eldred, Dale, c58
Elicson, Joe, S27.8*, S63/Ph
Elisofon, Eliot, S51/Ph
Elliot and Fry (London), W10/Ph
Elliot, Mitchell, a52
Elliott, Jane and Martyn (Austin),
    A32/Ph, N20/Ph
Ellison Studios (Austin), A32.11*,
    A86.8, P82/Ph
Embree, E. D., H76.24*, W20.63*
Emerson, Peter Henry, A86.117-120*,
    H64/Ph
Emrich, Ronald, A60/Ph
Engel, Morris, F34.13*, H64/Ph
England, William, A86/Ph
Englander, Joseph B., H73/Ph
Engle, Morris, S51/Ph
English, Owen, T58/Ph
Erdlen, C. W., F34.88
Erfurth, Hugo, A86/Ph
Ericson, O. T. (Vermillion SD),
    A16/Ph
Erwitt, Elliott, A86.211-212*, d46,
    F34.52*, H64.32-33*, H73.4*
Eskildsen, H52.115
Esquivel, T. R., Sr., l35
Eugene, Frank, A86/Ph, H64/Ph
Evans, Elliot A. P., N10/Ph
Evans, Frederick Henry, A86/Ph,
    H58/Ph
Evans, J. G., F34.77
Evans, Rodney, H64/Ph
Evans, Ron, F34/Ph
Evans, Walker, A86.58*, F34/Ph,
    H58.16*, H64/Ph, H73/Ph, S51.10*
Evans, H64/Ph

Fahrenberg, Albert, S51/Ph
Fairchild Aerial Photography, D30.24*
Falk, B. J. (New York), A88/Ph,
    D26.15, S51.6
Faller, Marion, H64/Ph
Falvella, J. W., A86.59*
Fannin, Hank, h70
Fardon, G. R., F34/Ph
Farm Security Administration, a20,
    a90*, S51.10

Farmer, Dennis, A60/Ph
Farraud, H64/Ph
Faurer, Louis, H64/Ph
Fay, John Spencer, H64/Ph
Faye, Gary, H64/Ph
Fehl, Fred, A86.1*; A88.7.2, 40.9
Feiler, Jo Alison, H64/Ph
Feininger, Lux, H64/Ph
Feldman, Fred, E40/Ph
Fellig, Arthur, see Weegee
Fennell, Linda, H64/Ph
Fennemore, J. , F34/Ph
Fenner, Phyllis, F34/Ph
Fenton, Roger, A86.2.20*, 122, 135,
    140; H64/Ph
Feresten, Peter Helms, A86.34,
    F34/Ph, H64/Ph
Ferguson, Jim, F34/Ph
Ferguson, John, A60/Ph
Ferrier, A., A86/Ph
Ferrier, G., A86.121
Fey and Braunig, S51/Ph
Fichter, Robert, H64/Ph
Fielder, A. M., S63/Ph
Figley (La Porte), W35/Ph
Fink, Larry, H64/Ph
Finklestein, Mel, D30/Ph
Finn, William, D30/Ph
Fiorillo, L., A86.188
Fisher, Larry Jene, b22
Fiske, George, F34.88, S51.25
Fiskin, Judy, H64/Ph
Fitch, Steve, F34/Ph, H64/Ph
Fitz, W. Grancel, F34/Ph
Flahive, Michael P., A32/Ph, a52
Flanagan, Sue, S24/Ph, S63/Ph
Flato, C. H., K30.2*
Fleming, Frederic, H64/Ph
Flick, Robert, H64/Ph
Flores, Arthur C. (Texon), M82.14
Flory, Linda, A60/Ph
Flukinger, Roy, A86.38
Flynn, J. T., D30/Ph
Fontana, Franco, H64/Ph
Foote, Elmer L., A86.8
Ford, B. A. (Braidwood IL), H37.14
Forster, Simon, A86.15*
Foster (Bonham), L65.34
Foster, Robert, D42/Ph
Fowx, Egbert Guy, F34/Ph
Fox Studio (San Antonio), P82/Ph
Fox, Dan, A60/Ph
Frampton, Hollis, H64/Ph
Franck, H64/Ph
Franco, Sergio (Ojinaga, Mexico),
    A16/Ph
Frank, Douglas, F34/Ph
Frank, Robert, F34/Ph, H64.34*,
    S51/Ph
Frank, Ruth, W20/Ph
Frashers Quality Photos, L65.62
Frazier, William, H64/Ph
Fredricks, Charles (New York),
    A86.48, L20/Ph, S63/Ph
Freeman, Alfred, D18/Ph, T82/Ph
Freeman, Charles M., A86.60*
Freeman, Joe, A60/Ph
Freeman, Martha, A60/Ph

A16/Ph, N20/Ph, S51/Ph, S63/Ph
Paris, A. C., S51/Ph, S63/Ph
Pariskas, A86.96
Park, Patricia, S51/Ph
Parker and Parker, F34.77
Parker, Bart, H64/Ph
Parker, F. , F34.77
Parker, Francis, E40/Ph
Parker, Maynard L., A74.5
Parks, S63/Ph
Parks, Gordon, H58/Ph, H64/Ph, H73/Ph
Parrish, W. H. (pub.), G40.29
Parvin, Bob, A54/Ph
Patiño, A80.18
Patterson, Elmer, h22
Patteson Harvey (San Antonio), C62/Ph, N20/Ph, S24/Ph, S51/Ph, s54, S63/Ph
Patton, W. H., h22
Paul, Susie, H64/Ph
Paxton, Herbert, A86.96
Payne, H. T., F34.77
Payne, Richard, H64/Ph
Peabody, Henry Greenwood, D26.2*
Peary, Robert, F34/Ph
Peck, Mary Elizabeth, A86.34, F34/Ph, H64/Ph
Peel, Michael, d46
Penn, Irving, F34/Ph, H64/Ph, S51/Ph
Penn, Russell, a52
Pennington, Harry, Jr., A86.6*
Peraire, Agtin (Mexico), F34.87
Perkins, Lyle C., l35
Perry, Garland, b52
Perry, W. E. (Perryton), C14.8
Peterson, Conradt (La Grange), L10/Ph
Petschler, H., and Company, A86/Ph
Petter, Charles, S63/Ph
Petteys, Diane, H64/Ph
Pevin, Michael, F34/Ph
Peyton's (New Orleans), N20/Ph
Pfahl, John, H64/Ph
Phelps, Brent, F34/Ph
Phillips, William Battle, A86.8
Pickwoad [Pickwood], Ed, D30/Ph
Pinderhughes, J. , H58/Ph
Pinkerton Studio (Monahans), M82/Ph
Piper, Stephen (Manchester NH), S13.10
Pipes, Richard, H73/Ph
Pittaway, f30
Pittman, Bill, h61
Plossu, Bernard, F34.61*
Plumb, E. S., E40.22*
Poindexter, John, S63/Ph
Polk, P. H., H64/Ph
Pollack, A86.140
Pollack (Baltimore MD), S13.5
Ponti, Carlo, A86/Ph
Ponting, Herbert G., A86/Ph
Porter, Eliot, F34.62*, H64.51*
Post, Helen, F34.23*
Potash, Mose L., S63/Ph, v30
Powell Studio, s54
Powell, L. T., S51.4
Powelson and Company, H64/Ph

Prather, Winter, F34.24*, 63*; H64/Ph
Pratt, Charles, H58/Ph, H64/Ph
Pratt, Francis Edward, A86.88*
Press Cliche, A86.96
Price, William Lake, A86.195
Prothro, m66
Provost, Herbert J., H52/Ph
Pumphrey, William, A86/Ph
Punch, Miss (Jacksonville), h16
Purcell (AL), N20/Ph
Puryear, Jack, S51/Ph
Putnam, Michael, H64/Ph
Putney, Harrison (Leavenworth KS), F34.83
Pyka, Charles, A86.44

Quesada-Burke, Carmen, H64/Ph
Quillan, Ellen Dorothy Schultz, O50.2*
Quinet, Achille, A86/Ph
Quinn, M82.4

Raba, Ernst (San Antonio), see also Brack and Raba; a36, A86.26, N20/Ph, S63/Ph, S45; S51.4, 17*
Rabor, N. (San Antonio), N20/Ph
Radabaugh, E. B. (Huntington IN), S13.11
Ragsdale, McArthur Cullen (San Angelo), h16, L65/Ph, S13/Ph, S63/Ph
Railroad Photo Car, h16
Rakoff, Penny, H64/Ph
Ramirez, Mario C., s42
Ramos, A80/Ph
Rand, Glenn, H64/Ph
Randolph, Ron, c70
Randolph, Rubin (Midland), M82/Ph
Ranney, Edward, F34/Ph
Ransom, Christopher, H64/Ph
Rathje, Julius (Lüneberg, Germany), L10.4
Ratliff, C. W., L65.76-77*
Rau, William H., F34/Ph
Ray, Man, A74.5, D26.6, F34.3, H58.27*, H64/Ph
Realistic Travels, A86.160-161*
Recknagel, Friederike, r60, S63/Ph
Rector, Ray, A86.29*
Redfield, Robert S., F34/Ph
Redin, Van, A32/Ph
Reece, Jane, F34/Ph
Reece, Mickey, r20
Reeves, Frank (Fort Worth), F74/Ph, L65.86*
Regal Studios (Corpus Christi), C62/Ph
Rehm, Jack, A32/Ph
Reidy, D30/Ph
Reilly, J. J., F34.77
Reingold, Mel, h61
Rejlander, O. G., A86.196-197*, 140, 180
Renger-Patzsch, Albert, A86.2.33*, H64/Ph
Resnick, Marcia, H64/Ph
Reutlinger, Charles, H64/Ph
Revelle, Barbara Jo, H64/Ph

Rexroth, Nancy, H64/Ph
Reynal, Key Bell, S51/Ph
Reynolds, Richard, A70, c70
Reynoso Castañeda, Antonio, H64/Ph
Rice, L. (Seguin), N20/Ph
Rice, L. T. (Wabash IN), A16/Ph
Rice, Paul, D30/Ph
Rice, Ted, III, F34/Ph
Richards, S. S. (Carthage NY), D76/Ph
Richie, Robert Yarnell, D42.6
Richter, A. (Maxwell), N20/Ph
Rickards, Constantine George, A80.23
Ricker, Norman Hurd, H76.16.3*
Rinehart, Frank A., F34/Ph
Rino, Frank, D30/Ph
Rivers, Charles, F34/Ph
Robbins, Al, D30/Ph
Roberson, Wayne, A60/Ph
Roberts, Paul (Odessa), M82/Ph
Robertson and Donaldson, W35/Ph
Robertson, James, A86/Ph
Robertson, Ogden, H58/Ph
Robeusne, H. F., F34.92
Robinson, Cervin, F34/Ph
Robinson, Henry Peach, A86/Ph
Robinson, Ralph Waldo, A86/Ph
Rocher, H. (Chicago), A88.5
Rodriguez (Paris), W20.12
Rössler, Jaroslav, H64.52
Roger-Viollet, H., H58.28*
Rogers (Brownwood), A16/Ph
Rogers, Byron, F34/Ph
Rogers, Frank, d10, D18/Ph, D30.45*
Rogers, Paul P., A80.25*
Rogovin, Milton, H64/Ph
Roh, Franz, H64/Ph
Rohde, Werner, H64/Ph
Roitz, Charles, H64/Ph
Rooker and Frasier, w60
Roper, A86.3
Rose, N. H., A18/Ph, d67, m42, S24/Ph, S63/Ph
Rose, P. H. (Galveston), A86.47, F34.77, G40.18, L20/Ph, L65.13.1, S63/Ph, W35/Ph
Rose [P. H.] and Zahn (Galveston), S63/Ph, W35/Ph
Rosenbaum, m66
Rosenberg, Sam, A86.97
Rosenblum, Walter, H64/Ph
Rosenthal, Zade, S51/Ph
Rosling, A86.140
Ross, Horatio, H64/Ph
Ross, Mungo, h70
Rosskam, Ed, F34/Ph, L65.47.5
Roszak, Theodore, H64/Ph
Rotan, Thurman, S51/Ph
Rotherwell, I. B., S51/Ph
Rothman, Henry, H64/Ph
Rothstein, Arthur, F34.65*, H64.53, H73/Ph
Rothwell, S63/Ph
Rotkin, Charles, F34/Ph
Rousse, George, H58/Ph
Rowe, Abbie, A42/Ph
Rubellin, S51.1
Rubenstein, Meridel, F34/Ph
Rubin, Janice, H64/Ph

SUBJECT INDEX

Entries in this index include proper names of nonpersonal subjects and headings for generic subjects. Subjects pertinent to a specific locale are not listed here; researchers should check the entries listed under those locales in the Collections List and in the Geographic Index for such subjects.

A few subjects are held in some quantity by virtually every collection. Those subjects are marked *passim* below, and only collections with extensive coverage or special focus on the subject are noted. An asterisk (*) indicates extensive coverage of a topic.

Abilene State School, A60.3, a10*
academia (passim), A35.36, A78.6; D30.17, 41; d64. Migrant worker A80.27
actors, A88, D26
agriculture (passim) C14, c38, C78.6, H52.1, L65. Grape, D18.11. Rice, A86.30
air pollution, a46
Alamo, A60.2-3, A78.54, S24/S*, S51/S, S63/S
All Church Press, F70.1*
American Field Service, L50.2
American Legion, A78.55, A86.3, H52.53
American Mayflower, D18.2*
animals (passim), f58. Bees, A68.25. Horses, F74.2*, Livestock, see ranching. Marine, A68.31, c82, s10. Zoo, b82.
anthropology (see People Index, ethnic), A92, d34, E60
Apollo space program, H67.2*
archaeology. Mexico, A80.15, 19, 23, 24. Petroglyphs, A92.3. Texas A60*.
architecture (passim, see also names of specific architects in People Index), A74, A76, A86. Ancient Egyptian, A86.2.7, 2.36, 64, 115, 123-129, 143. Ancient European, A86*. Brazilian, A80.5. Classical Roman and Greek, A86.2.16, 2.29. Commercial interiors, A36.22, C14.12, D18.13, F46.1, H52.49. Domestic interiors, S24.5. Furnishings, F34.10. Haciendas A80.4. Historical Texas, A60, A78, A86.9, D18, F34.94, S45. Historic American Building Survey, A60.2.3, A78.75, S24.6, G40.6. Log cabin, D76.8, F42. Public works, A54, D30.54, F50, F54, G40.13,

G50, O70, S70, W25. Pueblo, F34.9. South American baroque, A80.5. Spanish colonial in Mexico, D26.2.
Armadillo World Headquarters, A78.8
art reproduction, sculpture, A86.154, 192.
Ashland Oil Company, L65.43
astronomy, A86.2.17, 68, 144
Atomic Bomb Casualty Commission, H40.1*
automobile (passim) E40.3
aviation, f38, f66, h13, L65.6, R30*, s39, t50. Lighter-than-air craft, R30.15

ballet, see dance
Baptist Church, b70, F70*, l85, o30
barnstorming, R30.6, 9, 12
Bauhaus, H64.5
Beaumont Symphony Orchestra and Civic Opera, L50.48
beauticians, H52.6, L65.91
Beethoven Männerchor, S51.3
Belle Plain College, b10
Bell Helicopter, A26, h88
Bergdorff-Goodman, D26.6*
billboard advertising, H52.82
Bolshevik Revolution, A86.96
Boy Scouts of America, A32/S, A78.55; H52.53, 62
Braniff International Airlines, D30.45, R30.4
British Museum, A86.2.20, 122
Burnett Ranch, see 6666 Ranch

Calcasieu Lumber, A32/S
Camera Notes, F34.46
Camera Work, A86.146, F34.37
Camp Bowie, A68.56, W20.69
Camp Davis, D18.40
Camp Holland, A16/S
Camp Kent, A16/S

Camp La Noria, A16/S
Camp Logan, H52.40, 122; L65.63.2
Camp Mabry, A32/S, A78.5
Camp MacArthur, W20.16
Carr-Burdette College, s74
Catholic church, A34, d10, s21, s54
The Cattleman, F74.1*
Celanese Plant, A78.55, b46, C78
circuses, tent shows, and performers. A16/2, A32/S, A86.101; A88.6, 21; D18.5; L65.26, 35
Cities Service Company, L65.47
civil defense (nuclear warfare), A84
Civilian Conservation Corps, A16/S, A60.2.1, l75
civil rights, H52
Civil War, A86.56, 131; F34.37, h25; H76.10, 26; K30.15, L20.12, L50.14, L50.34, L65.8. Federal occupation of Brownsville, L20
Cold War, A84/S
Colonial Dames of the XVII Century, H52.3
Cowboy Artists of American, k10
cowboys (passim), A86.95
Crimean War, A86.2.5
Crystal Palace, A86.114*
Curtiss Aviation Company, R30.9

Dallas Little Theater, D26.13
Dallas Theatre Center, D26.14
dance, A88.8, 9; D26.4-5
Daughters of the American Revolution, H52.5
Daughters of the Republic of Texas, a38, S24*
Democratic Party, A26, H52.31
Demster Mill Manufacturing Company, C14.15
Décena Trágica, A80.17
diving, h70
Dow Chemical Company, A78.92, l25
Dr. Pepper, A60.2.7, W20

This book was prepared on a Compaq portable computer using Nota Bene software which produced camera-ready copy on a Hewlett-Packard LaserJet+ printer in 10-point TmsRmn with 1-point line spacing. The book was printed offset and bound by Thomson-Shore, Inc.

Texas A&M University Press : College Station